# PROFESSIONAL
# WINDOWS 7 DEVELOPMI

| INTRODUCTION | . . . . . . . . . . . . . . . . . . . . . . . . . . . . . . . . . . . . . . . . . . . . . xxv |
|---|---|
| ▶ **PART I** | **INTRODUCING WINDOWS 7** |
| **CHAPTER 1** | Windows 7 Improvements . . . . . . . . . . . . . . . . . . . . . . . . . . . . . . . . . . . 3 |
| **CHAPTER 2** | Developing a Windows 7 Strategy . . . . . . . . . . . . . . . . . . . . . . . . . . . .13 |
| **CHAPTER 3** | Understanding .NET 4.0 . . . . . . . . . . . . . . . . . . . . . . . . . . . . . . . . . . . .21 |
| ▶ **PART II** | **WORKING WITH THE WINDOWS 7 USER INTERFACE** |
| **CHAPTER 4** | Interacting with the Taskbar . . . . . . . . . . . . . . . . . . . . . . . . . . . . . . . . 37 |
| **CHAPTER 5** | Advanced Taskbar Techniques . . . . . . . . . . . . . . . . . . . . . . . . . . . . . . 57 |
| **CHAPTER 6** | Working with the Ribbon Interface . . . . . . . . . . . . . . . . . . . . . . . . . . . 85 |
| **CHAPTER 7** | Creating Custom Ribbon Interface Applications . . . . . . . . . . . . . . . . 105 |
| **CHAPTER 8** | Programming for Aero Glass Functionality . . . . . . . . . . . . . . . . . . . . 139 |
| **CHAPTER 9** | Working with the Multi-Touch User Interface . . . . . . . . . . . . . . . . . . 159 |
| ▶ **PART III** | **DEVELOPING SECURE APPLICATIONS** |
| **CHAPTER 10** | Using Standard NT Security Features in Windows 7 . . . . . . . . . . . . . . . 171 |
| **CHAPTER 11** | Understanding the User Account Control . . . . . . . . . . . . . . . . . . . . . . 201 |
| **CHAPTER 12** | Developing Applications with Enhanced Security . . . . . . . . . . . . . . . . 217 |
| **CHAPTER 13** | Interacting with the Built-In Security Features . . . . . . . . . . . . . . . . . . . 247 |
| ▶ **PART IV** | **ADVANCED WINDOWS 7 PROGRAMMING** |
| **CHAPTER 14** | Working in the Background . . . . . . . . . . . . . . . . . . . . . . . . . . . . . . . .293 |
| **CHAPTER 15** | Using the Windows 7 Libraries . . . . . . . . . . . . . . . . . . . . . . . . . . . . .329 |
| **CHAPTER 16** | Writing 64-Bit Applications for Windows 7 . . . . . . . . . . . . . . . . . . . . . 347 |
| **CHAPTER 17** | Using Parallel Programming in Windows 7 . . . . . . . . . . . . . . . . . . . . . 361 |
| **CHAPTER 18** | Using the Sensor and Location Platform . . . . . . . . . . . . . . . . . . . . . . 373 |
| **CHAPTER 19** | Using Windows XP Mode Effectively . . . . . . . . . . . . . . . . . . . . . . . . . 397 |

▶ **PART V** **WORKING AT THE COMMAND LINE**

**CHAPTER 20** Working with Windows PowerShell 2.0 . . . . . . . . . . . . . . . . . . . . . . . . 415
**CHAPTER 21** Creating Scripts . . . . . . . . . . . . . . . . . . . . . . . . . . . . . . . . . . . . . . . . . . 439
**CHAPTER 22** Creating Cmdlets . . . . . . . . . . . . . . . . . . . . . . . . . . . . . . . . . . . . . . . . . 455
**CHAPTER 23** Interacting Directly with PowerShell . . . . . . . . . . . . . . . . . . . . . . . . 469

**INDEX**. . . . . . . . . . . . . . . . . . . . . . . . . . . . . . . . . . . . . . . . . . . . . . . . . . . . . . . . . 483

PROFESSIONAL

# Windows 7 Development Guide

PROFESSIONAL

# Windows 7 Development Guide

John Paul Mueller

**Professional Windows 7 Development Guide®**

Published by
Wiley Publishing, Inc.
10475 Crosspoint Boulevard
Indianapolis, IN 46256
www.wiley.com

Copyright ©2011 by Wiley Publishing, Inc., Indianapolis, Indiana

Published simultaneously in Canada

ISBN: 978-0-470-88570-3
ISBN: 978-1-118-05795-7 (ebk)
ISBN: 978-1-118-05794-0 (ebk)
ISBN: 978-1-118-05793-3 (ebk)

Manufactured in the United States of America

10 9 8 7 6 5 4 3 2 1

No part of this publication may be reproduced, stored in a retrieval system or transmitted in any form or by any means, electronic, mechanical, photocopying, recording, scanning or otherwise, except as permitted under Sections 107 or 108 of the 1976 United States Copyright Act, without either the prior written permission of the Publisher, or authorization through payment of the appropriate per-copy fee to the Copyright Clearance Center, 222 Rosewood Drive, Danvers, MA 01923, (978) 750-8400, fax (978) 646-8600. Requests to the Publisher for permission should be addressed to the Permissions Department, John Wiley & Sons, Inc., 111 River Street, Hoboken, NJ 07030, (201) 748-6011, fax (201) 748-6008, or online at http://www.wiley.com/go/permissions.

**Limit of Liability/Disclaimer of Warranty:** The publisher and the author make no representations or warranties with respect to the accuracy or completeness of the contents of this work and specifically disclaim all warranties, including without limitation warranties of fitness for a particular purpose. No warranty may be created or extended by sales or promotional materials. The advice and strategies contained herein may not be suitable for every situation. This work is sold with the understanding that the publisher is not engaged in rendering legal, accounting, or other professional services. If professional assistance is required, the services of a competent professional person should be sought. Neither the publisher nor the author shall be liable for damages arising herefrom. The fact that an organization or Web site is referred to in this work as a citation and/or a potential source of further information does not mean that the author or the publisher endorses the information the organization or website may provide or recommendations it may make. Further, readers should be aware that Internet websites listed in this work may have changed or disappeared between when this work was written and when it is read.

For general information on our other products and services please contact our Customer Care Department within the United States at (877) 762-2974, outside the United States at (317) 572-3993 or fax (317) 572-4002.

Wiley also publishes its books in a variety of electronic formats. Some content that appears in print may not be available in electronic books.

**Library of Congress Control Number:** 2010942183

**Trademarks:** Wiley and the Wiley logo are trademarks or registered trademarks of John Wiley & Sons, Inc. and/or its affiliates, in the United States and other countries, and may not be used without written permission. Windows is a registered trademark of Microsoft Corporation in the United States and/or other countries. All other trademarks are the property of their respective owners. Wiley Publishing, Inc. is not associated with any product or vendor mentioned in this book.

*This book is dedicated to the newest member of our family, Shelby. She's already warmed our hearts and given us a great deal of joy.*

# ABOUT THE AUTHOR

**JOHN MUELLER** is a freelance author and technical editor. He has writing in his blood, having produced 87 books and over 300 articles to date. The topics range from networking to artificial intelligence and from database management to heads-down programming. Some of his current books include a Windows command line reference, books on VBA and Visio 2007, a C# design and development manual, and an IronPython programmer's guide. His technical editing skills have helped over 52 authors refine the content of their manuscripts. John has provided technical editing services to both *Data Based Advisor* and *Coast Compute* magazines. He's also contributed articles to magazines like *DevSource, InformIT, SQL Server Professional, Visual C++ Developer, Hard Core Visual Basic, asp.netPRO, Software Test & Performance,* and *Visual Basic Developer.*

When John isn't working at the computer, you can find him in his workshop. He's an avid woodworker and candle maker. On any given afternoon, you can find him working at a lathe or putting the finishing touches on a bookcase. He also likes making glycerin soap and candles, which come in handy for gift baskets. You can reach John on the Internet at JMueller@mwt.net. John is also setting up a Website at `http://www.mwt.net/~jmueller/`. Feel free to look and make suggestions on how he can improve it.

# ABOUT THE TECHNICAL EDITOR

**RUSS MULLEN** has been consulting and programming for more years than he cares to remember. He has tech-edited more than 70 books, ghost-written chapters, and co-authored several books.

# CREDITS

**ACQUISITIONS EDITOR**
Paul Reese

**PROJECT EDITOR**
William Bridges

**TECHNICAL EDITOR**
Russ Mullen

**PRODUCTION EDITOR**
Daniel Scribner

**COPY EDITOR**
William Bridges

**EDITORIAL DIRECTOR**
Robyn B. Siesky

**EDITORIAL MANAGER**
Mary Beth Wakefield

**FREELANCER EDITORIAL MANAGER**
Rosemarie Graham

**ASSOCIATE DIRECTOR OF MARKETING**
David Mayhew

**PRODUCTION MANAGER**
Tim Tate

**VICE PRESIDENT AND EXECUTIVE GROUP PUBLISHER**
Richard Swadley

**VICE PRESIDENT AND EXECUTIVE PUBLISHER**
Barry Pruett

**ASSOCIATE PUBLISHER**
Jim Minatel

**PROJECT COORDINATOR, COVER**
Katherine Crocker

**PROOFREADER**
Paul Sagan, Word One

**INDEXER**
Robert Swanson

**COVER DESIGNER**
LeAndra Young

**COVER IMAGE**
© iStock / Rubberball

# ACKNOWLEDGMENTS

**THANKS TO MY WIFE, REBECCA,** for working with me to get this book completed. I really don't know what I would have done without her help in researching and compiling some of the information that appears in this book. She also did a fine job of proofreading my rough draft and page-proofing the result. Rebecca also keeps the house running while I'm buried in work.

Russ Mullen deserves thanks for his technical edit of this book. He greatly added to the accuracy and depth of the material you see here, especially of some of the more difficult source code. Russ is always providing me with great URLs for new products and ideas. However, it's the testing Russ does that helps most. He's the sanity check for my work. Russ also has different computer equipment from mine, so he's able to point out flaws that I might not otherwise notice.

Matt Wagner, my agent, deserves credit for helping me get the contract in the first place and taking care of all the details that most authors don't really consider. I always appreciate his assistance. It's good to know that someone wants to help.

A number of people read all or part of this book to help me refine the approach, test the coding examples, and generally provide input that all readers wish they could have. These unpaid volunteers helped in ways too numerous to mention here. I especially appreciate the efforts of Eva Beattie and Osvaldo Téllez Almirall, who provided general input, read the entire book, and selflessly devoted themselves to this project.

Finally, I would like to thank Paul Reese, William Bridges, Dan Scribner, and the rest of the editorial and production staff at Wrox for their assistance in bringing this book to print. It's always nice to work with such a great group of professionals, and I very much appreciate the friendship we've built over the last few years.

# CONTENTS

| INTRODUCTION | xxv |
|---|---|

## PART I: INTRODUCING WINDOWS 7

### CHAPTER 1: WINDOWS 7 IMPROVEMENTS — 3

| Is Windows 7 Really Just Vista Fixed? | 4 |
|---|---|
| Considering the Major Improvements from a Developer Perspective | 4 |
|    Understanding the User Interface Improvements | 5 |
|    Considering the Security Improvements | 7 |
|    Developing Extended Applications | 8 |
| Considering Windows XP Mode | 9 |
| Developing for Windows PowerShell 2 | 9 |
| Moving Your Applications to Windows 7 | 10 |

### CHAPTER 2: DEVELOPING A WINDOWS 7 STRATEGY — 13

| Determining the User Windows 7 Comfort Level | 14 |
|---|---|
|    Defining Usage Requirements | 14 |
|    Considering Training Requirements | 16 |
|    Keeping the User Happy | 17 |
| Considering Whether to Move | 17 |
|    Testing Issues in Your Application | 17 |
|    Defining the Advantages of Moving to Windows 7 | 18 |
|    Working with Windows XP Mode | 19 |
| Moving Your Applications to Windows 7 | 20 |

### CHAPTER 3: UNDERSTANDING .NET 4.0 — 21

| Understanding Why You Need .NET 4.0 | 22 |
|---|---|
|    Defining Application Compatibility and Deployment | 22 |
|    Considering the New Core Features and Improvements | 24 |
|    Working with the Managed Extensibility Framework | 27 |
|    Implementing Parallel Computing | 27 |
|    Considering Networking | 28 |
|    Understanding the Data Improvements | 29 |
| Obtaining and Installing .NET 4.0 | 30 |
| Considering the Windows 7 Extended Functionality | 32 |
| Moving Your Applications to Windows 7 | 33 |

## PART II: WORKING WITH THE WINDOWS 7 USER INTERFACE

### CHAPTER 4: INTERACTING WITH THE TASKBAR — 37

**Viewing the New Taskbar in Windows 7** — 38
- Considering the Subtle Features — 39
- Understanding the Importance of Application Settings — 42

**Considering the Taskbar Updates** — 43
- Using the Taskbar as an Application Interaction Tool — 43
- An Overview of the New Taskbar Features — 44

**Creating the Basic Taskbar Application** — 45
- Obtaining the Windows API Code Pack for Microsoft .NET Framework — 46
- Creating the Solution — 48
- Adding the Jump List Code — 49
- Testing the Code Pack Result — 50

**Using the .NET 4.0 Approach** — 51
- Creating the Solution — 52
- Adding the Code — 52

**Avoiding Taskbar Overload** — 54
**Moving Your Applications to Windows 7** — 54

### CHAPTER 5: ADVANCED TASKBAR TECHNIQUES — 57

**Using Jump Lists** — 58
- Adding Common Categories — 58
- Adding Custom Categories — 67
- Performing Custom Tasks — 68
- Going Places Using a Jump List — 72

**Using Progress Bars** — 73
- Configuring the Progress Bar Application — 74
- Managing the Progress Bar — 74
- Changing States — 75

**Using Thumbnail Toolbars** — 77
- Defining the Thumbnail Toolbar Application — 78
- Drawing the Button Icon — 78
- Creating the Toolbar and Event Handler — 79

**Using Overlay Icons** — 80
**Combining Taskbar Controls** — 81
**Creating a Complete Interface** — 82
- Application Interaction Using Jump Lists and Thumbnail Toolbars — 82
- Displaying Status Using Overlay Icons and Progress Bars — 83

**Moving Your Applications to Windows 7** — 83

## CHAPTER 6: WORKING WITH THE RIBBON INTERFACE — 85

### Considering the Ribbon as a Whole — 86
- Precisely What Is the Ribbon? — 86
- Understanding How the Ribbon Can Help Novice Users — 89
- Viewing the Ribbon in Windows — 91

### Viewing the Ribbon in Office — 93
- Understanding the Office Document Connection — 94
- Considering How Office Technology Extends to Windows 7 — 98

### Defining the Ribbon Functionality in Windows 7 — 98
- An Overview of Ribbon Controls in Windows 7 — 99
- Understanding the Control Attributes — 102

### Moving Your Applications to Windows 7 — 103

## CHAPTER 7: CREATING CUSTOM RIBBON INTERFACE APPLICATIONS — 105

### Getting Started with the Ribbon — 106
- Obtaining the Windows 7 SDK — 106
- Obtaining RibbonLib — 108
- Configuring the Application — 110
- Defining a Ribbon Interface — 111
- Creating the Application — 121

### Using the Ribbon with WPF — 125
- Obtaining Microsoft Ribbon for WPF — 125
- Configuring the WPF Application — 126
- Defining the Ribbon Interface for the WPF Application — 127
- Creating the WPF Application — 132

### Moving Your Applications to Windows 7 — 137

## CHAPTER 8: PROGRAMMING FOR AERO GLASS FUNCTIONALITY — 139

### Considerations for Designing Applications for Aero Glass — 140

### Working with the Windows 7 Common File Dialogs — 141
- Considering the Common File Dialog Controls — 142
- Configuring the Common File Dialogs Example — 143
- Defining a File Open Dialog — 144
- Defining a File Save Dialog — 147

### Working with the Windows 7 Task Dialogs — 149
- Using the Task Dialog Effectively — 149
- Configuring the Task Dialog Example — 150
- Defining a Task Dialog — 151
- Making an Automatic Selection — 154

| Providing Extended Linguistic Services | 155 |
|---|---|
| Understanding the Role of Extended Linguistic Services | 155 |
| Configuring the Extended Linguistic Services Example | 156 |
| Adding Extended Linguistic Services to an Application | 156 |
| **Moving Your Applications to Windows 7** | **158** |

## CHAPTER 9: WORKING WITH THE MULTI-TOUCH USER INTERFACE — 159

| Considering Where Most Companies Use Multi-Touch | 160 |
|---|---|
| Defining the User Requirements for Multi-Touch | 161 |
| Adding Multi-Touch to Your Application | 162 |
| Obtaining the Multi-Touch Platform Interop Library | 163 |
| Configuring the Application | 163 |
| Adding Multi-Touch Interface Functionality | 164 |
| **Moving Your Applications to Windows 7** | **168** |

# PART III: DEVELOPING SECURE APPLICATIONS

## CHAPTER 10: USING STANDARD NT SECURITY FEATURES IN WINDOWS 7 — 171

| Considering Basic NT Security Feature Changes | 172 |
|---|---|
| Understanding Basic NT Security | 173 |
| Working with ACLs | 175 |
| Understanding the Security Descriptors | 176 |
| Understanding the ACEs | 177 |
| Working Directly with Windows NT Security | 178 |
| Checking User Permissions | 178 |
| Changing User Permissions | 183 |
| Auditing User Actions | 187 |
| Checking File and Directory Permissions | 192 |
| Changing File and Directory Permissions | 193 |
| Auditing Files and Directories | 195 |
| **Moving Your Applications to Windows 7** | **198** |

## CHAPTER 11: UNDERSTANDING THE USER ACCOUNT CONTROL — 201

| Understanding the UAC | 201 |
|---|---|
| Considering the Need for the UAC | 202 |
| Why It Isn't a Good Idea to Override the UAC | 202 |
| Developing Applications with Fewer Rights | 203 |
| Interacting with the UAC | 203 |

| Adding UAC Support to Your Application | 206 |
|---|---|
| Creating a Manifest | 207 |
| Executing as a Separate Process | 211 |
| Moving Your Applications to Windows 7 | 215 |

## CHAPTER 12: DEVELOPING APPLICATIONS WITH ENHANCED SECURITY — 217

| Considering Modern Application Security Requirements | 218 |
|---|---|
| Using Traditional NT Security | 218 |
| Using New NT Security Features | 218 |
| Working with Zones | 219 |
| Adding Security Roles | 221 |
| Adding Permissions | 221 |
| Working with Security Policies | 226 |
| Defining Your Application's Security Needs | 231 |
| Creating an Application with Enhanced Security | 233 |
| Developing for Zones | 234 |
| Developing for Security Roles | 236 |
| Developing for Permissions | 238 |
| Devising and Implementing a Security Policy | 242 |
| Configuring the ClickOnce Intranet Example | 242 |
| Debugging and Installing the ClickOnce Intranet Example | 243 |
| Configuring the ClickOnce Custom Example | 244 |
| Avoiding Too Much Security | 245 |
| Moving Your Applications to Windows 7 | 246 |

## CHAPTER 13: INTERACTING WITH THE BUILT-IN SECURITY FEATURES — 247

| Working with the Firewall | 248 |
|---|---|
| Interacting with the Firewall | 248 |
| Verifying the Firewall Status | 249 |
| Modifying a Setting | 255 |
| Adding and Deleting Ports | 258 |
| Adding Applications | 262 |
| Using the GPO Technique | 266 |
| Working with Automatic Updates | 274 |
| Configuring the Automatic Update Example | 275 |
| Writing the Settings Code | 275 |
| Writing the Update Code | 279 |

# CONTENTS

| | |
|---|---|
| **Accessing AppLocker** | **281** |
| Seeing the AppLocker Entries in the Registry | 281 |
| Configuring the AppLocker Demo Example | 282 |
| Reading AppLocker Entries | 282 |
| Creating an AppLocker Entry | 285 |
| **Moving Your Applications to Windows 7** | **290** |

## PART IV: ADVANCED WINDOWS 7 PROGRAMMING

### CHAPTER 14: WORKING IN THE BACKGROUND — 293

| | |
|---|---|
| **Advantages of Working in the Background** | **294** |
| **Developing Trigger-Start Services** | **296** |
| Triggering a Service | 297 |
| Obtaining the ServiceNative.CS File | 298 |
| Configuring the TriggerStartService Example | 299 |
| Writing Code for the TriggerStartService Example | 300 |
| Testing the TriggerStartService | 308 |
| **Providing Power Management** | **315** |
| Configuring the Power Management Example | 315 |
| Getting the Power Management State | 315 |
| Detecting a Change in Monitor State | 318 |
| **Implementing Application Restart and Recovery** | **319** |
| Configuring the Application Restart Example | 320 |
| Writing the Application Restart Example Code | 320 |
| **Working with the Network List Manager** | **323** |
| Configuring the Network List Manager Example | 324 |
| Writing the Network List Manager Code | 324 |
| **Moving Your Applications to Windows 7** | **327** |

### CHAPTER 15: USING THE WINDOWS 7 LIBRARIES — 329

| | |
|---|---|
| **Working with Known Folders** | **330** |
| Configuring the Known Folders Example | 332 |
| Writing the Known Folders Example Code | 332 |
| **Using Non-Filesystem Containers** | **335** |
| Configuring the Non-Filesystem Example | 336 |
| Writing the Non-Filesystem Example Code | 336 |
| **Considering User-Defined Collections** | **338** |
| Configuring the User-Defined Collection Example | 338 |
| Listing Libraries | 338 |
| Adding Libraries | 340 |

| | |
|---|---|
| Using the Explorer Browser Control | **341** |
|     Adding the Explorer Browser to Your Toolbox | 341 |
|     Configuring the Explorer Browser Example | 342 |
|     Writing the Explorer Browser Example Code | 343 |
| Moving Your Applications to Windows 7 | **345** |

## CHAPTER 16: WRITING 64-BIT APPLICATIONS FOR WINDOWS 7     347

| | |
|---|---|
| Considering the Advantages of 64-Bit Applications | **348** |
| Understanding the Requirements for 64-Bit Applications | **350** |
| Overcoming 64-Bit Development Issues | **351** |
|     Dealing with Programming Issues | 352 |
|     Accessing the Registry in Windows 7 | 352 |
|     Hosting Older DLLs | 353 |
| Writing a 64-Bit Application | **354** |
|     Configuring the Large-Number Example | 355 |
|     Working with the Configuration Manager | 356 |
|     Writing the Large-Number Example Code | 357 |
|     Running the Large-Number Test | 358 |
| Moving Your Applications to Windows 7 | **359** |

## CHAPTER 17: USING PARALLEL PROGRAMMING IN WINDOWS 7     361

| | |
|---|---|
| Considering the Advantages of Parallel Processing | **363** |
| Understanding the Requirements for Parallel Processing | **363** |
|     Evaluating the Task Length | 364 |
|     Evaluating the Task Type | 364 |
|     Considering Debugging | 365 |
|     Obtaining Required Resources | 365 |
|     Team Skills | 365 |
| Writing an Application that Relies on Parallel Processing | **366** |
|     Understanding the Parallel Class | 367 |
|     Configuring the Parallel Process Example | 368 |
|     Writing the Parallel-Process Example Code | 368 |
|     Debugging the Parallel-Process Example Code | 370 |
| Moving Your Applications to Windows 7 | **372** |

## CHAPTER 18: USING THE SENSOR AND LOCATION PLATFORM     373

| | |
|---|---|
| Defining the Sensor and Location Devices | **375** |
|     An Overview of the Sensor Categories | 375 |
|     Software Devices | 378 |

## Obtaining a List of Sensors — 379
Configuring the Get Sensors Example — 379
Writing the Get Sensors Code — 380
## Obtaining Specific Sensor Information — 385
Understanding the Geosense for Windows Data — 385
Configuring the Get Location Example — 386
Initializing the Sensor — 387
Creating and Handling Sensor Events — 388
Configuring Geosense for Windows Security — 390
Viewing Location Sensor Activity — 393
## Developing for Other Sensor and Location Devices — 394
## Moving Your Applications to Windows 7 — 394

## CHAPTER 19: USING WINDOWS XP MODE EFFECTIVELY — 397

### Considering Windows XP Mode — 398
Check for an Update — 398
Look for Third-Party Support — 399
Use the Compatibility Troubleshooter — 399
Change the Application Compatibility Settings Directly — 401
Use the Application Compatibility Toolkit — 402
Adjust User Account Control — 403
### Testing Your Application in Windows XP Mode — 404
Obtaining and Installing Windows XP Mode — 405
Configuring Windows XP Mode — 405
Using the Application in the Virtual Environment — 407
### Workarounds for Common Windows XP Mode Problems — 408
Resource Permission Issues — 408
Application Refuses to Use a Resource — 408
Virtual Environment Is Slow — 409
### Moving Your Applications to Windows 7 — 412

## PART V: WORKING AT THE COMMAND LINE

## CHAPTER 20: WORKING WITH WINDOWS POWERSHELL 2.0 — 415

### Replacing the Command Prompt — 416
Understanding the Need for Windows PowerShell — 416
Considering Why You Should Use PowerShell — 417
### Understanding PowerShell Command Basics for the Developer — 418
### Working with the Online Help — 421
### Understanding the Shell Property System — 424
### Moving Your Applications to Windows 7 — 438

## CHAPTER 21: CREATING SCRIPTS — 439

- Understanding When to Use Scripts — 440
- Using the PowerShell ISE — 441
- Writing a Basic Script — 444
- Performing Script Testing — 447
  - Using the PowerShell ISE Debugger — 448
  - Running the Script at the PS Prompt — 452
  - Defining a Company Policy for Scripts — 453
- Moving Your Applications to Windows 7 — 453

## CHAPTER 22: CREATING CMDLETS — 455

- Understanding When to Use Cmdlets — 455
- Creating a Shell Extension with the Make-Shell Utility — 457
- Writing a Basic Cmdlet — 460
  - Creating the Reverse-String.CS Example File — 460
  - Writing the Reverse-String.CS Example Code — 461
  - Compiling the Cmdlet Executable — 463
  - Using the Make-Shell Utility to Create the Shell — 464
  - Testing the New Shell — 465
- Moving Your Applications to Windows 7 — 467

## CHAPTER 23: INTERACTING DIRECTLY WITH POWERSHELL — 469

- Creating a Cmdlet Interface for Your Application — 470
  - Using the Built-In Cmdlets — 470
  - Using a Custom Cmdlet — 471
- Working with System Events — 472
- Using PowerShell for Application Status Information — 473
- Using PowerShell to Update Application Configuration — 475
- Performing Tasks from Remote Locations — 478
- Moving Your Applications to Windows 7 — 480

***INDEX*** — ***483***

# INTRODUCTION

**WINDOWS 7 HAS A CONSIDERABLE ARRAY** of new features to offer. Unlike some of the additions made to previous versions of Windows, these additions are substantial and not just eye candy. Using these features can make your application stand out. They make your application significantly easier to use and more responsive to user needs. In addition, many of the Windows 7 features also make your application more reliable and secure. Unfortunately, many of these features are also difficult to access and poorly documented, which is why you need the *Professional Windows 7 Development Guide*.

Did you know that Microsoft has made some substantial changes to the way some features work, but not really mentioned them? For example, Windows Management Instrumentation (WMI) has new functionality, and some older features no longer work because Microsoft has changed the security they depended on to function. The *Professional Windows 7 Development Guide* makes you aware of changes like this and provides the solutions you need to make your old applications work in the new Windows 7 environment.

You'll also find that Windows 7 is the first version of Windows 7 that truly feels comfortable to work with in the 64-bit environment. Of course, writing 64-bit applications requires a few changes to the way you write code. The *Professional Windows 7 Development Guide* provides the information you need to write 64-bit code from the Windows 7 perspective.

Of course, this book has a lot more to offer. You'll find all kinds of tips and techniques in this book that will make Windows 7 programming a lot easier and more productive. For example, you'll learn how to write code that uses multi-core processors efficiently in Windows 7 and discover how to make a progress bar appear on the Taskbar so that users know the status of a process in your application. Before long, you'll wonder why you didn't start moving your applications to Windows 7 even earlier.

## WHO SHOULD READ THIS BOOK

This book is for the professional developer. While it does include introductory sections, the pace of the introductory material is quite fast and the novice developer will tend to become lost. The book assumes that you have knowledge of the .NET Framework after working with C#. Some Windows 7 features don't work well with Visual Basic.NET, so this book is written to use C# as the base programming language. The examples do provide complete information on everything you need to include in the source code, so your knowledge of the .NET Framework doesn't have to be extensive, but some knowledge is helpful.

## HOW THIS BOOK IS ORGANIZED

The book is organized into Windows 7 functional areas, so that you can find the kind of application code you need quickly. Generally, each chapter covers one task or task group (such as Taskbar programming techniques). When a particular task or task group requires more than one chapter, the easier material normally appears first, followed by material that requires additional skills to understand. This book also requires use of a number of third-party libraries, the use of which is described in detail. You won't be left without the proper information on how to complete the example code. This book breaks the material into the following parts:

- **Introducing Windows 7:** This part of the book answers many of the questions that you probably expect, such as what features you'll find in Windows 7. You'll also find a guide that describes how to create a Windows 7 upgrade strategy. Windows 7 has so many new features that creating an upgrade strategy can prove daunting for many developers, so this book also provides some helpful tips on this process. Finally, this part of the book discusses the .NET Framework 4.0. Many of the Windows 7 features require that you use this new version of the .NET Framework.

- **Working with the Windows 7 User Interface:** The Windows 7 user interface is the first thing you'll notice when you boot up the operating system the first time. It looks gorgeous, but it's also quite functional. This part of the book helps you understand all these features and make use of new features such as Jump Lists. You may have noticed that right-clicking some Windows 7 applications displays a recent file list — you can add this functionality to your application, too, and this part of the book shows you how. This part also addresses new interface functionality such as the Ribbon interface, and it shows how to maximize use of Aero Glass in your applications. You'll even find a chapter about the Multi-Touch User Interface.

- **Developing Secure Applications:** Something the user will fail to notice but you can't miss are the significant changes in Windows 7 security. It's true that Microsoft relaxed security in some places to allow more applications to run unhindered, but that's only part of the story. In other areas, Microsoft has greatly tightened security or changed it altogether. You may suddenly find that your application doesn't work as well as it used to because it can't access resources or a resource isn't even available any longer. This part of the book makes you aware of all the latest security changes. In addition, you'll discover how to work with Windows 7 security features such as Windows Firewall. This part contains extensive code examples on adding, removing, and querying ports in the Windows Firewall that you won't find anywhere else.

- **Advanced Windows 7 Programming:** Many of the new Windows 7 features don't fit neatly into existing categories. You may have noticed the new Windows 7 Libraries feature, in which users can place documents and access them without consideration of the document's actual location. This part of the book includes code that shows how to add your application's files to the Libraries, so that you can place the document in a secure location, yet make it accessible to users who need it. You'll also discover new technologies such as trigger-start services,

64-bit application support, and parallel processing. This part even includes a chapter about the new sensor support that Windows 7 provides. Imagine being able to change the display so that it matches ambient lighting conditions. This is just one of many ways to use sensors, and this book tells you about the techniques for interacting with these sensors. Finally, you might have an application that simply doesn't like Windows 7, but you need to keep using it. There's also a chapter on using Windows XP Mode to keep that application running just a while longer.

➤ **Working at the Command Line:** The command line prompt that developers and administrators use today has been around since the days of DOS. In fact, the command line has commands that haven't changed since DOS was king. Unfortunately, the command prompt is hard to use and error-prone, so Microsoft has developed a new command prompt, Windows PowerShell. Windows 7 comes with Windows PowerShell 2.0, which fixes a lot of the problems with the first version. For example, Windows PowerShell 2.0 includes an editor so you can write code with greater ease and a debugger you can use to find errors in your code. This part of the book discusses Windows PowerShell in depth. In fact, you'll even learn how to create your own scripts and cmdlets.

## WHAT YOU NEED TO USE THIS BOOK

This is a Windows 7 programming book, so naturally, you need a copy of Windows 7. Using the Windows 7 Ultimate edition will give you access to the greatest number of features and let you use the greatest number of book examples. The Windows 7 Starter edition won't work for this book because it lacks Aero Glass functionality and most of the other features discussed in this book. If you want to write 64-bit examples, then you must have a 64-bit version of Windows 7. Otherwise, the 32-bit version of Windows 7 should work fine.

The book also assumes that you have a copy of Visual Studio 2010. You must have C# installed in order to work with the examples. The book was tested using Visual Studio 2010 Ultimate, but the examples should also work fine with Visual Studio 2010 Professional and Visual Studio 2010 Premium. The examples are unlikely to work with Express Edition products or special school edition products because these editions usually lack the required functionality.

You'll also need an Internet connection. Many of the examples require that you use third-party libraries that you'll need to download and install. Windows 7 has a lot of functionality that Microsoft only partially implemented in the .NET Framework 4.0, so these third-party libraries are essential to create working examples.

If you want to work with examples that require special hardware, such as sensors, then you need that hardware attached to your system. The sensor examples in Chapter 18 actually rely on a software sensor, so you can still work with that particular example if you don't have a special sensor attached to your system.

## CONVENTIONS USED IN THIS BOOK

To help you get the most from the text and keep track of what's happening, we've used some conventions throughout the book. Typical examples follow:

> Notes provide special information that you might find helpful. For example, a note might include a reference to a third-party product that will make your development efforts easier. In some cases, notes contain ancillary information that's nice to know, but not absolutely necessary. You can skip notes without losing anything — notes are simply there to provide a little extra information that you might not find elsewhere.

> A warning tells you that something terrible will happen should a particular event occur. For example, if you perform a task incorrectly, you might see data loss. Always read warnings carefully and think about them before you proceed in the book.

As for styles in the text:

- We *italicize* new terms and important words when we introduce them.
- We show keyboard strokes like this: Ctrl+A.
- We show filenames, URLs, and code within the text like so: persistence.properties.
- We show text you should type directly in this way: type **Hello** for regular text and type `MyFile.py` for code and filenames.
- We show text that you should replace with your own values in this way: *MyName* for regular text and `MyVariable` for code and filenames.
- We present code in the following way:

    ```
    We use a monofont type with no highlighting for most code examples.
    ```

- If some code is too long to fit on a single line in the book, but you need to type it in on a single line in your editor, we'll use a line continuation character like this:

    ```
    This code snippet is really very long and it won't fit on a single line in ↵
    the book so we use a line continuation character.
    ```

## SOURCE CODE

As you work through the examples in this book, you may choose either to type in all the code manually or to use the source code files that accompany the book. All the source code used in this book is available for download at http://www.wrox.com. Once at the site, simply locate the book's title (either by using the Search box or by using one of the title lists) and click the Download Code link on the book's detail page to obtain all the source code for the book. Code that is included on the Website is highlighted by the following icon:

 *Because many books have similar titles, you may find it easiest to search by ISBN; this book's ISBN is 978-0-470-88570-3.*

Once you download the code, just decompress it with your favorite tool. Alternately, you can go to the main Wrox code download page at http://www.wrox.com/dynamic/books/download.aspx to see the code available for this book and all other Wrox books.

## ERRATA

We make every effort to ensure that there are no errors in the text or in the code. However, no one is perfect, and mistakes do occur. If you find an error in one of our books, like a spelling mistake or faulty piece of code, we would be very grateful for your feedback. By sending in errata, you may save another reader hours of frustration and at the same time you will be helping us provide even higher quality information.

To find the errata page for this book, go to http://www.wrox.com and locate the title using the Search box or one of the title lists. Then, on the Book Search Results page, click the Errata link. On this page, you can view all errata that have been submitted for this book and posted by Wrox editors.

 *A complete book list including links to each book's errata is also available at www.wrox.com/misc-pages/booklist.shtml.*

If you don't spot "your" error on the errata page, click the Errata Form link and complete the form to send us the error you have found. We'll check the information and, if appropriate, post a message to the book's errata page and fix the problem in subsequent editions of the book.

## P2P.WROX.COM

For author and peer discussion, join the P2P forums at p2p.wrox.com. The forums are a Web-based system for you to post messages relating to Wrox books and related technologies and interact with other readers and technology users. The forums offer a subscription feature to e-mail you topics of interest of your choosing when new posts are made to the forums. Wrox authors, editors, other industry experts, and your fellow readers are present on these forums.

At http://p2p.wrox.com, you will find a number of different forums that will help you not only as you read this book, but also as you develop your own applications. To join the forums, just follow these steps:

1. Go to p2p.wrox.com and click the Register link.
2. Read the terms of use and click Agree.
3. Complete the required information to join as well as any optional information you wish to provide, and click Submit.
4. You will receive an e-mail with information describing how to verify your account and complete the joining process.

*You can read messages in the forums without joining P2P but in order to post your own messages, you must join.*

Once you join, you can post new messages and respond to messages other users post. You can read messages at any time on the Web. If you would like to have new messages from a particular forum e-mailed to you, click the Subscribe to this Forum icon by the forum name in the forum listing.

For more information about how to use the Wrox P2P, be sure to read the P2P FAQs for answers to questions about how the forum software works as well as many common questions specific to P2P and Wrox books. To read the FAQs, click the FAQ link on any P2P page.

# PART I
# Introducing Windows 7

- **CHAPTER 1:** Windows 7 Improvements
- **CHAPTER 2:** Developing a Windows 7 Strategy
- **CHAPTER 3:** Understanding .NET 4.0

# Windows 7 Improvements

**WHAT'S IN THIS CHAPTER?**

- Understanding the general perception of Windows 7
- Considering the developer-specific improvements in Windows 7
- Using Windows XP Mode to your advantage
- Working with Windows PowerShell 2
- Developing a process for moving your application to Windows 7

Many people are already hailing Windows 7 as the product Microsoft should have produced instead of Vista. It's true that Vista had more than a few problems, and that those problems remained even after several patches. Windows 7 is easier to use, more stable, and has more interesting features than Vista. In short, it's just a better version of Windows, and many users plan to upgrade. Of course, the user perspective doesn't tell the developer anything. Just because Windows 7 is a better product doesn't mean you should rush out a new version of your program to make use of Windows 7 functionality. In fact, many companies will take a wait-and-see approach — some of them to their detriment.

Windows 7 does include more than just a bit of a face lift and a few patches. As a developer, you'll find many of the changes in Windows 7 both exciting and necessary to robust application development. The new security features really do work, so using them in your application will make it more secure without affecting application performance and without garnering a host of hostile users, as Vista-specific applications have done. Features such as the ability to program the Taskbar are also much needed and helpful.

This chapter will provide you with an overview of what Windows 7 offers. It's not a Microsoft-sponsored essay on why you should upgrade to Windows 7, but rather something to consider as you make an informed decision about upgrading. For many developers, Windows 7 is a must-have upgrade because it truly does provide worthwhile functionality.

## IS WINDOWS 7 REALLY JUST VISTA FIXED?

One of the egregious features of Vista is the User Account Control (UAC). The feature is so terrible that you'll find more than a few articles devoted to disabling it (as an example, see `http://www.howtogeek.com/howto/windows-vista/disable-user-account-control-uac-the-easy-way-on-windows-vista/`). Vista used UAC as a bludgeon to coerce the user into senselessly clicking the OK button every time the permission-escalation dialog box appeared — the user ended up with a Pavlovian reaction — barely seeing the dialog box, just clicking it to get the application running. This makes the feature completely useless and counterproductive. (You can find more about Pavlov's experiments with conditioned response in dogs at `http://en.wikipedia.org/wiki/Ivan_Pavlov`.)

Windows 7 does fix this problem to a large degree. The UAC permission-escalation dialog box appears only when the user truly needs to approve an action by the operating system. This sort of change leads many developers to believe that Windows 7 is merely a patch to Vista. While Windows 7 does fix a number of interface, security, and development problems, and does contain all the latest patches, it provides significantly more functionality than a mere patch. Any thoughts you have of Windows 7 being the service pack that Microsoft should have released for Vista are simply wrong.

Many developers cringed at the compatibility issues present in Vista. In fact, application compatibility issues kept many organizations from even considering Vista as part of their upgrade path. Windows 7 does a significantly better job with compatibility. The built-in support provides better options for running existing applications. If your application won't run using this support, you can always download Windows XP Mode and run your application using a virtual machine (see the "Considering Windows XP Mode" section of this chapter for additional information). Most organizations are finding fewer applications that experience difficulty running under Windows 7, because Microsoft has relaxed a few of the security features and made other compatibility decisions that provide a friendlier environment. In short, Windows 7 provides more than a simple patch to the Vista compatibility problems — it provides a significant solution.

Developers rely on Windows to provide a certain level of application support out of the package. Vista often lacked support for proper drivers, and it had other issues that kept even well-behaved applications from running properly. Windows 7, even the 64-bit edition, comes with relatively complete drivers and other support for your applications. In fact, your users might not even notice that they're running on a 64-bit platform, should you choose the 64-bit edition.

## CONSIDERING THE MAJOR IMPROVEMENTS FROM A DEVELOPER PERSPECTIVE

Windows 7 provides significant new functionality that the developer will notice almost immediately. This chapter doesn't list every Windows 7 feature change. You can find a complete list at `http://windows.microsoft.com/en-US/windows7/products/features`. The following sections provide an overview of the features that most developers will want to at least consider adding or leveraging for their new applications and application updates.

## Understanding the User Interface Improvements

Windows 7 contains a significant number of user-interface improvements. For example, when you select an item on the Taskbar, you'll see a well-defined thumbnail for it, as shown in Figure 1-1. The functionality that Windows 7 provides for seeing what you need quickly is much improved over what Vista provided. Your application will have access to this kind of functionality even if you don't provide any additional code for it.

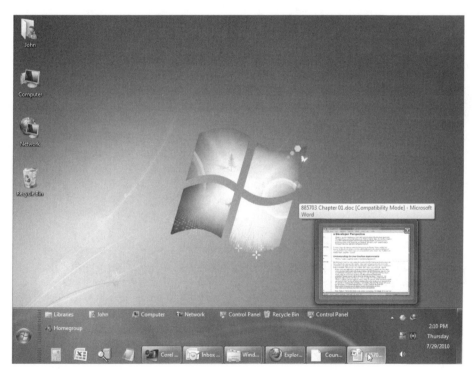

**FIGURE 1-1:** Windows 7 provides an improvement over the graphics in Vista.

In many cases, your application can use the Windows 7 graphics features automatically, but there are qualifications to consider. For example, the Snap feature described at http://windows.microsoft .com/en-us/windows7/products/features/snap helps users work more efficiently with applications. However, Snap won't work in many cases with applications that have custom window behaviors (see the caveat at http://windows.microsoft.com/en-us/windows7/Arrange-windows-side-by-side-on-the-desktop-using-Snap). Consequently, your application might work fine with Windows 7, yet the user might not be able to use all Windows 7 features when your application employs certain customizations. These customizations might appear helpful at first, but they can lead to inconsistent behavior that actually reduces user productivity. It's important to understand that the Windows 7 user interface adds gizmos the user will want to use but can only use when your application follows the rules. Check out the related URLs for Peek (`http://windows.microsoft.com/en-us/windows7/products/features/peek`) and Shake (`http://windows.microsoft.com/en-us/windows7/products/features/shake`).

Some Windows 7 user-interface features look automatic but aren't. For example, if you want your application to provide Jump Lists (`http://windows.microsoft.com/en-us/windows7/products/features/jump-lists`), you have to add the support to the application. In fact, there are a number of Windows 7 features that fall into this category, including, but not limited to:

➤ Jump Lists
➤ Progress Bars
➤ Custom Switchers
➤ Thumbnail Toolbars
➤ Overlay Icons

Chapters 4 and 5 provide the details needed to implement these features in your applications. These features and others fall into the Taskbar-improvement category that you can read about at `http://windows.microsoft.com/en-us/windows7/Whats-new-with-the-Windows-7-taskbar`. If you must select one area of improvement for your application, the Taskbar is the place to make the improvement because this makes the user significantly more efficient.

*Many of these new features require that you use the Aero Glass interface. Of course, that means having the required hardware support on your system. Unlike Vista, where Aero Glass was often eye candy and not much more, using Aero Glass in Windows 7 does provide opportunities to reduce user confusion, improve user efficiency, and reduce support costs. However, to get these improvements you have to make the required changes to your application.*

Another highly visible feature is the use of the Ribbon for many of the Windows 7 applications such as WordPad, shown in Figure 1-2. Chapter 7 also shows how to add the Ribbon to your applications. Support for using the Ribbon is built right into Windows 7, so it's always available to you. Many users find the Ribbon is easier and less confusing to use than the old menu and toolbar interface. (Power users often decry the Ribbon as a time waster, especially when working with applications that previously relied on a menu interface.)

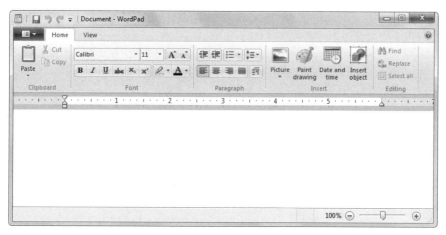

**FIGURE 1-2:** Adding a Ribbon interface to your applications is easier in Windows 7.

This has been an overview of some of the more popular user-interface additions. The rest of the book will show you how to incorporate a number of other user-interface features into your applications. For now, all you really need to know is that Windows 7 has a lot of new user-interface perks to offer.

## Considering the Security Improvements

Security is one of the more important topics today because there are more threats to your data, applications, network, and personal systems than ever before. Windows 7 adds more security to provide additional protection. However, it also takes a step back. Users found some of the security features in Vista draconian at best and impossible at worst. Microsoft has recognized that security features which users turn off because they dislike them aren't really security features. The current section of this chapter provides some highlights of the more important security improvements. You can see a complete overview of Windows 7 security at http://technet.microsoft.com/library/dd560691.aspx. Part III of the book focuses on security and how you can implement it in your applications.

Easing the number of times that the UAC asks the user for permission elevations is a priority for Windows 7. In reality, the UAC is a good feature because it alerts the user to potentially dangerous situations; you should encourage users to keep the UAC enabled. Smart programming on your part will keep the number of UAC requests to a minimum. In addition, you should ensure that your application doesn't request resources or access that it doesn't actually need. However, no matter how secure you make your application, there's a chance that someone will usurp control. If your application suddenly begins doing things you never designed it to do, you want the UAC to step in and alert the user to the problem. You'll discover more about the UAC in Chapter 11.

Enhanced auditing is another essential feature. The act of auditing provides you with information about user and application activity. Knowing what the system is doing helps you locate the source of security issues on a system, and auditing is a cornerstone of that process. You can add auditing features to your application. When your application tells the system what it's doing, it helps the system locate and destroy security threats.

Of course, your application still has access to standard Windows security (Chapter 10) and .NET-specific security (Chapter 12). In addition, your application will gain some security features automatically, including:

- Kernel patch protection
- Service hardening
- Data execution prevention
- Address space layout randomization
- Mandatory integrity levels

## Developing Extended Applications

Windows 7 allows you to extend your applications in some ways that users won't see directly, but which they will definitely appreciate as part of the usage experience. Extending your application isn't a requirement, of course, but once your organization begins to understand the power of Windows 7, you may decide that the benefits in speed and reliability are definitely worth the extra work. The following sections describe three kinds of extensions that many organizations are considering today.

### 64-bit Applications

Before Windows 7, you could work in a 64-bit environment, but it was painful. In fact, some people reported that the lack of device drivers and problems running older applications made the difficulties insurmountable. Windows 7 does provide a great 64-bit experience if your processor will support it. You can find a host of articles, such as the one at http://www.w7forums.com/windows-7-64-bit-vs-32-bit-t484.html, that describe the pros and cons of moving to 64 bits.

For the developer, the main reasons to move to 64 bits are memory and speed. A 64-bit application can access huge amounts of memory, up to 192 GB for most versions of Windows 7 (see http://msdn.microsoft.com/library/aa366778.aspx for the memory limits of each Windows 7 edition). In addition, using 64-bit registers makes it easier to optimize certain application activities, which means that your application runs faster. Chapter 16 tells you more about 64-bit programming.

### Parallel Processing

Most machines today come with multiple cores, which Windows treats as separate processors. The only problem is that most applications are still designed to use a single processor. Even if the application uses multiple threads, the method used to create it prevents Windows from executing the application on multiple processors. As a result, the application runs more slowly than it otherwise might if it could make use of those additional cores. This book doesn't provide you with a dissertation on exotic programming techniques such as functional programming (for details, see the article at http://www.devsource.com/c/a/Languages/Exploring-the-New-F-Language/).

However, Chapter 17 does get you started with parallel-programming techniques. You'll also want to check out the Parallel Computing Developer Center at http://msdn.microsoft.com/en-us/concurrency/default.aspx.

### Background Processing

Background processing is a technique developers have used for a while now to make the foreground task of an application run faster. While one thread prints a document in the background, another thread provides the user with continued access to application features in the foreground. Windows 7 provides improved functionality for creating and managing background processes. You can obtain white papers about these improvements at http://www.microsoft.com/whdc/system/pnppwr/powermgmt/backgroundprocs.mspx. Chapter 14 provides you with practical information about working with background tasks in Windows 7.

## CONSIDERING WINDOWS XP MODE

Some applications out there simply won't work in Windows 7. If you don't have the source code for all or part of the application, yet are tasked with making it work in Windows 7, you may have to resort to using Windows XP Mode. Essentially, Windows XP Mode is a virtual machine setup that you should avoid whenever possible. That said, real-world concerns often dictate that you need the application. When there isn't any alternative, you'll need to create a solution that incorporates Windows XP Mode to get your solution to run in Windows 7.

Windows XP Mode is a downloadable product and isn't part of Windows 7. You can find it at http://www.microsoft.com/windows/virtual-pc/download.aspx. Simply follow the steps on the site for obtaining your copy of Windows XP Mode and installing it on your system. You'll also want to review the resources on the Windows Virtual PC site at http://www.microsoft.com/windows/virtual-pc/. Of course, just getting Windows XP Mode installed and working with your application probably won't address the whole picture, especially if the older software you need is just part of an entire solution. Chapter 19 discusses techniques you can use to incorporate your Windows XP Mode application with the rest of Windows 7.

## DEVELOPING FOR WINDOWS POWERSHELL 2

Windows PowerShell has been an ongoing project. It first appeared as part of Vista, but you can download and add it to Windows XP as well. The main intent of Windows PowerShell is to provide a replacement for the aging command prompt. However, the command prompt has been around in some form since the days of DOS, and it's hard to overcome the prompt's incredible inertia simply because so many utilities are written for it. In fact, when moving from the 32-bit environment to 64 bits, you're far more likely to encounter a 16-bit command prompt utility that doesn't work on your system than you are to run into an aging Windows application. The command prompt continues to enjoy strong support with administrators because it provides the means to automate many tasks without a lot of effort. In addition, the command prompt can often accomplish tasks using a single command that would require many mouse clicks using the GUI.

Microsoft hopes to persuade more administrators to use Windows PowerShell in Windows 7 with the introduction of Windows PowerShell 2. This new version of Windows PowerShell offers a lot more in the way of utilities (called cmdlets). In addition, PowerShell now sports both a graphical interface and a debugger you can use to locate problems in cmdlets and scripts. Figure 1-3 shows the new Windows PowerShell Integrated Scripting Environment (ISE). If you work with multiple languages, Microsoft has provided multiple language support with the latest Windows PowerShell. In short, there's a lot to like with this release. You can find a complete list of the new features at http://technet.microsoft.com/library/dd367858.aspx.

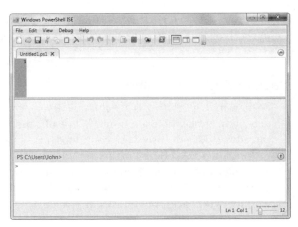

**FIGURE 1-3:** Windows PowerShell 2 now includes a graphical development environment.

Like administrators, developers will commonly use Windows PowerShell to automate tasks and perform standard tasks quickly. Developers will also like the idea of providing a command line interface to applications that use Windows PowerShell. Part V of this book focuses on tasks you can perform using Windows PowerShell. You'll see basic usage instructions in Chapter 20. Chapter 21 shows how to create scriptlets (a sort of batch file), while Chapter 22 shows how to build cmdlets. In Chapter 23 you'll find some advanced usage techniques, such as working with your cmdlets from a remote location. Although you won't get a full picture of everything that Windows PowerShell can do (you'd need an entire book to discover its full functionality), you'll obtain a basic understanding of the unique functionality it provides.

## MOVING YOUR APPLICATIONS TO WINDOWS 7

You'll definitely want to move your applications to Windows 7 at some point. Precisely when the move occurs depends on your organization's requirements. When you do make the move, you'll probably want to move to the 64-bit edition for a number of reasons. The most important is that the 64-bit edition provides access to additional memory. This edition truly is the path to the future, and it's probably a good idea to start working out any kinks in your application sooner rather than later. The main site to obtain information about moving your application to Windows 7 is at http://msdn.microsoft.com/en-us/windows/ee532070.aspx. Most developers will follow these steps to make the move to Windows 7 easier:

1. Review the Windows 7 and Windows Server 2008 R2 Application Quality Cookbook found at http://msdn.microsoft.com/library/dd371778.aspx. The Application Compatibility site at http://msdn.microsoft.com/library/bb757005.aspx discusses such topics as working in the 64-bit environment, UAC, and named pipe hardening. Your applications will need to address these requirements to work well within Vista and Windows 7. If your

application works on a server, make sure you pay special attention to the section on Issues Relevant to Windows Server 2008, especially the topic Application Compatibility: Windows Server 2008 Server Core. Server Core is a unique version of Windows Server 2008 that has special requirements — the tradeoff is that Server Core requires fewer resources and is both more reliable and more secure than other Windows Server 2008 editions.

2. Determine how to update your applications so they meet compatibility requirements. In some cases, you might decide to stop at this step because making the application compatible will prove difficult. In many cases, you can use the compatibility features provided by Windows 7 to run the existing application. Of course, if you're using the 64-bit edition, you won't be able to run any application that has any form of 16-bit support. This isn't a problem for Windows applications for the most part, but you might be surprised at the number of command line utilities that require 16-bit support and won't run any longer. If you encounter additional application compatibility questions during this process, check the Windows Application Compatibility site at http://msdn.microsoft.com/windows/aa904987.aspx. You can also ask questions on the Application Compatibility for Windows Development forum at http://social.msdn.microsoft.com/Forums/en-US/windowscompatibility/threads/. (The Windows 7 ISV Remediation Workshops site at http://readyset7.com/workshops/ is no longer available.) Chapter 2 provides additional information about developing a Windows 7 strategy. In some cases, you may want to remediate your application to use Windows XP Mode (see Chapter 19 for details).

3. Download or purchase the tools needed to rework your applications. You'll want these tools as a minimum:

    ➤ Windows SDK: http://msdn.microsoft.com/windows/bb980924.aspx

    ➤ Microsoft Application Verifier: http://www.microsoft.com/downloads/details.aspx?FamilyID=c4a25ab9-649d-4a1b-b4a7-c9d8b095df18

    ➤ Microsoft Application Compatibility Toolkit 5.5: http://www.microsoft.com/downloads/details.aspx?FamilyID=24da89e9-b581-47b0-b45e-492dd6da2971

    ➤ Microsoft Visual Studio 2010: http://www.microsoft.com/visualstudio

4. Install the tools on a Windows 7 test system. Use a test configuration of your application and not the production environment when developing the application update. It's important to have several accounts on your Windows 7 system. Make absolutely certain that you perform any testing using an account that has the same rights that your users will have. Otherwise, you won't find security and resource-access feature issues that could keep your application from running properly under Windows 7.

5. Work through each of the compatibility issues in your application. When you have an application that runs on a standard user account in Windows 7 without triggering any UAC messages (Chapter 11) or experiencing errors due to lack of resources or access (Chapter 10), it's time to perform your normal testing cycle with the update. At this point, you've completed a simple upgrade. Of course, you may decide to take advantage of special Windows 7 features, which means checking out Steps 6 and above.

6. (Optional) Update your application to use the new features in the .NET Framework 4.0. Chapter 3 helps you understand the advantages of working with this new version of the .NET Framework.

7. (Optional) Add new shell features such as programmable Taskbar support (Chapters 4 and 5).

8. (Optional) Add new interface features, such as a Ribbon interface (Chapters 6 and 7) and updated Aero Glass functionality (Chapter 8).

9. (Optional) Include an alternative user input such as the Multi-Touch User Interface (Chapter 9).

10. (Optional) Implement improved security functionality to keep your data and network safe (Chapters 12 and 13).

11. (Optional) Improve the functionality of your application in areas the user can't easily see. For example, consider using background tasks (Chapter 14), Windows 7 libraries (Chapter 15), and parallel-programming techniques (Chapter 17). Windows 7 is also a great 64-bit platform — consider making the move to 64 bits to gain the significant benefits that this environment can provide (see Chapter 16 for details). Even though the user won't directly see these improvements, the improved application performance will be obvious to everyone.

*Many organizations are placing increased emphasis on the command line. In many situations, the command line provides a fast method for configuring applications, managing users or system resources, and obtaining both application and system status. While it's possible to create perfectly acceptable applications that rely on the older CMD.EXE interface, Windows PowerShell has matured to the point that it provides a better command line environment. Part V of this book provides the information you need to work effectively with Windows PowerShell. This part of the book discusses techniques such as scripting and creating your own cmdlets to perform various application tasks.*

# Developing a Windows 7 Strategy

**WHAT'S IN THIS CHAPTER?**

➤ Defining a strategy that makes the user feel comfortable with the update

➤ Deciding how and when to move to Windows 7 from another version of Windows

Moving an application from an older version of Windows to Windows 7 might seem an obvious thing to do. However, making the move without a plan probably won't work very well. You have to create a strategy for moving the application, or you'll face delays and unexpected tensions. The source of most of these delays and tensions will be the people who actually benefit the most from the move: the users who work with the application every day. Most users don't care anything about your application — they care only about getting their work done. Any time you change something, it means they must focus attention away from their work to your application, and most are going to be hostile about the disruption of their schedules.

Another consideration is whether you should even move your application to Windows 7. You may find that the application is impossible to move, or that the amount of coding required to make the move is prohibitive. In some cases, it might actually be easier to create a new application, rather than attempt to recreate an existing application to work in the Windows 7 environment. This is especially true if you plan to make some major changes, such as moving from the 32-bit to the 64-bit environment.

This chapter provides an overview of some issues you need to consider as part of formulating a strategy to move your application. By the time you complete this chapter, you should have a better idea of how to accede to user demands and keep your project within budget. You may also have a compelling reason for persuading management to start from scratch or use an alternative strategy such as Windows XP Mode.

*You may very well decide to use any of a number of prescribed engineering approaches to moving the application. This chapter won't replace books devoted to the topic of software engineering approaches. If you already have a strategy in place, then you can easily skip this chapter and move on to the next topic. This chapter is designed to help anyone who doesn't already have a strategy in place and really needs to consider one before making any code changes.*

## DETERMINING THE USER WINDOWS 7 COMFORT LEVEL

Developers are constantly amazed that users don't really care about their applications. After all, the developer has put an enormous amount of effort into creating the application to meet user needs. Unfortunately for the developer's ego, what users care about is getting their work done, going home, and doing something (anything) other than work. If you try to move your application without considering the user's comfort level, the move is almost certainly doomed to failure. The following sections describe some issues you must consider before moving to Windows 7.

## Defining Usage Requirements

There's always something wrong with an application — something it fails to do or something it doesn't do quite right. Ask any five users what they feel is wrong with the application, and you'll receive five different answers. The users aren't being contrary. Humans tend to perceive things differently from each other, so it's no wonder that every user will have a different list of things that are wrong with an application. No matter how contrary your users may seem, addressing these perceived application deficiencies is important if you want to perform an upgrade properly. You can group common imperfections into the following categories:

➤ **Common problems:** Some applications have a common problem — one that everyone complains about. Perhaps it's how the application handles printing or saves data. In most cases, common problems are high priority because solving them has the potential to offer the greatest return in user satisfaction and efficiency. Some developers will write off these kinds of problems as not being worth fixing, but any common problem requires at least some consideration.

➤ **Innovative uses:** Users work with the application every day and often see ways to make the application more efficient — ways that would never occur to the developer. Even if the user doesn't know precisely how to present or implement an innovative feature, the developer should take time to work with the user and iron out innovative details when the feature truly presents a good application addition.

➤ **New requirements:** Everything grows and changes, including companies. As a company grows, the requirements for the applications it uses also change. It's important to differentiate between short-term and long-term changes, however, and make application updates that reflect long-term needs. Otherwise, you may find yourself removing the new feature a short time after you add it.

- **Antiquated functionality:** Museums love antiques, users don't. It's important to remove old features that users no longer require because these features often get in the way and make the user less efficient. In addition, older features can increase training costs and reduce application performance (reliability, speed, and security).

One problem with most requirement listings is that the authors tend to focus on the negative. In some cases, an upgrade can actually reduce user satisfaction by changing a feature that users really like. When defining usage requirements, you should consider asking users to define as many positive features for an application as negative features. Promoting a look at the positive will help users see the application as the complex undertaking it is and reduce failure potential by helping others see the upgrade as doable. Here are some common ways to group application strengths:

- **Easy keyboard usage:** It's amazing to see some users bang away at an application. The developer could never do things that quickly, even though the developer understands the inner workings of the application better. Most high-speed users rely on the keyboard — the mouse is way too slow. Any developer who changes the familiar keyboard combinations is likely to be hanged by bands of hostile users.

- **Reliable operation:** Users may not use the term "reliable" precisely, but a feeling of reliability is what you want to hear in the feedback. Make sure you understand the user's definition of reliable. For one user, reliable might mean that the application never breaks, but for another user it might mean that the application works consistently (even if it does break from time to time). Reliable application operation, no matter what form it takes, is always desirable because it makes the user happy, reduces support costs, and enhances user productivity.

- **Innocuous security:** Most users hate security because it gets in the way of accomplishing the task. Even entering a name and password is too much for some users. Anything that tends to keep the user from getting work done is unnecessary from the user's perspective. The best kind of security is the security that the user can't see, but that still keeps the data and user safe from harm. Upgrades should never disturb a security feature that already works well.

- **Feels peppy:** From the user perspective, speed is relative. It's possible to improve actual application speed, yet make it feel slower to the user. When this situation occurs, the developer says the application is faster, yet the user balks at the change the developer has made. It's important that applications feel fast to the user, even if the application isn't actually as fast as you could make it.

- **Understandable:** What's understandable to the developer probably isn't to the user. Most developers can simply look at interfaces and understand how they work because developers spend so much time creating them. A typical user doesn't spend any more time learning an interface than absolutely necessary because interfaces don't accomplish work. If a group of users tells you that they truly understand something, keep it in place because an understandable interface is truly rare.

## Considering Training Requirements

Training costs money. It sounds like a simple statement, but many developers don't take training into account. If you make a change to an application that requires additional user training, then the only way to make that update pay for itself is to make the user more efficient, productive, or reliable. In short, the company must gain something of value from the training time other than simply showing the user how to work with a new application feature. New isn't better unless it results in a tangible benefit, which usually means something you can put a dollar value on. In fact, some companies are now asking the developer to provide an estimate of how long it will take the new feature to pay for itself. If a new feature lets a user work twice as fast, then it will eventually pay for the cost of the upgrade, plus the cost of the training required to get the user up to speed.

When you consider training costs, you must also evaluate support requirements. Some users won't really attend training sessions, not even if you physically tie them up and drag them to the room where the training takes place (yes, the body is there, but the mind isn't). In some cases, users will simply think about the barbecue they're having this weekend or the next presentation they must make. They'll think of anything but the new feature you're trying to tell them about because they simply don't care about your application. As a result, the user is likely to call support for help with the new feature, usually five minutes after the training session that told how to use the new feature. You must add some amount of money into your estimate for support costs in addition to the training costs.

Even though you may not consider application help as part of training, it is. Every time the user accesses help, the help file presents a lesson that the user relies upon to perform a task. There is no physical teacher present, but the lesson that a help file writer has prepared is present. If the lessons the help file teaches don't match the application, then the user won't receive the required training and the costs of hiring someone to perform the training in person increase. Because a help file is an inexpensive means of training a user to perform certain tasks, updating the help file should be a priority for your team. Help files can't replace human trainers in many situations, but a great help file can significantly reduce training costs by freeing trainers to provide lessons on difficult or complex tasks.

*The easiest way to keep support costs down is to have interested users involved in the upgrade process. Even if a user's participation is limited to e-mail conversations about new features that the user would like to see, you'll get some feedback that makes the user feel like part of the process. With luck, users will tell you whether a feature works well for them and will perform other tasks as well (such as testing). In addition, users trained during the upgrade process will provide assistance to users who begin using the application after you move it to production. Try to have users from every area of the organization involved in the process. Use interested users, rather than dragging users into the process kicking and screaming. This gets better feedback and ensures that the users actually do use the upgrade as you've created it.*

## Keeping the User Happy

The bottom-line consideration for many updates is keeping the user happy, no matter what your other goals might be. It's certainly important to meet organizational goals and keep the application updated, but an application that doesn't receive some level of user approval won't work because the user won't use it. Some organizations have created absolutely amazing applications that never met any of the goals expected of them because users ended up using other applications that they liked better (or they simply sidestepped using the application at all). Most applications replace some process that's already in place, so the user always has the option of continuing to use the original process. Here are some techniques you can use to keep the user happy:

- Ask the user's opinion.
- Get user feedback as you create the update.
- Keep users informed about application progress in a way that excites them about it.
- Explain why certain updates are required and get user input on alternative implementations when necessary.
- Involve the user in testing the update.

## CONSIDERING WHETHER TO MOVE

There's little doubt that your organization will make the move to Windows 7 at some point, unless you decide to wait for Windows 8 (a definitely risky procedure, considering that Microsoft has dropped support for Windows XP). The point is that if you're using Windows XP today, you'll be using a newer version of Windows sometime in the near future. However, moving to a new version of Windows doesn't necessarily mean that an application will make the move or that you'll use new Windows features as the result of an upgrade. Your strategy might be to create a compatible environment for the existing application while you write a new application specifically designed for Windows 7. It's important to come up with a strategy that works best for your organization. The following sections discuss some Windows 7-specific issues you should consider before (and while) you make the move.

### Testing Issues in Your Application

Before you can formulate an update strategy, you need to know about the update challenges. Most developers will realize the need for testing immediately and begin working on a test suite to check the application. However, you must perform your tests under controlled conditions or the results you obtain will be suspect or misleading. For example, testing the application using a development account won't tell you anything because developers aren't commonly users. In order to test the application, you must create a realistic user account and use it for testing purposes. In fact, you need to create a list of user categories and test the application once for each category. A manager account could produce errors that a manufacturing user would never see. Here are some Windows 7 issues to consider as you test:

- **User interface:** The Aero Glass interface presents some challenges to the developer. For example, one developer relied on title bar hints to convey information to the user — these hints no longer worked in Windows 7. You need to check everything from icons to controls when performing your test. Don't assume that any element of the interface will work as intended, because Windows 7 definitely presents some surprises.

- **Accessibility:** Users with special needs shouldn't have any concerns when moving to Windows 7, but it pays to check. For example, your application may no longer size correctly when the user relies on a large font, or it may not look right when the user switches to one of the high-contrast themes. Make sure all the accessibility features still work as anticipated.

- **Security:** As the Internet has become less secure, and devious people have become more adept, Windows has had to become more secure. Some Windows 7 security is almost invisible, but other forms of security will definitely impede user progress. It's important to update your application to produce as little visible security as possible to keep users from simply ignoring it.

- **Resource access:** As part of the security update and because of some driver differences, you can't assume that your application will have the same access to resources it had when working with Windows XP. Make sure you check access to every type of resource as part of the testing process.

- **64-bit compatibility:** Your application may behave differently in the 64-bit environment than it does in the 32-bit one. It's important to test the application in both environments because Windows 7 is definitely headed toward 64-bit computer usage.

- **Help functionality:** One of the features that developers commonly fail to test (or test fully) is the Help system. Microsoft has made more than a few changes in Help over the years. In fact, some versions of Help that worked fine in Windows 95 and marginally in Windows XP won't work at all in Windows 7. Make sure you test the Help system for your application completely — both direct help and context-sensitive help.

- **Driver or hardware incompatibility:** Drivers and hardware support are less of an issue in Windows 7 than for upgrades such as Vista. Even so, Windows 7 relies on a new driver model, and users are bound to have new kinds of hardware attached to their systems. Consequently, you must test your application to ensure it works well in the new environment.

After developer testing is over, you need to create another test suite. In this case, you use the results of the developer testing to create a test procedure for real-world users. Make sure you have at least one user for each user category, or the test results won't be complete. Users work differently with applications than developers do. Consequently, users will likely find problems that a developer would never find, simply because the user lacks knowledge the developer has and the developer lacks knowledge the user has. For example, the developer might not realize that the user normally orders several parts together because one part is useless without the other. The combination of part orders could trigger an error that the developer would never see, but the user will always see because the user always orders the parts together.

## Defining the Advantages of Moving to Windows 7

Part of your Windows 7 application update strategy will probably involve using some new controls. Most developers will swoon over the new controls in Windows 7, but most users won't notice until you point them out, and then they're likely to say something like, "So what?" Features such as Jump Lists will definitely make applications easier to use, but don't expect users to get too excited about them. Instead of focusing on the control, what you really need to do is focus on how the control will accomplish work faster or with greater ease. In fact, it's probably a waste of time even to mention the control name. When users do react positively to the ways in which the new controls will help them, you can use their input to define how you plan to use Windows 7 features to your advantage.

Some new Windows 7 features won't require any input from users unless you use the feature in a way that will attract user notice. For example, you can easily add new security features to your application, and as long as the security is invisible (or nearly so) you probably won't need to mention it to the user. In fact, when it comes to security, the less the user knows, the better. The same holds true for parallel programming and other features the user won't normally see. In general, the less the user knows about these hidden features, the better. Sometimes, a simple mention of one of these background features will elicit negative feedback; even when the change isn't noticeable, some users will claim to see a negative effect.

Whether you use some new feature, such as the Ribbon, depends on how you plan to change the application. A new application could certainly use the Ribbon to good effect. However, based on the continued grousing by power users about the Ribbon in Office, it might be a good idea to avoid such a prominent change in your own application unless you truly love a good battle.

Whatever new features you plan to use, your strategy should define some tangible reason for using it. In most cases, a monetary return is the easiest reason to sell and the easiest to prove after you complete the project. However, whenever you can demonstrate a security, reliability, or speed improvement, management is likely to approve the change. Defining a change as simply looking nice will never prove successful. Even if management approves the change, you'll likely find that the user gripes later, placing you in the position of having to remove the change or trying to sell the user on it as well.

## Working with Windows XP Mode

You may decide not to move your application to Windows 7 at all. In this case, you can use Windows XP Mode to make it appear to the application that it still resides on a Windows XP machine. However, don't be fooled. The application is still running on a virtual machine with several additional layers between it and the resources it needs. You must test your application to ensure it actually works in Windows XP Mode. It's important to test the application using the same criteria described in the "Testing Issues in Your Application" section of the chapter.

Your users probably won't know how to work with a virtual machine. In addition to testing the application, you must determine how to configure user support for the new environment. It's important to consider training and support costs as part of the Windows XP Mode update. These are going to be a lot less than the cost of updating your application, but you still have to consider them as part of your determination of whether it's viable to update your application or not. In some cases, the costs of using Windows XP Mode may persuade you to make the update after all.

## MOVING YOUR APPLICATIONS TO WINDOWS 7

This chapter has provided a brief overview of the requirements for creating a Windows 7 application movement strategy. The most important fact you can take from this chapter is that moving your application without a concrete strategy, one that considers both the user requirements and current application status, is doomed to failure.

In addition to the information found in this chapter, you need to apply general software engineering principles. For example, you must consider the skills of your development team and have a great software design in place. Make sure you rely on a solid development methodology, such as Agile (http://en.wikipedia.org/wiki/Agile_software_development), to help ensure project success. *C# Design and Development*, by John Paul Mueller, Wrox 2009, provides the details you need to create a useful software design for your upgrade. Before you move to the next chapter, make sure you have a stable strategy in place.

Windows 7 development doesn't require use of the .NET Framework 4.0 (http://msdn.microsoft.com/library/w0x726c2.aspx), but it certainly helps to use the updated features that this new version of the .NET Framework provides. You'll want to spend some time considering use of the .NET Framework 4.0 as part of your upgrade process. In addition to making it easier to use new Windows 7 features, the .NET Framework 4.0 includes a number of patches, enhanced security, and other features you'll want to use when creating your new or updated application.

# 3
# Understanding .NET 4.0

**WHAT'S IN THIS CHAPTER?**

➤ Defining the reasons you want to use the .NET Framework 4.0

➤ Getting your own copy of the .NET Framework 4.0

➤ Installing the .NET Framework 4.0

➤ Understanding how the .NET Framework 4.0 extends Windows 7

All managed applications depend on some form of the .NET Framework. Early versions of the .NET Framework were quite limited, but as the library has matured, Microsoft has added more functionality to it until today you can create extremely complex applications using managed code. In addition, more languages than ever before rely on the .NET Framework for support. You can even combine multiple languages such as C# and F# in the same application. (For details about F#, see the article at `http://www.devsource.com/c/a/Languages/Exploring-the-New-F-Language/`.)

Microsoft naturally wants you to use the .NET Framework 4.0 for all your development efforts, so you'll find that it has provided the usual resources. The main .NET Framework 4.0 resource page is at `http://msdn.microsoft.com/library/w0x726c2.aspx`. This chapter also will provide you with a good overview of the .NET Framework 4.0, although it doesn't describe every feature. The emphasis of this chapter is on the features that you'll use when creating new Windows 7 applications and updating existing applications. With this in mind, the chapter begins with an overview of why you need the .NET Framework 4.0 on your system (assuming you don't already have it installed). The chapter also discusses how you can obtain and install your own copy of the .NET Framework 4.0.

The focus of this chapter — the most important part if you don't want to read everything — is the last section, which describes how the .NET Framework 4.0 extends Windows 7. There are four ways in which it extends Windows 7 with regard to this book:

- User interface
- Security
- New or updated features such as 64-bit programming and the use of sensors
- Added command line support for Windows PowerShell 2.0

## UNDERSTANDING WHY YOU NEED .NET 4.0

As with every version of the .NET Framework, Microsoft has made improvements in the .NET Framework 4.0 that offer some new features, added stability, improved support for Win32 API functionality, and backward compatibility with previous versions of the .NET Framework. From a Windows 7 perspective, the bottom line is that you need the .NET Framework to gain easy access to new Windows 7 functionality. The following sections provide an overview of the various .NET Framework 4.0 features. You'll find that many of these features are items that developers have requested from Microsoft.

*Even though you aren't required to use the .NET Framework 4.0 to create a Windows 7 application, there aren't any good reasons to expend the extra effort creating an application using an older version of the .NET Framework. In fact, it's quite likely that you'll have the .NET Framework 4.0 installed on your machine at some point. For example, installing Visual Studio 2010 automatically installs the .NET Framework 4.0 on your system as a prerequisite. Because this book relies on Visual Studio 2010 and Windows 7 as the development platform, it also assumes that you have the .NET Framework 4.0 installed. If you choose not to install the .NET Framework 4.0, some of the examples won't work. In addition, none of the downloaded code will work in older versions of Visual Studio without modification.*

### Defining Application Compatibility and Deployment

Microsoft strives to maintain backward compatibility whenever possible. If you compiled your application using an older version of the .NET Framework, Microsoft isn't going to suddenly insist that you run it using a new version of the .NET Framework. In fact, as any developer knows, an application designed to work with an older version of the .NET Framework will often encounter problems when running with a new version of the .NET Framework. As usual, the .NET Framework 4.0 has some potential application-breaking changes in these areas:

- Security
- Third-party standards compliance

➤ Framework standards adherence and compliance (correctness)
➤ Garbage collection
➤ Reliability
➤ Speed

*You may find that your application doesn't work after you rebuild it using the .NET Framework 4.0. In fact, Microsoft seems to be expecting that some applications will encounter problems. Most applications will run, but if you're doing something exotic, especially using P/Invoke, you should expect to perform some upgrades. If you find that your application doesn't work, make sure you tell Microsoft about the problem at Microsoft Connect (*`http://go.microsoft.com/fwlink/?LinkId=154815`*). However, don't just tell Microsoft the application doesn't work. Provide as many specifics as you can, including sample code that shows precisely how your application failed.*

Fortunately, Microsoft provides a technique for testing your application for compatibility with the .NET Framework 4.0. Simply use the process outlined in the article at `http://msdn.microsoft.com/library/dd889541.aspx`. Once you've determined the compatibility level of your application, you can make decisions about the upgrade process. There are a number of features not covered in this chapter, such as additional platforms for the Client Profile and in-process side-by-side execution (see `http://msdn.microsoft.com/library/cc656912.aspx` and `http://msdn.microsoft.com/library/ee518876.aspx` for details).

*Many developers have limited their definition of performance to speed. However, an application is more than simply speed. When an application performs well, it does so quickly, reliably, and securely. Consequently, this book uses the term "performance" to mean the combination of speed, reliability, and security within an application.*

Some of the application-breaking changes are interesting because you might never encounter them. For example, the .NET Framework 4.0 uses background garbage collection, rather than concurrent garbage collection, to obtain better performance from your system. Normally, your application won't encounter any problems when using the new form of garbage collection. However, if your application is one of the few that perform some garbage collection tasks manually, you could definitely see some compatibility issues. Unfortunately, the source of these compatibility issues won't be obvious. When faced with an odd or unknown compatibility problem, make sure you also explore new *core features* that Microsoft has added to the .NET Framework 4.0.

## Considering the New Core Features and Improvements

Microsoft has included a host of new core features. A core feature affects the .NET Framework as a whole. For example, changing the way garbage collection works would affect every application created with the .NET Framework. You'll also use most of these changes. The following sections describe some of the most interesting core features from a Windows 7 perspective.

*There are many core features that this chapter doesn't cover, such as globalization improvements and the culture-sensitive formatting found in* `System.TimeSpan`. *In addition, changes to classes such as* `System.IntPtr` *and* `System.UIntPtr` *are better covered in a discussion of P/Invoke programming techniques. There are also changes to ASP.NET and Windows Presentation Foundation (WPF). Make sure you review the Microsoft resources found in this chapter to obtain a complete listing of all of the .NET Framework 4.0 changes. A small change might make a big difference in how your application works or how you update it to improve its responsiveness to user requests.*

### Using the Performance and Diagnostics Features

The performance and diagnostic features will make it possible to monitor the application at the application domain level, rather than at the process level. This means you'll be able to locate problems with your application far easier and fine-tune it better. To ensure you get application domain monitoring only when you need it, there's a new `AppDomain.MonitoringIsEnabled` property (described at http://msdn.microsoft.com/library/system.appdomain.monitoringisenabled.aspx).

Diagnostic improvements also let you access Event Tracing for Windows (ETW) events. These events provide you with detailed diagnostic information that can help you locate everything from subtle errors to sources of content that keep your application from running as it should. You can read more about ETW events at http://msdn.microsoft.com/library/dd264810.aspx. The Controlling .NET Framework Logging article at http://msdn.microsoft.com/library/dd264809.aspx provides you with procedures for capturing and using ETW events.

### Understanding Updated Code Contracts

Code contracts are normally defined using the method's signature. However, in the .NET Framework 4.0, you can now use other criteria to define a contract, such as preconditions and post-conditions. Some of these contract conditions can become pretty exotic, and you should use them only when necessary. Of course, a change of this sort always makes your code .NET Framework 4.0-specific. You can read about code contracts at http://msdn.microsoft.com/library/dd264808.aspx.

## Ridding Your Application of PIAs

The Component Object Model (COM) will remain with Windows forever. Too many developers have created too many components for COM to go away unless Windows undergoes significant changes. For this reason, Microsoft is constantly changing the way COM interaction works in the .NET Framework to make things easier for the developer. In the past, developers always had to ship Primary Interop Assemblies (PIAs) with their applications for COM interaction. The .NET Framework 4.0 can now embed the COM-type information into the application, negating the PIA requirement. There's a good explanation of this feature at `http://msdn.microsoft.com/library/ee317478.aspx` and `http://msdn.microsoft.com/library/3y76b69k.aspx`.

## Working with the DLR

One of the most exciting additions to the .NET Framework is the Dynamic Language Runtime (DLR), which provides support for dynamic languages such as IronPython. Dynamic languages provide a number of benefits such as the ability to enter several statements and execute them immediately to obtain feedback. Using a dynamic language also provides easier refactoring and code modification because you don't have to change static definitions throughout your code. It's even possible to call functions you haven't implemented yet and add an implementation later in the code when it's needed. Don't get the idea that dynamic languages are new. In fact, they've been around for a very long time. Examples of other dynamic languages include the following:

- LISP (List Processing)
- Smalltalk
- JavaScript
- PHP
- Ruby
- ColdFusion
- Lua
- Cobra
- Groovy

Dynamic languages are also elegant when it comes to performing certain tasks such as processing lists. Let's look at a quick example. Say you want to create an array of names in a function and pass them back to a caller. Here's the C# code to perform the task:

```
public String[] GetNames()
{
    String[] Result = new String[4];
    Result[0] = "John";
    Result[1] = "Amy";
    Result[2] = "Jose";
    Result[3] = "Carla";
    return Result;
}
```

```
public void ShowNames()
{
    String[] TheNames = GetNames();

    foreach (String Name in TheNames)
    {
        Console.WriteLine(Name);
    }
}
```

The code in `GetNames()` creates an array of `String`, fills it with names, and returns those names to the caller, `ShowNames()`. At this point, `ShowNames()` uses a `foreach` loop to display each name individually. Now take a look at the same functionality written in IronPython:

```
def GetNames():
    return "John", "Amy", "Jose", "Carla"

def ShowNames():
    for Name in GetNames():
        print Name
```

The code performs the same task in both cases, but as you can see, the IronPython code is significantly shorter. In addition, the IronPython code is actually easier to read. Interestingly enough, dynamic languages mix quite easily with static languages such as C# and Visual Basic, so you can use each language to carry out the tasks that the language is best suited to perform.

This book isn't designed to tell you everything about working with dynamic languages. If you're truly interested in working with IronPython, see *Professional IronPython* by John Paul Mueller, Wrox 2010.

## Detecting 64-bit Operating Systems

If you really want to support 64-bit applications, you must:

➤ Create separate 32-bit and 64-bit versions of your application

➤ Support 64-bit platforms alone

➤ Configure your application to detect the underlying operating system and load the appropriate support

Two properties, the `Environment.Is64BitOperatingSystem` (http://msdn.microsoft.com/library/system.environment.is64bitoperatingsystem.aspx) and `Environment.Is64BitProcess` (http://msdn.microsoft.com/library/system.environment.is64bitprocess.aspx), make it significantly easier to detect and interact with the underlying operating system and other processes on the target machine. These properties are just one more example of Microsoft's emphasis on 64-bit applications in Windows 7.

Of course, when you're working with a 64-bit application, you also want to provide 64-bit access to resources. The registry is one of the resources that could prove problematic. Fortunately, the .NET Framework 4.0 also provides 64-bit access to the registry through the `Microsoft.Win32.RegistryView` enumeration (http://msdn.microsoft.com/library/microsoft.win32.registryview.aspx). You use this enumeration to control how the .NET Framework opens registry keys.

## Working with the Managed Extensibility Framework

The Managed Extensibility Framework (MEF) is a stimulating addition to the .NET Framework because it means that you can begin treating an application as a box or perhaps a host that accepts modules that define a personality. MEF is an extension of ideas such as the Microsoft Management Console (MMC), where the MMC application acts as a host for snap-ins. However, MEF performs its task without the usual baggage that solutions such as MMC have — you don't have to jump through hoops and resort to highly customized application development to realize your goal. You use the MEF to:

- Define points where someone else can extend an application
- Expose services that other applications can use to extend themselves
- Offer resources that other applications can consume as a resource

The `System.ComponentModel.Composition` namespace (http://msdn.microsoft.com/library/system.componentmodel.composition.aspx) contains the classes, interfaces, and enumerations you use to implement MEF. The article at http://msdn.microsoft.com/library/dd460648.aspx provides an overview of precisely what MEF can do for you. MEF is so important that it has a community site at http://mef.codeplex.com/, where you can obtain resources such as white papers to help you develop MEF solutions.

## Implementing Parallel Computing

Modern systems come with multi-core processors that Windows sees as a multi-processor platform. Users want to see a result, in the form of enhanced application speed, from these multi-core machines, but obtaining that result is difficult. Parallel programming is a tricky skill to acquire. The problem is simple — state. When you use two or more processors to accomplish a task, you can't depend on any processor having the state information your application requires to execute. Up until now, an application could execute procedural code and depend on the processor's knowing the location of the application's data in memory, the result of the last step, location of the application code, and so on. When working with multiple processors, you can no longer depend on any given processor having such information available. As a consequence, developers commonly have to worry about the preservation of state information in some other way by using various threading techniques, which are error-prone at best.

Fortunately, there are less error-prone solutions for the developer than threading. Newer programming techniques such as PLINQ (Parallel Language Integrated Query) can help in a parallel-programming situation (*LINQ for Dummies*, John Paul Mueller, Wiley 2008, tells you more about working with LINQ). You can also rely on dynamic languages such as IronPython to perform the task. Of course, both these solutions still run counter to the way most developers currently write code.

The .NET Framework 4.0 offers a new alternative to the problem of parallel programming, one that works with the developer, in the form of the `System.Threading.Tasks` namespace (http://msdn.microsoft.com/library/system.threading.tasks.aspx). As with PLINQ and dynamic languages, you create tasks without having to spend time considering how the application maintains state information. All you do is create an asynchronous task and let the .NET Framework do the heavy lifting for you. An article at http://msdn.microsoft.com/library/dd460693.aspx tells you more about how this new namespace works.

## Considering Networking

The .NET Framework 4.0 provides a significant number of networking improvements, some of which you get automatically when you update your code and others that you have to add manually to your code. The following list provides an overview of these networking enhancements.

- **Improved security:** As with all other parts of the .NET Framework and Windows 7 in general, security has taken center stage. Check out these classes for additional information:
    - `System.Net.HttpWebRequest` (http://msdn.microsoft.com/library/system.net.httpwebrequest.aspx)
    - `System.Net.HttpListener` (http://msdn.microsoft.com/library/system.net.httplistener.aspx)
    - `System.Net.Mail.SmtpClient` (http://msdn.microsoft.com/library/system.net.mail.smtpclient.aspx)
    - `System.Net.Security.SslStream` (http://msdn.microsoft.com/library/system.net.security.sslstream.aspx)
    - `System.Net.Security.NegotiateStream` (http://msdn.microsoft.com/library/system.net.security.negotiatestream.aspx)
- **Superior Network Address Translation (NAT) support:** The .NET Framework has had NAT support for a long time, of course, but the Internet is moving to IPv6, so the .NET Framework 4.0 makes working with IPv6 considerably easier (see the article at http://msdn.microsoft.com/library/ee663252.aspx). The support relies on Teredo (http://en.wikipedia.org/wiki/Teredo_tunneling), which is an IPv6 transition technology that grants IPv6 connectivity to nodes behind NAT devices that don't understand IPv6. The article at http://msdn.microsoft.com/library/aa965909.aspx tells you more about Microsoft's version of this technology.
- **Increased network performance monitoring:** You gain access to a number of new performance counters when working with the .NET Framework 4.0 (http://msdn.microsoft.com/library/70xadeyt.aspx).
- **Updated HTTP header support:** The updates include support for large byte range headers (64 bits), support for multiple HTTP headers using the `System.Net.HttpWebRequest` class (http://msdn.microsoft.com/library/system.net.httpwebrequest.aspx), and the ability to set a `Host` header value independently of the required URI.

- **Enhanced Secure Sockets Layer (SSL) support:** The .NET Framework now provides SSL support for the `System.Net.Mail.SmtpClient` (http://msdn.microsoft.com/library/system.net.mail.smtpclient.aspx) and related classes.

- **Renovated mail header support:** This update adds more support for mail headers in the `System.Net.Mail.MailMessage` class (http://msdn.microsoft.com/library/system.net.mail.mailmessage.aspx).

- **Added null cipher for encryption:** A null cipher is an old version of cryptography akin to steganography, except that it relies on hiding the text within a more complex textual passage (http://en.wikipedia.org/wiki/Null_cipher). You use a null cipher as you would any other encryption policy, by using the `System.Net.ServicePointManager` class (http://msdn.microsoft.com/library/system.net.servicepointmanager.aspx) and the `EncryptionPolicy` property (http://msdn.microsoft.com/library/system.net.servicepointmanager.encryptionpolicy.aspx).

- **Modified password handling:** The .NET Framework still supports basic, digest, NTLM, and Kerberos authentication through the `System.Net.NetworkCredential` class (http://msdn.microsoft.com/library/system.net.networkcredential.aspx). However, instead of handling the password using a `System.String` instance, the .NET Framework now uses a `System.Security.SecureString` instance (http://msdn.microsoft.com/library/system.security.securestring.aspx), making any use of the password more secure.

- **Changed percent value conversion and normalization:** It's now possible to define precisely how percent values are converted and normalized using the `System.Uri` (http://msdn.microsoft.com/library/system.uri.aspx) and `System.Net.HttpListener` classes (http://msdn.microsoft.com/library/system.net.httplistener.aspx). This change affects the following classes:

    - `System.Net.Configuration.HttpListenerElement` (http://msdn.microsoft.com/library/system.net.configuration.httplistenerelement.aspx)
    - `System.Configuration.SchemeSettingElement` (http://msdn.microsoft.com/library/system.configuration.schemesettingelement.aspx)
    - `System.Configuration.SchemeSettingElementCollection` (http://msdn.microsoft.com/library/system.configuration.schemesettingelementcollection.aspx)
    - `System.Configuration.UriSection` (http://msdn.microsoft.com/library/system.configuration.urisection.aspx)

## Understanding the Data Improvements

The data improvements provided with the .NET Framework 4.0 fall into three areas: Active Data Objects (ADO.NET) (http://msdn.microsoft.com/library/ex6y04yf.aspx), dynamic data (http://msdn.microsoft.com/library/s57a598e.aspx), and Windows Communication Foundation (WCF) Data Services (http://msdn.microsoft.com/library/ee373845.aspx). In most cases, the changes reflect requirements of a Windows 7-oriented emphasis. For example, ADO.NET requires additional features to work well with LINQ queries.

You probably haven't heard of WCF Data Services before. That's because someone in Microsoft marketing decided to rename ADO.NET Data Services. Consequently, if you've used ADO.NET Data Services in the past, you already know quite a bit about WCF Data Services. There are some new goodies in WCF Data Services that fall into the following groups:

- Allowing data binding to WPF controls using the `DataServiceCollection` class (http://msdn.microsoft.com/library/ee474331.aspx and http://msdn.microsoft.com/library/ee373844.aspx)

- Counting entities in an entity set using the new `$inlinecount` query option (http://www.odata.org/developers/protocols/uri-conventions and http://msdn.microsoft.com/library/dd673933.aspx)

- Relying on server-driven paging using a data service (http://msdn.microsoft.com/library/ee358710.aspx) or .NET Framework client library (http://msdn.microsoft.com/library/ee358709.aspx)

- Obtaining a subset of the query projections using the new `$select` query option (http://www.odata.org/developers/protocols/uri-conventions and http://msdn.microsoft.com/library/ee473425.aspx)

- Supporting new types of custom data service providers (http://msdn.microsoft.com/library/ee960143.aspx)

- Performing streaming of binary resources by implementing the `IDataServiceStreamProvider` interface (http://msdn.microsoft.com/library/system.data.services.providers.idataservicestreamprovider.aspx and http://msdn.microsoft.com/library/ee358709.aspx)

## OBTAINING AND INSTALLING .NET 4.0

Windows 7 comes with the .NET Framework 4.0 already installed, so if your development system relies on Windows 7, you don't need to do anything special. The 32-bit version of the .NET Framework 4.0 appears in `\Windows\Microsoft.NET\Framework\v4.0.30319`, while the 64-bit version (assuming you're using 64-bit Windows 7) appears in `\Windows\Microsoft.NET\Framework64\v4.0.30319`. Make sure you check to verify that your system actually has the required files installed.

There are two different methods to obtain the .NET Framework 4.0. First, you can use the Web installer found at http://www.microsoft.com/downloads/details.aspx?FamilyID=9cfb2d51-5ff4-4491-b0e5-b386f32c0992 (the filename is `dotNetFx40_Full_setup.EXE` and the size is 868 KB). This method requires that you maintain a live Internet connection during the installation process. It might not be the optimal approach if your Internet connection is flaky. Second, you can use the stand-alone installer found at http://www.microsoft.com/downloads/details.aspx?FamilyID=0a391abd-25c1-4fc0-919f-b21f31ab88b7 (the filename is `dotNetFx40_Full_x86_x64.EXE` and size is 48.1 MB). In this case, you download the entire file and then install it as you would any other application on your system. This second method has the advantage of not using bandwidth for every installation — you perform the download once and then install locally for each machine that requires a copy of the .NET Framework. The following steps help you install the .NET Framework 4.0:

1. Double-click the file you downloaded. If you're working with Vista or Windows 7, you'll see a UAC dialog box where you'll have to give approval to start the installation process. The UAC dialog box is normal because you're making a major system change.

2. Click Yes. The installer will check your system and determine whether you already have the .NET Framework 4.0 installed. If you see the dialog box shown in Figure 3-1, simply click Cancel because you already have the .NET Framework 4.0 installed. (As an alternative, you can always remove the existing installation and reinstall it.) Otherwise, you'll see a licensing dialog box.

**FIGURE 3-1:** This dialog box tells you that you already have the .NET Framework installed.

3. Check the I Have Read and Understand the Licensing Terms checkbox and click Install. You'll see an Installation Progress dialog box while the installation program installs the .NET Framework on your machine. When the installation is complete, you see an Installation Is Complete dialog box.

4. Click Finish. At this point, you can open Program Features (or Add and Remove Programs). You should see the Microsoft .NET Framework 4 Client Profile and Microsoft .NET Framework 4 Extended entries shown in Figure 3-2. The Microsoft .NET Framework 4 Multi-Targeting Pack is part of the Visual Studio 2010 installation.

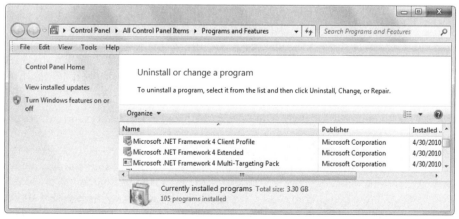

**FIGURE 3-2:** You'll actually see two entries as part of the .NET Framework 4.0 installation.

5. Reboot your machine to ensure that the .NET Framework is ready for use (the installation program won't tell you to reboot, but rebooting is a good idea).

*Some developers have reported problems getting the .NET Framework to install properly from the Visual Studio 2010 installation disks. In most such cases, the Microsoft .NET Framework 4 Multi-Targeting Pack fails to install or displays an error message when it does. If you encounter this problem, first try using the procedure in this section to install the .NET Framework 4.0, reboot your system, and then proceed with the Visual Studio installation.*

At some point, you might decide to uninstall the .NET Framework 4.0. Unfortunately, you can't simply open the original installation file and expect the uninstall to work. You must open the Program Features applet in the Control Panel and uninstall the Microsoft .NET Framework 4 Extended entry first. It's then possible to uninstall the Microsoft .NET Framework 4 Client Profile without rebooting first. After you uninstall both pieces, be sure to reboot your system to complete the task.

## CONSIDERING THE WINDOWS 7 EXTENDED FUNCTIONALITY

Windows 7 is a complex environment with functionality not enjoyed by earlier versions of Windows. The .NET Framework 4.0 plays to this improved functionality by making some features available only to Windows 7 developers. The foremost enhancement is in the area of security. You'll find that Microsoft has become ever more security-focused in recent years, in part due to the loss of market share that occurred when developers began to assume that Microsoft has poor product security. The fact that Microsoft products provide a bigger target doesn't help. Network security is an essential part of the new security umbrella that Microsoft provides to developers. You can get an overview of these security extensions at http://msdn.microsoft.com/library/dd582691.aspx.

Microsoft is also making it possible for developers to better monitor applications. The idea is that applications with better monitoring are less likely to present security and reliability problems. Of course, better monitoring also helps you tune the application to make it faster. Most of the monitoring comes in the form of performance counters that are exclusive to Windows 7, the .NET Framework 4.0, or both. There are examples of these performance counters throughout the chapter, and you'll encounter more of them as you progress through the book.

Another Windows 7 push is support for IPv6. The Internet is theoretically running out of usable IPv4 addresses at a rapid rate (http://en.wikipedia.org/wiki/IPv4_address_exhaustion and http://arstechnica.com/old/content/2008/08/were-running-out-of-ipv4-addresses-time-for-ipv6-really.ars). Because the Internet will soon have to rely on IPv6, Microsoft has made considerable efforts to make moving to IPv6 in Windows 7 as easy and as automatic as possible. Along with this push, you'll find considerable new IPv6 features in the .NET Framework 4.0 that will make your development efforts easier.

## MOVING YOUR APPLICATIONS TO WINDOWS 7

This chapter has provided an overview of the .NET Framework 4.0. Although you aren't absolutely required to use this version of the .NET Framework when creating your updated application, using the latest version will ease your development efforts by providing you with many of the elements you need without additional programming. If you use an older version of the .NET Framework, you'll need to expend additional effort creating the right connections to DLLs and performing your own low-level programming. Since development is hard enough without these additional tasks, you'll very likely use the .NET Framework 4.0.

Before you go any further in the book, verify that you have the .NET Framework 4.0 on your machine. If you don't have this version of the .NET Framework installed, make sure you read the instructions in the "Obtaining and Installing .NET 4.0" section of the chapter. Download and install the support required to build your update. If you're using Windows 7 as your development platform (always a good idea), then you'll likely have the .NET Framework 4.0 already installed. You also get the .NET Framework 4.0 as part of the Visual Studio 2010 installation, so there are many painless ways to obtain the support you require for your development efforts.

It also pays to familiarize yourself with the new features of the .NET Framework 4.0. Of course, there isn't any way to memorize the latest functionality, but having a good overview of the updated features will make your development efforts faster and more efficient. In addition, you'll probably spend a lot less time designing your application update. The new features of the .NET Framework 4.0 will save you development time.

Chapter 4 begins a new part of the book. In this part you discover how to use the user-interface elements supported by Windows 7 to make your application work better. You can improve your application in a number of ways, such as adding functionality to make finding data easier or to ease the selection process for the user. Chapter 4 specifically reviews the new features found at the Taskbar. Since every application relies on the Taskbar, this is one of the few chapters in the book that you should review even if you aren't planning on using Windows 7 functionality immediately. A small change in your application could make a big difference for the user.

# PART II
# Working with the Windows 7 User Interface

- **CHAPTER 4:** Interacting with the Taskbar
- **CHAPTER 5:** Advanced Taskbar Techniques
- **CHAPTER 6:** Working with the Ribbon Interface
- **CHAPTER 7:** Creating Custom Ribbon Interface Applications
- **CHAPTER 8:** Programming for Aero Glass Functionality
- **CHAPTER 9:** Working with the Multi-Touch User Interface

# Interacting with the Taskbar

**WHAT'S IN THIS CHAPTER?**

- ➤ Understanding the new Windows 7 Taskbar
- ➤ Defining the Taskbar updates you want for your application
- ➤ Creating your first Taskbar-enhanced application
- ➤ Creating a Taskbar-enhanced application using the .NET 4.0 approach
- ➤ Making good design decisions for the Taskbar

The Taskbar is one Windows component that affects every application you run. Because the Taskbar is so visible, Microsoft has been tweaking it for years. Vista received a few major Taskbar changes, but Windows 7 has made significant changes to the Taskbar. Yes, older applications work fine, but the new Taskbar contains a wealth of features that you may want to add to older applications to improve their functionality (modifying an existing feature) or make them more functional (adding new features).

> *You may not know it, but the Aero in Aero Glass is a bacronym for Authentic, Energetic, Reflective, and Open* (http://windowsteamblog.com/windows/archive/b/windowsvista/archive/2006/11/09/the-sounds-of-windows-vista.aspx). *What precisely is a bacronym? Well, it's a list of words used to define a term after the fact, as if the term started out as an acronym even though it was simply a word at one time* (http://en.wikipedia.org/wiki/Backronym). *Aero Glass didn't start out as an acronym; the phrase was created after the fact by Microsoft marketing to match the Aero Glass terminology already in use. You may run into this terminology on a Microsoft site from time to time. No one else seems to be using it and Microsoft may decide at some point to ignore the bacronym, but for now it does make for an interesting tidbit of information.*

## VIEWING THE NEW TASKBAR IN WINDOWS 7

The new Taskbar may be a little disappointing at first. It's nice to see thumbnails of your documents as shown in Chapter 1, in the section on "Understanding the User Interface Improvements." But let's face it, many developers, not to mention users, will yawn. However, many of the Taskbar enhancements are nothing to yawn at. Here's a quick list of what you can expect to see:

- **Pinned applications:** You can permanently attach any application to the Taskbar. This feature doesn't require any special programming on your part. However, to obtain the related Jump List functionality, you do have to provide special application code and the required control.

- **New controls:** The new controls perform tasks such as showing application progress, even if you can't see the main application display. This feature always requires special programming on your part, since the controls are part of your application and are simply displayed on the Taskbar, rather than controlled by the Taskbar.

- **Modifiable Taskbar buttons:** It's possible to modify the behavior of the Taskbar buttons to display new behaviors, such as in the method used to show multiple open documents. In addition, the Taskbar now includes organization features, such as the ability to rearrange the Taskbar so that applications appear in the order desired. Most of this feature doesn't require special programming on your part; but some behaviors, such as the display of multiple documents, work better with special application programming.

- **Application thumbnails:** The Taskbar displays a thumbnail of the active document within the application or a thumbnail for each of the open documents, depending on how the application is configured and the way the application is programmed. This feature isn't available in Windows Starter edition. It doesn't require any special programming on your part, but you can enhance the output using special programming.

- **Notification Area customization:** The Notification Area is fully customizable now. You can determine precisely which icons appear in the Notification Area and which icons are hidden. In fact, you can choose from several levels of icon display in the Notification Area. For example, an icon can display itself only when it has a notification to present. This functionality is under complete user control and you can't change it programmatically.

- **Action Center icon:** The Notification Area also includes a new Action Center icon, which is a central repository for notifications. The user can choose to ignore notifications until it's convenient to deal with them. These ignored notifications are stored in the Action Center until such time as the user opens the associated application and does something with them. You don't need to perform any special programming to make use of this feature.

- **Show Desktop button:** Microsoft has moved the Show Desktop button to the opposite end of the Taskbar. The button now appears as a captionless square. You actually have to hover the mouse over it to see its function. This is one of the less useful changes Microsoft has made. Naturally, you don't have to perform any special programming for this feature.

Now that you've had the quick overview, it's time to review the new Taskbar features in a little more detail. The following sections tell you more about these features and show where you can immediately see them in your copy of Windows 7. You'll get a demonstration of many of these features later in the chapter. For example, the new controls appear in the "An Overview of the New Taskbar Features" section of this chapter.

## Considering the Subtle Features

When you start working with Windows 7, you'll quickly notice that a few features are missing. For example, Windows 7 doesn't provide a Quick Launch toolbar, and you'll find that the Start ⇨ Recent Documents menu option is missing as well. These features still exist, but in a different way. The Quick Launch toolbar is replaced with the ability to pin an application to the Taskbar. Any application you pin remains on the Taskbar within easy reach, even after you close it. Likewise, the Recent Documents menu is now supported by Jump Lists that you see when you right-click the application.

It's important to understand that you get a different view of the Taskbar simply by looking at it, hovering the mouse over a particular icon, or right-clicking an icon. Figure 4-1 shows one way to arrange the Taskbar and Desktop, with favorite applications on the Taskbar and data folders on the Desktop. This isn't the way Microsoft sets the defaults; it simply displays a particular way of configuring the Taskbar and Desktop for optimal efficiency. Notice that some applications on the Taskbar, such as Word, have a box around them, while others, such as Excel, don't. Active applications are shown with boxes around them so that you know the applications are open.

**FIGURE 4-1:** Pinning places the applications you use most directly on the Taskbar.

When you hover the mouse over a particular icon, you see the windows open in that application. For example, Figure 4-2 shows that Windows Explorer has two windows open. You can choose how the Taskbar combines multiple open windows using settings on the Taskbar tab of the Taskbar and

Start Menu Properties dialog box (accessed by right-clicking the Taskbar and choosing Properties from the context menu), as shown in Figure 4-3.

**FIGURE 4-2:** Thumbnails give you a small view of the window.

Placing the mouse on one of the thumbnails will display that window on-screen, even if the window is currently minimized. This is called *peeking*. Figure 4-2 shows that the first thumbnail is selected, and you see it behind the Taskbar and thumbnail. Notice the red square in the upper-right corner of the first thumbnail. Clicking this box will close the window.

Right-clicking an icon displays options for that application. You'll always see options for selecting the application, unpinning the application from the Taskbar, and closing the window. Some applications include other features. To obtain these other features, you must write application code. For example, Figure 4-4 shows the options for Windows Media Player. In addition to the three standard entries, you also see options to resume playing the previous playlist and to play all the music currently found in the selected library.

**FIGURE 4-3:** The Taskbar and Start Menu Properties dialog box contains new options that reflect Windows 7 usage.

**FIGURE 4-4:** Context menus can contain any number of entries, but you must program them.

 *This chapter doesn't discuss a number of new Taskbar features that are user-specific and not programmable. For example, you can now rearrange the icons on the Taskbar in any order. Just drag and drop the icon into a new position.*

The thumbnails need not present a sterile appearance, either. For example, if you open Windows Media Player and begin playing some music, you can use controls in the thumbnail to control the player, as shown in Figure 4-5. Of course, you get these controls only if you add them into your application. Using controls within the thumbnail is just one example of how you can make your application significantly friendlier and reduce training costs. The user needs to know to look for the feature. This feature actually replaces the separate toolbar that used to contain controls for Windows Media Player.

Some of the features won't show up right away, and users might complain that they can't find them. For example, some organizations clear the options in the Privacy group on the Start Menu tab of the Taskbar and Start Menu Properties dialog box. If you clear these options, you'll find that some of the Jump List entries, such as the recent document list, are missing. Windows 7 actually maintains a recent document list for each application, so this feature is more useful than it was in previous versions of Windows. To see the recent document list, right-click the application icon on the Taskbar or view the application's entry in the Start menu.

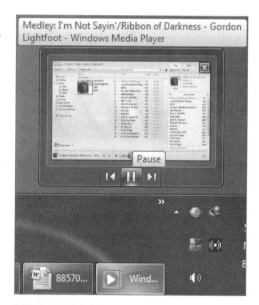

**FIGURE 4-5:** Add controls to the thumbnail to make it easier to control your application without maximizing it.

## Understanding the Importance of Application Settings

It's important to understand the interplay between Windows 7 settings, application settings, and the Taskbar appearance. Some applications provide you with settings that interact with Windows 7 in interesting ways. This section uses Microsoft Word 2007 as an example, but the same principles apply to a number of applications. It pays to spend some time looking at how various application settings affect Taskbar appearance. In short, you should take time to play with the application settings to determine whether there is a way you can enhance Taskbar functionality.

One of the more interesting application-setting differences is the ability to set the application to display a single icon on the Taskbar or one icon for each open document. For Word, this setting appears on the Advanced tab of the Word Options dialog box, as shown in Figure 4-6. If you clear the Show All Windows in the Taskbar option, then you see a single thumbnail for the active document when you hover the mouse over the Word application icon. The default is to show all the windows on the Taskbar. When you retain this setting, you see one thumbnail for each open document, as shown in Figure 4-7.

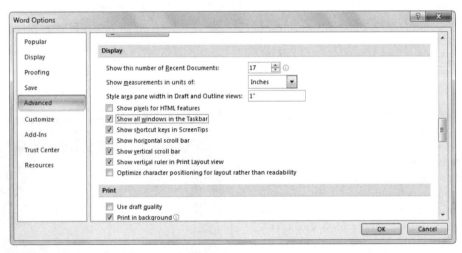

**FIGURE 4-6:** The Show All Windows in the Taskbar option controls how Word displays thumbnails.

Look again at Figure 4-3. Notice the Taskbar Buttons field. The setting for this field controls how the icons appear on the Taskbar and how these icons potentially affect the way your application behaves. The following list describes these actions:

- **Always Combine, Hide Labels:** The user is going to need to depend on the icon you use for your application because the Taskbar won't display a label for the application. Consequently, if you currently display several applications using approximately the same icon, there's a significant potential for user confusion and inefficiency at selecting the proper application.

- **Combine When Taskbar is Full:** The Taskbar always displays a label for your application, and it displays separate icons for each window when space allows. If the Taskbar becomes full, the user still sees the label, but the individual windows are combined into one icon.

This is probably the most efficient setting if you have a number of existing applications that don't necessarily follow the Windows 7 rules.

- **Never Combine:** Windows tries to get everything on the Taskbar, even if it won't fit. The icons get smaller and smaller until you can't see anything. This setting only works if the user is going to have just a few applications open at once.

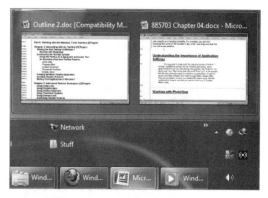

**FIGURE 4-7:** Some users find it easier to see just the active document, rather than all the documents.

There are subtle considerations you must make in updating your application for Windows 7, based on how the user interacts with the Taskbar. For example, you may have to change the application icon to ensure that it presents a unique appearance. You can't always assume the user will see an application label to help determine which icon to click. Even though these issues may seem minor, over time these little inefficiencies stack up and cost your organization real money in lost user productivity. In addition, you'll likely find that support costs increase when you make ill-advised decisions regarding application appearance, especially in the dramatically more graphic world of Windows 7.

## CONSIDERING THE TASKBAR UPDATES

The Taskbar takes on a greater importance to the developer in Windows 7 because of the features Microsoft has added to it. No longer is the Taskbar simply a method of presenting an icon for a running application. The Taskbar has become a central location for managing important applications (the term "important" here references the user's view of the application's use in that user's daily work). Depending on which features the Windows 7 installation has enabled, the Taskbar can suddenly become a one-stop shopping location for everything Windows — the user may reference the Start menu only on the rare occasion that a less commonly used application is needed. The following sections discuss these updates from the developer perspective.

## Using the Taskbar as an Application Interaction Tool

Most developers are going to have problems viewing the Taskbar as an application interaction tool (at least during the initial update research process). For most developers, the Taskbar will remain simply a place that displays an icon of the running application. To overlook the vast potential of the Taskbar in Windows 7 would be a mistake. The Taskbar has become an interactive environment for the user. In fact, with products such as Google Toolbar, most users are already looking at the Taskbar continually for information. If your application fails to use this resource, the user is likely not going to see other resources you've provided.

Getting the user's attention is a good reason to use the Taskbar as an interaction tool, but it isn't the only reason. You have to consider efficiencies gained by using the new Taskbar features. Users currently waste vast quantities of time trying to find what they need. Take some time to watch users in your organization perform their tasks — count the number of wasted steps in every activity. By using the Taskbar for interactivity, you remove one additional level of contact for the user and reduce the inefficiencies that most users experience today.

The new Taskbar features can also help the user avoid potential errors. Status information presented at the Taskbar lets the user monitor the application while doing something else. The ability to monitor without having to redisplay the application is important because many users look for ways to multitask. Even though the Taskbar provides this information, it does so in a non-intrusive manner, making the feature less cumbersome than message boxes, which appear from nowhere and derail the user's train of thought.

## An Overview of the New Taskbar Features

The biggest question is how you use the new Taskbar features to perform useful work. In some cases, such as Jump Lists, you probably have some good ideas already. The following sections include some recommendations for use, but as with anything, keep an open mind as to how your organization can use a particular feature.

### Jump Lists

A Jump List is essentially a new kind of context menu. You right-click an icon on the Taskbar, and you see some things you can do with the icon. For example, a recent-files list tells you about the files the user has opened in the past. The Jump List will also contain some basic tasks, such as pinning the application to the Taskbar. The basic idea is that the Jump List provides the user with quick ways to interact with the application.

Depending on the application, you might have some custom tasks that you want the user to be able to perform. For example, an application that needs to download information from another source could have an Update Status task. The task will execute in the background while the user does something else. The Taskbar can signal the user when the download is done.

Opening recent documents might not be the only way in which the user interacts with data on the Jump List. You could also provide a list of common templates the user can use to create new documents. It's also possible to send a recent document to another application and have that application open automatically with the document loaded — all without starting the original application. A single Taskbar click can perform the entire task quickly and easily.

Placing a destination on the Jump List is another way to improve user efficiency. For example, a browser Jump List can include a list of recent or standard destinations. The user can select a destination even when the application is closed. As soon as the selection is complete, the application will open and take the user to that location. Don't limit yourself to URLs. A destination can be a local hard drive, a network drive, or even a remote organization location through a Virtual Private Network (VPN). Given the way this feature works, the user need not even know the physical location of the destination.

### Progress Bars

The Progress Bar works much like progress bars everywhere — it shows the status of an ongoing process. For example, you can use a Progress Bar to show the status of a download or the progress of an installation. Any sort of ongoing process requires progress feedback, or the user will think the application has frozen. Adding a Progress Bar directly to the Taskbar makes it possible for the user to check application status without actually opening the application window. This is a quick and easy method for the user to track ongoing processes without affecting current work.

### Custom Switchers

A Custom Switcher allows you to change the way the Taskbar switches between windows. You might want to prioritize the windows in some way (such as alphabetically), and a Custom Switcher will allow you to do that. Unfortunately, Microsoft doesn't provide an example of a Custom Switcher as part of Windows 7. This feature could cause some problems because it changes the way in which the user normally interacts with the Taskbar — you'd need to provide special training in its use.

### Thumbnail Toolbars

Thumbnail Toolbars are extremely exciting because they provide the potential for major changes in the way the user interacts with the Taskbar. Instead of simply selecting the application or performing a task with it, the user can interact with major application features using the Thumbnail Toolbar. The Windows Media Player is the primary example of how this feature works in Windows 7. When working with a Thumbnail Toolbar, you can:

- Add a control with which the user interacts to perform application tasks
- Use a list of images to reflect button or application feature status
- Perform updates of the application status through the thumbnail image

### Overlay Icons

You use Overlay Icons as another means of communicating application status. In this case, the application icon receives an overlay — a small addition that reflects some type of status. These overlays work much like the status indicators in browser status bars. For example, you see an indicator showing that the site is using security to perform a transaction, or that the site is trying to store cookies on your machine. Everyone has seen these status indicators in browsers and other applications. (Word uses such status indicators to show when overtype is on or when you're in review mode.) By viewing the overlays, the user instantly knows the status of your application and can react appropriately.

## CREATING THE BASIC TASKBAR APPLICATION

Rather than overwhelm you with a complex application at the outset, the following sections create a simple Taskbar application. This first approach is best for application updates because you don't absolutely have to use the .NET Framework 4.0 to implement it (although using the .NET Framework 4.0 does help). In this case, the sections show what you need to do to add a simple Jump List item — the ability to launch Notepad — to the application. Even this simple addition would be impossible in earlier versions of Windows, so it does present a new feature for Windows 7. This technique comes in handy for launching applications associated with the current application or adding custom actions to your application (something best left for a future example). Chapter 5 will move to more complex examples, but for now it's time to view the process you'll use to build all your Taskbar updates.

## Obtaining the Windows API Code Pack for Microsoft .NET Framework

The code used to perform much of the Windows 7 magic is written in native languages such as C. Of course, the API access is always available to the intrepid developer willing to work at the command line and perform arcane feats of coding using P/Invoke. However, this book assumes that you really don't want to create more work for yourself. With this in mind, you'll want to download the Windows API Code Pack for Microsoft .NET Framework (version 1.0.1) from http://code.msdn.microsoft.com/WindowsAPICodePack. This library does all the hard work for you — you use it as you would any other managed library. The Home tab of the site tells you all the things you can do with this library, an impressive list. For the purposes of this book, you need to download the following items from the Download tab. (To download these files, you must click I Agree when you see the licensing agreement dialog box.)

- WindowsAPICodePack.ZIP
- WindowsAPICodePackHelp.EXE

After you download the files, you need to perform a few extra steps to obtain a working library. The following procedure will help you create the library used for the samples in this book:

1. Create a folder named \CodePack on your hard drive.
2. Double-click the WindowsAPICodePackHelp.EXE file. When you see the WinZip Self-Extractor dialog box (or equivalent), chose the \CodePack\Help folder in the Unzip to Folder field.
3. Click Unzip and the application will create the help file for you. It will also open the file for you in most cases.
4. Extract the WindowsAPICodePack.ZIP file to the \CodePack folder. You'll see two new subfolders:
   - Samples
   - WindowsAPICodePack
5. Open the \CodePack\WindowsAPICodePack folder, and you'll see a WindowsAPICodePack.SLN (solution) file.
6. Double-click WindowsAPICodePack.SLN to open it in Visual Studio. If you're using Visual Studio 2010, you'll see the Visual Studio Conversion Wizard. Click Finish to perform a standard conversion, and then click Close to close the Visual Studio Conversion Wizard.
7. Choose Release in the Solution Configurations dialog box.
8. Choose Build ➪ Build Solution to create the library. The output consists of four files:
   - \CodePack\WindowsAPICodePack\Core\bin\Release\Microsoft.WindowsAPICodePack.DLL

➤ \CodePack\WindowsAPICodePack\ExtendedLinguisticServices\bin\Release\Microsoft.WindowsAPICodePack.ExtendedLinguisticServices.DLL

➤ \CodePack\WindowsAPICodePack\Sensors\bin\Release\Microsoft.WindowsAPICodePack.Sensors.DLL

➤ \CodePack\WindowsAPICodePack\Shell\bin\Release\Microsoft.WindowsAPICodePack.Shell.DLL

9. Create a new `Lib` subfolder in the `\CodePack` folder as `\CodePack\Lib`. This new folder offers a central location to store the assemblies you just created.

10. Copy the four library files to `\CodePack\Lib` to make them easier to access. The projects in this book assume you've created such a library. You should now have the required help file and assemblies to access the Taskbar functionality.

*Microsoft constantly creates really long and cumbersome names for products and technologies. Rather than use Windows API Code Pack for Microsoft .NET Framework throughout the book, I've used the much simpler Code Pack.*

You'll probably want to make the Code Pack help file easy to access. Unfortunately, you can't easily add the help file to the Help menu, where it would be convenient to use. Rather, you can add it to the Tools menu using the following steps:

1. Choose Tools ⇨ External Tools to display the External Tools dialog box shown in Figure 4-8.

**FIGURE 4-8:** Add the Code Pack help file to the Tools menu to make it easier to access.

**2.** Click Add. Visual Studio creates a new entry for you.

**3.** Type the values shown in Figure 4-8 into the Title, Command, and Arguments fields. Make sure you change the paths for the `HH.EXE` and `WindowsAPICodePack.CHM` files to match your system setup.

**4.** Click OK. Visual Studio adds the new command to the Tools menu, where you can quickly access it as you need help with using the Code Pack.

## Creating the Solution

The example begins with the C# Windows Forms Application template. You should choose to use the .NET Framework 4.0 as the basis for the application. (However, you don't absolutely have to use the .NET Framework 4.0 because this example relies on the Code Pack approach.) In this case, the example uses a name of Simple Task Bar Sample, as shown in Figure 4-9. You don't absolutely have to create a directory for the solution, but it's a good idea to get used to doing so. Future examples will likely contain multiple projects, and using a separate directory for the solution makes it easier to organize the projects under it.

**FIGURE 4-9:** Create a Windows Forms Application for this example.

After you create the application, you need to add a reference to the `Microsoft.WindowsAPICodePack.Shell.DLL`. Right-click References and choose Add Reference from the context menu to display the Add Reference dialog box. Select the Browse tab and locate the `\CodePack\Lib` folder, as shown in Figure 4-10. Highlight the `Microsoft.WindowsAPICodePack.Shell.DLL` and click OK. You'll see the DLL added to the References folder of Solution Explorer.

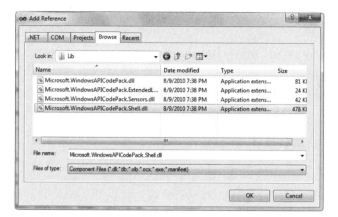

**FIGURE 4-10:** Add a reference to the Microsoft.WindowsAPI CodePack.Shell.DLL file.

Because of the nature of this application, you don't actually have to add anything to the form if you don't want to. The downloadable code includes some simple code and a few controls with it, but they're completely unnecessary for this example. The focus is on the Taskbar and what you can do with a Jump List.

There are many different ways and times at which you can add Jump List features to your application. In fact, Jump Lists can be quite fluid during application execution. The example application takes a simple approach; it modifies the Jump List once when the application first starts. With this technique in mind, highlight the form in the designer, click Events in the Properties window, and double-click the space next to the Shown event to create a Shown event handler. Your application is now ready to code.

## Adding the Jump List Code

This example has a number of coding elements. Of course, the first thing you'll want to add is `using` statements for the Code Pack, as shown here:

```
using Microsoft.WindowsAPICodePack.Taskbar;
using Microsoft.WindowsAPICodePack.Shell;
```

Notice that you must include both the `Taskbar` and `Shell` namespaces because you use elements of both for even a simple application. The Jump List is contained in a private field you define within the class like this:

```
// Define the JumpList.
private JumpList TheJumpList;
```

Now that you have both the required references and the private field to use, it's time to create some code. All the code appears within the `frmMain_Shown()` event handler as shown in Listing 4-1.

**LISTING 4-1:** Displaying a simple Jump List task

Available for download on Wrox.com

```
private void frmMain_Shown(object sender, EventArgs e)
{
    // Define the system path.
    String SysPath =
        Environment.GetFolderPath(Environment.SpecialFolder.System);

    // Create the JumpList.
    TheJumpList = JumpList.CreateJumpList();

    // Add a task to the JumpList.
    TheJumpList.AddUserTasks(
        new JumpListLink(SysPath + "\\Notepad.EXE", "Open Notepad")
        {
            IconReference = new IconReference(SysPath + "\\Notepad.EXE", 0)
        });

    // Display the addition on the JumpList.
    TheJumpList.Refresh();
}
```

The code begins by retrieving the system path and placing it in `SysPath`. You need to provide precise references to applications you want to access from a Jump List.

The next step is to create the `JumpList` variable, `TheJumpList`, using the `CreateJumpList()` static member of the `JumpList` class. At this point, the code uses `TheJumpList.AddUserTasks()` to add a new task to the Jump List. The `AddUserTasks()` method accepts a `JumpListLink` object and an `IconReference` as input. The `JumpListLink` constructor accepts two arguments as input: the path to the executable you want to add to the Jump List and the caption you want to associate with that executable. The `IconReference` simply provides the source of an icon to associate with the Jump List entry. In this case, the example uses the first icon found in `Notepad.EXE`.

At this point, the Jump List entry is complete. However, you won't see it on-screen until the code calls `TheJumpList.Refresh()`. It's possible to create a wealth of changes to the Jump List presentation and then display them all at once when necessary by calling `TheJumpList.Refresh()`. If you find that you don't see an expected change, make sure your code contains the required `Refresh()` method call.

## Testing the Code Pack Result

When you finish your application, build and start it as normal. When you right-click the icon on the Taskbar, you should see a new entry like the one shown in Figure 4-11. If you click on Open Notepad, you'll actually see a copy of Notepad open. Of course, a production application would probably have something specific to your organization or the application itself — you can start any application using this technique.

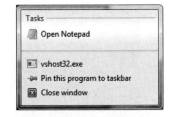

**FIGURE 4-11:** The example shows a new Jump List entry.

For now, select Pin this Program to the Taskbar. End the application. Surprisingly enough, you'll still see the application icon on the Taskbar. That's right, you can pin any application to the Taskbar, even applications that don't appear on the Start menu. Right-click the icon and you'll see the context menu shown in Figure 4-12. As you can see, you can still start Notepad from the context menu, even though the application isn't running. To get rid of the application icon, choose Unpin this Program from Taskbar.

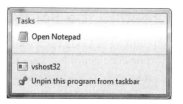

**FIGURE 4-12:** As long as the application icon is present, you can use items on its Jump List.

## USING THE .NET 4.0 APPROACH

You don't absolutely have to rely on the Code Pack to create the Jump List addition for your Windows 7 application. If you use the .NET Framework 4.0 exclusively (for example, when you create a new application from scratch), then you can use the .NET Framework features as an alternative approach. The Code Pack additions that we created earlier in the chapter also appear for .NET 4.0 developers in the System.Windows.Shell namespace located in the PresentationFramework.DLL file. You can use the .NET 4.0 approach when your application meets the following requirements:

➤ The application represents a new development or an update that will rely on the Windows Presentation Foundation (WPF) in place of the more familiar Windows Forms application.

➤ You'll use Visual Studio 2010 for development purposes.

➤ The application will use the .NET Framework 4.0 exclusively.

➤ The application will run only on Windows Vista or a newer version of Windows.

*For some reason, the approach in the following sections appears only to work in Visual Studio 2010, so if you don't want to update your IDE, the following sections won't help. (If someone can send me a working example of this approach in an earlier version of Visual Studio, it would be most helpful. Send your example to* JMueller@mwt.net.*)*

You can actually use two techniques to create the solution using the .NET 4.0 approach: eXtensible Application Markup Language (XAML) or standard code behind. The following sections show how to use both techniques to add a new task entry to a Task List.

*Space won't allow coverage of XAML and WPF in this book. If you need to brush up on your XAML skills, check out* WPF Programmer's Reference: Windows Presentation Foundation with C# 2010 and .NET 4, *by Rod Stephens, Wrox 2010. This book will get you started with XAML and show you some of the more interesting things you can do with WPF as a whole. You'll be impressed with the functionality you can achieve using WPF for your next application. Of course, upgrading an existing application to WPF will likely be a daunting task.*

## Creating the Solution

Unlike the Code Pack solution, you must create a WPF application to use the .NET 4.0 approach. The code could have possibly worked using older techniques, but the application requires a reference to System.Windows.Application.Current. This property is null in a Windows Forms application, so you can't use the .NET 4.0 technique with a Windows Forms application. Consequently, you select the WPF Application template in the New Project dialog box shown in Figure 4-9 and give the solution a name of Simple Task Bar Sample 2.

As with the Code Pack example, you don't have to provide any content on the application form if you don't want to. The purpose of this example is to show a simple Jump List addition. However, the downloaded source will have a few controls you can work with to fill out the example.

You do need to add a reference to the PresentationFramework assembly. However, because the PresentationFramework assembly appears as part of the .NET Framework, you simply look for it on the .NET tab of the Add Reference dialog box, as shown in Figure 4-13.

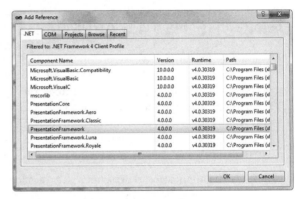

**FIGURE 4-13:** Add a reference to the PresentationFramework assembly.

## Adding the Code

You begin the coding by adding a using statement. In this case, you need only add a reference to the System.Windows.Shell namespace as shown here.

```
using System.Windows.Shell;
```

The .NET 4.0 approach can use a number of techniques to modify the Jump List. The technique you use depends on the kind of Jump List addition you want to make and your personal preferences. The first approach is to add the Jump List using XAML, as shown in Listing 4-2.

**LISTING 4-2:** Creating a Jump List using XAML

Available for download on Wrox.com

```
<Application x:Class="Simple_Task_Bar_Sample_2.App"
             xmlns="http://schemas.microsoft.com/winfx/2006/xaml/presentation"
             xmlns:x="http://schemas.microsoft.com/winfx/2006/xaml"
             StartupUri="frmMain.xaml">
    <JumpList.JumpList>
        <JumpList>
            <JumpTask
                Title="Open Notepad 1"
                Description="Open the Notepad Application"
                ApplicationPath="C:\Windows\Notepad.EXE"
                IconResourcePath="C:\Windows\Notepad.EXE"
```

# Using the .NET 4.0 Approach | 53

```
            IconResourceIndex="0">
        </JumpTask>
      </JumpList>
    </JumpList.JumpList>
</Application>
```

In this case, you simply add the `<JumpList.JumpList>` element to the `App.XAML` file and then define the Jump List as shown. The amount of information is the same as when you create a Jump List using the Code Pack approach, but the organization is different. Notice that a task is defined using the `<JumpTask>` element. This example shows just the basics — you can certainly add a lot more information if desired or needed.

The second approach relies on code, much like the Code Pack approach. However, in this case you create an event handler for the `Loaded` event, as shown in Listing 4-3.

**LISTING 4-3:** Creating a Jump List using the Loaded event

Available for download on Wrox.com

```csharp
private void Window_Loaded(object sender, RoutedEventArgs e)
{
    // Obtain the existing Jump List.
    JumpList TheJumpList = JumpList.GetJumpList(App.Current);

    // Create a new task for the Jump List.
    JumpTask TheTask = new JumpTask();

    // Define the task.
    TheTask.Title = "Open Notepad 2";
    TheTask.Description = "Open the Notepad Application";
    TheTask.ApplicationPath = @"C:\Windows\Notepad.EXE";
    TheTask.IconResourcePath = @"C:\Windows\Notepad.EXE";
    TheTask.IconResourceIndex = 0;

    // Add the task to the Jump List.
    TheJumpList.JumpItems.Add(TheTask);

    // Update the Jump List.
    TheJumpList.Apply();
}
```

There are some important differences. First, you don't define a new Jump List. Instead, you obtain the existing Jump List using the `JumpList.GetJumpList(App.Current)` method, where `App.Current` is a pointer to the current application. An application can have multiple Jump Lists, but generally, you use the existing Jump List and simply add to it. A Windows Forms application doesn't have a Jump List, so you must create it from scratch.

Creating a new task is somewhat different as well. The example creates the task as a separate item using a `JumpTask` object, `TheTask`. Configuring the task is about the same as working with a Code Pack application. You must provide the location of the application and a title for the application entry on screen.

After the code creates the task, it adds it to the Jump List using the `TheJumpList.JumpItems.Add()` method. The `JumpItems` collection also provides methods for enumerating, clearing, and otherwise manipulating the `JumpList` object. In order to see the change on-screen, the code calls `TheJumpList.Apply()`. The output of this application is similar to the Code Pack application, as shown in Figure 4-14.

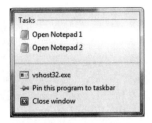

**FIGURE 4-14:** This example outputs two results, one for each technique.

## AVOIDING TASKBAR OVERLOAD

Sometimes a developer turns into "gadget boy" (or "gadget girl"). Gadget boy has a new technology that's the be-all and end-all of technologies — at least until the next technology comes along. The new technology must appear in everything and everywhere because it's just so cool. If you find yourself salivating over the luscious additions to the Taskbar at this point, you might want to take a step back. As with any good technology, you can overload and overwhelm the user with Taskbar functionality that the application doesn't require and the user certainly doesn't want. Your gadget may very well become the user's reason to stay as far away as possible from the updated application.

It's important to look at the usefulness of a Taskbar feature from the user's perspective. Right-clicking on the Taskbar icon and choosing Status Update, rather than having to navigate a series of menus, is helpful, so the user will probably like this feature. On the other hand, a feature called Print is probably not going to get a very good reception because the user won't know what's being printed or how. The user will probably want to preview the document anyway, which means using the application as a foreground task. When you think about the Taskbar, think about status information, background tasks, and efficient methods to manage data quickly.

The features you include at the Taskbar should be simple. If you decide to create a custom thumbnail, it shouldn't be packed with non-essential controls. Think about the Windows Media Player — the custom thumbnail contains a total of three essential controls. It's fast and simple to use. Users truly aren't interested in your application; they simply want to find the fastest and least error-prone method to get their work done in the simplest manner possible. If your application is completely invisible from the user's perspective, you've accomplished an amazing feat.

To avoid Taskbar overload, you should make sure users actually try it out. In fact, you should have them try several variations of your Taskbar features. The problem for developer and user alike is that most of these Taskbar features are so new that the user hasn't seen them before, much less used them to perform useful work. Consequently, you need to perform exhaustive testing and give the user a feel for what's possible, rather than giving just one choice that doesn't really help the user understand what can be achieved at the Taskbar.

## MOVING YOUR APPLICATIONS TO WINDOWS 7

This chapter has described the new features found on the Taskbar, shown how these new features appear, and provided you with an example of how to implement the new features. The Windows 7 Taskbar is a significant enhancement over the Taskbar found in previous versions of Windows.

Of course, any time you introduce something new, some people are going to find it awkward or difficult to use, while others will see it as a great improvement. The new Taskbar is an enhancement because it can do more, but you should also consider the need to train users how to use these new features, especially if you include them in your new or updated application.

Many developers will see the new Taskbar features as answers to questions asked long ago. The new features do make application use simpler and faster once you get used to working with them. There's a tendency among developers to overuse something new simply because it's the latest gadget. Because you can see all kinds of possibilities in the new Taskbar doesn't mean your users will see the same possibilities. In fact, many of them will be outright hostile to the new Taskbar. It pays to work through some mock-ups of how your application will change with the new Taskbar features and then present them to users before you actually implement them. The users might come up with some alternatives that you hadn't considered and will reject outright some changes as awkward or simply not useful. Listen to the user input with an open mind to ensure you use the new Taskbar features to the maximum benefit in your new or updated application.

This chapter is simply an introduction to the new Taskbar — not a complete treatment. Chapter 5 delves more deeply into the new Taskbar features and helps you understand the techniques required to implement them in an application. You'll discover how to use all the new controls in an application. The controls are treated one at a time, so that you can work with them in an application as separate controls. You can find some examples on the Internet, like the one at `http://windowsteamblog.com/windows/b/developers/archive/2009/04/03/windows-7-taskbar-net-sample-library-an-overview.aspx`, which show how to use the controls together. Although this is a nice example and you should take time to view it, make sure you understand each control in a stand-alone setting first; otherwise, you'll almost certainly become confused by the advanced Microsoft examples.

# 5

# Advanced Taskbar Techniques

**WHAT'S IN THIS CHAPTER?**

- Performing tasks, accessing documents, and going places using Jump Lists
- Showing application status using Progress Bars
- Controlling your application using a Thumbnail Toolbar
- Displaying immediate status using Overlay Icons
- Using control combinations to your advantage
- Defining a complete interface

This chapter looks at the various kinds of additions you can make to your application to help the user interact with it at the Taskbar. Of course, you won't want to add every possible feature to your application because that would overload the user and actually make the application less useful. Chapter 4 provides guidelines on how to use each of these features to best advantage.

You'll begin by using each of the Taskbar features individually. The chapter will then discuss how you can combine some Taskbar features to handle special needs. Finally, the chapter shows an application with several Taskbar features combined into a complete interface.

*You can use three different techniques to add Taskbar features to your application: Code Pack; Windows Presentation Foundation (WPF) eXtensible Application Markup Language (XAML); and WPF code behind. Chapter 4 demonstrates all three of these techniques using a basic Jump List task application as an example. This chapter relies on the Code Pack technique because it allows the maximum number of readers to work with the examples, and because most readers aren't yet relying on WPF for application development. Every one of these features is also available to WPF coders.*

## USING JUMP LISTS

Jump Lists are probably one of the more useful additions to the Taskbar. The user will already have a good idea of how to use a Jump List because it works much like a context menu, and context menus appear throughout Windows. Of course, the Jump List is tied directly to your application. You can use Jump Lists for three basic needs:

- Document and template listings
- Tasks
- Destinations

Some of the infrastructure required to accommodate these needs is already in place for you. All you need do is tell Windows to add a common category, such as a recent-files list, to your application. In other cases, you must describe precisely what you want, using a custom list of documents, templates, tasks, or destinations. The following "examples" describe how to work with both common and custom categories, as well as the three types of Jump List entry. (These and other topics are reflected in the folder organization for the code download at www.wrox.com.)

*The registry is highly susceptible to damage. Before you perform any coding that involves the registry, make a backup of the registry so that you can restore it later. As an alternative, you can create a restore point. However, the backup is always the better solution, in case the system becomes unbootable after a change.*

## Adding Common Categories

When you right-click an icon in the Taskbar, you may see separators between groups of items. These separators normally demarcate related items on the Jump List, or *categories* of items. A category is a group of items that perform in a consistent way and normally perform a related task. Microsoft groups categories into custom and common, with common categories being shared by all applications. The Jump List currently provides the following common categories, but you may eventually see more:

- **Recent:** Windows maintains a list of files that the application has opened in the order that the application has opened them. A Jump List will normally accommodate four files in the Recent common category, but some applications, such as Word, might accommodate more depending on the way you configure Word. If you open a new file, that filename goes to the head of the list. When a file appears at the end of the list and you open a new file, that filename falls off the list (but not necessarily out of the registry entry that contains the list of recent filenames). Use this Recent category when you expect the user to work on a file for a while, do something with the file, and then not work with that file again.

- **Frequent:** This list is populated by the names of files that the user opens frequently. If a user opens a file for the third time and another file has been opened only two times, then the file that has been opened only two times falls off the list. In other words, only files that the user opens frequently appear on the list, rather than files the user has opened recently. Use the Frequent category when you expect the user to work with a number of files for a long time, but not necessarily the same file every day. In short, you want to make it easy to find the files that the user commonly uses, rather than the files that the user has lately used.

It's possible to add both the Recent and Frequent common categories to a Jump List, and you might have reason to do so. However, Microsoft recommends that you choose either the Recent or Frequent common category because there's bound to be some overlap between the two, and you don't want to overwhelm the user with too many choices on the Jump List.

Now that you have a better idea of what you can do with common categories, it's time to look at an example of creating common categories for your application. The following sections describe the process you'll follow to add this feature to your application.

### Obtaining and Using RegistrationHelper

When your application requests that Windows open a file, Windows looks in the registry in the HKEY_CLASSES_ROOT hive for an entry for that extension. For example, if you want to open a file with a .TXT extension, then Windows follows this process to open it:

1. Locate the HKEY_CLASSES_ROOT/.txt branch in the registry.
2. Look at the OpenWithProgids subkey for a program identifier that it will use to open the file. For the sake of discussion, let's assume the program identifier is MyApp.
3. Locate the HKEY_CLASSES_ROOT/MyApp/shell/Open key.
4. Locate a command to open the file.
5. Open the file using the command.

This whole process is accomplished after your application registers itself as the file handler. A file can certainly have multiple handlers, but it has only one default handler, which is the point of the registration in this case. Now, you could easily write the code required to perform this task (you can find it in the \CodePack\Samples\Shell\TaskbarDemo\CS\RegistrationHelper\RegistrationHelperMain.cs file), but there isn't any reason to do so. Microsoft has already done all the heavy lifting for you. All you need do is use the RegistrationHelper application that Microsoft supplies to perform the task. The following steps tell how to obtain RegistrationHelper and where to place it for easy access:

1. Create a Bin folder in the \CodePack folder you created in Chapter 4.
2. Open the TaskbarDemo solution found in the \CodePack\Samples\Shell\TaskbarDemo\CS folder.
3. Perform a release build of the application (you don't have to run it if you don't want to).
4. Copy RegistrationHelper.EXE from \CodePack\Samples\Shell\TaskbarDemo\CS\TaskbarDemo\bin\Release to \CodePack\Bin. You're ready to begin using RegistrationHelper to register your application.

### Configuring the Common Categories Application

Before you can do anything, you need to configure the application. In this case, the form does have some functional controls. You need a method for adding new files to the Recent or Frequent category. In addition, when you open the application as the result of selecting an entry in either the

Recent or Frequent list, the application opens another copy of itself and shows which file you selected. Figure 5-1 shows the form used for this example.

You click Add Filename to add a file to the Filename List ListBox. The application actually opens the default program (Notepad in most cases) with the file, rather than handling the file itself. In fact, when you right-click the Taskbar icon and choose an entry in either the Recent or Frequent category, you simply see a copy of Notepad open, even though the application is still called upon to perform the work. The "Handling Recent and Frequent Category Clicks" section of this chapter describes this process in more detail.

After you create the form, you need to add references to the following DLLs. Use the same process as described in the "Creating the Solution" section of Chapter 4.

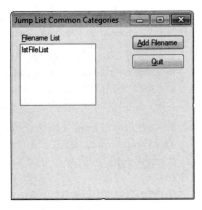

**FIGURE 5-1:** This form helps you open new files and displays a list of files opened.

```
Microsoft.WindowsAPICodePack.DLL
Microsoft.WindowsAPICodePack.Shell.DLL
```

This example uses a few more features of the Code Pack. In addition, you need to perform a little fancy programming to register the file extension and handle exiting the application properly. Add the following using statements to the beginning of your code and you'll have the project configured.

```
using Microsoft.WindowsAPICodePack.Taskbar;
using Microsoft.WindowsAPICodePack.Shell;
using Microsoft.WindowsAPICodePack.Dialogs;
using System.Diagnostics;
using System.Reflection;
using Microsoft.Win32;
```

## Registering the File Extension

In order for this example to work, Windows must know that your application wants to maintain a list of recently or frequently opened files of a certain type. To perform this task, you register the file extension. The registration consists of two parts. First, the application creates an entry in the HKEY_CLASSES_ROOT\.txt\OpenWithProgids key, as shown in Figure 5-2. The program identifier for the example application is CommonCategories, so that's the name of the value you add. The value need not contain any information.

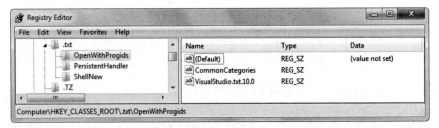

**FIGURE 5-2:** Register your application with the file extension you want to interact with.

Second, you must create an entry that describes your application. This description follows the same pattern as every other application in HKEY_CLASSES_ROOT, which means you define verbs for specific actions, such as opening the file. Figure 5-3 shows the hierarchy used for this application. In this case, the application can open only files using a command of ApplicationPath\Common Categories.exe %1, where ApplicationPath is the path to your application.

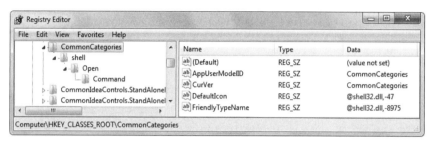

**FIGURE 5-3:** Create a description of your application.

To make the coding process and updates easier, it pays to create two global variables to hold the application identifier and program identifier. In this case, the application identifier and the program identifier are the same because the application supports only one program. However, you might need to create multiple program identifiers, one for each unique program within an application.

```
// Create variables that identify the application and program.
private String AppID = "CommonCategories";
private String ProgID = "CommonCategories";
```

There are many ways to handle the file extension registration. This book relies on the RegistrationHelper utility that ships with the Code Pack (as described in the "Obtaining and Using RegistrationHelper" section of this chapter). You could also create your own registration class or simply build the registry entries using procedural code. Listing 5-1 shows how you register your application using RegistrationHelper.

**LISTING 5-1:** Registering a file extension

Available for download on Wrox.com

```
private void RegisterFileExtension(String Extension, Boolean Unregister)
{
    // Create the execution path.
    String ExecPath = Assembly.GetEntryAssembly().Location;

    // Create a ProcessStartInfo structure for RegistrationHelper.
    ProcessStartInfo PSI =
        new ProcessStartInfo(@"D:\CodePack\Bin\RegistrationHelper.exe");

    // Calling RegistrationHelper requires some command line information.
    PSI.Arguments = String.Format("{0} {1} {2} \"{3}\" {4} {5}",
        ProgID,                 // Program Identifier
        false,                  // Register in HKEY_CURRENT_USER?
        AppID,                  // Application Identifier
        ExecPath + " %1",       // OpenWith Key Entry
        Unregister,             // Unregister this extension?
```

*continues*

**LISTING 5-1** *(continued)*

```
            " " + Extension);     // File Extension to Register

    // Use the operating system shell to execute this command.
    PSI.UseShellExecute = true;

    // Run this command using elevated privileges.
    PSI.Verb = "runas";

    // Attempt to register the file extension.
    try
    {
        Process.Start(PSI).WaitForExit();
    }
    catch (Win32Exception Except)
    {
        // Display error messages as needed.
        if (Except.NativeErrorCode == 1223)
            MessageBox.Show("User cancelled operation");
        else
            MessageBox.Show(Except.Message);
    }
}
```

RegistrationHelper requires a number of command line arguments to execute properly. The code begins by creating a `ProcessStartInfo` object, `PSI`, which contains the information that RegistrationHelper needs. You need the six bits of information shown in the code. If you register the application in `HKEY_CURRENT_USER`, then the settings become user-specific. This example doesn't require that level of flexibility, so it doesn't register itself in `HKEY_CURRENT_USER`.

One of the more important entries is the `OpenWith` key value argument. Most applications pass the name of the file to open as the first argument. Consequently, the `OpenWith` key value is often nothing more than the name of the application, followed by %1, which expands to the input filename. If your application requires additional inputs, be sure to include them with this entry.

The same command line can register or unregister the application, so the caller passes a Boolean value, `Unregister`, as part of the call to `RegisterFileExtension()`. Setting this value to `true` will unregister the application.

The final argument for RegistrationHelper is the file extension you want to register. A common mistake here is to use the wrong case or not include the period with the extension. For example, if you want to register the `.txt` extension, you must pass `.txt` and not `txt`, `TXT`, `.TXT`, or some other odd combination.

To execute RegistrationHelper properly, you must open a copy of the command process. The `PSI .UseShellExecute` property controls how Windows starts the process — setting this property to `true` opens a command processor.

Registry modification is a higher-level task — not everyone can do it. Because this application must have administrator privileges, the code sets the `PSI.Verb` property to `"runas"`, which opens the User Account Control dialog box to ask user permission to perform the task. Otherwise, the registry change could fail and the application won't work.

At this point, the code calls `Process.Start(PSI).WaitForExit()` within a `try` block. Normally, the process is going to start and perform its task unless one of the arguments is incorrect, you don't have proper rights, or you supply the wrong location for the RegistrationHelper utility. The `catch` code handles these possibilities. It's essential that the registry changes occur before the application continues, so the code uses `WaitForExit()` to ensure the task completes successfully before continuing.

### Creating the Common Categories Jump List

Creating the Jump List in this example is easy because Windows does most of the work for you. You begin by creating a global `JumpList` object, `TheJumpList`, as shown below:

```
// Define the JumpList.
private JumpList TheJumpList;
```

As with most Jump List additions, you create a `Shown` event handler, `frmMain_Shown()`, for the form, as shown in Listing 5-2. This event handler sets up the Recent category, but creating the Frequent category is just as easy. Notice that you don't add any actual category code.

**LISTING 5-2:** Adding a Recent or Frequent category to the Jump List

Available for download on Wrox.com

```
private void frmMain_Shown(object sender, EventArgs e)
{
    // Create the JumpList.
    TheJumpList = JumpList.CreateJumpList();

    // Display the Recent common category.
    TheJumpList.KnownCategoryToDisplay = JumpListKnownCategoryType.Recent;

    // Display the additions on the JumpList.
    TheJumpList.Refresh();
}
```

The code begins by instantiating `TheJumpList`. It then sets the `KnownCategoryToDisplay` property to `JumpListKnownCategoryType.Recent`. If you want to see the Frequent category instead, you set the property to `JumpListKnownCategoryType.Frequent`. Removing the list is accomplished by setting the property to `JumpListKnownCategoryType.Neither`. Make sure you call `Refresh()` after each change so it actually shows up on-screen. Figure 5-4 shows an example of the Recent list that you see after you add a few files to the list and right-click the application icon on the Taskbar.

**FIGURE 5-4:** Windows adds and manages the Recent or Frequent category as requested.

### Adding Files to the Jump List

Before your application will display any files on either a Recent or Frequent categories list, it must open some files. The application need not actually display the file — the act of sending the file to another application (as demonstrated in this example) also works. For that matter, you don't actually have to do anything with the file except open it in some way and then immediately close it. Listing 5-3 shows the file adding code for this example, which is purposely kept simple to maintain the Jump List focus.

Available for download on Wrox.com

**LISTING 5-3:** Adding a file to the Recent or Frequent category

```
private void btnAdd_Click(object sender, EventArgs e)
{
    // Create a common dialog box to allow file selection.
    CommonOpenFileDialog OpenDialog = new CommonOpenFileDialog();
    OpenDialog.Title = "Add a File to the Recent File List";
    OpenDialog.Filters.Add(
        new CommonFileDialogFilter("Text files (*.txt)", "*.txt"));

    // Display the dialog box on-screen.
    CommonFileDialogResult Result = OpenDialog.ShowDialog();

    // Save the result to the recent files list.
    if (Result == CommonFileDialogResult.OK)
    {
        // Add the file to recent files list.
        TheJumpList.AddToRecent(OpenDialog.FileName);

        // Show the selected file in the application's list box.
        lstFileList.Items.Add(OpenDialog.FileName);

        // Actually open the file.
        Process.Start(OpenDialog.FileName);
    }

    // Update the Jump List.
    TheJumpList.Refresh();
}
```

The code begins by creating a File Open dialog box like the one shown in Figure 5-5. The interesting part of this example is that you don't have to perform much coding to get it — the Code Pack provides it for you as part of the `Microsoft.WindowsAPICodePack.Dialogs` namespace. All this example does is supply a filter to define which kind of file to open. It then calls `OpenDialog.ShowDialog()` to display the dialog box on screen.

When the user clicks OK (`CommonFileDialogResult.OK`), the code adds the filename to the Jump List's Recent category by calling `TheJumpList.AddToRecent()`. It also adds the filename to the application's Filename List entry. Finally, the application

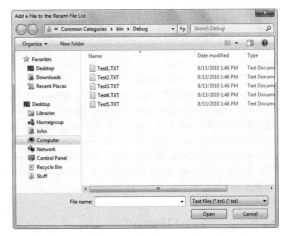

**FIGURE 5-5:** Windows adds and manages the Recent or Frequent category as requested.

calls `Process.Start()` with just the filename, which opens the file using the default application (normally Notepad unless you've changed it). To ensure the new file appears in the application's Jump List, call `Refresh()` before the `btnAdd_Click()` event handler exits.

## Handling Recent and Frequent Category Clicks

At this point, the application can add entries to either the Recent or Frequent categories. However, the application won't do anything when you select one of those entries. You must add some additional code to handle those Recent or Frequent category clicks. To begin this process, you add two global variables to the code as shown here.

```
// Create a reference to the Taskbar Manager.
private TaskbarManager Manager = TaskbarManager.Instance;

// Track the primary instance of the application.
private Boolean IsPrimary = true;
```

The first variable obtains a copy of the current `TaskbarManager` instance, which you use to register the application identifier (so the `TaskbarManager` knows your application). The second variable tracks whether the current application instance is the primary instance (the one that you interact with) or a secondary instance used to open a file in response to a user click on the Recent or Frequent category. Listing 5-4 shows how these two variables come into play.

**LISTING 5-4:** Handling incoming file requests

Available for download on Wrox.com

```
public frmMain()
{
    // Add the application identifier to the Taskbar Manager.
    Manager.ApplicationId = AppID;

    // Perform the normal initialization.
    InitializeComponent();

    // Check to see whether the extension is already registered.
    // Get the HKEY_CLASSES_ROOT\.txt\OpenWithProgids key.
    RegistryKey OpenWith =
        Registry.ClassesRoot.OpenSubKey(@".txt\OpenWithProgIds");

    // Obtain the program identifier value if it's available. If it is
    // available, it means that the file extension is registered.
    String IsReg = OpenWith.GetValue(ProgID, null) as String;

    // Register this application as a handler for the file extension if
    // necessary. If the application is already registered, then this isn't
    // the primary instance.
    if (IsReg == null)
        RegisterFileExtension(".txt", false);
    else
    {
        // Set this as a secondary instance.
        IsPrimary = false;

        // Open the file in Notepad.
```

*continues*

**LISTING 5-4** *(continued)*

```
            Process.Start(Environment.GetCommandLineArgs()[1]).WaitForExit();

            // Close this secondary instance.
            Environment.Exit(0);
        }
    }
```

The code begins by registering the application with the `TaskManager` using the `ApplicationId` property. You simply provide the `AppID` value created earlier for registering the application's file extension with Windows.

> `TaskManager` *functionality is one area that shows the new Taskbar features still require some tweaking. If you fail to assign an application identifier to the* `ApplicationId` *property, the error will show up as not having the file type registered with your application, even if you've performed the registration. Tracking the error down can take hours (if you think of looking at this issue at all). Make sure the* `TaskManager` *knows about your application to avoid potential odd error messages.*

The next step is to perform the usual initialization. You'll see the call to `InitializeComponent()` in every application.

A question that you might have is how the application determines whether it's the primary instance. The example performs this task using an interesting technique. The primary instance will always register the file extension when the application starts and unregister it when the application ends. Consequently, if the file extension is currently registered for this application, then the instance that Windows is creating is a secondary instance. The code checks for the file registration by calling `Registry.ClassesRoot.OpenSubKey()` with the `.txt\OpenWithProgIds` path and placing the result in `OpenWith`. If `OpenWith.GetValue()` can find a value that matches the application, then it fills `IsReg` with this value — otherwise, `IsReg` receives a `null`.

Once `IsReg` contains the current registry value, the code uses it to determine what to do. If this is a primary instance (`IsReg` is `null`), then the code calls `RegisterFileExtension()` to register the file extension (as a primary instance). Otherwise, the code sets `IsPrimary` to false, starts the default file processing application (usually Notepad) using `Process.Start()`, and finally exits.

There are a couple of interesting twists to note here. First, the application starts the default file processor, and then it calls `WaitForExit()` to wait until the user closes the application. If you don't wait for the application to exit, Windows will complain that your application has stopped working. The user won't actually see the secondary application instance, but the presence of the application instance is important. The second thing to notice is that the code calls `Environment.Exit(0)`, instead of `Close()`. The form isn't actually displayed at this point. Consequently, if you try to call `Close()`, you'll see an error message.

As part of the entire process, the application does need to unregister the file every time it exits. In a production application, you might leave the application registered, but for the purposes of this example, the code will leave your registry clean. Listing 5-5 shows how to unregister the code.

Available for download on Wrox.com

**LISTING 5-5:** Unregistering the file extension

```
private void frmMain_FormClosing(object sender, FormClosingEventArgs e)
{
    // Check for a primary application instance.
    if (IsPrimary)
    {
        // Clear the Recent common category so it doesn't appear when
        // the application is pinned.
        TheJumpList.KnownCategoryToDisplay = JumpListKnownCategoryType.Neither;
        TheJumpList.Refresh();

        // Unregister the .TXT file extension if this is the primary instance.
        RegisterFileExtension(".txt", true);
    }
}
```

The `frmMain_FormClosing()` event handler is called when the application closes. You don't want to do anything if this is a secondary instance, so the first thing the code checks is `IsPrimary` to determine the application instance status.

There's a final question to answer here of what happens when the user pins the application to the Taskbar. In order to prevent the user from trying to open a file with the application closed, the code sets `TheJumpList.KnownCategoryToDisplay` to `JumpListKnownCategoryType.Neither` and then refreshes the Jump List.

The code then calls `RegisterFileExtension()` with the second value set to `true`. This will unregister the file extension.

## Adding Custom Categories

Custom categories let you display a list of files or other items that meet special criteria. A category can be anything. You might want to create a list of special templates used by your organization for creating documents or a list of Help file topics that provide an overview of your application's inner workings. Using custom categories lets you decide precisely how the list appears to the user.

Creating a custom category follows many of the same techniques as creating a common category. You must register the file extension using precisely the same techniques. When the example is finished, it unregisters the file extension. The registry entries are precisely the same as well. In fact, this example uses exactly the same code as shown in Listing 5-1. Consequently, this example also relies on the same assembly references and `using` statements as the example in the "Adding Common Categories" section of this chapter does.

The biggest difference in the Custom Category example appears in Listing 5-6. Unlike using a common category, you must define precisely which files appear in the list and the order in which they appear.

**LISTING 5-6:** Creating a custom category

```
private void frmMain_Shown(object sender, EventArgs e)
{
    // Create the JumpList.
    TheJumpList = JumpList.CreateJumpList();

    // Add a custom category.
    TheJumpList.AddCustomCategories(MyCategory);

    // Create a filename and path.
    String FilePath =
        Path.GetDirectoryName(
            Assembly.GetEntryAssembly().Location) + @"\Test1.TXT";

    // Add a task to the custom category.
    MyCategory.AddJumpListItems(new JumpListItem(FilePath));

    // Refresh the JumpList.
    TheJumpList.Refresh();
}
```

In this case, the `frmMain_Shown()` event handler begins by creating the Jump List, `TheJumpList`. The next step is to add a custom category to `TheJumpList`. The custom category, `MyCategory`, is defined as a global variable like this:

```
// Define the custom category.
private JumpListCustomCategory MyCategory =
    new JumpListCustomCategory("My Custom Category");
```

When the custom category appears on the Jump List, it uses the string, My Custom Category, as its display name. The code then creates a string containing the path to the file you want to place on the custom category. A custom category that lacks an entry won't appear on the Jump List, even after you add it. In other words, the Jump List won't display just the category name. The entry you provide must be a full path, but only the filename appears on the Jump List. In this case, you'll see just `Test1.TXT` on the Jump List.

The entries in a custom category rely on the `JumpListItem` object. To add a new item to `MyCategory`, the code calls `AddJumpListItems()` with a new `JumpListItem` object whose constructor accepts `FilePath` as input. The code calls `TheJumpList.Refresh()` to display the new entry on-screen. The Custom Category example contains the remainder of the code for this example — be sure to compare it to the Common Categories example presented earlier in the chapter.

## Performing Custom Tasks

Up till now, the examples have focused on getting something displayed on the Jump List. Fortunately, you can do a lot more than simply stick something on the Jump List and hope the user clicks it at some point. It's possible to manage the Jump List much as you do any other part of your application. The Custom Task example shows some of what you can do simply by adding an array to your application and the proper management code. In this case, the example shows how to add and remove individual tasks from the Task list.

## Configuring the Custom Tasks Application

The user interface for this example is simple. All you really need is a button to add or remove Jump List entries as needed. The example uses a button named `btnTest` that switches captions between `&Remove Task` and `&Add Task`.

This example requires a reference to the Code Pack `Microsoft.WindowsAPICodePack.Shell.DLL` file. In addition, you need to add the following `using` statements.

```
using Microsoft.WindowsAPICodePack.Taskbar;
using Microsoft.WindowsAPICodePack.Shell;
using System.Reflection;
using System.IO;
```

## Creating the Custom Tasks Jump List

One of the secrets to working with Jump Lists is to rely on arrays. In most cases, you'll find a paucity of methods and properties for working with Jump List entities directly. Consequently, you must work with them indirectly. The example uses the following public variables to manage the `JumpList` object:

```
// Define the JumpList.
private JumpList TheJumpList;

// Define an array of tasks.
IJumpListTask[] TheTasks = new IJumpListTask[2];

// Create a number of tasks.
JumpListLink MyTask1;
JumpListLink MyTask2;
```

When you create a list of tasks on a Jump List, you actually use an `IJumpListTask` array to do it. The example creates an `IJumpListTask` array, `TheTasks`, which contains two elements. Of course, you can create an array of any size needed. The example fills this array using individual `JumpListLink` objects: `MyTask1` and `MyTask2`. You could just as easily reuse a single object — the example uses two for convenience.

Working with an `IJumpListTask` array and individual `JumpListLink` objects has a number of advantages beyond simple control, as shown in Listing 5-7. The example creates a Jump List with two Tasks entries in the `frmMain_Shown()` event handler.

**LISTING 5-7:** Defining a custom task Jump List

```
private void frmMain_Shown(object sender, EventArgs e)
{
    // Define the system path.
    String SysPath =
        Environment.GetFolderPath(Environment.SpecialFolder.System);

    // Create the JumpList.
```

*continues*

**LISTING 5-7** *(continued)*

```
    TheJumpList = JumpList.CreateJumpList();

    // Create the first custom task.
    MyTask1 = new JumpListLink(SysPath + @"\Notepad.EXE", "Open Test 1");

    // Configure the first custom task.
    MyTask1.IconReference = new IconReference(SysPath + "\\Notepad.EXE", 0);
    MyTask1.Arguments =
        Path.GetDirectoryName(
            Assembly.GetEntryAssembly().Location) + @"\Test1.TXT";

    // Create the second custom tsk.
    MyTask2 = new JumpListLink(SysPath + @"\Notepad.EXE", "Open Test 2");

    // Configure the second custom task.
    MyTask2.IconReference = new IconReference(SysPath + "\\Notepad.EXE", 0);
    MyTask2.Arguments =
        Path.GetDirectoryName(
            Assembly.GetEntryAssembly().Location) + @"\Test2.TXT";

    // Add tasks to the array of tasks.
    TheTasks[0] = MyTask1;
    TheTasks[1] = MyTask2;

    // Add the task array to the JumpList.
    TheJumpList.AddUserTasks(TheTasks);

    // Display the addition on the JumpList.
    TheJumpList.Refresh();
}
```

The code begins by obtaining the location of the system folder. It then creates `TheJumpList`.

The process of creating the tasks comes next. Unlike the example in Chapter 4 (see the "Adding the Jump List Code" section), this example defines `JumpListLink` objects and configures their arguments individually. Both `MyTask1` and `MyTask2` use similar arguments — one opens `Test1.TXT` and the other opens `Test2.TXT`. You have access to additional arguments for each of the `JumpListLink` objects, such as the working directory.

After the code configures the two `JumpListLink` objects, it places them in the `IJumpListTask` array using the standard technique. Each `IJumpListTask` array element is `null` when you first create it, and `null` values won't cause an error when the application executes. At this point, the code uses `TheJumpList.AddUserTasks()` to add the array to the Task List and calls `TheJumpList.Refresh()` to display the changes on-screen. Figure 5-6 shows how the Jump List appears to the user at this point.

**FIGURE 5-6:** The Jump List begins with two Tasks entries, but you can reduce it to one.

## Managing the Tasks Entries

The application is visible to the user at this point. However, you can change the appearance of the Jump List because this example works with arrays. In this case, the example uses a simple toggle mechanism to add or remove `MyTask2` as desired. Listing 5-8 shows the code required to perform this task.

**LISTING 5-8:** Managing the tasks entries on the Jump List

Available for download on Wrox.com

```
private void btnTest_Click(object sender, EventArgs e)
{
    // Determine which task to perform.
    if (btnTest.Text == "&Remove Task")
    {
        // Set the button to add a task.
        btnTest.Text = "&Add Task";

        // Remove a task from the task array.
        TheTasks[1] = null;

        // Add the task array to the JumpList.
        TheJumpList.ClearAllUserTasks();
        TheJumpList.AddUserTasks(TheTasks);

        // Update the Jump List.
        TheJumpList.Refresh();
    }
    else
    {
        // Set the button to remove a task.
        btnTest.Text = "&Remove Task";

        // Add a task to the task array.
        TheTasks[1] = MyTask2;

        // Add the task array to the JumpList.
        TheJumpList.ClearAllUserTasks();
        TheJumpList.AddUserTasks(TheTasks);

        // Update the Jump List.
        TheJumpList.Refresh();
    }
}
```

The code begins by testing the current state of `btnTest`. When `btnTest` displays Remove Task, the application removes `MyTask2` from the list. Likewise, when `btnTest` displays Add Task, the application adds `MyTask2` back to the list. The process is nearly the same for both toggles.

When the code removes the task, it sets `TheTasks[1]` to `null`. The difference in adding the task is that the code sets `TheTasks[1]` to `MyTask2`.

Before the code can modify the current list of tasks, it must remove the existing lists by calling `TheJumpList.ClearAllUserTasks()`. It then calls `TheJumpList.AddUserTasks()` to add the new version of `TheTasks` to the Jump List. As usual, the code ends by calling `TheJumpList.Refresh()`

to update the display. This technique lets you easily modify the list of tasks on the Taskbar at any time, which makes this approach more flexible than using a common categories approach.

## Going Places Using a Jump List

Microsoft classifies common category and custom category lists as destinations. Even though you might not consider them destinations, the Taskbar treats them as destinations, as contrasted to tasks, which are acts the user can perform. However, you can actually go places using either a list or a task simply by opening an URL rather than interacting with a file, or by opening an application to interact with the URL. The Go Places example shows one technique for accomplishing this task.

> *Usage differs on whether URL is pronounced like the name "Earl" or is sounded out by letter, "You-Are-Ell." This book follows the first style, so you will occasionally see "an URL" rather than "a URL."*

You configure this example the same way you do the Simple Task Bar Sample in Chapter 4. In addition, you add the same references and `using` statements. The difference is in how you create the `frmMain_Shown()` event handler. Listing 5-9 shows the code you need for this example.

**LISTING 5-9:** Going places using Jump Lists

```
private void frmMain_Shown(object sender, EventArgs e)
{
    // Define the system path.
    String ProgPath =
        Environment.GetFolderPath(Environment.SpecialFolder.ProgramFiles);

    // Create the JumpList.
    TheJumpList = JumpList.CreateJumpList();

    // Create the task.
    JumpListLink GoSomewhere =
        new JumpListLink(
            ProgPath + @"\Mozilla Firefox\Firefox.exe", "Visit APOD");

    // Configure the task.
    GoSomewhere.Arguments = "http://antwrp.gsfc.nasa.gov/apod/";
    GoSomewhere.IconReference =
        new IconReference(ProgPath + @"\Mozilla Firefox\Firefox.exe", 0);

    // Add a task to the JumpList.
    TheJumpList.AddUserTasks(GoSomewhere);

    // Display the addition on the JumpList.
    TheJumpList.Refresh();
}
```

The example begins by obtaining the location of the `\Program Files` folder (or of the `\Program Files (x86)` folder for 64-bit systems). If you're using a 64-bit browser, then you'll need to locate it on your hard drive because the `SpecialFolder` enumeration doesn't appear to contain a member for the 64-bit `\Program Files` folder. This example uses Firefox — you can just as easily use Internet Explorer or any other application capable of displaying Web pages.

After the code creates the Jump List, it begins defining a `JumpListLink`, `GoSomewhere`. In this case, the task will open a copy of Firefox (or other favorite browser) and load it with Astronomy Picture of the Day (APOD). You could just as easily load an HTML help file, take the user to the company's Website, or go anywhere else that makes sense for the application.

Configuring the task comes next. The `Arguments` property receives the URL. It pays to provide a full URL, including protocol. As usual, the code loads an icon to display on the Jump List. Once configuration is complete, the code calls `TheJumpList.AddUserTasks()` to add the task to the Jump List and `TheJumpList.Refresh()` to display it on-screen.

## USING PROGRESS BARS

Progress bars are somewhat misnamed. If you limit progress bars to simply showing the status of a task, then you're missing all kinds of opportunities. A progress bar can show the amount of something, such as the remaining disk space on a hard drive. You can also use progress bars to display distances or comparisons between two values. In fact, there are many creative ways to use progress bars in applications.

Now you can display your progress bar on the Taskbar. The application icon reflects the progress bar within your application. It actually displays a green, yellow, or red bar on top of the application's icon on the Taskbar, which means you can see the progress bar value without actually opening the application window. You could use this kind of display to track the status of a download or determine when a task is complete.

The Taskbar can track only one progress bar value at a time, but at least you now have this resource available for your applications. The Progress Bar example described in the following sections will help you understand how the Taskbar functionality works.

*Many of you will notice that the color of the bar on the Taskbar changes between green (normal), yellow (paused), and red (error). However, the `ProgressBar` control in the application doesn't do the same thing. In fact, changing the `ForeColor` property doesn't change the color of the bar, either. You seem to be stuck with a green bar, no matter what the state of the application might be. The reason for this problem is that your application is set to enable Windows XP visual themes by default. If you're using Visual Basic, there's an easy way to turn this feature off (see* `http://msdn.microsoft.com/library/y6kzhf8d.aspx`*). C# developers aren't provided with this option. If you want to disable visual styles, you can comment out the line that reads* `Application.EnableVisualStyles();` *in* `Program.CS` *for the project. However, turning off visual styles also gives you that flat look from Windows 2000; therefore, many developers aren't thrilled about this option. The only alternative is to create your own* `ProgressBar` *control and override the* `OnPaint()` *event handler to change the color of the bar (see* `http://support.microsoft.com/kb/323116` *and* `http://stackoverflow.com/questions/778678/how-to-change-the-color-of-progressbar-in-c-net-3-5`*).*

## Configuring the Progress Bar Application

The Progress Bar example provides some basic output so you can see how the Taskbar will appear in certain circumstances. First, there's the progress bar value itself that will determine the length of the bar on the Taskbar icon. A timer automatically updates the value so that you can see the bar move across the Taskbar icon. A Start button controls whether the timer is started or stopped. The Reset button changes the progress bar value back to zero. Figure 5-7 shows the basic layout for this application.

A progress bar can also have a state. The "Changing States" section of this chapter describes these states in further detail, but basically a state controls how the Taskbar icon interacts with the progress bar. For example, when the progress bar is in a normal state, the bar on the icon is green. An error state will produce a red bar, while a paused state will produce a yellow bar.

**FIGURE 5-7:** The Progress Bar example uses a timer to simulate progress.

You'll need to provide a reference to `Microsoft.WindowsAPICodePack.Shell.DLL`. In addition, the application requires the following `using` statement:

```
using Microsoft.WindowsAPICodePack.Taskbar;
```

## Managing the Progress Bar

The Progress Bar example performs four basic tasks: stop the progress bar, start the progress bar, reset the progress bar to zero, and update the progress bar value. Normally, you'd perform these tasks as part of some process, but this is a simulation after all. Listing 5-10 shows the code used for this part of the example.

**LISTING 5-10:** Starting, stopping, and resetting the progress bar

```
private void btnStart_Click(object sender, EventArgs e)
{
    // Determine the status of the Start button.
    if (btnStart.Text == "&Start")
    {
        // Set the State indicator to Normal.
        cbState.SelectedIndex = 0;
    }
    else
    {
        // Set the State indicator to Paused.
        cbState.SelectedIndex = 1;
    }
}

private void btnReset_Click(object sender, EventArgs e)
{
    // Reset the progress bar value.
    pbStatus.Value = 0;
```

```
    }

    private void UpdateStatus_Tick(object sender, EventArgs e)
    {
        // Increment the progress bar if the progress bar hasn't
        // exceeded its maximum value.
        if (pbStatus.Value < pbStatus.Maximum)
            pbStatus.Value += 1;

        // Set the Taskbar icon to reflect the progress bar.
        TheTaskbar.SetProgressValue(pbStatus.Value, pbStatus.Maximum);
    }
```

The `btnStart_Click()` event handler simply provides a toggle between the start and stop states. The "Changing States" section shows how changing the `cbState.SelectedIndex` value actually changes the progress bar state.

The `ProgressBar` control, `pbStatus`, will continue increasing its value until it reaches the maximum value it can show. At this point, it won't advance any further (since this is clearly impossible). The `btnReset_Click()` event handler simply sets the `pbStatus` `.Value` property to 0 to begin the update process over again.

To simulate a real progress bar, the example relies on a Timer control, `UpdateStatus`, to update `pbStatus`. The `UpdateStatus_Tick()` event handler simply increments `pbStatus.Value`, until `pbStatus.Value` is equal to `pbStatus.Maximum`. In addition, this event handler updates the Taskbar icon to match `pbStatus` by calling `TheTaskbar.SetProgressValue()`. The first argument contains the current progress bar value, while the second contains the maximum value. Figure 5-8 shows a typical view of the Progress Bar.

**FIGURE 5-8:** A Progress Bar places a colored bar over the icon to show status.

## Changing States

As with most controls, a *state* is simply the level of operation for the Taskbar Progress Bar. It can have five different states, as described in the following list:

- **Normal:** Progressing toward some final value. Displays a green bar.
- **Paused:** Stopped progressing temporarily, but will progress soon. Displays a yellow bar.
- **Error:** Encountered a condition that prevents progress. Displays a red bar.
- **Indeterminate:** Confused about the current status of the task. Doesn't display a bar.
- **NoProgress:** Stopped progressing toward the final value and the task isn't paused. Displays a non-moving green bar.

Of these five states, you'll use the Normal, Paused, and Error states most often. The Indeterminate state is really an indication that your application has no idea what its state is, which is something you should avoid. Listing 5-11 shows the implementation of the five states for this application.

**LISTING 5-11:** Testing the five progress bar states

```csharp
private void cbState_SelectedIndexChanged(object sender, EventArgs e)
{
    // Determine which option the user has selected.
    switch (cbState.SelectedIndex)
    {
        case 0: // Normal
            // Start the timer.
            UpdateStatus.Enabled = true;

            // Change the caption.
            btnStart.Text = "&Stop";

            // Set the Taskbar progress bar state.
            TheTaskbar.SetProgressState(TaskbarProgressBarState.Normal);
            TheTaskbar.SetProgressValue(pbStatus.Value, pbStatus.Maximum);

            // Set the progress bar state.
            pbStatus.Style = ProgressBarStyle.Continuous;

            break;

        case 1: // Paused
            // Disable the timer.
            UpdateStatus.Enabled = false;

            // Change the caption.
            btnStart.Text = "&Start";

            // Set the Taskbar progress bar state.
            TheTaskbar.SetProgressState(TaskbarProgressBarState.Paused);
            TheTaskbar.SetProgressValue(pbStatus.Value, pbStatus.Maximum);

            // Set the progress bar state.
            pbStatus.Style = ProgressBarStyle.Continuous;

            break;

        case 2: // Error
            // Disable the timer.
            UpdateStatus.Enabled = false;

            // Change the caption.
            btnStart.Text = "&Start";

            // Set the Taskbar progress bar state.
            TheTaskbar.SetProgressState(TaskbarProgressBarState.Error);
            TheTaskbar.SetProgressValue(pbStatus.Value, pbStatus.Maximum);

            // Set the progress bar state.
            pbStatus.Style = ProgressBarStyle.Continuous;

            break;

        case 3: // Indeterminate
```

```csharp
            // Disable the timer.
            UpdateStatus.Enabled = false;

            // Change the caption.
            btnStart.Text = "&Start";

            // Set the Taskbar progress bar state.
            TheTaskbar.SetProgressState(TaskbarProgressBarState.Indeterminate);
            TheTaskbar.SetProgressValue(pbStatus.Value, pbStatus.Maximum);

            // Set the progress bar state.
            pbStatus.Style = ProgressBarStyle.Marquee;

            break;

        case 4: // No Progress
            // Disable the timer.
            UpdateStatus.Enabled = false;

            // Change the caption.
            btnStart.Text = "&Start";

            // Set the Taskbar progress bar state.
            TheTaskbar.SetProgressState(TaskbarProgressBarState.NoProgress);
            TheTaskbar.SetProgressValue(pbStatus.Value, pbStatus.Maximum);

            // Set the progress bar state.
            pbStatus.Style = ProgressBarStyle.Continuous;

            break;
    }
}
```

In all five cases, the code follows a similar pattern. It begins by turning the timer off or on as needed for the simulation of progress. The next step is to set the `btnStart.Text` property to an appropriate value: `&Start` or `&Stop`.

The next step is important. First, the code sets the progress bar's state by calling `TheTaskbar.SetProgressState()`. The `TaskbarProgressBarState` enumeration provides all five of the values previously mentioned for setting the state. Second, the code sets the progress bar's value by calling `TheTaskbar.SetProgressValue()` with the current `pbStatus` value and maximum value.

Finally, the code sets the `pbStatus.Style` property to one of the `ProgressBarStyle` enumeration values. In most cases, you want `pbStatus` to display its current value by using `ProgressBarStyle.Continuous`. However, when the task is in an indeterminate state, you use `ProgressBarStyle.Marquee` to show a floating value. The Taskbar can't display this floating value (actually, a rotating bar displayed as a marquee), so it shows nothing at all.

## USING THUMBNAIL TOOLBARS

Windows 7 currently has just one example of a Thumbnail Toolbar, so naturally, everyone references it. The Windows Media Player provides controls directly on the thumbnail so that you can work with the application without displaying it. The controls are simple. You can start, stop, and pause the media you're playing. Two additional controls let you move between the previous and next selection when playing media with multiple selections. The example in this section is a little simpler. It simulates a Help button. There are times when a user wants to see Help while doing research without having to display the application. Of course, you can use a Thumbnail Toolbar for any purpose.

## Defining the Thumbnail Toolbar Application

The user interface for this example is very simple. The only required button is one named `btnTest` and labeled `Help`.

This example requires you to add a few assemblies that you might not have worked with in the past. In fact, you won't work with them in this example either, but the underlying Code Pack requires the assemblies to work. Begin by adding the following assembly as usual, using the Browse tab of the Add Reference dialog box.

```
Microsoft.WindowsAPICodePack.Shell.DLL
```

You also need to add the following assemblies from the .NET tab of the Add Reference dialog box:

```
PresentationCore
WindowsBase
```

The `PresentationCore` and `WindowsBase` assemblies are used when creating the Thumbnail Toolbar, and you won't actually use them directly. However, your application will fail to compile if you don't add them. In addition to the assemblies, you must also add the following `using` statement:

```
using Microsoft.WindowsAPICodePack.Taskbar;
```

## Drawing the Button Icon

Any button you add to a Thumbnail Toolbar is going to be added as a graphic image. Consequently, you must provide an icon that Windows uses to draw the image. Use the following procedure to add an icon to the example:

1. Right-click the project entry in Solution Explorer and choose Properties from the context menu. You'll see the project's properties window.

2. Select the Resources tab. You'll see any available resources as shown in Figure 5-9.

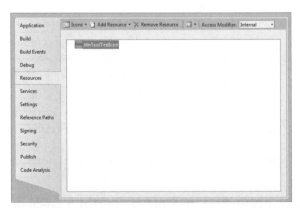

**FIGURE 5-9:** Provide a suitable icon for each of the buttons you want to add.

3. Choose Add Resource ➪ Add New Icon. You'll see a new icon added to the window.
4. Draw the icon you want to use. Figure 5-10 shows the icon used for the example.

## Creating the Toolbar and Event Handler

The Thumbnail Toolbar always exists for your application, but Windows doesn't display it unless it contains a button. Listing 5-12 shows the code used to add a button to the Thumbnail Toolbar.

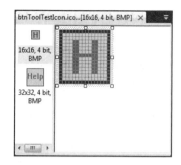

**FIGURE 5-10:** Make sure you include both 16 × 16 and 32 × 32 icons for your project.

**LISTING 5-12:** Creating the Thumbnail Toolbar control

```
private void frmMain_Shown(object sender, EventArgs e)
{
    // Create a button to display on the thumbnail.
    ThumbnailToolbarButton btnToolTest =
        new ThumbnailToolbarButton(
            Properties.Resources.btnToolTestIcon, "Request Help");

    // Configure the button.
    btnToolTest.Click +=
        new EventHandler<ThumbnailButtonClickedEventArgs>(btnTest_Click);

    // Add the button to the thumbnail.
    Manager.ThumbnailToolbars.AddButtons(this.Handle, btnToolTest);
}
```

The code begins by creating a `ThumbnailToolbarButton` object, `btnToolTest`. The constructor for this object requires an icon resource as input and a string that's used to display a tooltip when the user hovers the mouse over the control.

At a minimum, you must define a `Click` event handler for the button so that it can perform useful work. In this case, `btnToolTest` uses the same event handler as `btnTest` — the control on the form. Notice that this is a template call. You must provide `ThumbnailButtonClickedEventArgs` as the template, or the code won't compile. This particular aspect of the call differs from most of the examples you see online.

At this point, you can add the button to an instance of the `TaskbarManager`, `Manager`, using the `ThumbnailToolbars` `.AddButtons()` method. This call requires that you provide a handle for the window that you want to control with the button. Fortunately, you can easily obtain the handle using the `this.Handle` property. You must also provide the control you want to add to the Thumbnail Toolbar. Figure 5-11 shows how the example button (the one labeled Help) appears. Click the button and you'll see a simple message box.

**FIGURE 5-11:** Clicking the button displays a message box.

## USING OVERLAY ICONS

An Overlay Icon appears over the top of the Taskbar icon. You can use it to indicate some type of status information. For example, you might display an icon to show that the application is accessing a secure site or that the site has privacy issues that the user needs to know about. An icon can show that the application is experiencing some type of internal error or that a resource is unavailable. In short, you use Overlay Icons as a sort of graphic message to the user to indicate a condition that the user might want to investigate further or simply ignore until your application resolves it automatically. The following sections describe how to use the Overlay Icon example to work with Overlay Icons on the Taskbar.

Many aspects of using an Overlay Icon are the same as working with a Thumbnail Toolbar (see the "Using Thumbnail Toolbars" section of this chapter for details). For example, you must create an icon for each of the overlays you want to present. This example keeps things simple by presenting just one overlay. You perform the same setup as you do for the Thumbnail Toolbar example. In addition, you create an icon using the same technique as described in the "Drawing the Button Icon" section of this chapter. This example uses a yellow box with the word Yes! in it. Listing 5-13 shows the code for this example.

**LISTING 5-13:** Add an Overload Icon to the Taskbar

Available for download on Wrox.com

```csharp
private void btnShow_Click(object sender, EventArgs e)
{
    // Determine the icon status.
    if (btnShow.Text == "&Show")
    {
        // Set the button to hide the icon.
        btnShow.Text = "&Hide";

        // Add the overlay to the Taskbar icon.
        Manager.SetOverlayIcon(
            Properties.Resources.Exclamation, "Great, it's done!");
    }
    else
    {
        // Set the button to show the icon.
        btnShow.Text = "&Show";

        // Remove the overlay icon from the Taskbar icon.
        Manager.SetOverlayIcon(null, "");
    }
}
```

The example begins by determining the current `btnShow` status. The button toggles between Show and Hide so that you can see the Overlay Icon appear and disappear. In either case, the first step is to change the `btnShow.Text` property to display the alternate state.

Setting the overlay consists of calling the `TaskbarManager` instance, `Manager.SetOverlayIcon()` method. If you want to display an icon, you must provide an icon resource as the first argument and an accessibility string as the second argument. The accessibility string ensures that those with special needs can hear the status information when working with a screen reader. When you want the icon to disappear, simply pass a `null` value for the icon and an empty string. Figure 5-12 shows how the Taskbar icon appears with an overlay in it.

**FIGURE 5-12:** An Overlay Icon can show status information on the Taskbar.

## COMBINING TASKBAR CONTROLS

Through the examples in this chapter, you've experienced some of the tasks you can perform using the Taskbar controls. What's amazing is that these controls can greatly affect how the user perceives your application because the user is constantly viewing the Taskbar, even when interacting with other applications. Of course, because these controls can have such a big impact on the user's perceptions of your application, you need to choose the controls with great care.

One thing you should have noticed is that you don't always have to use the prescribed control to perform a given task. For example, you might immediately think that you must use a common category to retain a list of recently or frequently opened documents. However, you could just as easily maintain such a list using a custom category and thereby better control the presentation of the list to the user. The alternative to this form of list, however, is to create a list of tasks. You can easily use the example shown in the "Performing Custom Tasks" section of this chapter to manage a list of documents. Using this approach has the following advantages:

➤ Each document can have a custom icon associated with it, so that the user can rely on an icon, as well as the document name, to determine the document's purpose.

➤ The document can be opened by any of a number of applications, rather than simply the current or default application.

➤ There's no need to register a file association when using the task list approach because the application association is contained within the command you create.

➤ Using a task list approach may actually require less code and offer additional flexibility.

Using tasks does come with some disadvantages. For example, tasks aren't automatic in any form. You must configure and manage everything about them. Therefore, you must consider the benefit of each form of control in maintaining the lists of items you want to present to the user. In many situations, a combination of techniques will work best in displaying the choices the user needs, while reducing application complexity and coding requirements.

One of the issues you need to address is that most people are graphically oriented. That's the reason charts and graphs work better than tabular data to convey information at meetings. Consequently, you want to include graphics when you can on Jump Lists and on the Taskbar itself. An icon next to a Jump List item is likely to grab the user's attention long before the associated text. Likewise, a Progress Bar or Overlay Icon is going to help notify the user about status information long before any text you provide will. This said, text is always useful in passing on details that graphics can't provide. In some cases, you need to combine both graphical and textual controls to ensure the user understands the Taskbar presentation.

## CREATING A COMPLETE INTERFACE

A complete Taskbar interface isn't always about using the special features. Sometimes you must choose between features or select the right feature. However, before you can do anything at all, you must determine whether the platform even supports the features. After all, a user could try to run your application on an older version of Windows. In some cases, the user might use Mono (http://www.mono-project.com/Main_Page) to run the application on a non-Windows platform, so you can't know for sure whether the user has a platform that will work unless you conduct the simple test shown in the Check OS example. Listing 5-14 shows the simple code used to perform the check.

**LISTING 5-14:** Checking OS compatiblity

Available for download on Wrox.com

```
private void btnTest_Click(object sender, EventArgs e)
{
    // Get the application compatibility status.
    if (TaskbarManager.IsPlatformSupported)
        MessageBox.Show("This OS supports the features!");
    else
        MessageBox.Show("Sorry, tough luck.");
}
```

As you can see, all you need do is check the `TaskbarManager.IsPlatformSupported` property. When this property is true, you can use all the new Windows 7 features. Now that you have a better idea of how to check the functionality of your operating system, it's time to consider the interface decisions you must make.

## Application Interaction Using Jump Lists and Thumbnail Toolbars

When choosing between Jump Lists and Thumbnail Toolbars, you need to consider how the feature is used. A Jump List can contain both destinations and tasks, while a Thumbnail Toolbar is always used for tasks alone. In addition, you can add far more entries to a Jump List than you can to a Thumbnail Toolbar. In most cases, the practical limit for a Thumbnail Toolbar is four controls, although you could probably try to stuff one with additional controls if your application desperately needed them.

The significant advantage of the Thumbnail Toolbar is that it communicates graphically. As mentioned in the "Combining Taskbar Controls" section of this chapter, graphics communicate better to users than text ever will. The use of the right icon on a Thumbnail Toolbar could conceivably give your application an international appeal without requiring a ton of translation skills. In addition, using a Thumbnail Toolbar can reduce user training costs because you don't have to tell users constantly to read the text you've provided. Similar-sounding tasks and destinations on a Jump List can prove confusing for even the most advanced user.

In general, the best policy is to keep things simple. There are going to be some developers out there who will decide to try to put the entire application interface on the Taskbar, and it isn't going to work. It's important to remember that Taskbar controls, whether on a Jump List or a Thumbnail Toolbar, should consist of only those items that a user might change without displaying the application window. Keep the Windows Media Player example in mind because it's a good example of high-quality design practices.

Another concept to keep in mind is that Jump Lists are normally best for static choices, such as deciding which file you want to load or making the decision to perform a task such as downloading status information. A Thumbnail Toolbar works best for dynamic choices, such as pausing and restarting the status information download. The difference is often subtle, but it's best to keep this static versus dynamic orientation in mind as you design your application update.

## Displaying Status Using Overlay Icons and Progress Bars

Both Overlay Icons and Progress Bars can display status information. In addition, both these techniques place something over the top of the Taskbar icon. Consequently, you shouldn't use both techniques at the same time. In fact, it's probably a good idea to dedicate your application to one approach or the other to ensure they don't appear at the same time.

In most cases, you use Overlay Icons to display static status information, such as the presence of an application error or the loss of a needed resource. You can also use Overlay icons to display interaction information, such as the use of a high-security connection with a server.

Developers will typically use Progress Bars for dynamic information. While an Overlay Icon will show a definite state, the Progress Bar will show the progress of a task between start and finish — in short, you see a continuum of status information. When using a Progress Bar, you can indicate some types of static information using the three colors that a Progress Bar provides: green, yellow, and red. Although this chapter equated the colors with specific states, such as an error condition for red, you can assign any static value you want to the colors as long as the user understands these assignments.

## MOVING YOUR APPLICATIONS TO WINDOWS 7

This chapter demonstrates techniques for using various Taskbar features to enhance your application. Typically, you'll use just one or two of these features in a given application to avoid overloading the user with too much to think about. The features you choose to implement should flow with the application and work with it in a way that lets the user focus on work, rather than your application. Even if you're in the rare position of being able to use more features, make sure you use them correctly. A Jump List that covers the entire display is hardly helpful and will definitely confuse the user.

Now that you have some experience with the Taskbar features, it's time to decide which features to add to your application and the technique you want to use to add them. Remember that you actually have three techniques for adding the features to your application: Code Pack; WPF XAML; and WPF code behind. Try several combinations of features to determine which combinations make users most efficient and which combinations interfere least with users' work styles. As part of your decision, it's also important to consider the cost of the update and the amount of training users require to use the new features.

The Taskbar isn't the only place where your application can excel. In many cases, using the Ribbon interface will help less-experienced users learn the application faster and work with it more efficiently. (Some of your power users will most definitely complain that the Ribbon causes them to work slower and have to relearn the application.) Depending on how you use your application, you may decide to update it with a Ribbon interface, rather than continue to use the older menu and toolbar system. Chapter 6 starts the discussion of how to work with the Ribbon by presenting some guidelines and a basic example.

# Working with the Ribbon Interface

**WHAT'S IN THIS CHAPTER?**

➤ Understanding how the Ribbon can improve your application

➤ Working with Office, which currently uses the Ribbon interface

➤ Defining Ribbon functionality for application updates

The Ribbon interface has received more than a few comments from people. In the past, Microsoft relied on a menu and toolbar interface that new users seemed to find confusing and veteran users learned to love. For those who have learned to do everything with the keyboard using shortcuts, the Ribbon represents a new learning curve and a relatively steep one at that. On the other hand, new users are finally able to get up and running relatively fast, and smart developers have found ways to create task-oriented Ribbon additions that make it even easier to get the new user working quickly. This chapter isn't about politics, nor is it going to settle the question of which is best: Ribbon or menu and toolbar. The question is probably rendered moot anyway by whatever policies your organization has in place.

The news for Windows 7 is that the Ribbon has left Office and is now in the operating system. You'll see the Ribbon in all kinds of places (such as Wordpad), and it's a good bet that Microsoft will continue adding the Ribbon interface to other applications (such as Notepad). A few applications will probably retain their quirky interfaces (such as Windows Media Player) simply because there isn't a good alternative that works well. Whether you believe in the Ribbon or not, you'll probably encounter it at some point and will need to work with it. This chapter does discuss the Windows 7 view of the Ribbon so you'll have some idea of how the operating system handles it.

Windows 7 doesn't provide quite the same Ribbon functionality as Office does (where the Ribbon isn't quite fully integrated yet — for example, Outlook still partially uses the menu and toolbar interface). You can count on Microsoft improving Ribbon functionality in the next version of Windows. In fact, you can probably count on a Windows 7 service pack changing the way the Ribbon works in Windows 7. With this in mind (and to provide you with some ideas of how the Ribbon can work in your application), this chapter also looks at the Office 2007 implementation of the Ribbon. The reason this chapter doesn't look at Office 2010 is that Office 2010 takes the Ribbon to a new level that probably won't appear in Windows 7 at any time.

If your organization decides to use the Ribbon interface for an application update or a new application, you need to plan the update carefully. Users who haven't seen the Ribbon before won't know what to do with it. Veteran users are likely to treat the Ribbon with some level of contempt and animosity. However, moving to the Ribbon can pay off in some fantastic benefits if it's managed correctly and used for the correct reasons. This chapter also considers the planning you need to perform before moving to the Ribbon.

## CONSIDERING THE RIBBON AS A WHOLE

Before you can decide whether to add the Ribbon to your application, you need to know something about what the Ribbon looks like in Windows 7. There's a lot of misinformation about the Ribbon floating around on the Internet, and you might have heard horror stories of lost productivity from reviewers who haven't really used the Ribbon in the environment in which it's designed to work. Then again, you may have heard the opposite story — that somehow the Ribbon fixed every problem an organization had in training users, or that it increased productivity astronomically. Both viewpoints are absurd. The Ribbon is simply another tool. Like all tools, the Ribbon has correct uses — it has pros and cons. People misuse the Ribbon as they do just about every other tool. The following sections review the Ribbon from the Windows 7 perspective, which isn't precisely the same as the Office perspective.

### Precisely What Is the Ribbon?

The *Ribbon* is a tabbed interface that replaces the menu and toolbar system used by older applications. A Ribbon application relies on tabs to group like tasks together. The tasks appear within groups on the tab, and each group has one or more controls that help the user configure, view, and perform the task, and optionally review the task status. The Ribbon is generally viewed as a workflow mechanism where the user is engaging in a particular process to accomplish work. Figure 6-1 shows a typical Windows 7 Ribbon interface (this one is in Wordpad).

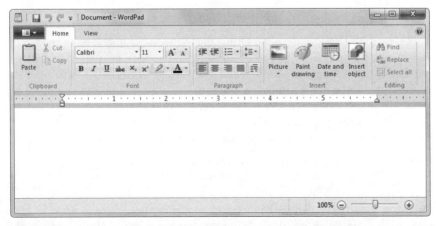

**FIGURE 6-1:** The Ribbon relies on a tabbed interface with groups of tasks.

Let's take one small example. If you want to find something, then you'll look at the Editing group on the Home tab, and you'll find a button named Find. Click Find and you'll see the Find dialog box, where you can enter the information for finding something and click Find Next. The process is very easy. Now, look at the same application with a menu and toolbar interface in Figure 6-2.

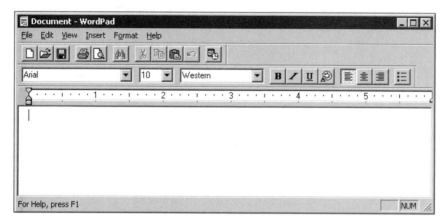

**FIGURE 6-2:** The menu and toolbar interface is less open than the Ribbon.

To find something, you must first know that you need to open the Edit menu. Nothing about the interface tells you to perform this step; you simply have to know to do it. On the Edit menu you see the Find and Find Next commands — it isn't apparent which one to use, so you select one at random and hope for the best. At this point, you see a Find dialog that contains essentially the same information as the Ribbon-based equivalent.

OK, so far it sounds as if the Ribbon is a lot easier to use. There's only one problem. Look again at the menu and toolbar version of Wordpad, and you'll notice that the Find Next entry has F3 next to it. That's right, if you want to repeat the search, you can simply press F3 to do it. The Ribbon equivalent doesn't provide this information. However, if you press F3 in the newer version of Wordpad, it also repeats the search, but now you need to know about F3 — nothing tells you about it.

Here in a nutshell is the problem between the Ribbon and the menu and toolbar interface. If you're a power user, pressing F3 is significantly faster than grabbing the mouse to click Find in the Editing group of the Home tab again. Unfortunately, nothing about the new version of Wordpad will ever tell you about this shortcut key, and there's no mandate to include such information on the Ribbon. In short, if you're a power user and you want to know about shortcut keys, you're out of luck unless you can find them in the Help file.

The Ribbon also tends to be slower for keyboard users. For example, let's look at the Find command from the keyboard user's perspective. You'll go through these steps:

1. Press Alt to see the next key you must click, as shown in Figure 6-3. Unlike the menu and toolbar interface, which underlines the speed keys, the Ribbon interface hides them. So you must press Alt, just to see the next key to press.

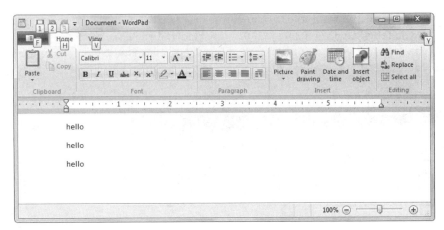

**FIGURE 6-3:** You must press Alt by itself to see the speed keys when working with the Ribbon.

2. Press H to access the Home tab. Now you see the Home tab shortcut keys, as shown in Figure 6-4.

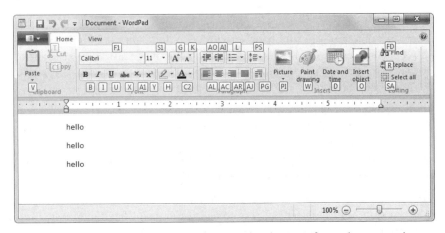

**FIGURE 6-4:** Access the appropriate tab to see the shortcuts for each command.

3. Press FD to access the Find command. So the total for the Ribbon is four key presses, and using the shortcuts is counterintuitive.

Now, look at the menu and toolbar version in Figure 6-2. You know that you press Alt+E to access the Edit menu because the E is underlined. You then press F to access the Find command. The menu and toolbar interface requires only two key presses to perform the same task, but one key press is compound (Alt+E), requiring some finger gymnastics. Of course, the Edit menu shows that you can do the same thing even faster by pressing Ctrl+F.

In fairness, compare mouse clicks for the Ribbon vs. the menu and toolbar interface. If you're using a mouse, the Ribbon offers one-click access to the Find command. On the other hand, the menu and toolbar interface requires two clicks — once on the Edit menu and again on the Find command. The Ribbon is inherently more mouse-friendly, and novices tend to use the mouse a lot.

Key presses and mouse clicks notwithstanding, the Ribbon has one undeniable appeal that the menu and toolbar interface lacks. The graphic interface makes it significantly easier for novices to understand and remember. For a company, the Ribbon interface can greatly reduce training costs now and support costs later. Common tasks appear in a larger font and rely on a larger icon than less-used tasks, so the Ribbon also has an implied preference for the commands. A user looking for a particular task finds it easier most of the time because common tasks are highlighted.

Position also makes a big difference on the Ribbon. Believe it or not, someone researched how users work and discovered that users are most likely to set the text font first, and then the paragraph format, so the Ribbon places them in that order. In fact, some of the best Ribbon applications create an actual workflow in which the user moves from left to right to accomplish the task. By the time the user gets to the right side of the Ribbon, the task is done — making the Ribbon a sort of mini-freeform-wizard.

By now you have a better feel for the Ribbon. It provides a friendly environment that isn't necessarily efficient to use. The focus of the Ribbon is to make things easy at the expense of speed. A Ribbon application is normally easier and faster to learn than an equivalent menu and toolbar application. However, power users tend to grouse at the inefficiencies of the Ribbon. The bottom line, though, is that an organization tends to have few power users and many novices, making the gains provided by the Ribbon concrete and quantifiable. Whether your organization fits in the Microsoft mold is up to you to decide.

## Understanding How the Ribbon Can Help Novice Users

The previous section answers some questions on how the Ribbon can help users. This section views how the Ribbon can help novice users to obtain more out of an application with less training and less support. Of course, as with everything, your results will vary with the quality and implementation of your design. The following list provides some ideas on how the Ribbon can help:

- Graphics make it easier for users to remember commands.
- Tabs normally group commands by major task area, making it easier to accomplish a particular task.
- Groups on tabs normally keep related commands together so that the user doesn't have to search for them.
- Using controls of different sizes places an emphasis on commonly used commands.
- Control variety means you can use the right control for a particular task. For example, you can use an actual checkbox when an option is either on or off. Drop-down list boxes make it possible to choose from a number of options. Special toggle buttons make it possible to execute the default command or a special command, such as Paste as the default or Paste Special as an alternative command.
- Complex controls (such as those with drop-downs) make it easier to create a default command and associated subordinate commands.

➤ Dialog box launchers make it easy for the user to see additional detail by using a full-fledged dialog when necessary, while normally ignoring the detail by using common commands within the group.

➤ Workflows make it easier for users to see the process they should follow when using the application.

➤ *Galleries* make it easy for users to select an option graphically, such as a typeface (by seeing an example of the typeface in the gallery) or a shape (by seeing how it appears in the gallery). A gallery can appear directly in the Ribbon (as it does for Word) or as a drop-down (as it appears in most Windows 7 applications).

There are other considerations with the Ribbon. For example, you can create the application to display the Ribbon as shown in the figures so far in the chapter. However, advanced users can regain some of their screen real estate by hiding the Ribbon. To do this, right-click in the tabbed area and choose Minimize the Ribbon from the context menu. Figure 6-5 shows an example of Wordpad with the Ribbon minimized. When you want to perform a task, you simply click the associated tab and the Ribbon reappears.

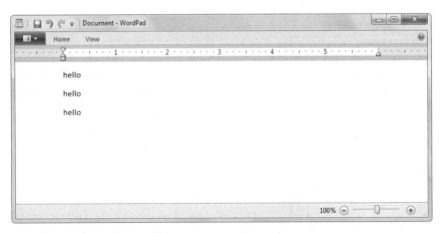

**FIGURE 6-5:** Minimizing the Ribbon can help advanced users save screen space.

One of the advantages cited for the Ribbon for Office 2007 is that users can't modify the interface, making it far easier to support the application (because commands will actually work the way support staff think they will). The one customization concession in Office 2007 is the *Quick Access Toolbar (QAT)*, where the user can place commonly used commands that are otherwise buried in the interface. The QAT appears in the upper left corner of the application — usually on the title bar. The placement of the QAT is a good idea because most users don't need a lot of customization. All they really need is to find a few commonly used commands. In the meantime, all the commands on the Home tab remain in place. When working with the menu and toolbar system, support staff would suddenly find that a command had gone missing because the user had removed it and now was wondering how to perform that task. If users find the current placement of the QAT won't work for them, they can place it below the Ribbon, as shown in Figure 6-6.

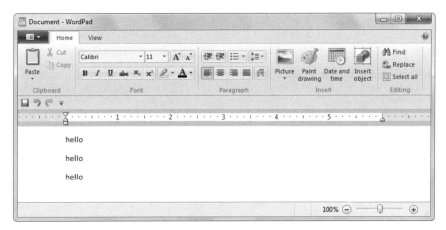

**FIGURE 6-6:** The QAT is the user customization area for a Ribbon application.

Even though it doesn't show too well in the figures so far in the chapter, the Ribbon is generally more accessible than the menu and toolbar system. The user doesn't have to go through any finger gymnastics to execute a command. Tooltips make it easier for users with screen readers to understand how the application works. The use of balloon letters makes it easier to see what to type next (Figures 6-3 and 6-4). In short, users with special needs will find working with the Ribbon interface easier.

## Viewing the Ribbon in Windows

A number of Windows 7 applications rely on the Ribbon interface. The two applications that you should pay most attention to, however, are Paint and Wordpad because these two applications use the Ribbon in a manner best suited for custom applications. You've already seen a number of examples of Wordpad in the book. Figure 6-7 shows an example of the Ribbon interface in Paint.

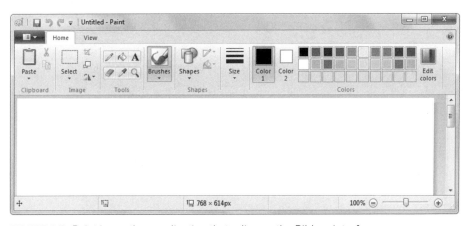

**FIGURE 6-7:** Paint is another application that relies on the Ribbon interface.

The Paint interface is interesting. You can't quite see it in the figure, but you start with what appears to be a sheet of paper and you draw on it, just as you would when working with a physical piece of paper. The workflow is stronger in Paint than it is in Wordpad. The user follows this process:

1. Select a command from either the Image or Tools group.
2. Perform a task with the Image group command (such as selecting an area of the drawing) or go to Step 4 for a Tools group command.
3. Go back to Step 1.
4. Select a brush or a shape from the associated drop-down gallery.
5. (Optional) When working with a shape, select options from the Shape Outline and Shape Fill drop-down list boxes.
6. (Optional) Select an outline or drawing size using an option from the Size drop-down list box.
7. (Optional) Select a foreground and background color using the appropriate options.
8. Create part of the drawing using the selected brush or shape.
9. Go back to Step 1.

As you can see, this workflow moves from left to right across the Ribbon. The user doesn't have to think too hard because the appropriate process is laid out as part of the Ribbon design. The options to save and print the resulting graphic appear on the File menu, which is that odd little button to the far left of the tabs. It follows the convention used by Office 2007 and its Office button.

The View tab contains commands for managing the view of the graphic, as shown in Figure 6-8. In this case, there isn't any workflow because the view is a matter of the user's own choice. However, the commands are still grouped in functional areas. For example, if you want to zoom into or out of the graphic, you can use the commands in the Zoom group, the last of which allows you to quickly move back to the 100 % zoom level.

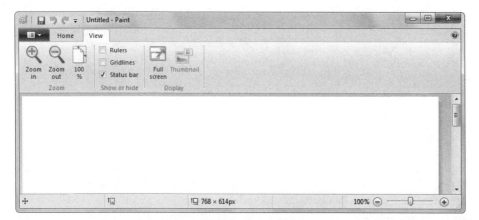

**FIGURE 6-8:** The View tab contains commands for managing the view of the graphic.

The Ribbon is also dynamic. For example, when you add a text element to a Paint graphic, Paint adds a new tab to the Ribbon, as shown in Figure 6-9. This dynamic addition applies only to the text element highlighted in the figure. If you move the cursor outside the text element, then the Text tab will go away.

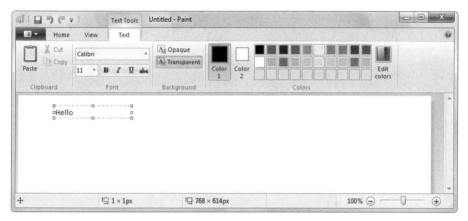

**FIGURE 6-9:** The Text tab illustrates the dynamic nature of the Ribbon.

Generally speaking, the Windows 7 applications are a good place to start your own research into the Ribbon because they're simple. The examples of Ribbon design you find in both Wordpad and Paint will get you started on your initial trials with the Ribbon and let everyone on your team get a feel for the next step. In fact, you should encourage your team to play with both Wordpad and Paint. Consider creating some exercises for them to try out. Make sure you get users interested in working with the Ribbon interface, too, so that they have some idea of what to expect when you start testing your own application.

You should also consider something in working with Windows 7. Microsoft hasn't added the Ribbon to Windows Media Player, because Windows Media Player doesn't easily fit within the Ribbon paradigm. Another application that's missing the Ribbon is Notepad. No one has provided a reason for this omission, but perhaps the application is too simple to require the Ribbon, or Microsoft felt that Notepad doesn't receive much serious use. It's important to view which applications don't employ the Ribbon because these omissions can tell you a lot about which applications are suitable for the Ribbon interface. It's an easy bet that Microsoft converted the most adaptable applications first.

## VIEWING THE RIBBON IN OFFICE

The Ribbon in Office presents a magnitude of complexity greater than the Ribbon interface you see in Windows 7 itself. Most production applications are going to be more complex than Wordpad or Paint. So even though these two applications represent a good starting place, they aren't really the end of the journey in discovering the Ribbon. The second place to look is Office 2007. Figure 6-10 shows a typical view of the Word 2007 Ribbon. As you can see, it contains significantly more tabs, and the interface itself is more complex.

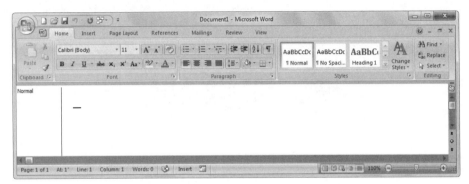

**FIGURE 6-10:** Word provides a relatively complex Ribbon interface.

As previously mentioned, Office 2010 has a lot of functionality changes that you won't see in Windows 7 — Office 2007 is a better choice to see what's possible in a complex application under Windows 7. In fact, even Office 2007 has some special tweaks that you probably won't be able to manage in your application because Microsoft hasn't made the implementation details fully available. The following sections look at how Office 2007 works with the Ribbon.

*As with Windows 7, it's a good idea to look at how Microsoft has used the Ribbon in Office 2007. For example, you'll quickly notice that Outlook doesn't use the Ribbon for its main interface — it still uses the menu and toolbar interface. However, when you create a message, the message window uses the Ribbon interface. One of the things you can do is discuss with colleagues why Microsoft would take this approach (the company hasn't put anything in print). One rumored reason is that the add-in developers need more time to produce Ribbon-friendly versions of their products, so Microsoft chose not to implement the Ribbon in Outlook.*

## Understanding the Office Document Connection

It may surprise you to learn that Office 2007 documents are actually ZIP files in disguise. For example, Word .DOCX, .DOCM, .DOTX, or .DOTM files are all .ZIP files. To see how this works for yourself, create a document in Word and save it to disk. Change the file extension from .DOCX or .DOCM to .ZIP. Open the resulting file with a product such as WinZIP and you'll see the file structure of the document file, as shown in Figure 6-11.

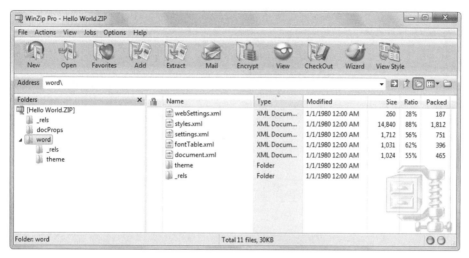

**FIGURE 6-11:** Many Office documents are simply ZIP files in disguise.

The content of the .ZIP file reflects all the elements of the documents, including any text you type into it. All this content appears within .XML files. For example, the Document.XML file shown in Figure 6-10 actually contains the content of this document. In fact, all the XML documents shown in Figure 6-11 affect the document in some way, and modifying them would change the appearance of the document in some way when you open it. In fact, this entire document structure is standardized as a European Computer Manufacturers Association (ECMA) standard (see http://www.ecma-international.org/publications/standards/Ecma-376.htm).

 *A single chapter can't present everything there is to know about the Office Ribbon. If you want a fuller, easy-to-understand treatment of the Office Ribbon, check out RibbonX for Dummies by John Paul Mueller, Wiley 2007 or VBA for Dummies by John Paul Mueller, Wiley 2007. Both books present the Ribbon simply and present techniques for working with it without having to use Visual Studio and Visual Studio Tools for Office (VSTO). It's actually quite easy to create complete Ribbon applications without resorting to advanced programming techniques, although using VSTO does present you with advanced capabilities for building complex add-ins. However, if your desire is simply to learn the details of Office support for the Ribbon, either of these books will do the job. (Both books do present a very simple VSTO application.)*

The Ribbon portion of a Word (or Excel) document or template comes as part of the CustomUI.XML file found in the \CustomUI folder. Figure 6-11 doesn't show such a folder because it doesn't contain its own interface. However, Figure 6-12 shows another document, OfficeMods2007.XLSM, that does contain custom Ribbon elements.

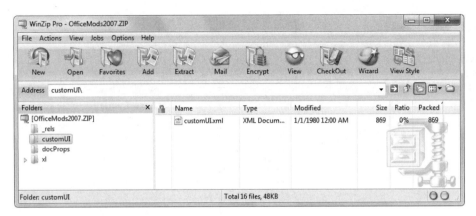

**FIGURE 6-12:** Any document or template can contain custom Ribbon elements when it has a CustomUI folder.

When you load this document, you may see a security warning telling you that macros have been disabled. To see how the example works, simply click Options, choose Enable This Content in the Microsoft Office Security Options dialog box, and click OK. You'll see a message box saying that the Ribbon has been loaded. Click OK. A new tab named My Tab will appear with a group and smiley button on it, as shown in Figure 6-13.

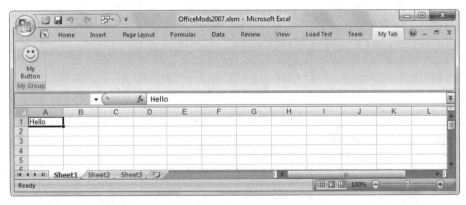

**FIGURE 6-13:** Adding the custom XML presents a new tab with custom controls on it.

Even though this book isn't about adding custom controls to Office, it's helpful to see the XML used to create the tab, group, and button shown in Figure 6-13. Listing 6-1 shows the XML found in the customUI.XML file. For the purposes of this book, you need only a general idea of what's going on, rather than a precise knowledge of all the details, so don't worry about the event handler code associated with this XML.

**LISTING 6-1:** Adding a tab, button, and control to an Excel worksheet

```xml
<?xml version="1.0" encoding="UTF-8" standalone="yes"?>
<customUI onLoad="RibbonLoaded"
  xmlns="http://schemas.microsoft.com/office/2006/01/customui">

  <commands>
    <command idMso="Underline" onAction="myUnderline"/>
  </commands>

  <ribbon>
    <tabs>
      <tab id="myTab" label="My Tab">
        <group id="myGroup" label="My Group">
          <button id="myButton" label="My Button" imageMso="HappyFace"
            size="large" onAction="myButton_ClickHandler"/>
        </group>
      </tab>
      <tab idMso="TabHome">
        <group id="BehaviorChange" label="Behavior" insertAfterMso="GroupFont">
          <toggleButton id="StopUnderline" label="Stop Underlining"
            onAction="StopUnderline_ClickHandler"
            getPressed="StopUnderline_GetPressed" size="large"
            imageMso="ShapeFillColorPicker"
            insertBeforeMso="UnderlineGallery"/>
        </group>
      </tab>
    </tabs>
  </ribbon>
</customUI>
```

This short piece of XML contains a lot of information. For example, the `<customUI>` element contains an `onLoad` attribute that defines which event to call when the Ribbon loads. In this case, the event is handled by VBA code within the Excel worksheet.

Office lets you modify existing commands on the Ribbon. To perform this task, you add a `<commands>` element and then describe which commands to change using `<command>` elements. The `Underline` command calls the `myUnderline` event handler in the VBA code for this worksheet, rather than performing the usual task.

As you can see, there's a hierarchy associated with the addition, beginning with the `<ribbon>` element. Below this element is the `<tabs>` element that contains one `<tab>` element for each new tab that you want to add to the worksheet. Each `<tab>` element can contain controls, groups, and other constructs, such as the `<group>` element shown in the example. Likewise, the `<group>` element acts as a container for the `<button>` element.

The example also modifies the content of the Excel Home tab. It adds a new `<group>` named `BehaviorChange`. In this group is a `<toggleButton>` named `StopUnderline`. Figure 6-14 shows the Home tab modification for this example. Compare this Home tab with the one you normally see when you open Excel.

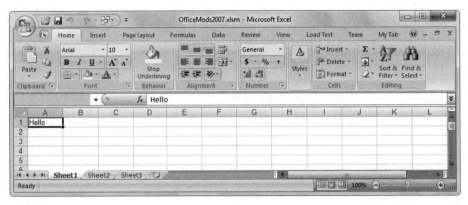

**FIGURE 6-14:** Office provides the means for modifying existing tabs as needed.

## Considering How Office Technology Extends to Windows 7

The same sorts of things that you see in the Excel example provided with this chapter are the things that you'll do when creating a Ribbon application of your own. For example, you'll create an XML file that contains the Ribbon interface you want to present. You'll then compile this file into binary form before incorporating it into your application. In sum, spending a little time with Office can be helpful because it helps you understand the XML portion of the Ribbon interface, using a product that's already debugged. If something doesn't work, it's more likely to be your XML than a bug in your application. With this in mind, you'll want to work through some interface scenarios using Office as a starting point. However, just worry about the interface — don't worry about the code behind at this point because the Office code behind is going to be completely different from what you use in your application.

Working with Office can also show you how the various controls work and give you ideas of what you can do with the interface you create. Fortunately, you don't have to do absolutely everything by hand. The Custom UI Editor (`http://openxmldeveloper.org/articles/CustomUIeditor.aspx`) makes the task of modifying the Office user interface significantly easier. If desired, you can look at the `customUI.XML` file to analyze precisely how the changes you make affect the Office user interface.

## DEFINING THE RIBBON FUNCTIONALITY IN WINDOWS 7

It's time to begin looking at some of the things you need to know to create a Ribbon interface for an application. One of the most important considerations at the outset is how to create the interface itself, which means knowing about tabs, groups, and controls. This section provides an overview of the controls and how you interact with them.

*This chapter discusses the actual markup contained in the* `UICC.XSD` *file that works with the UICC utility described in Chapter 7 to create a Ribbon binary. Don't confuse this markup with the Microsoft Office markup. Even though the two markups are similar, the Microsoft Office markup is richer in some respects. Normally, you'd use the UICC utility to create a Ribbon application with C++. Chapter 7 is going to use a special library named RibbonLib that makes things considerably easier for the Visual Studio developer. With this in mind, the following sections simplify the markup with an eye toward interoperability with the RibbonLib library found at* `http://windowsribbon.codeplex.com/releases/view/32943`*.*

## An Overview of Ribbon Controls in Windows 7

Windows 7 supports a number of components for use in Ribbon applications — essentially controls used for interaction, graphic display items, or structural objects. Many of these components are going to be familiar because you already use them in applications. There really isn't too much you can do to a checkbox to make it different from any other checkbox you've used in the past. The difference is that these components are optimized for use with the Ribbon. In addition, a few controls, such as `ToggleButton`, provide specific Ribbon functionality. Consequently, even if you've been developing applications for years, it pays to spend some time with the list of components in Table 6-1.

*You need to get used to the idea of working with a control or other object in context when creating a Ribbon application. For example, some controls must appear within another control, such as a structural element or a menu. Table 6-1 gives you a basic idea of which contexts a control can be used in. For now, it's only important to realize that a context is a situation in which you can use the control. If you want to see a complete description of all the Ribbon markup, check out the* `UICC.XSD` *file in the* `\Program Files\Microsoft SDKs\Windows\v7.1\Bin` *directory. You can load this file into Visual Studio to make it easier to explore the content of the file.*

**TABLE 6-1:** Types of Ribbon Components

| NAME | TYPE | DESCRIPTION |
| --- | --- | --- |
| Button | Control | Provides a basic execution function. Click the button and something happens within the Windows Ribbon. The Windows Ribbon provides eight different contexts in which you can use the Button control. |
| CheckBox | Control | Provides a basic selection function. The user enables or disables an option by clicking the control. The Windows Ribbon provides two contexts for the CheckBox control, including as a stand-alone control or as part of a menu. |

*continues*

**TABLE 6-1** *(continued)*

| NAME | TYPE | DESCRIPTION |
| --- | --- | --- |
| ComboBox | Control | Displays a list of options for the user. You create the list of options using the item control. Every ComboBox control must include at least one item control as a child. When working with a ComboBox control, the user can also type a value that doesn't appear in the list (a DropDown control requires the user to choose one of the options on the list). |
| DropDownButton | Control | Displays a list of options for the user. You create the list of options using the Item or Button control. The list must contain at least one of the two acceptable controls. The user must choose one of the options in the list that you provide. When the user chooses a Button, rather than an Item, control, the Windows Ribbon executes the requested action, rather than choosing the desired option. |
| HelpButton | Control | Provides a specialized form of the Button control used by the user to request help. |
| Spinner | Control | Defines a spinner used to increase or decrease the numeric quantity found in another control. |
| SplitButton | Control | Creates a button that has a default action and a list of alternative options. One of the best examples of the split button is the Paste button in the Clipboard group on the Home tab in Word and Excel. You must include a Button or ToggleButton for the default control. The optional actions appear within a Menu control, where you can add Button or ToggleButton controls. |
| ToggleButton | Control | Provides a combination of a CheckBox and a Button control. The user selects a state and performs an action by clicking the ToggleButton. |
| Command | Graphic Display and Structure | Defines the control attributes, such as name and identifier. This component also provides an extensive list of control modifiers used to change the display. For example, Command.LargeImages provides a list of large images used to display the control, while Command.SmallImages provides a similar list of small images. Additional attributes, such as ToolTipTitle and ToolTipDescription help define the user experience. |

| NAME | TYPE | DESCRIPTION |
| --- | --- | --- |
| DropDownColorPicker | Graphic Display and Structure | Displays a group of color settings from which the user can choose. The presentation is akin to a DropDownGallery, but is color-specific. |
| DropDownGallery | Graphic Display and Structure | Displays a group of controls in a drop-down structure to save space on the Ribbon. Word uses such a grouping in the Styles group of the Home tab. A DropDownGallery control differs from other grouping controls in that it provides drop-down lists that you can control in various ways. You can change the presentation of the controls using the rows and columns attributes. The ItemWidth and ItemHeight attributes help you control the size of each item in the group. You use the DropDownGallery control within a ButtonGroup or a Menu control, or as a stand-alone control. To display items in a gallery, you add code to the GetItemCount, GetItemImage, and GetItemLabel callbacks. |
| FontControl | Graphic Display and Structure | Presents an amalgamation of controls used to manage font selection. This is actually a complex control structure used to contain a series of other standard controls. |
| InRibbonGallery | Graphic Display and Structure | Provides an alternative form of the DropDownGallery where the most common options appear directly on the Ribbon. A DropDownGallery accommodates less common choices. This control works much like the Styles gallery found in Word does. |
| ContextMap | Structure | Creates a grouping of a ContextMenu and a MiniToolbar control. The two controls are linked and the user works with them together. This control can save you considerable time and effort when you need both a ContextMenu and a MiniToolbar. |
| ContextMenu | Structure | Defines a menu that you attach to some other object and use to define actions that the user can perform using the object. A ContextMenu has the same basic capabilities as a standard Menu control, but it works within a specific object context, rather than as a freeform listing of potential actions the user can perform at any time. |
| Group | Structure | Groups controls together. You can place any control within a Group and flow the set of controls either horizontally or vertically. |

*continues*

**TABLE 6-1** *(continued)*

| NAME | TYPE | DESCRIPTION |
| --- | --- | --- |
| Image | Structure | Provides the information used to access a single image that defines the control's appearance on-screen. |
| MenuGroup | Structure | Groups various types of buttons together. The buttons appear within a physical box and the Windows Ribbon places them closer together to show that they're associated in some way. You can use this grouping control with the Button, ToggleButton, DropDownGallery, Menu, and SplitButton controls. |
| Menu | Structure | Defines a menu that you create at design time. The Menu can contain controls such as the Button and CheckBox. You can use a Menu in stand-alone mode, or as part of a SplitButton control. Use the MenuSeparator control to place separations between Menu elements. Unlike a DropDownGallery, the Menu control presents all the options in a single column (much like the menu system in older versions of the Windows Ribbon). |
| MenuSeparator | Structure | Provides a means of separating elements within any control group. |
| MiniToolbar | Structure | Defines a toolbar that you attach to some other object and use to define actions that the user can perform using the object. A MiniToolbar has the same basic capabilities as a standard Windows toolbar, but it works within a specific object context, rather than as a freeform listing of potential actions the user can perform at any time. |

> *Tables 6-1 and 6-2 provide summaries of the various controls and attributes. The XML markup you use to create a Ribbon interface can become quite complex, and it's outside the scope of this book to discuss such markup in detail. You can find a complete listing of the markup for the Windows 7 Ribbon at* `http://msdn.microsoft.com/library/dd371591.aspx`.

## Understanding the Control Attributes

Controls have attributes that define how they appear to the end user, how you can access them, whether the control is active, and how the controls are organized. You'll commonly use attributes to change the default appearance and behavior of the Ribbon controls. Table 6-2 contains the most commonly used attributes (those that appear in at least four controls). It doesn't include some less-used attributes such as `showItemImage`, `showItemLabel`, `sizeString`, and `title`.

**TABLE 6-2:** Common Ribbon Control Attributes

| NAME | USAGE | DESCRIPTION |
| --- | --- | --- |
| Id | Access | Specifies the identifier for a custom control. Every control must have a unique Id value and you use this value to access the control in code behind. |
| Name | Access | Provides a name for the control that you use to access the control in the markup. |
| KeyTip | Activity | Adds a specific accelerator-key combination to the control. The KeyTip appears when the user presses Alt. You can specify any key combination, using from one to three letters. |
| LabelDescription | Display | Specifies the description text that the Windows Ribbon displays when the ItemSize attribute for a menu is set too large. |
| LabelTitle | Display | Specifies the text that appears as part of the control when it's displayed on-screen. |
| Size | Display | Determines the size of a control. You can choose between large and normal as values. |
| ToolTipTitle | Display | Provides a title for the information provided by the ToolTipDescription attribute. |
| ToolTipDescription | Display | Provides a short tip to help the user understand the purpose of a control. |
| Comment | Documentation | Provides a means for documenting the control and its functionality within the markup. |

# MOVING YOUR APPLICATIONS TO WINDOWS 7

This chapter has demonstrated some of the benefits and concerns of moving to the Ribbon as presented in Windows 7. It's important to remember that Windows 7 is behind Office in Ribbon functionality. Consequently, you should realize that you'll eventually see updates in Windows as well that could break your current application, change the way in which it works, or simply modify the way users view your application (perhaps viewing it as outdated because the Ribbon features don't match those found in Office 2010). The point is to plan your update carefully to match user requirements and the features that Windows 7 can provide to your application.

At this point, you should determine whether the Ribbon is the right choice for your application. If you have a lot of less qualified users and potentially a high turnover rate in your organization, then the Ribbon is probably a perfect match. On the other hand, organizations that have long-term employees with significant skills may be less well served by the Ribbon, especially if there's reluctance on the part of employees to embrace the Ribbon. Spend some time considering exactly what you plan to get out of the Ribbon interface. For example, the Ribbon provides a robust means of organizing workflows. A user can simply move from the left side of the Ribbon to the right to accomplish a given task. Of course, you're not implementing your upgrade just yet — make sure you spend enough time in the planning stage to ensure that your upgrade will work as anticipated.

Once you decide whether you're going to use the Ribbon interface in your application, you also need to decide on implementation details. For example, you need to decide whether the Ribbon interface will be hard-coded in your application. You may decide to use an Office-like setup to make the Ribbon more flexible in your application. Of course, using the Office approach also means changing your data formats to accommodate the additional information needed to configure the Ribbon. The Ribbon is a big departure from the menu and toolbar interface, and you should get all the changes you really need implemented in your application to ensure the Ribbon is also as flexible as you need it to be.

Chapter 7 adds to the information you've received in this chapter. While this chapter looked at what the Ribbon is, how it can benefit your organization, when you should use it, and how other developers have implemented it, Chapter 7 looks at several different application types so that you can see some actual Ribbon implementations. These implementations aren't precise answers, but they show you what's available. You need to make a decision then on precisely how you'll implement the Ribbon in your application.

# Creating Custom Ribbon Interface Applications

**WHAT'S IN THIS CHAPTER?**

➤ Developing a simple Forms application

➤ Developing a simple WPF application

As with many new technologies that Microsoft creates, the Ribbon technology designed for Windows 7 targets the C++ developer, not the managed-application developer. Even the tutorials Microsoft provides are for this group of developers (see `http://www.microsoft.com/downloads/details.aspx?FamilyID=F62039AD-A224-4979-AE7F-67B4E09CD81E`). Underlying the C++ support are Component Object Model (COM) DLLs. However, don't worry about the lack of material online. This chapter provides a good starting point for your Ribbon experience and then shows a few practical examples of how you can implement the Ribbon in your own application.

Adding the Ribbon to your applications is definitely worthwhile. Chapter 6 points out a number of advantages to using this new interface, especially in certain circumstances that are all too common in the corporate environment today (such as when you have a wealth of novice users who require extra hand-holding). Using the techniques in this chapter will provide you with two main methods of adding the Ribbon to your applications. (In neither case is Visual Studio ready to create a Ribbon-based application immediately.) Here are the methods:

➤ Rely on an interoperability (interop) module to provide access to the COM modules that C++ developers use to create their applications. Fortunately, there's a third-party library you can download to assist in this technique; otherwise, you'd have to rely on creating reams of difficult P/Invoke code to accomplish the task. This technique works great for Windows Forms applications that you want to update. In many cases, you can update an existing application with little disruption of the underlying code or data strategy.

➤ Use Windows Presentation Foundation (WPF) programming techniques. In this case, you can download managed application support directly from Microsoft, rather than rely on the interesting programming techniques provided for Windows Forms developers in this chapter. The WPF approach is useful for new application development.

No matter which technique you choose, you need to define the user interface using XML code. The Windows Forms approach relies on the XML code described in Chapter 6, while the WPF approach uses an eXtensible Application Markup Language (XAML) equivalent of the Chapter 6 discussion. There's no designer support for creating a Ribbon interface in Visual Studio. This means that you'll need a tool for viewing the interface as you create it. Fortunately, Microsoft supplies such a tool in the form of PreviewRibbon. This chapter shows how to work with PreviewRibbon. It also tells you how to get the utility working within Visual Studio 2010 (the code doesn't even compile when you first download it).

## GETTING STARTED WITH THE RIBBON

This first application, SimpleRibbon, uses the Windows Forms approach to adding Ribbon support to an application. In this application, you discover a number of fundamentals, such as how to use the Microsoft interop module to your advantage. You'll also obtain all the details needed to configure your system and create a simple Windows Forms application that employs the Ribbon. The example is purposely simple so that you can focus on setup, utilities, and technique.

*Whenever Microsoft introduces a technology that seems to make life difficult for the developer, a third-party vendor comes along to make things easier. Professional UI Solutions makes a set of Windows Forms controls called Elegant Ribbon (*http://www.prof-uis.com/elegant-ribbon/controls-framework-overview.aspx*) that you can use to create an Office-like environment for your application. You can even download and try the controls out free.*

### Obtaining the Windows 7 SDK

There isn't any easy way to obtain the support you need for working with the Ribbon. Unlike the Taskbar examples, you really do need the Windows 7 Software Development Kit (SDK) to create Ribbon-based applications for Windows 7. Even the Microsoft-supplied Ribbon example (see the example code and description at http://code.msdn.microsoft.com/PreviewRibbon) requires the Windows 7 SDK to run. It would be nice if there were a managed code approach you could take, but the Ribbon relies on Component Object Model (COM) technology that relies on a good deal of C++ code.

### GETTING MICROSOFT'S PREVIEWRIBBON EXAMPLE TO WORK

It's a good idea to at least view Microsoft's PreviewRibbon example before you perform much development work of your own, because managed code examples for the Ribbon are a bit scarce. In addition, getting Microsoft's example to work will also prepare your machine for your own development efforts and help you understand potential distribution problems for production applications. The following steps help you get the example to work properly:

1. Open the example using Visual Studio 2010. You'll immediately notice that you need to convert it for use with Visual Studio 2010. The conversion should proceed without error.

2. Try to compile the code to locate four errors within the application. The errors appear in the `ConfigOptions.CS` file.

3. Change each of the `val = ConfigurationSettings.AppSettings["String Value"];` lines to read `val = ConfigurationManager.AppSettings ["StringValue"];`. The code will compile at this point, but you still won't see the example work. That's because you haven't specified a Ribbon definition file for the example to use.

4. Copy the `BasicRibbon.XML` into the Debug folder for the application, so the application can easily access it.

5. Right-click the PreviewRibbon entry in Solution Explorer and choose Properties from the context menu.

6. Select the Debug tab and type **BasicRibbon.XML** in the Command Line Arguments field.

You should be ready to go now. Assuming you have the Windows 7 SDK installed, the example should run. Choose Start ➪ All Programs ➪ Microsoft Windows SDK v7.1 ➪ Windows SDK 7.1 Command Prompt. Windows will open a command prompt. Change directories to the Debug folder of the PreviewRibbon application (normally `\PreviewRibbon-src\source\bin`). Type **PreviewRibbon BasicRibbon .XML** and press Enter.

Of course, you might want to run the example from within Visual Studio. In this case, open the `App.CONFIG` file. You'll see four entries in the `<appSettings>` tag. Uncomment these entries and ensure that the paths point to the locations of the utilities that the application requires. Here are the entries for Visual Studio 2010 using the Windows 7 SDK version 7.1 on a 64-bit system (even though these entries appear on two or three lines in the book, they should appear on a single line in your source code):

```
<add key="UiccPath"
    value="C:\Program Files\Microsoft
        SDKs\Windows\v7.1\Bin\UICC.exe" />
```

*continues*

*(continued)*

```
    <add key="RCExePath"
        value="C:\Program Files\Microsoft
            SDKs\Windows\v7.1\Bin\RC.exe" />
    <add key="LinkExePath"
        value="C:\Program Files (x86)\Microsoft Visual Studio
            10.0\VC\Bin\Link.exe" />
    <add key="ColorizationValues"
        value="150, 127, 245; 25, 127, 245; 150, 71, 158" />
```

As an alternative to changing the `App.CONFIG` file, you can also change the paths provided by the `sdkBinPath`, `vsBinPath32`, and `vsBinPath64` variables found in `ToolHost.CS`. Changing either file will work.

The Windows 7 SDK comes in two forms: Web installer and an International Standards Organization (ISO) package used to create a DVD. You can obtain the Web installer from `http://www.microsoft.com/downloads/details.aspx?FamilyID=6b6c21d2-2006-4afa-9702-529fa782d63b` and the ISO version from `http://www.microsoft.com/downloads/details.aspx?FamilyID=35AEDA01-421D-4BA5-B44B-543DC8C33A20`. Whichever version you obtain, double-click the installer after the download to begin the installation. Follow the default setup instructions for installing the Windows 7 SDK on your system. A default installation will require 1.7 GB of hard-drive space.

*Make absolutely certain that you obtain the correct version of the Windows 7 SDK for your system. If you have a 64-bit version of Windows installed, you must download the 64-bit version of the Windows 7 SDK. Anyone using an Itanium system will need the Itanium version of the Windows 7 SDK. Attempting to install the incorrect version will result in a failure message that says the installer couldn't find a particular file (rather than telling you that you have the incorrect version of the SDK).*

## Obtaining RibbonLib

If you look at the PreviewRibbon example code, you'll find that it has a relatively large number of files containing complex code. Writing a COM wrapper for the Ribbon isn't for the faint of heart. With this in mind, you'll probably want to use a pre-written wrapper to make your Ribbon development easier. One such wrapper is RibbonLib at `http://windowsribbon.codeplex.com/releases/view/32943`.

After you download the ZIP file, extract it. You'll find .SLN files for both Visual Basic and C#. In addition, both Visual Basic and C# examples are included with the library. The solutions will require conversion for Visual Studio 2010. Simply follow the Visual Studio Conversion Wizard prompts as you normally would to perform the conversion. The conversion should proceed without error.

When you initially attempt to build the library and its examples, you'll be discouraged to see a number of errors (36 of them). The errors aren't due to any coding problem. The problem occurs when you use the latest version of the Windows 7 SDK. Use the following steps to correct the problem:

1. Right-click an example project entry in Solution Explorer and choose Properties from the context menu. You'll see the Properties window for that project.

2. Select the Build Events tab as shown in Figure 7-1. Notice that the Pre-Build Event Command Line field contains entries that compile the XML file containing the Ribbon code into a DLL. You must modify these entries to match the version of the Windows 7 SDK installed on your system (the book uses version 7.1).

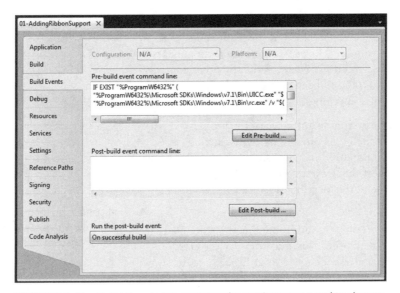

**FIGURE 7-1:** The Build Events tab contains the settings you need to change.

3. Click Edit Pre-Build. You'll see the Pre-Build Event Command Line dialog box shown in Figure 7-2.

**FIGURE 7-2:** This dialog box contains the pre-build events for the project.

4. Change each of the directory entries in the dialog box to match the directory setup on your machine. Be especially careful of the version numbers. The example is configured to use version 7.0 of the Windows 7 SDK.

5. Click OK.

6. Choose Build ⇨ Build Solution to build the application.

When the code compiles, you'll find Ribbon.DLL in either the \RibbonLib_v2.4\Ribbon\bin\Debug or \RibbonLib_v2.4\Ribbon\bin\Release folders, depending on the kind of build you performed. You'll use Ribbon.DLL for the Windows Forms examples in this chapter.

## Configuring the Application

The example begins with a Windows Forms application. You need to add a SplitContainer control to the form and set the Orientation property to Horizontal so that the form appears as shown in Figure 7-3. You don't need to add any other controls to the form at this point (and to keep things simple, it's probably better that you don't add anything).

At this point, you have an important piece of the puzzle, Ribbon.DLL. Create a reference to Ribbon.DLL by right-clicking References in Solution Explorer and choosing Add Reference from the context menu. Select the Browse tab in the Add Reference dialog box and browse to the location of Ribbon.DLL. Highlight Ribbon.DLL and click OK.

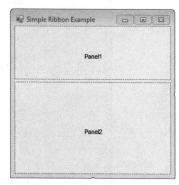

**FIGURE 7-3:** Configure the client area to contain two panes, one of which will contain the Ribbon.

The application requires only one additional using statement, using RibbonLib;. In addition, you must modify the class statement so that it includes a reference to IRibbonForm, as shown here:

```
public partial class frmMain : Form, IRibbonForm
```

After you add the interface, you can choose Implement Interface IRibbonForm from the drop-down list box, as shown in Figure 7-4.

The "Obtaining RibbonLib" section of the chapter discusses a Pre-Build Event Command Line (Figure 7-2). You must also add this script for building the Ribbon resources to the example application. The easiest way to perform this task is to copy it

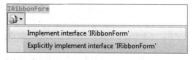

**FIGURE 7-4:** Implement the IRibbonForm interface in your application.

from one of the Ribbon-cs or Ribbon-vb projects. The same script works fine for every project you create. Listing 7-1 shows the script used for all the Windows Forms examples in this book (if you see a ↵ at the end of a line, it means that the next line is part of the current line).

**LISTING 7-1:** Script used to compile the Ribbon

Available for download on Wrox.com

```
IF EXIST "%ProgramW6432%" (
"%ProgramW6432%\Microsoft SDKs\Windows\v7.1\Bin\UICC.exe"
"$(ProjectDir)RibbonMarkup.xml" "$(ProjectDir)RibbonMarkup.bml"
/res:"$(ProjectDir)RibbonMarkup.rc"
"%ProgramW6432%\Microsoft SDKs\Windows\v7.1\Bin\rc.exe" /v
"$(ProjectDir)RibbonMarkup.rc"
) ELSE (
"%PROGRAMFILES%\Microsoft SDKs\Windows\v7.1\Bin\UICC.exe"
"$(ProjectDir)RibbonMarkup.xml" "$(ProjectDir)RibbonMarkup.bml"
/res:"$(ProjectDir)RibbonMarkup.rc"
"%PROGRAMFILES%\Microsoft SDKs\Windows\v7.1\Bin\rc.exe" /v
"$(ProjectDir)RibbonMarkup.rc"
)
cmd /c "("$(DevEnvDir)..\..\VC\bin\vcvars32.bat") &&
("$(DevEnvDir)..\..\VC\bin\link.exe" /VERBOSE /NOENTRY /DLL
/OUT:"$(ProjectDir)$(OutDir)$(TargetName).ribbon.dll"
"$(ProjectDir)RibbonMarkup.res")"
```

This script calls three utilities to create a DLL out of the `RibbonMarkup.XML` markup file you create in the "Defining a Ribbon Interface" section of the chapter. The UICC utility compiles the Ribbon markup that you create into a binary (.BML) file. The UICC utility also creates a resource (.RC) file based on the objects within the markup file. The RC utility compiles the resource file into a resource object (.RES) file.

At this point, the script calls on `VCVars32.BAT` to create an environment suitable for the linker. A linker (`Link.EXE`) takes object files and creates an executable from them. In this case, Link combines the two Ribbon files into a single executable native-code DLL. The DLL has your project name, followed by `.Ribbon.DLL`. For example, the DLL for this project is named `SimpleRibbon.Ribbon.DLL`.

To use RibbonLib, you must add a reference to `Ribbon.DLL` using the same procedure found in previous chapters. In addition, you must add the following using statements to your code:

```
using RibbonLib;
using RibbonLib.Controls;
using RibbonLib.Interop;
```

> *If you find that your application isn't executing as expected, make sure you verify that the directory containing the application has three files in it. The first,* `Ribbon.DLL`, *provides the interoperability layer between .NET and the Ribbon. The second,* `SimpleRibbon.Ribbon.DLL` *in this case, contains the native-code DLL that the Ribbon components use to display the Ribbon for your application on-screen. The third is the application executable, which is* `SimpleRibbon.EXE` *in this case.*

## Defining a Ribbon Interface

The Ribbon interface is actually an XML file containing special entries that are later compiled using the script shown in Listing 7-1. A Ribbon interface defies normal development procedures because it doesn't rely on a designer. You write the XML code directly when working with a Windows Forms application. The problem that most developers will encounter is finding a way to create the interface in an orderly manner. The following sections help you create the interface for the simple Ribbon application and also provide guidelines for creating the Ribbon interface in an organized way to reduce potential errors.

## Defining the Initial XML File

The process begins when you create an XML file. Use these steps to add an XML file to your project:

1. Right-click the project entry in Solution Explorer and choose Add ➪ New Item. You'll see the Add New Item dialog box shown in Figure 7-5.

**FIGURE 7-5:** Add an XML file to your application.

2. Highlight the XML File entry.
3. Type **RibbonMarkup.XML** in the Name field. The name you type is important because it has to match the name found in the script shown in Listing 7-1. If you use a different name, you'll have to change the script to match. Otherwise, your Ribbon won't compile and your application won't display the interface. Interestingly enough, Visual Studio will accept all this without displaying a single error message.
4. Click Add. Visual Studio will add the new XML file and automatically open it for you.

One way to stay out of trouble when you create the interface is to design the basic Ribbon structure before you add any details. Listing 7-2 shows a basic structure you can use for any application.

**LISTING 7-2:** Creating the basic Ribbon structure

```xml
<?xml version='1.0' encoding='utf-8'?>

<Application xmlns='http://schemas.microsoft.com/windows/2009/Ribbon'>
    <Application.Commands>
        <Command Name="cmdApplicationMenu" Id="1000" />

        <Command Name="cmdTabHome" Id="2000" LabelTitle="Home" />

        <Command Name="cmdQAT" Id="3000" />
    </Application.Commands>

    <Application.Views>
        <Ribbon>

            <Ribbon.ApplicationMenu>
                <ApplicationMenu CommandName='cmdApplicationMenu'>

                </ApplicationMenu>
            </Ribbon.ApplicationMenu>

            <Ribbon.Tabs>
                <Tab CommandName='cmdTabHome'>

                </Tab>
            </Ribbon.Tabs>

            <Ribbon.QuickAccessToolbar>
                <QuickAccessToolbar CommandName='cmdQAT'>

                </QuickAccessToolbar>
            </Ribbon.QuickAccessToolbar>
        </Ribbon>
    </Application.Views>
</Application>
```

The root node for a Ribbon interface is always `<Application>` and you must include the `xmlns` attribute that points to the version of the Ribbon schema you want to use for your application. The structure is further divided into two main areas: `<Application.Commands>` and `<Application.Views>`. Notice the dot syntax used for the node names. An *application command* is an action that you want the Ribbon to perform. You'll discover later that the command section contains property settings for each of the entries. An *application view* is the visual presentation of the Ribbon element. This section creates a connection between a visual element, such as a button, and a command that describes what to do with the visual element.

The basic Ribbon contains three areas: file menu, tabs, and QAT (Quick Access Toolbar). Consequently, the `<Application.Commands>` node has three child `<Command>` nodes for each of these areas. The areas don't actually do any work, so their definitions are simple. The file menu needs nothing more than a `Name` attribute (used to access the file menu in code) and `Id` attribute (used when creating the resource file — each resource must have a unique identifier). The same holds true for the QAT entry. Each of the tabs also requires a `LabelTitle` attribute that contains the name of the tab as it appears on the Ribbon. By convention, the first tab of a Ribbon application is always the Home tab, so the example labels it as such.

> The `Id` value you assign to each Ribbon element must be unique. However, there isn't any rule on how you number the Ribbon elements. The example uses values of 1000, 2000, and 3000 to make later numbering easier and more logical. The File ➪ New command will receive a value of 1010, while File ➪ Open will receive a value of 1020, and so on. A submenu, such as File ➪ New ➪ Document, will receive a value of 1011, and File ➪ New ➪ Template will receive a value of 1012. Using a numbering system like this isn't required, but it does make it easier to figure out the values of the Ribbon elements later when your structure becomes complex. Of course, you'll need to come up with a system that works for you. Using this approach lets you create up to 10 elements in each of the three areas, 99 menu items, and 10 submenu items, which will likely provide enough flexibility for any application.

When you begin working with the application views, you'll quickly find that they're highly structured, as contrasted with the commands, which tend to be flat. All three areas appear as children of the `<Ribbon>` node. The `<Ribbon.ApplicationMenu>` node contains all the file menu entries; the `<Ribbon.Tabs>` node contains all the tabs such as Home; and the `<Ribbon.QuickAccessToolbar>` node contains all the QAT entries which normally default to Save, Redo, and Undo. Within each of these areas, you begin to see controls. In this case, you see the `<ApplicationMenu>`, `<Tab>`, and `<QuickAccessToolbar>` controls, each with its associated commands. The sections that follow will concentrate, for the sake of simplicity, on specific commands and their associated Ribbon entries, but it pays to keep this overall structure in mind as you read.

## Developing a File Menu

The File menu (or the new term, Application menu) contains document management entries for the most part. Microsoft has been wishy-washy on just what to call the old File menu, and you'll find that Office 2010 actually returns to the File menu. No matter what you call the File menu, it contains entries such as New, Open, Save, Print, and Exit. You may find additional entries on this menu, but it's important to keep the File menu for document management functions and perhaps an application options entry.

The example contains just one entry on the File menu, Exit. A production application will have more entries, but this one entry is more than sufficient for now to show how to work with the File menu. You begin augmenting the File menu command shown in Listing 7-2 and add the Exit command as shown in Listing 7-3.

Available for download on Wrox.com

**LISTING 7-3:** Creating the File Exit command

```xml
<Command Name="cmdApplicationMenu"
         Id="1000"
         TooltipTitle="File Menu"
         TooltipDescription="Contains document management entries."/>
<Command Name="btnExit"
         Id="1010"
         LabelTitle="E&amp;xit"
         LabelDescription="End the Program"
         TooltipTitle="Exit"
         TooltipDescription="End the Program">
    <Command.LargeImages>
        <Image>Res/Exit32.bmp</Image>
    </Command.LargeImages>
    <Command.SmallImages>
        <Image>Res/Exit16.bmp</Image>
    </Command.SmallImages>
</Command>
```

The first thing you should notice is that there's no differentiation between menus, buttons, or any other visual presentations when it comes to commands. You simply use the `<Command>` node to define the actions and properties for the element. This example adds the `TooltipTitle` and `TooltipDescription` attributes. These attributes appear as balloon help when the user hovers the mouse over the entry. However, these attributes won't affect the QAT or an actual tab, such as Home. Keep the entries short and relevant. Anyone using a screen reader will hear these entries (in lieu of seeing them). Long entries take an unimaginable amount of time to read, and by the time the screen reader reads all the entries, the user has forgotten some of the initial entries. So short but precise is better.

The `btnExit` command contains an `Id` value of 1010 so you can quickly tell it belongs to the File menu. The `LabelTitle` attribute contains the text that appears on the menu. Notice the use of `&amp;` to represent an ampersand (&). As with all menus, placing an ampersand in front of a letter underlines that letter and creates a speed key. In this case, the speed key is the x in Exit. The `LabelDescription` attribute provides descriptive text for the label. As with the File menu, the `btnExit` command adds the `TooltipTitle` and `TooltipDescription` attributes for accessibility reasons.

A new addition is icons. The `<Command.LargeImages>` and `<Command.SmallImages>` nodes provide the Ribbon with images for the command. Because this is the File menu, the icon appears to the left of the word Exit in the menu. You normally supply two sizes of icons so that people who rely on a large-print screen can have an appropriately sized icon. The "Obtaining 32-bit Graphics" section of this chapter describes how to create these icons. You normally provide the name of the command along with the icon size (16×16 or 32×32). The icon must be in 32-bit `.BMP` format and appear within an `<Image>` node.

Now that you have the command part of the File menu, it's time to look at the view portion of the same menu. Listing 7-4 shows this part of the example.

## LISTING 7-4: Creating the File Exit view

Available for download on Wrox.com

```
<Ribbon.ApplicationMenu>
    <ApplicationMenu CommandName='cmdApplicationMenu'>
        <MenuGroup>
            <Button CommandName='btnExit' />
        </MenuGroup>
    </ApplicationMenu>
</Ribbon.ApplicationMenu>
```

You place entries on the File menu within `<MenuGroup>` nodes. If you use more than one `<MenuGroup>`, the Ribbon places separators between each group. The controls for a particular group appear within the `<MenuGroup>` node. In this case, there's only one entry, a `<Button>` control for Exit. All you need to provide is the `CommandName` attribute to create the association between the `<Button>` and the `<Command>`.

## Obtaining 32-bit Graphics

You'll very likely want to add icons to your Ribbon. All current Ribbon designs include graphics of various sorts. For most developers, the easiest way to obtain the required graphics is to draw them right in Visual Studio. The following steps get you started adding your first image to the project:

1. Right-click the project entry in Solution Explorer and choose Add ⇨ New Folder from the context menu. You'll see a new folder appear in Solution Explorer.

2. Type **Res** as the folder name and press Enter. The `Res` (resource) folder will contain all the graphics for your project.

3. Right-click the `Res` folder and choose Add ⇨ New Item from the Context menu. You'll see the Add New Item dialog box shown in Figure 7-5.

4. Highlight Bitmap File and type the filename in the Name field. Normally, you'll want to use a logical naming scheme, such as the control name followed by the icon size in pixels, such as `Exit32.BMP`.

5. Click Add. Visual Studio adds the bitmap and automatically opens it for editing.

6. Set the `Height` and `Width` properties to the icon size you want, such as 16.

7. Set the `Colors` property to 24-bit. Even though the drop-down list box shows 32-bit as an option and you can select it, Visual Studio won't allow the value on-screen. Unfortunately, Visual Studio produces 24-bit graphics as a maximum, not 32-bit graphics.

8. Draw the icon you want and save it to disk.

9. Close the graphics file.

At this point, you have a 24-bit bitmap that won't display on the Ribbon. In order to display graphics on the Ribbon, you must use 32-bit graphics, but as you just saw, Visual Studio doesn't support them. Use the following procedure to overcome this problem:

1. Download the `Convert2BMP.EXE` utility found at http://windowsribbon.codeplex.com/releases/view/32943.
2. Place the utility in an easily accessible location such as `C:\Convert2BMP`.
3. Open a command line and use the CD command to change directories to your project's `\Res` folder, such as typing **CD \SimpleRibbon\SimpleRibbon\Res** and pressing Enter.
4. Type **C:\Convert2BMP\Convert2BMP** *InputFilename* *OutputFilename* and press Enter, where *InputFilename* is the name of the original file and *OutputFilename* is the name of the modified file.

If you reopen the graphic at this point, you'll see that it is, indeed, 32 bits. However, don't make any additional changes to it. Simply close the graphic and use it on the Ribbon.

## Creating a Home Tab

The Home tab is probably the most complicated of the three areas you configure on the Ribbon. The reason is that you control the size and positioning of the controls, which means you must provide Windows with additional information. While the commands aren't much more complex than those used for the File (Application) menu, the setup of the Ribbon view can be significantly more complex. Given the goals of the Ribbon, size and positioning are important, so you can spend quite a bit of time getting the layout of the tabs just right. Listing 7-5 shows the Home tab command code.

**LISTING 7-5:** Creating the Home tab commands

Available for download on Wrox.com

```
<Command Name="cmdTabHome"
         Id="2000"
         LabelTitle="Home"
         TooltipTitle="Home Tab"
         TooltipDescription="Contains the main document settings."
         Keytip="H"/>
<Command Name="grpTest"
         Id="2010"
         LabelTitle="Test"
         TooltipTitle="Test Group"
         TooltipDescription="Test the Application" />
<Command Name="btnClickMe"
         Id="2011"
         LabelTitle="Click Me"
         TooltipTitle="Test Button"
         TooltipDescription="Click to see a dialog box."
         Keytip="C">
    <Command.LargeImages>
        <Image>Res/ClickMe32.bmp</Image>
    </Command.LargeImages>
    <Command.SmallImages>
        <Image>Res/ClickMe16.bmp</Image>
    </Command.SmallImages>
</Command>
```

The tabs require a bit more work because you need a different kind of presentation for the user. In addition to `btnClickMe`, which isn't that much different from `btnFileExt` described in the "Developing a File Menu" section of this chapter, you also have to create a group in which to place the button. The group is `grpTest` in this case. You create it much as you do a tab, but its visual presentation is different. A group gathers like controls together to make them easier to understand and find.

Both `cmdTabHome` and `btnClickMe` contain a new attribute, `Keytip`. The `Keytip` is one or more characters that identify the control for keyboard users. When a user presses Alt, the Ribbon displays the `Keytip` you provide. If you don't provide a `Keytip`, the Ribbon chooses a shortcut key for you that may not be a good match (such as selecting Y for the Home tab). Listing 7-6 shows the visual presentation of the Home tab.

**LISTING 7-6:** Creating the Home tab view

Available for download on Wrox.com

```
<Ribbon.Tabs>
    <Tab CommandName='cmdTabHome'>
        <Tab.ScalingPolicy>
            <ScalingPolicy>
                <ScalingPolicy.IdealSizes>
                    <Scale Group='grpTest' Size='Large' />
                </ScalingPolicy.IdealSizes>
            </ScalingPolicy>
        </Tab.ScalingPolicy>

        <Group CommandName='grpTest' SizeDefinition='OneButton'>
            <Button CommandName='btnClickMe' />
        </Group>
    </Tab>
</Ribbon.Tabs>
```

The Home tab view code begins with a new node, `<Tab.ScalingPolicy>`. A *scaling policy* defines how you want the controls to appear on the Ribbon. The default view is to show the controls in a small size. Using a small control lets the Ribbon display up to three buttons vertically before moving to the next horizontal position. Medium-sized controls are a little larger and will fit only two buttons vertically, while a large control consumes the entire vertical area.

You use the `<ScalingPolicy.IdealSizes>` tag to define the preferred size of the elements. The scaling policy is closely tied to the `SizeDefinition` attribute. When a group has just one button in it, the `SizeDefinition` is `OneButton`, which allows only `Size='Large'` controls. If you want to use some other size control, then you need to create a custom `SizeDefinition` node, which can get quite complex. For now, all you really need to know is that the scaling policy defines the size of the control and that the size you choose has to be consistent with the default `SizeDefinition` you choose, or you must create a custom `SizeDefinition` to accommodate special needs.

> You may wonder where the `OneButton SizeDefinition` *value comes from.* Microsoft has defined several default scaling policies for you. There is a listing of these scaling policies at http://msdn.microsoft.com/library/dd316927.aspx.

After you define a scaling policy, you can define the `<Group>` that holds the control you want to display (obviously, the Ribbon can contain as many groups as needed — the example uses just one group for the sake of simplicity). The `<Group>` associates the group with a suitable command and also defines the `SizeDefinition` for the controls in the group. All the controls will be the same size unless you create a custom `SizeDefinition`. Within the `<Group>` are one or more controls. The example uses a `<Button>` control, but you can use any mix of controls desired.

## Adding the QAT

The QAT, or Quick Access Toolbar, is actually the easiest part of the Ribbon to define, but you should define it last. The QAT makes controls used in other parts of the Ribbon easier for the user to access. For example, a user may want quick access to the File ➪ New command and place it on the QAT, rather than perform the extra steps required to actually access the File ➪ New command. In short, the QAT never introduces anything new — it uses features you've already defined. The QAT consists of two parts: the QAT itself and the customization component that appears as a drop-down list box of available items. Listing 7-7 shows the tags used to create the QAT and its associated customization.

### LISTING 7-7: Defining the QAT customization

```
<Command Name="cmdQAT"
         Id="3000"
         TooltipTitle="Quick Access Toolbar"
         TooltipDescription="Contains the user configurable settings."/>
<Command Name="CustomizeQAT"
         Id="3001" />
```

As you can see, the command portion of the QAT is extremely simple — nothing more than command declarations with appropriate tooltip information. The view is equally easy. Listing 7-8 shows the code used to create the QAT view.

### LISTING 7-8: Creating the QAT view

```
<Ribbon.QuickAccessToolbar>
    <QuickAccessToolbar CommandName='cmdQAT'
                        CustomizeCommandName='CustomizeQAT'>
        <QuickAccessToolbar.ApplicationDefaults>
            <Button CommandName="btnExit"
                    ApplicationDefaults.IsChecked="true" />
            <Button CommandName="btnClickMe"
                    ApplicationDefaults.IsChecked="true" />
        </QuickAccessToolbar.ApplicationDefaults>
    </QuickAccessToolbar>
</Ribbon.QuickAccessToolbar>
```

The `<QuickAccessToolbar>` node needs to contain a `CustomizeCommandName` attribute if you want the user to have the ability to change the QAT configuration. Because the QAT is there for the user to customize, you should always include this attribute.

The QAT will normally appear in a default state. You configure these defaults using the `<QuickAccessToolbar.ApplicationDefaults>` node. Each control that you want to appear on the QAT will appear as a child of this node. However, you don't define the control again — you simply provide its name. In addition, you provide the `ApplicationDefaults.IsChecked` attribute to control whether the control is visible when the user starts the application.

## Using PreviewRibbon to Test Your Design

At some point, you'll have enough Ribbon elements put together for your application that you'll want to start seeing what it looks like. You can simply start your application up and it will compile the Ribbon. Of course, you'll see just the visual display and it probably won't do anything because you haven't performed any code behind yet. An alternative to this approach is to use the PreviewRibbon utility to view the Ribbon you've created. This utility provides a number of useful diagnostics and helps you see how your interface works. To use this utility, copy the `RibbonMarkup.XML` and associated `\Res` folder to the PreviewRibbon executable folder, open a command prompt, type **PreviewRibbon RibbonMarkup.XML**, and press Enter. Figure 7-6 shows how the example application appears in PreviewRibbon.

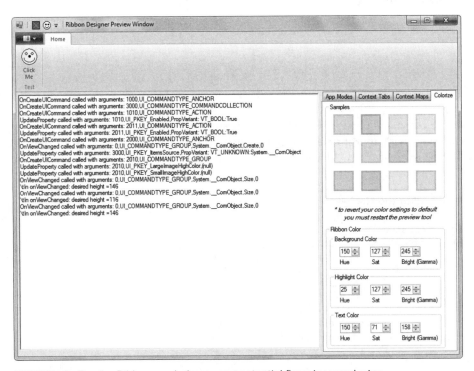

**FIGURE 7-6:** PreviewRibbon can help you see potential flaws in your design.

As your application becomes more complex, PreviewRibbon has more to offer. When working with the example application, you can obtain three benefits:

- Seeing the actual layout of the Ribbon to ensure it appears as you expect.
- Observing the message traffic that occurs when the user interacts with the Ribbon.
- Trying different Ribbon color combinations to ensure the colors you've chosen will work for the user. In some cases, color choices that seemed appropriate during the design phase don't work in reality.

The messages are the more interesting part at this point. For example, when you choose File ➪ Exit, you see the message, "Execute called with arguments: 1010,Execute,(n/a),(null)". Notice that the Ribbon uses the unique identifier you provided. The call executes an action. Finally, since this is a simple `Button` control, it doesn't pass any arguments to the event handler. When you click the Exit button on the QAT, it produces the same message, which tells you that everything is connected correctly. Now you can try the same actions with the Click Me button. In this case, you see a message of, "Execute called with arguments: 2011,Execute,(n/a),(null)", which corresponds to the identifier you assigned. Obviously, as an application becomes more complex, you can see more potential for performing QA checks on your design.

This utility also helps you discover some things about the Ribbon. For example, click the drop-down list box on the QAT. You'll see a message of "OnCreateUICommand called with arguments: 3001,UI_COMMANDTYPE_ACTION" as the Ribbon creates the menu shown in Figure 7-7. However, the Ribbon makes this call only once. If you open the drop-down list box again, it simply appears on-screen without an additional message.

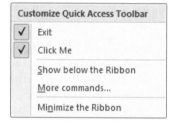

**FIGURE 7-7:** Explore your design to determine when it generates messages and how often it generates them.

It doesn't take long to figure out that the PreviewRibbon utility can tell you a lot about how the Ribbon works. All these messages are real Windows messages. Your .NET application receives these messages as a callback and then acts on them when you supply the required code. In fact, it's possible to create custom handlers to intercept and react to these messages, but working with RibbonLib is far easier.

## Creating the Application

The example application is only a front end at this point — the controls don't perform any useful work. It's time to add some code. Using RibbonLib does make things significantly easier, but you still need to add a few special pieces of code to make the application work properly. The following sections describe these special pieces of code, as well as the event handlers you use to react to user clicks.

### Implementing IRibbonForm

A Windows Forms application inherits from the `Form` class. However, in order to display a Ribbon, you need additional support in the form of the `IRibbonForm` interface. Using this interface is relatively easy, but you do need to provide support for two members as, shown in Listing 7-9.

**LISTING 7-9:** Implementing the required IRibbonForm members

```
public void RibbonHeightUpdated(int newHeight)
{
    // Update the height of the Ribbon.
    this.splitContainer1.SplitterDistance = newHeight;
}

public IntPtr WindowHandle
{
    // Return a handle to this window.
    get
    {
        return this.Handle;
    }
}
```

The Ribbon height can change when the user minimizes the Ribbon. If your application doesn't know about this change, you'll suddenly find that the user can't interact with this properly. The `RibbonHeightUpdated()` method receives the new height of the Ribbon and changes the size of the splitter used to allocate space for it. The result is that the second pane, the client area of the application, automatically resizes as needed to accommodate the Ribbon.

Before the Ribbon can even interact with your application, it needs to know which window to work with. The `WindowHandle` property returns an `IntPtr` with the handle for the current window. It's essential that you pass the correct handle. Normally, using `this.Handle` works just fine, but if you have an application with multiple windows, you'll want to pass the handle of the active window, rather than the main window.

## Defining the Application Framework

The Ribbon works within a specialized framework. If you were a C++ developer, you'd need to know all about this framework because you'd interact with it directly. However, as a C# developer working with RibbonLib, these details are already taken care of for you. If you want to know more about the framework, you can read about it at `http://msdn.microsoft.com/library/dd316910.aspx`. You still need to create and destroy the framework before you use it. Listing 7-10 shows the code used to perform this task.

**LISTING 7-10:** Creating and destroying the application framework

```
private void frmMain_Load(object sender, EventArgs e)
{
    // Create the Ribbon framework.
    MyRibbon.InitFramework(this);
}

private void frmMain_FormClosing(object sender, FormClosingEventArgs e)
{
    // Destroy the Ribbon framework.
    MyRibbon.DestroyFramework();
}
```

The code creates the framework when the form is loading through the `frmMain_Load()` event handler. All you do is call the `InitFramework()` method with a pointer to the form object. The framework is destroyed as the form is closing through the `frmMain_FormClosing()` event handler. In this case, the code calls the `DestroyFramework()` method. It may seem as if nothing too terrible will happen if you don't destroy the framework. However, if you don't destroy the framework, you'll create a memory leak at a minimum, and your application won't exit cleanly. Make sure you include both of these event handlers in your application.

### Accessing Ribbon Resources

Because of the way the Ribbon works, the resources on your form aren't immediately available. Yes, that seems very odd indeed. The controls are on the form, but they weren't put there by your application. A native-code DLL outside your application, `SimpleRibbon.Ribbon.DLL`, puts the controls there. In short, your application has no clue that these resources even exist until you create them using code. Many developers will have a hard time understanding how this can possibly work, which is why you really need to spend some time watching your application interface work using the PreviewRibbon utility (see the "Using PreviewRibbon to Test Your Design" section of this chapter for details).

The controls provided by the Ribbon aren't standard controls either. You need to use special Ribbon versions of the controls. The following code contains the declarations for each of the resources you need to access for this example.

```
// Define the Ribbon.
private Ribbon MyRibbon = new Ribbon();

// Access the main elements.
private RibbonApplicationMenu FileMenu;
private RibbonTab HomeTab;
private RibbonQuickAccessToolbar QAT;

// Access the controls on the main elements.
private RibbonButton FileExit;
private RibbonButton HomeClickMe;
```

Notice that the code begins by obtaining access to the Ribbon itself. You also need to access each of the major areas of the Ribbon: File menu, Home tab, and QAT. Finally, you need access to each of the buttons defined on the Ribbon. Each of these resources has a special type associated with it, and they don't have the same properties, methods, and events as Windows Forms controls.

The resources aren't initialized yet (except for `MyRibbon`, which is initialized when you create the application framework). Listing 7-11 shows the code used to initialize each of the resources.

**LISTING 7-11:** Initializing the application resources

```
public frmMain()
{
    InitializeComponent();

    // Gain access to the main elements.
```

*continues*

**LISTING 7-11** *(continued)*

```
    FileMenu = new RibbonApplicationMenu(MyRibbon, 1000);
    HomeTab = new RibbonTab(MyRibbon, 2000);
    QAT = new RibbonQuickAccessToolbar(MyRibbon, 3000);

    // Gain access to the File menu controls.
    FileExit = new RibbonButton(MyRibbon, 1010);

    // Create event handlers for the File menu controls.
    FileExit.OnExecute +=
        new RibbonLib.Controls.Events.OnExecuteEventHandler(
            FileExit_OnExecute);

    // Gain access to the Home tab controls.
    HomeClickMe = new RibbonButton(MyRibbon, 2011);

    // Create event handlers for the Home tab controls.
    HomeClickMe.OnExecute +=
        new RibbonLib.Controls.Events.OnExecuteEventHandler(
            HomeClickMe_OnExecute);
}
```

At this point, you should suddenly understand the need to use easily remembered identifiers for the controls on the Ribbon. In order to gain access to any of the controls, you must pass the instance of the Ribbon (`MyRibbon`) and an `Id` value to the constructor. Obtaining a reference to any Ribbon control works precisely the same way.

Once you have access to a control, you can begin using it. The two `Button` controls need to do useful work. To make this possible, the code creates `RibbonButton` objects and then accesses the `OnExecute` event for each of them. Only now do you have a callback between the Ribbon on the application and the code behind for your application. Fortunately, except for a few small wrinkles, there isn't anything mysterious about creating the event handler references. In fact, you can simply press Tab twice, as you normally would, to create both the remainder of the code after you type `OnExecute +=` and the event handler code.

## Handling Ribbon Events

The event handlers for this example are relatively simple since the focus of this example is on understanding the basics for creating an application with a Ribbon interface. Listing 7-12 shows the code for both event handlers.

**LISTING 7-12:** Handling the Ribbon Events

```
void FileExit_OnExecute(PropertyKeyRef key,
    PropVariantRef currentValue,
    IUISimplePropertySet commandExecutionProperties)
{
    // End the program.
    Environment.Exit(0);
}
```

```
void HomeClickMe_OnExecute(PropertyKeyRef key,
    PropVariantRef currentValue,
    IUISimplePropertySet commandExecutionProperties)
{
    MessageBox.Show("You clicked Click Me!");
}
```

The first thing you should notice is that the event handlers for a Ribbon control are different from the event handlers for Windows Forms controls. You get more information as input because you need it in order to perform some tasks. However, you can perform any required application-level task without accessing these properties. The properties generally affect access to the Ribbon in some way. For now, just realize that you have more information than normal at your disposal, and you'll probably need that information when creating a complex application.

The `FileExit_OnExecute()` event handler is called when the user clicks the Exit button in either of the locations (File menu or QAT). Notice that the code uses `Environment.Exit(0)` instead of the more standard `Close()`. The reason for this difference is that you're working with a Ribbon-based application. If you simply close the form, the application will exit without properly deallocating memory for the Ribbon. A return value of 0 indicates success to the system.

The `HomeClickMe_OnExecute()` event handler displays a simple message box. There isn't anything unique about this call.

## USING THE RIBBON WITH WPF

The Windows Presentation Foundation (WPF) is Microsoft's alternative to the Windows Forms application. This chapter won't debate the relative merits of WPF and Windows Forms. However, WPF does seem to attract the attention of developers developing a new application far more often than of developers performing upgrades, which is why this chapter views WPF in the light of new development. The following sections describe how to create a Ribbon-based application using WPF.

## Obtaining Microsoft Ribbon for WPF

As with Windows Forms development, Microsoft doesn't include any Ribbon development functionality for WPF in Visual Studio. You must instead download what you need and install it on your system before you begin your project. Fortunately, Microsoft does make a product available for WPF developers to use. You can find it at http://www.microsoft.com/downloads/details.aspx?FamilyID=2BFC3187-74AA-4154-A670-76EF8BC2A0B4. Make sure you download both `Microsoft Ribbon for WPF Source and Samples.MSI` and `Microsoft Ribbon for WPF.MSI` to obtain a complete setup.

First, double-click `Microsoft Ribbon for WPF.MSI` and follow the instructions to install Ribbon support for WPF. Second, double-click `Microsoft Ribbon for WPF Source and Samples.MSI` and follow the prompts to install the source and samples. The source code is nice, but what you really need are the Ribbon samples for later experimentation. Unfortunately, the Ribbon samples are stored in the `\Program Files\Microsoft Ribbon for WPF\v3.5.40729.1` or `\Program Files (x86)\Microsoft Ribbon for WPF\v3.5.40729.1` directory (depending on whether you have a

32-bit or 64-bit operating system) as `MicrosoftRibbonForWPFSourceAndSamples.ZIP`. In order to use the samples, you must open the `.ZIP` file and place it in a folder you have permission to access.

> *The Microsoft examples rely on their new Model-View-ViewModel (MVVM) design pattern. You can read about this design pattern at* `http://msdn.microsoft.com/magazine/dd419663.aspx`. *The MVVM approach probably works fine for large-scale development in corporations, but it isn't particularly friendly for learning a new development technique. With this in mind, the example in this chapter takes a much simpler approach to working with WPF and the Ribbon. The idea is to help you understand the underlying technology before you jump into the distinctly large learning curve of MVVM. However, once you master the basic Ribbon technology, you should at least look at MVVM for larger Ribbon projects where it can help you keep your application well ordered.*

## Configuring the WPF Application

Unlike the Windows Forms application found in the "Getting Started with the Ribbon" section of this chapter, your WPF application comes with a number of amenities. After you perform the installation, you'll see a new WPF Ribbon Application template in the Visual Studio New Project dialog box shown in Figure 7-8 (accessed by choosing File ➪ New Project or by clicking New Project on the Start page).

**FIGURE 7-8:** Adding WPF Ribbon support provides a new template for you to use.

The example application is named WPF Ribbon Example. Select the required project, enter a project name, and click OK. Visual Studio creates the project for you. The first thing you'll notice is that the new project includes everything needed to begin writing a Ribbon application, including a designer, as shown in Figure 7-9.

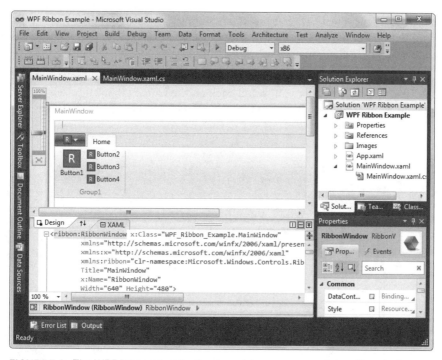

**FIGURE 7-9:** The WPF Ribbon Application template comes complete with a designer.

In fact, your application is ready to start designing. The only problem with using this template is that it relies on an entirely different technique for creating the Ribbon than any other programming strategy. In short, if you want to use WPF, then you need to learn yet another method of creating the Ribbon interface. All this said, at least the technique relies on graphic development methods using a designer instead of writing XML code.

## Defining the Ribbon Interface for the WPF Application

Having a designer to use is the nice part of working with WPF. Unfortunately, using the designer is a complex undertaking, and it's not even possible to set all the required configuration information using it. You have to perform some tweaks by working directly with the XAML, but you can create the basic layout using just the designer and the Properties window. As shown in Figure 7-9, the template automatically creates a Ribbon with a QAT (hidden, but there), a File menu with one menu entry, and a Home tab with four buttons on it. Everything that's supplied is generic, though, so you'll definitely want to change the interface. Fortunately, you have access to a full set of tools to perform the job, as shown in Figure 7-10.

This section shows how to modify the QAT, File menu, and Home tab so they appear the same as the example shown in Figure 7-6. In most cases, the example will use XAML so that you can easily see the required changes without spending hours clicking through the designer.

Begin by selecting the Home tab. It's not always obvious when you have a particular element selected. For example, you might think that you would click on the Home tab itself to select the Home tab, but what you really need to do is click within the Home tab client area, as shown in Figure 7-11.

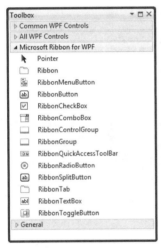

**FIGURE 7-10:** The Toolbox now contains a Microsoft Ribbon for WPF tab that holds Ribbon controls.

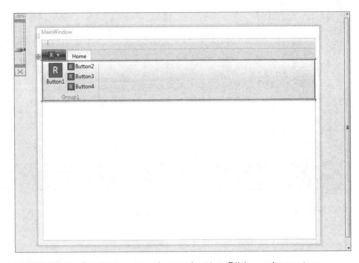

**FIGURE 7-11:** Exercise care when selecting Ribbon elements or you might modify the wrong object.

Locate the Items property in the Properties window and click the ellipsis next to it. You'll see the Collection Editor: Items dialog box shown in Figure 7-12. This dialog box contains a listing of the items within the Home tab. In this case, there's a single group. Change the Header property value to Test. In addition, change the KeyTip value to H.

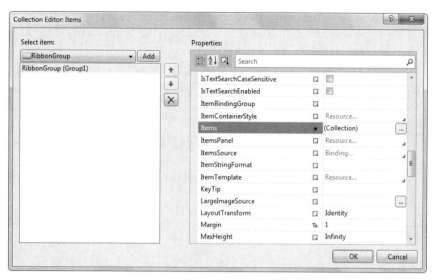

**FIGURE 7-12:** The Collection Editor: Items dialog box lets you drill down into the Ribbon in your application.

The application requires only one button for this example, so locate the Items property. Click the ellipsis next to it and you'll see another Collection Editor: Items dialog box. In fact, you can keep drilling down as needed to get to the level required in your application. Highlight RibbonButton (Button2) in the Select Item list and click Remove Item. Do the same thing for RibbonButton (Button3) and RibbonButton (Button4). You should now have a single large button in the Test group.

It's time to focus on the remaining large button. Copy the four graphics created in the "Obtaining 32-bit Graphics" section of the chapter to the `Images` folder of this project. Change the following properties to the values shown:

| PROPERTY NAME | VALUE |
| --- | --- |
| KeyTip | C |
| Label | Click Me |
| LargeImageSource | Images/ClickMe32.BMP |
| QuickAccessToolBarId | 2011 |
| SmallImageSource | Images/ClickMe16.bmp |
| ToolTipDescription | Click to see a dialog box. |
| ToolTipTitle | Test Button |

There are some properties you can't change using the Collection Editor: Items dialog box. One of these properties is the object name, which appears as x:Name in XAML. You need to change the XAML code directly to make this change.

Some of these settings take on increased importance when you're working with WPF. For example, there aren't any default KeyTip values. If you press Alt in a default WPF application, nothing happens — you don't see any letters at all. Therefore, if you want to accommodate keyboard users, you must define a KeyTip value for every object that requires one.

The QuickAccessToolBarId is also exceptionally important. If an object lacks this value, the user can't add it to the QAT. At this point, you've configured the Home tab. Listing 7-13 shows the XAML for this part of the application. If you compare this listing to Listing 7-5, you'll see many similarities, but also a few differences.

**LISTING 7-13:** WPF Home tab XAML code

Available for download on Wrox.com

```
<ribbon:RibbonTab x:Name="cmdTabHome"
                  Header="Home"
                  KeyTip="H">
    <ribbon:RibbonGroup x:Name="grpTest"
                        Header="Test">
        <ribbon:RibbonButton x:Name="btnClickMe"
                             LargeImageSource="Images/ClickMe32.BMP"
                             Label="Click Me"
                             KeyTip="C"
                             QuickAccessToolBarId="2011"
                             SmallImageSource="Images/ClickMe16.bmp"
                             ToolTipDescription="Click to see a dialog box."
                             ToolTipTitle="Test Button"
                             Click="btnClickMe_Click" />
    </ribbon:RibbonGroup>
</ribbon:RibbonTab>
```

One of the more important differences is that not every object receives a number. There's no Id attribute in XAML. XAML also uses different names for similar items. The Header and Label attributes replace the LabelTitle attribute. There are also similarities. Both XML and XAML use the ToolTipTitle and ToolTipDescription attributes to provide tooltips. Despite the differences, if you know how to work with the Windows Forms application XML, you also have a good idea of how to work with XAML.

You should also notice something else that differs when working with WPF. It's possible to create a direct connection to an event handler. Notice the Click attribute for btnClickMe. Notice that it points to btnClickMe_Click, which is discussed in the "Creating the WPF Application" section of this chapter. Listing 7-14 shows the XAML for the File (application) menu.

**LISTING 7-14: WPF File menu XAML code**

Available for download on Wrox.com

```
<ribbon:Ribbon.ApplicationMenu>
    <ribbon:RibbonApplicationMenu SmallImageSource="Images\SmallIcon.png"
                                  KeyTip="F">
        <ribbon:RibbonApplicationMenuItem
            Header="Exit"
            KeyTip="x"
            x:Name="btnExit"
            ImageSource="Images/Exit16.BMP"
            ToolTip="End the Program"
            ToolTipDescription="End the Program"
            QuickAccessToolBarImageSource="Images/Exit16.BMP"
            QuickAccessToolBarId="1010"
            ToolTipTitle="Exit"
            Click="btnExit_Click" />
    </ribbon:RibbonApplicationMenu>
</ribbon:Ribbon.ApplicationMenu>
```

The differences between the File (Application) menu for WPF and the File menu for Windows Forms are about the same as those for the Ribbon tab. You define the text that appears on the menu using the `Header` attribute and must define a `KeyTip` attribute if you want to support keyboard users. You must also define a `QuickAccessToolBarId` attribute value if you want the user to be able to place the menu on the QAT. As with btnClickMe, btnExit has a `Click` attribute to define the `Click` event handler, btnExit_Click().

*WPF development differs in another important way from Windows Forms development. The default graphics supplied with the template are .PNG (Portable Network Graphics) files and not .BMP files. In addition, these files are 24-bit, rather than the 32-bit files used by Windows Forms applications. While the UUIC utility requires that you provide 32-bit graphics, Visual Studio seems content to use 24-bit files. In short, you have one less conversion step to worry about.*

The QAT is part of the initial template, but you won't find an XAML entry for it, and without adding some code you have little control over how the QAT appears. In fact, unlike the Windows Forms application, most of the QAT functionality is controlled through the code behind. Listing 7-15 shows a basic QAT XAML entry.

**LISTING 7-15: WPF QAT XAML code**

Available for download on Wrox.com

```
<ribbon:RibbonQuickAccessToolBar
    Name="cmdQAT"
    ToolTip="Contains the user configurable settings."
    LayoutUpdated="cmdQAT_LayoutUpdated">
</ribbon:RibbonQuickAccessToolBar>
```

Unlike the Windows Forms application, you don't define members of the QAT as part of the markup. The members are defined in the code behind. However, as with other members of the Ribbon, the QAT does include an event entry. You need to define an event handler for the LayoutUpdated event, which is cmdQAT_LayoutUpdated() in this case.

## Creating the WPF Application

A WPF application has the potential to require a considerable amount of code behind, which contrasts somewhat to a Windows Forms application where a lot of the configuration is performed using XML. The most visible configuration requirement is the QAT. Although you could perform some configuration tasks in XAML, the QAT is far more reliant on events that you create in code behind. The following sections describe the code behind for this example.

### Handling the Button Events

Unlike a Windows Forms application, a WPF provides connectivity for you between the Ribbon and the code behind in the background — you don't have to create any special code as you do when working with a Windows Forms application. Consequently, all you really need to worry about are any event handlers that you described in the XAML, as shown in Listing 7-16.

**LISTING 7-16:** Creating the btnExit and btnClickMe event handlers

*Available for download on Wrox.com*

```
private void btnExit_Click(object sender, RoutedEventArgs e)
{
    // End the program.
    Close();
}

private void btnClickMe_Click(object sender, RoutedEventArgs e)
{
    // Display a message box.
    MessageBox.Show("You clicked Click Me!");
}
```

The btnExit_Click() and btnClickMe_Click() event handlers correspond to the Click attribute entries for the buttons in the XAML code. Unlike a Windows Forms application, the btnExit_Click() can actually call Close() without causing any sort of memory error. Again, all the connectivity requirements are handled for you in the background. The btnClickMe_Click() event handler code is precisely the same as its Windows Forms application counterpart.

### Handling the QAT

The QAT is handled completely differently when working with WPF. For one thing, you have to keep track of which elements are on the QAT. The QAT also works differently. When you right-click an item that has the QuickAccessToolBarId attribute defined, you see the Add to Quick Access Toolbar option on the Objects Context menu enabled as shown in Figure 7-13. Choose this option and the item appears on the QAT. Contrast this to the Context menu for the QAT in the Windows Forms application, where checking the item displays it on the QAT.

**FIGURE 7-13:** Each item has a Context menu entry that lets you add it to the QAT.

When you no longer want an item on the QAT, you right-click its entry on the QAT and choose the Remove from Quick Access Toolbar entry on the Context menu, as shown in Figure 7-14. The item is actually destroyed because it exists as a separate entity on the QAT. Consequently, you must always track objects you want to manage on the QAT.

**FIGURE 7-14:** Removing an item destroys its QAT entry.

One of the requirements for managing the QAT is a set of variables that track the object's existence on the QAT. There are only two buttons that have QAT access for the example. The following code provides the means for tracking their connected state:

```
// Create variables to hold QAT connectivity data.
private Boolean btnExitConnected = false;
private Boolean btnClickMeConnected = false;
```

The XAML for the QAT defines an event handler for the LayoutUpdated event. Updates occur in a number of situations, not just the addition or removal of objects on the QAT. Consequently, your code can't assume anything about the QAT; it must work as though the QAT could be performing some other task. Listing 7-17 shows the code used to manage QAT updates for the example.

### LISTING 7-17: Updating the QAT

```
private void cmdQAT_LayoutUpdated(object sender, EventArgs e)
{
    // Make sure the Ribbon is initialized.
    if (Ribbon.QuickAccessToolBar != null)

        // Determine whether there are any items on the Ribbon.
        if (Ribbon.QuickAccessToolBar.Items.Count > 0)
        {
            // Check the connectedness for each item on the Ribbon.
            foreach (var Item in Ribbon.QuickAccessToolBar.Items)
            {
```

*continues*

**LISTING 7-17** *(continued)*

```
            // Check the ID of each variable and set its connected
            // variable as appropriate.
            // Check for btnExit.
            if (((RibbonButton)Item).QuickAccessToolBarId.ToString() ==
               "1010")
            {
                // Only create a connective if we haven't done so already.
                if (!btnExitConnected)
                {
                    // Set the tracking variable so we don't make multiple
                    // connections.
                    btnExitConnected = true;

                    // Handle the Click event.
                    ((RibbonButton)Item).Click +=
                        new RoutedEventHandler(MainWindow_Click);

                    // Handle the Unloaded event.
                    ((RibbonButton)Item).Unloaded +=
                        new RoutedEventHandler(MainWindow_Unloaded);
                }
            }

            // Check for btnClickMe.
            if (((RibbonButton)Item).QuickAccessToolBarId.ToString() ==
               "2011")
            {
                if (!btnClickMeConnected)
                {
                    btnClickMeConnected = true;
                    ((RibbonButton)Item).Click +=
                        new RoutedEventHandler(MainWindow_Click);
                    ((RibbonButton)Item).Unloaded +=
                        new RoutedEventHandler(MainWindow_Unloaded);
                }
            }
        }
    }
}
```

The application can call `cmdQAT_LayoutUpdated()` a number of times before the QAT is even initialized. Therefore, the first check you must make is whether the QAT is `null`. You access the QAT using the `Ribbon.QuickAccessToolBar` object.

If the QAT has been initialized, it will contain information about itself that isn't used in this example, but the information is extensive and you should spend some time in the debugger reviewing it. The item of interest for this example is the `Ribbon.QuickAccessToolBar.Items` collection. When this collection has entries in it, you can process them to determine which items are on the QAT.

Both of the items you can place on the QAT are `RibbonButton` objects for this example, which simplifies the code. When you allow the user to place other kinds of objects on the QAT, you need to create relatively flexible code because you don't know what type of object is in a particular `Ribbon.QuickAccessToolBar.Items` collection item. To determine which button is being processed, the code coerces the generic object in `Item` to a `RibbonButton`. It then uses the `QuickAccessToolBarId` value to compare with the numbers assigned to each of the `RibbonButton` objects.

The first thing the code does is set the requisite tracking variable, such as `btnExitConnected`, to true. This variable ensures that the button doesn't create more than one event handler connection. Each button can call `cmdQAT_LayoutUpdated()` multiple times, so this step is extremely important.

The next step is to create a `RoutedEventHandler` object for the `Click` event, which connects to the `MainWindow_Click()` event handler. The `MainWindow_Click()` will route the call to the appropriate button event handler. When the user clicks the button on the QAT, the code calls `MainWindow_Click()` first.

A problem with the QAT is that you don't know when something is unloaded by monitoring the `cmdQAT_LayoutUpdated()` event handler. Monitoring is performed by the `Unloaded` event. So the code creates a `RoutedEventHandler` object for the MainWindow_`Unloaded()` event handler as well. This event handler takes care of any cleanup when the user removes an item from the QAT.

Now that you have some idea of how QAT layout monitoring occurs, it's time to look at how clicks are handled. Listing 7-18 shows the code used to handle QAT clicks.

**LISTING 7-18: Responding to QAT clicks**

Available for download on Wrox.com

```
void MainWindow_Click(object sender, RoutedEventArgs e)
{
    // Determine which button was clicked.
    switch (((RibbonButton)sender).QuickAccessToolBarId.ToString())
    {
        case "1010": // Exit

            // Call the standard click event.
            btnExit_Click(sender, e);
            break;

        case "2011": // Click Me
            btnClickMe_Click(sender, e);
            break;
    }
}
```

Routing clicks is relatively easy. All you need do is determine which `QuickAccessToolBarId` has fired the event. In both cases, the code simply calls the required `Click` event handler and passes both the `sender` and `e` values to it.

Cleanup is a little more involved than click routing. Listing 7-19 shows the last piece to this example, the `MainWindow_Unloaded()` event handler.

**LISTING 7-19:** Removing QAT members

Available for download on Wrox.com

```
void MainWindow_Unloaded(object sender, RoutedEventArgs e)
{
    // Determine which button was clicked.
    switch (((RibbonButton)sender).QuickAccessToolBarId.ToString())
    {
        case "1010": // Exit.
            // Remove the click event handler.
            ((RibbonButton)sender).Click -=
                new RoutedEventHandler(MainWindow_Click);

            // Remove the unloaded event handler.
            ((RibbonButton)sender).Unloaded -=
                new RoutedEventHandler(MainWindow_Unloaded);

            // Set the tracking variable to false.
            btnExitConnected = false;
            break;

        case "2011": // Click Me
            ((RibbonButton)sender).Click -=
                new RoutedEventHandler(MainWindow_Click);
            ((RibbonButton)sender).Unloaded -=
                new RoutedEventHandler(MainWindow_Unloaded);
            btnClickMeConnected = false;
            break;
    }
}
```

It's important to remember that the .NET Framework isn't magic. The example code you've examined still works with a native-code module. The fact that .NET hides it from you for a WPF application doesn't change things. When you debug this application, you'll see some sections of code where the Call Stack window (Figure 7-15) specifically mentions external code. This is your application's native module at work.

**FIGURE 7-15:** A WPF application doesn't magically get rid of the native module.

This is important because your application can still cause memory leaks when you don't handle things correctly. Consequently, you must perform cleanup for your application through the `MainWindow_Unloaded()` event handler. Every object you create, every event handler you define, everything that could have a memory connection to it, must be cleaned up before the object is unloaded.

In this case, the code determines which button is being cleaned up. It then removes the connection to the `Click` and `Unloaded` event handlers. After it performs these two cleanup tasks, the code sets the requisite tracking variable to `false` so that the process can begin anew the next time the user adds the object to the QAT.

## MOVING YOUR APPLICATIONS TO WINDOWS 7

This chapter has focused on techniques for adding the Ribbon to your application. Most developers will use the Windows Forms approach for application updates and the WPF approach for new development. Of course, you can always choose to use a third-party solution like Elegant Ribbon to reduce your workload. The one concept you should take away from this chapter is that using the Ribbon is going to require a lot of work from everyone, developer and user alike. In order to make using the Ribbon worthwhile, you must evaluate and quantify the benefits, using the concepts presented in Chapter 6. In short, you don't want to embark on a Ribbon adventure without a clear idea that you'll gain something in the end.

Now that you've seen a few Ribbon examples, you'll probably want to begin developing your own Ribbon application. That would be a mistake. Your first steps should be to obtain a copy of PreviewRibbon, get it working on your machine, and create some sample Ribbon setups for users, managers, and developers to see before you do anything else. It also pays to spend some time using debug to trace through the PreviewRibbon example so that you can better see how things work at a more advanced level (use the simple example in this chapter as your starting point, or you'll quickly go crazy).

After everyone agrees that the Ribbon truly is going to provide quantifiable benefits, start developing your application. However, start very simply. Because the Ribbon uses a callback mechanism, you want to be sure you develop the basic application first and get it working. After that, you can add the complete Ribbon interface, and then start making the features work one at a time as users test your application. The Ribbon is actually a forgiving environment to work in once you get the basic application working.

Chapter 8 takes the next logical step in the Windows 7 user interface environment — working with Aero Glass. Vista users often noted that Aero Glass was pretty much eye candy with a few helpful, but not essential, features. This perception has changed in Windows 7. Features such as Show Desktop and Peek make using Aero Glass more appealing. Of course, your application will look nicer running on Windows 7 if it supports Aero Glass, but Chapter 8 provides you with a lot of practical reasons for adding this support to your update or new application.

# Programming for Aero Glass Functionality

**WHAT'S IN THIS CHAPTER?**

- Defining Aero Glass design requirements
- Creating applications that use the Windows 7 common file dialogs
- Creating applications that use the Windows 7 task dialogs
- Developing applications that use extended linguistic services

The user is going to miss some important Windows 7 features without training because some of them are subtle and others are in places where the user won't naturally look. However, unless you specifically choose a theme that turns Aero Glass off, the user will notice it almost immediately, especially when you upgrade from Windows XP or older. For most users, the Aero Glass eye candy is going to be quite overwhelming at first — some may even declare that it's beautiful.

Of course, the Aero Glass functionality in Windows 7 is more than simple eye candy, as it tended to be in Vista. There's practical value in the Windows 7 version of Aero Glass. In fact, you've already seen some of this functionality in the examples shown in Chapter 5. Features such as Peek are part of the new Aero Glass functionality.

This chapter views some features that are uniquely tied to Aero Glass: common file dialogs, task dialogs (a sort of extended message box first developed for Vista), and extended linguistic services. Before you implement these features, you'll definitely want to ensure your application and users will support them, so the chapter begins with a planning session. Of course, you'll find the usual array of examples in this chapter that demonstrate how the features work.

*This chapter assumes that you've installed the Windows API Code Pack. You can find the instructions for installing the Code Pack in the "Obtaining the Windows API Code Pack for Microsoft .NET Framework" section of Chapter 4. The Code Pack contains everything you need to work with the new file dialogs, task dialogs, and extended linguistic features. This chapter relies on a Windows Forms application approach because many developers will be performing updates, rather than creating entirely new applications with the Windows Presentation Foundation (WPF).*

## CONSIDERATIONS FOR DESIGNING APPLICATIONS FOR AERO GLASS

Aero Glass is almost hypnotic. Working with this interface for any length of time makes you wonder how you got along without it. Using Aero Glass in Vista wasn't addictive because it was merely eye candy, for the most part. Windows 7 has added some real substance to Aero Glass, making its use a much harder decision for the developer. However, the developer really shouldn't be making the decision, nor should the design team. Aero Glass comes with some costs that developers will probably want to make management aware of before the project takes off, because the costs could be quite high. Aero Glass will affect your organization in the following areas:

- **Development costs:** This is the most obvious cost for Aero Glass. After all, the application update will cost money. However, Aero Glass comes with hidden costs. Implementing it in an application will require additional time, so you need to consider higher development costs from a longer project.

- **Developer training:** It's unlikely that the developers in your organization will know how to work with Aero Glass. Part of the training cost is in books like this one that show how to work with Aero Glass. However, even with good instructional materials, the developers in your organization will experience a high learning curve as they begin creating their first applications. Updates will cost more and take longer when you use Aero Glass because the developer requires additional support and time to code the updates.

- **User training:** Users always require training for an upgrade, to handle new interfaces, procedures, and data management. However, Aero Glass adds another level of training to the mix. Odd as it may seem, you have to train the user to look at the interface, rather than the glitz. At some level, the user gets distracted by the pretty interface and doesn't see the features that the interface is supporting. You need to set aside additional money for user training when using Aero Glass because the user won't be familiar with or even see some of the Aero Glass functionality.

- **Support:** This book has subtly (and sometimes not so subtly) introduced you to a number of new ideas. The concept of using Peek doesn't exist in Windows XP. Moving the mouse to the far right of the display to see the Desktop doesn't exist in any earlier version of Windows. Your support staff will require retraining to be able to discuss with the user these new concepts, some of which run counter to what the user has done before. Users from the past have no idea of what a Jump List is or why it's important, and support will need to know how to guide them through this process. Extra support training plus additional user support time equals increased costs.

➤ **Hardware updates:** At one time, PC hardware was extremely simple and low-powered. It needed to run only a character-mode interface. If you tried installing DOS on a modern machine, you'd find that some things occur so fast that "blink of an eye" is too slow. Adding graphics increases the required computing horsepower. Every layer adds to the requirements. Aero Glass is beautiful, but it's also graphics-intensive. At a minimum, you have to count on additional hardware for the graphics subsystem. Of course, additional graphics also require more memory, so you'll probably find that the systems also require more memory. The data used to power Aero Glass is larger, so your network may require an update. In short, Aero Glass is probably going to cost quite a bit in terms of hardware updates that you might not have expected.

➤ **Incompatibilities:** Every added processing layer adds another potential failure point to your application. At some point, something will fail. From a developer perspective, the failure occurs as an application incompatibility. After you get your update working, you'll find that some things don't work the way they did before and that some things don't work at all. The bad thing is that it's nearly impossible to determine during the planning process what will break, so you have to fix these issues during the debugging stage, which adds considerably to development time, cost, and frustration.

➤ **Accessibility:** Microsoft endeavors to make software that works well for those with special needs. However, accessibility for special-needs users takes a back seat to Aero Glass functionality. Try any of Microsoft's high-contrast themes and you'll quickly find that Aero Glass (and many of its features) is no longer available. If you need to support those with special needs in your organization, then using Aero Glass functionality might not be a good fit. Plan for these needs carefully.

*If you're developing a shrink-wrapped application, it's important to remember that Aero Glass doesn't appear in the Windows 7 Starter edition. Make sure you note the need to use a higher edition as part of your application requirements.*

## WORKING WITH THE WINDOWS 7 COMMON FILE DIALOGS

The common file dialogs, such as File Open and File Save, have been around since the earliest versions of Windows. The first versions of these dialog boxes were a bit clumsy and often didn't offer much flexibility. Configuring the dialog boxes could also be confusing or at least difficult, but with each version of Windows, Microsoft has sought to solve the most perplexing common file dialog problems. Windows 7 is no exception to the rule. The following sections describe the latest version of the common file dialogs and demonstrate how you can access them from your application using the Common File Dialogs example.

## Considering the Common File Dialog Controls

The `Microsoft.WindowsAPICodePack.Dialogs.Controls` namespace contains a number of controls you can use to interact with the common file dialogs. In most cases, you won't need to add to or subtract from the default configuration, but it's good to know that you have these controls available. The following list provides a quick overview of these controls:

- **CommonFileDialogButton:** Creates a pushbutton control.
- **CommonFileDialogCheckBox:** Creates a checkbox control.
- **CommonFileDialogComboBox:** Creates a combo box control. Every combo box must have at least one `CommonFileDialogComboBoxItem` object in it.
- **CommonFileDialogComboBoxItem:** Defines one `ComboBoxItem` for inclusion in a `CommonFileDialogComboBox` control.
- **CommonFileDialogGroupBox:** Creates a group box that can contain other controls. Grouping performs an important function both in the visual sense (putting like functionality together) and also in application functionality (such as radio buttons).
- **CommonFileDialogLabel:** Creates a label control.
- **CommonFileDialogMenu:** Creates a menu control. Each menu control must have at least one `CommonFileDialogMenuItem` object in it.
- **CommonFileDialogMenuItem:** Defines an individual menu item within a `CommonFileDialogMenu` object.
- **CommonFileDialogSeparator:** Provides a separator between menu items. You use this control to create menu item groupings.
- **CommonFileDialogRadioButtonList:** Creates a radio button list. Each radio button list must have at least one `CommonFileDialogRadioButtonListItem` object in it.
- **CommonFileDialogRadioButtonListItem:** Defines an individual radio button within a `CommonFileDialogRadioButtonList` object.
- **CommonFileDialogTextBox:** Creates a textbox control.

The interesting part about the new Windows 7 common dialog boxes is that you can add any of these controls to them and use those controls to perform special tasks (at least within limits). For example, if users are having a hard time understanding a particular dialog box, you can add a Help button with additional specialized instructions.

Unfortunately, you'll find that there are limits to what you can do with the dialog box itself. Many of the controls are locked down once you display the dialog box. For example, you can't modify the appearance of the dialog box after you display it. In addition, some properties aren't defined at the time you display the dialog box. As a result, you can't write code to clear the file selections the user has made.

All these controls have a complete selection of standard events. When a user clicks a button, you can monitor the event and handle it, if desired. The standard automation for creating event handlers also works, so you don't have to worry about defining the proper syntax. Simply press Tab twice as you normally would to create the event handler entries. The ability to modify the common dialog boxes provides great flexibility, yet you still obtain all the benefits of using a common dialog box in your application, including a standardized appearance.

In addition to the standard controls, you also have access to abstract container controls. Here are the controls you can access:

- **`CommonFileDialogControl`:** Provides an abstract class that contains all the shared functionality for the common file dialog controls.
- **`CommonFileDialogControlCollection<T>`:** Creates a collection of strongly typed dialog box controls.
- **`CommonFileDialogProminentControl`:** Specifies the properties and constructors for all prominent controls in common file dialogs.

## Configuring the Common File Dialogs Example

The example begins with a Windows Forms application. The example uses one `Button` control named `btnOpen` to demonstrate the File Open common dialog and a second `Button` control named `btnSave` to demonstrate the File Save common dialog. Of course, you can use any other suitable control, such as a menu, if desired.

Because this application relies on the Code Pack, you need to add references to it. In this case, you need to add references to the following DLLs using the Browse tab of the Add Reference dialog box:

```
Microsoft.WindowsAPICodePack.DLL
Microsoft.WindowsAPICodePack.Shell.DLL
```

In addition, this example requires use of the following references from the .NET tab of the Add Reference dialog box:

```
PresentationCore
PresentationFramework
System.Xaml
WindowsBase
```

Depending on the application requirements, you also need to add from one to three `using` statements. In most cases, it's best to add the following `using` statements to your application:

```
using Microsoft.WindowsAPICodePack.Dialogs;
using Microsoft.WindowsAPICodePack.Dialogs.Controls;
using Microsoft.WindowsAPICodePack.Shell;
```

## Defining a File Open Dialog

Sometimes it's hard to know precisely how to modify a common file dialog to make it easier to use. Microsoft has tried for years and still isn't happy. Because you know your users, you have a better chance of creating the perfect dialog box — one that precisely matches the needs of your users. The new `CommonOpenFileDialog` class makes it easier to make the modifications your users need in a File Open dialog box. Listing 8-1 shows some of the changes you can make and how to implement them.

**LISTING 8-1:** Defining a File Open dialog box

```
private void btnOpen_Click(object sender, EventArgs e)
{
    // Define the dialog box.
    CommonOpenFileDialog dlgOpen = new CommonOpenFileDialog("File Open");

    // Configure the File Open dialog box.
    // The user must select just one file.
    dlgOpen.Multiselect = false;
    // Treat .LNK files as their targets.
    dlgOpen.NavigateToShortcut = true;
    // Select a default starting location.
    dlgOpen.InitialDirectory = @"C:\Test";
    // Disallow read-only files.
    dlgOpen.EnsureReadOnly = false;

    // Add some alternative places to find data.
    ShellContainer Place = KnownFolders.DocumentsLibrary as ShellContainer;
    dlgOpen.AddPlace(Place, FileDialogAddPlaceLocation.Top);
    dlgOpen.AddPlace(@"C:\Test", FileDialogAddPlaceLocation.Top);

    // Add selection filters.
    dlgOpen.Filters.Add(new CommonFileDialogFilter("Text File", ".txt"));
    dlgOpen.Filters.Add(new CommonFileDialogFilter("HTML File", ".htm,.html"));
    dlgOpen.Filters.Add(new CommonFileDialogFilter("Document File", ".doc"));

    // Create a test button.
    CommonFileDialogButton btnHelp =
        new CommonFileDialogButton("btnHelp", "&File Selection Help");

    // Add an event handler for chkTest.
    btnHelp.Click += new EventHandler(btnHelp_Click);

    // Add a special control.
    dlgOpen.Controls.Add(btnHelp);

    // Show the dialog box.
    CommonFileDialogResult Result = dlgOpen.ShowDialog(this.Handle);

    // Check the selection results.
    if (Result == CommonFileDialogResult.OK)
```

```
            // Display the selected file.
            MessageBox.Show("The user selected: " + dlgOpen.FileName);
        else

            // The user clicked Cancel.
            MessageBox.Show("User clicked Cancel");
    }
```

The code begins by creating the File Open dialog box, `dlgOpen`, using the `CommonOpenFileDialog` class. If you really don't want to make any changes, you can call `dlgOpen.ShowDialog()` to obtain one or more file selections from the user at this point. However, you'll generally need to perform several kinds of tasks to optimize the File Open dialog box:

- Configure the existing features.
- Provide one or more custom locations to find files.
- Add one or more filters to define the kinds of files the user can open.
- Add one or more specialty controls.

The example doesn't begin to cover all the configuration options at your disposal, but it does show the options that you'll commonly change. For one thing, you'll want to set the File Open dialog box to specifically allow or disallow multiple file selections. When you want the user to open one file at a time, make sure you set `Multiselect` to `false`. Many organizations use .LNK (link) files to make it easier for users to find files without knowing where those files are located. If this is the case in your organization, you'll want to set `NavigateToShortcut` to `true` to ensure that the user opens the file pointed to by the link, rather than the .LNK file itself. It's also important to set an initial directory so the user always begins the search in a specific location. Finally, you'll want to decide whether the user should open read-only files. Nothing's more frustrating than to open a read-only file and later find that you can't save the changes you made. When you set `EnsureReadOnly` to `false` and the user selects a read-only file, the user sees the dialog box shown in Figure 8-1 automatically — no extra coding required on your part.

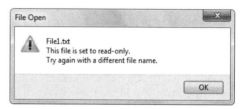

**FIGURE 8-1:** The new File Open dialog box helps ensure that users don't open read-only files inadvertently.

Even with a default directory and lots of help through .LNK files, users are apt not to find what they need. Fortunately, you can add other places the user can look for files. The `AddPlace()` method provides two techniques to accomplish the task, as shown in Listing 8-1. The first technique works with known locations, such as the user's Documents folder. The second technique works with non-standard locations, such as C:\Test. The user sees these added locations on the left side of the File Open dialog box along with the other standard locations, as shown in Figure 8-2.

**FIGURE 8-2:** Add new locations the user can rely on to find files as needed.

Every File Open dialog box should define standard filters the user can use to locate precisely the file type needed, even if one of the filters must be *.* to allow for all files. The code uses `dlgOpen.Filters.Add()` to add new filters to the list. Each filter entry is a `CommonFileDialogFilter` object, whose constructor requires two arguments: a common name for the file such as Text File and one or more file extensions. Notice that you separate multiple file extensions using commas:

```
dlgOpen.Filters.Add(new CommonFileDialogFilter("HTML File", ".htm,.html"));
```

which displays both `.HTM` and `.HTML` files for the user when the user selects the HTML File filter option.

The final addition that you'll commonly make is special controls. The example adds a special Help button to the File Open dialog box, but as described in the "Considering the Common File Dialog Controls" section of this chapter, you have a wide variety of controls from which to choose. You may be tempted to add the button as a global variable, but doing so can cause all kinds of problems the second time the user tries to open the File Open dialog box because the application will display an Invalid Operation error.

The `CommonFileDialogButton()` constructor requires the name of the control as the first argument because the application will send this information as the `sender` variable to the control's event handlers. After you create the variable, you can add event handlers to it. The example adds the event handlers as part of the form's constructor, as shown in Listing 8-2.

As with any other event handler, you can press Tab after you type +=, and the IDE will automatically add the proper event handler constructor for you. Press Tab a second time and the code automatically creates an event handler for you, like the one shown in Listing 8-2.

Available for download on Wrox.com

### LISTING 8-2: Creating the btnHelp event handler

```
void btnHelp_Click(object sender, EventArgs e)
{
    // Display a helpful message.
    MessageBox.Show(
        "Select the file type you want: text, HTML, or document." +
        " Then select a file from the resulting list.");
}
```

The event handler is simple in this case. All it does is display a help message. However, you can create event handlers of any required complexity. After you create the control, you add it to the File Open dialog box by calling `dlgOpen.Controls.Add()` with the name of the control as the argument.

The `btnOpen_Click()` event handler shown in Listing 8-1 displays the File Open dialog box next by calling `dlgOpen.ShowDialog()`. Notice the inclusion of `this.Handle` as an argument to tie the File Open dialog box to the application. If you don't provide this argument, the user could try to perform all kinds of other tasks and simply leave the File Open dialog box in limbo. When the user closes the dialog box by selecting either Open or Cancel, `Result` contains a `CommonFileDialogResult` enumeration value of either `OK` or `Cancel`. You can test for this value as shown in the example and do something. In this case, the example simply shows the name of the file that the user selected or displays a message stating that the user clicked Cancel. Figure 8-3 shows the File Open dialog box with all the additions made by the example.

## Defining a File Save Dialog

The new File Save dialog is every bit as flexible and programmable as the File Open dialog. Depending on what your application requires, you may create more or fewer additions to the File Save dialog. Getting users to put files in the right place and not overwrite existing files with completely different versions are two major

**FIGURE 8-3:** The modified File Open dialog box is truly helpful.

considerations when creating the File Save dialog box. Listing 8-3 shows the code used for this example. You'll find that the File Save dialog, like the File Open dialog, offers significantly more options than shown here.

**LISTING 8-3:** Defining a File Save dialog box

Available for download on Wrox.com

```
private void btnSave_Click(object sender, EventArgs e)
{
    // Define the dialog box.
    CommonSaveFileDialog dlgSave = new CommonSaveFileDialog("File Save");

    // Add some alternative places to find data.
    ShellContainer Place = KnownFolders.DocumentsLibrary as ShellContainer;
    dlgSave.AddPlace(Place, FileDialogAddPlaceLocation.Top);
    dlgSave.AddPlace(@"C:\Test", FileDialogAddPlaceLocation.Top);

    // Add selection filters.
    dlgSave.Filters.Add(new CommonFileDialogFilter("Text File", ".txt"));
    dlgSave.Filters.Add(new CommonFileDialogFilter("HTML File", ".htm,.html"));
    dlgSave.Filters.Add(new CommonFileDialogFilter("Document File", ".doc"));

    // Show the dialog box.
    CommonFileDialogResult Result = dlgSave.ShowDialog(this.Handle);

    // Check the selection results.
    if (Result == CommonFileDialogResult.OK)

        // Display the selected file.
```

*continues*

**LISTING 8-3** *(continued)*

```
        MessageBox.Show("The user saved the file as: " + dlgSave.FileName);
    else

        // The user clicked Cancel.
        MessageBox.Show("User clicked Cancel");
}
```

The code begins by creating the File Save dialog, `dlgSave`, as a `CommonSaveFileDialog` object. As with the File Open dialog, you supply a dialog box name as part of the `CommonSaveFileDialog()` constructor.

You should provide symmetry between the File Open dialog and File Save dialog locations. If you add special locations for the File Open dialog, you should provide the same locations for the File Save dialog, unless your company has a policy about precisely where the user saves files locally or on the network that would conflict with a symmetrical approach. Using a symmetrical approach tends to reduce user confusion, which reduces training and support costs.

The same consideration applies for filters. The example code adds precisely the same filters for both the File Open and File Save dialog boxes, using the `Filters.Add()` method. Make sure that you address any specifics as part of creating the filter sets. If one filter set allows both .HTM and .HTML files, then the other filter set should allow both of them as well.

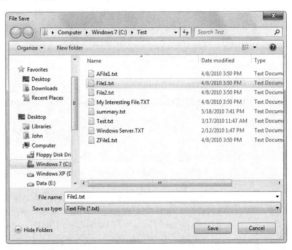

This example ends like the File Open dialog box by displaying the dialog box and then showing the result. As with the File Open example, the filename the user selects for saving the file appears as part of the Filename property. However, unlike the File Open example, the user can't ever save multiple files using a single save process. The user will always save one file at a time. Figure 8-4 shows how the File Save dialog box appears on-screen.

**FIGURE 8-4:** The File Save dialog box has many of the same features as the File Open dialog box.

The File Save dialog box includes a built-in feature to help prevent users from saving to an existing file. When the user selects an existing file and clicks Save, the application automatically displays the dialog box shown in Figure 8-5. You don't need to add this functionality; it comes as part of the dialog box. Of course, there's a property setting you can change, `OverwritePrompt`, if you want to override

**FIGURE 8-5:** The File Save dialog box comes with built-in functionality to prevent file overwrites.

this behavior. Simply set the `OverwritePrompt` property to `false` and the user won't see any overwrite warnings.

If the user tries to overwrite a read-only file, the application automatically displays a second message, as shown in Figure 8-6. In this case, the user isn't given an opportunity to bypass the protections. There isn't any way to override this behavior programmatically, either, unless you create an event handler for the `FileOK` event. You'd need to detect the file the user has selected, change the file's read-only status, allow the save to progress, and then change the file's status back to read-only. This could be a helpful technique

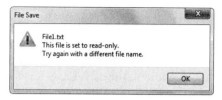

**FIGURE 8-6:** The user isn't allowed to save to a read-only file.

if you want to allow the user to write data to a file and then disallow changes to that file later except under certain conditions controlled by your application.

## WORKING WITH THE WINDOWS 7 TASK DIALOGS

A Task dialog is more advanced than a message box, but less complicated than a custom dialog. You generally configure a Task dialog using properties, but you can also add custom controls if desired. The Task dialog lets you communicate more information to the user than a message box does, and it provides considerable flexibility. Of course, you can't use it to replace custom dialog boxes. The Task dialog is meant to fill the middle ground between message boxes and custom dialog boxes. For example, many developers now use the Task dialog for privilege elevation needs. The following sections describe the Task dialog and show how to use it.

## Using the Task Dialog Effectively

Creating a Task dialog is a relatively simple process as long as you follow some basic rules. For one thing, you need to keep the purpose of the Task dialog in mind. The Task dialog was never meant to replace complex custom dialogs. It's also overkill for very simple information presentation needs. You don't want to replace your message boxes with Task dialogs because the Task dialog will then lose its meaning and you'll have a less useful application. Figure 8-7 shows the Task dialog created by the Task Dialog example.

**FIGURE 8-7:** A Task dialog provides a middle ground between message boxes and custom dialogs.

Notice that this dialog includes an icon, just as any message box can, along with three standard buttons: Yes, No, and Cancel. The Task dialog has a title and message text within it. Of course, there are differences, too. If you could see the dialog box in its original colors, you'd see that it has blue instructional text. In addition, it uses a larger font size than the message text. This dialog also includes details. Click the down arrow and you'll see some additional information, as shown in Figure 8-8.

This Task dialog includes a special feature, a progress bar. When time runs out on the progress bar, the dialog box automatically makes a selection for the user. Using this feature would let an application installation proceed using a default setting, or any other wizard for that matter. Coding this addition is easy because it's built right into the Task dialog. It's also possible to force the user to make a decision. You can set a Task dialog to disallow a cancel by the user. So you have both automation and concrete required action at your disposal.

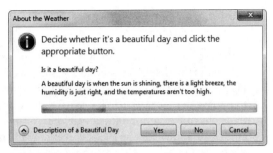

**FIGURE 8-8:** Task dialogs can provide amplifying information to the user.

A Task dialog comes with additional features not shown in the example. For example, you can add a hyperlink to the dialog. When the user clicks the hyperlink, the Task dialog passes control to the user's browser, where the user can obtain additional information. It pays to spend a little time playing with the Task dialog to obtain just the right appearance for your application.

The example doesn't include any custom controls. You can add them, but doing so can be tricky. There's no designer to help you, and you'll find that the number of available controls is limited — just push buttons and radio buttons. It's true that you can add a checkbox to the Task dialog's footer, but you don't have any control over position and you get only one checkbox. In short, the Task dialog does have limitations, just not as many as a message box does. With this in mind, here are some typical uses of the Task dialog (although you certainly shouldn't limit yourself to this list):

- Privilege elevation dialog
- Wizard step
- Installation program step
- Detailed reason dialog
- Application error dialog
- Simplified help
- Context-sensitive help

## Configuring the Task Dialog Example

The Task Dialog example begins with a Windows Forms application. The example adds a button to display the Task dialog. It requires use of the Code Pack. However, you need to add only one DLL to the project, as shown here:

```
Microsoft.WindowsAPICodePack.DLL
```

You'll also need to add the following `using` statement to complete the configuration:

```
using Microsoft.WindowsAPICodePack.Dialogs;
```

## Defining a Task Dialog

Because a Task dialog does so much more than a message box can, you can't create it as a single statement. As with many complex objects, you create the object first, and then configure it as needed before displaying it on-screen. Listing 8-4 shows the code used to create the Task dialog shown earlier in Figures 8-7 and 8-8.

LISTING 8-4: Create the Task dialog

```
private void btnTest_Click(object sender, EventArgs e)
{
    // Create the Task dialog.
    TaskDialog TD = new TaskDialog();

    // Configure the Task dialog.
    // Allow the user to cancel.
    TD.Cancelable = true;

    // Set the caption.
    TD.Caption = "About the Weather";

    // Set the inner text.
    TD.Text = "Is it a beautiful day?";

    // Add standard buttons to the dialog box.
    TD.StandardButtons |= TaskDialogStandardButtons.Yes;
    TD.StandardButtons |= TaskDialogStandardButtons.No;
    TD.StandardButtons |= TaskDialogStandardButtons.Cancel;

    // Add an icon to the dialog box.
    TD.Icon = TaskDialogStandardIcon.Information;

    // Add instructions to the dialog box.
    TD.InstructionText =
        "Decide whether it's a beautiful day and " +
        "click the appropriate button.";

    // Add some details.
    TD.DetailsCollapsedLabel = "What constitutes a beautful day?";
    TD.DetailsExpanded = false;
    TD.DetailsExpandedLabel = "Description of a Beautiful Day";
    TD.DetailsExpandedText =
        "A beautiful day is when the sun is shining, there is a " +
        "light breeze, the humidity is just right, and the " +
```

*continues*

**LISTING 8-4** *(continued)*

```
            "temperatures aren't too high.";

    // Set the host window.
    TD.OwnerWindowHandle = this.Handle;

    // Add a timing function so the user answers within
    // a specific interval.
    // Create the ProgressBar.
    TaskDialogProgressBar TimeIt =
        new TaskDialogProgressBar(0, 60, 0);

    // Add the ProgressBar to the dialog box.
    TD.ProgressBar = TimeIt;

    // Start the ProgressBar.
    TD.ProgressBar.State = TaskDialogProgressBarState.Normal;

    // Add a Tick event handler.
    TD.Tick += new EventHandler<TaskDialogTickEventArgs>(TD_Tick);

    // Display the Task dialog on-screen.
    TaskDialogResult Result = TD.Show();

    // Display the response on-screen.
    switch (Result)
    {
        case TaskDialogResult.Yes:
            MessageBox.Show("It's a beautiful day!");
            break;
        case TaskDialogResult.No:
            MessageBox.Show("The weather is bad.");
            break;
        case TaskDialogResult.Cancel:
            MessageBox.Show("The user didn't have an opinion.");
            break;
    }
}
```

The code begins by creating the `TaskDialog` object, `TD`. The constructor doesn't accept any input arguments.

The configuration process comes next. The `Cancelable` property lets you determine whether the user can cancel out of the dialog box. If you set `Cancelable` to `false`, the user can't click Cancel to exit the dialog box. Use the `Caption` and `Text` properties to set the same types of text that you normally associate with a message box. The `Text` property accepts control characters, so you can format the output for a pleasing presentation or simply let the text wrap from line to line as needed.

You aren't limited, as with a message box, to using certain combinations of buttons. As shown in the code, you select each of the standard buttons separately. Notice the technique shown in the code of working with the |= (or-equal) operator. It isn't possible to "or" the buttons together in a single line. For example, you can't use the following line of code:

```
TD.StandardButtons = TaskDialogStandardButtons.Yes ||
    TaskDialogStandardButtons.No || TaskDialogStandardButtons.Cancel;
```

*You can't use standard buttons and custom buttons together. The code will compile, but the dialog box will raise an error. In some cases, this limitation means that you must provide custom versions of standard buttons to make the application work properly.*

Most dialogs include an icon of some sort so the user knows what kind of dialog it is. The Task dialog has access to the full complement of standard Windows icons, but you can't create special icons for it. Assign the icon you want to the `Icon` property.

The next line of code shows one of the Task dialog special features. The `InstructionText` property accepts a string value that provides basic instructions to the user on what you want to happen next. The instruction text appears in blue in the dialog box and in a larger font so it attracts the user's attention immediately. You use the `InstructionText` property for a Task dialog that requires user interaction, such as a wizard or setup step, but you'd probably avoid using it for an informational dialog box. Users will generally figure out that they need to click OK to dismiss the dialog box after reading the message it provides. This particular feature could lose its appeal if developers begin overusing it for the wrong purposes, because the user will get used to seeing it and start ignoring it.

Another important Task dialog feature is detail information. The next section of code shows how to set up a detail, and you have already seen the detail displayed in Figure 8-8. The detail text is there to help novice users who just don't understand what the Task dialog is asking them to do. It helps alleviate the problem of too much information, without leaving out information for those who need it.

Many developers will miss the next step, and the user will see a confusing assortment of icons on the Taskbar as a result. You need to assign the Task dialog to the application using the `OwnerWindowHandle` property, or the user will see another icon added to the Taskbar. In addition, if you don't assign the Task dialog to the application, the user could simply ignore your request for additional information and continue working with the application in other ways. In most cases, you make the assignment using the `this.Handle` property, unless you want to assign the Task dialog to a child window (in which case, you need the handle to the child window instead).

The example includes code for a progress bar. Unlike many add-on controls, the progress bar requires special handling. You create the `TaskDialogProgressBar` object `TimeIt`, assign it to the `TD.ProgressBar` property, and then perform configuration as needed. To make the progress bar functional, you need to create an event handler for it. The most common event to handle is `Tick`. The "Making an Automatic Selection" section of this chapter explains how you can use the `Tick` event handler to cause the Task dialog to automatically make a selection for the user after a specified time interval.

Once you complete the required configuration, it's time to call `TD.Show()`. The user's selection (when using standard buttons) appears in the output as a `TaskDialogResult` enumerated value

(`Result`). A production application would continue at this point with some level of processing. The example merely displays the result of the user selection (the state of the weather for the user).

## Making an Automatic Selection

One of the problems with the message box is that it doesn't provide automation. You can display it, but that doesn't mean the user will ever figure out what to do next. Most developers have seen it happen at least once — you get a support call for a frozen application, only to find there's an open dialog box that the user is ignoring. If you haven't encountered this little user-support gem yet, you will. Fortunately, you can configure the Task dialog to make an automatic selection for users who are seemingly undecided, as shown in Listing 8-5.

### LISTING 8-5: Handle ProgressBar events

```
void TD_Tick(object sender, TaskDialogTickEventArgs e)
{
    // Create a copy of the Task dialog.
    TaskDialog ThisTask = (TaskDialog)sender;

    // Don't do anything if the ProgressBar is paused.
    if (ThisTask.ProgressBar.State !=
        TaskDialogProgressBarState.Paused)

        // Check the current value.
        if (ThisTask.ProgressBar.Value == ThisTask.ProgressBar.Maximum)
        {
            // Pause if the time is up.
            ThisTask.ProgressBar.State =
                TaskDialogProgressBarState.Paused;

            // Automatically select a value.
            ThisTask.Close(TaskDialogResult.Cancel);
        }
        else
            // Update the ProgressBar value.
            ThisTask.ProgressBar.Value += 1;
}
```

Unfortunately, you can't set the tick interval for a Task dialog. The tick occurs at a 200-millisecond interval. Consequently, the maximum value of 60 shown in Listing 8-4 creates a 12-second timer. The user has 12 seconds in which to make a decision, or the code shown in Listing 8-5 will automatically make the decision for the user.

The `TD_Tick()` event handler receives the Task dialog object in `sender`. To make it easier to interact with the Task dialog, the event handler code simply creates `ThisTask` to access the `TaskDialog` object.

The first check verifies that the `ProgressBar` is still in the `TaskDialogProgressBarState.Normal` state. Otherwise, the count is over and the Task dialog will be closing. This check is necessary to prevent possible race conditions (where the code starts another loop before the check is made). During testing, the example application would occasionally raise an exception before the Task dialog automatically closed because the code would attempt to update `ThisTask.ProgressBar.Value` beyond the maximum value or do something else that wasn't allowed. Using this check prevents the problem from occurring.

The second check determines what to do. If the `ThisTask.ProgressBar.Value` equals the `ThisTask.ProgressBar.Maximum` value, then it's time to pause the progress bar and close the Task dialog by calling `ThisTask.Close()`. The code automatically selects the most innocuous value, `TaskDialogResult.Cancel`, which means the user didn't have an opinion in this case. When `ThisTask.ProgressBar.Value` is less than `ThisTask.ProgressBar.Maximum`, the code simply increments the `ThisTask.ProgressBar.Value` property.

## PROVIDING EXTENDED LINGUISTIC SERVICES

Many applications today require support for more than one language. Even if you're writing an application that sees use only in a single country, the chances are high that people who speak other languages will use it and will require the prompts and other application features in another language. The following sections describe some of the principles of using the new Extended Linguistic Services (ELS) in Windows 7.

## Understanding the Role of Extended Linguistic Services

Over the years, developers have relied on a host of techniques for adding language support to their applications. For example, developers have used Local Identifiers (LCIDs) for many years. You can see a list of LCIDs at http://krafft.com/scripts/deluxe-calendar/lcid_chart.htm. Typically, the developer places the resources for a particular language in a subdirectory that uses the number of the language it supports, such as 1033 for American English or 2058 for Mexican Spanish. Of course, to get full LCID support, you also need to know that the hexadecimal equivalent for 1033 is 409 because Microsoft uses 409 for American English. In addition, you need to know that American English uses code page 1252. (Yes, it can get pretty confusing — see the charts at http://www.science.co.il/language/locale-codes.asp and http://www.i18nguy.com/unicode/codepages.html.)

The LCIDs go only so far in solving the problem of support for multiple languages, though, and they don't necessarily provide an overall solution. In fact, the solution is a hodgepodge because different developers will support different languages. Microsoft saw a need to add operating-system-level support for other languages and has done so using the National Language Support (NLS) functionality that developers have used up till now (see http://msdn.microsoft.com/library/dd319078.aspx for details). LCIDs are also abstract, so Microsoft has implemented Internet Engineering Task Force (IETF)-conformant string-based identifiers (see http://www.faqs.org/rfcs/rfc4646.html).

Even with NLS, though, the developer still encounters problems because simply providing prompts in the right language isn't enough. An application today needs to perform a number of tasks correctly for each language it supports, such as:

- ➤ Presentation of numeric data
- ➤ Presentation of dates and time

- Data sorting
- Keyboard layout support
- Printing support
- Translation between data formats (not necessarily the language itself, but the data presentation, such as the format of data or time)

Trying to code all these required tasks by hand can be error-prone and time-consuming. ELS is a new Windows 7 API that makes it easier to perform these tasks by reducing the amount of work the developer needs to do to obtain the desired result.

## Configuring the Extended Linguistic Services Example

The Extended Linguistic Services example starts with a Windows Forms application. To make it easy to see how the language detection features of ELS work, the example provides a textbox for entry and a list box for output. In some cases, such as detecting Spanish or Portuguese, you'll actually see multiple language possibilities as output, which makes the list box convenient. There's also a test button that initiates the language detection check. You'll use the Code Pack for this example and will need to add the following reference:

```
Microsoft.WindowsAPICodePack.ExtendedLinguisticServices.DLL
```

The example also requires the following `using` statement:

```
using Microsoft.WindowsAPICodePack.ExtendedLinguisticServices;
```

## Adding Extended Linguistic Services to an Application

There isn't any way a section of a chapter can discuss everything you need to know about working with other languages. However, there's one question that seems to vex developers everywhere: how to detect the language the user is speaking. It's a problem because the user often won't be able to communicate the language easily, or your application may not support the user's language directly. For that matter, the user may be another computer and not a human user at all. This particular service, language detection, is one that just about any developer can use. Listing 8-6 shows the code for this example.

### LISTING 8-6: Detect the user's language

Available for download on Wrox.com

```csharp
private void btnTest_Click(object sender, EventArgs e)
{
    // Clear the previous language list.
    lbOutput.Items.Clear();

    // Create a mapping service.
    MappingService LangDetect = new MappingService(
```

```
            MappingAvailableServices.LanguageDetection);

    // Perform language detection.
    using (MappingPropertyBag Bag =
        LangDetect.RecognizeText(txtInput.Text, null))
    {

        // Obtain the list of candidates as a string array.
        String[] Languages =
            Bag.GetResultRanges()[0].FormatData(
                new StringArrayFormatter());

        // Process each of the languages in the list.
        foreach (String Language in Languages)
            lbOutput.Items.Add(Language);
    }
}
```

The example begins by clearing the list box, `lbOutput`, so that you see just the languages associated with the current string, which appears in `txtInput`.

The next step is to create a `MappingService` object, `LangDetect`. The `MappingService()` constructor requires an input telling it what type of service to create. The available services appear in the `MappingAvailableServices` enumeration. The example uses the `LanguageDetection` service. The `MappingService` also supports script detection and a number of transliteration services.

Detecting a language involves creating a map of the language properties. The code creates a `MappingPropertyBag` object, `Bag`, to hold these properties. The `LangDetect.RecognizeText()` method outputs the properties it detects in the sample text found in `txtInput.Text` and places them in `Bag`.

At this point, you want to extract the data from `Bag`. The `GetResultRanges()` method outputs an array of `MappingDataRange` objects. When detecting a language, the output array contains only one element, which contains the list of detected languages.

To get these languages' output of the `MappingDataRange` array element, the code calls `FormatData()` with a new `StringArrayFormatter` object. The result is an array that you can then process using a `foreach` loop.

The detection is perfect in some cases. For example, if you type **Hello World**, you get en (English) as the only output. The language detector can't tell you what kind of English (such as en-US for American English), simply that it's English. On the other hand, if you type **Hola a todos**, the detector can't make a precise determination, as shown in Figure 8-9. In this case, you'd still need to select between Spanish and Portuguese. (The detector also provides both Spanish and Portuguese as output for **Olá Mundo**.) However, at least your list of choices is less than if you had to figure out the correct language from scratch.

**FIGURE 8-9:** ELS does an amazing job of correctly detecting most languages.

It's interesting to see how accurate the language detection is for ELS. For example, try typing **Hallo Welt** to see what language you get. ELS is still a little limited on what it can translate. It did handle this Chinese with aplomb: 您好世界, but failed miserably with this Hindi: नमस्ते विश्व. The point is that this tool is relatively easy to use, and it does a better job than the tools that most developers had in the past.

> *Theoretically, every one of the language examples in this chapter says, Hello World. However, I don't actually speak every one of these languages; if you're an accomplished linguist, you may find the translation less than perfect. For example, you might translate the Chinese characters as "How do you do, World, sir?" if you speak Chinese. Yes, these translations might make you laugh a bit, but they also get the point across to people who need the translation. If you'd like to create your own other language examples, try Google Translate at* `http://translate.google.com/`.

## MOVING YOUR APPLICATIONS TO WINDOWS 7

This chapter has provided you with examples of three more Windows 7 features. In this case, each of the features has a tie-in with Aero Glass. Because of the additional processing requirements for Aero Glass, many organizations will have to spend time looking at the cost vs. payoff for using these features. This time it's not just a case of updating the application or training the user — these features may also require hardware investments. Not only will the client systems require better graphics processors and more memory, but the network may require additional bandwidth and you might find there are other hidden expenses to consider.

Microsoft assumes that everyone is using the latest technology — in fact, they're counting on it. The only problem is that most companies still have a hand-me-down policy, with many users relying on older but still useful systems to perform less complex tasks such as word processing. You need to plan an application upgrade carefully if you plan to use Aero Glass. In some cases, it's actually better to bypass the productivity gains of the upgrade to avoid a large increase in costs. Now is the time to create a comprehensive budget for the upgrade to ensure it actually will produce a payoff at some point.

Make sure you spend some time playing with the various Windows 7 features found in this chapter. The examples didn't show every available property, method, and event for these new technologies, and some of them will prove interesting in solving your particular needs. The Task dialog is an especially welcome new feature — Microsoft should have introduced it quite some time ago.

Chapter 9 moves to an entirely new area of Windows, the Multi-Touch Interface. As with this chapter, the technology in Chapter 9 requires an investment in hardware, as well as updated software and user training. However, the hardware required for the Multi-Touch Interface is new enough that the vast majority of systems won't have it. The Multi-Touch Interface is for specialized needs today. The reason you want to learn about it now, even if you can't use it, is that this sort of technology can help you overcome some specific kinds of problems. For example, an industrial application will benefit from the Multi-Touch Interface, as will applications such as kiosks.

# Working with the Multi-Touch User Interface

**WHAT'S IN THIS CHAPTER?**

➤ Defining Multi-Touch Interface uses

➤ Understanding what the user needs to use the Multi-Touch Interface

➤ Working with the Multi-Touch Platform

Microsoft and other vendors have tried for years to get you to use something other than the mouse and keyboard to interact with your computer. Industry pundits constantly complain that these tools are antiquated at best (see John Dvorak's take on the topic at http://www.pcmag.com/article2/0,2817,2350895,00.asp). It's true, the keyboard has been around since the 1860s, but this only points out that the keyboard is a truly useful device that hasn't received its due as an important innovation.

To an extent, the vendors have been successful in moving you to other devices. Many people use their cell phones and other mobile devices with a combination of touch screens and keyboard substitutes. However, many mobile devices come with a keyboard simply because that's the way people are used to working. All these vendors have a vision of you interacting with your computer using a combination of voice and gestures at some point — the same vision that appears in many science fiction movies. Whether this vision materializes depends on how technology evolves. Products such as Dragon NaturallySpeaking (http://www.nuance.com/naturallyspeaking/products/) have made progress, but they don't work well for technical users, and at a 99 percent (maximum) comprehension rate, that means one in a hundred words will still be wrong, which may be one word too many.

The Multi-Touch Interface (originally called Windows Touch) is another in a series of alternative ways to interact with your computer. As with touch screens and other technologies, the Multi-Touch Interface will definitely appeal to some people. It also fulfills some specific needs. Whether it becomes the next keyboard remains to be seen. This chapter provides you with some ideas on how you can use the Multi-Touch Interface to create applications that users find both useful and helpful. In addition, it points out some of the ways in which the Multi-Touch Interface provides a unique experience that you can capitalize on in your development efforts.

*Microsoft uses a plethora of confusing terms for Multi-Touch, capitalizes it a few more ways, and even leaves out the hyphen sometimes. To avoid confusion in this chapter, the text uses Multi-Touch Interface to refer to the user experience — the actual use of Multi-Touch within an application. The developer part of the equation is called the Multi-Touch Platform. It consists of any tools, the Application Programming Interface (API), and any other developer-specific Multi-Touch functionality.*

You use the Multi-Touch Platform, the API Microsoft supplies, to add Multi-Touch functionality to your application. This chapter provides a short example of how to perform this task. As with many Windows 7 features, you'll find that you need to work a little to access the required functionality within the Visual Studio IDE. Unfortunately, this is one of the few areas the Code Pack doesn't address, so you need to rely on other techniques.

## CONSIDERING WHERE MOST COMPANIES USE MULTI-TOUCH

A number of uses for the Multi-Touch Interface come almost instantly to mind. The first is for tablet use. Someone driving a delivery truck or working with a tablet in some other way is an obvious candidate for this technology. However, at least as of this writing, there aren't any tablet devices that are compatible with the Multi-Touch Interface. Look for this to change, though, as more vendors release updated devices. At some point, the person working on a delivery truck will be able to make use of Multi-Touch for business purposes.

The second use is for mobile devices. Eventually, Microsoft will get into this area, too, but they aren't there today. As with the delivery truck scenario, look for vendors to provide Multi-Touch capability in some of the newer devices they produce.

A third use is industrial applications. In this case, you can use the Multi-Touch Interface today to good advantage. Imagine being able to zoom into a problem area so that you can see it better or pan left or right while wearing gloves or other special equipment. In fact, industrial applications could be considered the perfect use for Multi-Touch as it exists today and with the equipment currently available.

In some situations, a fourth use will be for artistic work — everything from creating a work of art to modifying a picture. The more precise the art, however, the less likely it is that the Multi-Touch Interface will prove productive. For example, you probably wouldn't use the Multi-Touch Interface for a CAD application, where precision is essential and the human finger much too wide to achieve it.

A fifth common use is for presentations of all types. Someone moving an object on-screen with a finger somehow looks more friendly than all that futzing with a mouse. It's easier for the presenter as well. The presenter can maintain focus on the presentation, rather than on the technology used to enhance the presentation.

> *You might not be sure how the Multi-Touch Interface affects Windows 7 at a technical level. An article at* http://msdn.microsoft.com/magazine/ee336016.aspx *provides a developer-level perspective on the Multi-Touch Interface.*

If you limit yourself to these obvious uses, you're missing the boat with the Multi-Touch Interface. It's important to consider innovative uses of touch technology. For example, people with special needs often find it easier to interact with a computer that's equipped with a touch screen. When you couple the touch screen with a Multi-Touch Interface, the application that seemed hard to use before suddenly becomes much easier to use. As the population ages, it will become more important to consider these alternative uses of a technology that might not seem so important today.

Using a Multi-Touch Interface could possibly reduce training costs as well. Teachers often point to the process of learning to use multiple senses as the most efficient way to learn. That's why teachers commonly incorporate visual, tactile, and verbal skills when they teach someone a new skill. Likewise, a user could possibly learn to use an application faster by applying more senses to interacting with it.

Of course, the Multi-Touch Interface will come in handy for schools and for presentations. Being able to grab precisely what you need on-screen without a lot of thought is important in real-time learning and discussion situations. No one wants to be lunging for a mouse or figuring out arcane keyboard shortcuts at such a time.

## DEFINING THE USER REQUIREMENTS FOR MULTI-TOUCH

Most businesses aren't going to want to update all their systems with touch devices immediately, but before you can use the Multi-Touch Interface, your system has to have a compatible touch device. Otherwise, users won't be able to perform tasks simply by touching the screen. The special screen makes it possible for the system to detect the user's touch and react accordingly.

It's easy to determine whether the device is compatible. Windows 7 is configured to let you start using Multi-Touch to perform operating-system-specific tasks immediately after it detects a compatible device. Unfortunately, as of this writing, there are only eight compatible devices; you can see them at http://www.microsoft.com/windows/compatibility/windows-7/Browse.aspx?type=Hardware&category=WindowsTouch&subcategory=All. Some users are almost certainly going to wonder why their touch device won't work with the Multi-Touch Interface, so it's important to determine at the outset which devices work.

Not all versions of Windows 7 support the Multi-Touch Interface. The user must have the Home Premium, Professional, Enterprise, or Ultimate edition of Windows 7 installed to use this feature. Because most businesses will likely use Windows 7 Professional, you shouldn't encounter a problem, but you should definitely check user systems for the correct operating system version. The Multi-Touch Interface won't work with older versions of Windows either, including Vista; you must have Windows 7 installed to use it.

As with many new technologies, the user will need to learn some new skills to work with the Multi-Touch Interface. Depending on your application, the user will need to learn a host of interesting gestures (and may get frustrated and use a few other gestures). You can see some of the required gestures at http://clubhouse.microsoft.com/public/post/659fa6d8-2d13-446e-ab80-a5a23bd4c9e9. The point is that the user may expect to become productive with the Multi-Touch Interface immediately, but the reality is that it's going to take time to practice the gestures in order to master them.

*One of the most interesting user needs is training on how to clean a screen. Most users today don't know how to properly clean their screens. The Multi-Touch Interface necessarily relies on screen contact, with the resulting smears and other dirt. You'll need to supply the user with appropriate cleaning supplies and training before you release a Multi-Touch application to production. Otherwise, you'll end up with a lot of hard-to-view displays. You can find cleaning instructions at* http://www.cleanlcds.com/.

## ADDING MULTI-TOUCH TO YOUR APPLICATION

Microsoft provides a number of interesting example programs, all of them complicated and all of them graphics-oriented. The examples are obviously designed to show off the capabilities of the Multi-Touch Interface, and they do a very good job of that. You can find these examples with the Windows 7 Multitouch .NET Interop Sample Library described in the "Obtaining the Multi-Touch Platform Interop Library" section of this chapter. However, most organizations don't really need complex graphics applications — they need a version of Multi-Touch that works with push buttons and the like. The Multi-Touch example is very simple. It demonstrates how you add the Multi-Touch Interface to a business application so that the user can interact with it using the keyboard, mouse, or the Multi-Touch Interface as desired. The example is purposely kept simple so that you can modify the code as needed for your application.

## Obtaining the Multi-Touch Platform Interop Library

As with most things Windows 7, Visual Studio doesn't provide the support required to access the features. In this case, the Code Pack won't help you either. Instead, download the Windows 7 Multitouch .NET Interop Sample Library from http://code.msdn.microsoft.com/WindowsTouch. When you open the Win7RC_MT.ZIP file to your root directory, you'll end up with a \Win7RC_MT folder that contains the source code you need to create the interoperability (interop) library. These steps will help you create the interop library used for the example in this chapter.

1. Open the Windows7.SLN solution using Visual Studio. Because this is an older solution, you'll need to convert it for use with Visual Studio 2010. Simply follow the Visual Studio Conversion Wizard prompts as usual.
2. Choose Build ➪ Build Solution. The build is going to fail with five errors.
3. Locate the error RC1004: unexpected end of file found error for Resource.H. Double-click this entry. Visual Studio will open the Resource.H file for you.
4. Go to the end of the Resource.H file and press Enter to add a linefeed. Save the file and close it.
5. Locate the \Win7RC_MT\Demo\Multitouch\MutlitouchWPF\mtWPFInertia\Images folder on your system.
6. Copy to the folder four JPG images named Pic1.JPG, Pic2.JPG, Pic3.JPG, and Pic4.JPG. The content of the images doesn't really matter, as long as you provide JPG files.
7. Choose Build ➪ Build Solution. The build should succeed this time.

After you're able to build the library, you'll find the Windows7.Multitouch.DLL library in the \Win7RC_MT\Release folder. This is the library you use to gain access to the Multi-Touch Platform when working with a Windows Forms application. If you want to create a Windows Presentation Foundation (WPF) application instead, you need the Windows7.Multitouch.WPF.DLL library found in the \Win7RC_MT\Mutitouch\Windows7.Multitouch.WPF\bin\Release folder.

## Configuring the Application

The Multi-Touch example begins with a Windows Forms application. The application has two push buttons, Test and Quit, that the user will be able to interact with, using keyboard, mouse, or touch (assuming the user's system has a touch device). You need to add the following reference using the Browse tab of the Add Reference dialog box. (The Multi-Touch interop library appears in the \Win7RC_MT\Release folder, as shown in Figure 9-1.)

```
Windows7.Multitouch.DLL
```

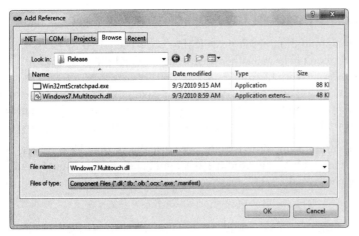

**FIGURE 9-1:** Add the required reference DLL to your project.

If you decided to create a debug version of the library, then you'll need to look in the \Win7RC_MT\Debug folder instead. You'll also need to add several using statements for this example, as follows:

```
using Windows7.Multitouch;
using Windows7.Multitouch.Win32Helper;
```

## Adding Multi-Touch Interface Functionality

The example application presents a typical business situation in that you'll use a similar process for any application you create. In many cases, you'll create the application first, test it, and then add a Multi-Touch Interface to it. The following sections describe a process you could use for new Windows Forms applications or updates to existing applications.

### Creating the Business Logic

The code begins with a pair of event handlers for btnTest and btnQuit. The example uses very simple code for these event handlers to keep the focus on the Multi-Touch Interface functionality. Listing 9-1 shows the event handler code.

**LISTING 9-1:** Creating some simple button event handlers

```csharp
private void btnQuit_Click(object sender, EventArgs e)
{
    // End the program.
    Close();
}

private void btnTest_Click(object sender, EventArgs e)
{
    // Display a message box.
    MessageBox.Show("This is a message box!");
}
```

As you can see, `btnQuit_Click()` closes the form (ending the application) and `btnTest_Click()` displays a simple message box. A production application would provide far more functionality, but these simple examples work fine for this example.

## Initializing the Multi-Touch Platform

The focus of the Multi-Touch Platform is the `TouchHandler` object. You need to create a global `TouchHandler` object, `ThisTouch`, to receive user touch events, as shown here:

```
private TouchHandler ThisTouch;
```

The example focuses on down touches. When the user touches the screen, the touch device generates a down-touch event. When the user lifts the finger, the touch device generates an up-touch event. There are a number of other gestures you can monitor as well, but for this example, all you really need to know about are down touches. Most business applications will need to detect the touch device and then create event handlers for the touch device as needed. Listing 9-2 shows a typical implementation of such logic.

**LISTING 9-2:** Performing TouchHandler initialization

```
public frmMain()
{
    // Perform the standard initialization.
    InitializeComponent();

    // Check for a touch device.
    if (TouchHandler.DigitizerCapabilities.IsMultiTouchReady)
    {
        // Create the touch handler object.
        ThisTouch = Factory.CreateHandler<TouchHandler>(this.Handle);

        // Add a touch event handler.
        ThisTouch.TouchDown +=
            new EventHandler<TouchEventArgs>(ThisTouch_TouchDown);
    }
    else
    {
        // Tell the user there is no touch device available.
        MessageBox.Show("No touch device is available.");
    }
}
```

The `TouchHandler.DigitizerCapabilities` property provides access to a number of values that help you discover the touch device capabilities. All that you really need to know to start is whether the touch device even exists. The `IsMultiTouchReady` property provides this information to you.

Once you know that the touch device exists, you can create the `TouchHandler`, `ThisTouch`. You don't use a standard constructor to perform this task. The code shows the proper technique of relying on a Factory to perform the task using the `CreateHandler<TouchHandler>` template. You must provide a handle to the appropriate window, which is going to be `this.Handle` in most cases for the current window.

## Handling Multi-Touch Events

Now that you have a local instance of the `TouchHandler`, you can use it to add event handlers. The example uses the `TouchDown` event to track events when the user presses the button on-screen. As with most event handlers, you type +=, press Tab once to create the event handler definition, and press Tab a second time to create the event handler method. The event handler method, `ThisTouch_TouchDown()`, appears in Listing 9-3.

**LISTING 9-3:** Handling touch events

```
void ThisTouch_TouchDown(object sender, TouchEventArgs e)
{
    // Convert the X and Y locations to a client window coordinate.
    Int32 XCoord = e.Location.X - this.ClientRectangle.Location.X;
    Int32 YCoord = e.Location.Y - this.ClientRectangle.Location.Y;

    // Check the location against btnTest.
    if ((XCoord >= btnTest.Location.X) &&
        (XCoord <= btnTest.Location.X + btnTest.Size.Width) &&
        (YCoord >= btnTest.Location.Y) &&
        (YCoord <= btnTest.Location.Y + btnTest.Size.Height))

        // Call the btnTest Click event.
        btnTest_Click(sender, null);

    // Check the location against btnQuit.
    if ((XCoord >= btnQuit.Location.X) &&
        (XCoord <= btnQuit.Location.X + btnQuit.Size.Width) &&
        (YCoord >= btnQuit.Location.Y) &&
        (YCoord <= btnQuit.Location.Y + btnQuit.Size.Height))

        // Call the btnQuit Click event.
        btnQuit_Click(sender, null);
}
```

The `ThisTouch_TouchDown()` method looks a little odd at first, but you need to consider how a touch device works. The user presses somewhere on the screen, which generates a touch event. Your code receives the event and calls `ThisTouch_TouchDown()`. The `TouchEventArgs`, e, contains a number of arguments, including the location of the press. However, the location information is in screen coordinates, not local client window coordinates. As a consequence, the code can't determine whether the user clicked `btnTest` or `btnQuit` without first converting the location to a client-based coordinate.

Let's pursue this a little more. For the sake of argument, the Multi-Touch client window's upper-left coordinate is currently at 80 pixels to the right of the display edge and 70 pixels from the top of the display, as shown in Figure 9-2. The user presses at a position of 280 pixels from the right of the display edge and 100 pixels from the top of the display. The actual client window coordinates then are 280 - 80 or 200 pixels from the right edge of the client window (`XCoord`) and 100 - 70 or 30 pixels from the top edge of the client window (`YCoord`).

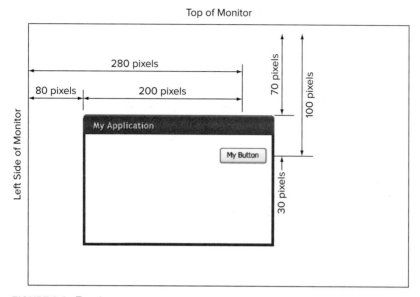

**FIGURE 9-2:** Touch measurements are converted to the client location.

 *It's essential that you use the* `this.ClientRectangle.Location` *property when determining the window's current location on-screen because* `this.Location` *points to the location of the entire window. The* `this.ClientRectangle.Location` *property takes the window border and title bar into account when making position calculations. If you find that the user presses are falling outside the expected range, check for this potential problem in your code.*

For this example, `btnTest` is located 197 pixels from the right edge of the client window and 23 pixels from the top edge of the client window. The button also has a width of 75 and a height of 23. So, let's take a look at the logic for the next section of code. The `XCoord` equals 200 and `YCoord` equals 30, so we have the following logic:

➤ 200 >= 197

➤ 200 <= 197 + 75

➤ 30 >= 23

➤ 30 <= 23 + 23

In short, all the statements are true. Therefore, the code calls `btnTest_Click()` and passes the current sender to it. The `btnTest_Click()` event handler doesn't use any of the event arguments, so the code sends `null` to it. The result is that the user sees the message box on-screen, just as if the user had pressed Alt+T or clicked Test. The code for `btnQuit` works precisely the same way as the code for `btnTest`.

## MOVING YOUR APPLICATIONS TO WINDOWS 7

This chapter has provided a good overview of the Multi-Touch Interface and provided you with some ideas on how to use it. Whether you can actually use the Multi-Touch Interface in your organization depends on the kinds of applications you create and the needs of your users. Working with the Multi-Touch Interface requires additional effort on everyone's part, and you also need special hardware to use it. In short, you need to be sure that your investment will have a payoff before you proceed with this technology. For some organizations, of course, the Multi-Touch Interface is an essential addition, and they will definitely welcome it with open arms.

One thing you need to do after a chapter like this is to explore the possibilities. Create a list of ways in which you can use the Multi-Touch Interface in your organization. You might be surprised to learn that you can use it in quite a few areas. Make sure you share your list with other people and ask for their input as well. If your list is large enough, try to put a value on the ways in which the Multi-Touch Interface can help your organization. Then start counting up the costs of implementing it. Make sure you include the cost of updated hardware, as well as the cost of replacing the hardware more often (touch screens have a habit of breaking because people are touching them all the time).

Even though the Multi-Touch Interface examples provided with the Windows 7 Multitouch .NET Interop Sample Library are somewhat complex, they're also interesting to study because they truly do demonstrate the Multi-Touch Interface features. Once you understand the example in this chapter, you'll want to spend some time working through these Microsoft examples. You may get ideas on how to spruce up your existing applications so they can do more with less effort on the part of the user.

This part of the book has concentrated on the basic concept of augmenting your applications. You've seen a number of ways in which you can incorporate Windows 7 features to make your applications better. In many cases, the features cost more money, but you also gain quite a bit in user productivity. The next section of the book discusses techniques you can use to secure your application. The gains you make by augmenting your applications are easy to lose when someone disrupts application usage, steals your data, or generally causes problems for your organization. Consider this next part of the book the next step you should take after you augment your application. Chapter 10 begins by looking at how you can use standard Windows security to make your applications better.

# PART III
# Developing Secure Applications

- **CHAPTER 10:** Using Standard NT Security Features in Windows 7
- **CHAPTER 11:** Understanding the User Account Control
- **CHAPTER 12:** Developing Applications with Enhanced Security
- **CHAPTER 13:** Interacting with the Built-In Security Features

# 10
# Using Standard NT Security Features in Windows 7

**WHAT'S IN THIS CHAPTER?**

- Understanding the changes to basic Windows NT security
- Considering how basic Windows NT security works
- Interacting with Windows NT security features

Applications can rely on many layers of protection in Windows. The basic layer of protection has been around since Windows NT, which is why it's called Windows NT security. This is the level of security that provides file and other resource security through settings you provide. It's also the level that provides basic login security and that controls which resources the user can access based on the access requirements for that resource. Most developers understand that Windows NT security (or simply NT security) uses a resource lock and user access key pattern.

NT security hasn't remained static over the years. For example, Microsoft has added and redefined permissions as needed over the years to keep pace with user computing requirements. One of the more important recent changes occurred in Vista where Microsoft decided to lock down (deny access to) the root directory and other important operating system directories on the hard drive. In many respects, these new security features reflect the way that other operating systems such as Linux are configured, rather than showing something new from Microsoft. Even so, you need to learn how to work around the new security requirements when creating an application. It's no longer allowable to place files in the root directory simply because it's convenient to do so.

>  *Security is an extremely complex subject in many respects and this chapter can't provide a complete treatment of the topic. Microsoft constantly adds new features to the .NET Framework to make security more complete and easier for the developer to implement. For example, if you want to implement pipe security for connections to resources, you can use the* `PipeSecurity` *class (*http://msdn.microsoft.com/library/system.io.pipes.pipesecurity.aspx*) and implement it using the* `PipeAccessRule` *class (*http://msdn.microsoft.com/library/system.io.pipes.pipeaccessrule.aspx*). Monitoring occurs using a* `PipeAuditRule` *object (*http://msdn.microsoft.com/library/system.io.pipes.pipeauditrule.aspx*). There is, in fact, an entire list of pipe-related security features at* http://msdn.microsoft.com/library/bb298714.aspx*. The point is that you can probably find a class for most security needs now without having to resort to using Platform Invoke (P/Invoke) to interact with the Win32 API directly.*

As with most versions of Windows, Microsoft tweaked NT security features in Windows 7. For example, Windows 7 includes enhanced auditing features to make it easier to discover the source of a breach or causes of other security problems. This chapter not only explores Windows NT security generally, but also helps you understand the latest changes in NT security for Windows 7. The point of this chapter is that you can't secure any application without first understanding the basic security features provided by NT security.

## CONSIDERING BASIC NT SECURITY FEATURE CHANGES

Windows 7 has a number of new security features. Some are internal. You won't use the following features directly, but they do affect the way in which your application executes.

- Kernel patch protection
- Service hardening
- Data execution prevention
- Address space layout randomization
- Mandatory integrity levels

These features change the way Windows 7 executes your application and the environment in which the application executes. In some cases, you may need to consider how these features work when writing your application, but managed application code developers, such as those who use C#, can probably forget these features even exist except to realize that they work in the background to secure the application environment.

Microsoft has also streamlined the User Account Control (UAC) functionality to make it less intrusive. Some security pundits have decried this action because it actually makes Windows 7 a little less secure. However, the other side of the coin is that users are less likely to ignore warnings that they see occasionally, rather than ones they see as part of nearly every action. Chapter 11 discusses the UAC changes in detail.

The most important NT security change for this chapter is enhanced auditing. Many developers have an extremely limited view of auditing. In fact, developers and administrators alike often see auditing as just another step along the road toward the world of Big Brother described in the book *1984*. See http://en.wikipedia.org/wiki/Big_Brother_(Nineteen_Eighty-Four) for details. However, auditing has many practical uses:

- Regulatory compliance requirements
- Business compliance requirements
- Application monitoring and debugging
- Trojan, virus, and other forms of malware detection
- Resource control
- Internal threat monitoring

## UNDERSTANDING BASIC NT SECURITY

Many developers view Windows NT security as difficult. However, the concepts behind Windows NT security are actually quite simple. When you leave your house, you close the door and lock it. The lock is a kind of security that you place on your house. Only someone with an appropriate key can access the house once you lock it (let's assume for a moment that intruders lack tools such as pry bars). The lock is a kind of access control, while the key is a right to access the house. Windows NT security works precisely this way. A resource, such as a file, has a lock on it that provides access control, while a user has a privilege (the key) that grants permission to use the resource in some way.

Let's take access to your house to the next level. The front door is only one level of access. You might have locked rooms, a safe, gun cabinet, or other elements in the house that require additional permissions to access. The main reason for these additional permissions is that the contents of the room or safe are especially valuable or perhaps unsafe. You might not want your children accessing them. To access these additional elements, you have a combination, additional keys, or other means of access. In other words, you have additional permissions not shared by everyone in the household. Windows NT security works in the same way. Most resources provide multiple levels of permissions that some users enjoy and others don't.

Access comes in two forms in Windows NT security. A user has personal rights that are assigned directly to that user — akin to the keys someone has on his or her key ring. In addition, a user can belong to a group of users who all share the same rights — akin to the key under the doormat that everyone in the house knows about and uses. It's important to understand that the user's access is limited to the combination of group and individual rights that the administrator assigns.

Rights are assigned by two parties. Administrators assign rights to users by changing the Windows configuration directly with a Microsoft-supplied utility, such as the security editor shown in Figure 10-1. Likewise, a developer can write code that sets Windows security for particular objects, calls, and portions of an application. When the developer couples this level of security with application settings, the administrator can achieve better security without losing any flexibility. In both cases, changes by the administrator or developer affect the rights required to perform specific tasks using resources such as a file. The right to write to a file is separate from the right to read from the file.

**FIGURE 10-1:** Administrators rely on utilities to change resource permissions.

User-level access depends on a Security IDentifier (SID, usually pronounced "Sid," like the name). When the user first logs in to the system, Windows assigns an access token to the user and places the user's SID (stored on the domain controller or other security database) within it. The user object carries around both the access token and the SID for the duration of the session. An access token also contains both a *Discretionary Access Control List* (DACL, pronounced "dackel") and a *System Access Control List* (SACL, pronounced "sackel"). The combination of Access Control Lists (ACLs) and SID within the access token is a key that allows the user access to certain system resources. Because this access lasts the entire session, the user must log out and then back in to the system whenever the administrator makes a change to security; otherwise, the user won't gain additional rights that the administrator provides.

A key is no good without a lock to open. The lock placed on Windows resources is called a security descriptor. In essence, a security descriptor tells what rights the user needs to access the resource. If the rights within the ACLs meet or exceed the rights in the security descriptor, then the lock opens and the resource becomes available. Figure 10-2 shows the contents of the ACL and the security descriptor used for token-based security. The following sections provide more details about how token-based security actually works, using Figure 10-2 as the point of discussion.

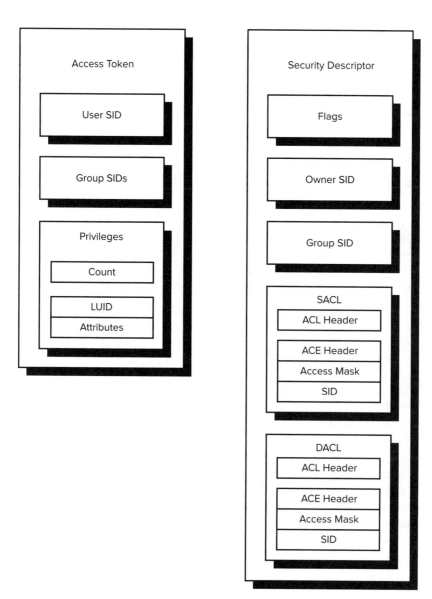

**FIGURE 10-2:** Token-based security relies on ACLs and security descriptors.

## Working with ACLs

There are two ways of looking at a user's rights under Windows: individual rights and group rights. The user's SID is the account number that Windows assigns to the user during login. The access token that holds the SID also contains other structures that identify the groups the user belongs to and what privileges the user has. Each group entry also has a SID. This SID points to other structures that describe the group's rights. To understand the user's rights, you need to know both the user's individual rights and the rights of the groups to which the user belongs. An administrator normally uses the Local Users and Groups or the Active Directory Users and Computers Microsoft Management Console (MMC) snap-in to change the contents of this access token, as shown in Figure 10-3. (To use this feature, right-click an entry, such as Guest, choose Properties from the Context menu, and select the Member Of tab to change the user's group affiliations.)

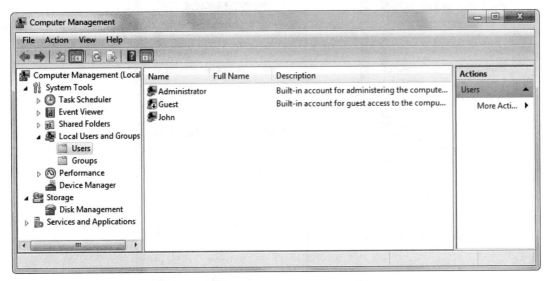

**FIGURE 10-3:** MMC snap-ins make it possible to change user access tokens.

The privileges section of the access token shown in Figure 10-2 begins with a count of the number of privileges the user has — the number of special privilege entries in the access token. This section also contains an array of privilege entries. Each privilege entry contains a Locally Unique IDentifier (LUID) — essentially a pointer to the entry object — and an attribute mask. The attribute mask tells what rights the user has to the object. Group SID entries are essentially the same. They contain a privilege count and an array of privilege entries.

One of the things you need to know as part of working with some kinds of objects is that object rights flow down to the lowest possible node unless overridden by another SID. For example, if you give the user read and write privileges to the \Temp directory on a hard drive, those rights will also apply to the \Temp\Stuff directory unless you assigned the user specific rights to that directory. The same holds true for containers. Assigning a user rights to a container object like a Word document gives the user the right to look at everything within that container, even other files in most cases. It's important to track a user's exact rights to objects on your server using security surveys, since you could inadvertently give the user more rights than needed to perform a certain task.

## Understanding the Security Descriptors

At this point, you have a better idea of how the access token (the key) works. It's time to look at the security descriptor (the lock). Figure 10-2 shows that each security descriptor contains five main sections. The following list describes each section.

- **Header and Flags:** The header consists of version information and a list of control flags. The flags tell you the descriptor status. For example, the SE_DACL_PRESENT flag indicates the presence of a DACL. If the DACL is missing, then Windows allows everyone to use the object. The basic security descriptors haven't changed since Windows 2000, so you can see a list of basic security descriptors at http://technet.microsoft.com/library/cc962005.aspx. The overview at http://technet.microsoft.com/library/cc961978.aspx provides additional information about Windows security flags.

- **Owner SID:** Tells who owns the object. This doesn't have to be an individual user; Windows allows use of a group SID here as well. The limiting factor is that the group SID must appear in the token of the person changing the entry. In other words, you can't assign ownership to a group where you don't have membership.

- **Group SID:** Tells which group owns the object. This entry contains only the main group responsible for the object and won't contain a list of all groups with access to the object.

- **SACL:** Controls the Windows auditing feature. Every time a user or group accesses an object when the auditing feature for that object is on, Windows makes an entry in the audit log. There's more than one entry in this section, in most cases, so Windows stores the information in an array.

- **DACL:** Controls object use. Windows assigns groups and users to a specific object. In most cases there's more than one entry in this section, so Windows stores the information in an array. A DACL can contain a custom value, a default value, or a null (empty) value, or it may not appear in the security descriptor at all (this last option is rare and dangerous). You'll normally find more objects with default values than any other DACL type.

## Understanding the ACEs

As previously mentioned, a security descriptor relies on a SACL and a DACL to control the security of an object. Both elements use the same basic ACL data structure, but for different purposes. An ACL consists of two entry types. The first is a header that lists the number of Access Control Entries (ACEs) in the ACL. Windows uses this number to determine when it's reached the end of the ACE list. (There isn't any end-of-structure record or other way to determine the size of each ACE in the structure.) The second entry is an array of ACEs.

An ACE defines the object rights for a single user or group. Every ACE has a header that defines the type, size, and flags for the ACE. It includes an access mask that defines rights a user or group has to the object. Finally, there's an entry for the user or group SID.

There are four main ACE header types (you can find the full list of ACE headers at http://msdn2.microsoft.com/library/aa374912.aspx). Windows currently uses three out of the four main ACE header types. The following list tells you about each of the main header types:

- **General Access:** This header type appears in the DACL and grants object rights to a user. Use it to add to the rights a user already has for an object on an instance-by-instance basis. For example, you might want to prevent the user from changing the system time so that you can keep the machines on the network synchronized. However, there might be one situation — such as daylight saving time — when the user would need this right. You could use an access-allowed ACE to allow the user to change the time in this one instance.

- ▶ **Object Access:** This header type appears in the DACL and helps Windows assign specific security to software objects and sub-objects. A developer must provide special code to provide this access. For example, the developer could use this type of ACE to assign security to the property of a COM object. To use this type of ACE, the developer needs to obtain or create a globally unique identifier (GUID) for the object in question. Once the developer adds the required code, application settings can allow the administrator to control access to particular application features at run time.

- ▶ **System Audit:** This ACE header type works with the SACL. It defines which events to audit for a particular user or group. There are system audit header types for both general and object use. The .NET Framework doesn't provide a specific auditing feature, so you can use this feature when you want to know who's accessing a particular Website feature and when they access it. This feature requires that the user log in to the system. Yes, it does work with anonymous access, but all you'll see is the anonymous user information.

- ▶ **System Alarm:** This is the currently unused ACE type. It enables either the SACL or DACL to set an alarm when specific events happen.

## WORKING DIRECTLY WITH WINDOWS NT SECURITY

If you aren't already assigning security to objects that your application creates, then you're missing out on a valuable Windows feature. Basic Windows NT security is the cornerstone of protection on every system that runs the Windows operating system. Newer features, such as Role-Based Security (RBS), are add-ons to this basic level of security. Think of role-based and other forms of security as the alarm system and other advanced security features in modern homes. Even though these advanced security features are welcome and extremely important, they can't replace the basic locks in a home. Likewise, you can't replace basic Windows NT security in your application. The following sections show how to perform some basic protection tasks using Windows NT security.

> *The .NET Framework 4 supplies the new* `System.Security.AccessControl` *namespace that gives you access to Windows NT security features. You can read about it at* http://msdn.microsoft.com/library/system.security.accesscontrol.aspx. *If you're using an older version of the .NET Framework, you must resort to using Platform Invoke (P/Invoke) programming techniques to gain access to Windows NT security. Using P/Invoke is somewhat cumbersome but not impossible. Books, such as .NET Framework Solutions: In Search of the Lost Win32 API, by John Paul Mueller, Sybex 2002, provide detailed instructions for performing such coding tasks. This chapter assumes that you'll use the simpler .NET Framework 4 approach for your applications.*

### Checking User Permissions

The factors that describe a user's permissions vary according to the user. A user will always have a SID and specific characteristics, such as an impersonation level. In addition, user permissions aren't always stored with the user token. Smart administrators use groups to help describe user permissions. Granting rights to groups (rather than individual users) saves time and effort when rights change to meet a new requirement. The following sections describe how to obtain information about user permissions.

## Configuring the User Permission Example

The User Permission example begins with the Windows Forms template. You need a button to call the code used to display the user's permissions, a label to mark the output, and a list box as shown in Figure 10-4.

The application doesn't require any special references. However, you do need to add the following using statement:

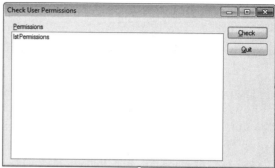

**FIGURE 10-4:** Define the User Permission interface as shown here.

```
using System.Security.Principal;
```

## Writing the User Permission Code

Microsoft doesn't make it hard to obtain the user permission entries. In fact, obtaining user permission settings is one of the items that the .NET Framework has supported for a long time. Microsoft does tweak the functionality, but the code in Listing 10-1 shows what you can typically expect to obtain as information from the .NET Framework without any special coding.

**LISTING 10-1:** Checking a user's permissions

```
private void btnCheck_Click(object sender, EventArgs e)
{
    // Get the current user.
    WindowsIdentity User = WindowsIdentity.GetCurrent();

    // Display the user's information.
    lstPermissions.Items.Add("Name: " + User.Name);
    lstPermissions.Items.Add("SID: " + User.User.Value);

    // Display the authentication information.
    lstPermissions.Items.Add(
        "Authenticated? " + User.IsAuthenticated.ToString());
    lstPermissions.Items.Add(
        "Guest? " + User.IsGuest.ToString());
    lstPermissions.Items.Add(
        "System Account? " + User.IsSystem.ToString());
    lstPermissions.Items.Add(
        "Authentication Type: " + User.AuthenticationType.ToString());
    lstPermissions.Items.Add(
        "Impersonation Level: " + User.ImpersonationLevel.ToString());
```

*continues*

**LISTING 10-1** *(continued)*

```
        // Get the group membership.
        lstPermissions.Items.Add("");
        lstPermissions.Items.Add("Group Membership:");
        foreach (IdentityReference Group in User.Groups)
            lstPermissions.Items.Add("\t" +
                Group.Translate(typeof(NTAccount)));
    }
```

The example begins by creating a `WindowsIdentity` object, User, that points to the current user by using the `GetCurrent()` method. The `WindowsIdentity` object doesn't provide any common constructor, but uses specialty constructors to help you obtain the right user identity. For example, you can just as easily obtain an anonymous account or impersonate another user.

The code displays the user's login name (as contrasted to the user's full name) and next the SID. Every user has a unique SID, so you can use a SID to ensure that the user you're working with is actually the user you want, even if there's a chance of having users with similar login names on the network.

After the code displays basic identification, it provides some authentication information. For example, you can determine whether the user is logged in to the system (authenticated) and whether the user is a guest. Your computer also has a number of system accounts that aren't meant for use by users, and you can detect system accounts as well. The three common system accounts are:

➤ **LocalSystem:** http://msdn.microsoft.com/library/ms684190.aspx

➤ **LocalService:** http://msdn.microsoft.com/library/ms684188.aspx

➤ **NetworkService:** http://msdn.microsoft.com/library/ms684272.aspx

Discovering group membership is extremely important. As you can see, the `WindowsIdentity` object makes this task quite simple. Unfortunately, you can use the `WindowsIdentity` object only to discover group affiliation — you can't use it to change group or any other information for that matter. Figure 10-5 shows typical output from this example.

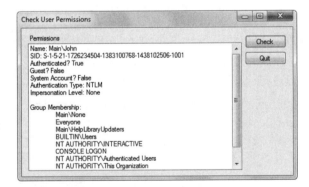

**FIGURE 10-5:** Discovering user permissions will help you interact with the user in an application.

## Using WMI for Permissions Example

Sometimes the .NET Framework will fall short in the information department. Another way to obtain the security information you need is to use Windows Management Instrumentation (WMI), as shown in the User Permissions Using WMI example in Listing 10-2. In this case, the example views user group affiliation from the group perspective, rather than from the user perspective. To begin this example, you create a Windows Forms application with controls similar to those shown in Figure 10-4.

In order to use WMI, you must add a reference to the `System.Management` assembly. You must also add the following `using` statement:

```
using System.Management;
```

It's important to realize that WMI isn't a managed interface — it relies on native code and Component Object Model (COM) interfaces. You can use WMI directly at the command line using the WMIC (Windows Management Interface Command line) utility. Because of the way WMI is constructed, you might find that you have to create some convoluted code in order to obtain the desired results. Listing 10-2 shows an example of a simple WMI application.

**LISTING 10-2:** WMI provides a secondary means of interacting with users and groups

Available for
download on
Wrox.com

```
private void btnCheck_Click(object sender, EventArgs e)
{
    // Create a query for the local group accounts.
    SelectQuery GroupQuery = new SelectQuery("Win32_Group");

    // Define the search object.
    ManagementObjectSearcher Searcher =
        new ManagementObjectSearcher(GroupQuery);

    // Look at each group.
    foreach (ManagementObject ThisGroup in Searcher.Get())
    {
        // Display the group's information.
        lstPermissions.Items.Add("Name: " +
            ThisGroup["Name"].ToString());
        lstPermissions.Items.Add("Domain: " +
            ThisGroup["Domain"].ToString());
        lstPermissions.Items.Add("Description: " +
            ThisGroup["Description"].ToString());
        lstPermissions.Items.Add("Local Group? " +
            ThisGroup["LocalAccount"].ToString());
        lstPermissions.Items.Add("SID: " +
            ThisGroup["SID"].ToString());
        lstPermissions.Items.Add("Status: " +
            ThisGroup["Status"].ToString());

        // Obtain a list of users for the group.
        SelectQuery UserQuery = new SelectQuery("Win32_GroupUser");
        ManagementObjectSearcher UserList =
            new ManagementObjectSearcher(UserQuery);

        // Display the list.
        lstPermissions.Items.Add("Users:");
        foreach (ManagementObject ThisUser in UserList.Get())
        {
            // Obtain the group information for each entry.
            String GroupPart = ThisUser["GroupComponent"].ToString();
```

*continues*

**LISTING 10-2** *(continued)*

```
            // When the group information matches the current group, output
            // it to the listbox.
            if (GroupPart.Contains(ThisGroup["Name"].ToString()))
            {
                // Obtain the user information for the entry.
                String UserPart = ThisUser["PartComponent"].ToString();

                // Extract the user name and output it.
                lstPermissions.Items.Add("\t" +
                    UserPart.Substring(UserPart.IndexOf("Name=")));
            }
        }

        // Add a space.
        lstPermissions.Items.Add("");
    }
}
```

The .NET Framework provides a number of ways to create a WMI query. The easiest method is to create a `SelectQuery` object, such as `GroupQuery`, and supply it with a WMI class. In this case, the example begins with the `Win32_Group` class. You can find a listing of WMI classes at http://msdn.microsoft.com/library/aa394554.aspx.

Creating the query is only the first step. You must now execute the query using a `ManagementObjectSearcher` object, `Searcher`. The .NET Framework will happily create any query you want, but the query can fail if it's incorrect. The failure will occur when you execute the query using the `ManagementObjectSearcher` object, so sometimes the errant code isn't where the debugger tells you it is.

The `for` loop is where the query actually executes. Calling `Searcher.Get()` obtains a single group entry and places it in the `ManagementObject`, `ThisGroup`. The `ThisGroup` object contains a wealth of helpful information, such as the group name, SID, and status.

At this point, you have a list of groups, but not of users who are members of the groups. In order to obtain the list of users, you must create another query for the `Win32_GroupUser` class. The output of this query is actually an object array consisting of two strings, as shown here:

```
{\\MAIN\root\cimv2:Win32_GroupUser.GroupComponent=
"\\\\MAIN\\root\\cimv2:Win32_Group.Domain=\"MAIN\",
Name=\"Administrators\"",
PartComponent="\\\\MAIN\\root\\cimv2:Win32_UserAccount.Domain=\"Main\",
Name=\"Administrator\""}
```

Even though this output appears on multiple lines in the book, you'll see it as a single line in the debugger. The two strings are the `GroupComponent` and the `PartComponent`. The `GroupComponent` contains the complete path to the group information, which is Administrators in this example. Likewise, the `PartComponent` contains the complete path to the user associated with the group, which is Administrator in this example. The two-part nature of this query complicates the code a bit, but you can easily locate the users associated with a particular group using a `for` loop and then comparing the group name to the name in the `GroupComponent` (represented by `GroupPart`).

*The UAC has an effect on WMI. In some cases, you obtain less data and other classes become inaccessible. For example, you won't obtain a complete list of user accounts when the WMI output is filtered by the UAC because the UAC hides sensitive accounts from view. The article at* http://msdn.microsoft.com/library/aa826699.aspx *provides details on what you can expect when an account is hobbled by UAC filtering.*

Once the code has located a user associated with the current group, it outputs the information from `PartComponent`. Because the output contains a complete path, you use the `Substring()` method to extract just the information needed. Figure 10-6 shows typical output from this example.

## Changing User Permissions

Viewing group and user information is relatively easy using either of the techniques described in the "Checking User Permissions" section of this chapter. In fact, you can use

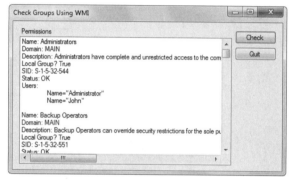

**FIGURE 10-6:** Using WMI has some significant advantages, but at the cost of additional code.

WMI to make some modifications to group or user content. However, the changes you can make are limited to simple modifications such as the user or group name. In order to make significant changes, such as creating a new group or user, or assigning an existing user to a group, you need to use the `DirectoryServices` namespace.

One of the first questions many developers ask about `DirectoryServices` is what they need to do when they aren't working on a domain. It turns out that the `DirectoryServices` namespace classes work just fine on any machine, even if you don't have a domain controller installed. In fact, the User Permission Modification example shown in the sections that follow will work just fine on a stand-alone machine.

### Configuring the User Permission Modification Example

The User Permission Modification example begins with a Windows Forms application. You need to add a button so that you can invoke the code used to make an association between an existing user and a new group that you'll create. In order to use the `DirectoryServices`, you must add a reference to `System.DirectoryServices`. The example also requires that you add the following `using` statement:

```
using System.DirectoryServices;
```

Before you can use this example, you need to create a group to experiment with. You don't want to experiment with a group that has any rights, so this group is simply an entry that has no rights whatsoever. Use the following steps to create the group on Windows 7:

1. Choose Start ➪ Control Panel ➪ Administrative Tools to display the Administrative Tools window.

2. Double-click Computer Management to display the Computer Management console shown in Figure 10-7.

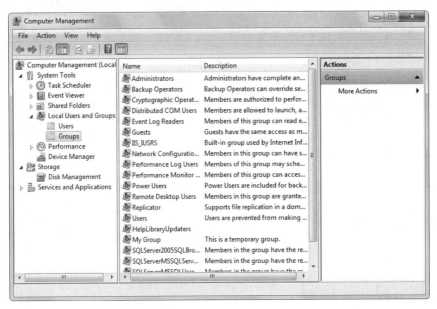

**FIGURE 10-7:** The Computer Management console helps you create new groups.

3. Open the `Computer Management\System Tools\Groups` folder as shown in Figure 10-7.

4. Right-click the Groups folder and choose New Group from the context menu. You'll see the New Group dialog box shown in Figure 10-8.

5. Type **My Group** in the Group Name field.

6. Type **This is a temporary group.** in the Description field.

7. Click Create. You'll see the new group added to the Groups folder of the Computer Management console. The group is now ready for use with the example.

**FIGURE 10-8:** Use the New Group dialog box to add a test group to your system.

## Creating the User Permission Modification Manifest

Windows 7 is particular about who can make system changes, such as assigning users to groups. Even if you're part of the Administrators group, you won't be able to make the change without elevating your permissions to the Administrator account. Chapter 11 explains the specifics of how the UAC works, but for the purposes of this example, you need to create a means of elevating the permissions so that the change can succeed. There are a number of ways to accomplish this task, but the easiest way is simply to add a .MANIFEST file to your application using the following steps:

1. Right-click the project entry in Solution Explorer and choose Add ➪ Add New Item from the context menu. You'll see the Add New Item dialog box shown in Figure 10-9.

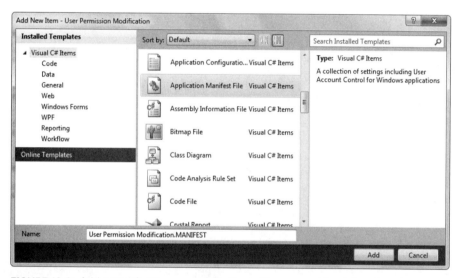

**FIGURE 10-9:** Add a manifest to your application with a request for rights elevation.

2. Highlight the Application Manifest File entry as shown in Figure 10-9.
3. Type **User Permission Modification.MANIFEST** in the Name field and click Add. Always use the name of the application, followed by .MANIFEST when creating this file, or the run time won't recognize the manifest requirements. For example, later in the chapter you'll use User Audit.MANIFEST when working with the User Audit example. Visual Studio adds the file to your project and automatically opens it for editing.
4. Locate the `<requestedExecutionLevel  level="asInvoker" uiAccess="false" />` entry in the file and change it to read:

    ```
    <requestedExecutionLevel level="requireAdministrator" uiAccess="false" />
    ```

5. Highlight the manifest file entry in Solution Explorer.
6. Change the Copy to Output Directory property to Copy if Newer. This change ensures that the manifest file appears with the application when you test it. Otherwise, you won't see any permission elevation and the example will fail to work.

## Writing the User Permission Modification Code

At this point, you've created an application shell, added a group to use for the test, and configured a manifest file. The actual code to assign a user to a group isn't hard. What you need to do is find the user and then the group you want to work with. You then use a simple method to add the user to the group, as shown in Listing 10-3.

**LISTING 10-3:** Modifying a user's permissions

Available for download on Wrox.com

```
private void btnAdd_Click(object sender, EventArgs e)
{
    // Create a directory object for the current machine.
    DirectoryEntry TheServer =
        new DirectoryEntry("WinNT://" + Environment.MachineName);

    // Locate the special group.
    DirectoryEntry TheGroup =
        TheServer.Children.Find("My Group", "Group");

    // Locate the user to add to the group.
    DirectoryEntry TheUser =
        TheServer.Children.Find("Guest", "User");

    // Add the user to the group.
    TheGroup.Invoke("Add", new Object[]{TheUser.Path.ToString()});

    // Display a success message.
    MessageBox.Show("User added to group successfully!");
}
```

The code begins by creating a `DirectoryEntry` object, `TheServer`, which points to the local machine. You need to supply a path such as `WinNT://MyMachine` to accomplish this task. The easiest way to create flexible code is to rely on the `Environment.MachineName` property for the name of the local machine.

At this point, you simply search for the group (`TheGroup`) and the user (`TheUser`), using the `Find()` method of `TheServer.Children` property. The application makes an assignment among the test group, My Group, and the Guest account, which shouldn't even be active on your machine.

To add the user to the group, the example calls `TheGroup.Invoke()` with the `Add` method and the path to `TheUser` object. The user information path is passed in an `Object` array. After you run the code, you see a success message box. However, the real results appear in the My Group Properties dialog box shown in Figure 10-10 (double-click the My Group entry in the Groups

**FIGURE 10-10:** Running the application adds the Guest account to My Group.

folder of the Computer Management console to see the results).

You need to know one final piece of information about this example. When you first start the debugger by choosing Debug ➪ Start Debugging, you'll see the message box shown in Figure 10-11. Click Restart Under Different Credentials. The system will then display the usual UAC dialog box, where you click Yes. Visual Studio will restart with the proper rights. Choose Debug ➪ Start Debugging again and the application will run as normal, but with elevated rights.

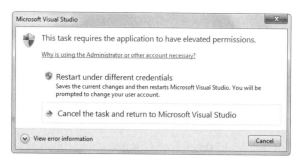

**FIGURE 10-11:** This example requires elevated rights to work properly.

 *If you try to run the example a second time, the code will fail. However, this time it fails because Guest is already a member of My Group. To run the example again, delete Guest from the Member list of My Group by highlighting its entry (shown in Figure 10-10) and clicking Remove.*

## Auditing User Actions

Windows 7 incorporates many forms of auditing. An audit simply tracks some system event and may not even have anything to do with the user specifically. For example, setting object access auditing tracks all access, not just the user's access. A virus could access an object, and auditing would make it possible to track the access. Incorrect object access by an errant application is also tracked. In short, auditing has all kinds of uses, not just reviewing user activity. The following sections describe how to build the User Audit example so you can see auditing in action.

### Configuring the User Audit Example

The User Audit example shows the current settings for any auditing on the system. The example begins with a Windows Forms application that looks much like the example shown in Figure 10-4. In addition, you must add the following `using` statement to your code:

```
using System.Security.AccessControl;
```

Unlike user security settings, auditing settings are quite sensitive, so you have to have administrator rights to view them. With this in mind, you must also add a manifest file to your application, as described in the "Creating the User Permission Modification Manifest" section of this chapter.

### Configuring the Registry for Audit Monitoring

The system auditing settings appear in the default value of the `HKEY_LOCAL_MACHINE\SECURITY\Policy\PolAdtEv` key of the registry. Microsoft is extremely paranoid about the auditing settings, so it takes even more precautions than usual. In this case, the registry actually blocks access to the settings, even to the administrator. The .NET Framework does provide methods for working with registry security, but it turns out that they don't work when the administrator is blocked from access. Your only option at this point is to manually set the required privileges using the following steps:

1. Locate `RegEdit.EXE` in your Windows folder (normally `C:\Windows`).

2. Right-click the file and choose Run as Administrator from the context menu. You'll see the normal UAC warning dialog box.

3. Click Yes. The system will start RegEdit as an administrator.

4. Right-click the `HKEY_LOCAL_MACHINE\SECURITY` key and choose Permissions from the Context menu. You'll see the Permissions for Security dialog box shown in Figure 10-12. Notice that the Administrators group has almost no permission — only the SYSTEM account can access this registry key.

5. Check Full Control and click OK. You now have access to the `HKEY_LOCAL_MACHINE\SECURITY\Policy\PolAdtEv` key.

6. Choose View ⇨ Refresh or press F5 to see the new keys you can access.

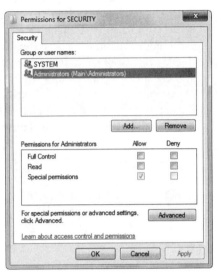

**FIGURE 10-12:** Change the Administrator privileges to allow full control.

## Writing the User Audit Code

This example shows how to read the audit settings from the registry. However, by knowing the locations of the registry settings, you can also write the audit settings. The audit settings are found in a `Byte` array. Each byte entry can have one of four values:

- 0: Disabled
- 1: Success auditing
- 2: Failure auditing
- 3: Both success and failure auditing

Some of the auditing settings have multiple `Byte` array entries, but the reason for the multiple entries isn't clear, and Microsoft has chosen not to document the Windows 7 settings. With this in mind, Table 10-1 shows the audit settings and the `Byte` array decimal indexes associated with each entry. You need to monitor only one of these bytes when reading the values, but you must set all of them when changing a value.

## Working Directly with Windows NT Security | 189

*Microsoft has documented the audit settings in the past. In fact, you can find a Knowledge Base article on the topic at* http://support.microsoft.com/kb/246120. *Unfortunately, this Knowledge Base article is incorrect for Windows 7, and there doesn't appear to be any documentation for the updated configuration. Therefore, the settings in this chapter are based on personal testing, rather than on direct Microsoft documentation. If anyone has a documented source of information for the audit settings in Windows 7, please contact me at* JMueller@mwt.net.

**TABLE 10-1:** Registry Index Values for Audit Settings

| AUDIT SETTING | BYTE ARRAY INDEXES (DECIMAL) | BYTE ARRAY INDEXES (HEXADECIMAL) |
| --- | --- | --- |
| Audit Account Logon Events | 110, 112, 114, 116 | 6E, 70, 72, 74 |
| Audit Account Management | 90, 92, 94, 96, 98, 100 | 5A, 5C, 5E, 60, 62, 64 |
| Audit Directory Service Access | 102, 104, 106, 108 | 66, 68, 6A, 6B |
| Audit Logon Events | 22, 24, 26, 28, 30, 32, 34, 36, 38 | 16, 18, 1A, 1C, 1E, 20, 22, 24, 26 |
| Audit Object Access | 40, 42, 44, 46, 48, 50, 52, 54, 56, 58, 60, 62 | 28, 2A, 2C, 2E, 30, 32, 34, 36, 38, 3A, 3C, 3E |
| Audit Policy Change | 78, 80, 82, 84, 86, 88 | 4E, 50, 52, 54, 56, 58 |
| Audit Privilege Use | 64, 66, 68 | 40, 42, 44 |
| Audit Process Tracking | 70, 72, 74, 76 | 46, 48, 4A, 4C |
| Audit System Events | 12, 14, 16, 18, 20 | 0C, 0E, 10, 12, 14 |

Now that you know where the information is located and what the byte values are, it's time to write some code to interact with the audit settings. Listing 10-4 shows the code used for this example.

**LISTING 10-4:** Performing a system-level user audit

```
private void btnCheck_Click(object sender, EventArgs e)
{
    // Clear the previous results.
    lstSettings.Items.Clear();

    // Get the required key.
    RegistryKey Policies =
```

*continues*

**LISTING 10-4** *(continued)*

```csharp
        Registry.LocalMachine.OpenSubKey(@"Security\Policy\PolAdtEv");

    // Obtain the default value.
    Byte[] AuditValues = (Byte[])Policies.GetValue("");

    // Output the auditing values.
    // Check account logon auditing.
    switch (AuditValues[110])
    {
        case 0:
            lstSettings.Items.Add(
                "Audit Account Logon Events Disabled");
            break;
        case 1:
            lstSettings.Items.Add(
                "Audit Account Logon Events Success");
            break;
        case 2:
            lstSettings.Items.Add(
                "Audit Account Logon Events Failure");
            break;
        case 3:
            lstSettings.Items.Add(
                "Audit Account Logon Events Success and Failure");
            break;
    }

    ... Other Cases ...

    // Close the registry.
    Policies.Close();
}
```

The code begins by clearing any information from the list box. It then opens the appropriate registry key using the `Registry.LocalMachine.OpenSubKey()` method and places a reference to it in Policies. The default value isn't named, so you call `GetValue()` with a null string. The output is a `Byte` array named `AuditValues`. Checking for each of the nine audit settings is a matter of looking at the correct byte value at this point. The example code shows one `switch` statement used for the task. Remember to call `Policies.Close()` when the application ends.

## Testing the User Audit Example

The audit policies checked by this example reside in the Security Settings\Local Policies\Audit Policy folder of the Local Security Policy console shown in Figure 10-13. You can find this console in the Administrative Tools folder of the Control Panel.

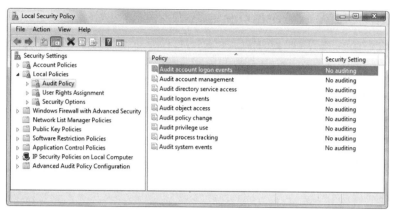

**FIGURE 10-13:** Use the Local Security Policy console to change audit settings for this example.

To change a setting, double-click its entry in the Local Security Policy console. You'll see a policy Properties dialog box similar to the one shown in Figure 10-14. The Explain tab tells you about the audit policy and what it monitors on your system. The dialog box has checkboxes that let you monitor successful events, failures, or both. Check the options that you want to try and click OK. Remember to return the settings to normal when you're done working with the example, or your event log will be filled with tons of unnecessary entries.

It's time to see how the application works. Because of the need for administrator privileges, you'll see the usual messages as you start the application. Click Check and you'll see the current audit policy settings. Change any setting and click Check again to see the change. Figure 10-15 shows typical output from this example.

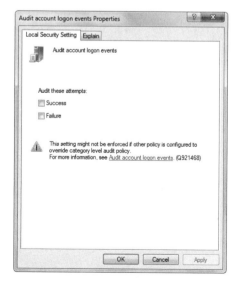

**FIGURE 10-14:** Modify the audit policies as necessary for testing.

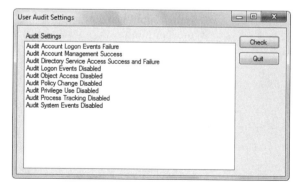

**FIGURE 10-15:** The example accurately reflects the current audit policy settings.

## Checking File and Directory Permissions

So far this chapter has focused on users. When all is said and done, however, the real issue is determining what rights a user has to a resource such as a file or directory. This section of the chapter uses a file for the simple purpose of demonstration. Nevertheless, the principles apply equally well to any resource. Before a user or other entity can access a resource, it's important to have the required rights. The following sections show an example of how to perform this task.

### Configuring the Check Permission Example

This example begins with a Windows Forms application. You add the controls shown in Figure 10-4. In addition, you need to provide the following `using` statements:

```
using System.Security.AccessControl;
using System.IO;
using System.Security.Principal;
```

### Writing the Check Permission Code

The principle behind this example is relatively simple. If a user has a particular permission, the system sets a flag within the DACL. The .NET Framework encompasses these flags within a structure called a `FileSystemAccessRule`. Listing 10-5 provides details on how this flag system works.

**LISTING 10-5:** Checking file or directory permissions

Available for download on Wrox.com

```
private void btnCheck_Click(object sender, EventArgs e)
{
    // Create a file security object for the target file.
    FileSecurity FS = new FileSecurity(
        Application.StartupPath + @"\Temp.TXT",
        AccessControlSections.Access);

    // Obtain the access rules for the file.
    AuthorizationRuleCollection AccessRules =
        FS.GetAccessRules(true, true,
            typeof(NTAccount));

    // Create a string that contains the rule data.
    String RuleHeading = "";

    // Process the access rules.
    foreach (FileSystemAccessRule AR in AccessRules)
    {
        // Add the principal name to the string.
        RuleHeading = AR.IdentityReference.Value.ToString();

        // Determine whether the permission is inherited.
        if (AR.IsInherited)
            RuleHeading += " (Inherited)";
        else
```

```
            RuleHeading += " (Not Inherited)";

        // Output the rule heading.
        lstPermissions.Items.Add(RuleHeading);

        // Obtain a list of permissions.
        if (AR.FileSystemRights.HasFlag(FileSystemRights.AppendData))
            lstPermissions.Items.Add("\tAppend Data");
        if (AR.FileSystemRights.HasFlag(FileSystemRights.ChangePermissions))
            lstPermissions.Items.Add("\tChange Permissions");
        if (AR.FileSystemRights.HasFlag(FileSystemRights.CreateDirectories))
            lstPermissions.Items.Add("\tCreate Directories");
        if (AR.FileSystemRights.HasFlag(FileSystemRights.CreateFiles))
            lstPermissions.Items.Add("\tCreate Files");

... Other Permission Statements Clipped ...

    }
}
```

The example begins by creating a new `FileSecurity` object, `FS`. The `FileSecurity` object contains information about a particular resource. In this case, it contains the `AccessControlSections.Access` flags. If you select one of the other values, such as `AccessControlSections.Audit`, you may have to have administrator privileges, but the access rules are open to anyone with the proper rights. The `FileSecurity()` constructor requires both the resource you want to use, `Temp.TXT` in this case, and the level of flags you want to access.

Within the `FS` are the flags you want to access. In order to access these flags, you create an `AuthorizationRuleCollection`, `AccessRules`. It's possible to format the rules in several ways. The example obtains both explicit rights and inherited rights using an `NTAccount` data type.

At this point, the example examines each of the rules within the `AuthorizationRuleCollection` individually using a `for` loop. Each of the `FileSystemAccessRule` objects, `AR`, provides a principal name (the account with access), whether the access is explicit (defined in particular for this object) or inherited, and a list of flags. The `HasFlag()` method makes it easy to determine whether the user has a particular right. Figure 10-16 shows typical output for this example.

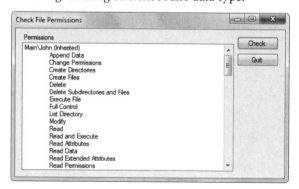

**FIGURE 10-16:** Rule structures help you manage both access and audits.

## Changing File and Directory Permissions

In general, an administrator is going to set resource permissions on a system, including file and directory permissions. However, there are times when an application needs to set permissions. Fortunately, changing file and directory permissions is another area that Microsoft has added to the .NET Framework to make it easier to manage this resource. The following sections describe the Modify Permission example, which shows the basics of changing a file permission. You can easily extend this example to work with other kinds of resources.

## Configuring the Modify Permission Example

This example begins with a Windows Forms application that has a single button, btnChange. You click the button to add a user to the permission list for the test file, Test.TXT. The example also requires that you add the following using statements to the code:

```
using System.Security.AccessControl;
using System.Security.Principal;
using System.IO;
```

## Writing the Modify Permission Code

Modifying a permission involves gaining access to the file and adding a rule to it. The rule provides an account, the kind of access, and whether to allow or deny the access. Listing 10-6 shows the code required for this example.

**LISTING 10-6:** Modifying file or directory permissions

Available for download on Wrox.com

```
private void btnChange_Click(object sender, EventArgs e)
{
    // Create a file security object for the target file.
    FileSecurity FS = File.GetAccessControl(
        Application.StartupPath + @"\Temp.TXT");

    // Create a new rule.
    FileSystemAccessRule Rule = new FileSystemAccessRule(
        new NTAccount(@"BUILTIN\Users"),
        FileSystemRights.Write,
        AccessControlType.Allow);

    // Add the rule to the file security object.
    FS.AddAccessRule(Rule);

    // Save the rule to the file.
    File.SetAccessControl(
        Application.StartupPath + @"\Temp.TXT", FS);

    // Display a success message.
    MessageBox.Show("Change Succeeded!");
}
```

The code begins by creating a FileSecurity object, FS, that provides access to the permissions for Temp.TXT. Remember that this code is actually changing the DACL for Temp.TXT. To provide better control over the process, you could include an `AccessControlSections.Access` enumeration member as a second argument.

To add a new user to the permissions, the code creates a `FileSystemAccessRule`, Rule, that includes the Users built-in account, the ability to write to the file, and an Allow permission. Notice that you must provide an account type, which is going to be `NTAccount()` in most situations. The code calls the `AddAccessRule()` method to actually add the rule to `FS`.

At this point, the code calls `File.SetAccessControl()` to change the DACL of `Temp.TXT`. This method requires that you provide the filename as the first input and the `FileSecurity` object as the second input. Because there isn't any notification that the process has succeeded, the code displays a simple success message. Figure 10-17 shows the modified permissions for `Temp.TXT`. Notice that the Write right has a dark checkmark, showing that it's explicitly set, while the Read & Execute and Read rights use lighter checkmarks to show that they're inherited.

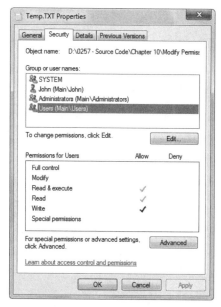

**FIGURE 10-17:** You can see the permissions change by looking at the file's Properties dialog box.

 *Never attempt to change file permissions while the file is open using a file object in Windows 7. You'll receive an "Attempted to perform an unauthorized operation" error message from the application. Absolutely nothing you can do will change the message or tell you the message source. Your code will look correct and you'll even find examples of it online (see* http://msdn.microsoft.com/magazine/cc163885.aspx*), but it won't work. Always change permissions with the file closed and using the* `File.SetAccessControl()` *static method directly.*

## Auditing Files and Directories

It's possible to audit many user (or other principal) activities by placing an audit directly on the user. However, the number of event log entries generated by such an action can be overwhelming. In many cases, you end up with too much information to process successfully. An alternative is to place an audit on the resource. This form of audit is targeted and generates just the messages you need. Of course, if you really do want to monitor all a user's activities, you still need to place an audit on the user. The following sections show how to place an audit on a file, but you can easily extend the techniques to work with other resource types.

## Configuring the Audit Activity Example

This example begins with a Windows Forms application that has a single button, `btnAudit`, which the user clicks to add or remove auditing. Because this application deals with auditing, you must add a manifest file to it using the procedure described in the "Creating the User Permission Modification Manifest" section of this chapter. You also need to add the following `using` statements:

```
using System.Security.AccessControl;
using System.Security.Principal;
using System.IO;
```

## Writing the Audit Activity Code

This example is a little fancier than some of the other examples in the chapter so far. It monitors the state of auditing on the file. If the file isn't audited, then the code adds auditing to it; otherwise, the code removes auditing from the file. The basic process is the same as adding an access rule to a file, except that you work with the SACL rather than the DACL. Listing 10-7 shows the code required for this example.

Available for download on Wrox.com

**LISTING 10-7:** Performing an audit of actions on a file or directory

```
private void btnAudit_Click(object sender, EventArgs e)
{
    // Create a file security object for the target file.
    FileSecurity FS = File.GetAccessControl(
        Application.StartupPath + @"\Temp.TXT",
        AccessControlSections.Audit);

    // Create a new rule.
    FileSystemAuditRule Rule = new FileSystemAuditRule(
        new NTAccount(@"BUILTIN\Users"),
        FileSystemRights.Write,
        AuditFlags.Failure);

    // Obtain a list of the existing rules.
    AuthorizationRuleCollection AuditRules =
        FS.GetAuditRules(true, true,
            typeof(NTAccount));

    // Check for the existence of the rule in the collection.
    Boolean FoundIt = false;
    foreach (FileSystemAuditRule AR in AuditRules)

        // Look for the rule.
        if ((AR.IdentityReference == Rule.IdentityReference) &&
            (AR.FileSystemRights.HasFlag(FileSystemRights.Write)) &&
            (AR.AuditFlags.HasFlag(AuditFlags.Failure)))
        {
            // Set FoundIt appropriately.
            FoundIt = true;
```

```
            // Exit the loop.
            break;
        }

    // Add or remove the rule as appropriate.
    if (FoundIt)

        // Remove the rule from the file security object.
        FS.RemoveAuditRule(Rule);

    else

        // Add the rule to the file security object.
        FS.AddAuditRule(Rule);

    // Save the rule to the file.
    File.SetAccessControl(
        Application.StartupPath + @"\Temp.TXT", FS);

    // Display a success message.
    MessageBox.Show("Change Succeeded!");
}
```

The code begins by creating a `FileSecurity` object, `FS`, using `Temp.TXT`. Notice that you must include the `AccessControlSections.Audit` argument in this case. The default is to provide a `FileSecurity` object for the DACL, so you must tell the system that you actually want to work with the SACL instead.

The next step is to create a `FileSystemAuditRule`, `Rule`, that provides the user account, right to monitor, and type of monitoring to perform as input. There are 23 different `FileSystemRights` values you can use to define the rights you want monitored, and you can "or" the values together as needed (such as `FileSystemRights.Write | FileSystemRights.Read` for both read and write access). The audit flags are `AuditFlags.Failure` and `AuditFlags.Success`. If you want to monitor both success and failure, you "or" the flags together (`AuditFlags.Failure | AuditFlags.Success`).

At this point, the code can begin checking for the presence of a particular auditing rule. It creates an `AuthorizationRuleCollection` object, `AuditRules`, which includes both explicit and inherited audit rules of type `NTAccount`. The code uses a `for` loop to review each of the `FileSystemAuditRule` entries, `AR`, in turn. To successfully find a particular rule, you must check the `IdentityReference`, `FileSystemRights`, and `AuditFlags` properties. The `HasFlag()` method makes it easy to find particular flags in the list. Once the code finds the entry of interest, it sets `FoundIt` to `true` and breaks out of the loop.

One of two events can happen at this point. The code can call `RemoveAuditRule()` to remove the rule from the list or `AddAuditRule()` to add the rule to the list based on the value of `FoundIt`. The code then calls `SetAccessControl()` to set the new rules in place.

Viewing the results is a little more complicated than viewing access rights. Use these steps to see the audit rights:

**1.** Right-click `Temp.TXT` and choose Properties from the Context menu.

**2.** Select the Security tab.

3. Click Advanced to display the Advanced Security Settings for Temp.TXT dialog box shown in Figure 10-18.

4. Select the Auditing tab as shown in Figure 10-18. Notice that even when using this editor, you must rely on privilege elevation to see the entries.

5. Click Continue. You'll see a second Advanced Security Settings for Temp.TXT dialog box open with just an Auditing tab, as shown in Figure 10-19. This time, you can see the audit rule the application created.

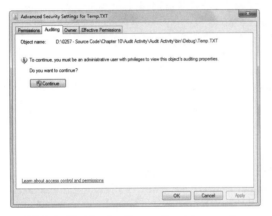

**FIGURE 10-18:** Viewing the audit entries requires administrator privileges.

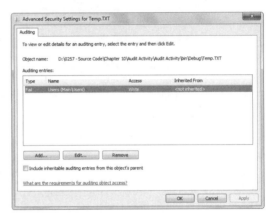

**FIGURE 10-19:** The example creates an audit rule for a failure to successfully write to the file by the Users account.

## MOVING YOUR APPLICATIONS TO WINDOWS 7

This chapter has described NT security under Windows 7. It isn't a detailed look at NT security because a detailed look would require an entire book. This chapter provides the highlights you need to write managed code properly and to diagnose problems induced by Windows 7 security features in your application. The one thing you should take away from this chapter is that NT security is an essential component of your Windows 7 application — it provides the basic level of security support needed to ensure that the application, user, and data remain safe. NT security can't fulfill every need, but you do need to rely on it as the starting point for security in your application.

At this point, you need to ask yourself the question, "How secure are my applications right now?" The policy in the past was to include as little security in applications as possible because the perception was that security degrades application performance and increases training costs. A user who spends more time thinking through security issues spends less time performing actual work. As users rely more heavily on the Internet, security becomes less of a nicety and more of a requirement. Virus writers and other nefarious individuals would just love to gain access to your network through an application that erroneously trades security for ease of use and raw speed. Since Windows 7 provides substantial tools to enhance application security, you need to re-evaluate application security in light of the threats against your organization and rewrite application code as needed. The bottom line rule of security is not to provide any more access than absolutely required.

You'll definitely want to explore a few issues this chapter has prepared you to explore, but hasn't explored in any detail. For example, the `System.Security.AccessControl` namespace contains a number of entries for registry security. Given the registry-based threats pointed at applications today, you might want to secure your registry entries to keep outsiders from damaging them. You'll also want to explore the directory-specific entries in the `System.Security.AccessControl` namespace.

Chapter 11 discusses one of the more controversial Windows security additions, User Account Control (UAC). Under Vista, the UAC is truly intrusive and can cause users to become less security-conscious because it constantly displays warnings about actions that the application is taking on the user's behalf. Whether you agree with Microsoft's latest actions or not, the UAC is less intrusive in Windows 7 and it's also easier for developers to work with. Because of the way Windows 7 works, you can't ignore the UAC when updating your application — some actions require the privilege elevation that the UAC provides. Chapter 11 adds to your basic NT security knowledge by addressing the UAC and showing you how to work with it.

# 11
# Understanding the User Account Control

**WHAT'S IN THIS CHAPTER?**

- Thinking about how the UAC works
- Working with the UAC
- Adding UAC support to an application

The User Account Control (UAC) was a new feature with Vista — one that most users maligned as a terrible nuisance at best. Windows 7 has a toned-down version of the UAC that's less likely to cause woe. In fact, you can now tune the UAC to provide the right level of protection for your particular needs. Some users will still likely turn the UAC off because they view it as an annoyance. The UAC does provide useful functionality, however, and discussing it from a developer perspective is part of the goal of this chapter.

This chapter also examines two techniques you can use to elevate user privileges as needed. The UAC places restrictions on your application. Even if some users turn the UAC off, others will have it on, so you need to assume that all users have it turned on to ensure your application works on all systems. As shown in Chapter 10, even users who are part of the Administrators group will require privilege elevation at times in order to perform some tasks, so group affiliation is no longer enough to ensure that all applications work as intended at all times.

## UNDERSTANDING THE UAC

At one time, PCs were stand-alone machines and had no security issues to speak of. Yes, a PC could get infected by someone with a floppy, but even that form of infection required direct user interaction and was easily stopped by leaving the floppies out of the machine. Early network connections weren't much of a problem either, as long as the administrator kept the system clean. The problems started when users started connecting to the Internet and the potential sources of contamination became many and varied. Today, a network administrator has to work hard simply to keep the infections under control, much less prevent them. Consequently, systems today need robust security, and the UAC is part of that solution. The following section provides a developer view of the UAC.

## Considering the Need for the UAC

Developers have become more careful about their programming strategies as technology has improved. Applications today are usually carefully planned and rely on a significant number of tools to make them more secure. The problem is complexity. Today's applications are considerably more complex than those early applications that ran on the original PC. In addition, bugs can exist in many places, many of them not under developer control. Consider these bug sources:

- Developer-created application code
- Code used from older projects and other developers
- The .NET Framework
- Third-party libraries
- Windows
- External application interactions
- Drivers and DLLs

Given that only the first of these sources is actually under the developer's control, it isn't surprising that lots of finger-pointing occurs when a bug results in an infection. There are more people looking for entrances into your application than there are developing that application. It's easier to find and exploit a bug than it is to fix it once it's discovered.

When an outsider wants to exploit a bug in your application or any of the support mechanisms on which it depends, it's all too easy to persuade the user to participate, which is where the UAC comes into play. In many cases, the best way to avoid infection is to look for unusual activities. The UAC alerts the user to possibly unusual activities that could result in an infection. Of course, the big thing is to train the user to recognize the UAC as a helpful aid and also to keep UAC alerts to a minimum so the user doesn't get desensitized to them.

## Why It Isn't a Good Idea to Override the UAC

Most users don't care anything at all about your application — their only concern is getting work done so they get paid and can go home each night on time. Anything else is an unwelcome disruption. It isn't too surprising, then, that security takes a back seat to the user's desire to get work done. Consequently, users often look for ways to disable the UAC because it disrupts their work.

Developers are almost as bad as users when it comes to the UAC. Chapter 10 shows that the UAC affects some of the output of Windows Management Instrumentation (WMI). In addition, the developer has to write additional code to implement the UAC. In short, the UAC is also a disruption to the developer who wants to get a working application out the door as quickly as possible.

Windows isn't known as a particularly secure operating system. In part, this reputation is warranted — Microsoft has made more than a few security mistakes over the years. Windows is also a complex operating system, and many of the concepts incorporated into it come from a time when security wasn't as big an issue as it is today. However, part of the reputation is simply a matter of Windows popularity. Everyone likes to attack the biggest target, and Windows is definitely a big target.

Because of the number of threats arrayed against it, Microsoft implements a number of security features in Windows. Of course, there's the application security that you should be adding to your application. (You are adding it, aren't you?) Windows itself provides security features, and there's the firewall that Windows supplies. The system should also have antivirus measures installed. The UAC is an essential piece of additional protection for a system that's almost certainly under daily attack. In most cases, it's also the only piece of protection that alerts you to unusual system activities (unless you have a third-party product installed that also provides this protection). Consequently, user and developer alike should make use of this important feature.

## Developing Applications with Fewer Rights

One way in which the UAC can actually help the developer is by providing an alert to excessive rights. When a user is going to read a file, there's no need to give that user the right to write to it as well. If your application needs to view access rights for the user to a file, there's no need to also obtain the audit rights. Every time your application needs to display a UAC dialog box, you need to consider whether the UAC alert is actually warranted. The UAC provides an important indicator to the developer that something is amiss with the application.

Developing applications with fewer rights is a good idea from a number of perspectives. A user who uses an application with fewer rights is less likely to invite various forms of contamination onto the machine, and there's less chance that the contamination, when it does occur, will cause problems such as data loss. Fewer rights also make it less likely that applications will face issues such as resource contention. For example, several applications can share a file in read-only mode; only one application can use a file in read/write mode. There are many ways in which fewer rights actually make application development easier, not harder.

A concern for most developers in creating applications with fewer rights is that users will complain. It's true that users will complain if they can't access the things they need to accomplish work. However, most users won't even notice having fewer rights when they can access everything they need. You'll make the application more secure and less resource-hungry, and all without raising any user ire as long as you test the application carefully using precisely the same rights that the user has to the application. Testing is the important part of the equation because the user's initial impression is important — an application that functions correctly from the outset won't attract any attention, even if the user has fewer rights than with the previous version.

## INTERACTING WITH THE UAC

Microsoft made a second fatal mistake with the UAC in Vista. Not only was the UAC obnoxious in presenting constant requests for privilege elevation, but Microsoft provided only one option for dealing with the UAC — turning it off. In fact, you'll find a number of sites that describe four methods for turning the UAC off, such as the one at http://www.petri.co.il/disable_uac_in_windows_vista.htm. Most users opted for the first method listed on this site because MSConfig is friendly and relatively easy to fix should the user make a bad choice. In addition, MSConfig is one of the utilities that many administrators let users work with.

Windows 7 takes a completely different approach to the UAC. When you open MSConfig now, you'll see a different option, as shown in Figure 11-1. Instead of simply disabling or enabling the UAC (it used to be called User Account Protection or UAP), the user sees an option to change the UAC settings.

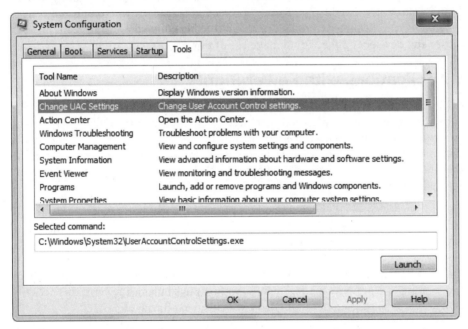

**FIGURE 11-1:** MSConfig used to contain settings to turn the UAC off, but now it launches a more measured approach.

When the user highlights Change UAC Settings and clicks Launch, Windows presents the window shown in Figure 11-2. The user now has four options from which to choose. The default setting is less obnoxious than in Vista, but still presents the UAC dialog box when necessary. You can still choose the Vista level of UAC interaction. A third setting presents UAC warnings, but does so without using the secure desktop. Only if the user is completely averse to any UAC interaction at all is it necessary to turn the feature completely off, but you shouldn't ever exercise this option because the UAC does provide a valuable service.

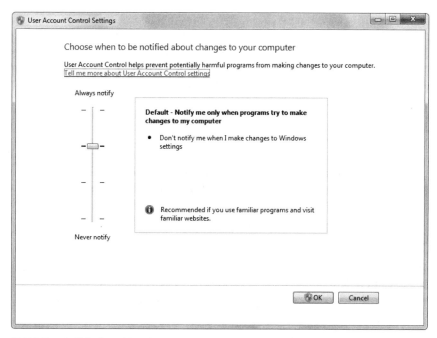

**FIGURE 11-2:** Windows 7 makes it possible to ease UAC restrictions.

The administrator still has a higher level of access to UAC functionality than the user does, through the User Account Control settings found in the `Security Settings\Local Policies\Security Options` folder of the Local Security Policy console shown in Figure 11-3. For example, the administrator can insist that only applications that are both signed and validated are candidates for privilege elevation. This setting is so restricted that it would tend to shut down most systems today — few third-party vendors currently sign their applications.

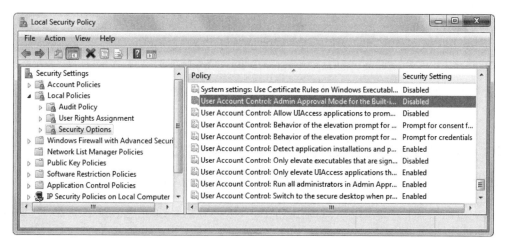

**FIGURE 11-3:** The administrator has the ultimate level of control over UAC configuration.

Of course, the important issue is to figure out what all this means to you as a developer. You normally want to develop your applications to support a Vista level of UAC interaction, unless you're absolutely certain that users will have Windows 7 installed on their systems. Make sure that your application actually supports the UAC fully, because new applications and application updates will run on systems that have the UAC on them, and you can't count on the user's disabling the UAC (in fact, the user is well advised not to disable the UAC).

If your application will run on mission-critical systems that have extra security requirements, then you'll also want to be sure that your application is signed before you send it anywhere. It may be that administrators will require signed and validated applications in the future as threats to current systems become more intense and widespread. In short, making your application UAC-friendly is going to be a requirement, so it's best to start planning for the support now. Use these steps in preparing your application for use with Vista and Windows 7:

1. Test your application for Windows compatibility using the Microsoft Application Compatibility Toolkit (http://www.microsoft.com/downloads/details.aspx?FamilyId=24DA89E9-B581-47B0-B45E-492DD6DA2971).

2. Classify your application and individual application elements as standard user, administrator, or mixed usage so that you can better define the security requirements.

3. Redesign the application functionality to provide UAC compatibility by reducing rights or requesting privilege elevation as needed.

4. Redesign the application interface to provide UAC-friendly tips and techniques to the end user.

5. If at all possible, redesign the application installer so it doesn't require administrator-level privileges.

6. Create a manifest for your application so that the application runs as planned.

7. Embed the manifest with the application if you don't expect the administrator to modify it at any point. External manifests can get lost or modified by the end user, resulting in undesirable side effects.

8. Test your application using precisely the same credentials and resource access as the end user. Otherwise, you can't be sure the application will work at all.

9. Authenticode signs your application so that it's easy to detect any modifications to it.

10. Get your application tested by Microsoft so it appears on the Windows 7 Compatibility Center (http://www.microsoft.com/windows/compatibility/windows-7/default.aspx).

## ADDING UAC SUPPORT TO YOUR APPLICATION

The .NET Framework is a little behind the curve when it comes to the UAC. This is surprising considering how hard Microsoft is pushing people to rely on the UAC as a security measure. Currently, you can't request privilege elevation in the .NET Framework for a thread or other useful work element. In fact, you have only two choices:

- Elevate the application to administrator level as a whole using a manifest.
- Call an external application element and elevate it as part of the calling process.

The following sections describe how to create an application that provides UAC support within the limits that the .NET Framework currently allows. In many cases, you'll have to make some decisions on how to break your application into pieces using the current strategies. Microsoft will probably make it possible eventually to perform in-place privilege elevations or allow some method of creating a thread that will support privilege elevation.

## Creating a Manifest

The first technique for working with the UAC is to elevate your entire application to administrator level. You should use this approach only when the application is designed exclusively for administrator use, won't see any use outside the network, and is extremely focused — performing just one or two small tasks. Using this technique to elevate the privileges of an application that should normally run at a lower level will leave huge security holes in your system. The following sections describe how to work with this kind of application.

### Defining the Manifest Application

The technique shown in this section will work with any .NET application. However, the example relies on a Windows Forms template application that has a single button, btnAudit, for testing purposes. The example doesn't require any additional references, but you do need to add the following using statements:

```
using System.Security.AccessControl;
using System.Security.Principal;
using System.IO;
```

### Adding the Manifest

This example uses the manifest approach to allowing administrator privileges. You can use the technique shown in the "Creating the User Permission Modification Manifest" section of Chapter 10 to add the manifest.

The <requestedExecutionLevel> tag accepts two inputs. The first, level, describes what type of execution you need. When working with the UAC, you always request requireAdministrator. However, there are situations where using highestAvailable may work for specific needs. Microsoft terms these scenarios as mixed mode, where a standard user and administrator work with the application. An article at http://msdn.microsoft.com/library/bb756929.aspx describes how these settings react when users have certain settings enabled on their systems.

The second setting, uiAccess, gives the application access to other windows on the desktop. Normally, the application can't drive output to other windows. Microsoft recommends setting this value to false normally. The only exception that Microsoft makes is for applications with accessibility (special needs) features. For example, an application might need to send output to an on-screen keyboard. There are probably other situations where you'll need to set this value to true, but doing so opens a potential security hole. Updating a simple status indicator probably isn't a good use for this feature — the security risk outweighs the benefit of the update.

## Creating the Application Code

The example application adds or removes auditing from a test file, Test.TXT, that appears in the output folder. In this case, the application adds or removes auditing for the write right of the BUILTIN\Users account. The event fires when the user fails to write to the file. This application relies on a simple toggle mechanism to perform its task after detecting the audit state of the file. Listing 11-1 shows the code you need for this example. The "Auditing Files and Directories" section of Chapter 10 describes how this application works.

**LISTING 11-1:** Performing an audit of actions on a file or directory

```
private void btnAudit_Click(object sender, EventArgs e)
{
    // Create a file security object for the target file.
    FileSecurity FS = File.GetAccessControl(
        Application.StartupPath + @"\Temp.TXT",
        AccessControlSections.Audit);

    // Create a new rule.
    FileSystemAuditRule Rule = new FileSystemAuditRule(
        new NTAccount(@"BUILTIN\Users"),
        FileSystemRights.Write,
        AuditFlags.Failure);
    // Obtain a list of the existing rules.
    AuthorizationRuleCollection AuditRules =
        FS.GetAuditRules(true, true,
            typeof(NTAccount));

    // Check for the existence of the rule in the collection.
    Boolean FoundIt = false;
    foreach (FileSystemAuditRule AR in AuditRules)

        // Look for the rule.
        if ((AR.IdentityReference == Rule.IdentityReference) &&
            (AR.FileSystemRights.HasFlag(FileSystemRights.Write)) &&
            (AR.AuditFlags.HasFlag(AuditFlags.Failure)))
        {
            // Set FoundIt appropriately.
            FoundIt = true;

            // Exit the loop.
            break;
        }

    // Add or remove the rule as appropriate.
    if (FoundIt)

        // Remove the rule from the file security object.
        FS.RemoveAuditRule(Rule);

    else
```

```
            // Add the rule to the file security object.
            FS.AddAuditRule(Rule);

         // Save the rule to the file.
         File.SetAccessControl(
            Application.StartupPath + @"\Temp.TXT", FS);

         // Display a success message.
         MessageBox.Show("Change Succeeded!");
      }
```

## Compiling the Manifest into the Application

In most cases, you won't use a separate manifest file as the examples in Chapter 10 do. The only exception is when you're absolutely certain the administrator will need to make changes to the application manifest at some point (and even then, using a separate manifest is a dangerous proposition). Compiling the manifest into the application prevents anyone from modifying (at least with any ease). In addition, compiling the manifest into the application means that the manifest won't get lost. To compile the manifest into the application, you use MT.EXE, a utility that comes with the Windows 7 SDK. The "Obtaining the Windows 7 SDK" section of Chapter 7 tells you how to obtain and configure the Windows 7 SDK for your system.

> *If you've decided to modify your example from Chapter 10 for this chapter, you need to change an* Audit Activity.MANIFEST *file setting. Highlight the* Audit Activity.MANIFEST *file entry in Solution Explorer. In the Properties window, change the Copy to Output Directory property value to Do Not Copy. You don't need to copy the manifest to the output directory when you embed it in the executable.*

You need to add a special command to the project before Visual Studio will compile the manifest file for you. Use these steps to configure the application to compile the manifest into the executable:

1. Right-click the project entry in Solution Explorer and choose Properties from the Context menu. You'll see the Audit Activity properties window.

2. Select the Build Events tab.

3. Click Edit Post-build to display the Post-build Event Command Line dialog box shown in Figure 11-4.

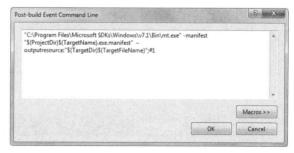

**FIGURE 11-4:** Add a special command line to compile the manifest file.

4. Type the following command in the dialog box (as a single line, rather than on multiple lines as shown in the book):

```
"C:\Program Files\Microsoft SDKs\Windows\v7.1\Bin\MT.EXE"
-manifest "$(ProjectDir)$(TargetName).exe.manifest"
-outputresource:"$(TargetDir)$(TargetFileName)";#1
```

You need to provide the actual path to `MT.EXE` as part of the command. The `-manifest` command line switch tells the Manifest Tool (MT) utility where to locate the manifest file you want to compile, which is normally the same folder as the source code for your application. The `$(ProjectDir)` macro points to this location, while the `$(TargetName)` macro provides the name of the application. The `-outputresource` command line switch provides the location of the executable that should receive the manifest. The `$(TargetDir)` macro provides the location of the executable (including whether the output is in the Release or Debug folder), and the `$(TargetFileName)` macro provides the name of the executable file.

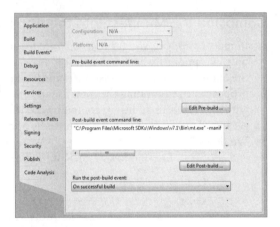

**FIGURE 11-5:** The Build Events tab contains pre-build and post-build command lines.

5. Click OK. The Build Events tab should now contain a command like the one shown in Figure 11-5.

6. Choose Build ➪ Build Solution. The application will build as normal. You should see a successful MT utility entry, as shown in Figure 11-6, in the Output window.

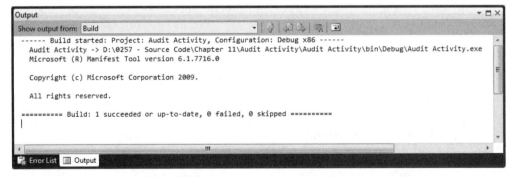

**FIGURE 11-6:** Make sure that the MT utility is successful in adding the manifest file to your executable.

### Executing the Application

The result of compiling the manifest into the executable is no different from working with the manifest file separately. When you start to debug the application, you'll still see the Visual Studio notification shown in Figure 11-7. The debugger will still start the application as normal and you'll still see a UAC dialog box. Everything will work as before. The only difference is that the manifest file is contained within the executable, rather than appearing as a separate file.

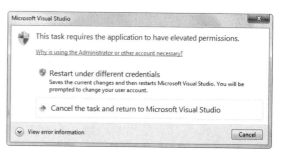

**FIGURE 11-7:** Visual Studio presents a notification when it needs to elevate your privileges.

## Executing as a Separate Process

Setting an entire application to execute in administrator mode is uncommon and unsafe. The more common scenario is to separate the application into pieces that can execute at one of three levels:

- With the rights used to invoke them
- With the highest privileges that the user natively has
- Administrator mode

The .NET Framework currently executes each level as a separate process, rather than using threads or some other convenient method. The following sections show one scenario that uses separate processes to execute in standard mode and in administrator mode.

### Defining the Separate Process Application

The example begins with a Windows Forms template application named Modify Permission that has a single button, `btnChange`. You can give the solution and project the same name, if desired. You don't need to add any special references for the example, but you do need to add the following `using` statement:

```
using System.Diagnostics;
```

### Creating the Secondary Project

You add the second process as a separate project. Use the following steps to create the secondary project:

1. Right-click the solution entry in Solution Explorer and choose Add ➪ New Project from the Context menu. You'll see the Add New Project dialog box shown in Figure 11-8.

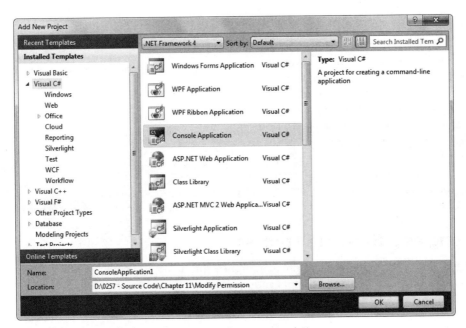

**FIGURE 11-8:** Add a console application to the current solution.

2. Highlight the Console Application template.

3. Type **SetPermission** (no spaces) in the Name field and click OK. Visual Studio adds the SetPermission project to the Modify Permission solution. You also see the SetPermission.CS file opened for editing.

## Configuring the Secondary Project

As a console application, SetPermission doesn't include any controls or other special interface needs. You also won't need to add any references to it. However, you do need to add the following using statements:

```
using System.Security.AccessControl;
using System.Security.Principal;
using System.IO;
```

The project needs a special setup as well. You want the output of the build process to appear with the Modify Permission.EXE file to make it easier for Modify Permission.EXE to find it. Use the following steps to configure the build output:

1. Right-click the SetPermission project entry in Solution Explorer and choose Properties from the Context menu. You see the SetPermission properties window.

2. Highlight the Build tab.

3. Select Debug in the Configuration drop-down list box.

4. Type **..\Modify Permission\bin\Debug\** in the Output Path field. Your Build tab should look like the one shown in Figure 11-9.

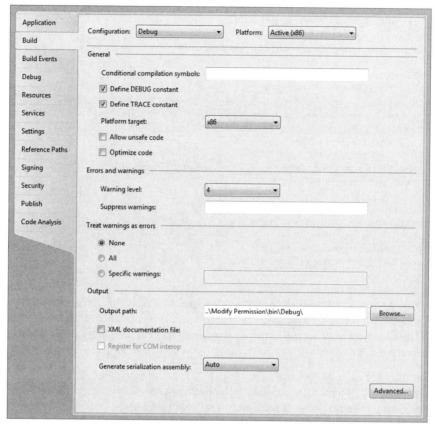

**FIGURE 11-9:** Make sure you configure the build to place the output with Modify Permission.EXE.

5. Select Release in the Configuration drop-down list box.
6. Type `..\Modify Permission\bin\Release\` in the Output Path field.

You also want to be sure that the correct project executes when you debug the application. Right-click the Modify Permission project in Solution Explorer and choose Set as StartUp Project from the context menu. The Modify Permission entry will appear in bold type to indicate that it's the startup project.

## Writing the Primary Application Code

It's time to add some code to the application. Begin with the primary application, Modify Permission. This application can perform any number of tasks that rely on the user's standard credentials. In fact, when working with a production application, it's likely to be the largest part of the application because there really are very few tasks that require administrator privileges. Listing 11-2 shows the code you need for the example application.

**LISTING 11-2:** Calling an external application

```
private void btnChange_Click(object sender, EventArgs e)
{
    // Obtain the application path.
    String ThePath = "\"" + Application.StartupPath + "\"";

    // Create a new process for changing the permissions.
    ProcessStartInfo PSI = new ProcessStartInfo(
        "SetPermission", ThePath);

    // Configure the process to run in an elevated state.
    PSI.Verb = "runas";

    // Run the process.
    Process.Start(PSI).WaitForExit();

    // Display a success message.
    MessageBox.Show("Change Succeeded!");
}
```

The code begins by creating a path to the secondary application. It then creates a `ProcessStartInfo` object, `PSI`, which accepts the secondary application name and path as arguments. The next step is to set the `PSI.Verb` property to `"runas"`. This step is very important because it tells the system to elevate the process rights to administrator mode.

At this point, the code calls `Process.Start()` with `PSI` as the argument. You want to be sure that you add `WaitForExit()` so that the secondary application exits before the primary application continues processing. The final step is to display a success message.

## Writing the Secondary Application Code

Unlike your production application, the secondary application does most of the work in the example. In this case, the secondary application receives the application path as an input and uses it to modify the rights for `Temp.TXT`, as shown in Listing 11-3.

**LISTING 11-3:** Modifying file or directory permissions externally

```
static void Main(string[] args)
{
    // Create a file security object for the target file.
    FileSecurity FS = File.GetAccessControl(
        args[0] + @"\Temp.TXT");

    // Create a new rule.
    FileSystemAccessRule Rule = new FileSystemAccessRule(
        new NTAccount(@"BUILTIN\Users"),
        FileSystemRights.Write,
        AccessControlType.Allow);
```

```
            // Add the rule to the file security object.
            FS.AddAccessRule(Rule);

            // Save the rule to the file.
            File.SetAccessControl(
                args[0] + @"\Temp.TXT", FS);
        }
```

The code begins by creating a `FileSecurity` object, `FS`, with the application path (passed as `args[0]`) and the filename, `@"\Temp.TXT"`, as an argument. The code then builds a new `FileSystemAccessRule` object, `Rule`, that contains the account name, rights, and type of access (allow or deny). The kind of identity, in this case, is an `NTAccount`, `@"BUILTIN\Users"`. The code is requesting the `FileSystemRights.Write` right and will allow (`AccessControlType.Allow`) the action.

Now, the code adds the new rule to `FS` using the `AddAccessRule()`. It then uses the `File.SetAccessControl()` method to actually change the rights on the file.

Make absolutely certain that you perform this task on a closed file to ensure that your application doesn't experience an error. Performing the task on an open file can cause conflicts, especially if the file is opened for write access, which locks it. To see the results of this example, right-click the file and choose Properties from the Context menu. Select the Security tab to see the results shown in Figure 11-10.

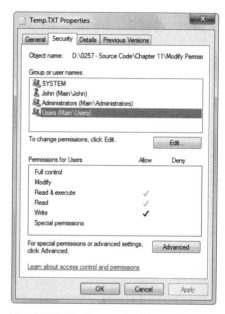

**FIGURE 11-10:** The result of this two-part application is to set the BUILTIN\Users account rights.

## MOVING YOUR APPLICATIONS TO WINDOWS 7

This chapter has discussed an important new Windows security feature, the UAC. Whether you like the UAC or not, you'll have to develop applications that work with it or you'll find that users aren't going to be able to use your application at some point. Creating an application that works with the UAC isn't hard, but you do need to test it fully using the same credentials and forms of access that the user will have. If you don't take this important step, it's almost guaranteed that your application will fail to work as intended. Security is only going to become stricter as time progresses, so getting used to creating secure applications now will definitely save you time and effort later.

One of the things that Microsoft hasn't been pushing very hard is performing a survey of your existing applications. You need to test every application that the user will rely on and then decide how to make each one work with the UAC. One technique you can use when you don't have the required source code to update an application, or the source code is so outdated you can't easily update it, is to write a wrapper application. The wrapper application will provide the means to elevate privileges in a reasonable way. It's a better solution than simply configuring the application always to run in administrator mode. The important point is to create such a list today so that you know which applications you must update or replace later.

At one time, Windows NT security was enough to secure a system because every system was essentially the same, and users didn't work in outside locations. Today, you have users who do their work in a library or coffee shop. Users often work at home or even in their cars. In many cases, users want to check their e-mail or perform simple tasks while on vacation. In short, you don't know where the user is going to be when it's time to interact with your application, so security has to be more flexible than Windows NT security alone provides. Chapter 12 adds to what you know already and provides some useful techniques for developing flexible applications that can work in a number of environments and avoid a wealth of potential threats.

# 12

# Developing Applications with Enhanced Security

**WHAT'S IN THIS CHAPTER?**

- ➤ Defining application security requirements for modern applications
- ➤ Considering security needs for a particular application
- ➤ Using enhanced security features in an application
- ➤ Creating and employing a security policy
- ➤ Avoiding overwhelming users with security

NT security was developed at a time of low threat. The Internet didn't even exist yet, except as an experiment. Many users didn't have a connection to the LAN, much less anything more dangerous. It's small wonder, then, that NT security really hasn't kept pace with modern threats. Yes, it's an important place to start (and many applications don't even utilize NT security as fully as they should), but you really need more to protect users, applications, and data from today's external threats.

The .NET Framework comes with a number of enhanced security features you can employ to make your application safer. These features restrict user access to resources, application functionality, and data as needed, but they do so in a different way than pure NT security does. For the most part, these features make it possible to create flexible security that considers a user's current role or place of work. A user can have more rights when acting as a manager, rather than as a standard user. In addition, the user will have more rights when working in the office than when working at the local coffee shop. The following sections describe these security features in more detail.

## CONSIDERING MODERN APPLICATION SECURITY REQUIREMENTS

Modern applications have a lot of security needs. Chapters 10 and 11, along with this chapter, describe them. It's important to put together a comprehensive view of these security needs, which is what you'll find in the sections that follow. As you read these sections, think about rings of security. Just as ancient cities relied on multiple rings of walls for protection, modern applications rely on multiple layers of security for safety. When one layer fails, another layer is there to at least partially make up for the loss.

### Using Traditional NT Security

Chapter 10 describes NT security as the basic security for every application. Windows 7 uses NT security in new ways to make the system even more secure. For example, you can't access the root directory for direct file manipulation any longer (unless you pull some interesting tricks). Applications must create subdirectories now, which are easier to control from a security perspective. Most applications created today don't even fully implement this basic level of security. It's important that you give users only the rights they actually need. When users only have to read files, then giving them write rights is a security violation, even if it does make writing your application easier.

### Using New NT Security Features

Many applications fail to work on Windows 7 because they don't implement new NT security features. For example, applications commonly place files in the `\Windows` or `\Windows\System32` directories, even when they don't need to do so. Always verify that the user has rights to directories other than those in the user's own `\Users\`*`UserName`* directory. In addition, use the `\Users\`*`UserName`* directory whenever possible to store user files.

Rely on shared folders next. Only use system directories when absolutely required (which is almost never with the Windows 7 setup). Rather than store application-wide information in the `\Program Files\`*`ApplicationName`* directory, store it in the `\Users\All Users\`*`ApplicationName`* directory. When using the `\Users\All Users\`*`ApplicationName`* directory, you must set security appropriate for your application because the security inherited from the `\Users\All Users` won't actually allow the user to do anything. This added security ensures that users can access application-wide data but can't create anything in the `\Users\All Users` directory itself.

For years now, developers have abused common storage areas such as the registry. Using the registry presents many problems, not the least of which is that the registry is hard to back up and prone to failure at the worst possible times. It's far better to use the `\Users\`*`Username`*`\AppData\Roaming` directory to store individual application settings as serialized XML. You can also store serialized XML settings in the `\Users\All Users\`*`ApplicationName`* directory as needed.

>  *XML serialization is a powerful data storage technique that's incredibly easy to implement, flexible, and less prone to errors than many other ways of storing data. In addition, it's easy to store both group and individual settings using XML serialization in a way that makes it less likely the group or individuals will lose their settings. You can read more about this technique at* http://www.devsource.com/c/a/Techniques/XML-Serialization-Better-than-the-Registry/.

It's important to remember that the User Account Control (UAC) severely limits the acquisition of certain information. For example, the UAC specifically limits the amount of information you can obtain from Windows Management Instrumentation (WMI). If your application counts on the availability of certain types of restricted WMI information, your application could fail, despite not having any issue that your debugger can easily detect. Look for these sorts of issues as you debug applications that suddenly stop working on Windows 7 (see http://msdn.microsoft.com/library/aa826699.aspx for details). On the other hand, Windows 7 also provides access to a number of new WMI features, as described at http://msdn.microsoft.com/library/aa394053.aspx.

## Working with Zones

The concept of security zones originated with Internet Explorer, and you can still see this concept at work in the Internet Options applet shown in Figure 12-1. In this case, selecting a particular zone for an Internet location changes the security for that site. Likewise, you can change the zone in which an application is operating to modify the privileges that the application (and by extension the user) enjoys. Zone-based security makes sense because you can preconfigure several scenarios and then select the scenario that matches the user's current location. For example, you can use one zone when the user works in a coffee shop and another when the user is at the office. The concept of a zone is also relatively easy to understand, so explaining the different security setups to end users is easier.

Modern software requires the use of zones. You can't be sure where a user is going to work. Users often work at a coffee shop, the library, the beach, or other unsecure locations. The .NET Framework currently recognizes six zones (in order of trustworthiness).

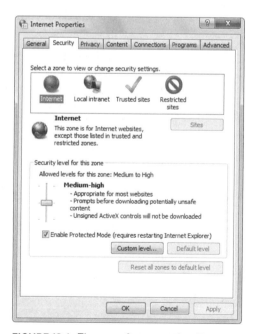

**FIGURE 12-1:** The use of zones makes it easy to change application functionality to match a situation.

- **MyComputer:** This is the local computer. The code isn't accessing anything outside the local computer, so it receives the highest trust level.
- **LocalIntranet:** This is the local network. The code is using a local server or other source for data and code. Because the risk of contamination is slightly higher, the code receives fewer permissions to perform tasks automatically.
- **Trusted:** This is an override zone that enables the developer to create a special configuration for trusted locations outside the local computer. Use this zone with care because it can cause untold woe when the code performs tasks that end up infecting the local computer, damaging data, or compromising the system in other ways.
- **Internet:** This is the external network. The Internet zone can include the actual Internet or simply locations outside the local network. You use the Internet zone to strictly control access to data and code, but not to cut it off completely.
- **Untrusted:** This is an external location that the code must access, but that you don't trust. The code can still execute, but with significant restrictions. In some cases, the code may not actually execute because it can't access most local resources. You use this zone when you must access something externally, but you can't validate the external access to meet company standards.
- **NoZone:** The default state of all .NET code that doesn't specify a zone. If you don't specify a zone, the code can do anything anywhere. In short, you should never use this zone.

Zones are part of Code Access Security (CAS). In fact, they form part of the evidence you receive about an assembly, and you can use this information to determine how to react to the code. Code can come from anywhere today, so knowing the code's origin and security features is important. You might normally execute a piece of code when it comes from the local drive, but not execute precisely the same piece of code when it originates on the Internet. Here's a listing of the evidence presented as part of CAS for an assembly:

- **Application directory:** The location of the code. You might decide that a local assembly is acceptable, but an assembly originating on a network drive isn't.
- **Hash:** The cryptographic hash used to encrypt the assembly. Some hashes are easy to compromise, while others aren't.
- **Publisher:** This is the signature of the publisher who created the assembly. You may decide that you'll accept assemblies signed by ABC Corporation but not those signed by XYZ Company.
- **Site:** The domain of origin for the code. For example, this evidence might be `www.abc_corporation.com`. You won't see both a site and an application directory presented as evidence.
- **Strong name:** The signed name of the assembly. This is the full identifier for the assembly and includes the public key used to sign the assembly, version number, and simple assembly name (among other items).

- **URL:** The actual download location for the code. In most cases, you'll see the site and URL used together. For example, this entry might be `http://www.abc_corporation.com/mydownload/simplestuff.dll`.
- **Zone:** The zone of origin for the code. For example, if the application obtains the code from the Internet, you'll see Internet in this category.

## Adding Security Roles

Role-Based Security (RBS) is the counterpart to CAS. While CAS strives to control security by controlling the tasks that code can perform (regardless of what the user can do), RBS places the user in a specific role to control what the application presents as functionality. A user can have several roles, depending on need, location, and task. For example, a user can easily be in the manager role when creating new accounts, but the standard user role when adding data to a database. The idea is to control what the user does based on the user's specific need. A user can also fill the roles of local user and remote user based on location. When the user works from a coffee shop, the application can place the user in the remote user role to help prevent possible data corruption. In addition, the remote user role may help prevent an outsider from eavesdropping on sensitive information. In short, RBS controls the user, while CAS controls the code. This two-pronged approach provides considerable flexibility.

RBS roles are completely free-form. You can create as many roles as needed to define an application completely (unlike zones, where the zones are predefined). The methods used to manage RBS appear in the `Principal` and `PrincipalPermission` classes. You use methods such as `IsInRole()` to determine the current user's role and configure the application appropriately. It's also possible to use RBS in several ways:

- **Imperative security:** As part of an in-code `Demand()`
- **Declarative security:** As part of an attribute-based `Demand()`
- **Directly:** Using code to examine the evidence presented by the `Principal` object

## Adding Permissions

The permissions granted or denied by NT security present one level of security; the permissions provided by the classes in the `System.Security.Permissions` namespace (`http://msdn.microsoft.com/library/system.security.permissions.aspx`) present a second level of security. This second level provides fine-grained control over specific kinds of tasks, rather than the coarse general control provided by NT security. For example, the `FileDialogPermission` class controls how a user can interact with a file dialog box — a fine level of control not provided by NT security.

In many cases, you have a choice between imperative or declarative security in implementing permissions. For example, the `FileDialogPermission` class provides a means of controlling file dialogs using imperative security, while the `FileDialogPermissionAttribute` class provides the same level of control using declarative security. The choice between imperative security and declarative security is a matter of personal choice and level of desired control. Declarative security, which relies on attributes, generally affects an entire assembly, class, or method, while imperative security works at the code level. You use imperative security when you need the utmost control of the permissions and don't mind writing a little more code to get it.

Many developers have gotten used to setting policies using CAS. Unfortunately, Microsoft has removed this capability in the .NET Framework 4. Consequently, methods you've used in the past, such as `FileIOPermission.Deny()`, no longer work without adding the `<NetFx40_LegacySecurityPolicy enabled="true"/>` tag to your application (the documentation at http://msdn.microsoft.com/library/system.security.codeaccesspermission.deny.aspx shows that the method is obsolete). You can see the `<NetFx40_LegacySecurityPolicy enabled="true"/>` tag documentation at http://msdn.microsoft.com/library/dd409253.aspx. The change makes sense. Virus code could simply use `FileIOPermission.Assert()` to override any denied privilege created by a lower level. You can read about this update at http://msdn.microsoft.com/library/ee191568.aspx.

You should understand that setting permissions is still important, and that you may need to use the outdated methods, such as `FileIOPermission.Deny()`, on some occasions. The CAS Policy example described in the following sections demonstrates a few important permissions features. First, you'll see how to use both declarative and imperative security. Second, the example demonstrates the dangerous nature of using these older permissions in some environments.

> One way to reduce the risk of using permissions to set policy is to sign your executable. Signing the executable makes it tough for someone to modify your code without the Common Language Runtime (CLR) detecting the change. This means that denying a permission will actually deny it as intended as long as your code is defined correctly.

## Configuring the CAS Policy Example

The CAS Policy example begins with a Windows Forms application. You add a single button called Test (`btnTest`). In addition, you must add the following `using` statements to the application:

```
using System.IO;
using System.Security;
using System.Security.Permissions;
```

## Creating a Legacy Security Configuration

Because this application is using outdated `Deny()` methods, you must also add a configuration file to the application that allows the use of legacy security. The following steps describe how to perform this task:

1. Right-click the project entry in Solution Explorer and choose Add ⇨ New Item from the Context menu. You'll see the Add New Item dialog box shown in Figure 12-2.

# Considering Modern Application Security Requirements | 223

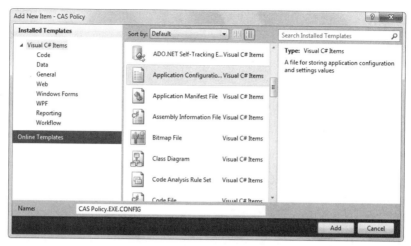

**FIGURE 12-2:** Add a configuration file to your application.

2. Highlight the Application Configuration File template.

3. Type `CAS Policy.EXE.CONFIG` in the Name field and click Add. Visual Studio adds the configuration file to your application and opens it for editing.

4. Type the following code within the <configuration> element:

   ```
   <runtime>
       <NetFx40_LegacySecurityPolicy enabled="true"/>
   </runtime>
   ```

5. Highlight the configuration file in Solution Explorer.

6. Choose Copy if Newer in the Copy to Output Directory property in the Properties window.

## Creating the CAS Policy Example Code

As previously mentioned, imperative security buries the security checks within the code, which means that you can perform the checks as needed. Listing 12-1 shows an example of imperative security.

**LISTING 12-1:** Using imperative security to control file access

Available for download on Wrox.com

```
// Use declarative security to restrict access to the
// test file.
[FileIOPermission(SecurityAction.Deny,
    AllLocalFiles=FileIOPermissionAccess.Read)]
private void btnTest_Click(object sender, EventArgs e)
{
    // Call the initial method for opening the file.
    UseSecurity();

    // Call the override method to try again.
    OverrideSecurity();
```

*continues*

**LISTING 12-1** *(continued)*

```
}

private void UseSecurity()
{
    Stream FS = null;   // A test file stream.

    // Try to access the object.
    try
    {
        FS = new FileStream(
            Application.StartupPath + @"\Temp.txt",
            FileMode.Open,
            FileAccess.Read);
    }
    catch (SecurityException SE)
    {
        // Display an error message if unsuccessful.
        MessageBox.Show("Access Denied\r\n" +
                    SE.Message,
                    "File IO Error",
                    MessageBoxButtons.OK,
                    MessageBoxIcon.Error);
        return;
    }

    // Display a success message.
    MessageBox.Show("File is open!",
                "File IO Success",
                MessageBoxButtons.OK,
                MessageBoxIcon.Information);

    // Close the file if opened.
    FS.Close();
}

// This method uses imperative security to override the
// previous permission denial.
private void OverrideSecurity()
{
    FileIOPermission FIOP;   // Permission object.
    Stream FS = null;        // A test file stream.

    // Create the permission object.
    FIOP = new FileIOPermission(
        FileIOPermissionAccess.Read,
        Application.StartupPath + @"\Temp.txt");

    // Allow access to the resource.
    FIOP.Assert();

    // Try to access the object.
    try
    {
        FS = new FileStream(
```

```
                    Application.StartupPath + @"\Temp.txt",
                    FileMode.Open,
                    FileAccess.Read);
            }
            catch (SecurityException SE)
            {
                // Display an error message if unsuccessful.
                MessageBox.Show("Access Denied\r\n" +
                            SE.Message,
                            "File IO Error",
                            MessageBoxButtons.OK,
                            MessageBoxIcon.Error);
                return;
            }

            // Display a success message.
            MessageBox.Show("File is open!",
                        "File IO Success",
                        MessageBoxButtons.OK,
                        MessageBoxIcon.Information);

            // Close the file if opened.
            FS.Close();
        }
```

The example begins with a declarative permission attribute, `FileIOPermission`. In this case, the `SecurityAction.Deny` value denies a permission, `AllLocalFiles` defines it as pertaining to all local files, and `FileIOPermissionAccess.Read` specifies that the read permission is denied. This declarative permission applies to the `btnTest_Click()` method and every method that `btnTest_Click()` calls.

To test out the permission, `btnTest_Click()` calls `UseSecurity()`. The `UseSecurity()` method creates a `Stream` object, `FS`, that it uses to open `Temp.TXT` for read access. Given that this action is denied, the open should fail. In this case, you do see the error message shown in Figure 12-3.

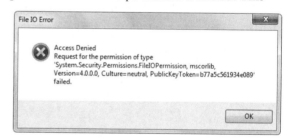

**FIGURE 12-3:** The declarative permission denies access to Temp.TXT.

At this point, `btnTest_Click()` calls `OverrideSecurity()`. However, this time the code begins by creating a `FileIOPermission` object, `FIOP`. This object is designed to request the `FileIOPermissionAccess.Read` permission for `Temp.TXT`. It demonstrates the imperative approach for setting permissions (as contrasted to the declarative approach used earlier in this section). When the code calls `FIOP.Assert()`, the system grants access to the file. The code then uses precisely the same technique as in the `UseSecurity()` method to create a `Stream` object, `FS`. In this case, the call is successful, so you see the success message. After the user clicks OK, the code simply closes the file by calling `FS.Close()`.

The point of this exercise is that permissions set using the classes in the `System.Security.Permissions` namespace are fluid. Code can easily change them as needed, which is why Microsoft is apparently abandoning at least the policy part of CAS. Still, this example shows how to implement the old-style code should you need it.

*This approach does come with some limitations, so you need to use it carefully. Native code images produced with the NGen utility can run slower. The basic reason for the performance loss is that the code marked with the* `<NetFx40_LegacySecurityPolicy>` *element must run as a Just-in-Time (JIT, pronounced "jit") assembly, rather than a native code image. In short, the CLR must compile the code every time before it can run it.*

## Working with Security Policies

Policies are an important part of working with security in the .NET Framework. The policy defines the security settings for one or more applications. When the CLR runs an application, it checks the application against the security policies and interacts with it appropriately. The .NET Framework actually supports four levels of policies, as shown in Table 12-1. (The version portion of the Configuration File Location entry is the version number of the .NET Framework that you're using.)

**TABLE 12-1:** Policy Levels Supported by the .NET Framework

| LEVEL | CONFIGURATION FILE LOCATION | DESCRIPTION |
| --- | --- | --- |
| Enterprise | %Systemroot%\Microsoft.NET\Framework\version\Config\enterprise.config | Defines policies that affect the organization as a whole. These policies are normally set as part of an Active Directory tree or forest. |
| Machine | %Systemroot%\Microsoft.NET\Framework\version\Config\security.config | Defines policies that affect all the users on a particular machine. This level has been eliminated in the .NET Framework 4. |
| User | %UserProfile%\Application Data\Microsoft\CLR Security Config\version\security.config | Defines policies that affect all the applications run by a particular machine user. |
| AppDomain | Normally, the application directory | Defines policies for a specific application. This level isn't enabled by default; you must create these policies as part of defining the application. |

You configure the enterprise, machine, and user policies using the Code Access Security Policy (CASPol.EXE) utility found in the %Systemroot%\Microsoft.NET\Framework\*version*\ directory of your system (where version is the version number of the .NET Framework you're using). The directions for using CASPol appear at http://msdn.microsoft.com/library/cb6t8dtz.aspx.

*At one time, Microsoft provided the* MSCorCfg.MSC *console to configure CAS policies. You can still obtain this tool by downloading the Microsoft Windows SDK for Windows Server 2008 and .NET Framework 3.5 from* http://www.microsoft.com/downloads/en/details.aspx?FamilyId=F26B1AA4-741A-433A-9BE5-FA919850BDBF. *However, the tool probably won't provide what you need when working with the .NET Framework 4 because Microsoft has eliminated many of the features that this tool supported in the past, such as machine-level policies. The new approach is to use security transparency. Check out the articles at* http://msdn.microsoft.com/library/2bc0cxhc.aspx *and* http://msdn.microsoft.com/library/dd233103.aspx *for further details.*

Within each of the security policy levels are code groups. Each code group defines a particular kind of code, such as all the code that runs on the system or a special application designed to meet mission-critical needs for your organization. The code groups are further divided by zones, such as MyComputer and LocalIntranet. Microsoft is slowly getting rid of the whole policy setup in favor of something new that works with Windows 7 features such as AppLocker (see http://technet.microsoft.com/windows/dd320283.aspx), but for now you'll still be working with policy levels.

One of the more interesting policy levels from a developer perspective is the AppDomain. The AppDomain policies are completely under developer control and make it possible for you to create a completely secure application without any administrator intervention. The following sections describe how to create an AppDomain application.

### Configuring the AppDomain Example

The AppDomain example consists of two applications: Main (the starting application) and Called (the application started with the AppDomain in place). The following steps help you create this solution:

1. Choose File ➪ New ➪ Project. You'll see the New Project dialog box.
2. Highlight the Windows Forms Application template.
3. Type **Main** in the Name field and **AppDomain** in the Solution field, as shown in Figure 12-4. Click OK. Visual Studio creates the AppDomain solution and Main project for you.
4. Right-click the solution entry in Solution Explorer and choose Add ➪ Add Project from the Context menu. You'll see the Add New Project dialog box shown in Figure 12-5.

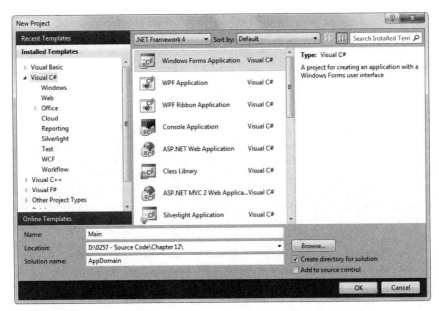

**FIGURE 12-4:** Create a Windows Forms application as the starting project.

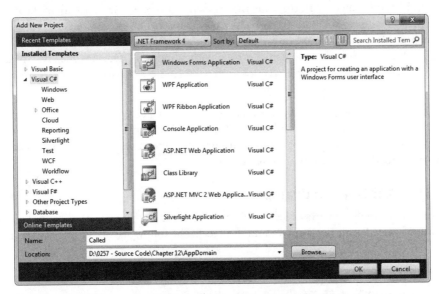

**FIGURE 12-5:** Define a second project to run using the AppDomain.

5. Type **Called** in the Name field and click OK. Visual Studio adds the secondary project to your solution.

6. Right-click the Called project in Solution Explorer and choose Properties from the Context menu. You'll see the project's Properties window.

7. Select the Build tab. You'll see the build options for the project.
8. Select the Debug option in the Configuration field.
9. Type `..\Main\bin\Debug\` in the Output Path field. Your properties window should look like the one shown in Figure 12-6.

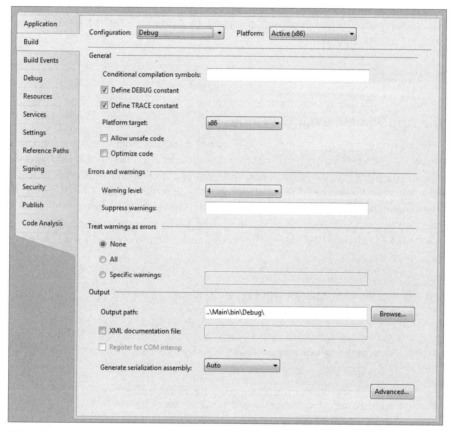

**FIGURE 12-6:** Define a second project to run using the AppDomain.

10. Select the Release option in the Configuration field.
11. Type `..\Main\bin\Release\` in the Output Path field. Visual Studio will now output the Called project's executable to the Main project's output directory.

The two applications will have one form each. The Main project will have two buttons on its form, one labeled Default (`btnDefault`), which performs a task using the default security settings, and the other labeled AppDomain (`btnAppDomain`), which performs a task using special security settings using the Called application. Because the AppDomain policy features provided by CAS were another in a long line of security casualties in the .NET Framework 4, you also need to add a configuration file using the procedure found in the "Creating a Legacy Security Configuration" section of this chapter. The Main project requires the following `using` statements:

```
using System.IO;
using System.Security;
using System.Security.Policy;
```

The Called application has a single button, Secure (`btnSecure`), which performs a task using the security settings imposed by the AppDomain created by Main. The Called application requires the following `using` statements:

```
using System.IO;
using System.Security;
```

## Creating the AppDomain Example Code

The idea behind this example is to create a sandbox in which another application operates. The standard security gives full access to all system resources, but you may not trust the code in an application, so you place it in an environment where it can do little harm. In this case, the example shows that full access allows the Main application to open a file, but the LocalIntranet policy restricts the Called application so it can't open the file. This example relies on the same file opening code shown for the `UseSecurity()` method in Listing 12-1 for both `btnDefault_Click()` and `btnSecure_Click()`. Listing 12-2 shows the special code used to create a sandbox in which the Called application executes.

**LISTING 12-2:** Creating an AppDomain to control file access

Available for download on Wrox.com

```
private void btnAppDomain_Click(object sender, EventArgs e)
{
    // Define a new AppDomain policy.
    PolicyLevel AppPolicy = PolicyLevel.CreateAppDomainLevel();

    // Define a membership condition for the policy.
    AllMembershipCondition Members = new AllMembershipCondition();

    // Create a permission set for the Called application.
    PermissionSet CalledPermissions =
        new PermissionSet(AppPolicy.GetNamedPermissionSet("LocalIntranet"));

    // Define a policy statement based on the permssions for
    // the Called application.
    PolicyStatement CalledPolicy = new PolicyStatement(CalledPermissions);

    // Create a code group for the Called application policy. The hierarchy
    // is AppPolicy->AllCodeGroup->CalledPolicy.
    CodeGroup AllCodeGroup = new UnionCodeGroup(Members, CalledPolicy);

    // Assign the code group to the application policy created earlier.
    AppPolicy.RootCodeGroup = AllCodeGroup;

    // Define an application domain that includes the policies for the
```

```
        // Called application.
        AppDomain CalledDomain = System.AppDomain.CreateDomain("CustomDomain");

        // Assign the domain policy to the new domain.
        CalledDomain.SetAppDomainPolicy(AppPolicy);

        // Use the domain to execute the Called application with the
        // appropriate rights.
        CalledDomain.ExecuteAssembly(Application.StartupPath + @"\Called.EXE");
    }
```

You'll remember from previous discussions that there are four policy levels: Enterprise, Machine, User, and AppDomain. The code begins by creating an AppDomain policy level, `AppPolicy`, by calling `PolicyLevel.CreateAppDomainLevel()`.

A policy level is worthless unless it has members and assigns permissions to those members. The next step in the code is to create members using an `AllMembershipCondition` object, `Members`. Essentially, this membership condition states that all the code that runs in the AppDomain policy is affected by the conditions of the membership — the permissions you assign to the policy. Therefore, the next step is to state the permission for the policy by creating a `PermissionSet` object, `CalledPermissions`. You can assign any permissions you want to the policy, but in this case, the code calls `AppPolicy.GetNamedPermissionSet()` to obtain the default permissions assigned to the LocalIntranet zone. This permission, and any other permissions you decide you want to add, are placed within a `PolicyStatement` object, `CalledPolicy`.

At this point, you have a policy level, a membership condition, and a set of permissions enclosed in a policy statement. The next step is to create a code group to contain the membership condition and its associated permissions, and then to assign the code group to the policy level. The code begins this step by creating a `CodeGroup` object, `AllCodeGroup`, using the `UnionCodeGroup()` constructor with `Members` and `CalledPolicy` as arguments. The code then assigns `AllCodeGroup` to the `AppPolicy.RootCodeGroup` property. You now have a complete AppDomain policy to work with.

The code needs to create a domain to implement the policy at this point, so it creates an `AppDomain` object, `CalledDomain`, using `System.AppDomain.CreateDomain()` and gives it a name of `CustomDomain`. A call to `CalledDomain.SetAppDomainPolicy()` applies `AppPolicy` to the AppDomain. The code ends with a call to `CalledDomain.ExecuteAssembly()` with the location of `Called.EXE`.

When you run this example, you can click Default to see that the Main application truly can access `Temp.TXT` without any problem. The example displays the expected success message. Click AppDomain and you'll see the Called application form appear. Click Secure and you'll see an error message (see Figure 12-3) — the Called application can't access `Temp.TXT` even though it uses the same code as the Main application. The reason is that the Called application executes within the LocalIntranet zone and lacks the required permission.

## DEFINING YOUR APPLICATION'S SECURITY NEEDS

Even though basic NT security is a good place to start your security for an application, modern applications need more, and you'll find this additional support in the .NET Framework. The emphasis of NT security is on the user or other principal. A resource has a lock on it that the user's rights unlock. The idea is simple, but it doesn't address a critical logic error that the .NET Framework addresses. Most of the .NET Framework additions address code — limiting what the code can do with a resource or data regardless of what rights the user might have. In short, the .NET Framework functionality balances the security picture and blocks another critical source of entry that nefarious individuals have relied upon in the past.

Table 12-2 describes the types of security that the .NET Framework makes available to you. You may not need every type within your application, but it's a good idea to use as many types as reasonable. The important issue is to consider how users work with your application and how the application interacts with system resources. For example, if your application communicates with a server or the Internet, it's a good idea to encrypt the communication to ensure that no one can listen in. Each .NET Framework type addresses a specific security need.

**TABLE 12-2:** Types of Security Provided by the .NET Framework

| SECURITY TYPE | PURPOSE | DESCRIPTION |
| --- | --- | --- |
| Evidence-based Security | This feature determines what rights to grant to code, based on information gathered about it. | The Common Language Runtime (CLR) examines the information it knows about an assembly and determines what rights to grant that code based on the evidence. The evidence is actually matched against a security policy, which is a series of settings that defines how the administrator wants to secure a system. |
| Code Access Security (CAS) | The CLR uses this feature to determine whether all the assemblies in a calling chain (stack) have rights to use a particular resource or perform a particular task. | All the code in the calling chain must have the required rights. Otherwise, CLR generates a security error that you can use to detect security breaches. The purpose of this check is to ensure that external code can't intercept rights that it doesn't deserve. Note that the policy portion of CAS has been removed in the .NET Framework 4. |
| Defined Verification Process | The verification process ensures that the code doesn't include any fatal flaws that would keep it from running. | Before the Just-in-Time (JIT) compiler accepts the Microsoft Intermediate Language (MSIL) assembly, it checks the code the assembly contains for type safety and other errors. The checks also determine if an external force has modified strongly named code. After these checks are performed, JIT compiles the MSIL into native code. The CLR can run a verified assembly in isolation so that it doesn't affect any other assembly (and more importantly, other assemblies can't affect it). |

| SECURITY TYPE | PURPOSE | DESCRIPTION |
| --- | --- | --- |
| Role-Based Security | This feature determines the user's current role and assigns rights appropriate to that role, rather than ones based on the user's login. | If you know how Role-Based Security works in COM+, you have a good idea of how it works in .NET. Instead of assigning security to individuals or groups, you assign it based on the role that an individual or group will perform. The Windows Security Identifier (SID) security is limited in that you can control entire files, but not parts of those files. Role-Based Security still relies on identifying the user through a login or other means. The main advantage is that you can ask the security system about the user's role and allow access to program features based on that role. An administrator will likely have access to all the features of a program, but individual users may only have access to a subset of the features. |
| Cryptography | The system uses this feature to keep outsiders (human or computer) from reading data in any location. | The advantages of cryptography are many. The concept is simple — you make data unreadable by using an algorithm, coupled with a key, to mix the information up. When the originator supplies the correct key to another algorithm, the original data is returned. Over the years, the power of computers has increased, making old cryptology techniques suspect. The .NET Framework supports the latest cryptographic techniques, which ensure your data remains safe. |
| Separate Application Domains | This feature keeps the code in an application separated into parts so that a less secure part can't interfere with a more secure part. | You can write .NET code in such a way that some of the pieces run in a separate domain. It's a COM-type concept, where the code is isolated from the other code in your program. Many developers use this feature to load special code, run it, and then unload that code without stopping the program. For example, a browser could use this technique to load and unload plug-ins. This feature also works well for security. It helps you run code at different security levels in separate domains to ensure true isolation. |

## CREATING AN APPLICATION WITH ENHANCED SECURITY

You've seen in previous sections that the .NET Framework provides a number of ways to secure applications using policies. However, that's just part of the picture. The .NET Framework also makes it possible to keep the application environment safe by examining the evidence that other assemblies provide. For example, knowing the zone that the assembly comes from is important.

Your application might trust an assembly from the MyComputer zone, but not one from the Internet zone. Likewise, you need to know the user's role. Remember that a user can wear several hats (have different roles) and that you need to tune the application to work within those roles. Finally, permissions, presented as evidence, tell you what the object at hand (assembly or user) can do. The following sections examine the use of zones, roles, and permissions in .NET applications.

## Developing for Zones

Zone membership is important because it gives you a quick, standardized indicator of the code's source. For example, if the code comes from the local machine, it'll be part of the MyComputer zone. The following sections describe how to check the zone for an assembly using code.

### Considering Evidence within an Application

The word "evidence" brings up the vision for many people of a court with judge and jury. The term is quite appropriate for the .NET Framework because any code that wants to execute must present its case before CLR and deliver evidence to validate any requests. CLR makes a decision about the code based on the evidence and decides how the evidence fits within the current policies (laws) of the run time as set by the network administrator. Theoretically, controlling security with evidence as CLR does allows applications built upon the .NET Framework to transcend limitations of the underlying operating system. This view is largely true. However, remember that CLR is running on top of the underlying operating system and is therefore subject to its limitations. Here's the typical evidence-based sequence of events:

1. The assembly demands access to data, resources, or other protected elements.
2. CLR requests evidence of the assembly's origins and security documents (such as a digital signature).
3. After receiving the evidence from the assembly, CLR runs the evidence through a security policy.
4. The security policy outputs a permission based on the evidence and the network administrator settings.
5. The code gains some level of access to the protected element if the evidence supports such access; otherwise, CLR denies the request.

Note that the assembly must demand access before any part of the security process occurs. When working with NT security, the system normally verifies and assigns security at the front end of the process — when the program first runs. (A program can request additional rights later or perform other security tasks.) CLR performs verifications as needed to enhance system performance.

Evidence includes a number of code features. CLR divides code into verifiable and non-verifiable types. Verifiable code is type-safe and adheres to all the policies defined by the .NET Framework. Consequently, code output by Visual Basic is always verifiable. Visual C# can output non-verifiable code because it includes direct pointer manipulation features. However, in general, CLR considers C# code verifiable. Visual C++ is a little less verifiable because it not only includes pointer support, but also such functions as `reinterpret_cast`. Older code, such as that found in most Windows DLLs and COM objects, is always non-verifiable. Interestingly enough, loading unverifiable code is a right that CLR grants to local applications only (as a default). Remote programs have to request this right.

CLR defines two kinds of evidence: assembly and host. You can create any number of custom evidence types by deriving from the `Evidence` class. Any custom evidence resides within the assembly as assembly evidence. CLR also ships with seven common evidence classes that cover most needs. These seven classes provide host evidence because Microsoft implemented them as part of the host (CLR).

- `ApplicationDirectory`
- `Hash`
- `Publisher`
- `Site`
- `StrongName`
- `URL`
- `Zone`

The `ApplicationDirectory`, `Site`, `URL`, and `Zone` classes show where the code came from. The `Publisher` and `StrongName` classes tell who wrote the code. Finally, the `Hash` class defines a special number that identifies the assembly as a unique entity — it shows whether someone has tampered with the content of the assembly.

### Configuring the Check Membership Example

The example begins with a Windows Forms application. You add a button, Test (`btnTest`), to test the example code. In addition, you need to add the following `using` statements:

```
using System.Reflection;
using System.Security;
using System.Security.Policy;
```

### Creating the Check Membership Code

Each of the host evidence classes has an associated membership condition class. For example, the `ApplicationDirectory` class, which is the evidence presented to the policy, uses the associated `ApplicationDirectoryMembershipCondition` class to determine its membership status. When CLR passes evidence to one of the membership classes, the object determines if the assembly in question belongs to a particular code group. If the assembly is a member of the code group, then CLR authorizes the assembly to perform code group tasks. Listing 12-3 shows a typical example of membership testing.

**LISTING 12-3:** Discovering code group membership

```
private void btnTest_Click(object sender, System.EventArgs e)
{
   // Get the current assembly.
   Assembly Asm;
```

*continues*

**LISTING 12-3** *(continued)*

```
    Asm = Assembly.GetExecutingAssembly();

    // Get the evidence from the assembly.
    Evidence EV;
    EV = Asm.Evidence;

    // Create a membership condition check.
    ZoneMembershipCondition ZoneMember;
    ZoneMember = new ZoneMembershipCondition(SecurityZone.MyComputer);

    // Check for application directory membership.
    if (ZoneMember.Check(EV))
        MessageBox.Show("Assembly is a member.");
    else
        MessageBox.Show("Assembly doesn't belong.");
}
```

The code begins by accessing the assembly to get the evidence needed for this check. The example gains access to the current assembly using the `GetExecutingAssembly()` method. However, you could also use calls such as `LoadAssembly()` to load an external assembly.

Once the code has access to the assembly, it uses the `Evidence` property to get all the evidence for the assembly. Most assemblies support four kinds of evidence as a minimum: `Zone`, `URL`, `StrongName`, and `Hash`.

This code checks for `Zone` class membership using the `ZoneMembershipCondition` object `ZoneMember`. As part of creating `ZoneMember`, you must define the `SecurityZone` enumeration member to check.

The `Check()` method returns a simple Boolean value indicating whether the assembly is part of the specified class, which is `SecurityZone.MyComputer` in this case. Because you're executing this program from your desktop, the check likely passes in this case. However, if you were to check for some other zone, the check would fail. Note that checking membership doesn't generate a permission object — all this check does is tell you when an assembly has a particular membership.

## Developing for Security Roles

Role-Based Security asks the question of whether some entity (a user, the system, a program) is in a particular role. If it's in that role, the entity can likely access a system resource or application feature safely. The concept of a role is different from something more absolute like a group. When you're a member of a group, you have the same access whether you access the system from a local machine or the Internet. A role does include the idea of group membership, but this is membership based on the environment — the kind of access requested in a given situation from a specific location. An entity's security role changes, rather than being absolute. The following sections describe how to check a user's role based on the evidence presented by the application's current domain.

### Configuring the Security Role Example

This example begins with a Windows Forms application. You add a Test button (`btnTest`). In addition, you need to add the following `using` statements:

```
using System.Security.Principal;
using System.Threading;
```

## Creating the Security Role Example Code

It may surprise you to learn how many roles a particular user fulfills at any given time. The example in this section obtains the identity of the current user — the one logged in to the system. It then discovers the roles that the user fulfills. Listing 12-4 shows the code required for this example.

**LISTING 12-4:** Using the IsInRole() method

```
private void btnTest_Click(object sender, System.EventArgs e)
{
   WindowsPrincipal  MyPrincipal;   // The role we want to check.
   AppDomain         MyDomain;      // The current domain.
   StringBuilder     Output;        // Example output data.
   Array             RoleTypes;     // Standard role types.

   // Set the principal policy for this application.
   MyDomain = Thread.GetDomain();
   MyDomain.SetPrincipalPolicy(PrincipalPolicy.WindowsPrincipal);

   // Get the role and other security information for the current
   // user.
   MyPrincipal = (WindowsPrincipal)Thread.CurrentPrincipal;

   // Get the user name.
   Output = new StringBuilder();
   Output.Append("Name: " + MyPrincipal.Identity.Name);

   // Get the authentication type.
   Output.Append("\r\nAuthentication: " +
      MyPrincipal.Identity.AuthenticationType);

   Output.Append("\r\n\r\nRoles:");

   // Create an array of built-in role types.
   RoleTypes = Enum.GetValues(typeof(WindowsBuiltInRole));

   // Check the user's role.
   foreach(WindowsBuiltInRole Role in RoleTypes)
   {
      // Store the role name.
      if (Role.ToString().Length <= 5)
         Output.Append("\r\n" + Role.ToString() + ":\t\t");
      else
         Output.Append("\r\n" + Role.ToString() + ":\t");

      // Store the role value.
      Output.Append(
```

*continues*

**LISTING 12-4** *(continued)*

```
                MyPrincipal.IsInRole(WindowsBuiltInRole.User).ToString());
    }

    // Output the result.
    MessageBox.Show(Output.ToString(),
                "User Role Values",
                MessageBoxButtons.OK,
                MessageBoxIcon.Information);
}
```

The code begins by obtaining the domain for the current thread. The "Working with Security Policies" section of this chapter shows how a domain is created programmatically — the example in Listing 12-4 reverses the process and views the domain as it already exists in the application. The program executes in an application domain, and we can obtain information about that domain. In this case, the code sets the security policy for this domain equal to the same policy used by Windows. The application is now executing with the same policy that the user has when working with Windows. You could theoretically change that policy depending on conditions such as user location.

Now that the code has set the security policy for the thread, it uses that information to create a `WindowsPrincipal` object, `MyPrincipal`. This object knows all kinds of security information about the user. The code shows how you can obtain the user name and the method of authentication used.

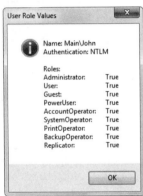

**FIGURE 12-7:** A view of the output from an IsInRole() method check.

The most important use for `MyPrincipal` is to determine which roles the user is in. You probably haven't defined any roles as part of a CASPol configuration process, so the example uses the `WindowsBuiltInRole` enumeration to check the standard types. If the user is in the requested role, the `IsInRole()` method returns `true`. This value is converted to a string and placed in `Output`. Figure 12-7 shows typical output from this example. Of course, the results will change when you run the program on your system because the dialog box will reflect your name and rights.

The important concept to take away from this example is that Role-Based Security performs a task similar to standard Windows security, but using a different and more flexible technique. Because of the differences between Windows security and Role-Based Security, you may need to rely on the groups provided by NT security, especially when working in an environment that has a mix of managed and unmanaged code. Chapter 10 discusses how to work with NT security within an application.

## Developing for Permissions

So far, the chapter has discussed the kinds of security you can use, how the system uses evidence, and how to determine membership in a particular code group. All these facts help you understand how security works, but your code still doesn't have permission to perform any tasks. When CLR loads an assembly, the assembly lacks any rights — it can't even execute code. Consequently, the first task CLR must perform with the assembly is to use the evidence and the code group memberships to determine what permissions the assembly has. To perform this task, CLR must run the evidence through the policies set up by the network administrator. The following sections discuss how to obtain two types of permissions within an application.

## Configuring the Obtain Permissions Example

The example begins with a Windows Forms application. Add two buttons, Test (btnTest) and URL Test (btnUrlTest). The first button checks the user's local permissions. The second checks the user's access to an URL. The application also requires access to a textbox, txtUrl, for the URL to check and txtOutput for the application output. Unfortunately, the SecurityManager is another .NET Framework 4 casualty, so you also need to add a configuration file using the procedure found in the "Creating a Legacy Security Configuration" section of the chapter. You must add the following using statements to the application:

```
using System.Reflection;
using System.Security;
using System.Security.Policy;
```

## Creating the Local Permissions Code

The first part of the application obtains a list of permissions for the user on the local machine. In most cases, unless the administrator has set policies using the CASPol utility, the output will simply say that the user has unrestricted rights. Listing 12-5 shows the code needed for this example.

**LISTING 12-5:** Getting a permission list using a policy

```
private void btnTest_Click(object sender, System.EventArgs e)
{
    IEnumerator       Policies;   // Security policies.
    PolicyLevel       Policy;     // A single policy.
    PolicyStatement   Statement;  // A list of permissions.
    Assembly          Asm;        // Current assembly.
    Evidence          EV;         // Security evidence.
    StringBuilder     Output;     // Output data.

    // Initialize the output.
    Output = new StringBuilder();

    // Get the current assembly.
    Asm = Assembly.GetExecutingAssembly();

    // Get the evidence from the assembly.
    EV = Asm.Evidence;

    // Get all of the policies.
    Policies = SecurityManager.PolicyHierarchy();
    while (Policies.MoveNext())
    {
        // Get the current policy.
        Policy = (PolicyLevel)Policies.Current;
```

*continues*

**LISTING 12-5** *(continued)*

```
        // Get the policy name.
        Output.Append("Policy: " + Policy.Label);

        // Determine the permissions for this policy.
        Statement = Policy.Resolve(EV);
        Output.Append("\r\n" + Statement.PermissionSet.Count +
            " Permissions:\r\n" + Statement.PermissionSet);

        // Get the attributes.
        Output.Append("Attributes: " +
            Statement.Attributes + "\r\n\r\n");
    }

    // Display the results.
    txtOutput.Text = Output.ToString();
}
```

The code begins by getting the executing assembly and the evidence it contains. It uses this information to create a list of policies using the `SecurityManager.PolicyHierarchy()` method. The `SecurityManager` is another of the CAS policy features, so it's obsolete in the .NET Framework 4. This method actually returns a list of policy objects you can enumerate using an `IEnumerator` object, `Policies`.

The `PolicyLevel` object, `Policy`, contains the individual policies associated with the assembly. Notice the `Policy.Resolve()` method call. This call sends the assembly evidence to the policy for evaluation. The output is a `PolicyStatement` object, which includes the permissions generated by the policy. Each `PolicyStatement` includes a `PermissionSet` property that defines the permissions for the assembly based on that policy. Figure 12-8 shows typical output for this part of the example on a machine that hasn't been configured by the administrator to use specific policies.

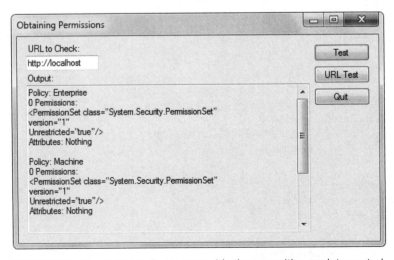

**FIGURE 12-8:** The default policy is to provide the user with complete control.

## Creating the URL Permissions Code

You can use other techniques to build a set of permissions. For example, you can determine the permissions for a Website. However, you must build the evidence because it doesn't already exist in a neat package. In addition, you need to consider which evidence to present to the policy. Listing 12-6 shows an example of building evidence to access a Website (you can supply any URL you wish).

**LISTING 12-6:** Building evidence to obtain permissions

```
private void btnUrlTest_Click(object sender, EventArgs e)
{
    PermissionSet Perms;    // A single policy.
    Evidence EV;            // Security evidence.

    // Create evidence based on the URL.
    EV = new Evidence();

    // Fill the evidence with information.
    EV.AddHostEvidence(new Url(txtUrl.Text));
    EV.AddHostEvidence(Zone.CreateFromUrl(txtUrl.Text));

    // Determine the current permissions.
    Perms = SecurityManager.ResolvePolicy(EV);

    // Create the output.
    txtOutput.Text = Perms.ToString();
}
```

This example still relies on evidence. However, you must build the evidence using the `AddHostEvidence()` method. The evidence consists of an URL and a Zone in this situation, but you can use any acceptable form of evidence. Notice that this example uses the `SecurityManager` object to resolve the policy. Figure 12-9 shows the output from this example.

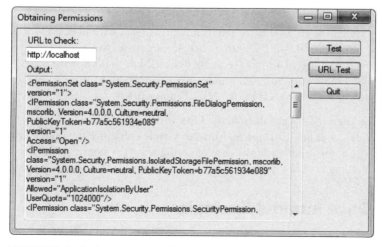

**FIGURE 12-9:** Code access permissions generally appear in XML format.

Notice that the information uses an XML format. Each of the permissions listed includes the full class information, which makes it easier to determine precisely what the permission means. For example, the first permission is `System.Security.Permissions.FileDialogPermission`. This permission controls access to the file dialog box. The Website in question can't access all the file dialog features, but it can open the file dialog, which is all that the user needs in order to open or save a file in most cases. One of the last items in the list (at least for this URL) is the `System.Security.Permissions.ZoneIdentityPermission`. This permission shows that the URL is within the Internet zone for my machine. Testing URLs on the Web correctly shows zone change.

> *You can find a complete list of standard permissions for the .NET Framework at* `http://msdn.microsoft.com/library/24ed02w7.aspx`. *It's also easy to find additional class resources on the .NET 247 site at* `http://www.dotnet247.com/247reference/System/Security/Permissions/System.Security.Permissions.aspx`.

Once you have access to permission objects, you can modify the permissions for the object by using the `PermissionSet` members. For example, you can add a permission using either the `AddPermission()` or the `Assert()` methods. Be aware, however, that the `Assert()` method can cause security vulnerabilities by giving an object rights that other objects in the hierarchy don't have. In addition, the `Assert()` method requires that the code have the `SecurityPermissionFlag.Assertion` permission, which CLR doesn't grant in some cases (making an `Assert()` method call harder to make than `AddPermission()`). Neither of these methods will allow you to add permissions that the current policy doesn't allow — you can't use these calls to circumvent security measures. You can also use the `FromXml()` method to load an XML formatted file that contains rights the object should have.

## DEVISING AND IMPLEMENTING A SECURITY POLICY

One of the cornerstones of security using .NET is to create a security policy. Many of the examples in this chapter have relied on the existing technique for performing this task, with updating to accommodate the missing functionality in the .NET Framework 4. Of course, this could leave you with the impression that Microsoft no longer supports security policies, but that's not the case. No matter which version of the .NET Framework you use, policies are essential and the actual names of the zones used for policies haven't changed — even in the .NET Framework 4.

What has changed is the method used to implement policies. One approach, the easiest of the techniques that Microsoft provides, is called ClickOnce. You can simply configure the policy as part of your application setup, and the application will take care of configuring the system when the user installs the application. The following sections describe the ClickOnce approach in more detail.

### Configuring the ClickOnce Intranet Example

The ClickOnce Intranet example begins with a Windows Forms application. You add a Test button (`btnTest`) for some test code to the form. This example relies on the same file opening code shown for the `UseSecurity()` method in Listing 12-1. After you add the button and its associated code, you need to configure the application to use ClickOnce as described in the following steps:

1. Right-click the project entry in Solution Explorer and choose Properties from the Context menu. You see the application's Properties window.
2. Select the Security tab.
3. Check Enable ClickOnce Security Settings. Visual Studio enables some additional security settings in the window.
4. Choose the This is a Partial Trust Application option.
5. Choose Local Intranet from the drop-down list box. Your configuration should look like the one shown in Figure 12-10.

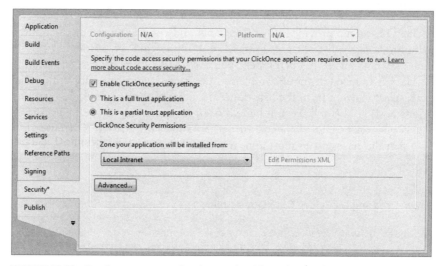

**FIGURE 12-10:** Configure your application so that it's no longer fully trusted.

## Debugging and Installing the ClickOnce Intranet Example

The default Visual Studio setup automatically configures the debugger to run within the zone that you've designated. Simply press F5 or click Start Debugging as usual. In this case, when you click Test, you'll see an error message because the application is running in the Intranet zone, but now go to the application's `Debug` directory in Windows Explorer and run the application there. You'll discover that the application can open the file as normal — as if the application is running with full rights (and it is).

The ClickOnce technology configures the user's machine when the user installs the application. You'll see a `ClickOnce Intranet.APPLICATION` file in the Debug folder. Double-click this file and you'll start the installation process. First, you'll see a verification dialog box. After the verification process is complete, you'll see the dialog box shown in Figure 12-11.

At this point, you can click Install. After a few moments, the application is installed and automatically starts for you. If you click Test now, you'll see the error message you had expected in the first place. The ClickOnce technique provides just another way to implement the security.

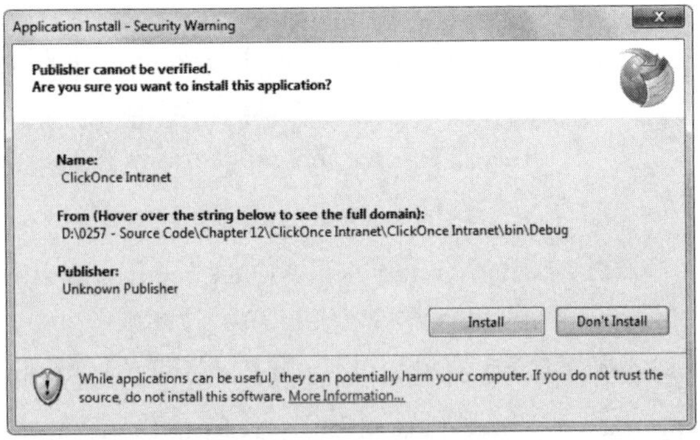

**FIGURE 12-11:** ClickOnce provides an installation file you can use for local or Internet installations.

## Configuring the ClickOnce Custom Example

The default ClickOnce setup provides a Local Intranet and an Internet setting, but nothing else. You might find that the list of rights granted your application is far from helpful. In fact, the application may not run at all. Fortunately, you can use the same process shown in the "Configuring the ClickOnce Intranet Example" section to configure your application in another way. This time, select Custom from the list, rather than one of the preconfigured options. Click Edit Permissions XML and you'll see another editor open where you can add permissions to the `<applicationRequestMinimum>` element. Listing 12-7 shows the custom XML used for this example. Note that the class entries must appear on one line, even though they appear on multiple lines in the book.

**LISTING 12-7:** Creating a custom ClickOnce policy

*Available for download on Wrox.com*

```
<PermissionSet class="System.Security.PermissionSet"
                    version="1" ID="Custom" SameSite="site">
    <IPermission
        version="1"
        class="System.Security.Permissions.SecurityPermission, mscorlib,
            Version=4.0.0.0, Culture=neutral, PublicKeyToken=b77a5c561934e089"
        Flags="Assertion, Execution, BindingRedirects" />
    <IPermission
        version="1"
        class="System.Security.Permissions.UIPermission, mscorlib,
            Version=4.0.0.0, Culture=neutral, PublicKeyToken=b77a5c561934e089"
        Unrestricted="true" />
    <IPermission
        version="1"
        class="System.Security.Permissions.FileIOPermission, mscorlib,
            Version=4.0.0.0, Culture=neutral, PublicKeyToken=b77a5c561934e089"
        Unrestricted="true" />
</PermissionSet>
```

This set of permissions reflects the minimum required to make the example run. The default Local Intranet actually provides more rights than those shown here (open the `ClickOnce Intranet.EXE .MANIFEST` file found in the `Debug` folder to see these rights for yourself).

A typical <IPermission> element contains the version attribute, which is always set to 1, the class attribute, which contains the class information for the permission you want to provide, and the Unrestricted attribute, which is set to true to allow the permission. Note the differing capitalization used for the attributes. You must use the proper capitalization for ClickOnce to work.

Notice that the System.Security.Permissions.SecurityPermission class doesn't use the Unrestricted attribute. Instead, it uses a Flags attribute. If you look at the documentation for this class, you'll find that Flags is one of the properties it supports. The list of flags shows which specific rights the user obtains. In many cases, it's possible to provide specific permissions by using class properties in place of the Unrestricted attribute.

When you run the ClickOnce Custom example, you'll find that the user can now access the file, just as if the application were run locally. However, this version of the application isn't running with full permissions. It has only the permissions shown in Listing 12-7, so application access is controlled.

## AVOIDING TOO MUCH SECURITY

You may think that it's impossible to secure your application too much, given the hostile nature of the application environment today, but it is. One of the major factors you have to consider is the balance between the user's getting work done and the need to keep users, applications, and data safe from external influences. The safest application in the world is one that does absolutely nothing at all — it has no interface, interacts with no files, and doesn't work with the process. Of course, such an application is completely useless and presents a kind of extreme example that no developer would ever create. However, it's possible to create something less egregious that's equally useless to the user. Simply denying access to all the files the user needs to accomplish a task is enough to make the application nearly useless. Therefore, you have to make a list of things the user needs and prepare the security to work around these items safely, rather than deny access to them.

Microsoft has provided the optimal example of another problem. If you make the security features of your application noticeable, especially if they become annoying, the user is going to find a way to disable them. It may surprise you to see just how inventive users can become when they're completely annoyed. When the user finally fails to find a solution to the annoyance, you can be sure the application won't be used. The user will simply find another way to accomplish the task. An application that provides annoying security isn't used. If nothing else, the user will run (not walk) to the nearest door and find another place to work.

> *Just so you don't think that Microsoft is the only culprit, many people find other products just as annoying from a security perspective. For example, some people install ZoneAlarm on their computers, but find that it's overly strict when fully operating. It questions a great many things and throws up a warning that the user has difficulty getting rid of. Some users leave it on in "learning" mode, which reduces its usefulness to them and which they have to click to renew periodically.*

Lack of access and annoying are two common and fairly obvious problems. Security also needs to provide its services without slowing the application down or making it useless on all the platforms the user works with. The need for speed is something all users have. If your application is slow or simply fails to work everywhere the user needs it, you'll definitely hear complaints. The user may also find some inconvenient ways of getting around the problem. In short, security can't encumber the application and remain useful.

Security can also backfire on the developer. Everyone might be happy with the application except for one really weird bug that pops up occasionally. It doesn't appear often enough to annoy the user, but it does appear often enough that you have to fix it. Unfortunately, your security has made it impossible to locate the bug, or perhaps the bug is the result of some odd security requirement. Perhaps the application fails when it tries to write settings to a particular part of the registry because you've blocked that part of the registry from access. Security really can become painful for the developer as well as the user. Look at security when you need to find those odd bugs that appear to defy any logical explanation. More than a few developers have caused their own woe by being overzealous with the security settings.

A final precaution on the overuse of security: be alert for instances when it begins to interfere with other applications. In general, you need to provide security that protects your application, but doesn't completely isolate it from the outside world. Most applications today have to interact with other applications to be useful. In short, you have to weigh the risks of interaction and determine whether the interaction will truly cause a problem.

## MOVING YOUR APPLICATIONS TO WINDOWS 7

This chapter has explored the enhanced security features that the .NET Framework provides and has placed them within the context of NT security. The most important bit of information you can take from this chapter is that it's possible to examine user activities in the context of the user's role and work environment. Making security flexible is extremely important in today's work environment. You don't know how users will interact with your applications or where, and the threats to the application and its data are greater than ever before, so it's important to put security in place that can keep everything safe without unduly restricting user access.

At this point, many developers are thinking that all the additional security the .NET Framework provides is just too much work. The reality is that there may not be enough security in place to keep at bay all the threats your application has to face. One of the reality checks that developers should perform is to talk with administrators and listen to the horror stories these professionals can relate. Developers are often surprised to hear just how many ways users can find to circumvent application security in the quest to get work done quickly and without disruption. It's also important to talk with users and really listen to what they have to say about how they plan to use the application you create. Once you have this information in hand, start planning for the worst-case scenario that your application will face. Create a security plan for your application that works with the user but still keeps the application and data safe.

Because modern systems are buttoned down so tightly, you often have to interact with the operating system features in order to accomplish certain tasks. Chapter 13 describes how to interact with some of the more important operating system features, such as the firewall. If your application interacts with the outside world, you might find a need to add an exception to the current firewall configuration. In some cases, you might simply need to know the current firewall configuration to ensure your application is compatible with the operating system. Chapter 13 also looks at features such as automatic updates and virus protection.

# 13
# Interacting with the Built-In Security Features

**WHAT'S IN THIS CHAPTER?**

- ➤ Building firewall interactivity
- ➤ Checking Windows Update
- ➤ Interacting with AppLocker

To this point, this part of the book has focused on security within the application. Internal security is extremely important. The better you can protect the application's internal workings, the less likely it is that you'll encounter problems normally associated with security issues, such as data loss. However, most applications today aren't islands unto themselves — they interact with the outside world. External interaction means working with Windows features that protect the system as a whole, such as the Windows Firewall. Because of the threats by external entities, if your application needs to communicate with the outside world using anything other than the standard ports, you need to know how to create entries for your application using the Windows Firewall.

Your application will also need to perform other checks in some situations. For example, you might want to ensure that the user has automatic updates enabled, and that the system has certain updates installed. Some applications fail to work when the application needs certain updates in place, and the user has failed to install them. Likewise, applications are more reliant on virus protection today. Your application may need to check the user's use of virus protection before it installs or performs other tasks. This chapter demonstrates how to interact with all these essential built-in security features.

*This chapter shows how to work with the Microsoft products supplied with Windows 7. Users install third-party firewalls and virus protection products in many cases, so you'll also need to consider these third-party products as part of an overall application strategy. In some situations, the best you can do is automate the Windows functionality that you know exists on the machine and then require the user to perform any manual interactions with a third-party product. In addition, this chapter focuses on Windows 7 functionality. The examples probably won't work with earlier versions of Windows because Microsoft is constantly changing product functionality. For example, Microsoft has deprecated certain firewall functions, such as* `INetFwProfile.put_FirewallEnabled()` *in Windows Vista, Windows 7, and Windows Server 2008 (see* http://msdn.microsoft.com/library/bb756912 .aspx *for details). In sum, if you want to support certain types of external functionality in your application, you need to research the target product, the host operating system, and any updates the user is likely to perform on both the operating system and the product.*

## WORKING WITH THE FIREWALL

The Windows Firewall is probably the most often used external feature because applications often have to define new ports to use to communicate with the outside world. In addition, applications need to know the firewall status so they can interact with Windows and the outside world correctly. With this in mind, the following sections demonstrate techniques you can use to access and interact with the Windows Firewall.

 *The techniques used in the following section rely on the* `dynamic` *keyword that appears as part of the .NET Framework 4. These techniques won't work with older versions of the .NET Framework. However, you can still access the Windows Firewall using standard COM techniques when using older versions of the .NET Framework.*

### Interacting with the Firewall

There are a number of ways to interact with the Windows Firewall. In the past, developers would often use Component Object Model (COM)-based code. You can see an example of such code at `http://blogs.msdn.com/b/joncole/archive/2005/12/06/managed-classes-to-view-manipulate-the-windows-firewall.aspx`. It doesn't take long to figure out that using COM-based code is time-consuming and error-prone. You have to write a lot of code to accomplish most tasks with the Windows Firewall using this approach, but it does admittedly work with older versions of the .NET Framework.

Fortunately, the .NET Framework 4 provides a better approach through the `dynamic` keyword. In this case, you can interact with the Windows Firewall much as you would using VBScript. The technique is simple and relatively straightforward, despite not looking very much like the standard C# code you've used in the past. To test this out for yourself, create a Windows Forms application and add a Check (`btnCheck`) button to it. You don't need to add any special references or `using` statements. Listing 13-1 shows the code you need to create the Access Firewall example.

Available for download on Wrox.com

**LISTING 13-1:** Creating firewall access using the dynamic keyword

```
private void btnCheck_Click(object sender, EventArgs e)
{
    // Create the firewall type.
    Type FWManagerType = Type.GetTypeFromProgID("HNetCfg.FwMgr");

    // Use the firewall type to create a firewall manager object.
    dynamic FWManager = Activator.CreateInstance(FWManagerType);

    // Check the status of the firewall.
    MessageBox.Show("The firewall is turned on: " +
        Convert.ToString(
            FWManager.LocalPolicy.CurrentProfile.FirewallEnabled));
}
```

As previously mentioned, this code really does look like something you'd create using VBScript, rather than C#, but it works extremely well. The code begins by creating a new `Type`, `FWManagerType`, defined using the `Type.GetTypeFromProgID()` constructor with `"HNetCfg.FwMgr"` as the object to create.

Now that the code has a `Type` to use, it can create an instance of the object defined by that `Type` using the `Activator.CreateInstance()` constructor. Just in case you've never seen the `Activator` class before, you can read more about it at http://msdn.microsoft.com/library/system.activator.aspx. At this point, the example has access to the firewall manager using the `FWManager` object that's described merely as type `dynamic`.

The code displays a simple on/off indicator in this case for the Windows Firewall using a message box. Of course, you're wondering where to obtain the list of objects to access the on/off state of the Windows Firewall. One such place is at http://technet.microsoft.com/library/cc737845.aspx. However, you'll find a wealth of VBScript examples on the Internet that will give you additional information that you can apply directly to your C# application with a little translation. You can see a few of these VBScript examples at http://msdn.microsoft.com/library/aa366415.aspx.

## Verifying the Firewall Status

The Windows Firewall has a lot of settings, many of which are useful for applications to know. The Firewall Status example provides a representative example of the available settings, but it doesn't show all of them. The example begins with a Windows Forms application. You need to add a Status button (`btnStatus`) and a list box (`lstOutput`). The example doesn't require any special references or `using` statements. However, you do need to add the constants shown in Listing 13-2. These constants are used within the application to show the state of items such as the IP version. The constant names and values come directly from the Windows SDK.

### LISTING 13-2: Defining the Firewall Status example constants

```
// Define Constants from the SDK and their associated string name
// Scope
const Int32 NET_FW_SCOPE_ALL = 0;
const String NET_FW_SCOPE_ALL_NAME = "All subnets";
const Int32 NET_FW_SCOPE_LOCAL_SUBNET = 1;
const String NET_FW_SCOPE_LOCAL_SUBNET_NAME = "Local subnet only";
const Int32 NET_FW_SCOPE_CUSTOM = 2;
const String NET_FW_SCOPE_CUSTOM_NAME = "Custom Scope (see RemoteAddresses)";

// Profile Type
const Int32 NET_FW_PROFILE_DOMAIN = 0;
const String NET_FW_PROFILE_DOMAIN_NAME = "Domain";
const Int32 NET_FW_PROFILE_STANDARD = 1;
const String NET_FW_PROFILE_STANDARD_NAME = "Standard";

// IP Version
const Int32 NET_FW_IP_VERSION_V4 = 0;
const String NET_FW_IP_VERSION_V4_NAME = "IPv4";
const Int32 NET_FW_IP_VERSION_V6 = 1;
const String NET_FW_IP_VERSION_V6_NAME = "IPv6";
const Int32 NET_FW_IP_VERSION_ANY = 2;
const String NET_FW_IP_VERSION_ANY_NAME = "ANY";

// Protocol
const Int32 NET_FW_IP_PROTOCOL_TCP = 6;
const String NET_FW_IP_PROTOCOL_TCP_NAME = "TCP";
const Int32 NET_FW_IP_PROTOCOL_UDP = 17;
const String NET_FW_IP_PROTOCOL_UDP_NAME = "UDP";
```

The use of each of these constants will become clearer as you work through the example code. The example shows many of the statistics for the Windows Firewall, but it leaves out a few items such as globally open ports and a list of services. Listing 13-3 shows the code used for this example.

### LISTING 13-3: Obtaining the Windows Firewall status information

```
private void btnStatus_Click(object sender, EventArgs e)
{
    // Clear the old settings.
    lstOutput.Items.Clear();

    // Create the firewall type.
    Type FWManagerType = Type.GetTypeFromProgID("HNetCfg.FwMgr");

    // Use the firewall type to create a firewall manager object.
    dynamic FWManager = Activator.CreateInstance(FWManagerType);

    // Obtain the firewall profile information.
```

```csharp
    dynamic FWProfile = FWManager.LocalPolicy.CurrentProfile;

    // Output the type of profile on the local machine.
    switch ((Int32)FWProfile.Type)
    {
        case NET_FW_PROFILE_DOMAIN:
            lstOutput.Items.Add("Profile Type: " +
                NET_FW_PROFILE_DOMAIN_NAME);
            break;
        case NET_FW_PROFILE_STANDARD:
            lstOutput.Items.Add("Profile Type: " +
                NET_FW_PROFILE_STANDARD_NAME);
            break;
    }

    // Check the status of the firewall.
    lstOutput.Items.Add("Firewall Enabled: " +
        Convert.ToString(FWProfile.FirewallEnabled));

    // Determine whether exceptions are allowed.
    lstOutput.Items.Add("Exceptions Not Allowed: " +
        Convert.ToString(FWProfile.ExceptionsNotAllowed));

    // Determine whether notifications are disabled.
    lstOutput.Items.Add("Notifications Disabled: " +
        Convert.ToString(FWProfile.NotificationsDisabled));

    // Verify whether unicast responses to multicast
    // broadcasts are disabled.
    lstOutput.Items.Add("Unicast Responses to Multicast " +
        "Broadcasts Disabled: " +
        Convert.ToString(
            FWProfile.UnicastResponsestoMulticastBroadcastDisabled));

    // Print the Remote Administration settings.
    lstOutput.Items.Add("");
    lstOutput.Items.Add("Remote Administration:");
    dynamic RASettings = FWProfile.RemoteAdminSettings;

    // Show whether Remote Administration is enable.
    lstOutput.Items.Add("\tRemote Administration Enabled: " +
        Convert.ToString(RASettings.Enabled));

    // Get the Remote Adminstration IP version.
    switch ((Int32)RASettings.IpVersion)
    {
        case NET_FW_IP_VERSION_V4:
            lstOutput.Items.Add("\tIP Version: " +
                NET_FW_IP_VERSION_V4_NAME);
            break;
        case NET_FW_IP_VERSION_V6:
            lstOutput.Items.Add("\tIP Version: " +
                NET_FW_IP_VERSION_V6_NAME);
            break;
        case NET_FW_IP_VERSION_ANY:
```

*continues*

**LISTING 13-3** *(continued)*

```
            lstOutput.Items.Add("\tIP Version: " +
                NET_FW_IP_VERSION_ANY_NAME);
            break;
    }

    // Obtain the Remote Administration scope.
    switch ((Int32)RASettings.Scope)
    {
        case NET_FW_SCOPE_ALL:
            lstOutput.Items.Add("\tScope: " +
                NET_FW_SCOPE_ALL_NAME);
            break;
        case NET_FW_SCOPE_CUSTOM:
            lstOutput.Items.Add("\tScope: " +
                NET_FW_SCOPE_CUSTOM_NAME);
            break;
        case NET_FW_SCOPE_LOCAL_SUBNET:
            lstOutput.Items.Add("\tScope: " +
                NET_FW_SCOPE_LOCAL_SUBNET_NAME);
            break;
    }

    // Display the Remote Administration addresses.
    lstOutput.Items.Add("\tRemote Administration Addresses: " +
        RASettings.RemoteAddresses);

    // Print the ICMP settings.
    lstOutput.Items.Add("");
    lstOutput.Items.Add("ICMP Settings:");
    dynamic ICMPSettings = FWProfile.IcmpSettings;

    // Obtain the ICMP settings.
    lstOutput.Items.Add("\tAllowOutboundDestinationUnreachable: " +
        Convert.ToString(ICMPSettings.AllowOutboundDestinationUnreachable));
    lstOutput.Items.Add("\tAllowOutboundSourceQuench: " +
        Convert.ToString(ICMPSettings.AllowOutboundSourceQuench));
    lstOutput.Items.Add("\tAllowRedirect: " +
        Convert.ToString(ICMPSettings.AllowRedirect));
    lstOutput.Items.Add("\tAllowInboundEchoRequest: " +
        Convert.ToString(ICMPSettings.AllowInboundEchoRequest));
    lstOutput.Items.Add("\tAllowInboundRouterRequest: " +
        Convert.ToString(ICMPSettings.AllowInboundRouterRequest));
    lstOutput.Items.Add("\tAllowOutboundTimeExceeded: " +
        Convert.ToString(ICMPSettings.AllowOutboundTimeExceeded));
    lstOutput.Items.Add("\tAllowOutboundParameterProblem: " +
        Convert.ToString(ICMPSettings.AllowOutboundParameterProblem));
    lstOutput.Items.Add("\tAllowInboundTimestampRequest: " +
        Convert.ToString(ICMPSettings.AllowInboundTimestampRequest));
    lstOutput.Items.Add("\tAllowInboundMaskRequest: " +
        Convert.ToString(ICMPSettings.AllowInboundMaskRequest));

    // Display the authorized applications.
```

```csharp
lstOutput.Items.Add("");
lstOutput.Items.Add("Authorized Applications:");

// Obtain each port in turn and display its characteristics.
foreach (dynamic Application in FWProfile.AuthorizedApplications)
{
    // Display the port name.
    lstOutput.Items.Add("\tName: " + Application.Name);

    // Display the port number.
    lstOutput.Items.Add("\tImage Filename: " +
        Application.ProcessImageFileName);

    // Display the IP version for the application.
    switch ((Int32)Application.IpVersion)
    {
        case NET_FW_IP_VERSION_V4:
            lstOutput.Items.Add("\tIP Version: " +
                NET_FW_IP_VERSION_V4_NAME);
            break;
        case NET_FW_IP_VERSION_V6:
            lstOutput.Items.Add("\tIP Version: " +
                NET_FW_IP_VERSION_V6_NAME);
            break;
        case NET_FW_IP_VERSION_ANY:
            lstOutput.Items.Add("\tIP Version: " +
                NET_FW_IP_VERSION_ANY_NAME);
            break;
    }

    // Display the scope for the application.
    switch ((Int32)Application.Scope)
    {
        case NET_FW_SCOPE_ALL:
            lstOutput.Items.Add("\tScope: " +
                NET_FW_SCOPE_ALL_NAME);
            break;
        case NET_FW_SCOPE_CUSTOM:
            lstOutput.Items.Add("\tScope: " +
                NET_FW_SCOPE_CUSTOM_NAME);
            break;
        case NET_FW_SCOPE_LOCAL_SUBNET:
            lstOutput.Items.Add("\tScope: " +
                NET_FW_SCOPE_LOCAL_SUBNET_NAME);
            break;
    }

    // Show the application's enabled state.
    lstOutput.Items.Add("\tEnabled: " +
        Convert.ToString(Application.Enabled));

    // Get the remote addresses for the application.
    lstOutput.Items.Add("\tRemote Addresses: " +
```

*continues*

**LISTING 13-3** *(continued)*

```
            Application.RemoteAddresses);

        // Add a space.
        lstOutput.Items.Add("");
    }
}
```

The example begins by creating a `HNetCfg.FwMgr` type definition, `FWManagerType`. It uses this `Type` to create an instance of the Windows Firewall Manager, `FWManager`, using `Activator.CreateInstance()`. At this point, the code creates a second `dynamic` variable, `FWProfile`, which contains the `FWManager.LocalPolicy.CurrentProfile` property values. You want to create this second `dynamic` variable to make it easier to interact with the Windows Firewall. In addition, you can now easily see the property values that the Windows Firewall supports using the debugger, as shown in Figure 13-1. In fact, you can use the debugger to expand the various property values to see what they contain — making it far easier to write your code.

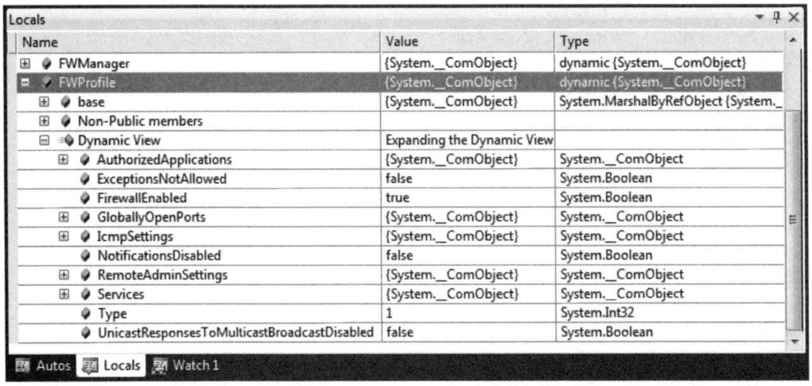

**FIGURE 13-1:** Use the debugger to view the dynamic data provided by the Windows Firewall.

There are a number of ways to determine the profile type for the machine, but using a `switch` is as convenient as any other method. When performing a comparison, you must coerce the data because the compiler won't know the type of the data until run time. In this case, `FWProfile.Type` is an `Int32` value.

Once the code lists the common profile settings, it begins work on the Remote Administration settings. These settings control whether an administrator can manage the firewall from a remote system, such as the administrator's machine. The code begins by obtaining the Remote Administration settings from the `FWProfile.RemoteAdminSettings` property using another `dynamic` variable, `RASettings`. There isn't any limit to the number of levels you can access using this technique. Debugging is easier when you use `dynamic` variables for each level so that you can easily see how each level is constructed. The Remote Administration settings require use of several `switch` structures that you create using the same approach as the profile type.

The Internet Control Message Protocol (ICMP) settings come next. In this case, all you see is a series of `Boolean` or `String` values that you access directly. The `FWProfile.IcmpSettings` provides full access to all the ICMP settings shown in the example.

The `FWProfile` object contains a number of collections that you process just as you would any managed collection. The code shows how to work with the `FWProfile.AuthorizedApplications` collection. In this case, each `Application` object is a `dynamic` variable that tells you a number of things about each application that's registered with the Windows Firewall, including:

- Name
- Executable filename and location
- IP version of the entry
- Scope of the entry
- Application's firewall entry enabled state
- Remote addresses the application has requested to access

The profile provides access to other kinds of information. In fact, you can discover anything you need to learn about the Windows Firewall using the techniques shown in this example. Figure 13-2 shows typical output from this example.

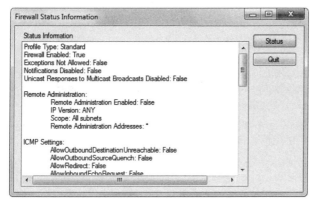

**FIGURE 13-2:** The example outputs a considerable amount of information about the Windows Firewall.

## Modifying a Setting

You can programmatically change the Windows Firewall settings. The Remote Administration example shows how to enable and disable the Remote Administration feature of the Windows Firewall, but the same principles hold true for any setting you want to change.

The example begins with a Windows Forms application. Add a button to change the setting (`btnChange`). The caption on this button actually changes to show the state of the feature — Enable when the Remote Administration feature is turned off and Disable when the Remote Administration feature is turned on. Because the Windows Firewall is a sensitive part of the system, you must also add a manifest to the example using the procedure found in the "Creating the User Permission Modification Manifest" section of Chapter 10. This example doesn't require any special references or using statements. However, the example does require that you create some global variables and constants as shown in Listing 13-4.

> **LISTING 13-4:** Defining the Remote Administration example global variables

```
// Create the firewall type.
Type FWManagerType = Type.GetTypeFromProgID("HNetCfg.FwMgr");

// Define a firewall manager object.
dynamic FWManager;

// Define a Remote Administration object.
dynamic RASettings;

// Scope
const Int32 NET_FW_SCOPE_ALL = 0;
const Int32 NET_FW_SCOPE_LOCAL_SUBNET = 1;

public frmMain()
{
    InitializeComponent();

    // Create the firewall manager.
    FWManager = Activator.CreateInstance(FWManagerType);

    // Get the Remote Administration settings.
    RASettings = FWManager.LocalPolicy.CurrentProfile.RemoteAdminSettings;

    // Check the Remote Administration status.
    CheckStatus();
}

private void CheckStatus()
{
    // Set the btnChange caption as needed.
    if ((Boolean)RASettings.Enabled)
        btnChange.Text = "&Disable";
    else
        btnChange.Text = "&Enable";
}
```

The global variables will require initialization as shown in the `frmMain()` constructor. In addition, you need to check the status of the Remote Administration feature to ensure the button has the correct caption on it.

As previously mentioned, this example uses a toggle for `btnChange`. The `CheckStatus()` method detects the current Remote Administration feature state and sets `btnChange` accordingly.

Changing the setting is relatively easy, but you need to follow a few rules when doing it. Listing 13-5 shows the code used to change the Remote Administration setting.

**LISTING 13-5:** Modifying the Remote Administration setting

Available for download on Wrox.com

```
private void btnChange_Click(object sender, EventArgs e)
{
    // Set the Remote Administration settings as needed.
    if ((Boolean)RASettings.Enabled)
    {
        // Turn Remote Administration off.
        RASettings.Enabled = false;
    }
    else
    {
        // Set the Remote Administration to a specific address.
        RASettings.RemoteAddresses = "12.1.1.64/255.255.255.240";

        // Set the Remote Administration to a scope that includes
        // all addresses within the scope.
        //RASettings.Scope = NET_FW_SCOPE_ALL;

        // Turn Remote Administration on.
        RASettings.Enabled = true;
    }

    // Check the status.
    CheckStatus();
}
```

The code begins by verifying the current Remote Administration setting. This is an important check because someone could have modified the setting externally. When you need to turn Remote Administration off, it's only necessary to set the `Enabled` property to `false`.

You can take several approaches when turning Remote Administration on. The default technique for the example is to supply a specific address for the `RemoteAddresses`. In this case, the example uses an IPv4 address of `12.1.1.64` and a mask of `255.255.255.240`. (If you want to allow multiple IP addresses, then separate them using commas.) Windows Firewall will automatically set the `Scope` property to a custom scope in this case. It's also possible to specify a `Scope` property value such as `NET_FW_SCOPE_ALL`. In this case, Windows Firewall automatically sets the `RemoteAddresses` property value to `*`. In either case, the code must set the `Enabled` property to `true` to turn the Remote Administration feature on. The code ends by changing the `btnChange` caption to match the current Remote Administration state.

At this point, you're probably wondering precisely how this change affects the Windows Firewall settings you can see in the Control Panel. Open the Windows Firewall applet in the Control Panel and click the Advanced Settings link. You'll see a Windows Firewall with Advanced Security window. Select the `Windows Firewall with Advanced Security\Monitoring\Firewall` folder, and you'll see three new entries for Remote Administration as shown in Figure 13-3.

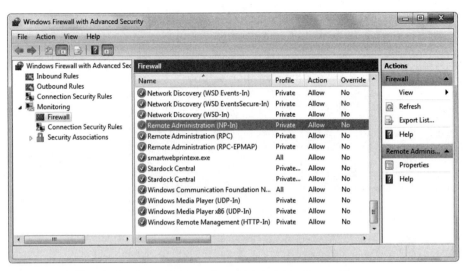

**FIGURE 13-3:** The application adds three Remote Administration entries.

The single change made by the application produces all three entries. If you double-click one of these entries, such as Remote Administration (NP-In), you'll see that the entry does in fact use the IPv4 address specified by the application, as shown in Figure 13-4.

Unfortunately, you don't have individual control over each of the entries. For example, you can't choose to include just Named Pipes (NP) as a potential avenue for making Windows Firewall changes from a remote location — you must accept both NP and Remote Procedure Call (RPC)/Transmission Control Protocol (TCP) as conduits. In addition, you can't set the protocols individually; a single change modifies all three protocol entries. Despite these limitations, you still have programmatic control over the entry configuration. If you want better control over the entries, then you must use the entries in the `Windows Firewall with Advanced Security\Inbound Rules` folder to make the change.

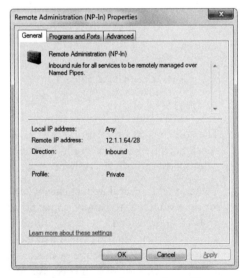

**FIGURE 13-4:** Each entry uses the settings you provided in the application.

## Adding and Deleting Ports

Unless you want to engage in some fancy programming, you're a bit limited on ports you can add to the Windows Firewall. For example, you can't easily create a port that provides specific user configuration information. The technique shown in the Add Port example will create a private port using any of the supported protocols (the example shows two, but many others are available). You can create ports for a given scope or a specific address as needed. Even with the limitations of this technique, it will answer most application needs.

The Add Port example begins with a Windows Forms application. You add two buttons: Add (`btnAdd`) to add the port and Delete (`btnDelete`) to remove the port. You must also add a manifest to the example using the procedure found in the "Creating the User Permission Modification Manifest" section of Chapter 10. The application will appear to work without the manifest, but the system won't actually add the port. The application doesn't require any special references or `using` statements. It does require that you add the following constants:

```
// Define Constants from the SDK
// Scope
const Int32 NET_FW_SCOPE_ALL = 0;
const Int32 NET_FW_SCOPE_LOCAL_SUBNET = 1;
const Int32 NET_FW_SCOPE_CUSTOM = 2;

// Protocol
const Int32 NET_FW_IP_PROTOCOL_TCP = 6;
const Int32 NET_FW_IP_PROTOCOL_UDP = 17;
```

Now that you have the basics in place, it's time to add the port. Listing 13-6 shows the code used to add a private port to the system.

**LISTING 13-6:** Adding a port to the Windows Firewall

*Available for download on Wrox.com*

```
private void btnAdd_Click(object sender, EventArgs e)
{
    // Create the firewall type.
    Type FWManagerType = Type.GetTypeFromProgID("HNetCfg.FwMgr");

    // Use the firewall type to create a firewall manager object.
    dynamic FWManager = Activator.CreateInstance(FWManagerType);

    // Obtain the firewall profile information.
    dynamic FWProfile = FWManager.LocalPolicy.CurrentProfile;

    // Create the port type.
    Type PortType = Type.GetTypeFromProgID("HNetCfg.FWOpenPort");

    // Define a new port instance.
    dynamic NewPort = Activator.CreateInstance(PortType);

    // Specify the port parameters.
    NewPort.Name = "MyPort";
    NewPort.Protocol = NET_FW_IP_PROTOCOL_TCP;
    NewPort.Port = 9999;

    // The port entry must also include either a scope or a
```

*continues*

**LISTING 13-6** *(continued)*

```
        // remote address entry, but not both.
        //NewPort.Scope = NET_FW_SCOPE_LOCAL_SUBNET;
        NewPort.RemoteAddresses = "10.1.1.1/255.255.255.255";

        // Enable the port.
        NewPort.Enabled = true;

        try
        {
            // Try adding the port.
            FWProfile.GloballyOpenPorts.Add(NewPort);

            // Display a success message.
            MessageBox.Show("Port successfully added!");
        }
        catch (Exception err)
        {
            // Display an error message.
            MessageBox.Show("Couldn't add the port!\n" +
                err.Message);
        }
    }
```

The code begins by creating the `HNetCfg.FwMgr Type` object and using it to create the Windows Firewall Manager object, `FWManager`. The code then gains access to the `LocalPolicy.CurrentProfile` property used to change the local policy (`FWProfile`). This part of the example is much like the other examples you've seen so far in the chapter.

This example creates another `Type`, `HNetCfg.FWOpenPort`, which is used to describe a Windows Firewall port. The code uses the `PortType` object to create a port object, `NewPort`, using the `Activator.CreateInstance()` method. At this point, the code begins defining the port characteristics. This port has a name of `MyPort` and it uses the TCP protocol on Port 9999. You also need to assign either a scope or a remote address, but not both. The example uses a remote address, so it assigns a value to the `RemoteAddresses` property. Finally, the code sets `NewPort.Enabled` to `true` so that the port is active after the system adds it.

A lot of examples on the Internet show that the `GloballyOpenPorts.Add()` method returns an error value. This isn't the case when working in a managed application. Make sure you place your call in a `try` block as shown. The `GloballyOpenPorts.Add()` method accepts just one argument, the `NewPort` object you created.

To see the port that the system has just added, you need to open the Windows Firewall with Advanced Security window and select the `Inbound Rules` folder. Figure 13-5 shows typical results for this example.

**FIGURE 13-5:** The port appears in the Inbound Rules folder.

Double-click the entry to display the port's Properties dialog box shown in Figure 13-6. The Properties dialog box displays everything you've configured for the port. It also displays information that you can't change programmatically using this technique, such as adding a port description. It's helpful to review the various properties on the tabs shown in Figure 13-6 to see if you need to change any options using some other method. Normally this requires that you create a Group Policy Object (GPO) or resort to some other means. The "Using the GPO Technique" section of this chapter explores one method of gaining further access using rules, but not all versions of Windows support rules are covered, and using rules is definitely more difficult than the technique shown in this section. Normally, you'll find the results of this technique satisfactory, and the coding is straightforward.

Removing the port is easier than adding it. In this case, you supply the port and protocol to uniquely identify the port. Listing 13-7 shows the code used to delete a port.

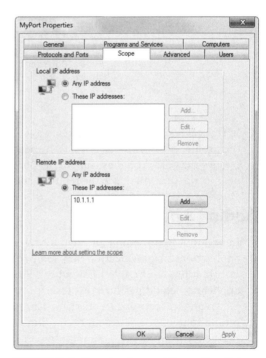

**FIGURE 13-6:** Opening the port Properties dialog box shows all the settings you've made.

Available for download on Wrox.com

**LISTING 13-7:** Removing a port from the Windows Firewall

```
private void btnDelete_Click(object sender, EventArgs e)
{
    // Create the firewall type.
    Type FWManagerType = Type.GetTypeFromProgID("HNetCfg.FwMgr");

    // Use the firewall type to create a firewall manager object.
    dynamic FWManager = Activator.CreateInstance(FWManagerType);

    // Obtain the firewall profile information.
    dynamic FWProfile = FWManager.LocalPolicy.CurrentProfile;

    try
    {

        // Delete the port based on the port name.
        FWProfile.GloballyOpenPorts.Remove(9999,NET_FW_IP_PROTOCOL_TCP);

        // Display a success message.
        MessageBox.Show("Port successfully deleted!");
    }
    catch (Exception err)
    {
        // Display an error message.
        MessageBox.Show("Couldn't delete the port!\n" +
            err.Message);
    }
}
```

In this case, you don't need to create a `HNetCfg.FWOpenPort` object. The code begins by accessing the profile, `FWProfile`, as normal. It then calls the `GloballyOpenPorts.Remove()` method to remove the port. You must supply the port number and protocol type as inputs. As with adding a port, make sure you place the removal code within a `try` block to catch any errors.

## Adding Applications

In addition to providing an exemption for a port, you can also provide exemptions for applications. An application may require direct access to a Website for updates or to obtain information. Normally, the Windows Firewall will try to prevent such access because the application could perform this task for wicked reasons, such as infecting your machine. When an application garners the trust required to interact directly with the Internet or other online source, it requires an exemption to do so. The Add Application example shows how to perform this task.

The Add Application example begins with a Windows Forms application. You add two buttons: Add (`btnAdd`) to add the application to the exemption list and Remove (`btnRemove`) to remove the application from the list. You must also add a manifest to the example using the procedure found in the "Creating the User Permission Modification Manifest" section of Chapter 10. The addition process will appear to work without the manifest, but the system won't actually add the application to the list. The example doesn't require any special references or using statements. It does require that you add the following constants:

```
// Define Constants from the SDK
// Scope
const Int32 NET_FW_SCOPE_ALL = 0;
const Int32 NET_FW_SCOPE_LOCAL_SUBNET = 1;
const Int32 NET_FW_SCOPE_CUSTOM = 2;

// Set constants
const Int32 NET_FW_PROFILE_DOMAIN = 0;
const Int32 NET_FW_PROFILE_STANDARD = 1;
```

Ports and applications vary in their intent. A port opens a gate for any application that knows about the port, while an application exception applies only to a specific application. Theoretically, it's safer to create an exception for an application than it is to open a new port, so you should use the application exception option whenever possible. Listing 13-8 shows the code used to add an application exception to the Windows Firewall.

Available for download on Wrox.com

**LISTING 13-8:** Adding an application exception to the Windows Firewall

```
private void btnAdd_Click(object sender, EventArgs e)
{
    // Create the firewall type.
    Type FWManagerType = Type.GetTypeFromProgID("HNetCfg.FwMgr");

    // Use the firewall type to create a firewall manager object.
    dynamic FWManager = Activator.CreateInstance(FWManagerType);

    // Obtain the firewall domain profile information.
    dynamic FWProfile =
        FWManager.LocalPolicy.GetProfileByType(NET_FW_PROFILE_DOMAIN);

    // Create the application type.
    Type AppType = Type.GetTypeFromProgID("HNetCfg.FwAuthorizedApplication");

    // Create an instance of the application type.
    dynamic NewApp = Activator.CreateInstance(AppType);

    // Supply the application specifics.
    NewApp.ProcessImageFileName = Application.ExecutablePath;
    NewApp.Name = Application.ProductName;

    // The application entry must also include either a scope
    // or a remote address entry, but not both.
    //NewApp.Scope = NET_FW_SCOPE_ALL;
    NewApp.RemoteAddresses = "10.1.1.1/255.255.255.255";

    // Enable the application.
```

*continues*

**LISTING 13-8** *(continued)*

```
    NewApp.Enabled = true;

    try
    {
        // Try adding the application.
        FWProfile.AuthorizedApplications.Add(NewApp);

        // Display a success message.
        MessageBox.Show("Application successfully added!");
    }
    catch (Exception err)
    {
        // Display an error message.
        MessageBox.Show("Couldn't add the Application!\n" +
            err.Message);
    }
}
```

The code begins by creating the Windows Firewall Manager `Type` and object (`FWManager`). It then accesses the profile. However, notice that the technique used in this example is different from the other examples in the chapter. The example uses the `GetProfileByType()` method to obtain the domain profile using the `NET_FW_PROFILE_DOMAIN` constant.

There are actually three levels of profile: domain, private, and public. The `NET_FW_PROFILE_STANDARD` constant provides access to the private profile, while the `NET_FW_PROFILE_DOMAIN` constant provides access to the domain profile. The SDK apparently doesn't provide a constant for the public profile. If you want to create a public-profile entry, you need to use the technique shown in the "Using the GPO Technique" section of this chapter. The vast majority of the application exceptions you create appear in either the private or domain profile. The public profile is generally reserved for applications and services such as File and Print Sharing and Network Discovery, to give two examples. Some services and low-level applications use a combination of profiles or sometimes all three. For example, Routing and Remote Access uses all three profiles for its exceptions.

To create an application exception, the code defines the `AppType` Type using the `HNetCfg.FwAuthorizedApplication` program identifier. It then creates the `NewApp` object using the `Activator.CreateInstance()` method with `AppType` as an argument. The code shows typical entries you need to provide to define an application. Make certain that you define either the `Scope` property or the `RemoteAddresses` property but not both.

At this point, the code calls `AuthorizedApplications.Add()` to create the new application exception. You supply the `AppType` object, `NewApp`, as input to the method. As with ports, creating a new application exception defines two entries, one for TCP and another for User Datagram Protocol (UDP). You'll want to place the `AuthorizedApplications.Add()` method call within a `try...catch` block to catch any errors generated by the addition. Figure 13-7 shows typical entries generated by this example.

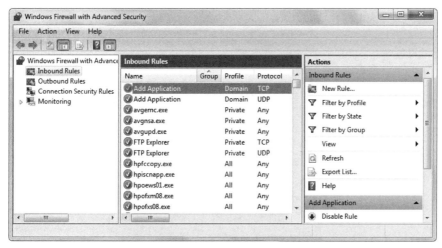

**FIGURE 13-7:** An application exception generates two entries: one for TCP and another for UDP.

Double-clicking either of these entries displays the Add Application Properties dialog box shown in Figure 13-8. Notice that the entries are much the same as a port entry. The big difference is the content differences for items such as the entries on the Programs and Services tab, where an application exception entry will have the This Program option selected and the name of a particular program defined.

At some point, you'll probably want to remove the application exception. Leaving an application exception in place after you uninstall the application is a big security risk, so you'll definitely want to remove the entry as part of your uninstall routine. Listing 13-9 shows the code used to remove an application exception from the Windows Firewall.

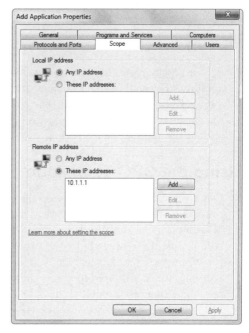

**FIGURE 13-8:** The application exception entries contain much of the same information as a port entry.

> **LISTING 13-9:** Removing an application exception from the Windows Firewall

*Available for download on Wrox.com*

```
private void btnRemove_Click(object sender, EventArgs e)
{
    // Create the firewall type.
    Type FWManagerType = Type.GetTypeFromProgID("HNetCfg.FwMgr");

    // Use the firewall type to create a firewall manager object.
    dynamic FWManager = Activator.CreateInstance(FWManagerType);

    // Obtain the firewall profile information.
    dynamic FWProfile =
        FWManager.LocalPolicy.GetProfileByType(NET_FW_PROFILE_DOMAIN);

    try
    {
        // Delete the application based on the application path.
        FWProfile.AuthorizedApplications.Remove(Application.ExecutablePath);

        // Display a success message.
        MessageBox.Show("Application successfully removed!");
    }
    catch (Exception err)
    {
        // Display an error message.
        MessageBox.Show("Couldn't remove the application!\n" +
            err.Message);
    }
}
```

As with the `btnAdd_Click()` code, the `btnRemove_Click()` method begins by creating a Windows Firewall Manager object, `FWManager`, and using it to access the domain profile using the `GetProfileByType()` method. The code then calls `AuthorizedApplications.Remove()` with the executable path of the application (`Application.ExecutablePath`) as an argument. As with adding the application exception, you want to place the removal code in a `try...catch` statement.

## Using the GPO Technique

Older versions of Windows rely on the techniques described in the previous sections of the chapter to manage the Windows Firewall. These techniques also work fine with the latest versions of Windows, including Windows 7. However, as the security threats have increased, so has the complexity of the firewall used to protect systems. Microsoft has created a new Windows Firewall for Windows 7 that has features you can't access using the older techniques shown in the previous sections. When you need to access these new features, you need to use an entirely different access technique that relies on GPO and a series of rules in place of the techniques used in the past. The following sections provide an overview of how to use these newer techniques.

### Configuring the Rule Technique Example

The Rule Technique example performs three tasks. First, it shows how to enumerate the rules used to configure the Windows Firewall exceptions and services. You need to be able to enumerate these rules to find entries that may be helpful to your application. The same rule configuration applies to ports, applications, and services, so you don't need to worry about any special objects when working with the various Windows Firewall elements. Second, the Rule Technique example shows how to add an application exception. The same technique works for adding ports or services as needed. Third, the Rule Technique example shows how to remove the application exception. To make things interesting, the application exception appears in the public profile that you can access using other techniques in this chapter.

The example begins with a Windows Forms application. You add three buttons: Get Rules (btnGetRules), Add (btnAdd), and Remove (btnRemove). The application also requires use of a list box control, lstRuleList. There isn't any need for special references or using statements. However, the application does require the following constants:

```
// Entries from ICFTypes.H
// Alternative Profile Type
const Int32 NET_FW_PROFILE2_DOMAIN = 1;
const Int32 NET_FW_PROFILE2_PRIVATE = 2;
const Int32 NET_FW_PROFILE2_PUBLIC = 4;
const Int32 NET_FW_PROFILE2_ALL = 2147483647;

// Protocol
const Int32 NET_FW_IP_PROTOCOL_TCP = 6;
const Int32 NET_FW_IP_PROTOCOL_UDP = 17;
const Int32 NET_FW_IP_PROTOCOL_ICMPv4 = 1;
const Int32 NET_FW_IP_PROTOCOL_ICMPv6 = 58;

// Direction
const Int32 NET_FW_RULE_DIR_IN = 1;
const Int32 NET_FW_RULE_DIR_OUT = 2;

// Action
const Int32 NET_FW_ACTION_BLOCK = 0;
const Int32 NET_FW_ACTION_ALLOW = 1;
```

Notice that these constants come from the ICFTypes.H file. Reviewing this file is helpful when you need other ideas for working with rules in the Windows Firewall. In this case, you see the constants for all three profiles and a special constant used when all three profiles are required by the rule. The list of protocols is a little short. A rule can employ any of the protocols shown in Figure 13-9. The problem is that the ICFTypes.H file only documents the TCP and UDP protocols — NET_FW_IP_PROTOCOL_ICMPv4 and NET_FW_IP_PROTOCOL_ICMPv6 are the result of experimentation. All the other constants do appear in the ICFTypes.H file.

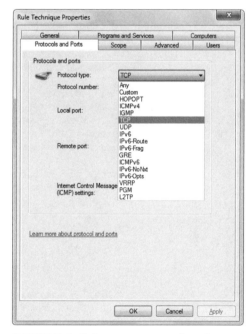

**FIGURE 13-9:** Rules can use a number of protocols.

## Obtaining a List of Rules

Before you can learn much about the rule technique for working with the Windows Firewall, you must know how to enumerate the rules. The rules provide considerably more information than older Windows Firewall techniques. For example, you can discover precisely which profile a rule appears in and determine both local and remote addresses. The code shown in Listing 13-10 doesn't include all the information you can obtain from a rule, but it gives you a good start on the most commonly used bits of information.

**LISTING 13-10:** Obtaining a list of Windows Firewall rules

```
private void btnGetRules_Click(object sender, EventArgs e)
{
    // Clear the old entries.
    lstRuleList.Items.Clear();

    // Define a GPO policy type.
    Type PolicyType = Type.GetTypeFromProgID("HNetCfg.FwPolicy2");

    // Create the policy object.
    dynamic Policy = Activator.CreateInstance(PolicyType);

    // Determine whether the firewall is enabled in specific profiles.
    lstRuleList.Items.Add("Domain Firewall is Enabled: " +
        Policy.FirewallEnabled(NET_FW_PROFILE2_DOMAIN));
    lstRuleList.Items.Add("Public Firewall is Enabled: " +
        Policy.FirewallEnabled(NET_FW_PROFILE2_PUBLIC));
    lstRuleList.Items.Add("Private Firewall is Enabled: " +
        Policy.FirewallEnabled(NET_FW_PROFILE2_PRIVATE));

    // Process each rule in turn.
    lstRuleList.Items.Add("");
    lstRuleList.Items.Add("Rules:");
    lstRuleList.Items.Add("");
    foreach (dynamic Rule in Policy.Rules)
    {
        // Use only the enabled rules.
        if (Rule.Enabled)
        {
            // Output the rule name.
            lstRuleList.Items.Add("Rule Name: " + Rule.Name);

            // Output the associated application.
            lstRuleList.Items.Add("Application: " + Rule.ApplicationName);

            // Display the rule's description.
            lstRuleList.Items.Add("Description: " + Rule.Description);

            // Output the rule's group.
            lstRuleList.Items.Add("Grouping: " + Rule.Grouping);

            // Determine the associated profiles.
```

```csharp
            if (Rule.Profiles == NET_FW_PROFILE2_ALL)
                lstRuleList.Items.Add("All Profiles");
            else
            {
                if ((Rule.Profiles & NET_FW_PROFILE2_DOMAIN)
                    == NET_FW_PROFILE2_DOMAIN)

                    lstRuleList.Items.Add("Domain Profile");

                if ((Rule.Profiles & NET_FW_PROFILE2_PRIVATE)
                    == NET_FW_PROFILE2_PRIVATE)

                    lstRuleList.Items.Add("Private Profile");

                if ((Rule.Profiles & NET_FW_PROFILE2_PUBLIC)
                    == NET_FW_PROFILE2_PUBLIC)

                    lstRuleList.Items.Add("Public Profile");
            }


            // Determine whether the rule is inbound or outbound.
            switch ((Int32)Rule.Direction)
            {
                case NET_FW_RULE_DIR_IN:
                    lstRuleList.Items.Add("Inbound Rule");
                    break;
                case NET_FW_RULE_DIR_OUT:
                    lstRuleList.Items.Add("Outbound Rule");
                    break;
            }

            // Determine whether the rule allows or blocks an action.
            switch ((Int32)Rule.Action)
            {
                case NET_FW_ACTION_ALLOW:
                    lstRuleList.Items.Add("Allow Action");
                    break;
                case NET_FW_ACTION_BLOCK:
                    lstRuleList.Items.Add("Block Action");
                    break;
            }

            // Determine the rule's protocol.
            switch ((Int32)Rule.Protocol)
            {
                case NET_FW_IP_PROTOCOL_ICMPv4:
                    lstRuleList.Items.Add("ICMP v4");
                    break;
                case NET_FW_IP_PROTOCOL_ICMPv6:
                    lstRuleList.Items.Add("ICMP v6");
                    break;
                case NET_FW_IP_PROTOCOL_TCP:
```

*continues*

**LISTING 13-10** *(continued)*

```
                lstRuleList.Items.Add("TCP");
                break;
            case NET_FW_IP_PROTOCOL_UDP:
                lstRuleList.Items.Add("UDP");
                break;
            default:
                lstRuleList.Items.Add("Other Protocol");
                break;
        }

        // Display the local addresses and ports.
        lstRuleList.Items.Add("Local Addresses: " + Rule.LocalAddresses);
        lstRuleList.Items.Add("Local Ports: " + Rule.LocalPorts);

        // Display the remote addresses and ports.
        lstRuleList.Items.Add("Remote Addresses: " + Rule.RemoteAddresses);
        lstRuleList.Items.Add("Remote Ports: " + Rule.RemotePorts);

        // Add a space between entries.
        lstRuleList.Items.Add("");
    }
  }
}
```

The example begins by clearing the old list entries. It then creates a new `Type`, `PolicyType`, using the `HNetCfg.FwPolicy2` program identifier. This technique doesn't rely on the Windows Firewall Manager; it uses policies instead, so you start with a `Policy` object. The next step is to create the `Policy` object using the `Activator.CreateInstance()` with the `PolicyType` as an argument.

One `Policy` object can work with multiple profiles. The code demonstrates this fact by obtaining the `FirewallEnabled` property value for all three profiles. To check this out, try turning off one of the firewall configurations in the Windows Firewall applet — the status will change for the appropriate profile in the application. You won't always use the technique shown for the `FirewallEnabled` property to work with a specific profile, but you'll use it in some cases, so keep it in mind.

The next step is to show the content of each of the enabled rules for the system. The example uses a `foreach` loop with a `dynamic` variable, `Rule`, to perform this task. Many of the standard Windows Firewall rules aren't enabled, so one of the first checks you'll normally perform is to verify the enabled status of the rule. The example uses an `if` statement with `Rule.Enabled` to accomplish this task.

Most of the `Rule` entries are straightforward. A rule has a name and description. Application exceptions will also include an application name with a full path to the application. A grouping is a method of ordering associated rules together. You need to create an application resource to accomplish this task, but the technique for doing so is outside the scope of this discussion.

Determining which profile a rule is part of is a little cumbersome. First, you need to determine whether the rule is part of all the profiles by checking the `Profiles` property against `NET_FW_PROFILE2_ALL`. If the rule doesn't exist in all the profiles, it must exist in at least one profile and could exist in two. The series of three `if` statements that comes next checks for each of these possibilities.

A rule is inbound (meaning it checks the incoming data stream) or outbound (meaning it checks the outgoing data stream), but never both. The next check verifies that the rule is either inbound or outbound. A rule can also allow or block an action, so that's the next check. Rules can use a host of different protocols, but they use only one protocol at a time. For example, a rule can't service both TCP and UDP. To provide both TCP and UDP support, you must create two rules. The example checks against four different common protocols. If none of these protocols is valid, the check simply reports that the rule is using some other protocol.

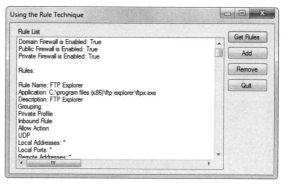

The last check determines the local and remote addresses and ports for the rule. Working with rules lets you assign both local and remote addresses and ports. However, you won't find any other advantages in working with rules — an address still must translate correctly as described in the "Adding a New Application Rule" section below. Figure 13-10 shows typical output from this example.

**FIGURE 13-10:** Rules provide a lot of detail but can prove complex to read.

## Adding a New Application Rule

This section describes how to create a new application rule. The approach works equally well for a port or service with a little tweaking of the example code. Rules generally provide a basis for creating an exception to the baseline rules. A rule is inbound or outbound and it either allows or blocks an action. The rule is focused on a specific port and could include addresses and specific application information. Listing 13-11 shows the code used to perform this task.

LISTING 13-11: Adding a new application rule to the public profile

```
private void btnAdd_Click(object sender, EventArgs e)
{
    // Define a GPO policy type.
    Type PolicyType = Type.GetTypeFromProgID("HNetCfg.FwPolicy2");

    // Create the policy object.
    dynamic Policy = Activator.CreateInstance(PolicyType);

    // Define a rule type for the policy.
    Type RuleType = Type.GetTypeFromProgID("HNetCfg.FwRule");

    // Create the rule object.
```

*continues*

**LISTING 13-11** *(continued)*

```csharp
        dynamic Rule = Activator.CreateInstance(RuleType);

        // Define the rule specifics.
        Rule.Name = Application.ProductName;
        Rule.ApplicationName = Application.ExecutablePath;
        Rule.Description = "This is a sample GPO entry.";
        Rule.Profiles = NET_FW_PROFILE2_PUBLIC;
        Rule.Direction = NET_FW_RULE_DIR_IN;
        Rule.Action = NET_FW_ACTION_ALLOW;
        Rule.Protocol = NET_FW_IP_PROTOCOL_TCP;
        Rule.RemoteAddresses = "10.1.1.1/255.255.255.255";
        Rule.RemotePorts = "*";
        Rule.LocalAddresses = "*";
        Rule.LocalPorts = "*";
        Rule.Enabled = true;
        Rule.InterfaceTypes = "All";

        try
        {
            // Add the rule to the list.
            Policy.Rules.Add(Rule);

            // Display a success message.
            MessageBox.Show("Application successfully added!");
        }
        catch (Exception err)
        {
            // Display an error message.
            MessageBox.Show("Couldn't add the Application!\n" +
                err.Message);
        }
    }
```

The example begins by creating a `Policy` object using the same approach as in the "Obtaining a List of Rules" section of this chapter. It then creates a `RuleType` object using the `Type.GetTypeFromProgID()` method with `HNetCfg.FwRule` as an argument. The next step is to create the Rule object using `Activator.CreateInstance()` with `RuleType` as the argument.

A rule must fully define the exception. Unlike older techniques shown in previous sections of this chapter, a rule doesn't make any assumptions. Consequently, it's far more likely that your code will fail when creating a rule, so you have to be prepared to provide full error trapping when working with rules. In addition, rules can sometimes have unpredictable results when you don't define them adequately.

This example shows typical entries for an application exception. Notice that you must define the rule's direction, the action it performs, and which profile it appears in. As with any other Windows Firewall entry, you must provide a protocol for the rule and any addresses it requires. A rule has both local and remote addresses and ports, so you need to define both. After the code defines the rule, it calls `Policy.Rules.Add()` to perform the task within a `try...catch` statement. If you make a mistake in defining the rule, the system will still accept it in many cases without any error (the errors will come later when you try to use the faulty rule to perform useful work). Figure 13-11 shows the result of this example.

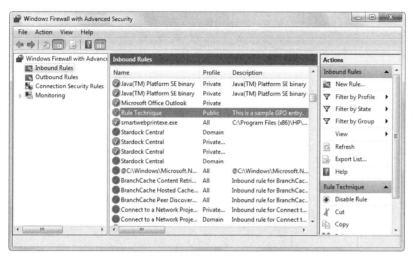

**FIGURE 13-11:** Using rules lets you add a single application entry in the public profile.

Notice that the output is a single rule. If you want an application exception for both TCP and UDP, then you must create two separate rules to do it. Unlike older Windows Firewall techniques, the rule technique doesn't assume that you want both protocols, which actually makes this approach a little safer, albeit more time-consuming and code-intensive. The actual rule output is the same as the example shown in the "Adding Applications" section of this chapter. Figure 13-12 shows the results.

## Removing an Application Rule

Removing an application rule using the rule technique is similar to removing a rule using the techniques shown in the "Adding Applications" section of this chapter. However, there are some subtle differences that could get you into trouble, as shown in Listing 13-12.

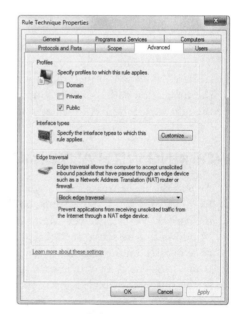

**FIGURE 13-12:** Rules make it possible to access all the application exception entries.

Available for download on Wrox.com

**LISTING 13-12:** Removing an application rule from the public profile

```
private void btnRemove_Click(object sender, EventArgs e)
{
    // Define a GPO policy type.
```

*continues*

**LISTING 13-12** *(continued)*

```
    Type PolicyType = Type.GetTypeFromProgID("HNetCfg.FwPolicy2");

    // Create the policy object.
    dynamic Policy = Activator.CreateInstance(PolicyType);

    try
    {
        // Delete the application based on the application path.
        Policy.Rules.Remove(Application.ProductName);

        // Display a success message.
        MessageBox.Show("Application successfully removed!");
    }
    catch (Exception err)
    {
        // Display an error message.
        MessageBox.Show("Couldn't remove the application!\n" +
            err.Message);
    }
}
```

The first difference is that you create a policy; the Windows Firewall Manager doesn't do it. You still use the `Remove()` method to perform the task, but notice that you use the rule name — not the application path. Some developers confuse the two techniques and later find that the rules they thought were gone are still entered in the Windows Firewall listing.

## WORKING WITH AUTOMATIC UPDATES

As part of the security setup for your application, you need to know whether Windows is up to date. In some cases, your application could actually fail because it depends on a fix being in place that the user hasn't installed yet. Many administrators and developers alike realized the need to check the Windows Update status and created code to perform that task. Unfortunately, most of the existing code is based on the techniques found on sites such as http://support.microsoft.com/kb/328010, which is outdated for Windows 7. In fact, the best approach may be to simply check the local system settings using the simple registry checks described in the sections that follow.

*This section of the chapter doesn't provide you with techniques for adding automatic updates to your application. Many developers today rely on Microsoft's ClickOnce technology (*http://msdn.microsoft.com/library/t71a733d.aspx*) to create applications that automatically update. You can read more about this technique at* http://msdn.microsoft.com/library/t71a733d.aspx*. The ClickOnce approach is a bit limited, however, so some developers rely on home-grown flexible solutions such as the one at* http://www.codeproject.com/KB/install/DDayUpdate_Part1.aspx *or third-party libraries such as the one at* http://wyday.com/wybuild/*.*

## Configuring the Automatic Update Example

The example begins with a Windows Forms application. It requires two buttons, Settings (`btnSettings`) and Updates (`btnUpdates`), and a list box, `lstResults`. You don't need to add any special references or `using` statements.

## Writing the Settings Code

One of the first things you'll want to do is view the Windows Update settings, but this task can prove difficult if you follow the clues online. A number of Websites discuss the contents of the `HKEY_LOCAL_MACHINE\SOFTWARE\Microsoft\Windows\CurrentVersion\WindowsUpdate\Auto Update` key. In fact, you can see this key in RegEdit as shown in Figure 13-13. As you can see, accessing this key would let you detect all the Windows Update settings and determine how the user has configured the system.

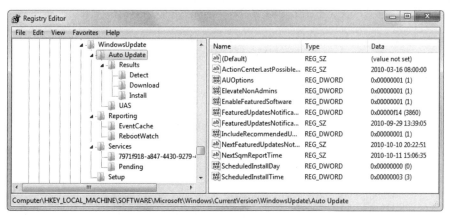

**FIGURE 13-13:** The WindowsUpdate subkey is inaccessible from your application.

The RegEdit utility can sometimes prove deceptive. When you run the following code, you'll find that the `WindowsUpdate` subkey is missing from the list.

```
// Track the results.
Boolean NotFound = true;

// Obtain the CurrentVersion registry key.
RegistryKey WU =
    Registry.LocalMachine.OpenSubKey(
        @"SOFTWARE\Microsoft\Windows\CurrentVersion");

// Get all of the subkeys and process them.
String[] Subkeys = WU.GetSubKeyNames();
foreach (String KeyName in Subkeys)
{
    // Look for the WindowsUpdate subkey.
    if (KeyName == "WindowsUpdate")
    {
```

```
        // Display a success message.
        MessageBox.Show("Found WindowsUpdate!");

        // Update the tracking variable.
        NotFound = false;
        break;
    }
}

// Check the tracking variable.
if (NotFound)

    // Display a failure message.
    MessageBox.Show("WindowsUpdate is Missing!");
```

As far as your .NET application is concerned, the `WindowsUpdate` subkey doesn't exist. Running in administrator mode won't help. Changing the key's permissions won't help either. This is a circumstance where RegEdit shows something your application can't access directly.

Fortunately, you can access the information you need using COM and the `dynamic` keyword. Listing 13-13 shows the code used to access the Windows Update settings for this example.

**LISTING 13-13:** Obtaining the current Windows Update settings

```
private void btnSettings_Click(object sender, EventArgs e)
{
    // Clear the list box.
    lstResults.Items.Clear();

    // Create the AutoUpdate type.
    Type SettingsType = Type.GetTypeFromProgID("Microsoft.Update.AutoUpdate");

    // Use the AutoUpdate type to create a settings object.
    dynamic Settings = Activator.CreateInstance(SettingsType);

    // Verify that the Windows Update service is running.
    if (Settings.ServiceEnabled)
        // Display the status.
        lstResults.Items.Add("Windows Update Service Enabled.");
    else
    {
        // Display the status and exit because the code can't
        // process any more information.
        lstResults.Items.Add("Windows Update Service Disabled.");
        return;
    }

    // Determine the update mode and output data accordingly.
    switch ((Int32)Settings.Settings.NotificationLevel)
    {
        case 1:
            lstResults.Items.Add("Update Mode: Never Check");
            break;
```

# Working with Automatic Updates | 277

```csharp
        case 2:
            lstResults.Items.Add("Update Mode: Check for Updates");
            break;
        case 3:
            lstResults.Items.Add("Update Mode: Download Updates/No Install");
            break;
        case 4:
            lstResults.Items.Add("Update Mode: Automatically Install Updates");

            // Get the automatic check day and time.
            switch ((Int32)Settings.Settings.ScheduledInstallationDay)
            {
                case 0:
                    lstResults.Items.Add("\tEvery Day: " +
                        Settings.Settings.ScheduledInstallationTime + ":00");
                    break;
                case 1:
                    lstResults.Items.Add("\tSunday: " +
                        Settings.Settings.ScheduledInstallationTime + ":00");
                    break;
                case 2:
                    lstResults.Items.Add("\tMonday: " +
                        Settings.Settings.ScheduledInstallationTime + ":00");
                    break;
                case 3:
                    lstResults.Items.Add("\tTuesday: " +
                        Settings.Settings.ScheduledInstallationTime + ":00");
                    break;
                case 4:
                    lstResults.Items.Add("\tWednesday: " +
                        Settings.Settings.ScheduledInstallationTime + ":00");
                    break;
                case 5:
                    lstResults.Items.Add("\tThursday: " +
                        Settings.Settings.ScheduledInstallationTime + ":00");
                    break;
                case 6:
                    lstResults.Items.Add("\tFriday: " +
                        Settings.Settings.ScheduledInstallationTime + ":00");
                    break;
                case 7:
                    lstResults.Items.Add("\tSaturday: " +
                        Settings.Settings.ScheduledInstallationTime + ":00");
                    break;
            }
            break;
    }

    // Check the kinds of updates allowed.
    if (Settings.Settings.FeaturedUpdatesEnabled)
        lstResults.Items.Add("Featured Updates Enabled");
    else
        lstResults.Items.Add("Featured Updates Disabled");

    if (Settings.Settings.IncludeRecommendedUpdates)
```

*continues*

**LISTING 13-13** *(continued)*

```
            lstResults.Items.Add("Include Recommended Updates");
    else
            lstResults.Items.Add("Don't Include Recommended Updates");

    if (Settings.Settings.NonAdministratorsElevated)
            lstResults.Items.Add("Non-administrators Automatically Elevated");
    else
            lstResults.Items.Add("Only Administrators Can Update System");

    // Get update search and installation information.
    lstResults.Items.Add("Last Successful Search Date:" +
            Settings.Results.LastSearchSuccessDate);
    lstResults.Items.Add("Last Successful Installation Date: " +
            Settings.Results.LastInstallationSuccessDate);
}
```

The example begins by clearing the old results. It then creates the `SettingsType` by calling `Type .GetTypeFromProgID()` with the `Microsoft.Update.AutoUpdate` program identifier. The code uses the `dynamic` keyword to create the `Settings` object by calling `Activator.CreateInstance()` with `SettingsType` as an argument. At this point, you have access to all the Windows Update settings.

It's important not to assume that the user has the Windows Update service enabled. In some cases, the administrator could turn the service off or the user might do so. The first check verifies that the service is enabled. If not, the code outputs text showing that the service is disabled and exits.

A user can select four levels of update. The next check determines the notification level — the amount of update information the user receives. At one end of the spectrum, the user can choose not to receive any update information at all (which means the user will have to manually request update information), and at the other end the updates can occur automatically without any user notification at all. When the user chooses the automatic update option, the system is also configured for a day and time to perform the update (usually when it's least likely to cause problems for the user's work schedule). The system can check for updates every day or on a specific day and at a specified time.

The user can also select a number of update features. The example doesn't review all these settings, but the user can choose whether to check for recommended updates in addition to critical updates. The most important entry for developers is whether users can install updates. In some cases, the system will be configured to allow only administrators to perform updates, which means that your application may have to wait until an administrator can install the required updates.

Finally, the example checks `Settings.Results` for two bits of information that help you understand system health. The `LastSearchSuccessDate` should be recent if the system at least checks for updates regularly. Of course, simply because the system checks for updates doesn't necessarily mean that the user is installing any of them, which is why you must also check the `LastInstallationSuccessDate` property to ensure it isn't too far out of date with the last search date. Microsoft constantly provides updates, so the two dates should be reasonably close. Figure 13-14 shows typical output from this portion of the example.

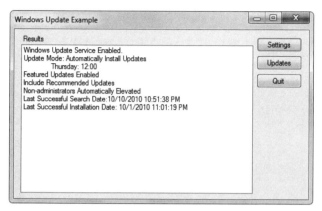

**FIGURE 13-14:** The example shows all the important Windows Update settings.

## Writing the Update Code

Once you know whether the user's system is healthy from an update check and download perspective, you need to know which updates the user has actually installed. For example, you might worry that your application won't work properly without the daylight saving time and time zone updates found in the Knowledge Base article at http://support.microsoft.com/kb/2158563. Using the technique shown in Listing 13-14, you can obtain the complete list of updates and search it for the appropriate update.

**LISTING 13-14:** Obtaining a list of installed updates

Available for
download on
Wrox.com

```
private void btnUpdates_Click(object sender, EventArgs e)
{
    // Clear the list box.
    lstResults.Items.Clear();

    // Create the Microsoft Update Searcher (MUS) type.
    Type MUStype = Type.GetTypeFromProgID("Microsoft.Update.Searcher");

    // Use the MUS type to create a searcher object.
    dynamic Searcher = Activator.CreateInstance(MUStype);

    // Access the entire history.
    dynamic Updates =
        Searcher.QueryHistory(0, Searcher.GetTotalHistoryCount());

    // Check each update in the history in turn.
    foreach (dynamic Update in Updates)
    {
        // Display only the successful updates.
        if (Update.ResultCode == 2)
        {
            // Display the update information.
```

*continues*

**LISTING 13-13** *(continued)*

```
            lstResults.Items.Add("Title: " + Update.Title);
            lstResults.Items.Add("Description: " + Update.Description);
            lstResults.Items.Add("Date (GMT): " + Update.Date);
            lstResults.Items.Add("Installation Method: " +
                Update.ClientApplicationID);

            // Add a blank line.
            lstResults.Items.Add("");
        }
    }
}
```

The code begins by clearing the previous results from the list box and creating a `Type`, `MUStype`, based on `Microsoft.Update.Searcher`. The code then creates the `Search` object using `Activator.CreateInstance()` with `MUStype` as an argument.

The `Searcher` object actually has access to a number of methods for querying the update database. The example uses the simplest of these techniques, `QueryHistory()`. You supply the starting record and number of records to return as inputs. The other methods are documented at http://msdn.microsoft.com/library/aa386530.aspx.

The next step is determining which updates to check. One of the most important properties for developers is the `ResultCode`. The example looks for updates that succeeded. A result code can have any of the following values:

➤ **2:** The update succeeded.

➤ **4:** The update failed for some reason other than that the user or system aborted it.

➤ **5:** The user or the system aborted the update. An update is aborted either manually or when the system detects an error in the update code or conditions.

➤ **Other:** There could be other update codes that aren't listed. A third-party vendor could provide an update code for a partial update or a pending update. In most cases, you aren't concerned about these alternate conditions and need to know only whether the update succeeded, failed, or aborted.

The output information also includes an update title, a description of what the update does, the date the user installed the update, and the technique used to install the update. Figure 13-15 shows typical output from this part of the example.

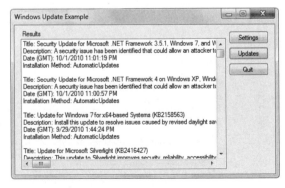

**FIGURE 13-15:** It's possible to search the update database for a particular update.

## ACCESSING APPLOCKER

AppLocker provides a significant new means of enforcing application execution policies. The emphasis is on code rights, not user rights as it is with NT security. You can attach AppLocker rules in a number of ways. For example, you can create AppLocker rules that affect a particular user or group. AppLocker rules can also affect an executable's publisher or even the version of a file. It's also possible to restrict particular application types. You can read more about the ways in which you can use AppLocker to control applications on a system at http://technet.microsoft.com/library/ee424367.aspx.

AppLocker doesn't work with all versions of Windows. In fact, you're limited to the following versions:

- Windows Server 2008 R2 Standard
- Windows Server 2008 R2 Enterprise
- Windows Server 2008 R2 Datacenter
- Windows Server 2008 R2 for Itanium-Based Systems
- Windows 7 Ultimate
- Windows 7 Enterprise

You can create AppLocker rules when working with Windows 7 Professional, but the operating system won't enforce the rules. So even though AppLocker is a marvelous new security feature, it does currently have some significant limitations. AppLocker does build on Software Restriction Policies (SRP) technology found in older versions of Windows, so you may have to rely on SRP for now and update to AppLocker later.

### Seeing the AppLocker Entries in the Registry

The AppLocker entries are part of a GPO. Unfortunately, in this case there isn't a convenient COM object you can use to access the information you need. What you need to do in this case is view the data using a registry entry. In fact, there are commonly eight or more registry entries you could use, but only one of the multitude of registry entries is always in a known place in the registry, the HKEY_LOCAL_MACHINE\SOFTWARE\Policies\Microsoft\Windows\SrpV2 key. Figure 13-16 shows how this key might appear on your system.

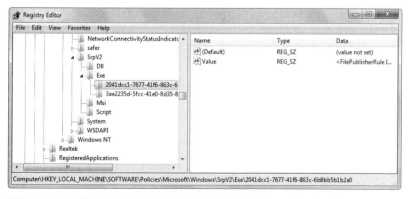

**FIGURE 13-16:** AppLocker relies heavily on the registry to store settings.

The SrpV2 key stands for Software Restriction Policy version 2, because that's what AppLocker really is. Beneath this key are four keys for DLL, executable, installer, and script files. Each policy key name appears as a Globally Unique Identifier (GUID), which is pronounced "gwid" (think of squid). Every policy has just one value, named Value. It consists of an XML description of the policy. Here's a typical example of a publisher policy.

```
<FilePublisherRule Id="2041dcc1-7677-41f6-863c-6b8bb5b1b2a0"
                   Name="My AppLocker Rule 2"
                   Description="Another sample AppLocker rule."
                   UserOrGroupSid="S-1-1-0"
                   Action="Allow">
  <Conditions>
    <FilePublisherCondition
      PublisherName="O=MICROSOFT CORPORATION, L=REDMOND, S=WASHINGTON, C=US"
      ProductName="MICROSOFT (R) VISUAL STUDIO (R) 2010"
      BinaryName="VSHOST32.EXE">
        <BinaryVersionRange LowSection="10.0.0.0" HighSection="*"/>
    </FilePublisherCondition>
  </Conditions>
</FilePublisherRule>
```

Of course, the entry won't appear nicely formatted in the registry — it appears as a single line of barely readable XML. Some information, such as the Id, Name, Description, UserOrGroupSid, and Action attributes, remains the same for every entry. The contents of the <Conditions> element vary by the kind of exclusion you create. For example, a path exclusion only requires a <FilePathCondition> element that contains a Path attribute.

## Configuring the AppLocker Demo Example

The AppLocker Demo example consists of a Windows Forms application. You need to add two buttons, List Entries (btnList) and Add Entries (btnAdd). The example also requires a list box for output, lstEntries. Because this example relies on the registry, you do need to add the following using statements, but you don't need to add any special references.

```
using Microsoft.Win32;
using System.Xml;
using System.Security;
```

Everyone can read the AppLocker entries, so you don't need to add a manifest if your only goal is to read the entries. However, only administrators can add new entries. Your application will need to add a manifest to the example using the procedure found in the "Creating the User Permission Modification Manifest" section of Chapter 10.

## Reading AppLocker Entries

Reading the AppLocker entries means locating the entries in the registry and then parsing them. You have no way of knowing how many entries the registry will contain (if it contains any entries at all). Listing 13-15 parses the entries using the assumption that the registry might not contain any entries.

**LISTING 13-15:** Reading the AppLocker entries from a known location

```
private void btnList_Click(object sender, EventArgs e)
{
    // Clear the previous entries.
    lstEntries.Items.Clear();

    // Open the AppLocker registry key.
    RegistryKey AppLock =
        Registry.LocalMachine.OpenSubKey(
            @"SOFTWARE\Policies\Microsoft\Windows\SrpV2");

    // Obtain the kinds of entries that the application can create.
    String[] EntryTypes = AppLock.GetSubKeyNames();

    // Process each entry in turn.
    foreach (String EntryType in EntryTypes)
    {
        // Display the entry type.
        lstEntries.Items.Add(EntryType);

        // Open the associated subkey.
        RegistryKey ThisType = AppLock.OpenSubKey(EntryType);

        // Obtain a list of entries within the type.
        String[] AppLockEntries = ThisType.GetSubKeyNames();

        // Process each of the individual entries.
        foreach (String AppLockEntry in AppLockEntries)
        {
            // Display the individual entry GUID.
            lstEntries.Items.Add("\t" + AppLockEntry);

            // Open the individual entry.
            RegistryKey ThisEntry = ThisType.OpenSubKey(AppLockEntry);

            // Obtain the XML value of the entry.
            XmlDocument Entry = new XmlDocument();
            Entry.LoadXml(ThisEntry.GetValue("Value").ToString());

            // Obtain the root element.
            XmlNode TheRule = Entry.FirstChild;

            // Display the overall rule values.
            lstEntries.Items.Add("\t\tName: " +
                TheRule.Attributes["Name"].Value);
            lstEntries.Items.Add("\t\tDescription: " +
                TheRule.Attributes["Description"].Value);
            lstEntries.Items.Add("\t\tGroup or User SID: " +
                TheRule.Attributes["UserOrGroupSid"].Value);
            lstEntries.Items.Add("\t\tAction: " +
                TheRule.Attributes["Action"].Value);

            // Obtain the condition element.
```

*continues*

**LISTING 13-15** *(continued)*

```
            XmlNode Conditions = TheRule.FirstChild;

            // Examine the conditions.
            foreach (XmlNode Condition in Conditions)
            {
                // Display the attributes for each condition.
                foreach (XmlAttribute Specification in Condition.Attributes)
                {
                    // Show the attribute information.
                    lstEntries.Items.Add("\t\t\t" + Specification.Name +
                        ": " + Specification.Value);
                }
            }

            // Close the individual entry.
            ThisEntry.Close();

            // Add a space.
            lstEntries.Items.Add("");
        }

        // Close the entry type.
        ThisType.Close();

        // Add a space.
        lstEntries.Items.Add("");
    }

    // Close the main key.
    AppLock.Close();
}
```

The example begins by clearing the previous list box entries. It then opens the one key that you can depend on to find AppLocker entries, assuming the target system supports AppLocker. The `AppLock` object contains a handle to the registry entry after the code calls `OpenSubKey()` using the `Registry.LocalMachine` property. The code calls `GetSubKeyNames()` to obtain a list of entries and places them in `EntryTypes` (the array should contain the `Dll`, `Exe`, `Msi`, and `Script` key names). Because Microsoft could decide to change the format of the registry entries, the code uses a `foreach` loop to parse through whatever entries appear in the `EntryTypes String` array.

At this point, the code opens a subkey, such as `Dll`, for processing by calling `OpenSubKey()`. The code uses the `GetSubKeyNames()` call to place a list of GUID entries in `AppLockEntries`. It uses a second `foreach` loop to process each of the GUID entries that appear as subkeys of `EntryType`.

As previously mentioned, each GUID entry contains a value named `Value` that contains XML describing the rule used to define an exception. The code begins by creating an `XmlDocument` object, `Entry`, and placing the XML in it by calling `LoadXml()`. The code processes the XML as you would any XML document. It begins by accessing the `<FilePublisherRule>` or other rule element, listing the attributes in this element, and then working through the `<Conditions>` element. The precise order of processing depends on the rule. Figure 13-17 shows typical output from this example.

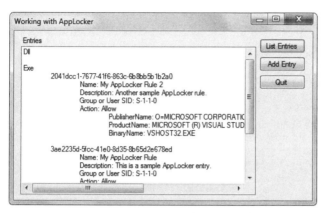

**FIGURE 13-17:** The example displays any AppLocker rules configured on your system.

## Creating an AppLocker Entry

Creating an AppLocker entry is a difficult and error-prone process because the entries appear in so many registry keys. You literally have to search the registry looking for the proper places to put the keys. Consequently, this part of the application starts with the recursive search routine shown in Listing 13-16.

**LISTING 13-16:** Using a recursive routine to search the registry

Available for download on Wrox.com

```
private List<String> SearchReg(
    RegistryKey StartHive, String StartPath,
    String SearchKey, List<String> Results)
{
    RegistryKey Start; // Defines a starting point for the search.

    // This operation will fail when processing certain users.
    try
    {
        // Open the specified registry key.
        Start = StartHive.OpenSubKey(StartPath);
    }
    catch (SecurityException SE)
    {
        // The application can't process this key.
        return Results;
    }

    // Start may be null after an attempt to open some user keys.
    if (Start == null)
        return Results;

    // Get a list of subkeys for that key.
```

*continues*

**LISTING 13-16** *(continued)*

```
        String[] Subkeys = Start.GetSubKeyNames();

        // If there aren't any subkeys to process, exit.
        if (Subkeys.Length != 0)

            // Process each of the subkeys in turn.
            foreach (String Name in Subkeys)

                // When the key is equal to the search term.
                if (Name == SearchKey)
                {
                    // Add the string to the list.
                    Results.Add(StartPath + @"\" + Name);
                }
                else
                    // Otherwise, keep searching.
                    Results =
                        SearchReg(
                            StartHive, StartPath + @"\" + Name,
                            SearchKey, Results);

    return Results;
}
```

The code begins by attempting to open a supplied registry key. In some cases, attempting to open the key will generate an error because the key isn't meant to be opened for any sort of use (such as the secure keys of the default user's account). It's actually easier to let the exception occur in this case and catch it, than it is to generate a list of keys that could cause problems. If the `OpenSubKey()` call succeeds, the result could still be a `null` entry, meaning the key doesn't exist. The example handles both issues by returning the current results to the caller.

If the supplied key is valid and it opens properly, the code generates a list of subkeys to check using the `GetSubKeyNames()` method. The code checks each of these subkeys in turn for the search key name. When the code finds a key that matches, it adds the key to `Results` for return to the caller. Otherwise, the code recursively calls `SearchReg()` to process the next level of subkeys.

Now that you know how the search routine works, it's time to look at the code for adding an AppLock entry. Listing 13-17 shows this code.

**LISTING 13-17:** Adding a new path AppLock entry

```
private void btnAdd_Click(object sender, EventArgs e)
{
    // Open the AppLocker registry key.
    RegistryKey AppLock =
        Registry.LocalMachine.OpenSubKey(
            @"SOFTWARE\Policies\Microsoft\Windows\SrpV2\Exe", true);

    // Create a new GUID.
```

```csharp
Guid EntryGuid = Guid.NewGuid();

// Use the new GUID to create a subkey and then open the subkey.
RegistryKey EntryKey = AppLock.CreateSubKey(EntryGuid.ToString());

// Create the XML required for the entry value.
XmlDocument TheRule = new XmlDocument();

// Define the condition.
XmlElement Condition = TheRule.CreateElement("FilePathCondition");
XmlAttribute Path = TheRule.CreateAttribute("Path");
Path.Value = Application.ExecutablePath;
Condition.Attributes.Append(Path);

// Add the condition to a list of conditions.
XmlElement Conditions = TheRule.CreateElement("Conditions");
Conditions.AppendChild(Condition);

// Create the root node.
XmlElement Root = TheRule.CreateElement("FilePathRule");

// Define the rule attributes.
XmlAttribute Id = TheRule.CreateAttribute("Id");
Id.Value = EntryGuid.ToString();
Root.Attributes.Append(Id);

XmlAttribute Name = TheRule.CreateAttribute("Name");
Name.Value = "My Generated AppLocker Rule";
Root.Attributes.Append(Name);

XmlAttribute Description = TheRule.CreateAttribute("Description");
Description.Value = "Test rule generated by an application.";
Root.Attributes.Append(Description);

XmlAttribute SID = TheRule.CreateAttribute("UserOrGroupSid");
SID.Value = "S-1-1-0";
Root.Attributes.Append(SID);

XmlAttribute Action = TheRule.CreateAttribute("Action");
Action.Value = "Allow";
Root.Attributes.Append(Action);

// Add the conditions to the root.
Root.AppendChild(Conditions);

// Add the root to the rule.
TheRule.AppendChild(Root);

// Set the value of the registry entry to the XML rule.
EntryKey.SetValue("Value", TheRule.OuterXml);

// Close the keys.
EntryKey.Close();
```

*continues*

**LISTING 13-17** *(continued)*

```
    AppLock.Close();

    // Check for the 64-bit key.
    AppLock = Registry.LocalMachine.OpenSubKey(
        @"SOFTWARE\Wow6432Node\Policies\Microsoft\Windows\SrpV2\Exe",
        true);

    // If the entry exists, add the data to it.
    if (AppLock != null)
    {
        // Use the GUID to create a subkey and then open the subkey.
        EntryKey = AppLock.CreateSubKey(EntryGuid.ToString());

        // Set the value of the registry entry to the XML rule.
        EntryKey.SetValue("Value", TheRule.OuterXml);

        // Close the keys.
        EntryKey.Close();
        AppLock.Close();
    }

    // Create a list of registry strings that require
    // the addition of the registry information.
    List<String> RegKeys = new List<string>();
    RegKeys = SearchReg(
        Registry.CurrentUser,
        @"Software\Microsoft\Windows\CurrentVersion\Group Policy Objects",
        "SrpV2", RegKeys);

    // Process each of the current user entries.
    foreach (String KeyString in RegKeys)
    {
        // Open the base key.
        RegistryKey Key = Registry.CurrentUser.OpenSubKey(KeyString + @"\Exe",
            true);

        // Create the new rule key.
        RegistryKey NewRule = Key.CreateSubKey(EntryGuid.ToString());

        // Set the value.
        NewRule.SetValue("Value", TheRule.OuterXml);

        // Close the keys.
        NewRule.Close();
        Key.Close();
    }

    // Clear the old entries.
    RegKeys.Clear();

    // Each user can have special entries, too.
```

```
            String[] UserList = Registry.Users.GetSubKeyNames();

        // Process each of the users in turn.
        foreach (String User in UserList)
            RegKeys = SearchReg(
                Registry.Users,
                User,
                "SrpV2", RegKeys);

        // Process each of the user entries.
        foreach (String KeyString in RegKeys)
        {
            // Open the base key.
            RegistryKey Key = Registry.Users.OpenSubKey(KeyString + @"\Exe", true);

            // Create the new rule key.
            RegistryKey NewRule = Key.CreateSubKey(EntryGuid.ToString());

            // Set the value.
            NewRule.SetValue("Value", TheRule.OuterXml);

            // Close the keys.
            NewRule.Close();
            Key.Close();
        }

        // Display a success message.
        MessageBox.Show("AppLocker Entry Successful!");
    }
```

This looks like a lot of code, but the process is repetitive. The code begins by opening the HKEY_LOCAL_MACHINE\SOFTWARE\Policies\Microsoft\Windows\SrpV2 key by calling `Registry.LocalMachine.OpenSubKey()`. Notice that you must add a second argument, `true`, to open the key for writing, or the code will fail. The next step is to generate a GUID because every AppLocker rule must have a unique identifier. The code creates the new entry by calling `CreateSubKey()` with the new GUID found in `EntryGuid`.

At this point, the example has a new key to use. The next step is to start creating the XML for the value, `Value`. The code begins by creating a new `XmlDocument` object, `TheRule`. It then uses `TheRule` to create the rule condition. The rule condition contains a `Path` attribute that includes the application's path information. The condition is encased in a `<Conditions>` element.

It's time to create the root element, which is a `<FilePathRule>` element in this case. The `<FilePathRule>` element contains all the expected attributes, such as `Id`. After creating all the required attributes, the code adds the `<Conditions>` element using `AppendChild()`. Finally, the code adds the `<FilePathRule>` element to `TheRule`. Now that the XML is complete, the code creates the `Value` value and assigns the XML to it using the `TheRule.OuterXml` property.

The next step is to create an entry for the HKEY_LOCAL_MACHINE\SOFTWARE\Wow6432Node\Policies\Microsoft\Windows\SrpV2\Exe key, which only appears on 64-bit systems. This second key is also always found in the same location. However, now you have to begin searching for `SrpV2` keys that could appear just about anywhere in these areas:

- `HKEY_CURRENT_USER\Software\Microsoft\Windows\CurrentVersion\Group Policy Objects\`
- `HKEY_USERS\`*`SID`*`\Software\Microsoft\Windows\CurrentVersion\Group Policy Objects\`

Not every `HKEY_USERS` subkey will have the required entry, which makes searching for user entries even harder. To make this process easier, the code uses `SearchReg()`, described earlier, to locate keys and place them in a `List`. A `foreach` loop makes the steps for creating the required keys and values easier. The process for creating the keys and values is the same each time. After running this part of the example, you must log out and then back into the system to actually see the results in AppLocker.

## MOVING YOUR APPLICATIONS TO WINDOWS 7

This chapter has explored some of the external security features you can add to your application. Of all the items in this chapter, the firewall material is probably what you'll use most often. Modern applications often require some sort of external access across the Internet or a local network. When your application relies on a special port or other configuration, you need to tell the firewall about it, or the communication will be blocked. Obviously, checking on the state of the user's machine will also help your application maintain a secure environment by ensuring that the host system has the required updates and virus protection.

Before you go to the next chapter, take some time to perform an application survey. Decide which internal and external elements you need to ensure that your application, the user, and the application data remain safe from external influences. It's important to make these security decisions as part of the design process. Bolt-on security, the kind that you add after the fact, no longer provides adequate application protection. You need security that's built into the application from the time you create the initial design. Make sure you spend time talking with both administrators and users about your design decisions. You'll find that your assumptions about what should work often don't reflect real-world application needs.

Chapter 14 begins a new part of the book. In this part, you'll discover some advanced Windows 7 programming techniques you can use to make your applications even better. Some of these programming techniques are exclusive to Windows 7 — making the application incompatible with earlier versions of Windows. Chapter 14 begins with techniques you can use to let your application work in the background. Using background processes is helpful for long-running tasks or tasks that don't require user interaction. For example, printing a document can be a long-running task that you perform in the background while the user continues to work in the foreground. Likewise, creating a search index is a task that doesn't require user interaction, so you can perform it in the background when the user isn't using all the processing cycles for foreground tasks. Of course, background processing has been around for a long time, but Windows 7 adds some interesting new twists that you'll discover in Chapter 14.

# PART IV
# Advanced Windows 7 Programming

- **CHAPTER 14:** Working in the Background
- **CHAPTER 15:** Using the Windows 7 Libraries
- **CHAPTER 16:** Writing 64-Bit Applications for Windows 7
- **CHAPTER 17:** Using Parallel Programming in Windows 7
- **CHAPTER 18:** Using the Sensor and Location Platform
- **CHAPTER 19:** Using Windows XP Mode Effectively

# 14
# Working in the Background

**WHAT'S IN THIS CHAPTER?**

- ➤ Considering why your application should work in the background
- ➤ Creating a trigger-start service
- ➤ Providing power management
- ➤ Adding restart and recovery to your application
- ➤ Accessing the network list manager

Applications can run either in the foreground, where the user interacts with them, or in the background, where they perform tasks independently. A word processor is an example of a foreground task. The user starts a new document, types some text into it, formats it, and performs other tasks with it. A service, such as Windows Time, is an example of a background application. Windows Time can maintain time synchronization just fine without any user interaction.

However, the lines between foreground and background tasks aren't absolute. A word processor can employ a background task to print a document upon user request. The user can continue working in the foreground with the document while the word processor prints it in the background. Likewise, the W32Tm utility lets you interact with the Windows Time service. You might choose to resynchronize the local machine with an Internet time source, which means requesting the action from the Windows Time service, using the W32Tm utility.

Many of the examples in the book are necessarily foreground tasks because you want to see how a particular Windows 7 feature works. This chapter takes another approach to working with Windows 7. The sections that follow discuss background tasks and how you can use them to enrich the application environment in Windows 7.

*None of the examples in this chapter are designed to work with earlier versions of Windows, and you must have Visual Studio 2008 as a minimum even to create most of the examples (the author relied on Visual Studio 2010 to write the examples, so you'd need to port the code to Visual Studio 2008). For example, trigger-start services aren't available on any version of Windows earlier than Windows 2008 R2. Theoretically, some examples, such as the power management example, could work on earlier versions of Windows, but you would need to do some tweaking to make them work in the earlier environments.*

## ADVANTAGES OF WORKING IN THE BACKGROUND

Most systems spend the majority of their time working in the background. If you look at the Task Manager display, you'll see that there are more than 60 processes running on any Windows 7 machine, most of them not even started by the user. To see this for yourself, right-click the Taskbar and choose Start Task Manager from the Context menu. Select the Processes tab and click Show Processes from All Users. Figure 14-1 shows a typical example of what you'll see. Notice the number of processes started by accounts other than the logged-in user, who is John in this case.

The idea of background processes isn't new. Long before Windows appeared on the scene, people were using background tasks. Early systems didn't have the computing horsepower to support many background tasks, but they did support some. In general, background tasks have the following advantages:

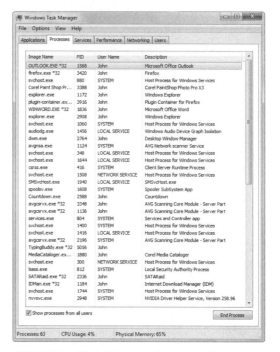

**FIGURE 14-1:** Task Manager shows that Windows has many processes running in the background.

- ➤ **Improved system efficiency:** They use processing cycles that the user doesn't employ.
- ➤ **Increased application responsiveness:** They perform such tasks as printing in the background while servicing user requests in the foreground.
- ➤ **Enhanced application functionality:** They provide the means for adding features that normally wouldn't work well in a foreground scenario, such as long-term searches against large databases.

- **Protocol support:** They create a conduit between applications or services that normally can't communicate with each other due to differences in data format, platform, structure, or processing requirements. In many cases, common functionality, such as LAN support, is nothing more than protocols used to create a conduit.
- **Specialized hardware interface:** They offer a way to use hardware that the operating system doesn't support natively. For example, Windows 7 offers support for special sensors. The Adaptive Brightness service monitors light sensors and automatically changes the display brightness to match current light conditions.

These uses of background processing can fit any environment, including Windows. However, Windows uses background processing in particular ways. You may find some of the following uses in other operating systems as well (and Microsoft likely borrowed a number of these ideas from older operating systems).

- **System monitoring:** Many forms of background processing do nothing more than monitor a particular part of the operating system. When a particular event occurs, the application does something, such as displaying a message or updating the system time. In some cases, the system-monitoring applications rely on a foreground application for configuration and manual request requirements.
- **System-level functionality:** Developers often place system-level code in services or other background applications. This code often runs under a different account than the user account and feeds the resources the user-level application requires in a safe manner.
- **General services:** The system uses background processing to support general services, such as providing Bluetooth support or a Web server. The service monitors the system for application requests and operates as necessary.
- **Security services:** As threats have increased, a special kind of software has developed that's specifically devoted to security needs. Everything from virus detection to firewalls runs as background processes that continually monitor the system for threats. Modern operating systems also provide data protection in the form of cryptographic services and whole-drive encryption.
- **System diagnostics:** The complexity of modern operating systems makes it harder for administrators to detect and fix problems that occur. Background processes can monitor the system for problems and automatically fix them in some cases, or provide diagnostic information to the administrator in others. Some of these diagnostic services also take the form of maintenance applications. For example, to keep the operating system working at peak efficiency, the Disk Defragmenter service defragments the hard drive.
- **Media support:** Windows provides a significant level of media support, most of which requires some form of background processing to accomplish. For example, streaming audio continues as long as the user desires it, even though the application that supports the streaming operates in the background.

## DEVELOPING TRIGGER-START SERVICES

Trigger-start services are an efficiency measure in Windows 7. The short story is that Windows currently uses too many resources because as user needs change it needs to support more and more software. One of the most common problems is too many services. Most services remain running while you work with Windows. The service constantly polls the system looking for work to do. Of course, this polling process wastes processing cycles. In addition, the service constantly uses resources such as memory because it must remain loaded at all times. Even though developers don't often use the service-start modes effectively, you do have several options for starting and stopping standard services.

➤ **Disabled:** The service is completely disabled and can't start on its own. However, a user can manually start the service as required using either the Services applet in the Control Panel or the Service Control (SC) command line utility.

➤ **Manual:** The operating system can start the service when it detects a need, or an application can start the service through a request. While the service is stopped, it doesn't use any system resources or processing cycles.

➤ **Automatic:** The service starts during system startup. This is the mode most developers use. Unfortunately, not every service needs to start immediately (and sometimes they don't need to start at all). Overuse of this mode is the reason Microsoft has developed trigger-start services. Windows start times constantly increase, in part, because of the use of automatic mode when a service doesn't actually require it.

➤ **Automatic Delayed:** Microsoft introduced this mode with Windows Vista as a sort of compromise. The service still starts automatically, but it waits until Windows is completely running to do so. The user can begin working with Windows faster, and the perception is that Windows starts faster. Because this is a newer mode, few developers use it, and use of this mode doesn't solve the basic problem with automatic mode — overuse of system resources and processing cycles.

Because few developers actually use manual or disabled mode, Microsoft had to come up with something different — something that developers would understand and use. In addition, developers have requested something more flexible than the four simple modes currently supported by standard services. A trigger-start service is akin to a manual standard service, except that it relies on the operating system to wake it up when a special event occurs. It's the use of a special event that makes trigger-start services more flexible than standard services. Using a trigger-start service means that the service uses processing cycles and resources only when there's something to do, making the service considerably more efficient. The following sections describe trigger-start services in more detail.

> *The example in this section relies on Platform Invoke (P/Invoke) to perform its task. Many developers dislike using P/Invoke because the code can be hard to read and even harder to understand. Normally, Microsoft or a third party will create a library to make Win32 API access easier, but such a library isn't available for working with trigger-start services at the time of this writing. If you hear of such a library, feel free to contact me about it at* `JMueller@mwt.net`.

## Triggering a Service

A trigger-start service isn't anything too strange. Don't think of it as an entirely new technology. Rather, it's simply a new way to start the service when needed. If you focus on the means of starting the trigger-start service, you'll find the entire process easier to understand. A trigger-start service can use any of these triggers as a source for starting:

- **Adding or removing a device:** Fires whenever the system sees a new device. For example, the user could attach a Universal Serial Bus (USB) device, such as a camera. This event also fires when a device is removed from the system, so you could handle a situation where the user attaches a printer, prints something, and then detaches the printer.

- **Joining or leaving a domain:** Fires whenever the system logs in to a domain or logs out of a domain. You can use this event to monitor the user's activities with servers.

- **Opening or closing a firewall port:** Fires whenever the system detects the opening or closing of a firewall port. A service that relies on this trigger could monitor application use of temporary Internet access. It could also look for unusual activities, such as those performed by viruses.

- **Changing a group policy:** Fires whenever anyone modifies a group policy on the system, even if the modification is automatic (such as through a login script). A service using this trigger could look for unusual activities or simply respond to changes in user rights.

- **Changing network availability:** Detects changes in the network configuration. For example, this trigger will detect when the first IP address for a TCP/IP stack becomes available. It also detects when a TCP/IP stack is no longer available (or is about to become unavailable), so that applications can terminate communication that relies on the TCP/IP stack.

- **Defining a custom event using Event Tracing for Windows (ETW):** Allows the developer to create custom event triggers. A custom event trigger could use any event you desire. For example, you might want to start the service only when an external utility makes a request. You could create a custom trigger to start the service when the system detects such a request. Generally, it's far easier to use manual or disabled mode whenever possible instead of creating a custom trigger.

> *Some trigger-start service methods are thwarted by third-party software. For example, if the user installs a third-party firewall and disables the Windows firewall, it's unlikely trigger-start services that rely on the opening or closing of a port will work. This particular trigger relies on the Windows Firewall to detect changes in port configuration. It's not likely that third-party vendors will add the required support to their firewalls unless Microsoft mandates the change as part of a conformance criterion.*

In order to create a trigger, you must provide the operating system with the information it needs to detect the event and then start the appropriate service. A trigger description consists of the following pieces of information:

- **Trigger event type:** The major type of the trigger event, as previously described in this section.

- **Trigger event subtype:** A subtype that better describes the trigger event. Not all trigger types have subtypes. For example, there aren't any subtypes associated with joining or leaving a domain, but there are subtypes associated with adding or removing a device (in this case, you supply the Universally Unique Identifier, or UUID, of the device).

- **Action:** The task to perform when the event occurs. In general, the trigger either stops or starts a service.
- **Data:** Information to provide to the service as part of the action. The data you supply depends on the trigger event type, subtype, and action. Some trigger types don't require any additional data. For example, a trigger based on the opening of a port requires that you specify the port number, but joining or leaving a domain doesn't.

Windows supplies two methods of registering a trigger-start service. The first technique is to use the SC utility with the TriggerInfo command. For example, if you want to set the example service to start when it detects a change in Port 23 using the TCP protocol, you type **SC TriggerInfo TriggerStartService Start/PortOpen/23;TCP** and press Enter. Let's take that command apart.

- SC is the name of the utility.
- TriggerInfo is the command that defines a trigger-start service.
- TriggerStartService is the name of the example service (not the display name, but the actual service name).
- Start is the action you want Windows to perform.
- PortOpen is the trigger event type (port) and subtype (open).
- 23;TCP is the data for the trigger — Port 23 and the TCP protocol.

Unfortunately, the manual technique doesn't work well because it relies on the administrator to know about the TriggerInfo command and manually register the service after installation. The second technique is to programmatically register the service as a trigger-start service. In this case, the installation routine automatically provides the required trigger-start information to the operating system. The problem with this approach is that you must work with P/Invoke to use it. In short, there aren't any easy methods for creating a trigger-start service using managed code, but you can do it.

## Obtaining the ServiceNative.CS File

As previously mentioned, there's currently no third-party library or direct .NET Framework support for trigger-start services. However, Microsoft does supply the Knowledge Base article at http://support.microsoft.com/kb/975425. When you download the sample provided as part of the Knowledge Base article, you get some code and a confusing ReadMe.TXT file that doesn't really help you understand how trigger-start services work.

The example also includes the ServiceNative.CS file (when you download the C# version of the example; you can also download Visual Basic and C++ versions of the example). This file has useful code in it that makes the job of creating a trigger-start service significantly easier. You still have to deal with P/Invoke, but at least you don't have to create all the data structures from scratch. In addition, the ServiceNative.CS file correctly defines the AdvAPI32.DLL calls used to create a trigger-start service.

Because the `ServiceNative.CS` file is so helpful, the example in this section relies on it to reduce the amount of code you must write. Download the C# version of the example to your hard drive. Double-click the resulting `CSWin7TriggerStartService.EXE` file and follow the prompts to place the example on your hard drive in a location that you can easily find later.

> *The TriggerStartService example shows how to work with a firewall port trigger. You can find other examples of trigger-start services online. The Microsoft support example at* `http://support.microsoft.com/kb/975425` *shows how to create a trigger-start service that responds to a device event. The example at* `http://www.codeproject.com/KB/cs/Trigger_Start_Service.aspx` *demonstrates how to work with changing network availability triggers.*

## Configuring the TriggerStartService Example

The TriggerStartService example begins with a Windows service, so you'll select the Windows Service template in the Windows folder of your favorite language, as shown in Figure 14-2. Of course, the Windows Service template is only the starting point. You can compare the process of creating a standard service with the trigger-start service in this section by reviewing the article at `http://www.devsource.com/c/a/Architecture/Writing-a-Managed-Windows-Service-with-C/`.

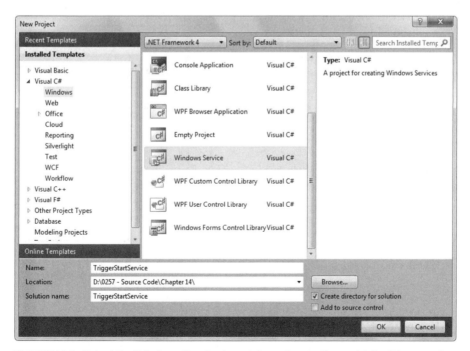

**FIGURE 14-2:** Select the Windows Service template as the starting point for this example.

Now that you have a Windows Service project to use, you can begin configuring it. The following steps will get you started:

1. Right-click the `Service1.CS` entry in Solution Explorer and choose Rename from the Context menu. Change the filename to `TriggerStartService.CS`. The filename change is necessary to ensure you don't end up with a service named Service1 installed on the system.

2. Right-click the project entry in Solution Explorer and choose Add ⇨ Existing Item from the Context menu. You'll see an Add Existing Item dialog box.

3. Locate the `ServiceNative.CS` file on your hard drive (see the "Obtaining the ServiceNative.CS File" section for details), as shown in Figure 14-3. Adding this file provides P/Invoke support for the trigger-start features found in `AdvAPI32.DLL`.

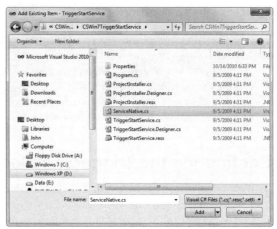

**FIGURE 14-3:** Add the ServiceNative.CS file to your application.

4. Right-click anywhere in the Design View window and choose Add Installer from the Context menu. The installer makes it possible to install the service on Windows later. You'll see several new files added to the project. Finally, you'll see a ProjectInstaller Design View window open.

5. Right-click the `ProjectInstaller.CS` file entry in Solution Explorer and choose Rename from the Context menu. Rename the installer to `TriggerStartServiceInstaller.CS`.

6. Select `serviceInstaller1` in the Design View window.

7. Change the `(Name)` property to `TriggerStartServiceInstall`, as shown in Figure 14-4.

8. Change the `ServiceName` property to `TriggerStartService`, as shown in Figure 14-4.

9. Select the `serviceProcessInstaller1` entry in the Design View window.

10. Change the `Account` property to `LocalSystem`.

**FIGURE 14-4:** Set the service installer name and the installed name of the service.

## Writing Code for the TriggerStartService Example

The example service must perform a number of tasks to ensure reliable operation. For example, because this is a trigger-start service, the service must ensure that it gets installed only on an operating system that supports trigger-start services. Of course, the example must perform some useful task. In this case, the service will detect the opening and closing of a particular port and log it in the System event log. The following sections describe the various code elements of this example.

## Creating the Trigger

The trigger code appears as part of the `TriggerStartServiceInstaller.CS` file. To add this code, right-click the `TriggerStartServiceInstaller.CS` file in Solution Explorer and choose View Code from the Context menu. You'll see the code editor for the `TriggerStartServiceInstaller.CS` file. To begin this process, add the following using statements to this file:

```
using System.ServiceProcess;
using System.Runtime.InteropServices;
```

Now that the file is configured, add the method and variables shown in Listing 14-1. This method creates a trigger object that the system uses to start and stop the service at the right time.

**LISTING 14-1:** Defining the service trigger

Available for download on Wrox.com

```
// Define the GUIDs used for the trigger subtype. You can obtain the GUIDs from
// http://msdn.microsoft.com/library/dd405512.aspx.
Guid FIREWALL_PORT_OPEN_GUID =
    new Guid("b7569e07-8421-4ee0-ad10-86915afdad09");
Guid FIREWALL_PORT_CLOSE_GUID =
    new Guid("a144ed38-8e12-4de4-9d96-e64740b1a524");

private Boolean ConfigurePortTrigger(String ServiceName)
{
    // Obtain access to the service controller for this service.
    using (ServiceController SC = new ServiceController(ServiceName))
    {
        try
        {
            // Create a string to hold the port information.
            String PortNumber = "23\0TCP\0\0";

            // Define a pointer to the port information.
            IntPtr PortNumberPtr = Marshal.StringToHGlobalUni(PortNumber);

            // Define the port data.
            SERVICE_TRIGGER_SPECIFIC_DATA_ITEM PortData =
                new SERVICE_TRIGGER_SPECIFIC_DATA_ITEM();
            PortData.dwDataType =
                ServiceTriggerDataType.SERVICE_TRIGGER_DATA_TYPE_STRING;
            PortData.pData = PortNumberPtr;
            PortData.cbData = (uint)(PortNumber.Length * 2);

            // Create a pointer to the port data.
            // Begin by allocating the required memory from the global heap.
            IntPtr PortDataPtr = Marshal.AllocHGlobal(
                Marshal.SizeOf(typeof(SERVICE_TRIGGER_SPECIFIC_DATA_ITEM)));
```

```csharp
// Next, place the pointer to the GUID in FirewallPortOpen.
Marshal.StructureToPtr(PortData, PortDataPtr, false);

// Create the port open trigger.

// Create a pointer to the FIREWALL_PORT_OPEN_GUID GUID.
IntPtr FirewallPortOpen =
    Marshal.AllocHGlobal(Marshal.SizeOf(typeof(Guid)));
Marshal.StructureToPtr(
    FIREWALL_PORT_OPEN_GUID, FirewallPortOpen, false);

// Create the start service trigger.
SERVICE_TRIGGER StartTrigger = new SERVICE_TRIGGER();

// Place data in the various start trigger elements.
StartTrigger.dwTriggerType =
    ServiceTriggerType.SERVICE_TRIGGER_TYPE_FIREWALL_PORT_EVENT;
StartTrigger.dwAction =
    ServiceTriggerAction.SERVICE_TRIGGER_ACTION_SERVICE_START;
StartTrigger.pTriggerSubtype = FirewallPortOpen;
StartTrigger.pDataItems = PortDataPtr;
StartTrigger.cDataItems = 1;

// Create the port close trigger.

// Create a pointer to the FIREWALL_PORT_OPEN_GUID GUID.
IntPtr FirewallPortClose =
    Marshal.AllocHGlobal(Marshal.SizeOf(typeof(Guid)));
Marshal.StructureToPtr(
    FIREWALL_PORT_CLOSE_GUID, FirewallPortClose, false);

// Create the stop service trigger.
SERVICE_TRIGGER StopTrigger = new SERVICE_TRIGGER();

// Place data in the various stop trigger elements.
StopTrigger.dwTriggerType =
    ServiceTriggerType.SERVICE_TRIGGER_TYPE_FIREWALL_PORT_EVENT;
StopTrigger.dwAction =
    ServiceTriggerAction.SERVICE_TRIGGER_ACTION_SERVICE_STOP;
StopTrigger.pTriggerSubtype = FirewallPortClose;
StopTrigger.pDataItems = PortDataPtr;
StopTrigger.cDataItems = 1;

// Create an array of service triggers.
IntPtr ServiceTriggersPtr =
    Marshal.AllocHGlobal(
        Marshal.SizeOf(typeof(SERVICE_TRIGGER)) * 2);
// Add the start service trigger.
Marshal.StructureToPtr(StartTrigger, ServiceTriggersPtr, false);
// Add the stop service trigger.
Marshal.StructureToPtr(StopTrigger,
    new IntPtr((long)ServiceTriggersPtr +
        Marshal.SizeOf(typeof(SERVICE_TRIGGER))), false);
```

```
        // Create a pointer to the service's trigger information
        // structure.
        IntPtr ServiceTriggerInfoPtr =
            Marshal.AllocHGlobal(
                Marshal.SizeOf(typeof(SERVICE_TRIGGER_INFO)));

        // Define the service trigger information structure.
        SERVICE_TRIGGER_INFO ServiceTriggerInfo =
            new SERVICE_TRIGGER_INFO();

        // Fill the structure with information.
        ServiceTriggerInfo.cTriggers = 2;
        ServiceTriggerInfo.pTriggers = ServiceTriggersPtr;

        // Place a pointer to the structure in ServiceTriggerInfoPtr.
        Marshal.StructureToPtr(
            ServiceTriggerInfo, ServiceTriggerInfoPtr, false);

        // Change the service's configuration to use triggers.
        Boolean Result = ServiceNative.ChangeServiceConfig2(
            SC.ServiceHandle.DangerousGetHandle(),
            ServiceConfig2InfoLevel.SERVICE_CONFIG_TRIGGER_INFO,
            ServiceTriggerInfoPtr);

        // Get any errors.
        int ErrorCode = Marshal.GetLastWin32Error();

        // Clean up from all of the allocations.
        Marshal.FreeHGlobal(PortNumberPtr);
        Marshal.FreeHGlobal(PortDataPtr);
        Marshal.FreeHGlobal(FirewallPortOpen);
        Marshal.FreeHGlobal(FirewallPortClose);
        Marshal.FreeHGlobal(ServiceTriggersPtr);
        Marshal.FreeHGlobal(ServiceTriggerInfoPtr);

        // Check for an exception.
        if (!Result)
        {
            Marshal.ThrowExceptionForHR(ErrorCode);
            return false;
        }
        else
            return true;
    }
    catch
    {
        return false;
    }
}
```

The code begins by defining two Guid objects, FIREWALL_PORT_OPEN_GUID and FIREWALL_PORT_CLOSE_GUID. These objects correspond to constants used within C++ to provide values to the Win32

API call, `ChangeServiceConfig2()`. If you look at any of the trigger-start service examples, you'll see a confusing list of GUIDs and wonder where the developer obtained them. These GUIDs appear at http://msdn.microsoft.com/library/dd405512.aspx. In short, you can't use just any GUID value; you must use the specific GUIDs that Microsoft has defined for trigger event types. The reason these objects are defined globally is that you may need to use them in more than one location (unlike this example, where they're used only once).

The `ConfigurePortTrigger()` method begins by creating a `ServiceController` object, `SC`, that uses the name of the service, `ServiceName`, to access the example service. Everything within the `using` block applies to the example service. Because P/Invoke code is less stable than managed code, you want to place it all within a `try...catch` block (or even several `try...catch` blocks) to provide more granular error control.

It's important to remember that there's a boundary between native code and managed code. This example is working in both worlds. In order to make managed code and native code work together successfully, you must marshal data between the two environments. Consequently, you see a number of uses of the `Marshal` class within this example. C++, and therefore the Win32 API, also relies on null-terminated strings. The P/Invoke code for this example begins by creating a *multi-string*, a single string that contains multiple substrings. The `String`, `PortNumber`, contains two substrings — 23 is the first string and `TCP` is the second string. Each of these strings is null-terminated using the `\0` escape character, and the string as a whole is null-terminated by another `\0` escape character.

This string exists in managed memory, so the Win32 API can't access it. To make `PortNumber` available to the Win32 API, the code calls `Marshal.StringToHGlobalUni()`, which copies the string to native memory and returns a pointer to the native memory as an `IntPtr`, `PortNumberPtr`. The `SERVICE_TRIGGER_SPECIFIC_DATA_ITEM` documentation at http://msdn.microsoft.com/library/dd405515.aspx specifies that the multi-string you supply must be in Unicode format and not ANSI format, which is why this example uses the `Marshal.StringToHGlobalUni()` method to perform the marshaling.

Remember from the discussion in the "Triggering a Service" section that a trigger can contain a data element. The `SERVICE_TRIGGER_SPECIFIC_DATA_ITEM` structure is used to create that data element, `PortData`. As with many Win32 API structures, you must specify the kind of data that you're supplying in `PortData.dwDataType`, which is a `SERVICE_TRIGGER_DATA_TYPE_STRING` in this case. The `PortData.pData` element contains a pointer to the native memory location that holds the string you created. You must also supply the length of that string as a `uint` (not an `int`). Because the string is in Unicode format, you must multiply the value of `PortNumber.Length` by 2 in order to obtain the correct data length.

Interestingly enough, the data structure `PortData` is also in managed memory, so again, the code must marshal it to native memory where the Win32 API can access it. Unlike strings, it's not easy to determine the size of the native memory structure pointed to by `PortDataPtr`. The code calls `Marshal.AllocHGlobal()` to allocate the memory required by the native memory structure from the global heap, but it has to tell the method how much memory to allocate. The code calls `Marshal.SizeOf()` to determine the native memory size of `SERVICE_TRIGGER_SPECIFIC_DATA_ITEM`. You absolutely must not call the standard `sizeof()` method to determine the size of the data structure, because `sizeof()` returns the managed size.

Allocating the memory required by `PortData` is only the first step. The memory doesn't contain any data yet. The `Marshal.StructureToPtr()` method moves the data in `PortData` to native memory and then places a pointer to that memory in `PortDataPtr`. The third argument is set to `false` because you don't want to delete any old content.

All these steps have created a data element for the trigger and marshaled it to native memory. Now it's time to create an actual trigger. The first step is to marshal the trigger subtype described by `FIREWALL_PORT_OPEN_GUID` to native memory. Because a `Guid` is a structure, the code uses the same technique as it did for `PortData` — it allocates the memory by calling `Marshal.AllocHGlobal()` and then moves the data to that memory by calling `Marshal.StructureToPtr()`.

You create a trigger by defining a `SERVICE_TRIGGER` object. In this case, the code creates `StartTrigger` and then begins filling it with data. Remember that a trigger consists of four elements: trigger type, trigger subtype, action, and data. The trigger, `StartTrigger.dwTriggerType`, is a simple enumerated value, `SERVICE_TRIGGER_TYPE_FIREWALL_PORT_EVENT`. The action, `StartTrigger.dwAction`, is also an enumerated value, `SERVICE_TRIGGER_ACTION_SERVICE_START`. The trigger subtype, `StartTrigger.pTriggerSubtype`, is a pointer to the previously marshaled data pointed to by `FirewallPortOpen`. Likewise, the data, `StartTrigger.pDataItems`, is a pointer to the previously marshaled data pointed to by `PortDataPtr`. The structure also requires that you tell the Win32 API how many data items `PortDataPtr` contains, using the `StartTrigger.cDataItems` element.

The process for creating the stop trigger is the same as the process for the start trigger. At this point, the code has two managed triggers. The triggers point to native memory, but the data itself, the enumerated values and pointers, resides in managed memory. The code must create an array of triggers and place it in `ServiceTriggersPtr`. You would normally use a managed code process to create the array, but creating the array for native code use is completely different.

The code begins by allocating memory on the global heap for the array. Notice that the call to `Marshal.AllocHGlobal()` allocates enough memory for two `SERVICE_TRIGGER` data structures. As before, allocating the memory doesn't magically transfer the data. Transferring the first data structure, `StartTrigger`, is easy. The code simply calls `Marshal.StructureToPtr()` as usual for any data structure. The second transfer is a little harder because `StopTrigger` must end up after `StartTrigger` in the array. The technique the code uses to accomplish this task is to call `Marshal.StructureToPtr()` again, with a pointer to the native memory version of `StartTrigger` and a space allocated for `StopTrigger`. You can create an array of any size using this approach. If you had another trigger to add, you'd still call `Marshal.StructureToPtr()` with `ServiceTriggersPtr` as the first item of the second argument.

At this point, the code has created two triggers and placed them in an array. However, in order for the Win32 API to work with just about any data, it has to be placed in a package. The package, in this case, is a `SERVICE_TRIGGER_INFO` structure, `ServiceTriggerInfo`. The code fills `ServiceTriggerInfo.cTriggers` with the number of triggers and then places the pointer to the native memory trigger array, `ServiceTriggersPtr`, in `ServiceTriggerInfo.pTriggers`. `ServiceTriggerInfo` is in managed memory, so the code creates `ServiceTriggerInfoPtr`, which points to the same data in native memory, by calling `Marshal.StructureToPtr()`.

All the configuration is now completed. The code calls `ServiceNative.ChangeServiceConfig2()` with the handle to the service (`SC.ServiceHandle.DangerousGetHandle()`), an enumerated value that tells what kind of change to make (`SERVICE_CONFIG_TRIGGER_INFO`), and a pointer to the required data (`ServiceTriggerInfoPtr`). Notice the call to `DangerousGetHandle()`. A dangerous handle is essentially a native code handle to the service. It's dangerous because the handle is outside the control of the managed environment, which means that odd things can happen to it, like getting de-allocated while still in use. Unfortunately, there isn't any alternative to providing the handle in this case. You can find a list of other tasks that you can perform using `ChangeServiceConfig2()` at http://msdn.microsoft.com/library/ms681988.aspx.

The `ServiceNative.ChangeServiceConfig2()` call returns a `Boolean` value, `Result`, that indicates success or error, but doesn't tell you what error occurred. To obtain the actual error information, the code calls `Marshal.GetLastWin32Error()` and places the value in `ErrorCode`. The error code is a simple number. You can look up the text version of the number using the `ErrLook.EXE` utility found in the `\Program Files\Microsoft Visual Studio 10.0\Common7\Tools` folder of your setup. The code also calls `Marshal.ThrowExceptionForHR()` to create a managed exception that should include human readable information for the error.

The code has allocated a lot of native memory. None of this memory is automatically cleaned up. In fact, if you don't manually clean it up, Windows will continue to think that the memory is allocated. The memory will remain inaccessible until the next reboot, creating a memory leak. In order to prevent a memory leak, your code must call `Marshal.FreeHGlobal()` for each memory allocation as shown in the example code.

### Detecting the Operating System Version

Because a trigger-start service doesn't run under older versions of Windows, you want to be sure that users install it as a trigger-start service under only the right version of the operating system. The service will still work with other versions of Windows, but not as a trigger-start service. Consequently, you can still install it with older versions, but you can't configure it for a trigger-start service. To accommodate this need, the example handles the `AfterInstall` event. Use these steps to create the event handler:

1. Select the `TriggerStartServiceInstall` entry in the `TriggerStartServiceInstaller` Design View window.

2. In the Properties window, click Events. You'll see a list of events associated with the `TriggerStartServiceInstall` object.

3. Double-click the `AfterInstall` event entry. Visual Studio automatically creates the required event handler for you.

Now that you have the event handler in place, it's time to add some code to it. Listing 14-2 shows the event handler code.

**LISTING 14-2:** Checking the operating system version

Available for download on Wrox.com

```
private void TriggerStartServiceInstaller_AfterInstall(
    object sender, InstallEventArgs e)
{
    // Check the operating sytem version.
    if (Environment.OSVersion.Version >= new Version(6, 1))
```

```
            // Configure the trigger for the service.
            this.ConfigurePortTrigger(TriggerStartServiceInstall.ServiceName);
        else

            // This is the wrong version of the operating system.
            throw new NotSupportedException("Wrong OS Version");
    }
```

The code begins by checking the operating system version supplied by `Environment.OSVersion` `.Version` against a `Version` object that has a major version number of 6 and a minor version number of 1, which works for either Windows 7 or Windows Server 2008 R2 (but not the original version of Windows Server 2008). You can see a list of version numbers at http://msdn.microsoft .com/library/ms724832.aspx.

When the operating system version is new enough, the code calls `ConfigurePortTrigger()`, which is described in Listing 14-1, to create the required trigger-start service changes for the service. The `TriggerStartServiceInstall.ServiceName` property supplies the required service name. Otherwise, the code raises a `NotSupportedException()` exception and exits.

### Defining the Service Code

The emphasis of this example is on creating a trigger-start service, so the service code isn't much to look at. In this case, the service code outputs one of two messages to the event log to describe the state of Port 23. The service code appears in `TriggerStartService.cs`. Listing 14-3 shows the code used in this case.

**LISTING 14-3:** Adding event log entries to monitor the port

Available for download on Wrox.com

```
protected override void OnStart(string[] args)
{
    // Add a starting event log entry.
    WriteEventLog("Telnet Port 23 Opened");
}

protected override void OnStop()
{
    // Add a stopping event log entry.
    WriteEventLog("Telnet Port 23 Closed");
}

private void WriteEventLog(String Message)
{
    // Use the System event log.
    EventLog.Log = "System";

    // Send a message to the event log.
    EventLog.WriteEntry(Message, EventLogEntryType.Information);
}
```

The code needs to override two event handlers: `OnStart()` and `OnStop()`. In both cases, the event handlers call `WriteEventLog()` with the message to place in the event log.

The default configuration for writing event log entries is to use the Application log. However, service entries normally appear in the System log, so the `WriteEventLog()` method begins by setting the `EventLog.Log` property to System. The code then calls `EventLog.WriteEntry()` with the message and the type of entry to create, which is `EventLogEntryType.Information` in this case.

## Testing the TriggerStartService

At this point, you have a trigger-start service you can use to monitor Telnet utility Port 23. Of course, before you can use Telnet, you need a Telnet server and the proper system setup. Once you do have a Telnet setup installed and tested, you need to install and check the service. Finally, after all this effort, you can open a Telnet connection, check something simple, and then close the Telnet connection. Viewing the event log shows the result of all the work to date. The following sections help you configure and test the service. You can skip the "Configuring Telnet" section if you already have a Telnet setup to use.

### Configuring Telnet

Many networks don't use a Telnet setup any longer because Telnet can become a security liability if it isn't managed correctly. You can find a host of articles on the Internet about Telnet security — one of the better articles is at `http://www.interwork.com/blog/2008/11/18/qa-how-to-eliminate-the-security-risks-associated-with-telnet-ftp/`. Telnet is still a useful protocol because it works on nearly any system, it's reliable, and it's simple. Even if you don't currently have a Telnet setup to use, you can still configure Windows 7 to provide localized Telnet services using the following steps:

1. Open the Programs and Features applet in the Control Panel. You'll see the Programs and Features window.

2. Click Turn Windows Features On or Off. You'll see the Windows Features dialog box, shown in Figure 14-5.

3. Check the Telnet Server option and click OK. Windows will install the Telnet Server feature on your system. However, the Telnet Server won't be available immediately because the Telnet service is installed in a disabled state.

4. Open the Services console found in the Administrative Tools folder of the Control Panel. Locate the Telnet service.

**FIGURE 14-5:** Install the Telnet Server feature to provide Telnet support.

5. Double-click the Telnet service entry, and you'll see the Telnet Properties dialog box shown in Figure 14-6. The figure shows the Telnet service as it will appear after Step 7.

6. Select Manual in the Startup Type field and click Apply. This action will enable the Start button near the bottom of the Telnet Properties dialog box.

7. Click Start and click OK. Windows will start the Telnet service. However, you still can't access Telnet because Windows has placed a security obstacle in your way.

8. Open the Computer Management console found in the Administrative Tools folder of the Control Panel.

9. Open the `Computer Management\System Tools\Local Users and Groups\Users` folder.

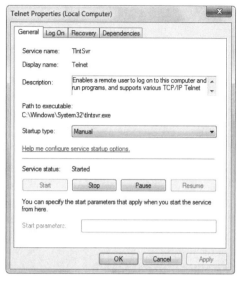

**FIGURE 14-6:** Configure and start the Telnet service to provide access to Telnet.

10. Double-click your account in the `Users` folder. You'll see the Properties dialog box for your account.

11. Select the Member Of tab. You see the list of groups that you're a member of.

12. Click Add. You'll see the Select Groups dialog box.

13. Type **TelnetClients** in the Enter the Object Names to Select field. Click OK. Your Properties dialog box should look similar to the one shown in Figure 14-7 (with TelnetClients in the Member Of list).

14. Click OK to close the Properties dialog box.

15. Choose Start ➪ All Programs ➪ Accessories. Right-click the Command Prompt entry and choose Run As Administrator from the Context menu. You'll see a command prompt open.

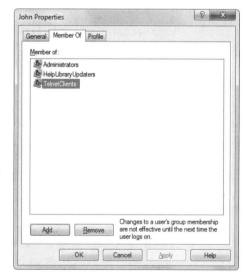

**FIGURE 14-7:** Add your account to the TelnetClients group.

16. Type `Telnet MachineName` and press Enter, where `MachineName` is the name of your system. You'll see a prompt that tells you about a potential security risk of using Telnet (sending your password over the network). Because this is a localized test, you shouldn't have anything to worry about — no information is actually going across the network.

17. Type **Y** and press Enter. You'll see a command prompt like the one shown in Figure 14-8. This is a command prompt accessed using Telnet. If you see this command prompt, you know your Telnet setup is configured and working properly.

18. Type **Exit** and press Enter to end the Telnet session. Telnet will display the "Connection to host lost" message in the command prompt.

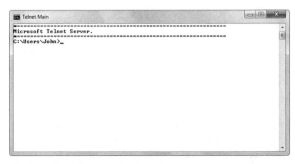

**FIGURE 14-8:** This command prompt is the result of a working Telnet setup.

19. In the Services console, right-click the Telnet entry and choose Stop from the Context menu. This action closes Port 23.

## Installing the Service

After you build the service, you need to install it before you can use it. Because this is a trigger-start service, you also need to verify that the service installed correctly. You want to be sure that the service installed as you intended it to install, rather than as a standard service. The following steps help you install the service:

1. Choose Start ➪ All Programs ➪ Microsoft Visual Studio 2010 ➪ Visual Studio Tools. Right-click the Visual Studio Command Prompt (2010) entry and choose Run As Administrator from the Context menu. You'll see a command prompt window open.

2. Change directories to the directory that contains the service. For example, if your service appears in the \Chapter 14\TriggerStartService\TriggerStartService\bin\Debug folder, you type **CD \Chapter 14\TriggerStartService\TriggerStartService\bin\Debug** and press Enter.

3. Type **InstallUtil TriggerStartService.EXE** and press Enter. You'll see a number of messages appear as InstallUtil installs the service. Your command prompt will look similar to the one shown in Figure 14-9. The important message appears at the end: "The Commit phase completed successfully."

4. Open the Services console found in the Administrative Tools folder of the Control Panel. Locate the TriggerStartService entry, as shown in Figure 14-10. Notice that the TriggerStartService is set to start manually, not automatically. In addition, the service should log in using the LocalSystem account, as shown in the figure. If you see these entries, then you'll know that the TriggerStartService has at least installed successfully. However, you still don't know whether it has installed as a trigger-start service.

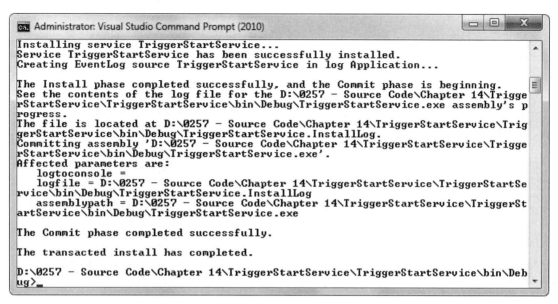

**FIGURE 14-9:** Install the TriggerStartService.EXE file as a service.

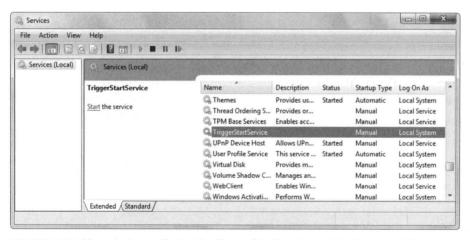

**FIGURE 14-10:** You need to verify that the TriggerStartService installed successfully.

5. At the command prompt, type **SC QTriggerInfo TriggerStartService** and press Enter. The SC utility will tell you the trigger-start service status of a service when you use the QTriggerInfo command. Figure 14-11 shows the results you should see. If you see this output, then you know that the service has installed as a trigger-start service. Notice that the output tells you that this service is waiting for a firewall port event, and that it's looking at Port 23 — precisely what you had programmed into the service.

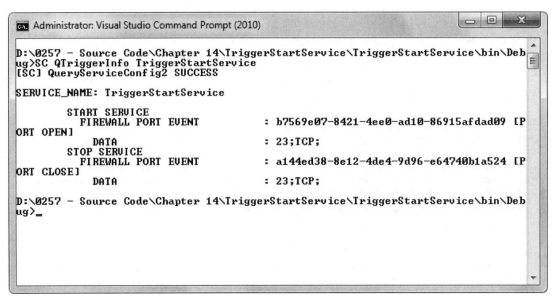

**FIGURE 14-11:** You need to verify that the TriggerStartService installed as a trigger-start service.

## Performing the Telnet Test

At this point, you have Telnet installed and configured, and the service is installed and configured. Follow these steps to test the functionality of the trigger-start service:

1. Open the Event Viewer console in the Administrative Tools folder of the Control Panel. You'll see the Event Viewer window.

2. Open the `Event Viewer\Windows Logs` folder.

3. Right-click the System log entry and choose Clear Log from the Context menu. You'll see an Event Viewer dialog box.

4. Click Clear to clear the events in the Event Viewer.

5. Open the Services console in the Administrative Tools folder of the Control Panel. Right-click the Telnet entry and choose Start from the Context menu. The Telnet service will start. Starting the Telnet service opens Port 23. You can verify this fact by typing **NetStat -a** at the command prompt and pressing Enter. The NetStat utility shows that the system is listening on Port 23, as shown in Figure 14-12. (Notice the 0.0.0.0:23 address entry on the first line of the output — the :23 part of the entry signifies Port 23.)

6. Wait at least 60 seconds. Windows doesn't guarantee that a trigger-start service will respond immediately to an event. In fact, you'll find that the documentation makes a vague reference to a 60-second response time, but Microsoft never makes it very clear. Depending on system load, a trigger-start service may not even respond within 60 seconds, but it will respond.

7. Choose Action ➪ Refresh. You'll see that TriggerStartService has started. It will remain started as long as the Telnet service is running, as shown in Figure 14-13.

Developing Trigger-Start Services | 313

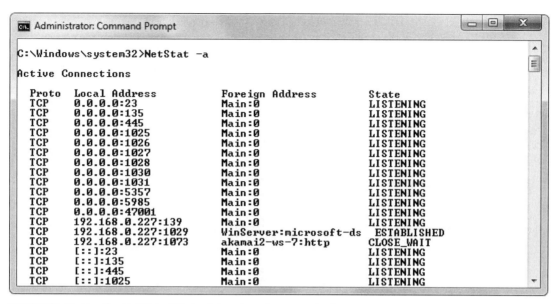

**FIGURE 14-12:** Use the NetStat utility to determine when a particular port is open.

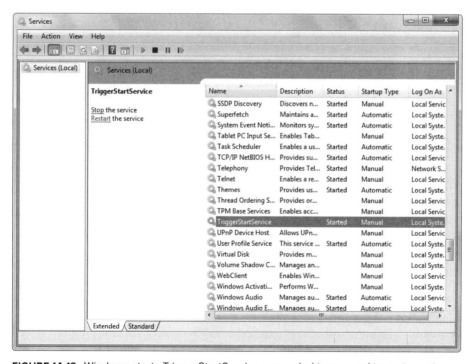

**FIGURE 14-13:** Windows starts TriggerStartService as needed to respond to port events.

8. Right-click the Telnet service and choose Stop from the Context menu. The Telnet service will stop. Verify that Port 23 is no longer open by typing `NetStat -a` at the command prompt and pressing Enter.

9. Wait at least 60 seconds.

10. Choose Action ➪ Refresh. You'll see that TriggerStartService has stopped.

11. In the Event Viewer, make sure the System log is selected and choose Action ➪ Refresh. You'll see a series of event log entries like those shown in Figure 14-14.

**FIGURE 14-14:** The exercise you just completed creates a number of event log entries.

12. Beginning with the oldest entry, view the entries one at a time. You'll see the sequence of events that you've just tested with this procedure. The event log will tell you that Telnet started, then TriggerStartService. One of the entries will tell you that Port 23 has opened. Keep following the entries, and you'll eventually see one where Port 23 closes after the Telnet service stops. Notice that the trigger-start service starts and stops as the port opens and closes, but that Windows doesn't act immediately — the action always requires some amount of time.

At this point, you might want to uninstall TriggerStartService. To perform this task, type InstallUtil /U TriggerStartService.EXE and press Enter. You'll see a series of messages similar to the ones shown in Figure 14-9 as InstallUtil removes the TriggerStartService from the system.

## PROVIDING POWER MANAGEMENT

The entire computer industry is under significant pressure to become greener, to use less power, and to use power more efficiently. Microsoft has continued to address this need by updating the power management features in every version of Windows. You can read about these updates for Windows 7 at http://www.microsoft.com/windows/windows-7/features/power-management.aspx.

Like many parts of Windows, power management works in the background by monitoring the system in various ways. Applications can interact with power management functionality in a number of ways. The most common interaction is to query power management about the current configuration, so that the application knows how to run in a low-power environment, such as a laptop. An application can also subscribe to power management events to discover when certain events occur, such as a low-battery alarm. The Power Management example shows how to perform basic power management monitoring.

*This chapter assumes that you've installed the Windows API Code Pack. You can find the instructions for installing the Code Pack in the "Obtaining the Windows API Code Pack for Microsoft .NET Framework" section of Chapter 4. The Code Pack contains everything you need to work with the new power management, application restart recovery manager, and network list manager features. This chapter relies on a Windows Forms application approach because many developers will be performing updates, rather than creating entirely new applications with the Windows Presentation Foundation (WPF).*

### Configuring the Power Management Example

This example begins with a Windows Forms application. You'll need to add a button (btnGet) to obtain data about the current power management functionality and a list box (lstData) to output the results of the query. In addition, you'll need to add a reference to Microsoft.WindowsAPICodePack.DLL and provide the following using statement:

```
using Microsoft.WindowsAPICodePack.ApplicationServices;
```

### Getting the Power Management State

It used to be difficult to get a substantial amount of information from Windows regarding the status of the power management system. An application could start to perform a long task when battery power was low, resulting in lost data, corruption, or other problems in at least a few cases when the battery suddenly decided to fail. Windows 7 makes it possible to monitor the power state so that your application can interact with the host system appropriately. For example, it's now possible to anticipate a low-battery state and to reserve disk operations to those that are essential to data protection, rather than use the disk as normal. Listing 14-4 shows the incredible amount of information you can now obtain from Windows 7.

Available for download on Wrox.com

**LISTING 14-4:** Outputting the power management state

```
private void btnGet_Click(object sender, EventArgs e)
{
    // Clear any existing data.
    lstData.Items.Clear();

    // Obtain the current power source.
    lstData.Items.Add("Power Source: " + PowerManager.PowerSource);

    // Check for a battery.
    if (PowerManager.IsBatteryPresent)
    {
        // Display a battery present message.
        lstData.Items.Add("Battery Present");

        // Get the battery state.
        BatteryState BattState = PowerManager.GetCurrentBatteryState();

        // Display the battery statistics.
        lstData.Items.Add("\tBattery Life %: " +
            PowerManager.BatteryLifePercent);
        lstData.Items.Add("\tBattery Life (mw): " +
            BattState.CurrentCharge);
        lstData.Items.Add("\tMaximum Charge (mw): " +
            BattState.MaxCharge);
        lstData.Items.Add("\tShort Term Battery? " +
            PowerManager.IsBatteryShortTerm);
        lstData.Items.Add("\tSuggested Battery Warning Charge (mw): " +
            BattState.SuggestedBatteryWarningCharge);
        lstData.Items.Add("\tSuggested Battery Critical Charge (mw): " +
            BattState.SuggestedCriticalBatteryCharge);

        // Check the current battery usage.
        if (BattState.ACOnline)
            lstData.Items.Add("\tAC Online");
        else
        {
            lstData.Items.Add("\tSystem Using Battery");
            lstData.Items.Add("\t\tDischarge Rate: " +
                BattState.DischargeRate);
            lstData.Items.Add("\t\tEstimated Time Remaining: " +
                BattState.EstimatedTimeRemaining);
        }
    }
```

```csharp
        // Display the monitor information.
        lstData.Items.Add("Monitor On? " + PowerManager.IsMonitorOn);
        lstData.Items.Add("Monitor Required? " +
            PowerManager.MonitorRequired);

        // Display the UPS status.
        lstData.Items.Add("UPS Attached? " +
            PowerManager.IsUpsPresent);

        // Display the current power personality.
        lstData.Items.Add("Current Power Personality: " +
            PowerManager.PowerPersonality);

        // Display an indicator that shows if the system will
        // block the sleep state.
        lstData.Items.Add("Will System Block Sleep State? " +
            PowerManager.RequestBlockSleep);
    }
```

The example begins by checking the current power source using `PowerManager.PowerSource`. You'll normally see one of three values as output: AC, UPS, or Battery. The `PowerManager` class is `static`, so you don't have to create any objects to use it, as shown in the listing.

Theoretically, you can query any `PowerManager` property or method any time you want. However, some properties and methods make sense only at specific times. The next section of code works with the battery. It begins by checking the battery state using `PowerManager.IsBatteryPresent`. If the battery is present, the code begins checking the battery status.

The `PowerManager` class provides direct access to some battery information, such as whether the battery is present. You can also determine the percentage of battery life left, using the `PowerManager.BatteryLifePercent` property. However, to get the maximum amount of information, you must create a `BatteryState` object, which is `BattState` in this example. The information you can receive about the battery is much improved from previous versions of Windows. For example, you can now query the precise amount of battery life left in milliwatts (mw) by accessing the `CurrentCharge` property.

A special property, `IsBatteryShortTerm`, tells you whether the battery lasts a short time. This particular property is extremely useful in determining just how much you should depend on the battery to fuel your application. It's even possible to determine how fast the battery is being used by querying the `DischargeRate` property, and Windows will estimate how much time the battery has left when you access the `EstimatedTimeRemaining` property. In short, there's no longer any good reason for your application to run out of power, because Windows 7 provides you with great statistics for monitoring battery life.

The remaining `PowerManager` statistics fill in gaps from earlier versions of Windows. The `PowerManager.IsMonitorOn` property tells you whether the monitor is currently on, while the `PowerManager.MonitorRequired` tells you whether the system actually requires a monitor (it could be in a closet somewhere and not even have a monitor attached).

*It isn't always the best idea to depend on some* `PowerManager` *statistics unless you know the machine configuration (perhaps it's for a custom program in your organization). Some monitors have their own power-off feature, so the monitor could be off even when Windows thinks that it's on. The same holds true for an Uninterruptible Power Supply (UPS). Many vendors supply their own software, which replaces the native Windows software and doesn't generate the UPS properties.*

There are actually two places with a use for Windows 7 battery information. The first is a laptop battery. The second is an Uninterruptible Power Supply (UPS). You can determine whether a UPS is attached by using the `PowerManager.IsUpsPresent` property. One caveat for Windows 7 is that if your UPS relies on a serial cable, all you can determine is whether the UPS is attached. You need a newer UPS that has a USB cable to determine the UPS battery statistics.

The output of the `PowerManager.PowerPersonality` is a little confusing. If you have your system set for the Balanced option in the Power Options applet, the output says Automatic. There isn't any output for a custom setup. However, you can determine whether the system is using the Power Saver or High Performance option. Except for the plan name, there doesn't appear to be any way to obtain the settings for the power plan using the `PowerManager` class.

Most of the `PowerManager` properties are read-only. The `PowerManager.RequestBlockSleep` property is read/write. When set to `true`, it blocks requests for the system to go into sleep mode. You can use this setting when the system needs to perform a long task that doesn't require user intervention. The default setting doesn't block sleep requests. It's important that you not use this setting on a laptop running on the battery. Using this setting could cause data loss when the laptop battery runs out of power, and the current system state isn't saved to the hard drive in the `HiberFil.SYS` file. Figure 14-15 shows typical output from this application for a desktop machine.

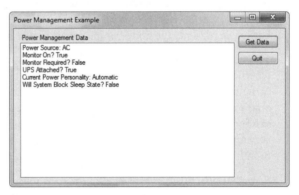

**FIGURE 14-15:** The Windows 7 power management features provide a lot of information.

## Detecting a Change in Monitor State

The `PowerManager` class supports a number of events that help your application react to specific power conditions. For example, the `BatteryLifePercentChanged` event lets you monitor the battery state and close the application before power runs out. You can also keep track of the power source using the `PowerSourceChanged` event and suggest the user close your application when the system is running on the battery, in order to conserve battery power for more important tasks.

An extremely useful event is `IsMonitorOnChanged`. If your application monitors this event, it won't try to interact with the user when the user clearly can't see the output of your application. Listing 14-5 shows how to use this event.

**LISTING 14-5:** Handling a monitor state change event

```
public frmMain()
{
    // Perform standard initialization.
    InitializeComponent();

    // Add an event handler for monitor state changes.
    PowerManager.IsMonitorOnChanged +=
        new EventHandler(PowerManager_IsMonitorOnChanged);
}

void PowerManager_IsMonitorOnChanged(object sender, EventArgs e)
{
    // Just show the monitor state.
    if (PowerManager.IsMonitorOn)
        lstData.Items.Add("The monitor is on!");
    else
        lstData.Items.Add("The monitor is off!");
}
```

As with all events, Visual Studio helps you create the code in the `frmMain()` constructor. As soon as you type +=, the IDE displays a message that tells you to press Tab to create the event handler code. You press Tab a second time to create the event handler itself, `PowerManager_IsMonitorOnChanged()`.

The example code simply outputs a message in this case. It outputs one message when the monitor is on and another when the monitor is off, as shown in Figure 14-16. All you need do to see the results of this example is set Windows to turn the monitor off after a minute and then wait for the monitor to turn itself off. The code uses the `PowerManager.IsMonitorOn` property to determine the current monitor state.

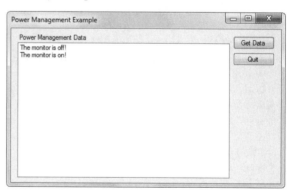

**FIGURE 14-16:** Using events makes it possible to automatically respond to power events.

## IMPLEMENTING APPLICATION RESTART AND RECOVERY

It's now possible to tell Windows that you want your application to automatically restart if it fails. In this case, *restart* means to start the application over again, not to do anything else. You can also tell Windows to start your application in a *recover* mode. The recover mode calls a special method in your application to recover any data that the application was working on when it failed.

The restart and recover features are completely independent. There isn't any reason you can't simply implement a recover mode if so desired. The recovery will simply take place when the user restarts the application at some time in the future. Likewise, if your data isn't performing any data manipulation (it might simply be a status indicator), then you can define restart only.

The Code Pack examples show a relatively complex application that implements both restart and recover modes in the `\CodePack\Samples\AppRestartRecoveryDemo` folder. The example can be a little hard to digest in one big chunk. The example in this section takes just the first step; it demonstrates how to implement a restart feature. After you see how the Application Restart example works, you'll likely want to spend time looking at the Code Pack example to get a better idea of precisely how you could implement both features in your application.

## Configuring the Application Restart Example

This example begins with a Windows Forms application. You'll need to add a Crash button (`btnCrash`) to cause the application to crash unexpectedly. Unlike most examples, you'll want to set the `btnCrash.Enabled` property to `false` because you can't click Crash immediately after starting the application. In addition, you'll need to add a reference to `Microsoft.WindowsAPICodePack.DLL` and provide the following `using` statement:

```
using Microsoft.WindowsAPICodePack.ApplicationServices;
```

## Writing the Application Restart Example Code

The Application Restart example performs a basic task — it crashes. When a user clicks `btnCrash`, the application simply stops working. At that point, the user sees a somewhat familiar dialog box, the restart dialog box shown in Figure 14-17. This dialog box is specific to Application Restart, but a number of applications on a Windows 7 system display the same dialog box. When the user clicks Restart, the application restarts. The example application knows it has restarted and displays a dialog box saying so. While all this sounds simple, it wasn't simple at all to implement until Windows 7.

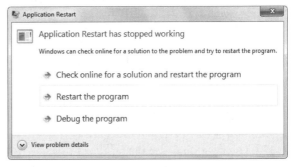

**FIGURE 14-17:** A crashing application can display a restart dialog box like this one.

Windows 7 won't display the restart dialog box for an application that crashes before it has run for 60 seconds. Microsoft hasn't stated why it placed this particular limit on the restart mechanism, but you need to work around it for the example application. To make this task easier, the example displays a countdown timer on `btnCrash`. You can see the time tick down, and then the code enables the Crash button so you can click it. Listing 14-6 shows the supporting code to perform this task.

**LISTING 14-6:** Defining the timer

```csharp
// Define a countdown variable.
private Int32 Countdown;

// Define a timer to use for the countdown.
System.Timers.Timer WaitToCrash;

// A delegate to update the btnCrash.Text property.
private delegate void SetTextCallback(String Value);

// The method called to perform the actual update.
private void SetText(String Value)
{
    btnCrash.Text = Value;
}

// A delegate to update the btnCrash.Enabled property.
private delegate void SetEnabledCallback(Boolean Value);

// A method called to enable the button.
private void SetEnabled(Boolean Value)
{
    btnCrash.Enabled = Value;
}

// A delegate to disable the counter.
private delegate void SetCounterCallback(Boolean Value);

// A method called to disable the counter.
private void SetCounter(Boolean Value)
{
    WaitToCrash.Enabled = Value;
}

void WaitToCrash_Elapsed(object sender, System.Timers.ElapsedEventArgs e)
{
    // Check the countdown.
    if (Countdown == 0)
    {
        // Modify the enabled state using a thread-safe method.
        SetEnabledCallback Enable = new SetEnabledCallback(SetEnabled);
        this.Invoke(Enable, new Object[] { true });

        // Modify the caption using a thread-safe method.
        SetTextCallback Update = new SetTextCallback(SetText);
        this.Invoke(Update, new Object[] { "&Crash" });

        // Disable the counter.
        SetCounterCallback NoCount = new SetCounterCallback(SetCounter);
        this.Invoke(NoCount, new Object[] { false });

        // Display a message.
        MessageBox.Show("Time to crash the system!");
    }
```

*continues*

### LISTING 14-6 *(continued)*

```
        else
        {
            // Change the countdown value.
            Countdown--;

            // Modify the text using a thread-safe method.
            SetTextCallback Update = new SetTextCallback(SetText);
            this.Invoke(Update, new object[] { Countdown.ToString() });
        }
    }
}
```

The code begins by defining an `Int32` value, `Countdown`, which maintains the current countdown value, starting with 60 seconds. The actual timer is a `System.Timers.Timer` object, `WaitToCrash`.

The example has to change three properties during the process of displaying the countdown timer. It has to update `btnCrash.Text` with the latest counter value (so you can see it count down), set `btnCrash.Enabled` to `true` when the countdown reaches 0 (so you can click the button), and disable the counter by setting `WaitToCrash.Enabled` to `false`. If you try to change any of these values directly, the system will complain. The code creates a delegate and event handler for each property change to handle the changes in a code-safe manner.

The `WaitToCrash_Elapsed()` event handler processes each `WaitToCrash` tick event. Normally, the event handler will decrement `Countdown` and display the new value on `btnCrash` by invoking its thread-safe `SetText()` event handler. When `Countdown` reaches 0, the code enables `btnCrash`, sets its `Text` property to `&Crash`, and disables the counter. The user also sees a message box saying it's time to crash the application.

Now it's time to look at the restart code. The application needs to tell Windows to offer to restart the application when it crashes and place limits on when a restart occurs. In this case, it also requires some method of crashing the application. Listing 14-7 shows the required code.

### LISTING 14-7: Restarting an application

```
public frmMain()
{
    // Perform the standard initialization.
    InitializeComponent();

    // Register the application for restart. We don't want to restart
    // the application if it failed as the result of a reboot or a
    // patch.
    ApplicationRestartRecoveryManager.RegisterForApplicationRestart(
        new RestartSettings("/Restart",
            RestartRestrictions.NotOnReboot |
            RestartRestrictions.NotOnPatch));

    // Set the countdown.
    Countdown = 60;

    // The application can't crash immediately. The system won't restart an
    // application that crashes within 60 seconds of starting. Set a timer
```

```csharp
        // to alert the user to the ability of the system to crash.
        WaitToCrash = new System.Timers.Timer(1000);
        WaitToCrash.Elapsed +=
            new System.Timers.ElapsedEventHandler(WaitToCrash_Elapsed);
        WaitToCrash.Enabled = true;

        // Display a message when the system has restarted the application,
        // rather than starting from scratch.
        if (System.Environment.GetCommandLineArgs().Length > 1 &&
            System.Environment.GetCommandLineArgs()[1] == "/Restart")
            MessageBox.Show("Application is restarted!");
    }

    private void btnCrash_Click(object sender, EventArgs e)
    {
        // Cause the application to crash.
        Environment.FailFast("Application Restart example has crashed!");
    }
```

The code begins with the form constructor, `frmMain()`. Registering the application for restart comes first, with a call to `ApplicationRestartRecoveryManager.RegisterForApplicationRestart()`. Part of registering the application is to tell Windows how and when to restart it. The `RestartSettings()` constructor accepts two arguments. The first is a string that defines the command line arguments you want passed to the application during a restart. The second is a list of `RestartRestrictions` enumeration values that defines situations where you don't want the application restarted, such as after a reboot or after someone patches the system.

The next few steps initialize the timer. The code sets `Countdown` to 60 seconds and configures `WaitToCrash`. The `System.Timers.Timer()` accepts an interval in milliseconds — a value of 1,000 configures the timer for one-second intervals.

The last part of `frmMain()` is potentially the most interesting. Normally, the application won't receive any command line arguments (or, if it does, you'll need to handle them appropriately). Checking for a command line argument with the `System.Environment.GetCommandLineArgs().Length` property is the first step. When there's a command line argument to process, the application verifies that it's `/Restart`, which is the command line argument passed as part of the `RestartSettings()` constructor. When both conditions are satisfied, the application can perform any required restart tasks, such as recovering any data that could have been lost when the application crashed. In this case, the application simply displays a message box.

The `btnCrash_Click()` event handler sets all the restart events in motion. When the user clicks btnCrash, the code calls `Environment.FailFast()`, which causes the application to crash. Because the debugger will try to catch and handle this situation, you can't test the application using the debugger. Instead, you must choose Debug ⇨ Start Without Debugging or press Ctrl+F5 to start the application.

## WORKING WITH THE NETWORK LIST MANAGER

In times past, developers often had to restore Windows Management Instrumentation (WMI) queries and direct Win32 API access using P/Invoke to discover details about the network. Yes, the .NET Framework does tell you a lot of useful information, such as the drive setup, but there are additional details, such as the network identifier and whether there's an Internet connection available, that can prove elusive to obtain. The Network List Manager makes it significantly easier to discover these details about your network. The Network List Manager example shows how to perform this task.

## Configuring the Network List Manager Example

This example begins with a Windows Forms application. You'll need to add a Get Data button (btnGet) to obtain data about the current network connectivity and a list box (lstData) to output the results of the query. In addition, you'll need to add a reference to Microsoft.WindowsAPICodePack.DLL and provide the following using statement:

```
using Microsoft.WindowsAPICodePack.Net;
```

## Writing the Network List Manager Code

The Network List Manager can provide a wealth of information about the network. It's easy to discover every connection and every network attached to a machine. Some of the information, such as the network identifier, is read-only. However, you can change other information, such as the network name. Listing 14-8 shows the statistics you can obtain about the connections and network attachments for a machine.

**LISTING 14-8:** Obtaining network connectivity information

```csharp
private void btnGet_Click(object sender, EventArgs e)
{
    // Remove any previous results.
    lstData.Items.Clear();

    // Obtain the current connected state.
    if (!NetworkListManager.IsConnected)
    {
        // Display an error message.
        MessageBox.Show("No network detected!");

        // Exit the method.
        return;
    }
    else
        lstData.Items.Add("Network Connection Detected");

    // Check for an Internet connection.
    lstData.Items.Add("Internet Connection Available? " +
        NetworkListManager.IsConnectedToInternet);

    // Check the connectivity status.
    lstData.Items.Add("Connectivity State: " +
        NetworkListManager.Connectivity);
```

```csharp
// Obtain a list of all of the network connections.
NetworkConnectionCollection Connections =
    NetworkListManager.GetNetworkConnections();

// Check each network connection in turn.
foreach (NetworkConnection ThisConnection in Connections)
{
    // Get the basic connection information.
    lstData.Items.Add("Connection:");
    lstData.Items.Add("\tAdapter ID: " +
        ThisConnection.AdapterId);
    lstData.Items.Add("\tConnection ID: " +
        ThisConnection.ConnectionId);

    // Check its connected state.
    if (!ThisConnection.IsConnected)
    {
        // If the network isn't connected, exit.
        lstData.Items.Add("\tNot Connected");
        break;
    }

    // Display the connection information.
    lstData.Items.Add("\tConnected");

    // Display some connection specifics.
    lstData.Items.Add("\tConnectivity: " +
        ThisConnection.Connectivity);
    lstData.Items.Add("\tDomain Type: " +
        ThisConnection.DomainType);

    // Get the network-specific information.
    Network ThisNetwork = ThisConnection.Network;

    // Display general network information.
    lstData.Items.Add("Network:");
    lstData.Items.Add("\tName: " +
        ThisNetwork.Name);
    lstData.Items.Add("\tNetwork ID: " +
        ThisNetwork.NetworkId);

    // Get specifics if the network is connected.
    if (ThisNetwork.IsConnected)
    {
        lstData.Items.Add("\tConnected");
        lstData.Items.Add("\tInternet Connection? " +
            ThisNetwork.IsConnectedToInternet);
        lstData.Items.Add("\tCategory: " +
            ThisNetwork.Category);
        lstData.Items.Add("\tConnected Time: " +
            ThisNetwork.ConnectedTime);
        lstData.Items.Add("\tConnectivity: " +
            ThisNetwork.Connectivity);
```

*continues*

**LISTING 14-8** *(continued)*

```
                lstData.Items.Add("\tCreated Time: " + 
                    ThisNetwork.CreatedTime);
                lstData.Items.Add("\tDescription: " + 
                    ThisNetwork.Description);
                lstData.Items.Add("\tDomain Type: " + 
                    ThisNetwork.DomainType);
            }
            else
                lstData.Items.Add("\tNot Connected");
        }
    }
}
```

The code begins by checking the connected state of the machine, using the `NetworkListManager` `.IsConnected` property. If the machine isn't connected, the code displays an error message and exits. When the code finds a connection, it displays the overall network information for the machine, such as the presence of an Internet connection.

A single machine can (and often does) have multiple connections. Each connection is associated with a physical network adapter. The user must enable the network adapter for it to show up with this check. The `NetworkConnectionCollection` object, `Connections`, contains all the connections for the machine. If the `NetworkListManager.IsConnected` property is `true`, there's always at least one `NetworkConnection` object to process.

The code relies on a `foreach` loop to process `Connections` as individual `NetworkConnection` objects, each identified as `ThisConnection`. As a minimum, each `NetworkConnection` has a valid `AdapterId` and `ConnectionId` property, so the code displays this information on-screen. The next step is to check `ThisConnection.IsConnected` to determine whether the `NetworkConnection` is actually connected to the network (it may be enabled but not connected to anything at all, or may be in an error state). If the code doesn't find a connection, it displays this fact and moves on to the next connection. The connection is associated with the lower levels of the network protocol, including the physical adapter.

After the code displays the connection statistics, it moves on to the network statistics. The network is associated with the higher-level software settings. As shown in the example, you can check the network identifier and name even if the network isn't connected (which would likely indicate an error condition). The `Network` object, `ThisNetwork`, is what you use to check the amount of time that the user has remained connected and is also where you can get human-readable information about the network, including a description. Figure 14-18 shows typical output from this example.

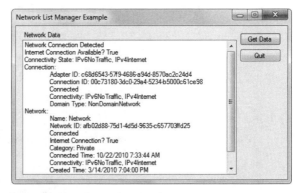

**FIGURE 14-18:** The network information presented here can be useful in digging further into the network structure.

## MOVING YOUR APPLICATIONS TO WINDOWS 7

This chapter has demonstrated several uses of background tasks specifically designed for Windows 7. Of course, there are many other forms of background processing that this chapter doesn't cover. For example, you haven't seen an example of how to make your application print in the background. The one fact you should take away from this chapter is that most processing occurs in the background, since only one task can run in the foreground at any given time. Even though Windows normally gives the foreground task priority, the vast majority of system processing occurs when the user isn't even looking at the machine.

Background processing represents one way to use system resources more efficiently and to make it appear that your application is more responsive to user needs. However, because background processing occurs without user interaction, you must also plan it carefully. Part of your application update planning should include how you can use new Windows 7 background processing features to make your application better. For example, you might want to determine how you can use a trigger-start service to perform tasks that don't require user interaction. Now is also a good time to start planning how to react to background tasks. For example, you need to consider how your application reacts to power management events.

Chapter 15 looks at another Windows 7 feature that helps create efficient applications, Windows 7 Libraries. The Libraries feature is actually an offshoot of the original My Documents folder. However, instead of using a known folder location, the Libraries feature helps bring together information from a number of disparate locations. The user no longer cares where something is located, but rather that the document contains what's needed to perform a task. An application developer can use the Libraries feature to make it easier for the user to focus on the data, rather than on the underlying hardware used in searching for the data.

# 15

# Using the Windows 7 Libraries

**WHAT'S IN THIS CHAPTER?**

- Interacting with known Windows 7 folders
- Working with non-filesystem containers
- Creating user-defined collections
- Adding the Explorer browser control to an application

Windows 7 comes with a number of new features that are loosely called Libraries. From the user's perspective, the Library feature offers a way to centralize document management. The user accesses all documents from a central location without regard to the document's actual location. Of course, if you stuffed all the user's documents into one huge folder, finding any one item would be a nightmare, so the library relies on a set of known folders, such as Documents, Music, Pictures, Downloads, and Videos to organize the information. Known folders also include system folders, such as the Recycle Bin. Of course, each of these known folders can have subfolders. The idea is that the user accesses everything from a central organized location. Your application can also place items in the Library to make them easier to access. The Library concept makes it possible for you to add items the user should access without revealing each item's true location, which is a form of data hiding.

It's also possible to create collections of items that don't exist as part of the filesystem. For example, the Library can contain a list of printers or a list of security certificates. All these items are registered in the registry, just like filesystem objects, but they don't belong to the filesystem, so Windows 7 handles them as non-filesystem containers. From the user's perspective, there isn't any difference between a known folder and a non-filesystem container, but you do need to handle them differently programmatically.

A user can also create custom collections. These custom collections might relate to a specific project or contain resources for a particular application. The purpose of a custom collection is to make it possible for the user to create additions to the Library so that the Library can change to meet user needs. Likewise, you can create custom collections for the user that reflect a particular need for your application or for the organization as a whole. Custom collections fill a need when one of the known folders or non-filesystem containers isn't suitable.

You can work with the Library feature using the standard techniques you've used in the past. However, the Explorer Browser control can make it easier to display the hierarchy of known folders and non-filesystem containers that the system supports. Using the Explorer Browser control also lends a Windows 7 appearance to your application. Of course, the choice of display techniques is entirely up to you.

> *This chapter assumes that you've installed the Windows API Code Pack. You can find the instructions for installing the Code Pack in the "Obtaining the Windows API Code Pack for Microsoft .NET Framework" section of Chapter 4. The Code Pack contains everything you need to work with the new Library feature and the associated Explorer Browser control. This chapter relies on a Windows Forms application approach because many developers will be performing updates, rather than creating entirely new applications with the Windows Presentation Foundation (WPF).*

## WORKING WITH KNOWN FOLDERS

Known folders are essentially those folders that the system already knows about — they're the folders that the system is designed to provide. The `KnownFolders` class contains a host of these folder listings as individual properties. For example, if you want to access a list of entries in the Administrative Tools folder of the Control Panel, you use the `KnownFolders.AdminTools` property. In fact, you might be surprised at just how many folders it contains. Here's a list of the folders you can access (including a special `All` property that accesses all the known folders):

| | | |
|---|---|---|
| AddNewPrograms | AdminTools | All |
| AppUpdates | CDBurning | ChangeRemovePrograms |
| CommonAdminTools | CommonOEMLinks | CommonPrograms |
| CommonStartMenu | CommonStartup | CommonTemplates |
| Computer | Conflict | Connections |
| Contacts | ControlPanel | Cookies |
| Desktop | DeviceMetadataStore | Documents |

| | | |
|---|---|---|
| DocumentsLibrary | Downloads | Favorites |
| Fonts | Games | GameTasks |
| History | ImplicitAppShortcuts | Internet |
| InternetCache | Libraries | Links |
| LocalAppData | LocalAppDataLow | LocalizedResourcesDir |
| Music | MusicLibrary | NetHood |
| Network | OriginalImages | OtherUsers |
| PhotoAlbums | Pictures | PicturesLibrary |
| Playlists | Printers | PrintHood |
| Profile | ProgramData | ProgramFiles |
| ProgramFilesCommon | ProgramFilesCommonX64 | ProgramFilesCommonX86 |
| ProgramFilesX64 | ProgramFilesX86 | Programs |
| Public | PublicDesktop | PublicDocuments |
| PublicDownloads | PublicGameTasks | PublicMusic |
| PublicPictures | PublicRingtones | PublicVideos |
| QuickLaunch | Recent | RecordedTV |
| RecordedTVLibrary | RecycleBin | ResourceDir |
| Ringtones | RoamingAppData | SampleMusic |
| SamplePictures | SamplePlaylists | SampleVideos |
| SavedGames | SavedSearches | SearchCsc |
| SearchHome | SearchMapi | SendTo |
| SidebarDefaultParts | SidebarParts | StartMenu |
| Startup | SyncManager | SyncResults |
| SyncSetup | System | SystemX86 |
| Templates | TreeProperties | UserPinned |
| UserProfiles | UserProgramFiles | UserProgramFilesCommon |
| UsersFiles | UsersLibraries | Videos |
| VideosLibrary | Windows | |

The purpose of the `KnownFolders` class is to provide you with quick access to every common folder on a system. You obtain a substantial amount of information about the entries as well. For example, you can determine whether an entry is simply a link or a real file. It's also possible to obtain a list of properties for the entry. Although the Known Folders example described in the sections that follow works exclusively with the `KnownFolders.Documents` property, it does show you what you can achieve using any of the `KnownFolder` properties.

*Many of the applications in this book require use of special icons. Unless you have access to a full-time artist or you're one of the few developers with artistic talent, it's nearly impossible to obtain aesthetically pleasing icons for applications that aren't used in a hundred other places. The Windows Guides site at* http://mintywhite.com/customize/icons/43-application-program-pngico-icon-packs-windows-customization/ *provides a good alternative to using truly horrible icons in your application. You'll find a wealth of beautifully rendered icons that will make your application look as professional as the code it contains.*

## Configuring the Known Folders Example

This example begins with a Windows Forms application. You'll need to add a List button (btnList) to obtain a list of the known folders and their content, and a list box (lstOutput) to output the results of the query. In addition, you'll need to add a reference to Microsoft.WindowsAPICodePack.Shell.DLL and provide the following using statement:

```
using Microsoft.WindowsAPICodePack.Shell;
```

## Writing the Known Folders Example Code

The Known Folders example provides you with a view of the kinds of information you can obtain from the `KnownFolders.Documents` property — it doesn't describe every kind of information you can obtain. All the `KnownFolders` properties will provide similar sorts of information. Listing 15-1 shows the code you need for this example.

**LISTING 15-1:** Displaying known folder information

```
private void btnList_Click(object sender, EventArgs e)
{
    // Clear the previous information.
    lstOutput.Items.Clear();

    // Display generic information about the Documents
    // known folder.
    lstOutput.Items.Add("Documents Known Folder:");
    lstOutput.Items.Add("\tCanonical Name: " +
        KnownFolders.Documents.CanonicalName);
    lstOutput.Items.Add("\tCategory: " +
```

```csharp
        KnownFolders.Documents.Category);
lstOutput.Items.Add("\tDefinition Options: " +
    KnownFolders.Documents.DefinitionOptions);
lstOutput.Items.Add("\tFile Attributes: " +
    KnownFolders.Documents.FileAttributes);
lstOutput.Items.Add("\tFolder ID: " +
    KnownFolders.Documents.FolderId);
lstOutput.Items.Add("\tLocalized Name: " +
    KnownFolders.Documents.LocalizedName);
lstOutput.Items.Add("\tLocalized Name Resource ID: " +
    KnownFolders.Documents.LocalizedNameResourceId);
lstOutput.Items.Add("\tPath: " +
    KnownFolders.Documents.Path);
lstOutput.Items.Add("\tRelative Path: " +
    KnownFolders.Documents.RelativePath);

// Add a space prior to enumeration.
lstOutput.Items.Add("");

// Enumerate the content of the Documents known folder.
foreach (var Document in KnownFolders.Documents)
{
    // Output generic object information.
    lstOutput.Items.Add("Document Type: " + Document.GetType());
    lstOutput.Items.Add("Document Name: " + Document.Name);
    lstOutput.Items.Add("Display Name: " +
        Document.GetDisplayName(DisplayNameType.Url));
    lstOutput.Items.Add("Is this a FileSystem object? " +
        Document.IsFileSystemObject);
    lstOutput.Items.Add("Is this a link? " + Document.IsLink);

    // If this is a ShellFileSystemFolder, output some
    // additional information.
    if (Document.GetType() == typeof(ShellFileSystemFolder))
    {
        // Convert to a specific type.
        ShellFileSystemFolder ThisFolder =
            (ShellFileSystemFolder)Document;

        // Display the ShellfileSystemFolder information.
        lstOutput.Items.Add("Parsing Name: " +
            ThisFolder.ParsingName);
        lstOutput.Items.Add("Path: " + ThisFolder.Path);

        // Enumerate the documents in the folder.
        lstOutput.Items.Add("Contents:");
        foreach (var FolderDoc in ThisFolder)
        {
            lstOutput.Items.Add("\tName: " + FolderDoc.Name);
        }
    }

    // Add a space between items.
    lstOutput.Items.Add("");
}
}
```

Each `KnownFolders` property provides some basic information about the folder as a whole, so the application begins by displaying this information. Some information, such as `KnownFolders.Documents.Path`, appears as a simple string, while other information appears as part of an enumeration, such as `KnownFolders.Documents.DefinitionOptions`. These top-level properties are always enumerable because they contain other elements such as files and folders. So after the code displays the basic information about the folder, it begins displaying information about the folder content using a `foreach` loop.

Notice that the code defines `Document` as type `var`. That's because `Document` can be of several different types, depending on the content of the selected folder. In this case, the two most common content types are `ShellFile` (for files) and `ShellFileSystemFolder` (for folders). You could also see a `ShellLink` object in this case. The point is that you can't assume anything about the content of `Document`.

The IDE is smart enough to provide you with a list of basic properties common to all the objects that `Document` contains. The code displays a number of these items on-screen. Most of the properties are simple strings. However, at least one property, named `Properties`, is extremely complex, as shown in Figure 15-1. In this case, there are 43 properties used to define the `ShellFile`, `AccessODBC.DSN`, and Figure 15-1 shows just two of them. You can use `Properties` to discover significant details about the object in question.

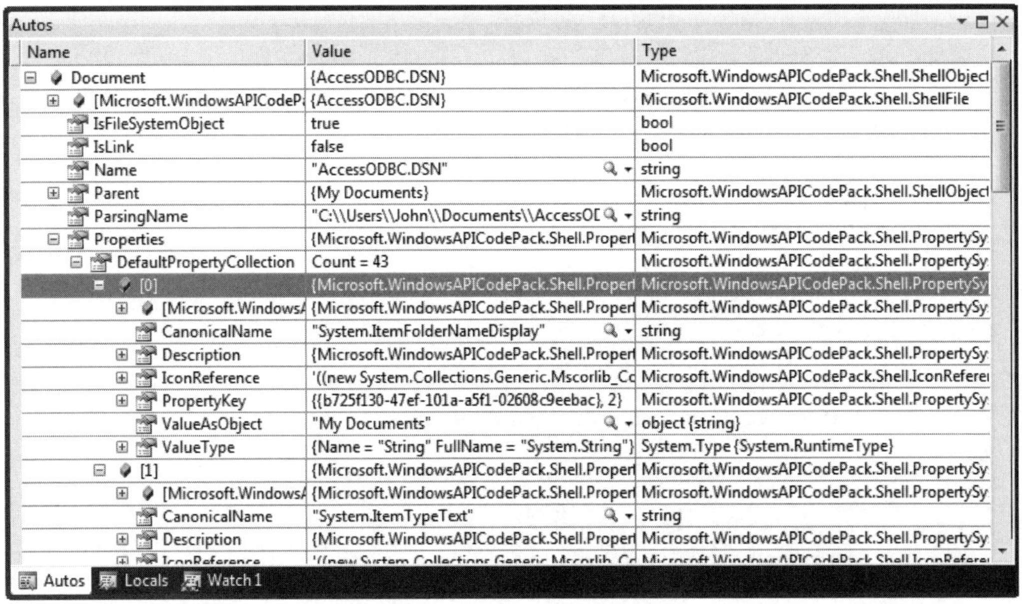

**FIGURE 15-1:** Some properties, such as the one named Properties, are extremely complex.

Most of the entries provided as output in this example are properties. However, there's one method you need to know about, `GetDisplayName()`. This method comes in handy because it lets you present the display name for an object using a special format. In this case, the example presents the display name using the `DisplayNameType.Url` format.

You need to become familiar with the objects that a particular `KnownFolders` property can contain. For example, the `KnownFolders` `.Documents` property can contain objects of type `ShellFileSystemFolder`, which has some special properties. In order to process this special information, the code first compares the type of the current `Document` object to `typeof(ShellFileSystemFolder)`. If the object types are the same, the code displays properties that are special for a `ShellFileSystemFolder` object, such as `Path`.

A `ShellFileSystemFolder` object is a container that can hold other objects. The example only processes one level of objects. Normally, you'd build a recursive routine to parse the entire folder tree. In this case, the output simply contains the name of each object within the `ShellFileSystemFolder` object. Figure 15-2 shows typical output from this example.

**FIGURE 15-2:** Known folder listings tell you a lot about the structure of data on a system.

## USING NON-FILESYSTEM CONTAINERS

As previously mentioned, non-filesystem containers are simply entries that aren't part of the filesystem. Because these entries aren't part of the filesystem, the `IKnownFolder.GetKnownFolder()` method actually creates these entries using the `NonFileSystemKnownFolder` type. You won't actually use the `NonFileSystemKnownFolder` type, though, or work with the `IKnownFolder` `.GetKnownFolder()` method. The `KnownFolders` class presents these objects using the `ShellNonFileSystemItem` type, which is how you detect them. The Non-Filesystem example demonstrates how to work with this entry type.

 *Even though this chapter provides you with good starter examples and the Code Pack also comes with good samples, sometimes you need additional help to get your application working. Special controls, such as the Explorer Browser, can prove especially troublesome if you don't quite understand how they work. You can obtain some great help with any issues you encounter from the discussion group found at* `http://code.msdn.microsoft.com/WindowsAPICodePack/` `Thread/List.aspx`.

## Configuring the Non-Filesystem Example

This example begins with a Windows Forms application. You'll need to add a List button (btnList) to obtain a list of the non-filesystem containers and their content, and a list box (lstOutput) to output the results of the query. In order to see the content this example has to provide, you'll want to make the dialog box bigger than normal to accommodate the extra text (set the form's Size.Width property to 600 and the Size.Height property to 750 if possible). In addition, you'll need to add a reference to Microsoft.WindowsAPICodePack.Shell.DLL and provide the following using statement:

```
using Microsoft.WindowsAPICodePack.Shell;
```

## Writing the Non-Filesystem Example Code

A number of non-filesystem containers are provided with the KnownFolders class. For example, the KnownFolders.Connections property is a non-filesystem container. The example relies on another non-filesystem container, KnownFolders.Games. This isn't the actual Games folder on your system, but rather a description of the games on your system, such as their Entertainment Software Rating Board (ESRB) rating. The site at http://www.esrb.org/ tells you more about these ratings. Listing 15-2 shows the code needed for this example.

**LISTING 15-2:** Displaying non-filesystem container information

```
private void btnList_Click(object sender, EventArgs e)
{
    // Clear the previous entries.
    lstOutput.Items.Clear();

    // Process each of the entries.
    foreach (var Entry in KnownFolders.Games)
    {
        // Verify that the entry is the correct type.
        if (Entry.GetType() == typeof(ShellNonFileSystemItem))
        {
            // Coerce the entry type.
            ShellNonFileSystemItem Item = (ShellNonFileSystemItem)Entry;

            // Output information about the entry.
            lstOutput.Items.Add("Name: " + Item.Name);
            lstOutput.Items.Add("Parsing Name: " + Item.ParsingName);
            lstOutput.Items.Add("Is File System Object? " +
                Item.IsFileSystemObject);
            lstOutput.Items.Add("Is Link? " + Item.IsLink);

            // Process the default properties for the item.
            lstOutput.Items.Add("Default Properties:");
            foreach (var Property in
                Item.Properties.DefaultPropertyCollection)
            {
                // List the property name and value.
                lstOutput.Items.Add("\t" + Property.CanonicalName +
```

```
                ": " + Property.ValueAsObject);

            // Process some of the system properties for the item.
            lstOutput.Items.Add("System Properties:");
            lstOutput.Items.Add("\tApplication Name: " +
                Item.Properties.System.ApplicationName.Value);
            lstOutput.Items.Add("\tAuthor: " +
                Item.Properties.System.Author.Value);
            lstOutput.Items.Add("\tCompany: " +
                Item.Properties.System.Company.Value);
            lstOutput.Items.Add("\tCopyright: " +
                Item.Properties.System.Copyright.Value);

            // Add a blank line for each item.
            lstOutput.Items.Add("");
        }
    }
}
```

The example begins by accessing the entries in the `KnownFolders.Games` property using a `foreach` loop. In this case, you know that the entries are going to be type `ShellNonFileSystemItem`, but it pays to verify that they're the correct type to avoid errors later in the code.

As with known folders, a non-filesystem container has properties like `Name`, `ParsingName`, and `IsFileSystemObject`. The `Path` property also exists, but is usually blank because a non-filesystem container doesn't have a place on the filesystem (local hard drive or network).

When working with a non-filesystem container, the `Properties` property takes on added significance. You want to check `Properties.DefaultPropertyCollection` for entries that define the non-filesystem container. The example simply enumerates through all the properties so you can see what's available. The properties will vary by the kind of non-filesystem container.

The `Properties` property also contains `System`. Unlike `Properties.DefaultPropertyCollection`, you can't enumerate `Properties.System`. Consequently, you must individually query values such as `Properties.System.ApplicationName.Value`. Unfortunately, `Properties.System` seldom contains any actual values, so you'll want to use `Properties.DefaultPropertyCollection` instead. Figure 15-3 shows typical output from this example.

**FIGURE 15-3:** Non-filesystem containers work with data outside the filesystem.

## CONSIDERING USER-DEFINED COLLECTIONS

The Libraries folder provided with Windows 7 holds user-defined collections of resources. Placing projects, files, pictures, sounds, and other items in this folder means that the user can find them with ease, organize them, search within them, and generally access the things needed to conduct business, without having to consider where the resource is actually located. The following sections describe how to interact with the user-defined collections.

### Configuring the User-Defined Collection Example

This example begins with a Windows Forms application. You'll need to add a List button (btnList) to obtain a list of the known folders and their content, an Add button (btnAdd) to add a new item to the collection, and a list box (lstItems) to list the contents of the user-defined collection. In addition, you'll need to add a reference to Microsoft.WindowsAPICodePack.Shell.DLL and provide the following using statement:

```
using Microsoft.WindowsAPICodePack.Shell;
```

Because this example also needs a special folder to add to the library you're creating, you need to create it. For the purpose of this example, use Windows Explorer to create a C:\Example folder. In the C:\Example folder, create a text file named Temp.TXT. You don't need to worry about any content; you won't be using it in this case.

### Listing Libraries

The default Libraries folder contains four items: Documents, Music, Pictures, and Videos. However, it can contain any number of items, depending on what the user chooses to add to it. A user adds an item to the Libraries folder by right-clicking any open area and choosing New ➪ Library from the Context menu. When the user opens the library, it asks the user to start adding folders to it. Unlike general purpose folders, a user can also optimize a library to hold specific types of information such as music or pictures. In short, a library is a special kind of folder.

The User-Defined Collection example performs two tasks. First, it lists the content of the Libraries folder. Second, it adds a new library to the folder. These two tasks represent the kinds of things you'll normally do programmatically. An application can add special entries to the Libraries folder to do things like make project handling automatic or help the user automate the optimizing of library content. Listing 15-3 shows the code needed to perform the first task, listing the library content.

**LISTING 15-3:** Listing the user-defined collections

```
private void btnList_Click(object sender, EventArgs e)
{
    // Clear the old entries.
    lstItems.Items.Clear();

    // Obtain access to the Libraries folder.
```

```
    IKnownFolder Libraries = KnownFolders.UsersLibraries;

    // Output the individual library entries.
    foreach (ShellLibrary Library in Libraries)
    {
        // Display information about each library.
        lstItems.Items.Add("Name: " + Library.Name);
        lstItems.Items.Add("Default Save Folder: " +
            Library.DefaultSaveFolder);
        lstItems.Items.Add("Is File System Object? " +
            Library.IsFileSystemObject);
        lstItems.Items.Add("Is Link? " + Library.IsLink);
        lstItems.Items.Add("Is Pinned to Navigation Pane? " +
            Library.IsPinnedToNavigationPane);
        lstItems.Items.Add("Is Read-Only? " + Library.IsReadOnly);
        lstItems.Items.Add("Library Type: " + Library.LibraryType);
        lstItems.Items.Add("Library Type ID: " +
            Library.LibraryTypeId);

        // Display a list of folders in the library.
        lstItems.Items.Add("Folder List:");
        foreach (ShellFileSystemFolder Folder in Library)
            lstItems.Items.Add("\t" + Folder.Name);

        // Add a blank line between entries.
        lstItems.Items.Add("");
    }
}
```

Each of the types handled by `KnownFolders` has different capabilities and properties — the `ShellLibrary` type is no different. Every entry in `KnownFolders.UsersLibraries` is of the `ShellLibrary` type, so you can use that type directly when enumerating the user-defined collections.

The `ShellLibrary` type does contain familiar properties such as `Name` and `IsFileSystemObject`. However, notice some of the differences in this case, such as `IsPinnedToNavigationPane` and `LibraryType`. These properties make sense only when working with a library entry. Especially important is the `LibraryType` because it tells you what kind of data the user expects to see in that library.

A library will also contain some type of content or it isn't useful. The top-level content is always a list of `ShellFileSystemFolder` items (folders). A user always adds an entire folder, not individual files, to a library. Each of the `ShellFileSystemFolder` entries can contain a mix of folders and files. Figure 15-4 shows typical output from this example.

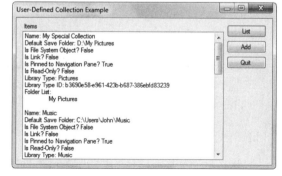

**FIGURE 15-4:** Listing the entries shows standard and user-defined entries.

## Adding Libraries

At some point you'll probably want to create some type of custom library for the user, especially if your application supports projects. The application can create a project library that gathers all the resources for the project into one place. The user need not know where any of these resources are stored (and probably doesn't care to know either). Adding a library is straightforward, as shown in Listing 15-4.

**LISTING 15-4:** Adding a new library

```
private void btnAdd_Click(object sender, EventArgs e)
{
    // Create a new library.
    ShellLibrary NewLibrary = new ShellLibrary("A New Library", true);

    // Add a folder to the new library.
    NewLibrary.Add(@"C:\Example");

    // Define the library type.
    NewLibrary.LibraryType = LibraryFolderType.Documents;

    // Close the library when finished.
    NewLibrary.Close();

    // Tell the user the library is added.
    MessageBox.Show("Library Successfully Added!");
}
```

There are a number of ways to create a new library, but the most common method is to define a new `ShellLibrary` object, `NewLibrary`, and specify a name for it using the first `ShellLibrary()` constructor argument. The second `ShellLibrary()` constructor argument specifies whether the application can overwrite an existing library of the same name. Because you're apt to run this example multiple times and the library doesn't contain any real data, it's just fine to overwrite it. In a real-world application, you'll probably set this second argument to `false` to avoid overwriting valuable information.

A library isn't much good without content. The example adds the folder you created earlier to `NewLibrary` using the `Add()` method. You can add as many folders as needed using this approach. The `Add()` method provides several overrides so you can add folders of various types, but remember that you can add only folders to a library, not files.

It's important to optimize a library whenever possible. The most basic optimization is to set the `LibraryType` property using a `LibraryFolderType` enumeration member. The example optimizes the library we've created to hold documents.

Always close a library before you exit the method that creates it, even if you have to reopen it later. Otherwise, it's possible you could lose some of the library configuration information. Once the library is added, you can see it in the Libraries folder, as shown in Figure 15-5.

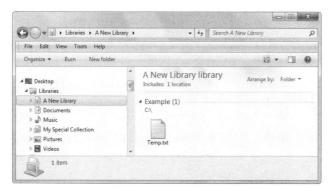

**FIGURE 15-5:** The new library contains the expected content.

## USING THE EXPLORER BROWSER CONTROL

Explorer Browser is another in a long line of controls that Microsoft has provided for making it easier to create interesting applications using less code. As the name implies, it's a browser-like control that you can place on a form and use to explore various resources, including any known folder, non-filesystem container, or user-defined collection. You could also use it to explore the filesystem, the Internet, or any other resource desired. As you might imagine, the actual presentation you see depends on the kind of resource you explore and the presentation you choose to code as part of the control. The following sections describe how to work with the Explorer Browser control.

 *The examples in this chapter provide a simple look at specific features so that you can see how each feature works individually. Of course, you'll likely want to put several of these features together to create a single application. The ExplorerBrowser example found in the* `\CodePack\Samples\ExplorerBrowser` *folder of your Code Pack installation provides a good (albeit somewhat complex) example of how these features can work together.*

### Adding the Explorer Browser to Your Toolbox

Before you can use the Explorer Browser control in an application, you need to add it to your Toolbox. The following steps help you get the Explorer Browser control set up for use with the example application. You can then use it for any application you want to create.

1. Open the Toolbox by choosing View ➪ Toolbox or by pressing Ctrl+Alt+X.
2. Right-click in any clear area of the Toolbox and choose Add Tab from the Context menu. You'll see a new tab added to the Toolbox.
3. Type **Explorer Browser** as the tab's name.

4. Right-click within the Explorer Browser tab and select Choose Items from the Context menu. You'll see the Choose Toolbox Items dialog box, as shown in Figure 15-6.

5. Click Browse. You'll see an Open dialog box.

6. Locate the `Microsoft.WindowsAPICodePack.Shell.DLL` file and click Open. Visual Studio automatically selects and highlights two controls for you, `CommandLink` and `ExplorerBrowser`, in the Choose Toolbox Items dialog box.

7. Click OK. You'll see the two controls added to the Explorer Browser tab of the Toolbox, as shown in Figure 15-7.

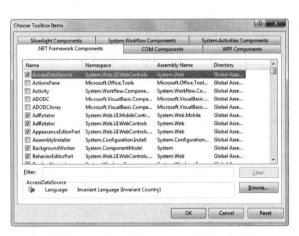

**FIGURE 15-6:** Use this dialog box to add the Explorer Browser control.

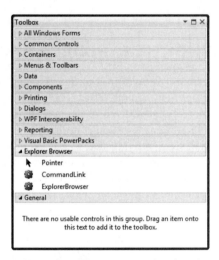

**FIGURE 15-7:** The two controls related to the Explorer Browser appear in the Toolbox.

## Configuring the Explorer Browser Example

This example begins with a Windows Forms application. You'll want a larger form, so set the `Size.Width` property to `700` and `Size.Height` property to `500`. The setup for this example is a little more extensive than for other examples so far. Begin by adding a `SplitContainer` control. You won't need to rename it. However, set the following properties to make the `SplitContainer` control provide the containers required for the example:

➤ Dock: Fill
➤ IsSplitterFixed: True

- Orientation: Horizontal
- SplitterDistance: 21

Add a `ComboBox` control, `lstFolders`, to the upper split container. Set its `Sorted` property to `True` and its `Dock` property to `Fill`. Add an `ExplorerBrowser` control, `Browser`, to the lower split container and set its `Dock` property to `Fill`. Your dialog box should look like the one shown in Figure 15-8.

Adding the `ExplorerBrowser` control automatically adds the required references to your application. However, you do need to provide the following `using` statement:

**FIGURE 15-8:** The example requires a little more configuration than normal.

```
using Microsoft.WindowsAPICodePack.Shell;
```

## Writing the Explorer Browser Example Code

The Explorer Browser example doesn't contain a lot of code, yet you can do quite a bit with it because the `ExplorerBrowser` control provides a lot of functionality by itself. When you start this example, you can choose any of the `KnownFolder` entries and see where this takes you in the right `Browser` pane. Listing 15-5 shows the code needed for this example.

**LISTING 15-5:** Using the Explorer Browser control to create an interesting interface

```
public frmMain()
{
    // Perform the standard initialization.
    InitializeComponent();

    // Initialize the folder list.
    foreach (IKnownFolder Folder in KnownFolders.All)
        lstFolders.Items.Add(Folder.CanonicalName);

    // Choose an initial folder.
    lstFolders.SelectedItem = KnownFolders.Documents.CanonicalName;
    Browser.Navigate(ShellFileSystemFolder.FromFolderPath(
        KnownFolders.Documents.Path));
}

private void lstFolders_SelectedIndexChanged(object sender, EventArgs e)
{
    try
    {
```

*continues*

**LISTING 15-5** *(continued)*

```
            // Locate the selection.
            foreach (IKnownFolder Folder in KnownFolders.All)

                // Compare the folder name to the selected name.
                if (Folder.CanonicalName == lstFolders.Text)
                {
                    // Change the selected folder.
                    Browser.Navigate(
                        ShellFileSystemFolder.FromFolderPath(
                            Folder.Path));

                    // Exit the loop.
                    break;
                }
        }
        catch
        {
            // Display an error message.
            MessageBox.Show("Can't select the specified item.");
        }
    }
}
```

The code begins with the `frmMain()` constructor. The example performs the standard initialization. It then fills `lstFolders` with the names of all the `KnownFolder` entries using a `foreach` loop. The `CanonicalName` property provides the most readable entries. The `ComboBox` control automatically sorts the names for you.

It's also important to provide an initial selection. The example uses the `KnownFolders.Documents` entry for this purpose. Setting `lstFolders` means changing the `SelectedItem` property to the appropriate `CanonicalName` value. To set the Browser display, the code relies on the `Navigate()` method. You must provide a `ShellFileSystemFolder` or a `ShellFile` object in most cases (any appropriate `ShellObject` should work). The example uses the `ShellFileSystemFolder` `.FromFolderPath()` method to obtain the appropriate value. In this case, the value is from `KnownFolders.Documents.Path`. At this point, the application presents an initial display similar to the one shown in Figure 15-9.

When the user clicks the drop-down list box, `lstFolders` displays all the available `KnownFolder` entries. From previous sections of this chapter, you know that some of those entries are non-filesystem containers that don't have a path. The example isn't designed to show the content of these containers — navigating to them will fail. However, all other entries should display without any problem in the right pane of the `Browser`.

After the user makes a selection, the example calls `lstFolders_SelectedIndexChanged()`. The `lstFolders.Items` collection contains a list of canonical names, not paths. The first task the code performs is to match the canonical name in an `IKnownFolder` object, `Folder`, with the canonical name the user has selected. When the two `CanonicalName` property values match, the code extracts a path from `Folder`. It then calls `Browser.Navigate()` to set the `Browser` display.

**FIGURE 15-9:** The initial display shows the user's personal folders.

## MOVING YOUR APPLICATIONS TO WINDOWS 7

This chapter has explored the Library feature of Windows 7, which serves to centralize data management for the user and hide the actual sources of that data. The Library can hold both folders (and associated files) and non-folder content such as security certificates. The goal of the Library is to provide one place the user can look to find needed resources of nearly any type. If you take one thing away from this chapter, it should be that the Library does require a little more work on your part and represents a new way of doing things, but that it also reduces support requirements because users can more easily find the data they need regardless of its actual location.

Before you begin creating your first Library application, you need to consider how you'll use the Library and whether you're willing to use it in place of other techniques that you've used in the past. The Library is a Windows 7 technology, so using it means moving beyond older versions of Windows. You need to weigh the cost of the move against the benefits gained by making data easier for users to access. Once you do decide to move to the Library, it's important to spend time figuring out precisely how you plan to implement your application. For example, you need to consider whether your application will use the Explorer Browser control or present the data in some other way.

Previous versions of Windows provided some form of 64-bit support, but the support was often less than useful. For example, the 64-bit support in Windows XP left you with a system that used only part of the available hardware due to a lack of drivers. Vista didn't improve on matters a lot. Windows 7 is the first version of Windows 64-bit applications to become truly practical. Chapter 16 provides an overview of the 64-bit support provided with Windows 7.

# 16

# Writing 64-Bit Applications for Windows 7

**WHAT'S IN THIS CHAPTER?**

➤ Using 64-bit applications to your advantage

➤ Defining the requirements for building and using 64-bit applications

➤ Considering 64-bit application development issues

➤ Creating a 64-bit application

Windows 7 is the first version of Windows in which a 64-bit setup is not only practical but actually a good idea. As Windows has become more complex, and users do more with their systems, the old 3 GB memory limit of 32-bit Windows presents too many limitations. (You may have thought that 32-bit Windows had a 2 GB limit because that's the limit Microsoft usually presents, but the site at http://msdn.microsoft.com/library/aa366778.aspx tells the whole story.) When you use 64-bit Windows, the system has a 7 TB or 8 TB limit, depending on which processor you use. Unfortunately, to gain access to all this memory you must combine 64-bit Windows with 64-bit applications. There are other advantages to working with 64-bit Windows, and this chapter begins by telling you about them.

> *You must exercise caution when discussing Windows 7 memory support. For example, while an application can access 3 GB memory maximum using 32-bit Windows 7, the physical memory limit is 4 GB. Likewise, the physical memory limit for 64-bit Windows 7 is 192 GB when using Windows 7 Ultimate, but only 8 GB when using Windows 7 Home Basic. The site at* http://msdn.microsoft.com/library/aa366778.aspx *discusses physical memory limits in more detail.*

Most people have forgotten the upsets created when the world moved from 16-bit applications to 32-bit applications, because systems have relied on a 32-bit architecture for so long. The 32-bit architecture has served well (and will likely continue to serve well for a while longer), but it's time to move on to 64 bits when the situation allows. The move to 64 bits isn't going to be any easier than the move to 32 bits was. You need to consider the requirements for making the move before you begin an update of your application.

Once you consider the requirements, you have to determine how to implement the requirements as part of a development strategy. A 64-bit application will present all kinds of issues. For example, the simple act of writing data to the registry is no longer so simple. Look at the various registry types presented by RegEdit — they reflect a 32-bit strategy for the most part. Now you'll need to work with QWORD values rather than the DWORD values of the past. Data storage will have to reflect 64-bit application needs, which means that even registry settings will introduce compatibility issues that your update will need to address. In addition, you may not have access to some older DLLs.

Of course, this chapter wouldn't be complete if you didn't see a 64-bit application in action. The example in this chapter shows how you can work with larger numbers in a 64-bit application. It's not the only thing you can do, but large-number handling is one reason businesses are considering the move to 64 bits. The following sections only introduce you to 64-bit programming, but the introduction is from a Windows 7 perspective, rather than the more general perspective you may have considered in the past.

*You may not feel that moving to a 64-bit environment is necessary, and it isn't necessary today. However, at some point 32-bit applications will disappear from the market, just as 16-bit applications are extremely uncommon today. In fact, some IT experts have surmised that Windows 8 may appear only in 64-bit form, which would make a move to 64-bit applications advantageous. Even if you don't plan to move your application to the 64-bit environment today, make sure you keep the necessity of the move in mind for the near future.*

## CONSIDERING THE ADVANTAGES OF 64-BIT APPLICATIONS

You may not see many 64-bit applications today — at least not publicly available applications. Most of the current 64-bit application development is for custom applications. Of course, there's the Office 2010 64-bit version. You can read about this version at http://technet.microsoft.com/library/ee681792.aspx. As you can see from the Advantages section of this white paper, the main reasons to use the 64-bit version are:

- Access to more memory
- Larger Excel workbooks
- Improved Microsoft Project capacity
- Enhanced security through hardware Data Execution Prevention (DEP)

The list of advantages doesn't mention anything about things that users will notice immediately, such as improved application speed. If you look at the list, the majority of the advantages seem to revolve around size — more memory, bigger workbooks, and larger projects. Still, users will notice these advantages quite quickly if they've been complaining about size as an issue.

Creating a 64-bit application can result in improved application performance, which is the combination of speed, reliability, and security. Here's how those three elements will likely play out for you:

- **Security:** Of course, the Office 2010 Website already mentions the security part of the performance picture in the form of DEP. Unfortunately, outside of DEP, 64-bit applications aren't inherently more secure than 32-bit applications. Only the fact that there are fewer 64-bit coded exploits will keep outsiders at bay for the short term, but you can be sure that these nefarious individuals are even now writing 64-bit exploits designed to crack your security.

- **Speed:** The speed part of the equation comes from the potential to access more memory. Accessing memory is always going to be faster than accessing the hard drive. With the greatly enhanced memory potential of a 64-bit application, it's possible to read an entire document into memory and access it there, rather than keep reading it from the hard drive. Code access is also faster — you can load DLLs into memory and keep them there, rather than load and unload DLLs to keep memory usage to a minimum. However, any speed gain you want to obtain has to be within the limits of the system's hardware. A 64-bit application won't make the hard drive run any faster or supply the processor with any additional clock cycles.

- **Reliability:** You can gain reliability in several ways. By reading a document stored on the network to local memory, you not only improve access speed, but you also insulate the application from intermittent network failures, making it more reliable. Reliability is inversely proportional to the number of parts in an application. Because you can create larger application pieces, it's possible to reduce the application's part count and improve reliability in that manner. Reliability is also inversely proportional to iterations. The fewer the number of iterations, the higher the application reliability. By reading larger pieces of data from the hard drive, for example, you can reduce the probability that an iteration will fail.

*There's always a potential for false savings when considering speed or reliability in an application. Reading an entire document from disk when you only intend to use half of it still wastes processing cycles whether you're working with a 32-bit or 64-bit application. Using resources with efficiency in mind is always the best way to improve application speed and reliability.*

Some types of application actually require 64-bit support today. For example, if your application uses memory-mapped files, you'll definitely want to upgrade to 64 bits at some point because files are quickly becoming large enough to overwhelm a 32-bit application. It doesn't take long to create a file 4 GB or larger. A 32-bit application simply can't handle the large files that users create today.

Processor-intensive applications greatly benefit from 64 bits because the application can often make use of the larger 64-bit registers to decrease the number of steps required to complete a task. This is especially true when the processor-intensive task is data-oriented. A cryptography routine can run three to five times faster on a 64-bit machine simply by making use of the larger registers to process data more quickly.

> Some users express disappointment with the 64-bit environment because their applications don't run any faster. It's important to consider the application load. A Web browser will run only as fast as its Internet connection allows. Switching to a 64-bit environment won't change the speed of the application because the Internet connection speed remains the same. Likewise, a 64-bit word processor won't run any faster because its speed is largely limited by how fast the user can type — most word processors already spend considerable time waiting for the user to do something.

Graphics applications also run considerably faster in a 64-bit environment because graphics applications tend to move huge amounts of data in memory. A 64-bit processor can move data twice as fast for a given clock speed because its registers are twice as large. In the case of graphics applications, the actual application code isn't working much faster, but the data used to feed the application code is able to arrive twice as fast, so the application code spends less time waiting. Given that the amount of graphics in applications is increasing, a 64-bit application will offer significant benefits.

Many applications today also rely heavily on XML. It's interesting to note that developers largely see XML as a disk-intensive task, but it really isn't. XML is a mixed task that requires substantial amounts of processing in certain situations. According to sites like Altova (the makers of XMLSpy), 32-bit systems are limited to opening XML files no larger than 200 MB (see http://www.altova.com/64-bit.html). The world is quickly moving to larger XML files to store everything from application settings to complete databases.

## UNDERSTANDING THE REQUIREMENTS FOR 64-BIT APPLICATIONS

Moving to a higher-level processor is a painful experience in most cases because many people underestimate the requirements for such a move. After all, simply increasing the size of the registers in the processor doesn't seem to be such a big deal. However, changing the size of the registers is only part of the move. A 64-bit processor has additional registers, larger memory access, increased speed, additional operating modes, and a host of other features that only a hardware engineer will care about. All these differences don't look like much until you start writing native code to access them. Of course, as a .NET developer you won't actually write native code in most cases, but Microsoft has to change Windows to work with the 64-bit processor, which is going to change your application.

Changes in the operating system tend to snowball. The 64-bit operating system requires 64-bit drivers. The new drivers require updated support software, and so on. Moving to 64 bits isn't simply a matter of updating your application; it's also a matter of understanding all the changes that surround the application. What the user perceives as a change that improves application speed or reliability is likely a massive change in some respects for your application. The following list describes some of the requirements you should consider when updating your application:

- **Operating system:** You must have a 64-bit operating system to run a 64-bit application. There are no 64-bit emulators for 32-bit systems (even if there were, they would run incredibly slowly). One issue that developers sometimes forget is whether application users run the .NET application using Mono (http://www.mono-project.com/Main_Page). Make sure the user has access to the proper 64-bit version of an operating system for Mono (see http://www.mono-project.com/Supported_Platforms).

- **Drivers:** Older versions of Windows were somewhat lenient on the drivers you were allowed to use. Due to security issues, Microsoft has greatly tightened the driver requirements for Windows 7. You must make sure that any special equipment comes with a 64-bit Windows 7-compatible driver before moving your application to 64 bits.

- **Support software:** Yes, you can use that older 32-bit support application if you really must with your 64-bit application, but the use of 32-bit software will cost performance and reliability. The "Hosting Older DLLs" section of this chapter discusses this issue in more detail.

- **Assemblies and libraries:** Try to upgrade all 32-bit assemblies to 64 bits if possible. Microsoft has created a 64-bit version of the .NET Framework. You might have to install this version separately (see the note in the "Writing a 64-Bit Application" section of the chapter).

- **Memory:** Depending on how you write your application, you may find that it consumes considerably more memory than it did in 32-bit form. Using 64-bit memory types may help make your application faster or add new features, but at the expense of higher memory usage. It's important to re-evaluate memory requirements for your application after making the move to 64 bits to ensure that the application isn't memory-starved.

- **Supporting hardware:** You need a 64-bit system to work with 64-bit applications. The motherboard, processor, and other hardware must provide the required 64-bit support. Obviously, you can't install a 64-bit operating system on a platform that doesn't support it.

One of the potential problems for developers has been persuading management to move to the 64-bit environment. There are many reasons cited, but often it comes down to time and money. Moving to 64 bits costs a lot of money, and businesses want to see a definite return on that investment. The problem is severe enough that Microsoft even put together a white paper for 64-bit SharePoint Server (http://technet.microsoft.com/library/dd630755.aspx) to persuade businesses to make the move. One requirement for your upgrade is to ensure that you've addressed management concerns in addition to the software and hardware requirements listed in this section. Make sure you have a good plan in place before you talk with management about making the move.

## OVERCOMING 64-BIT DEVELOPMENT ISSUES

As with any new technology, development issues must be overcome when you move to 64-bit programming. You need to consider these issues as part of any plan to move your application to a 64-bit environment. When creating a new application, you need to take these development issues into consideration in defining the application requirements, creating the application design, and assembling your development team. The following sections aren't meant as an inclusive list of every development issue you'll encounter. However, these sections do touch on some of the major issues you must deal with when working with Windows 7.

## Dealing with Programming Issues

No matter which operating system or development platform you use, there are going to be programming issues when moving from 32 bits to 64 bits. For example, the size of variables matters. When working with .NET variables such as Int32, you at least know right from the type name that the variable is 32 bits in size. What you may not remember is that many Windows 7 features require 64 bits when you work with 64-bit code. For example, if you perform any P/Invoke calls, the handle you receive from the Win32 API is 64 bits, not 32 bits. In order to find such information, you'll normally have to resort to C++ sites such as http://msdn.microsoft.com/library/3b2e7499.aspx because Microsoft doesn't readily make the information available for C# or VB.NET developers.

It's extremely important to consider the requirements of methods and functions you call. In some cases, methods and functions require variables of a specific size. You need to address this requirement as you code because it will become all too easy to try to pass a 64-bit variable to a method or function that expects a 32-bit variable. The method or function might simply truncate the 64-bit value, which will lead to data loss and unexpected results from your application.

Programming issues can sneak into the developer's life without notice. For example, if your 64-bit application interacts with the 64-bit version of Office 2010, you'll have some nasty surprises to consider. Strictly speaking, the 32-bit and 64-bit versions of Office 2010 aren't completely compatible, a situation described here: http://msdn.microsoft.com/library/ee691831.aspx. Even though the information on this site discusses problems with VBA, those same problems will affect your Visual Studio Tools for Office (VSTO) applications as well. Unfortunately, Microsoft doesn't provide a ready resource for these issues, so you have to ferret them out in other ways. You should be prepared for similar problems with other 64-bit applications — Office 2010 isn't alone in this regard.

## Accessing the Registry in Windows 7

Developers are likely to have some terrible surprises when accessing the registry in the 64-bit version of Windows 7. The 64-bit version of the registry contains both 32-bit and 64-bit keys, many of which have the same names. In other words, there's a 32-bit and a 64-bit version of the same key, so you need to know which key you're accessing. In fact, the problem is significant enough that Microsoft provides a Knowledge Base article that instructs administrators and developers alike how to view the registry when working with the 64-bit version of Windows. This article can be found at http://support.microsoft.com/kb/305097.

An article at http://msdn.microsoft.com/library/ms724072.aspx describes in more detail some of the differences in data storage. The use of registry redirection makes it likely that the 64-bit version of your application will actually rely on a physically different key from the 32-bit version. Even if your code uses precisely the same key, the physical key is different because the Registry Redirector will redirect the 64-bit key to a different location than the 32-bit key.

Let's say you create a 32-bit version of your application and run it on a 64-bit system. The 32-bit application needs to access the key at `HKEY_LOCAL_MACHINE\SOFTWARE\CompanyX`. The key is physically located at `HKEY_LOCAL_MACHINE\SOFTWARE\Wow6432Node\CompanyX`, but the Registry Redirector makes it look as if the key is at `HKEY_LOCAL_MACHINE\SOFTWARE\CompanyX`. A 64-bit version of the same application will physically store its data at `HKEY_LOCAL_MACHINE\SOFTWARE\CompanyX`. The 32-bit and 64-bit version of the application will use different physical locations for their data, so you can't assume that data sharing will take place. The way to overcome this issue is to target the Any CPU setting when creating your application, but then you lose some benefits of using a 64-bit application because the compiler can't perform the required optimizations.

To make matters even more confusing, older versions of Windows (including Windows Server 2008, Windows Vista, Windows Server 2003, and Windows XP/2000) use registry reflection. Your older code might use P/Invoke to call the `RegDisableReflectionKey()`, `RegEnableReflectionKey()`, and `RegQueryReflectionKey()` functions to control registry reflection. Starting with Windows Server 2008 R2 and Windows 7, you'll note that WOW64 (Windows 32-bit On Windows 64-bit) no longer relies on registry reflection, which means that you have to change any existing 64-bit code to reflect this change. Keys that were formerly reflected are now shared instead.

## Hosting Older DLLs

You don't have to toss out the older 32-bit DLLs in your arsenal when moving to a 64-bit application. However, it's important to know that you also can't load a 32-bit DLL in a 64-bit address space. Windows and .NET may hide the details from you, but the effects are clear. When you access a 32-bit DLL from your 64-bit code, the .NET Framework must marshal the data and calls between the two environments. Consequently, your application will use more resources, run slower, and experience more reliability problems because there's now a layer of marshaling code between your 64-bit application and the 32-bit DLL.

The key to hosting 32-bit code in the 64-bit environment is WOW64, which is an emulation layer that runs in 64-bit versions of Windows. The document found at http://www.microsoft.com/whdc/system/platform/64bit/wow64_bestprac.mspx provides you with some great information about how WOW64 works. Most of these issues are hidden from view for the .NET developer, but you still need to be aware of them. Unfortunately, WOW64 has limitations that you can't avoid, even as a .NET developer. Here are some of the limitations you need to consider:

➤ **Memory:** Your application is limited to 2 GB of address space. Although C++ developers can rely on the `/LARGEADDRESSAWARE` switch to gain access to 4 GB of address space, there isn't any corresponding switch for .NET developers. This limitation may mean breaking up larger pieces of code before making the move to 64 bits and loading each piece as needed.

➤ **DLL loading:** A 32-bit process can't load a 64-bit DLL (except for certain system DLLs). Consequently, your main application must load and manage all subordinate DLLs. If a 32-bit DLL requires support DLLs, you must ensure that you have the correct 32-bit support DLLs available and not rely on 64-bit DLLs that may be available with Windows.

➤ **Physical Address Extension (PAE) support:** There isn't any PAE support available. You may not think of it immediately, but this particular issue can affect SQL Server, which means your application may suddenly encounter database problems. The Knowledge Base article at http://support.microsoft.com/kb/274750 discusses how you configure SQL Server to use 3 GB of memory through PAE. The article at http://blogs.technet.com/b/beatrice/archive/2008/08/29/3gb-pae-and-awe-taking-away-some-confusion.aspx describes how PAE works. Make certain your 32-bit version of SQL Server doesn't rely on PAE before making the 64-bit move.

- **DirectX hardware acceleration:** Your application may not use DirectX directly, but some third-party libraries rely on it. There isn't any support for hardware acceleration, which means that your application can slow considerably. If your application relies on a third-party graphics library, make sure you check into any DirectX requirement before you make the move to 64 bits.

- **16-bit processes:** Once you move to a 64-bit version of Windows, you can't load any sort of 16-bit process — not even processes that would normally run at the command prompt when using 32-bit Windows. This particular limitation can mean recoding scientific and other older application code.

- **Virtual DOS Machine (VDM) support:** There isn't any form of VDM API support provided. This means that older command line utilities won't run.

- **Page-size-dependent APIs:** You won't be able to use any of the page-size-dependent APIs, such as Address Windowing Extension (AWE). Although this limitation probably won't affect your .NET application directly, it could affect support code, so you need to check any support requirements.

## WRITING A 64-BIT APPLICATION

Writing a 64-bit application using the .NET Framework is straightforward. You don't need to write any odd code, and you'll find that your old managed code will usually work fine. In fact, as long as you perform a few configuration tasks properly, you might not notice any differences at all. On the other hand, you might not immediately think about all the tasks you need to perform in order to obtain a true 64-bit application. The following sections help you create a true 64-bit application that works with some larger numbers using the Int64 type.

*This example assumes that you're using a 64-bit version of Windows 7 and have the 64-bit version of the .NET Framework available. The 64-bit .NET Framework assemblies normally appear in the* \Windows\Microsoft.NET\Framework64 *folder of your system. Before you begin this example, verify that you have the 64-bit version of the .NET Framework installed. You can download a combined x86/x64 version of the .NET Framework from* http://www.microsoft.com/downloads/en/details.aspx?FamilyID=0a391abd-25c1-4fc0-919f-b21f31ab88b7. *However, you still won't be able to test any 64-bit examples you create on a 32-bit system.*

*After you spend time reviewing this example, you might think that you can simply change some settings in the Configuration Manager and rebuild your application to move it from the 32-bit to the 64-bit environment. The reality is that you probably won't want to make that assumption because you can encounter some tricky situations when making the move. For example, if you work with variables that aren't type-safe, then their values may change in size when making the move. This problem is especially true when working with P/Invoke because the Windows API is terrible about maintaining any sort of mapping. However, you don't have to worry about an* int *suddenly changing its mapping to an* Int64; *an* int *will always map to an* Int32 *value. The article at* http://msdn.microsoft.com/library/ms973190.aspx *provides details about migrating 32-bit code to the 64-bit environment.*

## Configuring the Large-Number Example

The example begins with a Windows Forms application. You must also add an Add button (btnAdd) and three textboxes (txtValue1, txtValue2, and txtResult), as shown in Figure 16-1. Set the txtValue1.Text property to 4000000000000000000 and the txtValue2.Text property to 2000000000000000000 so that you don't have to keep typing the values for each test. The values are well outside the range of an Int32 value and truly test an Int64.

**FIGURE 16-1:** You can use this simple form for the 64-bit application.

One of the most common problems with a 64-bit .NET application is that the developer hasn't used 64-bit .NET assemblies. The default assemblies that come with a project are 32-bit ones. You won't find the 64-bit assemblies in the usual place either. The following steps help you configure your application to use 64-bit assemblies:

1. Open the References folder of Solution Explorer.
2. Highlight each reference in turn and press Delete to remove it.
3. Right-click the References folder and choose Add Reference from the Context menu. You'll see the Add Reference dialog box.
4. Select the Browse tab (normally, you'd select the .NET tab to add standard assemblies).
5. Locate the \Windows\Microsoft.NET\Framework64\v4.0.30319 folder on your system and highlight the System.Windows.Forms.DLL, System.DLL, and System.Drawing.DLL files, as shown in Figure 16-2. (The Microsoft.CSharp.DLL and System.Core.DLL files are automatically referenced as part of the build, so you don't need to add them.)

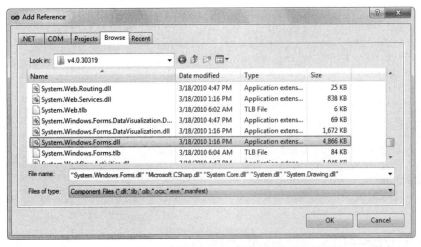

**FIGURE 16-2:** You must replace all 32-bit assemblies with their 64-bit counterparts.

6. Click OK. Visual Studio adds the 64-bit assemblies to your project.

This example doesn't require the full set of default `using` statements. All you need are the `using` statements listed here:

```
using System;
using System.Drawing;
using System.Windows.Forms;
```

## Working with the Configuration Manager

Microsoft assumes that you want to build a 32-bit project, so the configuration options reflect a 32-bit environment. In fact, you can't choose a 64-bit environment without modifying the configuration. The following steps describe how to modify the Configuration Manager to support a 64-bit build process.

1. Choose Build ▷ Configuration Manager. You'll see the Configuration Manager dialog box.
2. Click the Active Solution Configuration drop-down list and choose <New . . . >. You'll see the New Solution Configuration dialog box shown in Figure 16-3.
3. Type **Debug 64-Bit** in the Name field.
4. Choose Debug in the Copy Settings From field and click OK. Visual Studio creates the new solution configuration for you.

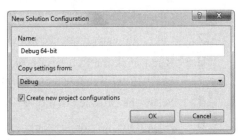

**FIGURE 16-3:** Create a new solution configuration to use in building your application.

*You might wonder why you would want to create a new solution configuration when you could just as easily modify the existing solution configuration. Modifying a default solution configuration proves confusing for other developers who need to work with your code. It's far less confusing to create a new and clearly worded solution configuration.*

5. Choose <New> in the Platform column drop-down list box. You'll see the New Project Platform dialog box shown in Figure 16-4.

6. Choose x64 in the New Platform field. Click OK. Your Configuration Manager dialog box should now look like the one shown in Figure 16-5.

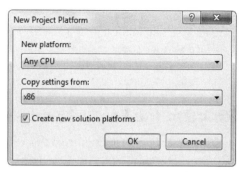

**FIGURE 16-4** Define the platform you want to support with this solution.

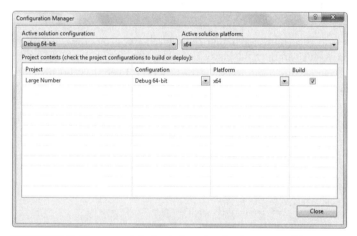

**FIGURE 16-5:** The completed solution clearly shows an x64 output.

7. Repeat Steps 2 through 6 for the Release build and name this new solution configuration Release 64-bit.

## Writing the Large-Number Example Code

The focus of this example is the setup for a 64-bit application, so the example code is quite simple. All the code does is read the two input values into local variables, add them, and produce an output as shown in Listing 16-1.

Available for download on Wrox.com

**LISTING 16-1: Adding two large numbers**

```
private void btnAdd_Click(object sender, EventArgs e)
{
    // Perform the addition.
    Int64 Value1 = Int64.Parse(txtValue1.Text);
    Int64 Value2 = Int64.Parse(txtValue2.Text);
    txtResult.Text = (Value1 + Value2).ToString();
}
```

The default values are too large to hold in an Int32 type, so the example uses an Int64 type. An Int64 data type can hold values ranging from –9,223,372,036,854,775,808 to 9,223,372,036,854,775,807. The code uses Int64.Parse() to convert the text value in txtValue1.Text and txtValue2.Text to numbers. It then adds the numeric values together, converts the result to a string, and outputs it to txtResult.Text.

## Running the Large-Number Test

You won't find the output from this example in the usual directory. Instead, you'll need to look in the \Large Number\Large Number\bin\x64\Debug 64-bit or \Large Number\Large Number\bin\x64\Release 64-bit folder of your system. The assembly will still be called Large Number.EXE. In fact, except for the fact that it's in a 64-bit folder, you won't see any difference between this assembly and a 32-bit assembly. The only time you'll see an immediate difference is when you try to run the application on a 32-bit system and discover that it won't work.

Of course, the question you should ask at this point is whether there really are any differences except for the fact that the 64-bit application won't run on a 32-bit system. The application does indeed have all the benefits of a 64-bit application. You won't see them directly, however. Even if you disassemble the 64-bit application, as shown in Figure 16-6, and compare it to a 32-bit counterpart, you won't see a difference. That's because the .NET Framework relies on byte code that's later interpreted by the Common Language Runtime (CLR). In order to see a real difference, you'd need to compile the example into a native image and perform a comparison at the assembler level.

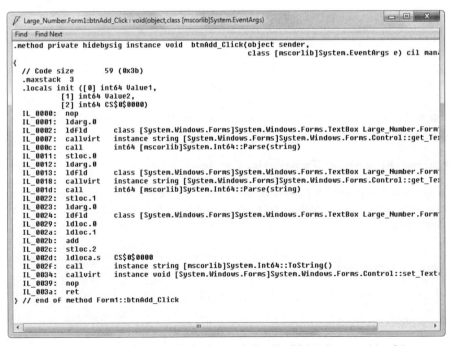

**FIGURE 16-6:** The 64-bit disassembly looks much like the 32-bit disassembly of the same application.

> **DISASSEMBLING THE LARGE NUMBER.EXE ASSEMBLY**
>
> You may want to check out the difference between a 32-bit compilation and a 64-bit compilation of this example for yourself. If that's the case, you'll need to create two versions of the example, one 32-bit and another 64-bit. Follow these steps to open a disassembly of either version:
>
> 1. Open a Visual Studio Command Prompt (2010).
> 2. Change directories to the folder that holds the application you want to disassemble using the CD (change directory) command. For example, to change directories to `\Large Number\Large Number\bin\x64\Debug 64-bit`, you type **CD \Large Number\Large Number\bin\x64\Debug 64-bit** and press Enter.
> 3. Type **ILDasm "Large Number.EXE"** and press Enter. The Intermediate Language Disassembler (ILDasm) utility creates a disassembly of the application for you. Note the use of double quotes around the filename. You must include the double quotes because of the space in the filename.
> 4. Open the `Large Number.EXE\Large_Number\Large_Number.Form1` entry.
> 5. Double-click the `btnAdd_Click` entry to display the disassembly.

The fact remains that there's a real difference, even with this example. If you were using a 32-bit version of the program, the application couldn't load the entire `Int64` value into a register because the register would be too small. However, when working with a 64-bit version, the entire value fits into a single processor register. The bottom line is that at the native-code level, the code performs less work, making it run faster. Because there's also a smaller amount of native code, the code is inherently more reliable as well. So there are very real differences, even with an example this small.

## MOVING YOUR APPLICATIONS TO WINDOWS 7

This chapter has helped you discover the wonders of 64-bit applications. To some extent, it may almost seem as if they're more trouble than they're worth right now unless you need something that a 64-bit application can provide, such as additional memory access. If you're a gadget freak, you might find the promise of 64-bit applications more than you can bear. At some point, 64-bit applications will become the standard, but that probably won't happen for some time yet because of the huge installed base of 32-bit applications that still do their job just fine.

It's important not to upgrade your application simply because a 64-bit architecture is the wave of the future. On the other hand, you shouldn't dismiss 64-bit applications as being too difficult or complex either, without first considering the potential benefits. Because progressing to a 64-bit architecture is such a big move, it's important to think about the pros and cons carefully.

Make sure you'll be getting a payback from the upgrade and that the incompatibilities the move introduces won't cripple your organization.

Another beneficial way to upgrade your application is to use parallel programming techniques. Most systems today come with multi-core processors in which Windows treats each core as an individual processor. The problem with parallel programming to date is that few programming languages support it, and many developers are unaware of the required techniques. Up until Windows 7, Windows didn't provide the best support for parallel applications either. Chapter 17 provides a good overview of parallel-programming techniques as viewed from the Windows 7 perspective.

# 17
# Using Parallel Programming in Windows 7

**WHAT'S IN THIS CHAPTER?**

➤ Understanding why parallel processing can improve your applications

➤ Defining the requirements for parallel processing

➤ Creating your own application with parallel processing

Most systems today come with multi-core processors. Each of those cores is treated as a separate processor by Windows. (It doesn't matter whether you have an Intel or AMD processor — multiple cores work the same with both vendors from a Windows perspective.) If you have four core processors, what Windows sees are four processors. Unfortunately, most applications today use just a single processor. The system has more to offer, but the application works with just one of the processors because it's not designed to do anything more. Consequently, even though the user and developer both want improved speed, and there's additional speed to be had, the application simply can't provide it. Using more than one processor has a number of other advantages, and this chapter explores them.

Before you can write a parallel-processing application, you need to define the requirements for such an application. For example, you need some technique for synchronizing the efforts of multiple processors. Otherwise, the application will end up scrambled and won't produce the desired result. In fact, it's the need to synchronize things in some way that has prevented many developers from even attempting to create a parallel-processing application in the first place. The "Understanding the Parallel-Processing Problem" sidebar discusses the problem in more depth. The rest of the chapter focuses on actual requirements to get you started.

This chapter also provides a simple example of an application that uses parallel processing. The application isn't very impressive — the focus is on technique, rather than on doing something fancy. By the time you finish working through the example application, you'll have a much better idea of how to create a parallel-processing application of your own.

### UNDERSTANDING THE PARALLEL-PROCESSING PROBLEM

It may seem incredibly easy to perform parallel processing within an application. All you really need to do is break the application into threads and assign each thread to a different processor. Unfortunately, that tactic will never work. Nor will other seemingly straightforward approaches to the problem, and all for one basic reason called *state*, which is the mutable condition of the data.

Most programming languages in existence today rely on state in some fashion to make the application function. For example, when adding two numbers, the programming language loads the first number into a register, then the second number into another register, and then uses the add microcode within the processor to perform the task. Finally, the code moves the result from the processor register to memory. All of these elements include state. The code can't move to a different processor because the current processor has stored the state of the procedure and only that processor can complete the task.

Another problem is resource contention. It's one thing to juggle resources using one processor, but coordinating the resource usage of multiple processors can become problematic. Without the proper safeguards, code in one processor could potentially modify the content of data being manipulated by code in another processor.

Older languages are created with a single processor environment in mind. They let the developer create variables, change the state of these variables, and work with each variable as if any code within the application has exclusive access to that variable. These *imperative* languages (languages that change application state) don't work well in the parallel programming environment without significant help. This chapter overcomes the deficiencies of imperative languages by using the `Parallel` class described at http://msdn.microsoft.com/library/system.threading.tasks.parallel.aspx to provide needed application functionality.

Newer *functional* languages, such as F# and IronPython, treat code as mathematical equations and avoid both state and mutable data. Functional languages are a subgroup of *declarative* languages, which also include query and logic languages. Once you assign a value to a variable in F# or IronPython, you can't change it — the data can move between processors because the data never changes. You can read about F# at http://www.devsource.com/c/a/Languages/Exploring-the-New-F-Language/. The book *Professional IronPython* by John Mueller, Wrox 2010, provides a full dissertation on how functional languages work, and how you can use them with imperative languages such as C# and Visual Basic.NET. When the `Parallel` class doesn't provide the functionality you need, you can always rely on a functional language to perform the required work in tandem with the imperative language of your choice.

## CONSIDERING THE ADVANTAGES OF PARALLEL PROCESSING

The one undeniable advantage of parallel processing is speed. If you use multiple processors to solve a problem, the problem will be solved more quickly. However, it's important to understand that using two processors won't solve a problem twice as fast. Parallel processing incurs some level of *overhead*, the resources used to manage the multiple processors. Depending on the efficiency of the management software, processing can approach being twice as fast, but never quite attain it. Another misconception is that the application will approach being twice as fast overall. Only the compute-intensive portion of the application will approach twice as fast. The application will still function at the same speed for network and disk operations; it will also continue to wait on the user to provide required input. So overall you'll see a speed benefit using parallel processing, but you won't see anything approaching twice as fast when working with two processors.

Some applications today lack needed functionality because adding the functionality would make the application run too slowly. For example, you might want to include specialized graphics-smoothing routines in your application. However, after adding these routines, you can visually see the application add the smoothing to the output. In fact, you can go to lunch and come back in the time it takes for the application to finish rendering the display. Obviously, users will never tolerate anything that slow. At one time, developers would solve issues of this sort by using a processor with a higher clock speed, but heat and other issues have made this solution obsolete. Using parallel processing techniques can solve these sorts of issues at a reasonable price and by using technology available today.

A less-understood advantage of parallel processing is that it lends a certain amount of security to your application. Most naughty applications designed to peek at your application do so based on a single processor. The assumption is that the Trojan application will find what it needs based on the application's using a single processor because that's how applications generally work. When an application uses multiple processors, it has an advantage because it's considerably harder to peek at it. The application is using multiple processors, each of which is using different areas of memory. A Trojan writer has to work much harder to gain any valuable information about your application, and the random nature of using multiple processors means that a sneak-peek trick that works today probably won't work tomorrow.

## UNDERSTANDING THE REQUIREMENTS FOR PARALLEL PROCESSING

As with any advanced programming technique, parallel processing has special requirements. You can't simply write some code and expect it to work. Adding multiple processors necessarily complicates the development scenario, which means that you must understand how to accommodate multiple processors as part of the application development plan. The following sections describe the requirements you should consider before you begin using multi-processing techniques in your application.

## Evaluating the Task Length

The time it takes to perform a task is important when evaluating the suitability of an application for parallel processing. Short tasks don't typically prove worthwhile because the overhead of managing the parallelism outweighs the benefits of using multiple processors. In some cases, the overhead can actually overcome the benefits and make the resulting application work slower.

Of course, there's a difference between long tasks that can be done efficiently and tasks that are so long they become unwieldy. The common wisdom is to break long tasks into smaller pieces when possible in order to make the tasks more granular and produce a better result with multi-threading. This principle still applies when creating an application that relies on parallel processing. In fact, you want the tasks evenly sized if possible, so that each task completes at the same time and you can maximize processor throughput, but the reality is that achieving a strict balance is nearly impossible. Some threads will undoubtedly end up waiting for other threads to complete.

## Evaluating the Task Type

Don't get the idea that parallel processing will magically fix your disk-bound database application. Parallel processing typically works best on compute-intensive applications. Of course, database applications do have compute-intensive sections where parallel processing will work fine, but the overall application may not be that much faster if the problem is actually the need to update the drive system on the host machine. When you target an application to use parallel processing, make sure you understand the types of tasks that the application performs and target those parts of the application that can benefit most.

It's important to consider the individual tasks carefully. For example, by using queries in parallel you can obtain the data needed for the application faster. However, you can also improve application execution speed by accessing only the data you need. Wasted resources are a major problem in most applications today. Combining parallel processing with reduced queries can garner the truly impressive results that most developers want, but you must think the process through carefully.

> *Some developers think that parallel processing will perform miracles with poorly written applications. The reality is that well-written, tightly implemented code will always work better than sloppy code that wastes resources. Nothing can replace well-written code. Before you convert an existing application to realize the benefits of parallel processing, make sure you've squeezed all the wasted processing cycles out of it and that the application uses resources wisely. Otherwise, the parallel processing will simply add another potential source of frustration when you finally do work through the original performance problems and correct them.*

## Considering Debugging

Parallel applications can be difficult to troubleshoot. After all, the code is executing on multiple processors and your debugger doesn't really track that sort of execution well. What you really get is a type of thread-based debugging as described in an article at http://msdn.microsoft.com/magazine/ee410778.aspx. The theory of such debugging sounds great, but the reality is quite different. A parallel application can introduce errors that are non-repetitive. The environment is no longer a constant because you now have multiple processors in play. Consider the issues you encounter when debugging a multi-threaded application and square them because you now have multi-threading and multi-processing at the same time. Even so, Visual Studio 2010 does provide some tools in the form of thread-based debugging to help you with your parallel-processing needs.

## Obtaining Required Resources

Some parallel-processing applications fail despite careful implementation and thorough analysis of the problem domain. Even if the developer squeezes out every last bit of resource-wasting processing, the application can still fail to perform as expected when the application becomes starved for resources. If your system is currently working hard to obtain access to memory for a single processed version of your application, it's going to fail when you turn to parallel processing. For example, if the application currently requires 1 GB of RAM to run effectively, it will require 2+ GB of RAM to run effectively when you use two processors. Each processor will require 1 GB of RAM and then you must also add RAM for the overhead generated by the parallel-processing requirements. In short, it's absolutely essential to profile your application in advance and determine the resources it requires before you move to parallel processing.

The problem is that the application won't necessarily show that it's resource-starved. The operating system will rely on virtual memory when it runs out of the physical equivalent. In some cases, the only clue you'll have is that the hard drive starts staying on all the time as the system thrashes. The system will constantly transfer data between RAM and the hard drive as it tries to comply with the requirements of parallel processing. In the end, your application will actually run slower if you don't have the resources required to implement parallel processing effectively.

## Team Skills

Parallel processing is significantly harder to understand and implement than any other new technology. Other transitions aren't nearly as difficult. For example, moving to the 64-bit environment can be difficult, but only because the 64-bit environment requires some interesting code changes due to the change in handle sizes and so forth. The transition is manageable, though, if you rely on checklists to ensure that all the required changes take place. When you work in a parallel-processing environment, it's important to consider the change in viewpoint that the environment requires. The application is no longer working on a single processor — multiple processors are now truly doing things simultaneously. The timing issues that you experience when working with threads are now multiplied by the number of processors that you use because things truly do happen at the same time.

Most developers today are trained in procedural coding techniques. A few developers have used declarative languages, and an even smaller percentage understand how these languages work, but for the most part, most developers see applications as a procedural process. In order to work with parallel processing effectively, the development team as a whole must move beyond relying on procedures to a perspective where nothing is assumed about when or where the code will execute. You literally don't know — you know only that it will execute at some point, assuming the application doesn't crash. Such a viewpoint requires a team with special skills.

## WRITING AN APPLICATION THAT RELIES ON PARALLEL PROCESSING

It would be difficult to include examples in a single chapter of every sort of parallelism that Windows 7 and the .NET Framework 4 support. In fact, it could be difficult to cover the topic extensively in a single book because the topic is relatively complex. The example in this section demonstrates just one technology, the `Parallel` class, which provides support for multiple processors. This particular example appears in the chapter because the `Parallel` class is straightforward, it's relatively easy to implement, and it provides a good starting point for anyone who wants to begin working with multiple processors. In addition, the example works just fine on systems that have only one processor. The following sections describe the Parallel Process example in more detail.

> **USING THE PLINQ ALTERNATIVE**
>
> There are many ways to add parallel processing to your application and this chapter covers just a few of them. Another technique that many developers use is to apply Parallel Language-Integrated Query (PLINQ) to the problem. Of course, this solution is specialized for various kinds of queries, but you can apply it to any source. There are obvious queries to databases, such as requesting information from SQL Server. However, you can also apply PLINQ to the content of a list box. You can obtain an overview of PLINQ at `http://msdn.microsoft.com/library/dd460688.aspx`.
>
> Of course, PLINQ is actually based on a simpler technology called Language-Integrated Query (LINQ), which is a generally useful technique for queries of all sorts. LINQ is a *query* language that's part of the same declarative language tree as F# and IronPython. When working with a query language, you define what you want as output from the query, rather than how to accomplish the task, as you would with an imperative language. The PLINQ technology relies on the generalized LINQ to Objects technique (`http://msdn.microsoft.com/library/bb397919.aspx`) rather than a more specific technology such as LINQ to SQL (`http://msdn.microsoft.com/library/bb386976.aspx`). You can read about all of the various kinds of LINQ technology in *LINQ for Dummies* by John Mueller, Wiley 2008.

## Understanding the Parallel Class

Microsoft recognizes the need to provide simple methods of adding parallelism to applications. Of course, parallelism is a type of multi-threading in that you create multiple threads that execute on separate processors. However, parallelism is more than simply creating a multi-threaded application. The threads must be able to execute in an independent manner. The `Parallel` class is part of the effort to create an environment in which applications can execute using more than one processor without adding undue complexity to the application itself. The concept is simple, but the implementation can be difficult. In this case, the application executes tasks within a special `for` loop. Each task can execute using a different processor.

The `Parallel` class is part of a much bigger experiment in parallelism, the Task Parallel Library (TPL) that's part of the .NET Framework 4. The components of the TPL appear as part of the `System.Threading` (http://msdn.microsoft.com/library/system.threading.aspx) and `System.Threading.Tasks` (http://msdn.microsoft.com/library/system.threading.tasks.aspx) namespaces. The `Parallel` class is just one technology in these classes, which also include the following concepts.

- **Data parallelism:** When an application must work on multiple bits of independent data, as in database records, it's usually faster to work on each bit in parallel. Instead of updating each record individually, the database application can update multiple records simultaneously. Of course, the key word is "independent." You can't update dependent data in parallel without terrible consequences. Read more about data parallelism at http://msdn.microsoft.com/library/dd537608.aspx.

- **Task parallelism:** Applications must often perform multiple independent tasks. In some cases, the tasks are similar, but different in a small way. For example, a scientific application can perform the same check using multiple instruments, or a security application can check the status of multiple intrusion sensors. As with data parallelism, the key word is "independent." The tasks must be independent of each other to succeed in a parallel-processing environment. You can read more about task parallelism at http://msdn.microsoft.com/library/dd537609.aspx.

- **Parallelism using asynchronous patterns:** The common element of both data and task parallelism is the concept of asynchronous processing. It's possible to create a pattern that describes multiple independent elements of some sort. The TPL supports asynchronous patterns in various ways. You can read about these types of processing at http://msdn.microsoft.com/library/dd997405.aspx.

- **PLINQ:** Most types of parallelism rely on the concept of doing something. An application processes multiple bits of independent data or checks multiple independent sensors. It's also possible to use parallelism when asking something. The sidebar, "Using the PLINQ Alternative," describes how to use PLINQ to perform multiple query tasks at once.

When working with the `Parallel` class, you have access to a number of `For()` and `ForEach()` loop structures that are implemented as methods (note the difference in capitalization from the standard C# `for` and `foreach` loops). In addition, the `Parallel` class supports an `Invoke()` method that accepts an array of actions to perform. All these methods can be executed in parallel if the `Parallel` class detects an opportunity to do so, and hardware resources are available to complete the action.

## Configuring the Parallel Process Example

The example begins with a Windows Forms application. You need to add a Test (btnTest) button and a list box (lstColors). The list box will contain a list of items to process. The example uses colors, but you can use any set of strings desired. Add as many strings as you want, but you'll want to keep the number of unique items low to ensure you can see them in the dialog box that appears after the data is processed. Figure 17-1 shows a typical setup for this example.

You don't need to add any special references for this example. However, you do need to add two special using statements as shown here:

**FIGURE 17-1:** The example requires a list box that contains items to process.

```
using System.Threading.Tasks;
using System.Text;
```

## Writing the Parallel-Process Example Code

The example code focuses on performing a task on multiple processors, rather than doing something elegant that you'd normally perform in a production application. In this case, the example processes a list of colors. It counts each color string and adds a new entry for each unique string. When the code completes, it outputs a dialog box with the results. Listing 17-1 contains the code needed for this example.

**LISTING 17-1:** Processing data items using multiple processors

Available for download on Wrox.com

```
private void btnTest_Click(object sender, EventArgs e)
{
    // Initialize the Colors array that is used to
    // hold the number of times each color appears.
    Dictionary<String, Int32> Colors = new Dictionary<String, Int32>();

    // Copy the list box object collection to an array for
    // processing.
    String[] ColorList = new String[lstColors.Items.Count];
    lstColors.Items.CopyTo(ColorList, 0);

    // Process each of the entries in the color list.
    Parallel.ForEach(ColorList, ThisItem =>

        // Create the lambda expression.
        {
            // Check the current color against those already
            // in the list.
            if (Colors.ContainsKey(ThisItem))

                // Update the color count if the color is
                // in the list.
```

```csharp
                Colors[ThisItem]++;
            else

                // Otherwise, add the color.
                Colors.Add(ThisItem, 1);
        }
    );

    // Create an output variable.
    StringBuilder Result = new StringBuilder();

    // Process the result.
    foreach (KeyValuePair<String, Int32> Item in Colors)
        Result.Append("Color: " + Item.Key + " appears "
            + Item.Value + " times.\n");

    // Display the result on-screen.
    MessageBox.Show(Result.ToString());
}
```

The code begins by creating a `Dictionary` object, `Colors`, that has a key of type `String` and a value of type `Int32`. Note that `Colors` will hold the summary of unique string names in `lstColors` and the number of times that the strings appear. For example, if red appears six times, the key will be red and the value will be 6.

Processing a `ListBox.ObjectCollection` can prove tricky, so the example creates a `String` array, `ColorList`. It uses the `CopyTo()` method to copy the list of colors found in `lstColors.Items` to `ColorList` for processing.

The next step is the actual parallel code for the example. The code calls `Parallel.ForEach()`, which is a parallel form of the `foreach` statement. The first argument is the list of items to process, which is contained within `ColorList`. The code then uses a *lambda expression* to process each element within `ColorList`. Lambda expressions are part of the LINQ technology. Each `ColorList` element appears within `ThisItem`.

The action for the lambda expression appears within the curly braces. When the color already appears in `Colors`, the code simply updates count value. Otherwise, the code uses the `Add()` method to add a new entry to `Colors` for the color in question. When the `ForEach()` method loop is complete, `Colors` will contain an entry for each unique color value and a count of the number of times this color appears in `lstColors`.

The final steps of this example are output-related. The code begins by creating a `StringBuilder` object, `Result`. It then uses a standard `foreach` processing loop to add each of the entries in `Colors` to `Result` as a `String`. When `Result` is complete, the code uses `Result.ToString()` to display the message box shown in Figure 17-2.

**FIGURE 17-2:** The example outputs a list of colors and the number of times each color appears.

## Debugging the Parallel-Process Example Code

There are some problems debugging the example as it exists right now — problems that have nothing to do with the code. Try setting a break point on the

```
if (Colors.ContainsKey(ThisItem))
```

line of the example code. Choose Debug ⇨ Start Debugging or press F5. You'll find that the example does stop at the right line, but not the first time through the loop in most cases. In some cases, the debugger will stop when Colors has nine items in it; at other times it will stop when Colors has only two items in it. If you try single-stepping through the code, you'll find that it lurches between steps. The odd behavior appears to be a problem with using multiple processors.

It's possible to obtain more consistent behavior from the debugger, but the logic of selecting a break point isn't always clear. Remove the previous break point and add a new one at the

```
Parallel.ForEach(ColorList, ThisItem =>
```

line of the example code. Choose Debug ⇨ Start Debugging or press F5 again. This time, you'll be able to single-step through each of the items as it's added to Colors. At least the debugger seems to work more consistently. The lesson here is that placing a break point inside the lambda expression may not work as expected. Microsoft hasn't documented why, and no reason for this behavior is stated online, apparently. The point is that if one break point doesn't appear to work for you, try setting one a little earlier in the code to see if it will work better. You should be able to find a break point that will let you see your code in action.

You'll also want to know how you can tell that the example is actually using threads to process the information. Choose Debug ⇨ Windows ⇨ Parallel Tasks or press Ctrl+Shift+D,K to display the Parallel Tasks window shown in Figure 17-3. In this case, the example is running four parallel tasks and has another one scheduled to run. Your window will very likely look different from the one shown, and it will also vary each time you run the application.

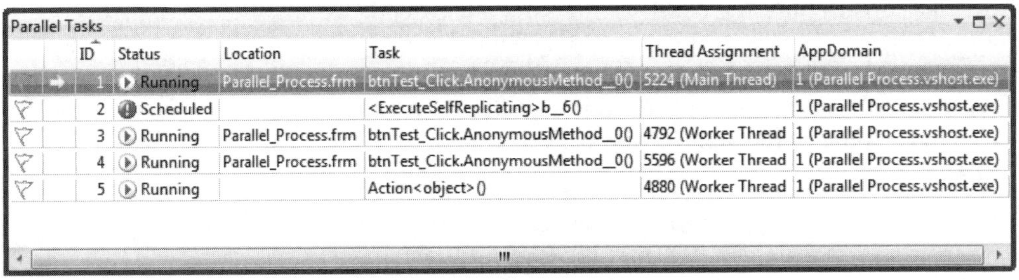

| | ID | Status | Location | Task | Thread Assignment | AppDomain |
|---|---|---|---|---|---|---|
| ➡ | 1 | ▶ Running | Parallel_Process.frm | btnTest_Click.AnonymousMethod_0() | 5224 (Main Thread) | 1 (Parallel Process.vshost.exe) |
| ▽ | 2 | ⏺ Scheduled | | <ExecuteSelfReplicating>b_6() | | 1 (Parallel Process.vshost.exe) |
| ▽ | 3 | ▶ Running | Parallel_Process.frm | btnTest_Click.AnonymousMethod_0() | 4792 (Worker Thread) | 1 (Parallel Process.vshost.exe) |
| ▽ | 4 | ▶ Running | Parallel_Process.frm | btnTest_Click.AnonymousMethod_0() | 5596 (Worker Thread) | 1 (Parallel Process.vshost.exe) |
| ▽ | 5 | ▶ Running | | Action<object>() | 4880 (Worker Thread) | 1 (Parallel Process.vshost.exe) |

**FIGURE 17-3:** Visual Studio makes it possible to see which tasks are running within your application.

It's important to note that the window in Figure 17-3 shows the parallel tasks, not all the threads running on the system. If you want to see all the threads, then choose Debug ➪ Windows ➪ Threads or press Ctrl+Alt+H instead. Figure 17-4 shows how the Threads window appears in comparison. Notice that the application uses a number of threads, but not all of them are running in parallel.

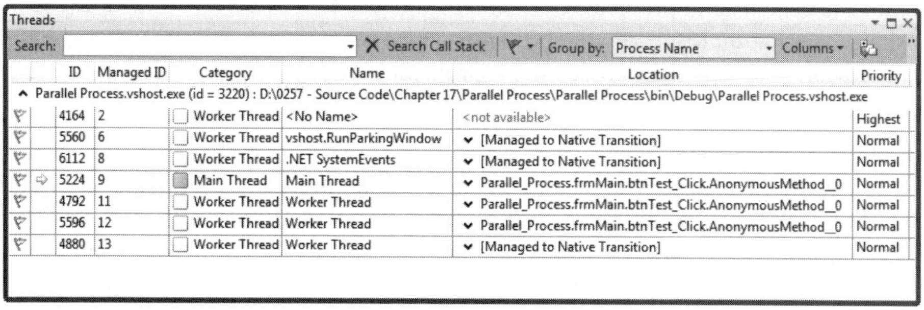

![Threads window screenshot showing columns for ID, Managed ID, Category, Name, Location, and Priority with several worker threads listed]

**FIGURE 17-4:** Parallel tasks differ from the threads your application uses.

It's also possible to get a pictorial view of the parallel processing using the Parallel Stacks window. Choose Debug ➪ Windows ➪ Parallel Stacks or press Ctrl+Shift+D,S to display the Parallel Stacks window shown in Figure 17-5. This pictorial view gives you a better understanding of precisely how your application is working. Hover your mouse over the entries to see the thread numbers and to obtain more information about them.

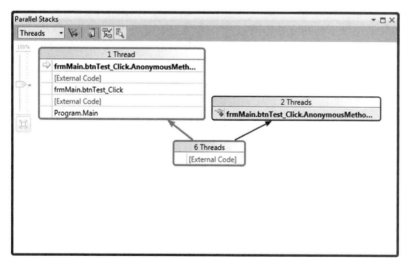

**FIGURE 17-5:** The pictorial view presented by the Parallel Stacks window tells you a lot about your application.

## MOVING YOUR APPLICATIONS TO WINDOWS 7

This chapter has provided a quick overview of parallel-programming techniques you can use in Windows 7 to make your applications run faster. The applications don't simply appear to run faster through threading techniques; they actually are faster because you use multiple processors to perform the work. Each processor works independently and simultaneously. Even though the definitions for multi-threading and multi-processing are well understood, some developers still get confused about the benefits and problems of each technology. If you take one thing away from this chapter, it should be that multi-processing produces a true increase in application speed by using multiple processors, but that such processing is problematic due to the nature of imperative languages (which require worrying about state).

Before you begin making plans to use parallel-programming techniques for your next application upgrade or new application, you need to have a plan. Parallel programming can be time-consuming to implement, hard to debug, and not very noticeable when implemented poorly. You need to consider what you'll get out of the parallel programming first. Think about how your application works and whether it even lends itself to parallel programming techniques. Once you have goals in place, define how to achieve those goals. It may be that using the `Parallel` class won't achieve your goals, and you'll actually need to use a functional language like IronPython or F#.

Chapters 14 through 17 discussed conventional programming enhancements available in Windows 7. They're conventional because these enhancements are also available in some form on other platforms, including other Windows platforms. Chapter 18 takes a further step — one that isn't necessarily available on other platforms without special libraries or third-party products. In Chapter 18 you'll discover how to use sensors to automate certain activities on a system. Of the various sensors, the most interesting and universally applicable is the light sensor. Imagine your monitor automatically changing its brightness and contrast to accommodate lighting conditions. A properly implemented interface promises to greatly reduce eyestrain and make users significantly more productive as well. Interestingly, users are likely to ignore this particular innovation, which is actually a compliment of sorts. When a user stops noticing your application and pays closer attention to work, you've achieved a significant goal.

# 18
# Using the Sensor and Location Platform

**WHAT'S IN THIS CHAPTER?**

➤ Understanding the sensor types and location devices

➤ Getting a list of installed sensors

➤ Getting specific sensor information

➤ Working with other sensor and location devices

For many years now, specialty hardware designers have created special drivers and other software to make their hardware accessible from Windows. It's possible to obtain special scientific sensors for Windows that rely on the RS422 and other standard interfaces. These sensors help scientists of all sorts to gather information and analyze it. Sensors also play a role in industrial automation. However, the fact that sensors are now in many homes is probably what prompted Microsoft to begin adding sensor support to Windows 7. Homes now have Windows-based security systems. You can obtain products to monitor the weather outside your home or to check on your children as they play. At some point, you'll probably be able to turn on your stove and tell it to cook dinner before your arrival home. The refrigerator will eventually tell you that you're out of milk. All these applications rely on sensors of various sorts, and they all require specialized device drivers and software.

> *This chapter assumes that you've installed the Windows API Code Pack. You can find the instructions for installing the Code Pack in the "Obtaining the Windows API Code Pack for Microsoft .NET Framework" section of Chapter 4. The Code Pack contains everything you need to work various types of sensors (as described in the "An Overview of the Sensor Categories" section of this chapter). This chapter relies on a Windows Forms application approach because many developers will be performing updates, rather than creating entirely new applications with the Windows Presentation Foundation (WPF).*

It would be quite easy to write an entire book about the sensors that you can use with Windows and still not cover them all. In fact, it would be possible to write a rather larger book just about the various sorts of industrial sensors. Home security would require an entirely separate book because the number and variety of sensors have increased so greatly. For example, many people don't realize it, but there's a special sort of sensor that can detect the sound of breaking glass and report it to you. If someone threw a rock through your window, you'd know about it long before you arrived home. Consequently, this chapter gives you just a taste of the sorts of things you can do in Windows 7 with various kinds of sensors.

Although theoretically there's no limit to the number of device types that Windows 7 can support, you can currently place the devices in three major groups: environmental, position, and light. The following sections provide an overview of these three major areas and demonstrate how you'd write code to work with external sensors. (If you have a specially equipped PC, you might find that some of these sensors are installed internally — the physical location doesn't matter for the purpose of writing the code.) Of course, you must have the device in order to test the code.

> *In order to code for a specific device, you actually need to have the device attached to your system or network. Because devices differ in their interfaces, functionality, user interface, and other specifics, code written for one device won't necessarily work for any other device. For example, writing code for one scanner won't necessarily help you create code for a different scanner. The non-standard features of devices have been the bane of developers since someone decided to attach a printer to a computer. Manufacturers sell products based on differences, and consumers purchase products because they deem a particular set of features important. As a consequence, developers generally need to test code with each supported device to ensure it actually works. Because of these differences, the code in this chapter will likely require tuning to work with the specific device attached to your system — don't assume any of the code will work without modification.*

## DEFINING THE SENSOR AND LOCATION DEVICES

Sensors and location devices are two separate kinds of input for a computer system. Sensors provide environmental information of some sort, while location devices tell you where you are. Combining these two elements is often the stuff of robotics, but this chapter won't even broach that topic. The following sections describe the kinds of devices that Windows 7 can interact with and tell you a bit about them.

## An Overview of the Sensor Categories

Sensors provide special functionality to computer systems. The term specifically applies to a device that mimics our own senses in some way. For example, sensors can detect light or sound. A special sensor may provide some type of tactile feedback. Of course, sensors can go well beyond human senses. A light detector can see into the infrared or ultraviolet ranges, neither of which is detectable by human eyes. So sensors can also augment human senses to let us detect things that are normally undetectable. No matter what the sensor does, however, it must convert what it detects into an electrical signal that the computer can interpret. The software you create assigns value to the electrical impulses and presents the resulting information in a form that the human viewer can understand.

Location devices are completely different from sensors. The vast majority of location devices today work on the Global Positioning System (GPS), which is an array of satellites that provides positional information in the form of radio waves. In sum, the location device is a special sort of radio receiver in most cases. When working with a GPS device, Windows receives actual satellite data, not electrical impulses. Your software accepts this data and formats it in a way that the human viewer can understand.

Another category of location device performs some sort of measurement and presents that measurement in the form of data or electrical impulses, depending on the characteristics of the device. For example, a location device could use a laser to measure the distance from the device to a wall. The output could be in the form of data (so many feet) or electrical impulse (a voltage level that falls within a minimum to a maximum value). The difference between the two categories of location devices is absolute versus relative position. A GPS device provides an absolute position, while the second location device category provides relative position.

The `SensorCategories` class provides a listing of sensor categories you can interact with. Table 18-1 provides a listing of these categories and describes them. The examples in this chapter will use a number of the categories.

**TABLE 18-1:** Categories of Sensors Supported by Windows 7

| CATEGORY | GROUP | DESCRIPTION |
| --- | --- | --- |
| All | N/A | Accesses all the sensors, no matter what category each sensor is in. This is the category you use to perform tasks such as obtaining an inventory of the system. |
| BioMetric | Environmental | All biometric devices, such as fingerprint or retina readers. The biometric device need not be security-related. For example, biometric devices can interpret a person's condition and locate potential health issues. |
| Electrical | Environmental | Any electrical device that doesn't fit in some other category. This category would include devices actually used to measure electricity. |
| Environmental | Environmental | Any device used to measure environmental conditions, such as temperature and humidity. Some unusual devices might fit into this category, such as a device used to measure static electricity based on environmental conditions. |
| Light | Light | Any device used to measure light. The device could simply measure the amount of light, but there could also be devices used for detecting certain kinds of light. |
| Location | Position | Any GPS device used to measure an absolute position based on satellite information. Theoretically, this category could also include input from LOng RAnge Navigation (LORAN) devices (see `http://www.navcen.uscg.gov/?pageName=loranMain`), but such devices are outdated and GPS is probably the only input device you'll see in use. |
| Mechanical | Environmental | Either an output or an input device used to measure something mechanically. For example, a device of this type could measure how far a door is opened or the amount of force applied to a test frame. |
| Motion | Position | Any device used to measure direction and velocity. These devices normally employ accelerometers, but could also rely on other means of detecting motion. See `http://www.dimensionengineering.com/accelerometers.htm` for a description of how accelerometers work. |

| CATEGORY | GROUP | DESCRIPTION |
| --- | --- | --- |
| Orientation | Position | Any device used to measure angular rotation about a center of mass. The measurements are normally made in terms of roll, pitch, and yaw. Even though these terms are normally applied to ships and airplanes, they can apply to anything. See http://en.wikipedia.org/wiki/Flight_dynamics for a description of roll, pitch, and yaw. |
| Scanner | Light | Any device that captures an image of some type. These devices naturally include scanners, but cameras could also appear in this category, as could telescopes configured to connect to a computer. Generally, this category includes any device that contains a Charge-Coupled Device (CCD) or its equivalent. |

The sensors are also categorized by how they're accessed. The SensorConnectionType enumeration tells you how the sensor is connected to the system. You'll see one of the following options:

- **Invalid:** Essentially, the system doesn't know how the device is connected. There might be something wrong with the device configuration. More likely, the device has been turned off so the system can't see how it's connected.

- **Integrated:** The device is built into the computer. Normally, this means that the device is part of the motherboard or is a peripheral directly attached to the motherboard.

- **Attached:** The device is attached to the computer indirectly. In most cases, the device attaches through a peripheral device or through an external port. The device may be connected through the USB port.

- **External:** The device uses an external connection. In many cases, this means that the device is attached through a network connection. The device may be on an external system and shared. The device could also be network-capable and have its own network connection.

*It's one thing to understand the mechanics of sensors, but quite another to see them in action. One of the more interesting uses of sensors in Windows 7 is adjusting monitors to match ambient light conditions. This feature is especially useful for laptops and other mobile devices. The article at* http://www.windows7news.com/2008/10/29/windows-7-sensors-explained/ *shows the effect of using ambient light sensors to adjust the monitor output.*

## Software Devices

You might not think that software can provide sensor capabilities, but it can. Windows 7 can work with software that performs analysis and creates sensor-like output. For example, you need not rely on a physical GPS to determine your position. It's possible to obtain a reasonably precise location using Wireless Fidelity (WiFi) connections (IEEE 802.11b wireless networking). For that matter, if you're willing to entertain a little less precision, you can use your IP connection as a means of determining location.

The example in the "Obtaining a List of Sensors" section of this chapter checks your system for any sort of sensor that Windows 7 detects. You might think that your system contains a wealth of sensors, but Windows 7 has shown itself extremely picky about what it considers a sensor. Only device drivers written as sensors actually appear as sensors when you check them. Consequently, your system filled with sensors might actually report that it has no sensors at all, as shown in Figure 18-1, when you run the example application.

**FIGURE 18-1:** Many people are surprised to find that their system doesn't have any detectable sensors.

Fortunately, you can add a usable sensor for experimentation and testing purposes that works just fine even on a desktop system. The Geosense for Windows driver is a free download from http://www.geosenseforwindows.com/. Download either the 32-bit or 64-bit driver as required for your machine. Follow these steps to install the software sensor on your system:

1. Double-click the `Geosense_1.2_x86.MSI` or `Geosense_1.2_x64.MSI` file. You'll see a rather humorous licensing agreement and its equally silly condition.

2. Check I Authorize You to Slap Me if I Violate the Terms Above and click Install. After a few seconds, you'll see the usual UAC warning.

3. Click Yes. The installation will proceed, and you'll eventually see a success message.

4. Click Finish. At this point, you can run the example in the "Obtaining a List of Sensors" section of this chapter and see the sensor, but the sensor won't do anything because it isn't enabled. If your only goal is to determine how Windows installs sensors, you can stop now. However, if you want to see how sensors work, you'll need to proceed to Step 5.

5. Open the Location and Other Sensors applet in the Control Panel. You'll see a list of sensors installed on your system, as shown in Figure 18-2 (the Geosense for Windows sensor might be the only entry on the list).

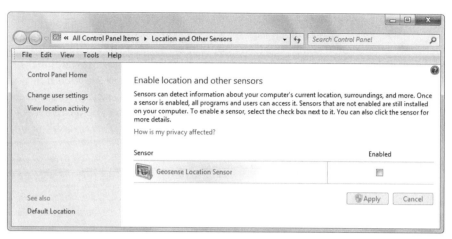

**FIGURE 18-2:** The Geosense for Windows sensor is disabled by default.

6. Check Enabled and click Apply. The Geosense for Windows sensor is now enabled.

## OBTAINING A LIST OF SENSORS

Before you can do anything with the sensors on a system, you need to know which sensors are installed. Fortunately, the `SensorManager` class makes getting the list relatively easy. The Get Sensors example described in the following sections shows how to use this class to query the sensors on a system.

> *The physical presence of a sensor on your system doesn't mean that Windows will recognize it. As with any piece of hardware, your sensor must come with an accompanying driver. Unfortunately, many vendors haven't released a version of their driver that works with the Windows 7 sensor functionality. For example, the Dell D series Latitude comes with a light sensor, but there isn't a Windows 7 driver for it, and therefore Windows 7 doesn't recognize the light sensor.*

### Configuring the Get Sensors Example

This example begins with a Windows Forms application. You'll need to add a List button (`btnList`) to obtain a list of the sensors, and a list box (`lstOutput`) to output the results of the query. In addition, you'll need to add references to `Microsoft.WindowsAPICodePack.DLL`, `Microsoft.WindowsAPICodePack.Shell.DLL`, and `Microsoft.WindowsAPICodePack.Sensors.DLL`. You must also provide the following `using` statements:

```
using Microsoft.WindowsAPICodePack.Sensors;
using Microsoft.WindowsAPICodePack.Shell.PropertySystem;
```

## Writing the Get Sensors Code

You can obtain a considerable amount of information about the sensors on your system. However, because the sensors vary quite a bit, writing generic code can be difficult. There are a number of hurdles to overcome, and sometimes you need to use generic types, such as Object, that don't provide the best information while writing the code. Of course, there are times when you'll need to take the generic approach because you need to inventory the devices that a system can access. Listing 18-1 shows one approach to handling this situation.

**LISTING 18-1:** Displaying a list of installed sensors

```
private void btnList_Click(object sender, EventArgs e)
{
    // Define a variable to hold the sensor list.
    SensorList<Sensor> AllSensors;

    // The system will raise an error if there aren't
    // any sensors to query.
    try
    {
        // Obtain a list of all the sensors.
        AllSensors = SensorManager.GetAllSensors();
    }
    catch (SensorPlatformException SensorErr)
    {
        MessageBox.Show(SensorErr.Message,
            "Error Obtaining Sensors",
            MessageBoxButtons.OK,
            MessageBoxIcon.Error);
        return;
    }

    // Clear the previous entries.
    lstOutput.Items.Clear();

    // Display the total number of sensors.
    lstOutput.Items.Add("Number of Sensors: " + AllSensors.Count);

    // Display the sensor information.
    foreach (Sensor ThisSensor in AllSensors)
    {
        // Output common elements.
        lstOutput.Items.Add("Name: " + ThisSensor.FriendlyName);
        lstOutput.Items.Add("Category ID: " + ThisSensor.CategoryId);
        lstOutput.Items.Add("Type ID: " + ThisSensor.TypeId);
        lstOutput.Items.Add("Description: " + ThisSensor.Description);
        lstOutput.Items.Add("Device Path: " + ThisSensor.DevicePath);
        lstOutput.Items.Add("Manufacturer: "
            + ThisSensor.Manufacturer);
        lstOutput.Items.Add("Model: " + ThisSensor.Model);
```

```csharp
        lstOutput.Items.Add("Serial Number: "
            + ThisSensor.SerialNumber);
        lstOutput.Items.Add("Sensor State: " + ThisSensor.State);

        // Check the connection type.
        try
        {
            // The device may not have a physical connection, so
            // you must place this code in a try block.
            lstOutput.Items.Add("Connection Type: "
                + ThisSensor.ConnectionType);
        }
        catch
        {
            // The most common device lacking a connection is a software
            // device driver.
            lstOutput.Items.Add("Connection Type: Software Device");
        }

        // Determine whether the sensor provides a data report.
        if (ThisSensor.AutoUpdateDataReport)
        {
            // Output the common data.
            lstOutput.Items.Add("Automatic Data Update");
            lstOutput.Items.Add("\tMinimum Report Interval: " +
                ThisSensor.MinimumReportInterval);
            lstOutput.Items.Add("\tCurrent Report Interval: " +
                ThisSensor.ReportInterval);

            // Try updating the data.
            ThisSensor.TryUpdateData();

            // Process the data report if there is data available.
            try
            {
                lstOutput.Items.Add("\tData Report Source: " +
                    ThisSensor.DataReport.Source);
                lstOutput.Items.Add("\tData Report Timestamp: " +
                    ThisSensor.DataReport.TimeStamp);
                lstOutput.Items.Add("\tNumber of Report Values: " +
                    ThisSensor.DataReport.Values.Count);

                // Enumerate the values.
                foreach (Guid Key in ThisSensor.DataReport.Values.Keys)
                {
                    // Display the key.
                    lstOutput.Items.Add("\t\t" + Key);

                    // Obtain the values for the key.
                    IList<Object> ValueEntries;

                    if (ThisSensor.DataReport.Values.TryGetValue(
                        Key, out ValueEntries))
```

*continues*

**LISTING 18-1** *(continued)*

```
                // Display the values associated with the key.
                foreach (Object ValueEntry in ValueEntries)
                    lstOutput.Items.Add("\t\t\t" + ValueEntry);
            }
        }
        catch
        {
            lstOutput.Items.Add("\tNo Data Available");
        }
    }
    else
        lstOutput.Items.Add("No Automatic Data Update");

    // Get the sensor properties.
    IList<PropertyKey> SuppList = ThisSensor.GetSupportedProperties();

    // Display the sensor properties.
    lstOutput.Items.Add("Properties:");
    foreach (PropertyKey PropKey in SuppList)
    {
        try
        {
            // This call will error out on software devices in
            // most cases.
            object Property = ThisSensor.GetProperty(PropKey);

            // The actual output property type depends on the device.
            // You'll need to add special handling for each device type
            // you expect to see.
            lstOutput.Items.Add("\tKnown Property: " +
                "Property ID: " + PropKey.PropertyId +
                " Format ID: " + PropKey.FormatId);
        }
        catch
        {
            // Display the unknown property type information.
            lstOutput.Items.Add("\tUnknown Property: " +
                "Property ID: " + PropKey.PropertyId +
                " Format ID: " + PropKey.FormatId);
        }
    }

    // Add a space between items.
    lstOutput.Items.Add("");
    }
}
```

The application begins by retrieving a list of sensors on the system. You have to place the check within a `try...catch` block because the code will create a `SensorPlatformException` exception if there aren't any sensors installed on the system. The `SensorManager.GetAllSensors()` method retrieves generic information about all the sensors on the system. If you want more specific information, you'll need to obtain a list of particular sensors as described in the "Obtaining Specific Sensor Information" section of this chapter. On successful return from the `GetAllSensors()` method call, `AllSensors` will contain a list of sensors installed on the system. There are a number of failure modes that will return an error message similar to the one shown in Figure 18-1 at this point.

The code begins displaying information by telling you how many sensors the system found using `AllSensors.Count`. This value will always be greater than 0 when the `GetAllSensors()` method call succeeds. The number of sensors found on your system depends in part on the number of Windows 7 device drivers you've installed that provide sensor information. The `AllSensors.Count` value is unlikely to reflect the actual number of sensors installed on your system, since many hardware vendors haven't updated their drivers to provide this information.

At this point, the code uses a `foreach` loop to begin processing each generic `Sensor` object in `AllSensors`. Even though this is a generic object, you can still obtain considerable information from it. The code begins by listing a number of elements common to all sensors, such as the sensor name, description, manufacturer, model, serial number, and so on. The `State` property tells you the status of the sensor. When a sensor is disabled, as shown in Figure 18-3, you're limited as to how much information the system will actually provide. In this case, the sensor simply outputs `AccessDenied` as its status to show that it has been disabled.

**FIGURE 18-3:** The example displays a list of sensors installed on the system.

It's also possible to detect the connection type. This is one of the first tricky pieces of data you can obtain, because a sensor may not have a connection. The most common reason for a lack of a connection is that the sensor is software-based like the Geosense for Windows sensor. Trying to access the `ConnectionType` property for a sensor that doesn't have a connection will raise an exception that you must catch. In this case, the code doesn't perform a lot of analysis; it simply assumes that the sensor is software-based.

The `AutoUpdateDataReport` property tells you whether the sensor will automatically update its data for you. When working with a generic sensor, you don't have many options for interacting with the sensor. If the `AutoUpdateDataReport` is `false`, the best you can do is say that there isn't any data to process.

When the `AutoUpdateDataReport` property is `true`, you can obtain some general information about how the sensor collects data, such as the minimum allowable report interval and the current report interval. Some sensors have to have a minimum report interval to avoid data overruns, which result in lost data.

Because this is a generic query of the sensor and not a specific interaction with it, you'll probably want to see sample data, but you won't need specific data for processing. The code calls `ThisSensor.TryUpdateData()` to attempt to get a data update from the sensor. This call automatically overwrites any existing data that the sensor might possess, so you want to use this call carefully when you're actually processing data.

If the sensor has data to process, the code can retrieve the data source, the time that the data was collected, and the number of values that the sensor can provide. A call to any of these properties when there's no data present will cause an exception that you must catch. In this case, the exception simply indicates that there's no data to process.

The `DataReport` property includes three sub-properties of interest. The `Source` property contains the source of the report information. The `TimeStamp` property tells you when the data was collected. The `Values` property is actually a collection of key/value pairs. The `Key` member is a `Guid` object that uniquely identifies a particular set of values. The `Values` member is an `IList<Object>` collection of values associated with the `Key`. For example, the Geospace for Windows sensor has a `Key` of `{055c74d8-ca6f-47d6-95c6-1ed3637a0ff4}` that represents the location information as shown in Figure 18-4. The associated `Values` member contains a list of entries that define the location, including longitude, latitude, city, state, and even ZIP code. However, you can't access the Values member directly — doing so raises an exception. Instead, the code uses the `TryGetValue()` method with the `Key` as the first argument and a buffer, `ValueEntries`, as the second argument. Notice that you must use the `out` keyword. The return from `TryGetValue()` is a `Boolean` that indicates success or failure. After the code obtains the values, it uses a `foreach` loop to display them.

**FIGURE 18-4:** Enabling the Geosense for Windows sensor returns good results even for an IP address.

In addition to the other information you can obtain about sensors, each sensor has a list of properties that it supports. The properties you obtain depend on the sensor, and with a software sensor the properties are going to be an unknown type for the most part unless you can get a matching list of Globally Unique IDentifiers (GUIDs) from the vendor.

The example shows how to obtain a list of properties using the `GetSupportedProperties()` method. The output of this method is an `IList<PropertyKey>` object, `SuppList`. The code relies on a `foreach` loop to process `SuppList`. Each entry is a `PropertyKey` object, `PropKey`. The code next tries to determine the kind of property by calling `GetProperty()` with `PropKey` as the argument.

If there's a method to turn the `PropKey` into a property value, the call succeeds. Otherwise, the code throws an exception, and you must process it as an unknown property, as shown in the example. Theoretically, even if the system can't find the `PropKey`, you should be able to provide custom processing of the property information using the vendor's documentation.

*Each kind of sensor has different property identifiers. You can see the list of these sensors at* http://msdn.microsoft.com/library/dd318969.aspx. *For example, when working with the Geosense for Windows sensor, you use the property identifiers found at* http://msdn.microsoft.com/library/dd318981.aspx *to discover the meaning of each property. Many of the GUIDs you see in the listings and output in this chapter appear in the* Sensors.H *file provided with the Windows 7 SDK in the* \Program Files\Microsoft SDKs\Windows\v7.1\Include *folder. Reviewing this header file can solve a number of the problems you'll encounter trying to decipher some types of sensor data.*

## OBTAINING SPECIFIC SENSOR INFORMATION

An application may begin by performing an inventory of a system looking for particular sensors. However, in order to perform useful work, the application will eventually need to look for a specific sensor. For example, if you want to obtain location information, you'll need to locate a `Location` sensor. The following sections move on to the next step by using the Geosense for Windows sensor, working directly with the sensor to obtain location information.

### Understanding the Geosense for Windows Data

If you're going to work with a specific sensor, it's a good idea to know what type of information you'll receive. This means knowing the values that you'll obtain from the `DataReport.Values` property. The Geosense for Windows sensor outputs two keys. The first contains a timestamp, as shown in Figure 18-4. The second contains a list of 10 values, as shown in Table 18-2.

**TABLE 18-2:** Geosense for Windows Sensor Data

| ELEMENT | DATA TYPE | DESCRIPTION |
| --- | --- | --- |
| 0 | Double | Latitude |
| 1 | Double | Longitude |
| 2 | Double | Altitude |
| 3 | Double | Accuracy (a value of 0 means that the accuracy level is unknown) |
| 4 | String | Street Number |

*continues*

**TABLE 18-2** *(continued)*

| ELEMENT | DATA TYPE | DESCRIPTION |
|---|---|---|
| 5 | String | Street |
| 6 | String | City |
| 7 | String | Region |
| 8 | String | State |
| 9 | String | Postal Code |

## Configuring the Get Location Example

This example begins with a Windows Forms application. You'll need to add a series of textboxes to hold the data results, as shown in Figure 18-5, and a Get button (btnGet) to output the results of the query. Name the textboxes: txtLatitude, txtLongitude, txtAltitude, txtAccuracy, txtStreetNumber, txtStreet, txtCity, txtRegion, txtState, and txtZIP.

**FIGURE 18-5:** Provide some textboxes to hold the output data, as shown here.

In addition, you'll need to add references to Microsoft.WindowsAPICodePack.DLL, Microsoft.WindowsAPICodePack.Shell.DLL, and Microsoft.WindowsAPICodePack.Sensors.DLL. You must also provide the following using statements:

```
using Microsoft.WindowsAPICodePack.Sensors;
using Microsoft.WindowsAPICodePack.Shell.PropertySystem;
```

## Initializing the Sensor

Before you can use the sensor, you need to create an object to access it. The code in Listing 18-2 creates a global object used to access the Geosense for Windows sensor. It also performs some initialization tasks for working with the sensor.

**LISTING 18-2:** Configure the sensor for use

```
// Storage for the location sensors.
SensorList<Sensor> LocationSensors;

// Storage for the Geosense for Windows sensor.
Sensor Geosense;

public frmMain()
{
    // Perform the standard initialization.
    InitializeComponent();

    // Obtain a list of location sensors.
    LocationSensors =
        SensorManager.GetSensorsByCategoryId(SensorCategories.Location);

    // Access the Geosense sensor.
    if (LocationSensors.Count == 1 &&
        LocationSensors[0].FriendlyName == "Geosense Sensor")
        Geosense = LocationSensors[0];
    else
        foreach (Sensor ThisSensor in LocationSensors)
            if (ThisSensor.FriendlyName == "Geosense Sensor")
                Geosense = ThisSensor;

    // Verify that we found the sensor.
    if (Geosense == null)
    {
        MessageBox.Show("Geosense for Windows sensor not installed!" +
            "\nClosing Application");
        Environment.Exit(1);
    }

    // Set an event handler for state changes.
    Geosense.StateChanged +=
        new StateChangedEventHandler(Geosense_StateChanged);

    // Set an event handler for data updates.
    Geosense.DataReportChanged +=
        new DataReportChangedEventHandler(Geosense_DataReportChanged);
}
```

The `SensorList<Sensor>` object, `LocationSensors`, contains a list of specific sensors. In this case, it contains those sensors used to obtain location data. The `Sensor` object, `Geosense`, contains the reference to the Geosense for Windows sensor.

The form's constructor begins with the usual call to `InitializeComponent()`. It then obtains a collection of location sensors by calling `SensorManager.GetSensorsByCategoryId()` with an argument of `SensorCategories.Location`. Notice how this call differs from the `SensorManager.GetAllSensors()` method call shown in Listing 8-1. The output is specific, and only the location sensors will appear in the output collection, `LocationSensors`.

The presence of a location sensor doesn't mean that you've found the Geosense for Windows sensor. The code performs two different checks for the sensor using an `if...else` structure. In the first case, there's only one sensor available, so the code checks its `FriendlyName` property value, which must be `"Geosense Sensor"`. In the second case, the code uses a `foreach` statement to check all the sensors returned for a sensor that has a `FriendlyName` property value of `"Geosense Sensor"`. In both cases, the result is to set `Geosense` to a reference of the sensor.

The code verifies that the Geosense for Windows sensor is present by checking `Geosense` for a `null` value. If the value is `null`, the code outputs an error message and exits using the `Environment.Exit()` method. This approach allows the example to return an error code of 1 in this case.

When the sensor does exist, the code creates event handlers for the two events that the sensor supports: `StateChanged` and `DataReportChanged`. Remember that you can use the IDE to help you create the event handlers. Press Tab after typing += to create the remainder of the event handler statement. Press Tab a second time to create the event handler methods. This process is quick and easy.

## Creating and Handling Sensor Events

After you create a reference to the Geosense for Windows sensor, you can begin interacting with it. The first step is to check the sensor and then initiate a request, as shown in Listing 18-3.

**LISTING 18-3:** Perform sensor updates as needed to check the position

```
private void btnGet_Click(object sender, EventArgs e)
{
    // Verify that the Geosense sensor is on.
    if (Geosense.State != SensorState.Ready)
    {
        MessageBox.Show("Please enable the Geosense sensor.");
        return;
    }

    // Perform an update.
    Geosense.UpdateData();
}
```

The code begins by checking the `Geosense.State` property. If this property doesn't have a value of `SensorState.Ready`, the code displays an error message and exits without initiating a request. Otherwise, it initiates a request by calling `Geosense.UpdateData()`.

As previously mentioned, the Geosense for Windows sensor supports two events. Listing 18-4 shows the handlers for these events.

**LISTING 18-4: Use events to respond to sensor changes**

```
void Geosense_DataReportChanged(Sensor sender, EventArgs e)
{
    // Create a location Guid.
    Guid Location = new Guid("{055c74d8-ca6f-47d6-95c6-1ed3637a0ff4}");

    try
    {
        // Update the timestamp.
        txtTime.Text = Geosense.DataReport.TimeStamp.ToString();

        // Update the location.
        txtLatitude.Text =
            Geosense.DataReport.Values[Location][0].ToString();
        txtLongitude.Text =
            Geosense.DataReport.Values[Location][1].ToString();
        txtAltitude.Text =
            Geosense.DataReport.Values[Location][2].ToString();
        txtAccuracy.Text =
            Geosense.DataReport.Values[Location][3].ToString();
        txtStreetNumber.Text =
            Geosense.DataReport.Values[Location][4].ToString();
        txtStreet.Text =
            Geosense.DataReport.Values[Location][5].ToString();
        txtCity.Text =
            Geosense.DataReport.Values[Location][6].ToString();
        txtRegion.Text =
            Geosense.DataReport.Values[Location][7].ToString();
        txtState.Text =
            Geosense.DataReport.Values[Location][8].ToString();
        txtZIP.Text =
            Geosense.DataReport.Values[Location][9].ToString();
    }
    catch
    {
    }
}

void Geosense_StateChanged(Sensor sender, EventArgs e)
{
    MessageBox.Show(
        "Geosense state changed to: " + Geosense.State.ToString());
}
```

The `Geosense_DataReportChanged()` event handler is the more important of the two event handlers for this example. In this case, the code begins by creating a `Guid` object, `Location`, which uses the GUID shown in Figure 18-4 to access the location data values shown in Figure 18-4.

The output code begins by displaying the time of the data report using the `TimeStamp` property. It then displays all the data values listed in Table 18-2 on-screen by accessing each of the `DataReport.Values[Location]` entries in turn. Figure 18-6 shows typical output from this example. Of course, your display will show the data for your location.

The `Geosense_StateChanged()` event handler responds to changes in the Geosense for Windows sensor state. You can use this event handler to ensure that the user doesn't turn off the sensor between calls. In this case, the event handler simply displays a message box with the new sensor status, as shown in Figure 18-7. The only two states available appear to be Ready and AccessDenied.

**FIGURE 18-6:** Typical output data from Geosense for Windows

**FIGURE 18-7:** The application tells you when the sensor status changes.

## Configuring Geosense for Windows Security

It's important to understand that not everyone on a system needs access to every sensor. You may, in fact, want to strictly limit access to some sensor types, depending on their function. For example, you'll notice that the Geosense for Windows sensor comes with a privacy warning as described at http://www.google.com/privacy-lsf.html. In addition, Windows provides the privacy information shown in Figure 18-8 (click the How Is My Privacy Affected? link in the Location and Other Sensors applet to see it).

Everyone can automatically access a sensor after you install it. In order to control access to the sensor, you must manually change its security settings or locate the appropriate entry in the registry. To accomplish this task, click the Geosense Location Sensor link in the Location and Other Sensors applet. You'll see the Sensor Properties window shown in Figure 18-9. This window provides access to all the sensor settings. In this case, you can change the sensor description, modify the security settings, or uninstall the sensor.

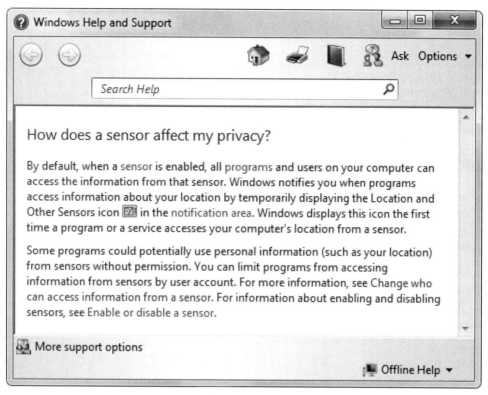

**FIGURE 18-8:** Sensors can incur privacy issues when you use them.

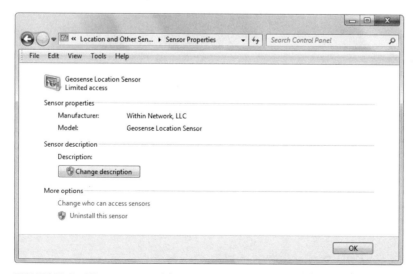

**FIGURE 18-9:** All sensors provide properties that you can modify.

*Locating the appropriate entry in the registry can be a bit tricky. Begin by polling every numbered subkey of the* `HKEY_LOCAL_MACHINE\SYSTEM\CurrentControlSet\Enum\Root\SENSOR` *key. Check the* `HardwareID` *value of each of these numbered subkeys for the name of the sensor you want to change (the Geosense for Windows sensor appears as a multi-string entry of* `Sensors\GeosenseSensor`*). You must then check the* `Device Parameters\SensorPermissions` *subkey. For example, if the Geosense for Windows sensor is the only sensor installed on your system, you can see the security settings in the* `HKEY_LOCAL_MACHINE\SYSTEM\CurrentControlSet\Enum\Root\SENSOR\0000\Device Parameters\SensorPermissions` *key. When everyone has access to the sensor, you'll see a DWORD value entry for the S-1-1-0 well-known Security IDentifier (SID) with a value of 1, which enables it (see the list of well-known SIDs at* http://support.microsoft.com/kb/243330*). When you clear the Everyone entry, this SID value entry will equal 0. Allowing services access to the sensor will add entries for the following SIDs: S-1-5-18, S-1-5-19, and S-1-5-20. Theoretically, you can provide finer-grained security control by modifying the registry entries for the particular sensor, but then you need to worry about potential side effects. The sensor may not work correctly if all services can't access it, but you'll find out only through experimentation.*

Click the Change Who Can Access Sensors link and you'll see the User Settings window shown in Figure 18-10. Make sure the correct sensor is selected (the Geosense Location Sensor in this case), then clear or check entries as needed to provide secure access to the sensor. The example shows that the Administrator, John, and three services accounts can access the Geosense for Windows sensor, but not the Guest account.

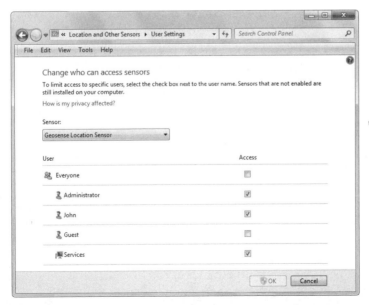

**FIGURE 18-10:** Configure the sensor to provide the level of security you feel is necessary.

An interesting thing will happen in the example application when you change access. You'll actually see two messages. First, you'll see a message box telling you that the sensor access is denied. Second, you'll see another message box telling you that the sensor is ready. When you change the sensor access, Windows appears to remove permissions first and then add them back in. The example application will also receive an update event, even though you haven't clicked Get. You can verify this update by starting the application and making the security changes without clicking Get first. The blanks will automatically fill with information after you clear the second message box telling you that the sensor is ready to use.

## Viewing Location Sensor Activity

Privacy is a concern when using sensors, including the Geosense for Windows sensor. You may be curious as to who is using the sensor on the system. Fortunately, there's a quick way to find out. Click the View Location Activity link in the Location and Other Sensors applet. Windows will display a message that it's adding a snap-in for a few moments, and then you'll see the Event Viewer applet displayed with the Location Activity entry highlighted, as shown in Figure 18-11.

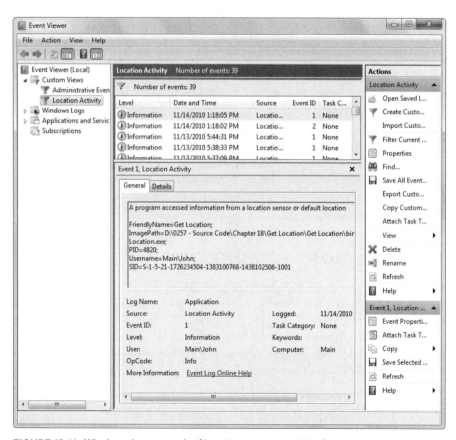

**FIGURE 18-11:** Windows keeps track of location sensor activity for you.

The event viewer logs tell you everything you need to know about the location sensor access, including the name of the application performing the access and the account name used to run the application. Of course, you get all the normal event log entries, such as the time the access occurred. In addition, you can even determine details such as the Program IDentifier (PID) and Thread IDentifier (TID), which is helpful in deciding how often the application accessed the sensor during a single session. The event log entry won't tell you precisely what kind of access was performed when working with sensors that have multiple functions, but at least you know about the sensor access.

## DEVELOPING FOR OTHER SENSOR AND LOCATION DEVICES

The example in this chapter shows how to work with one type of sensor — a location sensor. However, you can develop applications to work with any sort of sensor that Windows 7 supports, and there's a host of them. It would be nice if Microsoft provided a sensor emulator for developers, but such an emulator isn't available at the time of this writing. You may find some third-party products online that will prove useful. For example, Validity provides a biometric sensor demo at http://www.validityinc.com/post.aspx?id=186.

The Code Pack comes with two additional sample sensor applications in the \CodePack\Samples\Sensors folder. The first shows how to work with accelerometers and the second shows how to work with ambient light sensors. These two examples are a little more complex than the one in this chapter — they provide a good next step in learning how to work with sensors. Of course, you must have the required sensors installed on your system, with the requisite sensor-aware device drivers. Otherwise, you won't see anything happen when you run the example code.

As with all the other Code Pack examples, you need to convert the code for use with Visual Studio 2010. However, the code won't compile in this particular case without error. You'll see four errors appear on-screen that probably won't make much sense. Fix the first two errors by opening the Settings1.Designer.CS file in the AccelerationMeasurement project. Highlight all the functional code in that file and click Comment Out the Selected Lines. Perform the same task for the Settings1.Designer.CS file in the AmbientLightMeasurement project. The solution will now compile as expected.

## MOVING YOUR APPLICATIONS TO WINDOWS 7

This chapter has taken you a bit into the future. Windows 7 supports a host of external devices today, and you probably have at least a few of them, but the day of the talking refrigerator is still in the future for most people. The idea is an interesting one, though. If you take nothing else away from this chapter, it should be that Windows 7 is the first version of Windows to make it possible to attach a range of sensors and actually use them to develop practical applications. Just how you use this feature depends on your organization's needs.

The reality is that you might be tasked today with updating applications to use at least a few sensors. A monitor that automatically adjusts to the ambient light is probably going to be a specialty item today, but it will eventually hit the mainstream. Like anything else, monitoring sensors requires system resources. The more sensors your system monitors, the slower it will get. As part of your update planning, you need to consider where to obtain the resources used to monitor sensors, how often to monitor the sensors, and what to do with the data once you obtain it. Applications could become more efficient in some cases by partially relying on historical data instead of constantly monitoring sensors. It pays to plan the use of sensors carefully. For example, make sure you obtain spare sensors as future replacements, so that you don't need to write new code to accommodate replacements.

Chapter 19 moves in another direction, but it has something in common with this chapter — it also is working on the fringe of existing programming needs. In Chapter 19 you'll discover how to work with Windows XP Mode effectively. Windows XP Mode is a special virtual environment for applications that just don't work well with Windows 7, no matter how you configure them. Of course, Microsoft prefers that you update the application to work with Windows 7, but this isn't always practical. Organizations often have a huge investment in existing code and can't afford to simply throw that investment away. If you have a reliable application, but don't own the source code, you might find that you absolutely must rely on Windows XP Mode — at least for the short term.

# 19

# Using Windows XP Mode Effectively

**WHAT'S IN THIS CHAPTER?**

- ➤ Defining uses for Windows XP Mode
- ➤ Analyzing an application using Windows XP Mode
- ➤ Overcoming potential problems using Windows XP Mode

Windows 7 goes a long way toward making it possible to use older applications in a more secure environment. Of course, you still have access to the compatibility mode settings that Vista supported, along with a few others. However, Microsoft went a few steps further in Windows 7. You don't get complete backward compatibility, of course, but you can tone down the User Account Control (UAC) as a starting point. The combination of various tweaks does make it possible to run a few more applications in Windows 7 that simply wouldn't run in Vista. In fact, Windows 7 users generally feel that this version of the operating system is significantly better than Vista.

The problem still occurs that some applications won't run. The majority of this book has discussed upgrade techniques you can use to make your code more compatible with Windows 7. In addition, this book has discussed a wealth of new features you can add to your application during the upgrade process. The problem is that you might not have all the source code for your application — it could rely on third-party modules for which you don't have the source code. If those modules are essential, you can't replace them, and if the modules are the source of the compatibility trouble, you may have to simply accept using Windows XP Mode (a fully functional version of Windows XP operated as a virtual machine) to run your application. This chapter provides you with the techniques for doing so.

Even Windows XP Mode won't fix every compatibility problem. The reason is simple — you're running a virtual machine on top of Windows 7. Using a virtual machine isn't precisely the same as using the native operating system. Most applications can't tell the difference, but you may have the one application on the planet that can. This chapter also provides some troubleshooting techniques you can use to make Windows XP Mode work a little better. These techniques can help, but even so they can't fix absolutely every problem. In some cases, you'll have to simply retire the old application and all its modules, and start from scratch in order to obtain satisfactory results from Windows 7. This chapter has a few pointers in that regard as well.

## CONSIDERING WINDOWS XP MODE

Windows XP Mode is a virtual machine. It's software that runs on top of Windows 7 to make it appear that you have a system running Windows XP. Of course, you don't really have a system running Windows XP — the underlying operating system is still Windows 7. It's possible to fool yourself into believing that simply because the virtual machine looks and feels like Windows XP, it really is Windows XP. The reason it's so important to keep this in mind is that you may have to troubleshoot your installation later with Windows 7 issues in mind.

The best way to get your application running is to try to make it work with Windows 7. The previous chapters of this book all assume that you have the source code for your application and plan to update it. Of course, many applications rely on third-party modules. In some cases, these modules are libraries that integrate with your application. All you really have is a black-box version of the library where certain input produces a certain output for a given call. However, when working with libraries you can possibly create your own black box to replace the third-party library.

Some modules are actually stand-alone applications. You create the data the application requires to run and then execute that application from your own application. This scenario is actually more problematic than the third-party library because now you have an entire application's worth of black box and far less information on how it works. This second scenario is even more problematic when the stand-alone application does something special, such as interact with external hardware. On top of the usual software issues, you also have the hardware to consider. Hardware is notoriously difficult to work with when you don't have the documentation required to understand its interfaces.

No matter what situation you find yourself in, it's important to take time to consider the alternatives before you move directly to using Windows XP Mode. Sometimes using Windows XP Mode to fix the problem is akin to swatting a fly with a mallet. The fly may be dead, but so is whatever you hit with the mallet. The following sections provide some ideas on how you can fix the non-functional component of your application.

### Check for an Update

While it may seem silly to mention this particular option, you might be surprised at the number of people who don't actually consider it before they embark on the Windows XP Mode solution. It's important to realize that an update need not come from the vendor that originally created the library or stand-alone application. Sometimes motivated outsiders create solutions. In fact, these solutions often come from developers who are just as frustrated as you are with a perceived lack of solutions from the library or application vendor.

## Look for Third-Party Support

It's amazing to see the ingenuity of some people. A group will find that there's a problem with a particular piece of software and that the vendor has no desire to fix it. For that matter, the vendor might not even exist any longer. The world is packed with orphaned software that has third-party volunteers as its sole source of support. Often, someone will complain on a forum somewhere and someone else will answer that he or she has the problem, too. A third party will join in with some ideas that seem to work at least some of the time. Someone else will chime in with potential fixes for those ideas to make them work more often. By the time the message thread is a mile long, someone has found just the right set of software tweaks, configuration changes, and bits of additional code to make the application or library work.

Unfortunately, the solution isn't going to appear on the vendor site (assuming the vendor is still around). You'll need to search through messages trying to find this particular solution — the one that works. It's time-consuming, messy, and frustrating, but third-party solutions can prove viable as well. Of course, it's up to you to decide whether you want to spend the time looking for this sort of solution.

*Book authors and magazine writers often spend hours looking for solutions of this sort. They'll either provide a pointer to the message thread or rewrite it to make it more understandable. Of course, finding the right book or article can also be quite time-consuming and frustrating, but a careful search with Google can make things easier. The point is not to forget these formal sources of information when you need a solution for your application or library issue. Books and articles make good sources of information for potential fixes if you happen to look in the right place at the right time.*

## Use the Compatibility Troubleshooter

There's a perception by some developers that user aids aren't necessarily for them. However, user aids help everyone. Unfortunately, the Compatibility Troubleshooter only works with stand-alone applications and not third-party libraries for the most part. To try the Compatibility Troubleshooter, right-click the application in question and choose Troubleshoot Compatibility from the Context menu. You'll see the Program Compatibility dialog box appear. The Program Compatibility application will check your application and then present the dialog box shown in Figure 19-1.

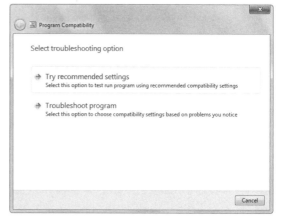

**FIGURE 19-1:** Select the troubleshooting option that you think will fix the problem.

## Using the Recommended Settings

Your first option is Try Recommended Settings. Based on the analysis the Compatibility Troubleshooter performed, it displays recommended settings for your application such as those shown in Figure 19-2. In this case, the recommended setting is to change the application to use the Windows XP (Service Pack 2) compatibility mode. Click Start the Program. If the application starts, you may have solved your problem.

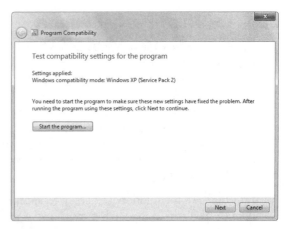

**FIGURE 19-2:** The Compatibility Troubleshooter will display recommended settings for you.

### COMPATIBILITY MODE OPTIONS

Windows 7 actually offers a considerable number of compatibility modes for your application. Each of these compatibility modes provides a slightly different environment for your application, so you need to try them all. Here are the options you have available:

- Windows 95
- Windows 98/Windows Me
- Windows NT 4.0 (Service Pack 5)
- Windows 2000
- Windows XP (Service Pack 2)
- Windows XP (Service Pack 3)
- Windows Server 2003 (Service Pack 1)
- Windows Server 2008 (Service Pack 1)
- Windows Vista
- Windows Vista (Service Pack 1)
- Windows Vista (Service Pack 2)

You'll want to test the application thoroughly to make sure it actually is working. Just because the application starts doesn't mean you have fixed anything. Make sure you test the functionality with which your application was encountering issues and use a variety of test data to look for potential problems (such as range issues). After you've worked with the application for a while, click Next. The wizard will display the options list shown in Figure 19-3.

If the recommended settings fixed the problem, click Yes and the wizard will apply the settings to the application. Otherwise, click one of the two No options. You can also try using the process in the "Troubleshooting the Application" section below.

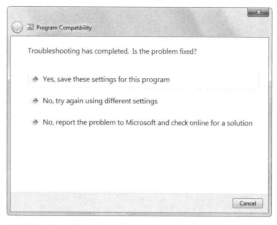

**FIGURE 19-3:** In many cases, the recommended settings fix the problem.

## Troubleshooting the Application

If the Try Recommended Settings option doesn't work for you, restart the Compatibility Troubleshooter and select the Troubleshoot Program option instead. You'll see a list of common application ailments, as shown in Figure 19-4.

Depending on the options you select, the wizard will ask a series of questions. These questions will fine-tune the settings and potentially create a compatibility environment that works for the application. Of course, the wizard may fail to find the right solution. In this case, you can always try working with the settings manually as described in the "Change the Application Compatibility Settings Directly" section below.

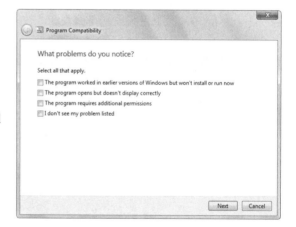

**FIGURE 19-4:** Choose one or more of the options shown in the list.

## Change the Application Compatibility Settings Directly

The Compatibility Troubleshooter wizard doesn't always select the best settings to make an application work with Windows 7. In some cases, an odd selection of settings can make a big difference. You may also need to work with the application. For example, some older applications work fine as long as you don't use their sound features. It may be a difficult choice whether to keep using the application without the feature or to get rid of the application entirely. To see the compatibility settings for an application, right-click the application and choose Properties from the Context menu. Select the Compatibility tab and you'll see the list of settings shown in Figure 19-5.

It may be tempting to try a number of settings at once, just to see what happens. The best course of action is to try the settings one at a time. Try each of the settings in turn before you use any combinations. The reason for this careful approach is that the settings all come with a cost in application speed, reliability, or security. A setting can affect application functionality or make it impossible to use certain features. You may even find that a setting prevents the application from working, which is the thing you're trying to overcome. In short, taking things slow and moving carefully are essential to making sure your application works with the fewest possible compatibility settings in place.

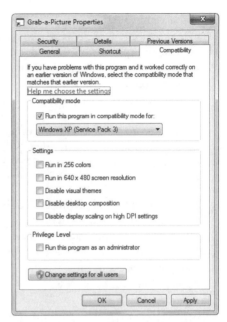

**FIGURE 19-5:** It's possible to adjust the compatibility settings directly so you can try different combinations.

## Use the Application Compatibility Toolkit

Most developers associate the Application Compatibility Toolkit (ACT) with upgrade planning. In fact, that's the major reason to use this particular tool, but it also comes in handy for finding potential problems with a supplementary application or a third-party library. In some cases, an environmental issue can keep the application or library from working as intended. Microsoft could even have a solution to the problem that you don't know about.

You begin working with the ACT by installing it on a test system. Most of the ACT downloads do deal with planning. All you really need to get is `ApplicationCompatibilityToolkitSetup.EXE` from http://www.microsoft.com/downloads/en/details.aspx?FamilyId=24DA89E9-B581-47B0-B45E-492DD6DA2971. Make absolutely certain that you use version 5.6 or above of the ACT.

After you install the application, choose Start ➪ All Programs ➪ Microsoft Application Compatibility Toolkit ➪ Application Compatibility Manager. The first time you start the tool, you'll need to perform some configuration tasks related to your particular system. If you experience problems connecting to the SQL Express copy of SQL Server on your system, make sure the SQL Server Browser service is running (otherwise, ACT can't find the server). You'll need to create an analysis package, install it, and collect data for the test system while someone uses it. The Application Compatibility Manager will help you sort through the data collected and come to some compatibility decisions for the environment as a whole that may result in a working application or library. Although this process is time-consuming (the standard collection process is three days), it can provide some useful suggestions on making the application or library work within the Windows 7 environment.

## Adjust User Account Control

The UAC is an extremely useful part of Windows 7. You don't want to remove it unless absolutely required to. Many of the threats today rely on the user's being uninformed about system events. The UAC keeps this from happening. However, you also want to be able to eliminate the UAC as a potential source of problems for your application, so turning it off long enough for testing can be helpful. To adjust the UAC, open the User Accounts applet of the Control Panel. You'll see the window shown in Figure 19-6.

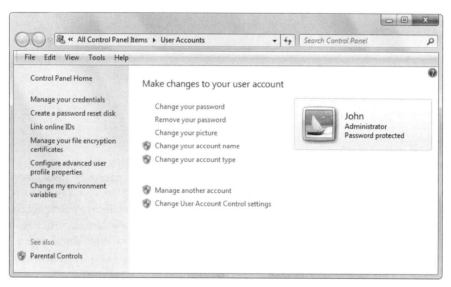

**FIGURE 19-6:** The User Accounts applet provides access to the UAC settings.

Click the Change User Account Control Settings link and you'll see the settings shown in Figure 19-7. Try moving the level down just one notch before you turn the UAC off completely. Test your application. If you really need to turn UAC off, try that setting and test your application again. The point is to keep trying various techniques to ensure you absolutely must run the application using Windows XP Mode.

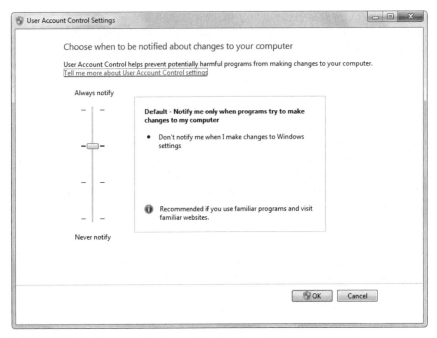

**FIGURE 19-7:** Test your application with various levels of UAC support.

In many cases, a UAC issue actually points to a permissions problem. Running the application or using the library in administrator mode can help (see the "Executing as a Separate Process" section of Chapter 11 for the technique on performing this task). However, the problem could be one of allowing access to a particular part of the system. Perhaps the application or library needs access to the \Windows\System32_ folder. Permissions problems can be difficult to locate, but they're not impossible to fix. Take time to look for resource or account issues as part of the troubleshooting process. The vendor documentation could even point out the need for permissions in a particular area, or you might find an application file in an unexpected location on a system where the application or library does work.

## TESTING YOUR APPLICATION IN WINDOWS XP MODE

At some point, you'll decide that no amount of tweaking will help the application or third-party library you need to use to make your application work. You also find there are no updates, special software remedies, or grass-roots support to make the application or library work. So you've come to the end of the line. You have two options now — replace the application or library with new code or try to make it work using Windows XP Mode. Of course, you'll need to use the entire application in Windows XP Mode, not just the supporting application or library. The following sections describe how to install and use Windows XP Mode.

## Obtaining and Installing Windows XP Mode

It's time to obtain and install Windows XP Mode. Before you do anything else, you need to download the Windows XP Mode installer from http://www.microsoft.com/windows/virtual-pc/download.aspx. After you select a platform and language, you'll see three buttons. As described on the download site, download the components in this order:

1. Windows XP Mode
2. Windows Virtual PC
3. Windows XP Mode Update

You can read about the Windows XP Mode update at http://support.microsoft.com/kb/977206. Windows Update will let you know about any other patches needed to make Windows XP Mode work properly.

Double-click in turn each of the files you've downloaded. The installation for Windows XP Mode isn't hard. There aren't even any options to select. All the Windows XP Mode installation file does is install a virtual hard-disk file for Windows XP Mode.

The Windows Virtual PC installation comes next. The first part of this installation checks for updates. You may not even realize some of these updates are available because they affect Windows Virtual PC and not your Windows installation as a whole. At a minimum, you'll be asked about installing the KB958559 update (http://support.microsoft.com/kb/958559), which is actually the Windows Virtual PC. Click Yes. You'll see the usual licensing terms dialog box, which you'll need to accept before the installation can proceed. The installation process can take a while. You'll see a progress dialog box like the one in Figure 19-8 during this time.

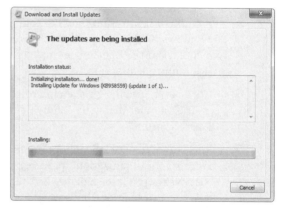

**FIGURE 19-8:** The Windows Virtual PC installation will display a progress dialog box.

Before you can install the patch, you must restart your PC. Click Restart on the Installation Complete dialog box that appears when the Windows Virtual PC installation is complete. During the restart process you'll see several configuration messages. Just be patient and wait for the installation to complete. Once your system restarts, you can install the Windows XP Mode Update. Of course, you'll have to restart your system yet again for the patch to take effect.

## Configuring Windows XP Mode

You're finally ready to use Windows XP Mode. The following steps get you started:

1. Choose Start ➪ All Programs ➪ Windows Virtual PC ➪ Windows Virtual PC. You'll see a licensing agreement.

2. Read the agreement and accept it. Click Next. You'll see an Installation Folder and Credentials dialog box like the one in Figure 19-9.

3. (Optional) Change the Installation Folder field, if desired, by clicking Browse and choosing a new location. Generally, you want to use the default installation folder to keep things simple and standardized. However, if your boot drive is short on space and you want to use a secondary drive for the virtual PC, you'll want to change the Installation Folder field.

4. Type a password in the Password field and type it again in the Confirm Password field.

5. (Optional) If you want to make your Windows XP Mode installation more secure, clear the Remember Credential (Recommended) option.

6. Click Next. You'll see the Help Protect Your Computer dialog box shown in Figure 19-10.

7. Select an automatic update option that reflects your organization's policy and click Next. You'll see a dialog box that contains information about starting the Windows XP Mode setup process. Make sure you read this information carefully.

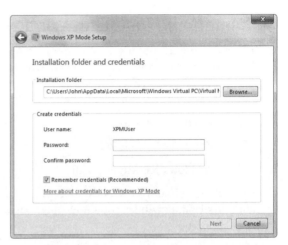

**FIGURE 19-9:** Select an installation folder and provide credentials for Windows XP Mode.

**FIGURE 19-10:** Keep your Windows XP Mode installation updated by choosing automatic updates.

*Windows XP Mode shares drive space with your Windows 7 installation to make it easier for Windows XP Mode applications to share data with your Windows 7 applications, so all the Windows 7 drive rules apply to your Windows XP Mode installation. You can turn off drive-sharing later if you want. The dialog box contains a link you can click to learn the details about changing drive-sharing.*

8. Click Start Setup. The setup process can take a while to complete. When the setup process is complete, you'll see a virtual PC environment like the one in Figure 19-11.

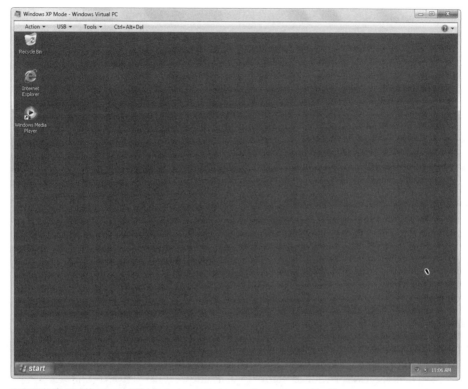

**FIGURE 19-11:** Windows XP Mode is ready to use for your application.

## Using the Application in the Virtual Environment

Windows XP Mode is a fully functional virtual machine. The default configuration allows the Windows XP Mode virtual machine to share resources with your Windows 7 drive. However, the first drive for Windows XP Mode is a virtual drive — the Windows XP Mode drive. This drive plays by the rules that Windows XP uses, not those of Windows 7.

It's important to remember that this virtual machine lacks any installed functionality, including the .NET Framework. You also won't have a development environment available or any of the other tools you're used to using. Consequently, before you can do anything else, you need to install the .NET Framework and any development tools you want to use. Make sure you install the Windows XP version of those tools. Any Windows 7-specific tools you own won't work in the Windows XP virtual environment. This limitation might seem obvious, but sometimes a developer will get in a hurry and not keep the Windows XP nature of the setup in mind.

If you want to use Windows XP Mode to see how the user will interact with the application, you may only want to install the application along with the .NET Framework. When working with Windows XP Mode from a user perspective, make sure your configuration has the same security and resource rules that the user will have, or you won't obtain useful results. The point is to configure the environment as if you're working with a newly installed operating system because that's what you have to work with.

## WORKAROUNDS FOR COMMON WINDOWS XP MODE PROBLEMS

Your Windows XP Mode installation will normally run without problems. When it does encounter a problem, the virtual environment makes it possible to restart Windows XP Mode without bothering anything else running on Windows 7. In fact, the ability to restart an errant operating system without rebooting the entire system is one of the reasons virtual operating systems are so popular. However, just because Windows XP Mode is flexible doesn't mean you'll never encounter problems with it. There are situations where you'll encounter things you'll want to fix. The following sections describe a few of these scenarios and offer a few solutions.

### Resource Permission Issues

It's important to remember that Windows XP Mode is running on a Windows 7 installation. The rules that normally apply to Windows 7 also apply to shared resources for Windows XP Mode. For example, you can't access the root directory of a Windows 7 drive from Windows XP Mode any more than you can access it from Windows 7. Consequently, if your application is especially unruly about using Windows 7 shared resources using the Windows 7 rules, make sure you work with the virtual drive exclusively.

### Application Refuses to Use a Resource

The virtual nature of the environment becomes a little more obvious as you begin working with the application and discover that it can't find a resource that you know your machine has to offer. The problem is that the virtual machine is isolated from your real machine — it can see only the resources that you let it see. The first thing you should check is whether integration is turned on. Choose Tools. If you see an Enable Integration Features option, select it. It's also possible to disable integration features, when you need to completely isolate the virtual machine to prevent possible contamination, by choosing Tools ➪ Disable Integration Features.

Even if the integration features are turned on, it doesn't mean that a particular feature is accessible. To check the availability of features, choose Tools ➪ Settings. You'll see the Windows XP Mode – Windows Virtual PC Settings window. Select Integration Features and you'll see a list of settings, as shown in Figure 19-12.

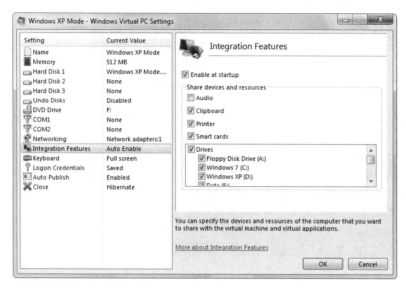

**FIGURE 19-12:** Verify that the integration feature you want to use is accessible.

In this case, most integration features are available. However, notice that the Audio option is cleared. If your application provides audio output, you won't hear it unless this option is checked.

## Virtual Environment Is Slow

The virtual environment will never be as fast as a native Windows XP installation, so you'll need to get used to Windows XP Mode running a little slower on your system than a native installation would. However, you can do things to speed up the virtual environment a bit so it doesn't run so slowly that you fall asleep at the keyboard.

One of the more important changes you can make is to provide Windows XP Mode with additional memory. The default value of 512 MB is too small for many business configurations. Even a native Windows XP installation requires more memory than that. The following steps help you configure Windows XP Mode to provide additional memory:

   **1.**   Click Ctrl+Alt+Del (at the top of the virtual machine display — don't press the actual key combination). You'll see the Windows XP version of the Windows Security dialog box, as shown in Figure 19-13.

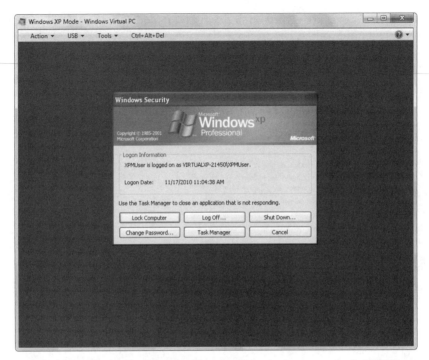

**FIGURE 19-13:** Display the Windows Security dialog box so you can shut Windows XP Mode down.

2. Select Shut Down. When you see the Shut Down Windows dialog box, select Shut Down and click OK. Windows XP Mode shuts down.

3. Choose Start ➪ All Programs ➪ Windows Virtual PC ➪ Windows Virtual PC. You'll see a list of virtual machines installed on your system, as shown in Figure 19-14.

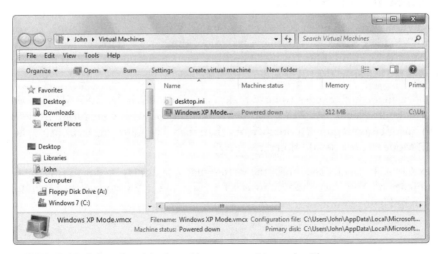

**FIGURE 19-14:** Select the virtual machine you want to work with.

4. Right-click the Windows XP Mode entry and choose Settings from the Context menu. You'll see the Windows XP Mode – Windows Virtual PC Settings window.

5. Highlight the Memory option. You'll see the current memory allocated for this virtual machine, as shown in Figure 19-15. Notice that this display also shows the maximum available memory.

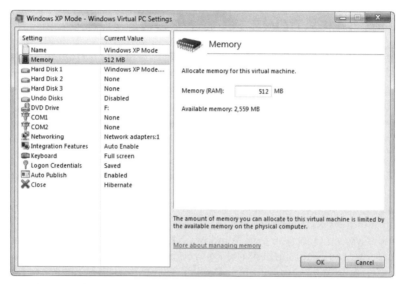

**FIGURE 19-15:** The memory display shows how much memory is allocated for the virtual machine.

6. Set the Memory (RAM) field for a value that's larger than the current value, but less than the Available Memory field value.

*Setting the Memory (RAM) field value too high can starve your Windows 7 applications or cause thrashing, in which the system is constantly exchanging data between RAM and the hard drive. A good rule of thumb is to use no more than half the Available Memory field value for your virtual machine. However, you can try different values to see what works best with your system.*

7. Click OK to accept the new value.

8. Double-click the Windows XP Mode entry to restart the virtual machine.

There are other ways to get a more responsive Windows XP Mode session. Removing integration features will enhance overall responsiveness because the virtual machine will have to do less work to interact with Windows 7. Anything that you'd normally do to tune Windows XP, such as shutting down unneeded services and reducing the number of visual effects, also works with Windows XP Mode. In short, Windows XP Mode responds much as any Windows XP setup does within the confines of the virtual machine environment.

## MOVING YOUR APPLICATIONS TO WINDOWS 7

This chapter has presented Windows XP Mode. If you take anything away from this chapter, it should be that Windows XP Mode is the option to try last. Working with a virtual machine environment adds complexity to the system setup and presents a few challenges of its own. In addition, you have to obtain and install Windows XP Mode before you can use it. Even so, Windows XP Mode does provide a viable option for getting some older applications to work and is worth the effort when you don't have the source code to perform an update of the entire application.

Before you jump right into using Windows XP Mode, go through the various ideas in the rest of the book to determine if there isn't something you can do to make that application work without resorting to Windows XP Mode. You'll also want to do some planning on implementing your solution using Windows XP Mode. Make sure you spend the time going through the suggestions in the "Considering Windows XP Mode" section of this chapter even before you install Windows XP Mode on your test system. Once you have Windows XP Mode installed, test the application thoroughly to ensure it works as anticipated. Use the troubleshooting techniques found in the "Workarounds for Common Windows XP Mode Problems" section of this chapter to work out any glitches.

Chapter 20 begins a new part of the book. Many developers focus their attention on the Windows GUI and using the Visual Studio IDE to perform the majority of their work. It's true that these graphical environments can reduce complexity by letting the developer work through a set of valid choices at each phase of the development process. However, using the GUI environment can also slow you down. In addition, it's not always possible to perform every task using the GUI. The command line requires that you memorize at least the techniques used to complete tasks. However, the less intuitive interface can make the developer incredibly efficient as well. Chapter 20 gets you started with Windows PowerShell — the new command line for Windows.

# PART V
# Working at the Command Line

- **CHAPTER 20:** Working with Windows PowerShell 2.0
- **CHAPTER 21:** Creating Scripts
- **CHAPTER 22:** Creating Cmdlets
- **CHAPTER 23:** Interacting Directly with PowerShell

# 20
# Working with Windows PowerShell 2.0

**WHAT'S IN THIS CHAPTER?**

- ➤ Using Windows PowerShell in place of the old command prompt
- ➤ Working with PowerShell from a developer perspective
- ➤ Getting help when you need it
- ➤ Working with the shell property system

Many developers have used the command prompt to perform tasks. In fact, you've used the command prompt in the form of batch commands for several of the examples in this book. However, the command prompt comes from the days of DOS, the Disk Operating System, many years ago. Some people consider it outdated or at least too difficult to use, so Microsoft has come up with a command prompt replacement, the Windows PowerShell. In many respects, Windows PowerShell is just like the old command prompt. For example, you still type commands to perform tasks, and you also use scripts to execute multiple commands. However, Windows PowerShell also comes with a much nicer Help system and it's considerably easier to use.

Windows PowerShell hasn't received a great amount of attention, and some developers haven't even tried it yet because it's different from what they've used in the past. The old command prompt still works. However, at some point you'll probably have to at least entertain the thought of using Windows PowerShell, because Microsoft has started using it with some of its products. For example, you can't perform some tasks with Exchange Server without using Windows PowerShell — just how much Microsoft intends to use Windows PowerShell remains to be seen.

*Microsoft continuously updates Windows PowerShell to include new functionality. For example, you now have access to a debugger when working with Windows PowerShell, and your script can listen to events and react to them. You can see a complete list of these changes at* http://technet.microsoft.com/library/dd367858.aspx. *Along with the changes, however, you'll probably notice a few script-breaking issues with Windows PowerShell 2.0. For example, Microsoft has added new keywords that add functionality, but that could also conflict with variables and other names in your existing scripts. You can see these changes at* http://technet.microsoft.com/library/dd871148.aspx#BKMK_PS20.

This chapter also exposes you to the Windows PowerShell commands. It provides you with a quick overview of them, so you can see what's available, and how you might start working Windows PowerShell into your daily activities. The overview is helpful because you'll find it a good quick reference to things you can do with Windows PowerShell. You may even find that you prefer using Windows PowerShell to perform certain tasks once you get used to using it. However, the four chapters in this part won't discuss Windows PowerShell in detail — you'll need to seek out books dedicated to this topic to learn about Windows PowerShell in depth.

## REPLACING THE COMMAND PROMPT

As IT has shrunk in size, time-strapped administrators and developers alike have begun moving from the GUI environment to the command prompt. The reason is simple: working with a GUI is intuitive and easy, but it's also time-consuming. A process that might require 10 or so mouse clicks in a GUI can require as little as one command at the command prompt. Typing the command is considerably faster than using the GUI, and today speed is everything. The tradeoff is that the person working at the command prompt must memorize the commonly used commands and have a great reference available for discovering less-used commands quickly, or the speed advantage of the command prompt quickly diminishes.

Windows PowerShell represents a compromise of sorts for those time-strapped administrators and developers. Yes, you still type commands, but Windows PowerShell makes it easier to discover those commands and how to use them. It doesn't precisely lead you through the process of typing the command as a GUI would, but it does make working with the command straightforward. The following sections describe this, and other reasons for replacing the command prompt, in detail.

## Understanding the Need for Windows PowerShell

One of the problems with a new technology is that the technology has to address a need before people will accept it. A new command line is no different. Developers will wonder why they should use a new command line when there's a perception that the existing command line works fine. The following list provides some good reasons to use Windows PowerShell in place of the older command line:

- The Windows PowerShell provides a greater level of reliability than the command line.
- Using the Windows PowerShell improves security because you need the required credentials to execute commands.

➤ Windows PowerShell helps anyone obtain the full resources of the .NET Framework without becoming a programmer. For a developer, using the Windows PowerShell can simplify tasks that would normally require a full-fledged application.

➤ In many cases, the commands are easier to remember and use because they use human-readable terms (the older commands are also available, for the most part, should you decide to use them).

➤ Scripting is considerably more powerful in Windows PowerShell, albeit not always as easy as working at the old command prompt. Windows PowerShell 2.0 fixes some of the problems people faced when working with earlier versions of Windows PowerShell by providing a script editor with full debugging capabilities.

➤ Instead of using plain text for data, Windows PowerShell uses .NET objects, which means you can obtain consistent output of complex data.

These basic reasons for using Windows PowerShell also tell you what Microsoft is trying to accomplish. If you take a hard look at Windows 7, many of the low-level operating system features still don't rely on the .NET Framework, but many of the higher-level features do. For example, you can no longer talk about IIS without also talking about the .NET Framework. The .NET Framework also makes an appearance in security, graphics, and communications. Consequently, it isn't any surprise that the Windows PowerShell also has a very heavy connection to the .NET Framework. In general, you're going to find Microsoft moving more and more in the direction of using the .NET Framework for the majority of operating system features. This change in focus means that today you really do need a .NET Framework connection at the command prompt to get useful work done, and that the connection will only get stronger as time passes.

*Although Microsoft hasn't made a statement on the matter, many industry experts view Windows PowerShell as a highly extensible equivalent to many Unix shells on the market. Under Unix, many graphical utilities simply provide a convenient way to use the well-defined command line utilities. Working at the command line is the main event, and the graphical environment serves to make working with the command line utilities easier for those who need it. If this is the direction Microsoft is taking, you may eventually see all the old poorly documented and virus-prone utilities disappear from Windows, replaced by Windows PowerShell equivalents. Of course, this won't happen in Windows 7 or perhaps even the next version of Windows, but because of the security problems with current utilities, Microsoft may feel forced to move in this direction.*

## Considering Why You Should Use PowerShell

The fact that the .NET Framework hasn't taken over yet may leave some people considering not using Windows PowerShell today. It's true; you can work at the command line with versions of Windows from Windows XP to Windows 7 without ever looking at Windows PowerShell. In fact, you'll very likely be able to work with Windows 8 with nary a glimpse at Windows PowerShell. Microsoft doesn't throw out old technology very quickly. However, they do throw it out. Fortunately, there are many other personal reasons to use Windows PowerShell, some of which follow:

- It provides better automation features so you can do more with less effort.
- You can create scripts more quickly in many cases.
- Scripts created with Windows PowerShell tend to execute faster for a given task than the task could be performed at the old command line.
- Using Windows PowerShell reduces potential mistakes.
- You get more information from Windows PowerShell than you did from the command line utilities of the past.
- It's easier to obtain usable help in Windows PowerShell than it is at the command prompt (which sometimes doesn't provide any help at all).
- Windows PowerShell provides a script debugger, which makes it far easier to find errors than when you worked with batch files at the old command prompt.

Of course, you may now wonder whether you should just throw away that old command prompt. Unfortunately, you can't do that either. Many individuals and most companies have a significant base of existing batch files and scripts that they aren't going to be willing to throw away. This established base might not run very well under Windows PowerShell for the very reasons that you want to use it — improved security and reliability. Consequently, during this transitional phase, you'll probably have to use both the command line and Windows PowerShell for maximum productivity. To make the transition smoother, you may want to begin moving those old batch files and scripts to Windows PowerShell as time permits.

## UNDERSTANDING POWERSHELL COMMAND BASICS FOR THE DEVELOPER

Unlike earlier versions of Windows, you don't have to install Windows PowerShell on Windows 7 — it comes as a standard feature of the operating system. To start a copy of Windows PowerShell, choose Start ➪ All Programs ➪ Accessories ➪ Windows PowerShell ➪ Windows PowerShell. If you're using a 64-bit version of Windows 7, this will open a 64-bit version of Windows PowerShell. If you have older cmdlets that you want to use with Windows PowerShell, you may have to open a 32-bit PS prompt. In this case, choose the Windows PowerShell (x86) command instead. It's also helpful to pin the Windows PowerShell command to the Start menu, since Microsoft chose to bury it so deeply in the menu structure. Simply right-click the Windows PowerShell command and choose Pin to Start Menu from the Context menu.

*You'll see Windows PowerShell abbreviated as PS in more than a few locations. When you see PS, think PowerShell. This is especially important when opening the PS prompt. The PS prompt appears in the Windows PowerShell window. You type commands at the PS prompt.*

Working at the Windows PowerShell command line is intrinsically different from working at the CMD.EXE command line. One of the first things you'll notice is that using the /? command line switch doesn't work for many commands and utilities. For example, if you want to find out about the Dir command, you must type Help Dir and press Enter. The command line help is also significantly different. Some people will feel they're reading a programming manual rather than a help listing. Figure 20-1 shows a typical example. You'll see immediately that Windows PowerShell doesn't provide the same command line help you used in the past.

**FIGURE 20-1:** Windows PowerShell provides a different sort of help than you used in the past.

*Windows PowerShell uses a relatively large font and a 120-character screen size by default. The figures in this chapter use a somewhat smaller font and an 80-character screen size to ensure you can see the text within the book. What this means to you is that your screen won't precisely match the one in the book — the text will wrap differently and the screen may contain a little less information. However, the overall content will be the same.*

Most commands and many utilities don't work the same when using Windows PowerShell. For example, say you want to locate all the temporary files on your system and place the results in the Temp.TXT file. Using the old method, you would type Dir *.TMP /S >> Temp.TXT and press Enter. This technique doesn't work under Windows PowerShell. Instead, you type Get-ChildItem -Include *.TMP -Recurse >> Temp.TXT and press Enter. The results are similar; the syntax is completely different. You can substitute Dir for Get-ChildItem, but that's about the limit of the similarities. The Dir command does work differently under Windows PowerShell. The output of both the Dir *.TXT and Get-ChildItem *.TXT commands appears in Figure 20-2. Notice that both commands produce the same results, but that these results aren't the same as you'd get using the Dir *.TXT command at a command prompt, which is shown in Figure 20-3.

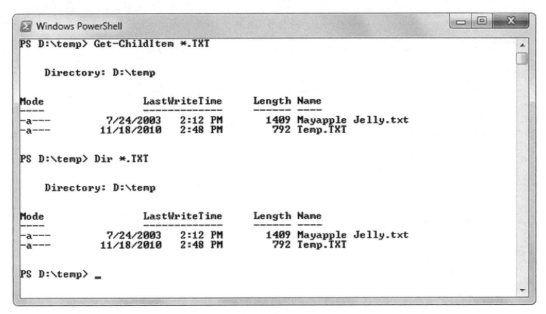

**FIGURE 20-2:** The output of the directory command, no matter which syntax you use, differs in Windows PowerShell.

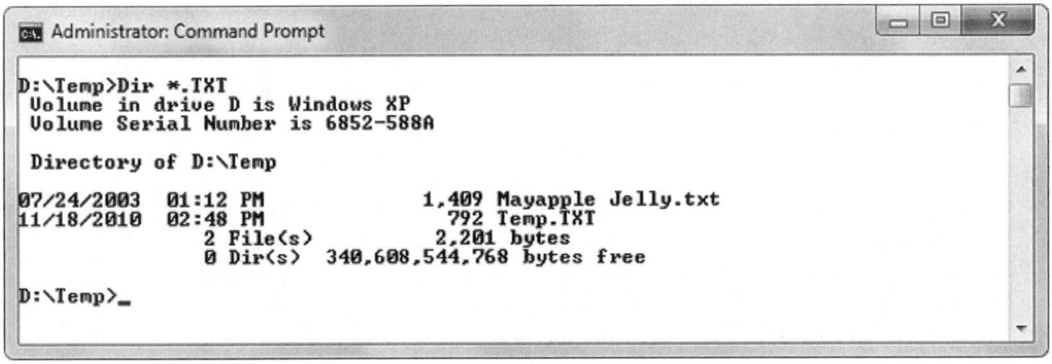

**FIGURE 20-3:** Here's the result of the Dir *.TXT command at the command prompt.

Windows PowerShell uses a wealth of new names for old commands. For example, the CD command from days past is now the Set-Location command. The "Working with the Online Help" section below describes how to obtain help for either standard Windows PowerShell commands or the old command line alternatives.

## WORKING WITH THE ONLINE HELP

Windows PowerShell features an extensive Help system that the old command line can't match. Of course, it helps to know what commands are available. You can see a list of the Windows PowerShell commands by typing Help * and pressing Enter. Figure 20-4 shows part of the list (PowerShell automatically truncates the command descriptions to allow more of them to fit on the screen). This list might look a little daunting at first. However, it represents a major change in the way the command shell works with commands, from ancient Unix to a more modern object-oriented methodology. The bottom line is that Windows PowerShell provides a vast wealth of commands, many of which don't appear in the old command prompt, but which require you to learn a new way of working with those commands.

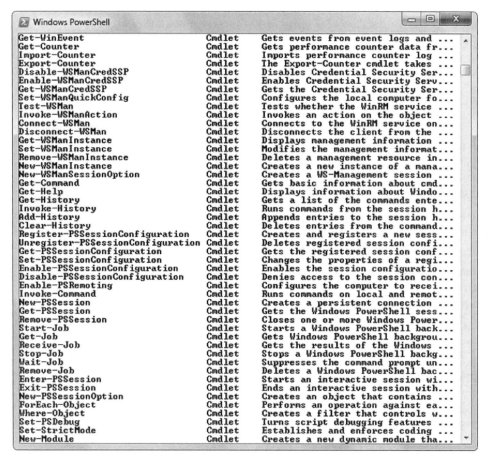

**FIGURE 20-4:** Before you begin using Windows PowerShell in earnest, you'll want to review the command list.

Microsoft has also standardized help at the PS prompt. For example, when you type `Help Dir` and press Enter, you see the help information shown in Figure 20-1. If you type `Help CD` and press Enter, you'll see the same categories of information. Of course, the information in each section will relate to the `CD` command (or more precisely, the Set-Location command). You'll always see the following categories of information when seeking help:

- **Name:** The Windows PowerShell name of the command. You won't ever see the old command line equivalent name for the command (which is why you need Table 20-1 in the "Understanding the Shell Property System" section of this chapter). For example, if you type `Help Set-Location` and press Enter, you'll still see `Set-Location` as the name, not `CD`.

- **Synopsis:** A one- or two-line description of the purpose of the command. Sometimes the description is less than helpful to the developer who has worked at the command prompt for a long time. For example, the synopsis for the `Dir` command is, "Gets the items and child items in one or more specified locations." A developer would probably find a synopsis of "Lists the files and directories in the specified location" more helpful, but Windows PowerShell doesn't work that way. (You'll find out later in this section that the Microsoft-supplied synopsis is actually more correct.)

- **Syntax:** Provides a Backus-Naur Form (BNF) presentation of the various ways you can use the command. Optional elements appear in square brackets ([]). Command line switches appear with a short dash (–) followed by the command line switch in initial caps. Variables appear in angle brackets (<>) in lowercase. The variable name, such as `string`, tells you the kind of data the command expects. If you see a variable with [] after it, such as `string[]`, it means that you can supply multiple variables of that type as an argument.

- **Description:** If you find the synopsis a little hard to understand, the longer description section will generally help clear things up. The description usually contains several paragraphs of information about the command. It never contains usage examples, however. In order to obtain usage examples, you use the `-Examples` command line switch. For example, to get `Dir` command usage examples, you type `Help Dir -Examples` and press Enter.

- **Related Links:** Sometimes the Help system won't provide enough information, especially when multiple commands can interact with each other. The Related Links section provides a list of other commands and URLs you can use to obtain additional information.

- **Remarks:** In most cases, you'll see a list of command extensions you can use to obtain additional information. However, the Remarks section can contain all sorts of useful information that doesn't fit in one of the other categories.

When you add command line switches to the `Help` command, you'll see other information. For example, when you type `Help Dir -Detailed` and press Enter, you'll see a Parameters section that describes each of the parameters in detail as shown in Figure 20-5. Not shown in the figure is a list of examples. The examples are enlightening because they help you make sense of the confusing synopsis presented earlier. Unlike the command line version of the `Dir` command, you can type `Dir Registry::HKLM\Software` and obtain a listing of the keys in the HKEY_LOCAL_MACHINE\Software branch of the registry.

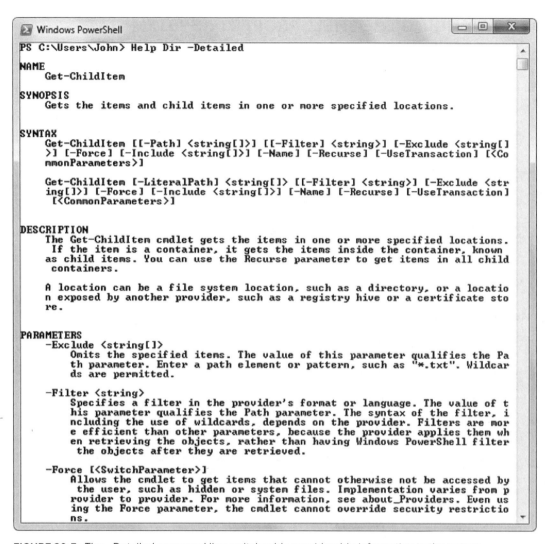

**FIGURE 20-5:** The –Detailed command line switch adds considerable information to the output.

If you still don't have enough information after using the -Detailed command line switch, you can use the -Full command line switch, which gets quite detailed. Not only is the parameter information more detailed, but the -Full command line switch adds even more sections: Inputs (information that you can pipe to the command), Outputs (the type of information you receive as output), and Notes (interesting additional information that doesn't fit anywhere else, such as a list of aliases for the command). Before you leave this section, you should take time to work through a few commands in the Help system to truly understand the considerable flexibility and level of information it provides.

## UNDERSTANDING THE SHELL PROPERTY SYSTEM

Using Windows PowerShell is a different experience from working with the command line in a number of ways, not the least of which is how Windows PowerShell provides functionality. Instead of individual utilities, Microsoft is placing a strong emphasis on cmdlets and scripts, which let you access the power of the .NET Framework in a secure manner. The Windows PowerShell interface is significantly different, as described in the "Understanding the Windows PowerShell Difference" section of this chapter. Table 20-1 shows a general list of the commands available as part of Windows PowerShell as of the time of writing (the list isn't complete — it focuses on commands that most developers will use).

> *Not every command line command has a PS equivalent. Likewise, there are many PS commands that you can't perform at the command prompt. The crossover between the two is mainly common commands.*

**TABLE 20-1:** Commands Available in Windows PowerShell

| PS COMMAND | COMMAND LINE EQUIVALENT | DESCRIPTION |
| --- | --- | --- |
| Add-Computer | N/A | Adds the local computer to the domain or workgroup. |
| Add-Content | N/A | Adds the content of one or more objects to another object. For example, you could use this command to add the content of one or more files to a master file. |
| Add-History | N/A | Adds an entry to the session history even though you haven't actually executed the command. |
| Add-Member | N/A | Adds the user-defined custom member to an existing object. |
| Add-PSSnapin | N/A | Adds the requested Windows PowerShell snap-in to the current console. A snap-in is a set of features for manipulating a particular application or system resource such as a snap-in for Microsoft Exchange. |
| Add-Type | N/A | Adds a .NET Framework class to a Windows PowerShell session, which means that you can expand Windows PowerShell to include any class, even those you've created. This particular feature is especially handy for making unmanaged functionality available to Windows PowerShell through P/Invoke. |

| PS COMMAND | COMMAND LINE EQUIVALENT | DESCRIPTION |
| --- | --- | --- |
| Checkpoint-Computer | N/A | Creates a restore point on the local computer, assuming that the functionality for creating the restore point is enabled. |
| Clear-Content | N/A | Removes the content from a file or other object. The file or other object remains intact; it simply doesn't have any information stored in it. |
| Clear-EventLog | N/A | Removes all the entries from the specified event log. You can use this feature on local and remote computers. |
| Clear-History | N/A | Removes all the entries from the command history. |
| Clear-Host | Cls | Clears the screen and sets the cursor in the upper-left corner of the display area. |
| Clear-Item | N/A | Sets an item to contain a specific value that represents a clear condition. |
| Clear-ItemProperty | N/A | Removes the value from an object property. The system sets the property to a blank value, rather than a null (nothing) value. |
| Clear-Variable | N/A | Removes the value from a variable. The variable still exists; it simply doesn't contain any information. |
| Compare-Object | Compare | Performs a comparison of two objects. |
| Complete-Transaction | N/A | Completes the current transaction. A transaction-based system lets you roll back commands when a failure occurs. When the transaction is committed, all the changes performed by commands in the transaction are finalized. |
| ConvertFrom-CSV | N/A | Converts variable-length strings created by the `ConvertTo-CSV` command into .NET objects. |
| ConvertFrom-SecureString | N/A | Converts a secure string into an encrypted standard string. The most common reason to perform this conversion is to save the standard string to a file for later use. Use the `ConvertTo-SecureString` cmdlet to convert the string from a standard string to a secure string. You can learn more about the `SecureString` class at http://msdn.microsoft.com/library/system.security.securestring.aspx. |

*continues*

**TABLE 20-1** *(continued)*

| PS COMMAND | COMMAND LINE EQUIVALENT | DESCRIPTION |
| --- | --- | --- |
| ConvertFrom-StringData | N/A | Converts a string that contains one or move key/value pairs into a hash table. |
| Convert-path | N/A | Converts the path to the specified object from an MSH path to a provider path. Normally, this means creating a full path specification, including the drive letter. |
| ConvertTo-CSV | N/A | Converts .NET Framework objects into CSV variable-length format strings. It transmits these CSV strings to another command or utility through a pipeline. You'll normally use this feature to perform object analysis or process a number of objects that include the same properties, such as a directory listing. |
| ConvertTo-Html | N/A | Converts the input information into an HTML table. For example, you could use this command to convert a directory listing into an HTML format. |
| ConvertTo-SecureString | N/A | Converts an encrypted standard string into a secure string. You can also use this cmdlet to convert plain text strings into secure strings. |
| ConvertTo-XML | N/A | Converts .NET objects and structures to XML format. |
| Copy-Item | Copy | Copies the contents of one item to another item. |
| Copy-ItemProperty | N/A | Copies the contents of one object property to another object property. |
| Export-Alias | N/A | Exports a command alias that you've created for the current session to a file. For example, the alias of the `Dir` command is `Get-ChildItem`. |
| Export-CliXml | N/A | Creates an XML representation of one or more MSH objects. |
| Export-Console | N/A | Exports the changes made to the current console so that you can import them later to another console. Any changes you save overwrite the content of any existing console file. |
| Export-CSV | N/A | Exports the requested data to a CSV format. |
| Foreach-Object | Foreach | Performs a `foreach` looping function. This command normally appears in a script. |

| PS COMMAND | COMMAND LINE EQUIVALENT | DESCRIPTION |
|---|---|---|
| Format-Custom | N/A | Displays output data using a custom format. You specify the output format as part of a formatter file that describes the format. |
| Format-List | N/A | Displays the output data in a list format where each data element appears on a separate line. |
| Format-Table | N/A | Displays the output data in a tabular format where each element appears in a separate column. |
| Format-Wide | N/A | Displays objects as a list of the properties that contain the object's data. |
| Get-Acl | N/A | Obtains an Access Control List (ACL) for the specified object. |
| Get-Alias | N/A | Obtains the alias for the specified command. |
| Get-AuthenticodeSignature | N/A | Obtains the signature object (the digital signature) associated with a file. |
| Get-ChildItem | Dir | Displays a list of the children for a particular object. This command is normally associated as the alias for the Dir command and used to display a directory. However, you can use it for any object. |
| Get-Command | N/A | Obtains information about a specified command. The information is different from Help in that you receive a short synopsis of the command and its command line switches. |
| Get-Content | Type | Displays the content for an object. When used for a file, this command displays the file contents in a manner similar to the Type command. |
| Get-Credential | N/A | Obtains a credential object based on a particular password. |
| Get-Culture | N/A | Obtains the culture information for the current command line session. |
| Get-Date | Date Time | Displays the current date and time. There's no Time alias supplied with Windows PowerShell; the Date command does both date and time manipulation. |

*continues*

**TABLE 20-1** *(continued)*

| PS COMMAND | COMMAND LINE EQUIVALENT | DESCRIPTION |
|---|---|---|
| Get-Drive | CD | Obtains the specified drive object. Unlike CMD.EXE, you don't provide the colon after the drive letter. The current utility version doesn't support UNC drive specifications. When working with the old CD command, you supplied CD alone to obtain the current drive and directory. |
| Get-EventLog | N/A | Obtains the specified event log. |
| Get-ExecutionPolicy | N/A | Obtains the current execution policy for Windows PowerShell. The default setting is Restricted. Potential values include: Restricted, AllSigned, RemoteSigned, and Unrestricted. The execution policy determines the requirements for running code on a system, with Restricted providing the most protection and Unrestricted providing the least. |
| Get-Help | Help /? | Obtains help information about a specific command. You can also use this command to obtain a list of matching commands by using wildcard characters. |
| Get-History | N/A | Displays the command line history for the session. You can also use this command to select a command from the list to execute. |
| Get-Host | N/A | Displays information about the current host, including the session identifier and basic cultural information. |
| Get-Item | N/A | Displays information about the specified item. |
| Get-ItemProperty | N/A | Obtains the content of an object property. |
| Get-Location | N/A | Displays the current hard-drive location on the system. |
| Get-Member | N/A | Displays specifics about the supplied object including properties, methods, type information, and property sets. |
| Get-PfxCertificate | N/A | Obtains the Personal Information Exchange (PFX) certificate information. You can learn more about the PFX certificate at http://msdn.microsoft.com/library/ee416211.aspx. |
| Get-Process | N/A | Displays a list of the processes running on the machine. |
| Get-PSDrive | N/A | Returns information about the Windows PowerShell drives. The default output information includes the drive name, provider, and root directory. |

| PS COMMAND | COMMAND LINE EQUIVALENT | DESCRIPTION |
|---|---|---|
| Get-PSProvider | N/A | Obtains information about the specified provider. |
| Get-PSSnapin | N/A | Displays a list of the existing Windows PowerShell snap-ins loaded within the current session. The information includes the name, version, and description. |
| Get-Service | SC | Displays a list of all the services installed on a machine along with the service status. The command line version of SC doesn't exist in Windows PowerShell. |
| Get-TraceSource | N/A | Lists the properties for a given trace source. You can learn more about the TraceSource class used for creating a trace source at http://msdn.microsoft.com/library/system.diagnostics.tracesource.aspx. |
| Get-Transaction | N/A | Obtains information about the current transaction. A transaction-based system lets you roll back commands when a failure occurs. When the transaction is committed, all the changes performed by commands in the transaction are finalized. |
| Get-UICulture | N/A | Displays the culture information used for the user interface. |
| Get-Unique | N/A | Displays a list of unique items in a collection. This command lets you remove repeated entries from the list. You normally use this command as part of a script. |
| Get-Variable | Set | Displays the content of one or more variables. You can use this command while diagnosing errors in scripts or as a means of saving state information for later use. |
| Get-WinEvent | N/A | Obtains the specified event from all event logs, even the classic event logs. This is a kind of super-search command. If you use this command without specifying either an event or a log, you see all events from all logs. Press Ctrl+C to stop the event log display. You can use this command on both local and remote computers. |
| Get-WMIObject | WMIC | Obtains the Windows Management Interface (WMI) object for the machine. You can use this object to perform a broad range of tasks, such as obtaining information about the network. |

*continues*

**TABLE 20-1** *(continued)*

| PS COMMAND | COMMAND LINE EQUIVALENT | DESCRIPTION |
| --- | --- | --- |
| Group-Object | N/A | Groups objects that contain the same value for a given property. You can use this command to compare objects. |
| Import-Alias | N/A | Imports an alias from a file. This feature lets you use aliases that you've stored for later use. |
| Import-CliXml | N/A | Imports an XML representation of one or more MSH objects. |
| Import-CSV | N/A | Obtains objects from a CSV listing and transmits them to another command or utility through a pipeline. You'll normally use this feature to perform object analysis or process a number of objects that include the same properties, such as a directory listing. |
| Invoke-Expression | N/A | Executes the specified expression, normally a cmdlet. This is one of the default command line actions, so you won't use this command at the command line in most cases. However, you can use it within a script to execute a supplementary command. |
| Invoke-History | N/A | Executes a previously executed command based on its position in the history list. |
| Invoke-Item | N/A | Invokes an executable or opens a file. Essentially, this command performs the default actions associated with a file. |
| Join-Path | N/A | Creates a single path element from several path elements. |
| Limit-EventLog | N/A | Limits the size of the specified event log. You can use this feature on local and remote computers. |
| Measure-Command | N/A | Tracks the running time for scripts and cmdlets. You can use this command to measure system performance while performing a task. However, a more common use is to track the time that a task is running and when to terminate it when it takes too long. Many people will associate the functionality of this command with the watchdog timer used to reset hardware. Generally, you'll use this feature in a script to keep the script from freezing the system. |

| PS COMMAND | COMMAND LINE EQUIVALENT | DESCRIPTION |
| --- | --- | --- |
| Measure-Object | N/A | Measures the specified element of an object or object property. For example, you could count the number of directory entries using this command. You always use the output of another command as input to this command through a pipe. |
| Move-Item | Move | Moves an item from one location to another. For example, you can use this command to move a file from one location to another. |
| Move-ItemProperty | N/A | Moves a property from one object to another. |
| New-Alias | N/A | Creates a new alias for an existing cmdlet. The cmdlet must exist or this command will fail. |
| New-EventLog | N/A | Creates a new event log. You can use this feature on local and remote computers. |
| New-Item | MD<br>MkDir | Creates a new item in the specified namespace. |
| New-ItemProperty | N/A | Sets a new property for an item at a specific location. For example, you could use this feature to set a cmdlet property value. |
| New-Object | N/A | Creates a new .NET Framework object. You can create any object within the .NET framework. Even though you could use this command at the command line, you'll normally use it within a script to create objects necessary to manipulate data, show status information, or perform other tasks. |
| New-PSDrive | MountVol | Mounts a new drive on the system. |
| New-Service | SC | Installs a new service on the system. |
| New-Timespan | N/A | Defines a time span using a `TimeSpan` object. Normally, you'll use this feature within a script to track the time span required to perform a task or to create other time-related statistics. You can learn more about the `TimeSpan` object at http://msdn.microsoft.com/library/system.timespan.aspx. |

*continues*

**TABLE 20-1** *(continued)*

| PS COMMAND | COMMAND LINE EQUIVALENT | DESCRIPTION |
| --- | --- | --- |
| New-Variable | Set | Creates a new variable that you can use either at the command line or within a script. Variables act as storage containers for data that you want to retain in memory. |
| Out-Default | N/A | Specifies the default controller of output data. |
| Out-File | N/A | Specifies the output device to use for file information. This file receives the output of the specified command, script, or pipeline. |
| Out-Host | Echo<br>> Con | Sends the pipelined output of a series of commands to the console. |
| Out-Null | > Nul | Sends the output to the null device. Essentially, this places the output in the bit bucket. This command takes the place of the NUL: device used in older versions of the command line. |
| Out-Printer | > Lpt<br>> Prn | Sends the output to the printer. If you don't specify a printer, the system uses the default printer. |
| Out-String | N/A | Sends the pipelined output of a series of commands to a string variable. |
| Pop-Location | PopD | Removes a path from the top of the stack. |
| Push-Location | PushD | Adds a directory path to the stack. |
| Read-Host | N/A | Reads a line of input from the host console. Normally, you'll use this command within a script to query the user for input. |
| Remove-EventLog | N/A | Removes the specified event log. You can use this feature on local and remote computers. |
| Remove-Item | Del<br>Erase<br>RD<br>RmDir | Requests that a provider remove the specified item. Generally, this command works with directories and files. |
| Remove-ItemProperty | N/A | Removes the specified property value from an object. |
| Remove-PSDrive | N/A | Dismounts a drive currently attached to the system. See the new-drive command for details. |

| PS COMMAND | COMMAND LINE EQUIVALENT | DESCRIPTION |
|---|---|---|
| Remove-PSSnapin | N/A | Removes the specified Windows PowerShell snap-in from the current session. |
| Remove-Variable | Set | Removes a variable from the current session. This action deletes the variable. |
| Rename-Item | Ren<br>Rename | Requests that a provider rename the specified item. Generally, this command works with directories and files. |
| Rename-ItemProperty | N/A | Renames the specified property in the requested location. |
| Resolve-Path | N/A | Resolves the wildcards in a path so that you can see the actual path information. You can also use this feature within a batch file to provide actual path information to utilities that require it. The command line performed this task using variable expansion. |
| Restart-Service | SC | Restarts the specified Windows service after you stop it. Don't use this command with paused services. |
| Resume-Service | SC | Resumes the specified Windows service after you pause it. Don't use this command with stopped services. |
| Select-Object | N/A | Selects an object based on the arguments you provide to a cmdlet. |
| Select-String | Find<br>FindStr | Searches through strings or files for data with a specific pattern. |
| Set-Acl | N/A | Modifies the contents of an ACL. Use this command to change user, group, or machine security. |
| Set-Alias | N/A | Modifies an existing alias. Use the new-alias command to create a new alias for an existing command. |
| Set-AuthenticodeSignature | N/A | Modifies the Authenticode signature of an object such as a file. |
| Set-Content | N/A | Changes the content of the specified object at the requested location. For example, you could use this command to output data to a file. |
| Set-Date | Date<br>Time | Changes the system time and date. There's no Time alias supplied with Windows PowerShell; the Date command does both date and time manipulation. |

*continues*

**TABLE 20-1** *(continued)*

| PS COMMAND | COMMAND LINE EQUIVALENT | DESCRIPTION |
| --- | --- | --- |
| Set-ExecutionPolicy | N/A | Changes the current execution policy for Windows PowerShell. The default setting is `Restricted`. Potential values include: `Restricted`, `AllSigned`, `RemoteSigned`, and `Unrestricted`. The execution policy determines the requirements for running code on a system, with `Restricted` providing the most protection and `Unrestricted` providing the least. |
| Set-Item | N/A | Requests that a provider set the value of an item using the specified pathname. For example, you can use this command to set the value of a variable. |
| Set-ItemProperty | N/A | Sets an object property to the specified value. |
| Set-Location | CD<br>ChDir | Sets the working directory to the specified location. The working directory is where Windows looks for data files and places output when you don't specify a particular location as part of the output argument. |
| Set-PSDebug | N/A | Places the command line in a debug state. You use this feature to debug your scripts. Unlike previous versions of the command line, Windows PowerShell includes built-in debugging support to go with the built-in scripting support. |
| Set-Service | SC | Sets the properties of a service. For example, you can use this command to set a service to start automatically. You can also use it to change the description or the login account. This command lets you modify any editable service property. Note that some services offer more editable features than others do based on the design features included by the developer. |
| Set-TraceSource | N/A | Sets or removes the specified trace listeners and options from the requested trace source. See the `Get-TraceSource` command for additional information. |
| Set-Variable | Set | Changes the value of a variable. |
| Show-EventLog | N/A | Displays the Event Log console found in the Administrative Tools folder of the Control Panel. You can use this feature on local and remote computers. |

| PS COMMAND | COMMAND LINE EQUIVALENT | DESCRIPTION |
| --- | --- | --- |
| Sort-Object | Sort | Sorts the data provided. For example, you could use the command to sort a directory listing by the length of the file. However, this command works with any sortable object, such as files. |
| Split-Path | N/A | Separates one or more paths into a qualifier, parent path, or leaf item and places the result in a string. You'll normally use this feature from within a script to ensure you can locate specific places on the hard drive, determine the current hard-drive location, process or access files, or perform other path-related tasks. |
| Start-Process | Start | Starts the specified process. |
| Start-Service | SC | Starts a stopped service. Don't use this command with a service that's paused. |
| Start-Sleep | N/A | Places the console, script, cmdlet, or other executable code into a sleep state for the specified amount of time. You can use this feature within a script to stop script execution while you wait for the system to perform a task. For example, you might use this feature when waiting for a download to complete from the Internet. |
| Start-Transaction | N/A | Creates a new transaction, which starts an activity logging process. A transaction-based system lets you roll back commands when a failure occurs. When the transaction is committed, all the changes performed by commands in the transaction are finalized. |
| Start-Transcript | N/A | Creates a log of the console session. You can use this feature to keep track of tasks performed at the command line or diagnose the sequence of events used by a script to complete a task. The log file contains a complete record of the session from the time you use the start-transcript command until you issue the stop-transcript command or end the current session. |
| Stop-Process | TaskKill | Stops the specified process. The process terminates, which means that you could lose data. |
| Stop-Service | SC | Stops the specified service. You must use the start-service command to restart the service. |

*continues*

**TABLE 20-1** *(continued)*

| PS COMMAND | COMMAND LINE EQUIVALENT | DESCRIPTION |
|---|---|---|
| Stop-Transcript | N/A | Ends the logging of console input. See the Start-Transaction command for additional information. |
| Suspend-Service | SC | Pauses the specified service. The service is still in memory and retains any property values. You must use the Resume-Service command to restart a paused service. |
| Tee-Object | N/A | Sends input object to two places. In short, this command creates a copy of the specified input object so you can use it for multiple commands. |
| Test-Path | N/A | Provides a method for testing a path. The command returns true when the path exists. Although you could use this command at the command line, you'll generally use it in a script to ensure a path exists before you attempt to perform tasks that involve the path. |
| Trace-Command | N/A | Enables you to track trace sources for the duration of the command. This is a debugging feature. See the `Set-TraceSource` and `Get-TraceSource` commands for additional information. |
| Undo-Transaction | N/A | Rolls back the current transaction by reversing each of the logged transaction entries. A transaction-based system lets you roll back commands when a failure occurs. When the transaction is committed, all the changes performed by commands in the transaction are finalized. |
| Update-FormatData | N/A | Updates and appends format data files. These files let you format data using custom parameters. See the Format-Custom command for additional information. |
| Update-TypeData | N/A | Updates the `Types.MSHXML` file with additional type information for objects. |
| Use-Transaction | N/A | Adds a script block to the current transaction that allows you to perform scripted transactions. A script block may contain only transacted .NET Framework classes, such as `Microsoft.PowerShell.Commands.Management.TransactedString`. A transaction-based system lets you roll back commands when a failure occurs. When the transaction is committed, all the changes performed by commands in the transaction are finalized. |

## Understanding the Shell Property System | 437

| PS COMMAND | COMMAND LINE EQUIVALENT | DESCRIPTION |
|---|---|---|
| Where-Object | Where | Filters the data from a pipeline so the recipient receives only the data required to execute a command or manipulate data. |
| Write-Debug | N/A | Sends debugging information to the console display. You use this command to debug scripts and cmdlets by viewing information about specific objects and variables. |
| Write-Error | N/A | Sends error information to the console display. You use this feature to perform debugging and when you need to know the error status of both scripts and cmdlets. Errors are coding mistakes that cause the script or cmdlet to stop working, seriously degrade performance, damage data in some manner, or cause other serious damage. |
| Write-EventLog | N/A | Adds a new entry to the specified event log. You can use this feature on local and remote computers. |
| Write-Host | N/A | Displays a list of the objects supported by the current host. |
| Write-Object | N/A | Sends an object to the pipeline. This command lets you use objects with a series of cmdlets. |
| Write-Output | Echo | Sends one or more objects to the next command in a pipeline. If the current command is the last command in the pipeline, the objects are displayed on-screen. |
| Write-Progress | N/A | Sends a progress indicator to the console display. Using this command lets you track script or cmdlet progress and ensure that the script or cmdlet hasn't stopped. This feature is also useful for scripts and cmdlets to let the user know that the command is working during an interactive session. |
| Write-Verbose | N/A | Displays maximum information about any command. |
| Write-Warning | N/A | Sends warning information to the console display. You use this feature to perform debugging and when you need to know the warning status of both scripts and cmdlets. Warnings are coding mistakes that cause the script of a cmdlet to perform in a manner other than intended by the developer. A warning usually indicates a problem that isn't serious, but that you still need to know about in order to take any required repair action. |

## MOVING YOUR APPLICATIONS TO WINDOWS 7

This chapter has gotten you started with Windows PowerShell. You've probably noted some things you like and other things that seem too strange for words. Microsoft continues to improve Windows PowerShell — often without mentioning these changes in its promotional material. The version of Windows PowerShell in Windows 7 is a huge improvement over the original version that you had to download and install. Still, there's room for continued improvement. The one thing you should take away from this chapter is that Windows PowerShell is simply a new kind of command processor, one that's a bit easier to use and a little more secure than the older command processor that you've worked with since the days of DOS.

Now that you have some idea of how to use Windows PowerShell, take time to experiment. Execute some commands to see how this environment works. Work with the Help system for a while so that you can discover new commands and new ways to use Windows PowerShell. The best way to start with Windows PowerShell is to use it to obtain information. Informational commands are less threatening than any other command because they won't harm your system in any way.

This book assumes that as a developer you've probably spent more than a little time working through the intricacies of the command prompt (or at least, you've been exposed to it). Chapter 21 moves past the basic introduction found in this chapter and goes right into working with *scripts*, which are the equivalent of the batch files you created for the old command processor. You use scripts to issue a series of commands in an automated fashion. The new Windows PowerShell Integrated Scripting Environment (ISE) makes creating and debugging scripts considerably easier, and Chapter 21 shows how to use this new feature.

# 21
# Creating Scripts

**WHAT'S IN THIS CHAPTER?**

- Using scripts at the right time
- Working with the PowerShell ISE
- Creating a basic script
- Using and testing the script

The old command line allows a number of different kinds of automation. Of course, the oldest form of automation is the batch file. The script was introduced later, and it provides considerably more flexibility than working with batch files. The scripts provided by Windows PowerShell are even more powerful. You can perform a significant number of tasks using them. For the most part, you can access any managed portion of the .NET Framework using a script, which means you have access to just about everything in Windows.

>  *Windows PowerShell supports both scripts and cmdlets. A script is a series of commands contained in a text file that PS interprets. It's possible to execute scripts from the command line or make them part of the shell using the* Make-Shell *utility. A cmdlet is a compiled executable in DLL format. As with the script, you begin with a text file containing commands that the C# Compiler (CSC) turns into an executable. To use a cmdlet, you must make it part of the shell. Chapter 22 discusses cmdlets in more detail.*

This chapter isn't a complete guide to Windows PowerShell scripts, but it does provide an excellent start. Not only will you discover when to use scripts, but you'll also see a new feature, the PowerShell Integrated Scripting Environment (ISE). PowerShell ISE is a special kind of editor that makes working with scripts significantly easier than ever before.

The chapter also provides you with an example script so that you can see how one is created. As part of the scripting section, you'll discover how to run scripts directly at the PS prompt. You'll also receive information about some scripting essentials, such as setting a company policy about the use of scripts so that everyone uses them in the same way and in a secure environment. Even though Windows PowerShell does provide significantly more security than the old command prompt, it's still possible to use scripts in a way that opens security holes and could cause problems for your system.

## UNDERSTANDING WHEN TO USE SCRIPTS

Windows PowerShell scripts are quite powerful, so you can create complete applications with them if desired. In fact, there are a number of times when using scripts is better than any other automation technique. Here are some times when you might want to use a script in place of other automation, such as cmdlets:

- **Experimental code:** Using scripts is a good way to test experimental code. You can modify scripts with greater ease, which makes experimentation much faster. Scripts also provide nearly instant results, so you don't spend as much time between iterations.
- **Short-use code:** Sometimes you need to perform a task automatically, but only for a short time. For example, you might need to perform some changes to files after upgrading your system. The files only need to be updated once, but there are far too many files to update manually, so you create a script to perform the task.
- **Flexible applications:** You may create an application that will require tweaks from time to time. Recompiling a cmdlet or application is a painful process that you won't want to perform continuously because it's time-consuming. Scripts are relatively easy to modify, so they make a great choice for applications that require modifications from time to time to remain useful.
- **Less-skilled developer:** Scripts are a good way for the less-skilled developer to build proficiency.

However, scripts aren't a perfect solution. You'll encounter times when scripts are definitely the wrong way to solve a problem. The following list describes some of the times you want to avoid scripts:

- **User editing:** If you create a script, then place it somewhere on the network, and use it to perform user tasks, you can be sure that some user will look at the code. In fact, users may be tempted to play with your code, just to see what will happen when they do. Some users are like that — they like to play with things they really shouldn't.
- **Speed:** Because scripts are interpreted, they aren't a good solution when you need the code to run quickly. The compiled nature of cmdlets makes them a better choice when speed is essential.
- **Low-level access:** Scripts can access nearly all, but not quite all, of the .NET Framework. You definitely can't use a script to access code that requires P/Invoke. Cmdlets or full-fledged applications are a better choice when you need low-level access to Windows functionality.

## USING THE POWERSHELL ISE

The Windows PowerShell ISE is a new addition to Windows 7 that makes life significantly easier for the developer. When you open this application, you see a window with three panes, as shown in Figure 21-1. The panes from top to bottom are:

➤ **Script:** You use the Script pane to write your script. Later you can save this file to disk with a .PS1 extension and execute it from the PS prompt. This is also the pane where you perform debugging of your script. You can read more about the debugging features of Windows PowerShell in the "Using the PowerShell ISE Debugger" section of this chapter.

➤ **Output:** The Output pane displays the results of any script you execute in the Script pane or any command you type in the Command pane. It acts as the output portion of the normal PS prompt.

➤ **Command:** Whenever you have a question about how a command works, type it in the Command pane to try it out. You can then copy and paste the completed command from the Command pane to the Script pane. It's also possible to use the Command pane to obtain help. Simply use the Help command with whatever command you want to use to obtain the required help (see the "Working with the Online Help" section of Chapter 20 for details on using the Help command).

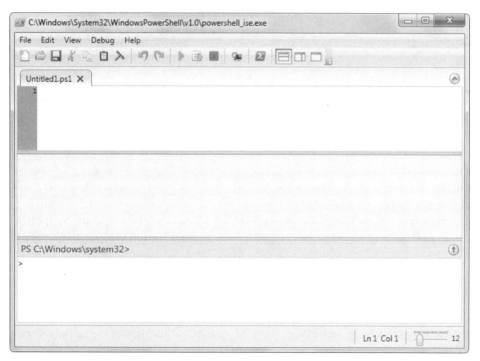

**FIGURE 21-1:** The Windows PowerShell ISE is a scripting editor that makes life easier for the developer.

To see how these various panes work together, place your cursor in the bottom pane. Type **Dir *.DLL**. Notice that the PowerShell ISE color-codes the text as you type it. (Sometimes the color coding is a bit hard to see, but Dir should appear in blue and *.DLL should appear in purple.) Press Enter. The result of the command appears in the Output pane, as shown in Figure 21-2.

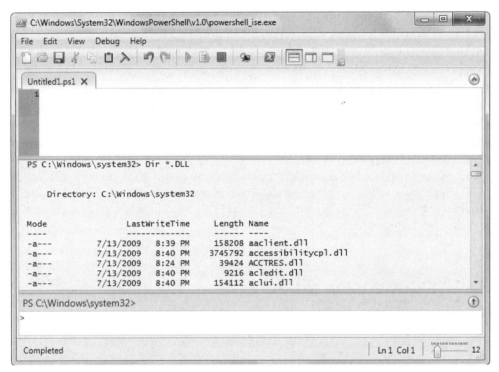

**FIGURE 21-2:** Typing a command and pressing Enter in the Command pane produces results in the Output pane.

As you can see, the command appears at the top of the Output pane, so you can copy and paste it should you desire to do so. The results of the command appear afterward, just as if you were looking at the PS prompt instead of the PowerShell ISE. To copy a command, highlight its entry in the Output pane, choose Edit ➪ Copy or press Ctrl+C, place the cursor in the Script pane, and then choose Edit ➪ Paste or press Ctrl+V. You now have a tested version of the command in the Script pane, so you know that the command should work.

At this point, you no longer need the text in the Output pane. Click Clear Output Pane on the toolbar (the icon looks like a little squeegee). You can also type **Cls** in the Command pane and press Enter to clear the Output pane.

The Script pane contains a single command. You pasted it there from the Output pane, so you're pretty sure it will work fine, but you don't know that for certain. Click Run Script on the toolbar or press F5. The results of running the script appear in the Output pane, as shown in Figure 21-3.

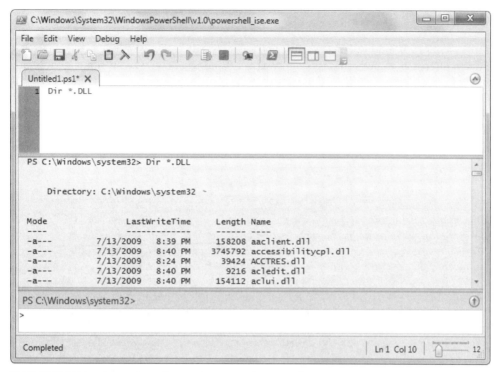

**FIGURE 21-3:** Running scripts also produces results in the Output pane.

Your first script is ready to go now, so it's time to save it. Choose File ⇨ Save or press Ctrl+S. You'll see a Save As dialog box. The default save directory is the Libraries folder on your machine. Type **ShowDLLs** in the File Name field and press Enter. The PowerShell ISE saves the new script to the hard drive for you.

 *As with any other Windows file, a Windows PowerShell script file can contain spaces in the name. However, adding a space tends to make the script a lot harder to use at the PS prompt. Generally, you want to avoid spaces in the filename unless you have an overwhelming reason to add one.*

It's possible to double-check the script you just created by opening a PS prompt and running the script. To open a PS prompt, click Start PowerShell.EXE on the toolbar. You'll see a PS prompt open. The instructions in the "Running the Script at the PS Prompt" section of this chapter describe how to run a script.

## WRITING A BASIC SCRIPT

As with most scripts, a Windows PowerShell script is simply a series of executable statements that the system interprets to perform tasks. However, a Windows PowerShell script is built on a combination of the C# language, special objects that the Windows PowerShell developers create for you, the .NET Framework, and any special cmdlets that you create. You can find a great overview of the language on the ars technica Website at `http://arstechnica.com/guides/other/msh.ars`. If you want the short version, check out the basic list of elements on Arul Kumaravel's WebLog at `http://blogs.msdn.com/arulk/archive/2005/02/24/379732.aspx`.

> *This chapter isn't going to provide a description of the Windows PowerShell scripting language or its programming elements, but will show you how to use them to create a script. Microsoft provided downloadable documentation for Windows PowerShell 1.0 and you can still get it at* `http://www.microsoft.com/downloads/details.aspx?FamilyId=B4720B00-9A66-430F-BD56-EC48BFCA154F`. *Windows PowerShell 2.0 uses online documentation. The authoritative resource for the Windows PowerShell scripting language is the current documentation available at* `http://technet.microsoft.com/library/bb978526.aspx`. *If you have questions you can't find answers to, try the newsgroup at* `http://www.microsoft.com/communities/newsgroups/list/en-us/default.aspx?dg=microsoft.public.windows.powershell`. *The blog at* `http://blogs.msdn.com/b/powershell/` *will keep you updated on the latest developments. You can find a host of development tools at* `http://msdn.microsoft.com/library/aa830112.aspx`. *When all else fails, try the main Windows PowerShell site at* `http://technet.microsoft.com/scriptcenter/powershell.asp`.

Script files are text files with a `.PS1` (PowerShell) file extension. In the past, if you tried to edit a file with a `.PS1` extension, the system would display an error message. You had to rename the file to have a `.TXT` or other editable file extension and perform any required changes. Microsoft has changed the rules in Windows 7. It's now possible to open a `.PS1` file directly without any trouble. A PowerShell script can also use these file extensions:

- **.PSM1:** The PowerShell Module file contains part of a script. Unlike a `.PS1` file, which contains a whole script or the main module for a script, a `.PSM1` file contains functions or other entities that you use as part of a number of scripts.

- **.PSD1:** The PowerShell Data file doesn't contain any script code. Instead, it contains translated strings that are used as data for a script. One use for these data files is to allow internationalization of your scripts to support multiple languages. See the article at `http://technet.microsoft.com/library/dd315390.aspx` for details on this process (along with a sample script).

➤ **.PS1XML:** The PowerShell XML file doesn't contain script code, but it can affect how script code executes. For example, you can use this sort of file to define how scripts format data for display on-screen (see the article at http://technet.microsoft.com/library/dd315396.aspx). These XML files can also control how PowerShell works with data types (see the article at http://technet.microsoft.com/library/dd347581.aspx).

A Windows PowerShell script can include a wealth of features. As with any command line script, you can include any command that the command interpreter supports, as well as calls to utilities. In addition, Windows PowerShell scripts support all the same statements that full-fledged programming languages do, including both conditional and looping statements. Unlike JavaScript, Windows PowerShell scripts also include the concept of data type.

> *Windows PowerShell scripting has taken off. You can find sample scripts on many Websites. However, some samples are better than others. The first place you should look for sample scripts is on the Microsoft site at* http://gallery.technet.microsoft.com/scriptcenter/. *You'll also want to check out the community scripts at* http://www.powershellcommunity.org/Scripts.aspx. *The blog site at* http://pshscripts.blogspot.com/ *provides some excellent scripts, and the third-party scripting site at* http://psobject.codeplex.com/ *is an excellent place to look as well.*

The "Using the PowerShell ISE" section of this chapter shows a truly basic scripting example. The example in the present section looks at something a little more advanced and practical. In this case, the example demonstrates how to map a network drive using a script. It's something that developers and administrators alike need to do on a regular basis. Listing 21-1 shows the code you need for this example.

**LISTING 21-1:** Mapping a network drive with Windows PowerShell

Available for download on Wrox.com

```
#Input arguments Local Drive and Network UNC location.
Param ($DriveLtr = "", $UNCName = "")

# Detect the correct number of input arguments.
if (($DriveLtr -eq "") -or ($UNCName -eq ""))
{
   # Detect a request for command line help.
   if ($DriveLtr -eq "/?")
   {
      # Display the help information
      [system.console]::Out.WriteLine(
         "Usage: MapNetwork <letter> <UNC target>")

      # Exit the script and provide an error level of 1 to
```

*continues*

**LISTING 21-1** *(continued)*

```
      # indicate a help request.
      return(1)
   }
   else
   {
      # Ask whether the user wants to continue.
      [system.console]::Out.WriteLine(
         "No input provided! Provide it interactively? [Y | N]")
      $Answer = [system.console]::In.ReadLine()

      # If the user doesn't want to continue, display help and exit.
      # Use an exit code of 2 to indicate a data entry error.
      if ($Answer -eq "N")
      {
         [system.console]::Out.WriteLine(
            "Usage: MapNetwork <letter> <UNC target>")
         return(2)
      }

      # Input the drive letter.
         [system.console]::Out.WriteLine(
            "Type the local drive letter (X:).");
         $DriveLtr = [system.console]::In.ReadLine();

      # Input the UNC drive on the remote machine.
         [system.console]::Out.WriteLine(
            "Type the UNC location (\\MyServer\MyDrive).");
         $UNCName = [system.console]::In.ReadLine();
   }
}

# Define the network object used to map the drive.
$oNetwork = new-object -COM WScript.Network

# Attempt to create the connection.
Trap [Exception]
{
   # Display an error when the task fails.
   [system.console]::Out.WriteLine("Couldn't map the drive!")
   [system.console]::Out.WriteLine($_.Exception.Message)
   return 3
}

# Perform the drive mapping function.
$oNetwork.MapNetworkDrive($DriveLtr, $UNCName);
```

You should notice a few things about this example. It uses a unique scripting language to perform tasks such as creating an if...then structure. The example uses the pound sign (#) for comments. In addition, you might notice the odd method of performing logical operations with -eq (for equals) and -or (for or). You'll find a complete list of these logical operators in the Windows PowerShell documentation. All variables in a Windows PowerShell script must begin with the dollar sign ($), as shown in the example.

For anyone who has worked with the .NET Framework, the `[system.console]::Out.WriteLine()` method call will look familiar, and it's precisely that — familiar. The example makes a call to the console class of the system namespace. The console class contains an `Out` property that's actually a container for the standard output stream. The stream object includes the `WriteLine()` method that the example uses to output text. You can use any .NET Framework feature in precisely the same way, which means that Windows PowerShell has a very large list of language features from which to choose.

One feature that differs from standard .NET application coding is the lack of a `try...catch` structure. When working with Windows PowerShell, you use a `Trap` instead. The `Trap` relies on the .NET Framework exception classes. Once you set a trap, it remains in effect until it either goes out of scope or you set another trap. To access the data that the exception provides, you use the `$_.Exception` property, followed by the exception property that you want to access. The example simply displays the `Message` property so that the user knows what happened during an attempted drive mapping.

Windows PowerShell can use COM objects. In this example, the script creates the `WScript.Network` object. To perform this task in Windows PowerShell, you must use the `New-Object` command and call it with the `-COM` command line switch. The result is the `$oNetwork` object that calls the `MapNetworkDrive()` method. The `Trap` statement that appears before the `MapNetworkDrive()` method call provides error trapping in this case.

*Now that you have a taste for Windows PowerShell scripting, you might want to obtain some additional tutorial type resources. The best place to start is the tutorial at* http://xahlee.org/powershell/index.html. *In addition, you can use an older series of articles about Windows PowerShell scripting on ComputerWorld.* The four-part scripting series begins at http://www.computerworld.com/softwaretopics/os/windows/story/0,10801,107669,00.html. *The second part is at* http://www.computerworld.com/softwaretopics/software/story/0,10801,107673,00.html. *You'll find the third part at* http://www.computerworld.com/softwaretopics/os/windows/story/0,10801,107681,00.html. *The fourth part is at* http://www.computerworld.com/softwaretopics/os/windows/story/0,10801,107683,00.html.

## PERFORMING SCRIPT TESTING

You're ready to try a script. However, running a script with Windows PowerShell is nothing like running a script under the old command line. The following sections describe how to work with Windows PowerShell scripts.

## Using the PowerShell ISE Debugger

The easiest way to run the script shown in Listing 21-1 is to load it in the PowerShell ISE. You can then click Run Script on the toolbar or press F5, and the script will start. However, the moment you try to execute the script, you get the nasty message shown in Figure 21-4. That's because you're no longer executing simple commands as you did with the simple script in the "Using the PowerShell ISE" section of this chapter.

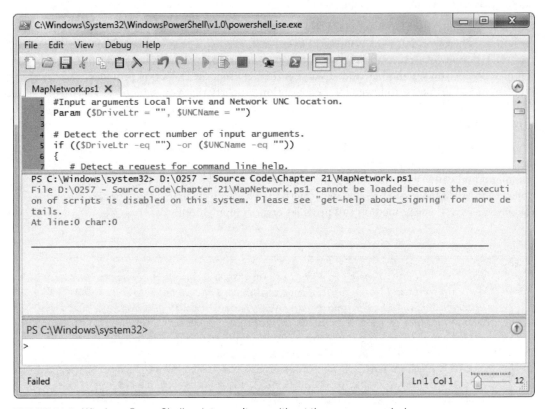

**FIGURE 21-4:** Windows PowerShell scripts won't run without the proper permission.

You have to make a decision now. The issue is what level of script to allow on your system. Before you disable the protection that Windows PowerShell provides, consider using the security to your advantage and set the system to execute only signed scripts. To set the system to use any script, type **Set-ExecutionPolicy Unrestricted** in the Command pane and press Enter (see the "Defining a Company Policy for Scripts" section of this chapter for a description of the various policies you can use for scripts). You'll see an Execution Policy Change dialog box that warns about the consequences of your action. Click Yes and you'll see another error message, as shown in Figure 21-5.

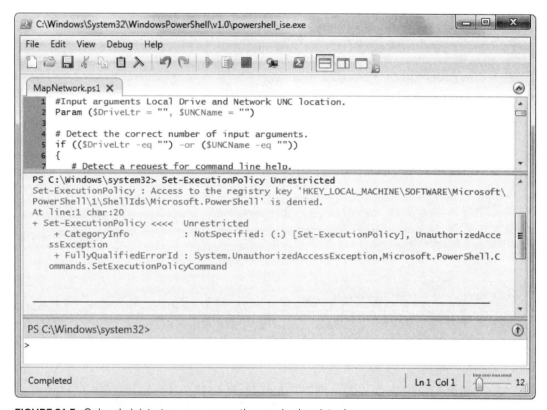

**FIGURE 21-5:** Only administrators can access the required registry key.

Before you start pulling your hair out, consider the fact that you don't want just anyone to change the script permissions on your system, and that Windows 7 automatically logs you in as a standard user. Close the copy of PowerShell ISE you have running right now. Open a new copy with administrator privileges by right-clicking the Windows PowerShell ISE icon and choosing Run As Administrator from the Context menu. The new PowerShell ISE window title will show that you've opened it with administrator privileges. Reopen your script file, type **Set-ExecutionPolicy Unrestricted** and press Enter in the Command pane, and click Run Script again. You'll immediately run into another problem, as shown in Figure 21-6.

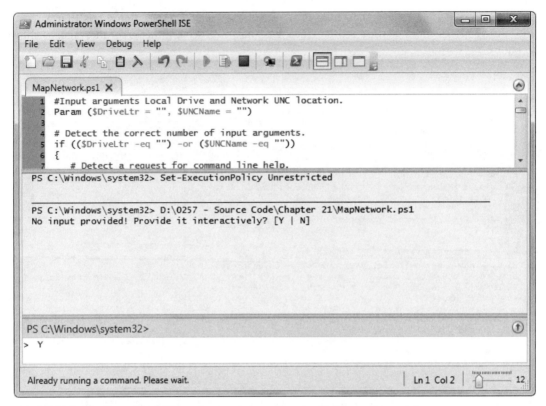

**FIGURE 21-6:** The PowerShell ISE environment doesn't work with interactive scripts.

There isn't any way to respond to the interactive script. You can't type the required **Y** in the Command pane — PowerShell ISE displays the message shown in the status bar of Figure 21-6. Because the interpreter is already processing a command, you can't enter a new one (to answer the question in the Output pane). There also isn't any way to enter this information in the Output pane. Click Stop Execution or press Ctrl+Break. You'll find that PowerShell ISE is now non-functional. In short, the debugger doesn't work for every situation without some help. To fix the debugger, add the following code immediately after the Param ($DriveLtr = "", $UNCName = "") line from Listing 21-1:

```
# Create test arguments when debugging.
if ($Debugging)
{
    $DriveLtr = "Z:"
    $UNCName = "\\Winserver\Drive_D"
}
```

You'll need to change the $UNCName variable to match a location on your network. For this example, the test system has access to a server named Winserver that exposes a resource called Drive_D. Let's test the example again. In the Command pane, type **$Debugging = $True** and press Enter. Place your cursor on the if ($Debugging) line. Press F9 or choose Debug ➪ Toggle Breakpoint. You'll see the line highlighted in red. Now click Run Script or press F5. The debugger will stop at the desired line, as shown in Figure 21-7. Notice that the Output pane shows that the debugger has detected a break point.

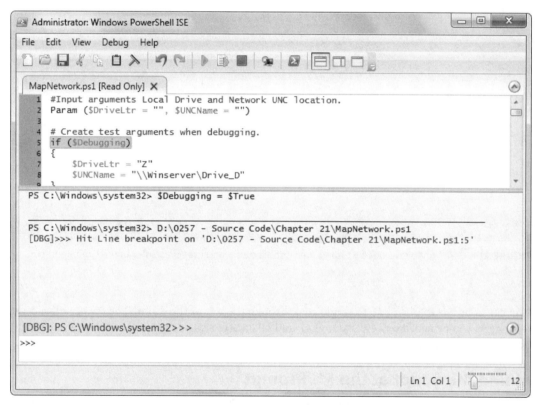

**FIGURE 21-7:** The debugger will work now that you've added a little code for it.

Press F10 to single-step to the next line of the code. Because you've defined a variable called $Debugging, the code defines test values to the **$DriveLtr** and **$UNCName** variables. To see the value of these variables after the assignment, type $DriveLtr and press Enter in the Command pane, followed by typing $UNCName and pressing Enter in the Command pane. Your results should be similar to the ones shown in the Output pane in Figure 21-8 for the example program.

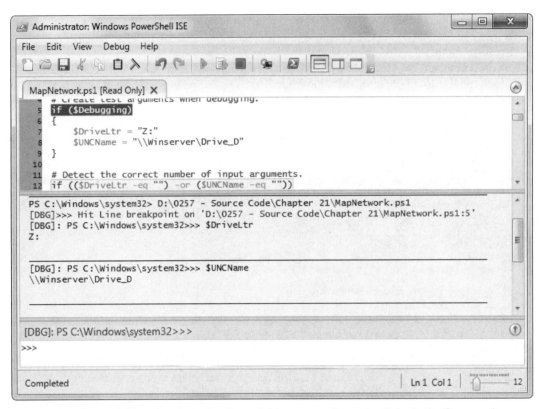

**FIGURE 21-8:** See variable values by typing the variable name and pressing Enter in the Command pane.

You can continue to press F10 to single-step through the rest of the script. The script will succeed (as long as you provided correct $DriveLtr and $UNCName variable values), and your system will have a new mapped drive.

## Running the Script at the PS Prompt

At some point, you'll want to test the script in Listing 21-1 at the PS prompt. Of course, you'll first want to disconnect the mapped drive you created with the debugger, by right-clicking its entry in Windows Explorer and choosing Disconnect from the Context menu.

Accessing the script is going to be a little different at the command prompt. Use the CD command to get to the folder that contains the script. Type **./MapNetwork** and press Enter. The script will tell you that it requires input. You can add the required input and map a drive.

The script also accepts the input arguments from the command line. Try the command line arguments by typing **./MapNetwork Z: \\WinServer\Drive_D** (where \\WinServer\DriveD is a drive resource on your system) and pressing Enter. Try entering incorrect arguments, and you'll find that the exception handling works fine, too. The one thing you should notice is that the debugging code added in the "Using the PowerShell ISE Debugger" section doesn't interfere with the normal operation of the script from the PS prompt.

## Defining a Company Policy for Scripts

You might think that the default Windows PowerShell setup of not running any scripts is terrible. However, consider how many users have downloaded scripts from the Internet and run them without having any idea of what the script could do or even that they were downloading a script. It's important to consider how scripts running amok on user machines create infections that waste everyone's time and energy, not to mention damaging both systems and data. In fact, you might have been involved in cleaning up such a problem at some time in the past. Consequently, you need to weigh this factor against the few minutes required to sign your script so the system knows that it's safe to execute. Most companies today have a zero-tolerance policy regarding executable content because it's become too expensive to continually clean infected machines.

Generally speaking, you should maintain the default Restricted policy of not running any scripts for all the users on the network. If users don't run scripts, you don't need to worry about them loading something that will destroy their machines even accidentally.

When you must allow the user to run scripts, set the policy to AllSigned. At the AllSigned level, the user can't run a script unless someone you trust signs it. You could set the policy so that only scripts signed by someone at your company run on the user machine. Using only signed scripts on user machines ensures that you know who created the script and understand the potential pitfalls of using the script.

Administrators and developers will likely want to share code from time to time. You should still ensure that someone has signed the code. Consequently, setting the policy to RemoteSigned could make sense for those who have more knowledge about Windows and need to execute code that someone else created. In most cases, you want to use this level with care because anyone can send you a signed script and your system will execute it, even if the individual used fake credentials.

The final policy level is Unrestricted. Using the Unrestricted level is returning to previous versions of Windows where you don't have any protection. Windows PowerShell will allow you to shoot yourself in the foot, but why do it? Always keep your system safe by using signed code.

## MOVING YOUR APPLICATIONS TO WINDOWS 7

This chapter has examined Windows PowerShell scripts. Unlike batch files and command line scripts, PS scripts have the whole .NET Framework at their disposal, making it possible to create complex automation scenarios. Many developers will be able to use the scripting features of Windows PowerShell to create successful applications without resorting to working with cmdlets, which are considerably harder to create. The one thing you should take away from this chapter is that scripts are quite powerful and you shouldn't ignore them simply because some people associate scripts with user-level programming.

Now that you know a little bit more about scripting with Windows PowerShell, take some time to create a few scripts of your own. Working with scripts that display information is probably the safest option for the first few scripts. For example, try creating a script that lists all the mapped drives on a system in tabular format. Another good script to create would be one that lists all the Run and RunOnce key entries in the registry for the HKEY_CURRENT_USER\Software\Microsoft\Windows\CurrentVersion and HKEY_LOCAL_MACHINE\SOFTWARE\Microsoft\Windows\CurrentVersion keys. Remember from Chapter 20 that the Dir command does a lot more in Windows PowerShell than it does at the command line.

Scripts are extremely interesting, but they can have problems. A user can easily change a script. Because scripts are interpreted at run time, they can run more slowly than you'd like. Cmdlets can solve these problems, but they're harder to put together than scripts. Chapter 22 shows how to work with cmdlets. After you finish this chapter, you can better decide how you'd like to automate tasks in Windows PowerShell. Most developers end up using a combination of scripts and cmdlets because each form of automation has advantages.

# 22
# Creating Cmdlets

**WHAT'S IN THIS CHAPTER?**

- Using cmdlets effectively
- Using the Make-Shell utility to create a shell extension
- Creating a basic cmdlet

Scripting works fine for a wide variety of needs. However, just as an interpreted language doesn't always provide what's needed for a successful application, scripts sometimes fall short, too. When this occurs, you really need to have something compiled, which in Windows PowerShell is a cmdlet. There's a balance you must consider when deciding between scripts and cmdlets, so that's the first topic this chapter covers.

Writing a basic cmdlet isn't much different from writing a typical application. There are some special rules you need to follow, however, and this chapter discusses them. The biggest change you'll notice is that cmdlets aren't directly usable from the command line. You must make them part of the Windows PowerShell shell in order to use them, which requires the use of a special utility. This chapter discusses the entire process for creating and using a cmdlet successfully in Windows PowerShell.

## UNDERSTANDING WHEN TO USE CMDLETS

Cmdlets have some significant advantages over scripts. They're the best solution for many practical needs. The following list describes some of the best uses for cmdlets. Of course, you'll probably be able to come up with a few of your own reasons for using them as well.

- **Application interfaces:** Although there aren't a lot of applications that currently rely on cmdlets, there are some out there that do. For example, you'll find that Microsoft Exchange comes with its own set of cmdlets. You can learn more about these cmdlets and how Microsoft Exchange uses them at http://technet.microsoft.com/library/bb123778.aspx.

- **Complex shell extensions:** A cmdlet has access to far more than a script does. For example, it's possible to use P/Invoke with a cmdlet, so you can access Windows features that don't currently appear as part of the .NET Framework or a COM interface. Because you have better access to every bit of Windows functionality, you can create cmdlets that do far more than a script can.

- **Enhanced security:** It's very hard to secure a script because scripts are written using simple text. The compiled nature of cmdlets makes it far less likely that someone can tamper with them. This added security makes your system more secure as a whole and reduces the risk to anyone using the PS prompt enhancements you create.

- **Specialized security:** A script uses the default Authorization Manager (read about the Authorization Manager at http://technet.microsoft.com/library/cc726036.aspx), which means that you can't control the use of roles with a script. A cmdlet can override the default Authorization Manager, making it possible to create specialized security functionality with a cmdlet.

- **Speed:** Cmdlets are compiled, which means they're ready to run. Generally, a cmdlet will run much faster than a script of the same functionality.

- **Ease of access:** Cmdlets are part of the Windows PowerShell shell, which means you invoke them using precisely the same techniques you use for any other command at the PS prompt. This built-in nature of cmdlets makes them easier for most users to understand.

- **Resource usage:** Although it isn't always the case that cmdlets use fewer resources to perform a given task than a similar script, it's generally true. At the very least, a cmdlet will use the same number of resources as a corresponding script, so from a resource perspective you have nothing to lose by working with a cmdlet instead of a script.

It's important not to overestimate the value of cmdlets. There are times when a cmdlet is overkill and will cost valuable time when time counts the most. In addition, not everyone has the skill required to create a good cmdlet. The following list describes some of the issues that you should consider when deciding to create a cmdlet:

- **Incredible complexity:** When compared with a script, creating a cmdlet is significantly more complex. Not only do you have to compile cmdlets, but then you must also make them part of the Windows PowerShell shell. Testing is more involved as well, with a longer test, fix, and rebuild cycle than scripts enjoy.

- **Distribution issues:** A cmdlet is part of the shell, so you need to distribute a new shell to distribute a cmdlet or you must rely on complex build scenarios to install the cmdlet on the user's machine. Meanwhile, a script requires that you send a file to someone with a few added instructions on proper usage.

- **Larger investment:** The complexity of a cmdlet is only one component that contributes toward a larger investment. Creating a cmdlet requires more time, more intensive testing, and a longer test, fix, compile cycle. Plan on a cmdlet costing quite a bit more to develop than a script.

➤ **Skill level:** There are many people who can create a script. A power user can easily create one, as can an administrator. However, cmdlets require a skilled developer to create. Even a novice developer will experience problems trying to jump all the hurdles presented by a cmdlet. In short, you have to leave cmdlets to the professionals.

## CREATING A SHELL EXTENSION WITH THE MAKE-SHELL UTILITY

You can create extended command shells for the Windows PowerShell environment. Essentially, you create a new version of the Windows PowerShell executable with your code added as part of the executable. The `Make-Shell` utility helps you create these extensions. You use this utility to add the cmdlets you create to the shell so that you can execute them directly from the command line as you would any other command. The `Make-Shell` utility always creates an executable file as output. This utility uses the following syntax:

```
make-shell
    -out n.exe
    -namespace ns
    [ -lib libdirectory1[,libdirectory2,..] ]
    [ -reference ca1.dll[,ca2.dll,...] ]
    [ -formatdata fd1.format.ps1xml[,fd2.format.ps1xml,...] ]
    [ -typedata td1.type.ps1xml[,td2.type.ps1xml,...] ]
    [ -source c1.cs [,c2.cs,...] ]
    [ -authorizationmanager authorizationManagerType ]
    [ -win32icon i.ico ]
    [ -initscript p.ps1 ]
    [ -builtinscript s1.ps1[,s2.ps1,...] ]
    [ -resource resourcefile.txt ]
    [ -cscflags cscFlags ]
    [ -verbose]
    [ -? | -help ]
```

*The `Make-Shell` utility used to appear as part of the Windows PowerShell installation program. However, Microsoft moved this utility to the Windows SDK because most users will create scripts for Windows PowerShell, rather than create their own shell. The `Make-Shell` utility (`Make-Shell.EXE`) appears as part of the Windows SDK in the \Program Files\Microsoft SDKs\Windows\v7.1\ Bin folder. The "Obtaining the Windows 7 SDK" section of Chapter 7 tells you how to obtain and configure the Windows 7 SDK for your system.*

The following list describes each of the command line arguments:

➤ **-out n.exe:** Specifies the name of the shell that you want to produce. You must specify the path as part of this argument. The `Make-Shell` utility automatically appends .EXE to the filename if you don't specify it. You must provide this command line switch or the `Make-Shell` utility will fail.

➤ **-namespace ns:** Specifies the namespace to use for the `RunspaceConfiguration` table and the `main()` function that the `Make-Shell` utility generates and compiles for you. The `main()` function is the entry point for the executable. You must provide this command line switch or the `Make-Shell` utility will fail.

- **-lib *libdirectory1*[,*libdirectory2*,..]**: Specifies the directories to search for .NET assemblies that your cmdlet requires to run. You don't need to specify this command line switch for assemblies that appear in the Global Assembly Cache (GAC) or in the same directory as the cmdlet's executable. You may need to use this command line switch for any Windows PowerShell assemblies that you reference. Always include this argument for assemblies that you access with the `-reference` command line switch unless the assemblies appear in the GAC. You must also provide directory entries for any assemblies that a main assembly references, but that don't appear in the GAC.

- **-reference *ca1.dll*[,*ca2.dll*,...]**: Specifies the assemblies that you want to include in the shell. Don't include system or .NET Framework assemblies in this list; the `Make-Shell` utility finds these assemblies automatically. Reserve this command line switch for special assemblies that the cmdlet requires to run, that contain the cmdlet code, and that contain resources used by the cmdlet. If you don't include this command line shell, the resulting executable contains only the intrinsic cmdlets (those produced by the Windows PowerShell team). You may specify the references using a full path. Otherwise, use the `-lib` command line switch to provide the path information as needed.

- **-formatdata *fd1.format.mshxml*[,*fd2.format.mshxml*,...]**: Provides a comma-separated list of format data to include as part of the shell. If you don't include this command line switch, then the resulting shell contains only the intrinsic format data (that produced by the Windows PowerShell team). The current shell provides formatting for text and serialized XML.

- **-typedata *td1.type.mshxml*[,*td2.type.mshxml*,...]**: Provides a comma-separated list of type data to include as part of the shell. If you don't include this command line switch, then the resulting shell contains only the intrinsic format data (that produced by the Windows PowerShell team).

- **-source *c1.cs* [,*c2.cs*,...]**: Specifies the names of the source files to use to create the shell additions. The source code must appear as C# code. The code can provide any functionality that you want to include at the command line. In addition to the code required to provide the new shell functionality, the code may include an Authorization Manager implementation that overrides the default Authorization Manager. You can also supply the Authorization Manager information (when you want to override the Authorization Manager) using the `-authorizationmanager` command line switch. The code can also include a number of assembly informational declarations, including the overrides in the following list:

    - `AssemblyCompanyAttribute`
    - `AssemblyCopyrightAttribute`
    - `AssemblyFileVersionAttribute`
    - `AssemblyInformationalVersionAttribute`
    - `AssemblyProductAttribute`
    - `AssemblyTrademarkAttribute`

- **-authorizationmanager *authorizationManagerType*:** Defines the type in a source code (C#) file or a compiled assembly that the new shell should use as an Authorization Manager. The new shell will use the default Authorization Manager when you don't specify this command line switch or include an Authorization Manager as part of the shell source code. When you do specify a new type, you must include the full type name, including any required namespaces.

- **-win32icon *i.ico*:** Specifies the name of the file containing the icon you want to use for the new shell. (The icon file can contain multiple icons, one for each major resolution, if desired.) The new shell will use the icon provided as part of the cmdlet assembly (if any) when you don't specify this command line switch. If the Make-Shell utility can't find any icon, it uses a generic internal icon.

- **-initscript *p.PS*:** Specifies the startup profile for the new shell. The Make-Shell utility doesn't verify this file in any way. Consequently, a faulty profile can prevent the new shell from running. A user can always override the default shell profile that you provide using the -NoProfile command line switch for the PS utility. Therefore, you shouldn't assume that the profile you provide is absolute, even when the profile works as anticipated.

- **-builtinscript *s1.PS[,s2.PS,...]*:** Defines a list of built-in scripts for the shell. The new shell discovers these scripts before it discovers scripts in the path. The scripts you provide as part of this command line switch are absolute; the user can't change them. The Make-Shell utility doesn't validate the scripts in any way. Consequently, even though an errant script won't keep the new shell from running, it will cause problems when the user attempts to run the script.

- **-resource *resourcefile.txt*:** Specifies a text file containing the resources that the shell uses. The resource file must contain a minimum of two resources. You must name the first resource ShellHelp. This resource contains the help text that the user sees when using the -help command line argument. The ShellHelp resource doesn't affect the output of the Help command used to display help for a particular shell command. The second resource is ShellBanner. This resource contains the text and copyright information that appear when the user invokes the shell in interactive mode. The new shell uses a generic help and banner when you don't provide these overrides.

- **-cscflags *cscFlags*:** Determines which flags the C# compiler (CSC.EXE located in the .NET Framework directory) receives as part of compiling the new shell. The Make-Shell passes these command line switches to the compiler unchanged. Always surround this command line switch with quotes. Otherwise, the Make-Shell utility may not pass all the C# compiler command line switches and the compilation process will fail.

- **-verbose:** Displays detailed information during the shell creation process. The Make-Shell utility created the detailed information, so the output won't include any details of the C# compilation. If you want to see details of the C# compilation as well, you need to include additional command line switches for the C# compiler. (This command line switch is undocumented and Microsoft may remove it in future versions of the Make-Shell utility.)

## WRITING A BASIC CMDLET

A cmdlet can literally do anything you want it to do. If you want to create a cmdlet to project the fuel used to travel to the moon, you can do it. A cmdlet could open a copy of your browser and display a particular site for you, or it could open an application and load the files you specify for you. The only thing a cmdlet won't do is display a graphical interface directly. However, even in this case you still have some flexibility because you can display a graphical interface indirectly. You can create an external module to display graphics or spawn a process to create the graphical interface. Generally speaking, however, cmdlets are more utilitarian than fanciful. The example in the sections that follow is a good illustration. In this case, the cmdlet does something simple — it reverses the content of a string and outputs it backward.

### Creating the Reverse-String.CS Example File

Unlike many other projects in this book, all you really need to create a cmdlet is a C# file. You don't need to create a project unless you really want to do so. This example doesn't even require one of the newer versions of the .NET Framework. Any version of the .NET Framework 2.0 or above will work just fine. With all this in mind, open any version of Visual Studio 2005 or above (the book uses Visual Studio 2010 as it has for all the examples so far) and choose File ➪ New ➪ File to display the New File dialog shown in Figure 22-1. Select the Visual C# Class template and click OK. Visual Studio will create a new C# class file for you.

**FIGURE 22-1:** Create a new C# file to hold your cmdlet code.

At this point, save the file as Reverse-String.CS. You'll want to change the class name to ReverseStringCommand. The class doesn't require any internal references. In addition, you'll need to add the following using statements (Visual Studio automatically adds using System; for you):

```
using System.Text;
using System.Management.Automation;
```

You don't have to add these references, but doing so makes your code considerably easier to read. It's possible to write a cmdlet using just two namespaces, System and System.Management.Automation. The first provides basic .NET Framework functionality, while the second provides access to the special features you need for creating a cmdlet. The example includes the System.Text namespace to provide access to the text manipulation features of the .NET Framework.

## Writing the Reverse-String.CS Example Code

It's important to note that a cmdlet isn't supposed to be a full application in most cases, and it's never a stand-alone executable. You won't be using the built-in compiler, nor will you use any of the other features of Visual Studio for the most part. Microsoft doesn't supply any special cmdlet templates to make creating a cmdlet easier. Theoretically, you can also write the code for a cmdlet using a simple editor such as Notepad. Of course, if you use Notepad you won't have the benefit of the Visual Studio editor features. Listing 22-1 shows an example of the code for a cmdlet.

**LISTING 22-1:** Creating a cmdlet for the Microsoft command shell

Available for download on Wrox.com

```
// Define a Cmdlet class to hold the code for the new cmdlet.
// This class will let the user reverse a string on-screen.
[Cmdlet("reverse", "string")]
public class ReverseStringCommand : Cmdlet
{
   // Create a private variable to hold the string the user passes.
   private string _initString;

   // Create a property to request the string from the user.
   [Parameter(Mandatory=true, Position=0)]
   public string InitString
   {
      get
      {
         return _initString;
      }
      set
      {
         if (value.Length == 0)
            _initString = "Empty";
         else
            _initString = value;
      }
   }
```

*continues*

**LISTING 22-1** *(continued)*

```
    // Perform the string reversal and return a value.
    protected override void ProcessRecord()
    {
        // Create a variable to hold the reversed results.
        StringBuilder Output = new StringBuilder();

        // Create a Char array to hold the characters.
        Char[] Characters = _initString.ToCharArray();

        // Reverse the String.
        for (Int32 Count = Characters.Length - 1; Count >= 0; Count--)
            Output.Append(Characters[Count]);

        // Output the result.
        WriteObject(Output.ToString());
    }
}
```

Every cmdlet must include the `[Cmdlet]` attribute, which is written as `[Cmdlet("reverse", "string")]` for this example. In this case, the attribute includes just the cmdlet name, `reverse-string` (the dash between words is supplied automatically — you provide each term for the cmdlet name as a separate string). When you type this value at the command line using the new shell, you'll execute the `reverse-string` cmdlet. The name of the class comes next. You can use any name you want, but using something close to the name of the cmdlet usually works best. You must inherit the `Cmdlet` class as part of creating a cmdlet, as shown in the example.

You don't have to include custom parameters with your cmdlet, but most cmdlets will require one or more parameters. This cmdlet includes one parameter named `InitString`. As shown in the code, it's good coding practice to define a parameter that relies on a local `private` variable. The code places the `public` input from the user into the `private` variable after testing it for any problems. In this case, the `InitString` parameter (actually a C# property) places the value in the private variable `_initString` only after checking to verify the input is meaningful. If the input isn't meaningful, then the `set()` method automatically creates a default value.

To make this property visible at the command line, you must include the `[Parameter]` attribute. The arguments shown are optional. These arguments tell the command line that it must display this parameter first (`Position=0`) and that the user must provide a value (`Mandatory=true`).

Every cmdlet has three opportunities to work with the data the user provides at the command prompt. The following list describes each of these opportunities.

➤ **BeginProcessing():** Lets you modify the data before the system sees it. It's also possible to perform any required startup tasks in this method, such as creating objects you need. Normally, you won't perform any data manipulation in this method.

➤ **ProcessRecord():** Performs the main processing tasks. This is the heart of the cmdlet, where all the data manipulation normally occurs. You'll always override this method to perform processing within the cmdlet.

➤ **EndProcess():** Performs any shutdown tasks for the cmdlet, such as releasing objects you no longer need. This part of the cmdlet can also output any post-processed data, but you won't use it as the main output of the cmdlet.

In all three cases, you must override the existing methods provided by the Cmdlet class, as shown in the listing, to accomplish tasks in your cmdlet. Each of these methods begins with protected override void.

The actual code for this example appears in the ProcessRecord() method. It converts the input data the user provides into a character array. This technique allows the code to access the characters in the input string one at a time. The for loop starts at the end of the character array and adds one character at a time to the StringBuilder object, Output. The result is that the loop reverses the string elements from their original order.

It's important to remember that a cmdlet isn't free-standing code. You don't have access to the console, for example, so you need to rely on the WriteObject() method to output data to the screen. In this case, the example converts Output to a string and sends the value to the display.

## Compiling the Cmdlet Executable

Before you can do anything with the cmdlet, you must create an executable. A cmdlet doesn't use the normal build process, so you can forget about using any of the Visual Studio build features. In fact, you can close your copy of Visual Studio as soon as you finish writing the code.

You can compile a cmdlet using the Make-Shell utility described in the "Creating a Shell Extension with the Make-Shell Utility" section of this chapter, but it's actually easier to perform the compilation as a separate step. Start this section at the Windows PowerShell command line in the folder that holds the C# code you created in the "Writing the Reverse-String.CS Example Code" section.

The first task you need to perform is to create an alias for the C# compiler. This compiler appears in the .NET Framework folder on your machine. You can use any version of the .NET Framework 2.0 or above. Creating an alias makes the compiler accessible by typing a simple command, CSC, at the command line. Here's the command for creating the alias on my system; you'll need to change the directory for CSC.EXE to match your system:

```
Set-Alias CSC C:\Windows\Microsoft.NET\Framework\v2.0.50727\CSC.EXE
```

The compiler must have access to all the libraries required to create the cmdlet. If a library exists in the GAC, then you don't need to worry about creating a reference to it. However, if the library isn't in the GAC, then you must reference it before you can use it. The next step is to create a variable to reference the System.Management.Automation.DLL library used in this example, which resides in the C:\Program Files\Reference Assemblies\Microsoft\WindowsPowerShell\v1.0 folder on my system (you'll need to check where it resides on your system). Complex examples can use multiple libraries, and you can include them all in one variable. Here's the command for creating a reference variable (type the entire command on a single line, even though it appears on more than one line in the book):

```
$ref = "C:\Program Files\Reference Assemblies\Microsoft\WindowsPowerShell\
v1.0\System.Management.Automation.DLL"
```

At this point, you can compile the executable using the C# compiler. You need to tell the compiler what kind of output you want to create, a library (DLL), the name of the input file, the name of the output file, and any libraries that the cmdlet needs, as shown here.

```
CSC /Target:library /Out:Reverse-String.DLL Reverse-String.CS /Reference:$ref
```

The compiler will display a logo as a minimum. If the file contains errors or you miss a library reference, you'll also see error messages. In general, you can now create a new shell with the resulting library. The compiling session will look similar to the one shown in Figure 22-2.

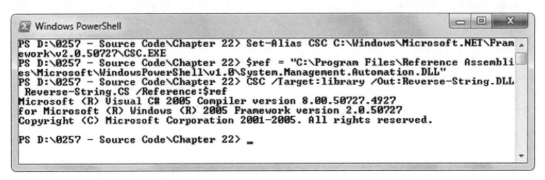

**FIGURE 22-2:** Compile the cmdlet code to create a library.

## Using the Make-Shell Utility to Create the Shell

It's time to create the new shell. You use the Make-Shell utility to perform this task. As with the compiling process, you begin by creating an alias for the Make-Shell utility using the following command. Make sure you change the path to match your system — the command provided in the book shows a typical location. In addition, you need to type the entire command on one line, even though it appears on multiple lines in the book.

```
Set-Alias Make-Shell "C:\Program Files\Microsoft SDKs\Windows\v7.1\Bin\
Make-Shell.EXE"
```

The Make-Shell utility must be able to find any libraries used to create the cmdlet, including the Reverse-String.DLL file. In order to do this, you create a variable holding the library directory like this (again, this command should appear on a single line):

```
$libdir = "C:\Program Files\Reference Assemblies\
Microsoft\WindowsPowerShell\v1.0;D:\0257 - Source Code\Chapter 22"
```

The following command line will create the new shell for this example:

```
Make-Shell -Out NewShell -NS DataCon.Demos -Lib $libdir -Reference Reverse-
String.DLL
```

This command line represents a minimal implementation. You must specify the output filename, the namespace for the shell, and the list of any DLLs you want to add as cmdlets. The output is an executable named `NewShell.EXE`. The new shell creation process should look similar to the one shown in Figure 22-3.

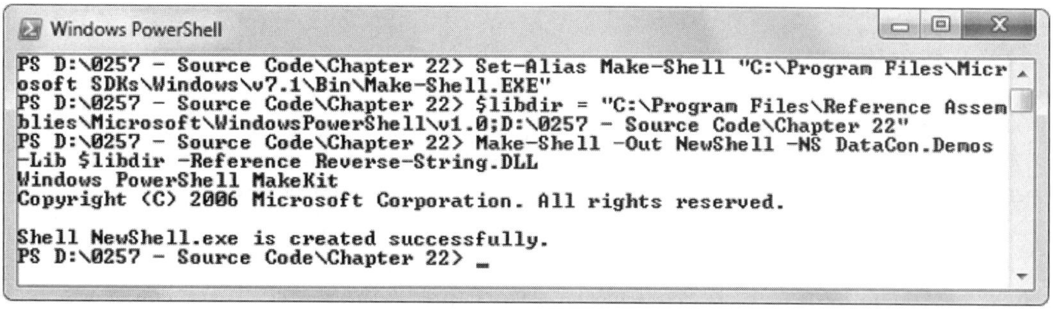

```
PS D:\0257 - Source Code\Chapter 22> Set-Alias Make-Shell "C:\Program Files\Micr
osoft SDKs\Windows\v7.1\Bin\Make-Shell.EXE"
PS D:\0257 - Source Code\Chapter 22> $libdir = "C:\Program Files\Reference Assem
blies\Microsoft\WindowsPowerShell\v1.0;D:\0257 - Source Code\Chapter 22"
PS D:\0257 - Source Code\Chapter 22> Make-Shell -Out NewShell -NS DataCon.Demos
-Lib $libdir -Reference Reverse-String.DLL
Windows PowerShell MakeKit
Copyright (C) 2006 Microsoft Corporation. All rights reserved.

Shell NewShell.exe is created successfully.
PS D:\0257 - Source Code\Chapter 22> _
```

**FIGURE 22-3:** Create a new shell containing the cmdlet you developed.

## Testing the New Shell

A Windows PowerShell shell requires a host of files that the example hasn't created. In fact, you won't normally need to create these files as long as you follow a simple rule — place your new shell in the same folder as the Windows PowerShell implementation. Perform this task by copying `NewShell.EXE` and `Reverse-String.DLL` files to the `\Windows\System32\WindowsPowerShell\v1.0` folder if you're working with a 32-bit system. Because we've created a 32-bit cmdlet and shell, you need to copy these files to the `\Windows\SysWOW64\WindowsPowerShell\v1.0` folder on a 64-bit system.

Before you can use the new shell, you must provide a registry entry for it. You can perform this task at the command line, but it's easier to use the Registry Editor to perform the task in this case. Select Start. Type **RegEdit** in the Search Programs and Files field, and press Enter. You'll see the Registry Editor.

You need to add a new key to the `HKEY_LOCAL_MACHINE\SOFTWARE\Microsoft\PowerShell\1\ShellIds` key. In fact, you have to add a new key every time you create a new shell. For the purposes of this example, create a key named `DataCon.Demos.newshell`. This key contains two values, both of which are strings. The first value, `ExecutionPolicy`, contains one of the values described in the "Defining a Company Policy for Scripts" section of Chapter 21. For the purposes of this example, set this value to `Unrestricted`. The second value, `Path`, contains the path to the new shell you just created. For the purposes of the example, this value will probably be `C:\Windows\System32\WindowsPowerShell\v1.0\NewShell.EXE` or `C:\Windows\SysWOW64\WindowsPowerShell\v1.0\NewShell.EXE`.

Figure 22-4 shows what your registry entries should look like.

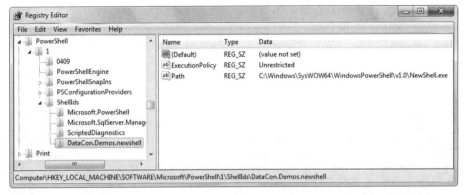

**FIGURE 22-4:** Define registry entries that tell the system how to use your new shell.

Now that you have the registry values in place, you can start the new shell. You can choose one of two techniques. The first is to double-click the executable for the new shell you created. The second method is to type the name of the shell at an existing command line prompt. The system will create a new shell and you can begin using it immediately. In either case, you should be able to execute the reverse-string cmdlet as you would any other cmdlet on the system. Begin by typing **Help Reverse-String** and pressing Enter. You'll see the help information shown in Figure 22-5. This help entry is incomplete because the cmdlet doesn't include all the required help information, but it provides enough information that someone could experiment with the cmdlet.

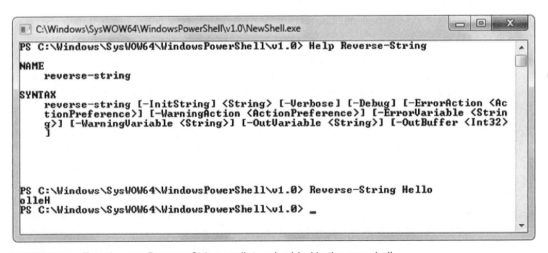

**FIGURE 22-5:** Test the new Reverse-String cmdlet embedded in the new shell.

Figure 22-5 also shows the results of using the cmdlet. In this case, type **Reverse-String Hello** and press Enter to see the results shown.

## MOVING YOUR APPLICATIONS TO WINDOWS 7

This chapter has discussed the benefits and issues of working with cmdlets. You've also created an extremely simple cmdlet that you can use for further experimentation. The essential information you should take from this chapter is that you typically use cmdlets in situations where speed is essential or a script simply won't work. Cmdlets can be difficult to create and complex to test. However, they also provide significantly more flexibility to the developer than working with a script. A cmdlet always requires that you create a new shell to use it, which can impose distribution problems on the developer.

The example cmdlet isn't quite complete. For example, it doesn't provide a complete help system. One of the first tasks you might want to accomplish is adding more substantial help by creating a Reverse-String.DLL-Help.XML file and placing it in the C:\Windows\System32\WindowsPowerShell\v1.0\en-US\ or the C:\Windows\SysWOW64\WindowsPowerShell\v1.0\en-US\ folder of your test system. You can find instructions for creating such a file at http://blogs.msdn.com/b/powershell/archive/2006/09/14/draft-creating-cmdlet-help.aspx.

Chapter 20 began the process of working with Windows PowerShell by describing the fundamentals of this new command line. Chapters 21 and 22 showed you two methods for extending Windows PowerShell to do the things you need to do with it. Chapter 23 will complete the presentation by discussing a few advanced topics. For example, you'll discover how to perform tasks from remote locations using Windows PowerShell, much as you do with the old command line. This final chapter is more theoretical than a code-oriented treatment of the various topics. The purpose is to help you understand some of the ways in which you can extend Windows PowerShell.

# 23
# Interacting Directly with PowerShell

**WHAT'S IN THIS CHAPTER?**

- ➤ Using cmdlets to interact with an application
- ➤ Handling system events
- ➤ Obtaining application status information
- ➤ Updating an application configuration
- ➤ Accessing remote locations

Executing commands directly at the PS prompt is one way to use Windows PowerShell. In fact, that's the way you used Windows PowerShell throughout Chapters 20, 21, and 22. However, Microsoft intends for you to do a lot more than simply issue commands at the PS prompt and see something happen. Windows PowerShell is designed to interact with applications in various ways. In fact, one of the biggest uses for Windows PowerShell today is Microsoft Exchange, which relies on the PS prompt for configuration purposes and to obtain application information.

At some point, you can bet that Microsoft will begin using Windows PowerShell extensively for all kinds of tasks. For example, read the article at `http://blogs.msdn.com/b/powershell/archive/2008/04/15/iis-7-0-powershell-support.aspx` for a discussion of the near miss of Windows PowerShell support for Internet Information Server (IIS) 7.0. The current version of IIS does have Windows PowerShell support in the form of cmdlets. There isn't any reason why you can't use Windows PowerShell for all sorts of tasks with your application today. You'll gain the security, ease of use, and reliability features of Windows PowerShell in the bargain.

You can also use Windows PowerShell for a number of standard tasks that the previous chapters didn't really discuss. For example, it's possible to access a system remotely using Windows

PowerShell, but only if you perform the required setup on the remote system first. This chapter discusses the required setup and the limitations that you'll experience when using remote access. Because most administrators do need to perform some level of remote access, it's important that you at least try to set up two systems and try out the remote access configuration described in this chapter.

## CREATING A CMDLET INTERFACE FOR YOUR APPLICATION

One of the ways in which Microsoft envisions developers using Windows PowerShell is as a means to interact with applications. For years now, developers have created applications that have a command line interface. In order to do this, the developer adds functionality to the application's `Main()` function. You can see an example of this kind of coding at http://www.devsource.com/c/a/Add-Ons/Win-Command-of-the-Command-Line-Interface/.

The problem with creating applications that work at the command line is that they suffer from the same problems that other command line commands do. It's easy to use the wrong command line switch or provide an invalid argument that ends up corrupting data. Sometimes a user won't even realize the command line interface exists and will complain that using the GUI is too slow. In short, controlling an application using the command line is possible, but it's far from foolproof, reliable, or secure. The following sections describe how to work with applications using Windows PowerShell features.

### Using the Built-In Cmdlets

The command line provides utilities such as `Start`, `TaskList`, and `TaskKill` to interact with applications. There are limits to this interaction, but the utilities are quite useful. Windows PowerShell also provides built-in cmdlets to interact with applications:

- **Start-Process:** Creates a new process (similar to the `Start` utility). You can perform all the standard tasks, such as passing a list of arguments to the application. However, the Windows PowerShell version also lets you do things like control the credentials used to interact with the application. It's even possible to start the application and interact with it without displaying a window that the user can see (something that's impossible using the command prompt, where the window always shows the user that a command line application has started).

- **Get-Process:** Obtains a list of running processes (similar to the `TaskList` utility). You can filter the list using various criteria, such as file version information, the process identifier, or a process name. This cmdlet even accepts wildcard characters, so you can obtain a range of processes based on a search string.

- **Stop-Process:** Stops one or more processes (similar to the `TaskKill` utility). A special switch forces processes to stop, even if they aren't responding. You can use wildcard characters and search criteria to stop a range of processes. A special `-WhatIf` command line switch lets you see what would happen if you actually executed the command. The `-WhatIf` command line switch performs this task without stopping any processes.

- **Wait-Process:** Waits for a process to stop before executing the next line in a script. You can use this cmdlet to ensure proper script timing. It's possible to set a timeout to ensure the script doesn't become hopelessly blocked.

➤ **Debug-Process:** Attaches a debugger to a running process so that you can debug it. You can use the process name or identifier. If more than one process fits the criteria you provide, `Debug-Process` will attach a debugger to each matching process.

The Windows PowerShell versions of the process manipulation utilities are significantly more flexible. In addition, you can perform tasks, such as waiting for a task to complete, that aren't readily available at the command line. This extra functionality may make it possible to use a script to interact with your application without adding any additional functionality. However, you always have the option of creating a custom cmdlet as described in the "Using a Custom Cmdlet" section below.

## Using a Custom Cmdlet

Creating a cmdlet to manage your application isn't difficult. In fact, you could add a cmdlet to an existing command line interface. The following steps describe what the cmdlet would need to do:

1. Build up a command line syntax that provides all the data required to start and control the application.
2. Create a `System.Diagnostics.ProcessStartInfo` structure with the acquired data.
3. Use the `System.Diagnostics.Process.Start()` method to start the application with the appropriate input.

The process is straightforward, and it results in an interface that's more reliable and less likely to cause security problems. Instead of relying on a finicky command line interface that will potentially accept incorrect data, you can verify each of the data inputs before you create the process. In addition, because you now have access to a `Process` object from the `Start()` method, it's possible to create a listener setup that will continue to accept commands from a remote source — the resulting environment can be interactive in ways that a command line interface could never accommodate.

As of this writing, there isn't any way to build the cmdlet directly into the application. Microsoft will likely update Visual Studio 2010 (or later) with the required templates at some point in the future when Windows PowerShell becomes more popular. Consequently, you build the cmdlet using the same techniques shown in Chapter 22.

*The example in Chapter 22 describes the standard method for creating an extension to Windows PowerShell. Essentially, you create an updated version of the shell that incorporates the code you want to provide. This technique is the most effective means of adding code that won't easily break, operates securely, and works reliably. However, Windows PowerShell 2.0 also incorporates the concept of a module. These modules work much like the modules found in other environments, such as Java or Python, with some Microsoft-specific twists. Because of the way modules are implemented, you'll encounter some breakage problems (the module gets moved or part of it is deleted by the user), and it isn't nearly as secure or reliable as the technique shown in Chapter 22. The article at* http://msdn.microsoft.com/library/dd878310.aspx *provides more details about working with modules.*

## WORKING WITH SYSTEM EVENTS

It often helps to monitor system events when working at the PS prompt. Knowledge of system events can help you avoid potential problems, and these events can also alert you to potential application problems. One of the most common ways to obtain system event information is to monitor the event logs. You can find a script for performing this very task at http://thepowershellguy.com/blogs/posh/archive/2007/02/26/hey-powershell-guy-how-can-i-monitor-event-log-messages-for-specific-words.aspx. (Yes, this is one really long URL; you can also use the TinyURL version at http://tinyurl.com/37dfa8b). The focus of this script is the System.Management.ManagementEventWatcher class (http://msdn.microsoft.com/library/system.management.managementeventwatcher.aspx), which is a great class to keep in mind because it works well for many different Windows Management Instrumentation (WMI) queries. For example, you could just as easily create an event watcher for new processes by modifying the code at http://msdn.microsoft.com/library/s4acy5e2.aspx. Every time the system starts a new application, your watcher will know about it.

The System.Management.Automation namespace (http://msdn.microsoft.com/library/system.management.automation.aspx) is another good place to look for interesting event mechanisms. You can use the various classes to interact with Windows PowerShell in various ways, including setting traps for specific exceptions such as the ApplicationFailedException (http://msdn.microsoft.com/library/system.management.automation.applicationfailedexception.aspx).

Windows PowerShell 2.0 even introduces a new event as part of the System.Management.Automation namespace, the PSEventReceivedEventHandler delegate. You can create an event handler for it and discover when specific events occur. For example, you could discover when a FileSystemWatcher discovers a change that you specify in the file system. A number of cmdlets are associated with events as described in the following list:

- **Get-Event:** Obtains a list of events currently in the PowerShell event queue (as contrasted to the event logs or system event queues). In order for the PowerShell event queue to receive events, you must register for an event using one of the Register* cmdlets described later in this list. Getting an event doesn't clear it from the PowerShell event queue — you must use the Remove-Event cmdlet to perform this task.

- **Register-ObjectEvent:** Subscribes to an event generated by any .NET Framework capable of generating events. For example, if you want to create a Timers.Timer object and subscribe to its Tick event, you can do so using this cmdlet.

- **Register-EngineEvent:** Subscribes to an event generated by the Windows PowerShell engine or by the New-Event cmdlet. For example, you can monitor events such as the start of a new session or the creation of a new PowerShell process.

- **Register-WmiEvent:** Subscribes to an event generated by WMI, which includes most system activities. For example, if you want to detect when specific process activities occur, you can use WMI to do it.

- **Unregister-Event:** Clears any subscription created by one of the Register* cmdlets. In order to use this cmdlet, you must provide a subscription or a source identifier.

- **New-Event:** Creates a new event and places it in the PowerShell event queue. You can use this cmdlet to create custom events for your scripts or cmdlets. The event can contain elements such as sender information and a specialized message.

- **Remove-Event:** Deletes events from the PowerShell event queue. You must provide an event or source identifier to remove an event from the PowerShell event queue.

- **Wait-Event:** Causes a script to wait until the PowerShell event queue receives a particular event before continuing. This cmdlet also supplies a `-Timeout` command line switch so that you can set a timeout value that keeps the script from freezing while waiting for an event that will never occur.

- **Get-EventSubscriber:** Obtains a list of event subscribers for the current session. This cmdlet won't obtain a list of all of the event subscribers on the system, nor is there any way to perform this task. Each PowerShell window creates a separate session, so a single machine can have multiple sessions running on it, and you can't depend on this cmdlet to tell you about these other sessions.

## USING POWERSHELL FOR APPLICATION STATUS INFORMATION

The kind of information you need about your application determines how you use Windows PowerShell. For example, you can obtain simple execution status information using any of the existing cmdlets, such as those described in the "Using the Built-in Cmdlets" section of this chapter. These cmdlets will let you start, stop, and check the execution of your application. In fact, they offer considerable flexibility in just how you perform these tasks. If you find the standard cmdlets don't provide everything needed, you can always control execution using a custom cmdlet as described in the "Using a Custom Cmdlet" section of this chapter.

This section assumes that you really do want to do something more than simply check the execution of an application. Of course, you can always rely on events and even the Windows message system to output data about your application to outside sources. The article at http://www.devsource.com/c/a/Using-VS/Working-with-Windows-Messages-in-NET/ tells you how to work with messages in a .NET application. You can get some more advanced information about messaging in the article at http://www.devsource.com/c/a/Using-VS/Hooking-Windows-Messages-in-NET/. If you haven't seen enough messaging techniques in the first two articles, a third article at http://www.devsource.com/c/a/Using-VS/Globally-Hooking-Windows-Messages-in-NET/ discusses global message-hooking techniques. However, events and messages have limits because they don't deal in data.

Windows PowerShell has a solution to this problem as well in the form of the provider. A provider lets you look at application data directly from the command line. You can learn more about providers at http://msdn.microsoft.com/library/ee126192.aspx. The basic premise behind a provider is that you can offer access to essential application data. In fact, Windows PowerShell provides a number of default providers that you can use to interact with your application. The following list contains the default providers:

- **Alias provider:** Gives you complete access to the list of Windows PowerShell aliases. For example, when you type `Dir` instead of `Get-ChildItem`, you're using an alias that's managed by the alias provider.

- **Certificate provider:** Lets you access the X.509 certificates (see http://www.ietf.org/rfc/rfc2459.txt for details) on a system, so that you can learn more about the digital signatures associated with an application.

- **Environment provider:** Provides access to the Windows environment variables. Often, applications store settings in environment variables to make behavior changes easy to perform.

- **FileSystem provider:** Allows access to the file system, which includes both directories and files.

- **Function provider:** Furnishes access to all the Windows PowerShell functions.

- **Registry:** Grants access to the Windows registry, where most applications store configuration data (despite Microsoft's best efforts to persuade developers to use any other means). The registry is also where most Windows settings reside, as well as a considerable amount of information about the system hardware and outside connectivity.

- **Variable:** Affords access to all the Windows PowerShell variables.

- **WS-Management:** Makes it possible to create connections to remote systems and use PowerShell commands on those systems. See the "Performing Tasks from Remote Locations" section of this chapter for more information about this particular provider.

*Sometimes, it helps to turn a problem inside out. Instead of interacting with your application from the outside using Windows PowerShell, you can have Windows PowerShell work within your application by creating a host application. In this case, the application loads the Windows PowerShell engine and then uses the engine to perform various tasks. This is similar to applications that create a command prompt as a process and interact with it using batch files or command line switches. However, Windows PowerShell provides considerably greater functionality and flexibility. You can read how to create an application to host Windows PowerShell at* http://msdn.microsoft.com/library/ee706563.aspx.

By combining various existing Windows PowerShell features with cmdlets, providers, and hosting that you create, it's possible to gain access to application status information from a number of perspectives. In short, you gain access to the following types of application status information:

- Execution state
- Events
- Messages
- Data
- Configuration

## USING POWERSHELL TO UPDATE APPLICATION CONFIGURATION

One of the reasons that Microsoft is so interested in developing Windows PowerShell further is that it provides a great method for discovering and updating application configuration information. Microsoft already uses Windows PowerShell to help you manage the configuration of these large applications:

- **Microsoft Exchange:** http://technet.microsoft.com/library/bb123778.aspx
- **Microsoft SharePoint:** http://technet.microsoft.com/library/ee806878.aspx
- **Internet Information Server (IIS):** http://technet.microsoft.com/library/ee790599.aspx
- **SQL Server:** http://msdn.microsoft.com/library/cc281954.aspx

There isn't any reason that your application can't use Windows PowerShell for application management. In fact, you might not have to even code the required support if your application relies on the registry to store settings. All you may need to do is document procedures for making the required changes. Table 23-1 shows the various commands you can use to work with the registry in Windows PowerShell.

**TABLE 23-1:** Registry-Related Commands in Windows PowerShell

| COMMAND | TYPE | DESCRIPTION |
| --- | --- | --- |
| Clear-ItemProperty | Value Management | Removes the content of the specified registry value without removing the value. You use the -Path command line switch to define the registry key. Use the -Name command line switch to specify which value to clear within the registry key. |
| Copy-Item | Key Management | Copies an existing registry key to another location. You use the -Path command line switch to define both the source and target registry keys. |
| Copy-ItemProperty | Value Management | Copies the specified value to a new location in the registry. You use the -Path command line switch to define the registry key. Use the -Name command line switch to specify which value to copy within the registry key. The -Destination command line switch determines the new location of the registry value. A copied registry value has the same name as the original value. |
| Get-ACL | Key Management | Obtains the Access Control List (ACL) for the specified registry key. You use the -Path command line switch to define the registry key. |

*continues*

**TABLE 23-1** *(continued)*

| COMMAND | TYPE | DESCRIPTION |
| --- | --- | --- |
| Get-ChildItem | Key Management | Displays the content of the specified registry key. You use the `-Path` command line switch to define the registry key. Using the `-Recurse` command line switch lets you obtain all the subkeys of the specified registry key. |
| Get-ItemProperty | Value Management | Displays the content of the specified registry value. You use the `-Path` command line switch to define the registry key. Add the `-Name` command line switch if you want to obtain the content of a specific value, rather than all the values for a particular registry key. |
| Get-Location | Navigation | Obtains the current location. The location depends on the last Set-Location command. The default location is the current directory on the hard drive, which is the user's personal directory when you open Windows PowerShell. |
| Move-Item | Key Management | Moves an existing registry key from one location in the registry to another location. You use the `-Path` command line switch to define the initial location. Use the `-Destination` command line switch to define the new location. |
| Move-ItemProperty | Value Management | Moves a value from one location to another. You use the `-Path` command line switch to define the source registry key. Use the `-Name` command line switch to specify which value to move within the registry key. The `-Destination` command line switch determines the new location of the registry value. |
| New-Item | Key Management | Creates a new key in the specified registry location. You use the `-Path` command line switch to define the registry key. |
| New-ItemProperty | Value Management | Creates a new registry value within the specified registry key. You use the `-Path` command line switch to define the registry key. Use the `-Name` command line switch to specify which value to add within the registry key. The `-Value` command line switch defines the new value for the registry value and the `-PropertyType` command line switch defines the value type. |

| COMMAND | TYPE | DESCRIPTION |
|---|---|---|
| Remove-Item | Key Management | Removes an existing key from the specified registry location. You use the -Path command line switch to define the registry key. |
| Remove-ItemProperty | Value Management | Removes a value from within the specified registry key. You use the -Path command line switch to define the registry key. Use the -Name command line switch to specify which value to remove from the registry key. |
| Rename-Item | Key Management | Changes the name of an existing registry key. You use the -Path command line switch to define the registry key. Use the -NewName command line switch to define the new key name. |
| Rename-ItemProperty | Value Management | Renames the specified value. You use the -Path command line switch to define the registry key. Use the -Name command line switch to specify which value to change within the registry key and the -NewName command line switch to specify the new value name. |
| Set-ItemProperty | Value Management | Changes the content of the value within the specified registry key. You use the -Path command line switch to define the registry key. Use the -Name command line switch to specify which value to change within the registry key. The -Value command line switch defines the new value for the registry value, and the -Type command line switch defines the value type. |
| Set-Location | Navigation | Lets you set the current working location within the registry to make it easier to issue subsequent commands. |

Some of the registry manipulation cmdlets require that you specify a data type for the data you want to insert. Table 23-2 shows the acceptable data types for registry entries based on the Microsoft.Win32.RegistryValueKind enumeration.

**TABLE 23-2:** Registry Data Types

| VALUE | REGISTRY TYPE | DESCRIPTION |
| --- | --- | --- |
| String | REG_SZ | Creates a null-terminated string. |
| ExpandString | REG_EXPAND_SZ | Creates a null-terminated string that includes unexpanded references to environment variables such as directories. These values are expanded when you retrieve the data from the registry. |
| Binary | REG_BINARY | Defines binary data in any form. |
| DWord | REG_DWORD | Specifies a 32-bit number. |
| MultiString | REG_MULTI_SZ | Creates an array of null-terminated strings. The array is terminated by two null characters. |
| QWord | REG_QWORD | Specifies a 64-bit number. |
| Unknown | N/A | Defines an unsupported registry data type such as REG_RESOURCE_LIST. Microsoft doesn't provide any guidance on just how you should define the data type, except to say that the data type is unknown. |

Windows PowerShell is equally adept at working with XML-based configuration information. You do need to use some relatively complex command combinations to work with XML data, but it's possible to make any changes required. The article at http://www.codeproject.com/KB/powershell/powershell_xml.aspx shows some of what you can do with the built-in cmdlets.

Theoretically, you can use the same techniques you use to access XML files with other file types, such as an .INI file. The key to accessing any file is to understand the file format completely. You can find additional XML access articles at http://www.pluralsight-training.net/community/blogs/dan/archive/2006/11/25/42506.aspx and http://technet.microsoft.com/library/ff730921.aspx. There's even a continuing miniseries on the topic at http://powershell.com/cs/blogs/news/archive/2009/02/02/master-xml-with-powershell-new-miniseries.aspx.

## PERFORMING TASKS FROM REMOTE LOCATIONS

Many people mistakenly believe that Windows PowerShell works only on the local system because there are no obvious command line switches to allow for remote access. After all, when working with the old command prompt, you could specify the name of the remote system, your username, and a password to gain access. Remote access at the old command prompt was extremely easy, but it was also unreliable and a huge security hole. Many people found out the hard way that remote access through the old command prompt caused them untold woe and many hours of rework. Windows PowerShell greatly improves on remote access, making it both more reliable and more secure.

It isn't possible to perform tasks remotely using Windows PowerShell until you perform some configuration tasks. You must perform a setup on both the local and remote systems because Windows PowerShell uses special Simple Object Access Protocol (SOAP) messaging to communicate. The following steps describe the configuration process:

1. Right-click the Command Prompt entry in the Start menu and choose Run As Administrator from the Context menu. You'll see a command prompt opened with administrator rights.

2. Type **WinRM QuickConfig** and press Enter. The WinRM command automatically configures the remote system to send and receive remote management messages. In general, configuring a system for remote management requests means:

   a. Creating a WinRM listener on HTTP://* to accept WS-Management requests to any IP on this machine.

   b. Enabling the WinRM firewall exception.

3. Ensure the Windows Remote Management (WS-Management) service is started. The service name is actually WinRM if you want to use a command line utility to start it instead by typing **SC Start WinRM** and pressing Enter. You can see this service in the Services console found in the Administrative Tools folder of the Control Panel as shown in Figure 23-1.

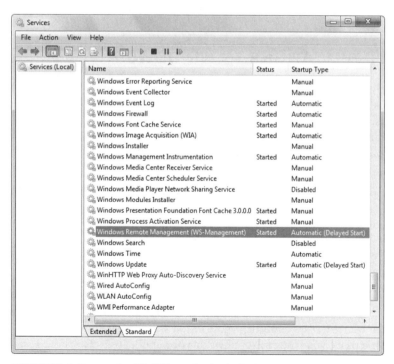

**FIGURE 23-1:** Ensure the WinRM service is started.

4. (Optional) If you plan to allow constant remote access to a particular system, make sure you configure the WinRM service to start automatically using a delayed start as shown in Figure 23-1.

5. Right-click the Windows PowerShell shortcut in the Start menu and choose Run As Administrator from the Context menu. You can verify that the WinRM service is running properly by typing `Get-Service WinRM` and pressing Enter.

6. At the PS prompt, type `Enable-PSRemoting -force` and press Enter. This command forces Windows PowerShell to allow remote queries. You can only perform remote management tasks when you open Windows PowerShell as an administrator.

Let's say you want to test a command after performing this configuration. You want to get the status of the Automatic Updates service (`WuAUServ`) on a remote system named WinServer. To accomplish this task, you type `Get-Service WuAUServ -ComputerName WinServer` and press Enter. If you're working at a PS prompt with administrator privileges, you'll see the results of the query on-screen. Notice that you don't have to supply credentials as part of the query.

Sometimes the method of accessing information remotely is less clear. For example, you might want to obtain a directory listing of the C drive on WinServer. In this case, the C drive would need to be shared so that you could gain access to it using the Universal Naming Convention (UNC). An administrative share will work just fine. To obtain the listing of the Drive C share on WinServer, you type `Get-ChildItem "\\WinServer\Drive C"` and press Enter.

## MOVING YOUR APPLICATIONS TO WINDOWS 7

The chapter has explored some of the more advanced uses of Windows PowerShell. The most important idea to take away from this chapter is that Windows PowerShell doesn't present any limits on how you use it to interact with applications, hardware, and other systems. The only limitations are your imagination, programming skill, and the resources required to build the scripts or cmdlets you need. The exciting thing about Windows PowerShell is that it makes the full functionality of the .NET Framework available to anyone in a relatively easy-to-use form.

One of the most important tasks that a developer can master is accessing a remote system. Administrators will commonly want to access systems remotely. That way, they can remain at their desks and answer more calls in a given timeframe. In addition, working from their desks means they have access to all the documentation and software required to respond to a problem. If you don't test your solutions using a remote system setup, the administrators who rely on your code are likely to experience problems.

Of course, you'll need to decide in the first place whether to implement special functionality for your application using Windows PowerShell. Doing so will require additional system resources, but the dividends can be great, especially as organization size increases. Make sure you plan out the kinds of interactivity you want to support for your application. Consider issues such as creating file-based configuration to make it easier to access the configuration information using a script or cmdlet.

Congratulations! You've reached the end of the book. It's my personal wish that you have found this book both helpful and entertaining. Please be sure to contact me at `JMueller@mwt.net` with your book-related questions and comments, and requests for future updates to this book. Make sure you always send complete information with requests for help, such as the page number, listing number, or figure number in question. I don't provide free consulting or the answers to questions about your personal project because time simply doesn't permit me to do so.

# INDEX

## A

AccelerationMeasurement projects, 394
Access Control Entries (ACEs), 177–178
   general access, 177
   object access, 178
      GUID, 178
   system alarms, 178
   system audits, 178
Access Control Lists (ACLs), 174–176
   LUID, 176
   MMC, 176
      snap-ins, 176
   user rights, 175
ACEs. *See* Access Control Entries
ACLs. *See* Access Control Lists
ACT. *See* Application Compatibility ToolKit
action center icons, 38
Active Data Objects network (ADO.NET), 29–30
Address Windowing Extension (AWE), 354
administrative folders, 330
ADO.NET. *See* Active Data Objects network
Aero Glass, 139–158
   accessibility, 141
   API Code Pack, 140
   developer training, 140
   development costs, 140
   dialogs, 139
   ELS, 155–158

      application additions, 156–157
      configurations, 156
      data extraction, 157
      IETF, 155–156
      LCIDs, 155
      map creation, 157
      NLS, 155–156
      purpose, 155–156
      tasks, 155–156
      user language detection, 156–157
   file dialogs, 139, 141–149
      common, 143
      configurations, 143, 145
      controls, 142–143
      custom locations, 145
      default directories, 145
      definitions, 144–147
      event handlers, 146
      filters, 145–146
      limits, 142–143
      overwrites, 148–149
      read-only, 145, 149
      save, 147–149
   functionality, 139
   hardware updates, 141
   incompatibility, 141
   support, 140–141
      Jump Lists, 141
      Peek, 140
   task dialogs, 139, 149–155
      automatic selections, 154–155
      buttons, 153
      configurations, 150–154
      creation, 151–152

      custom controls, 150
      definitions, 151–154
      effective uses, 149–150
      icons, 153
      information amplification, 150
      progress bars, 150, 153
      testing, 154–155
      tick intervals, 154
      uses, 150
   user training, 140
   WPF, 140
Aero interface, 17–18
   taskbars, 37
Agile, 20
alias providers, 473
AmbientLightMeasurement, 394
API. *See* Application Programming Interface Code Pack
APOD. *See* Astronomy Picture of the Day
AppDomains, 227–231, 233
   Called applications, 230
   example code creation, 230–231
   second project definitions, 228–229
Application Compatibility ToolKit (ACT), 402–403
   installation, 402–403
application development, Windows 7, 3
Application Programming Interface (API) Code Pack, 160
   Aero Glass, 140
   Background power management, 315

Application Programming Interface (API) Code Pack (*continued*)
  DLL hosting, 354
  Explorer Browser control installation, 341
  libraries, 330
  location platform, 374
  non-filesystem containers, 335
  sensor platform, 374
  taskbar application creation, 46–48
    file access, 47
AppLocker, 281–290
  configurations, 282, 285
  creating entries, 285–290
    new path additions, 286–289
    recursive routines, 285–286
  GPO, 281
  GUID, 282, 284, 289
  HKEY users, 289–290
  reading entries, 282–285
    from known locations, 283–284
    target systems, 284
  registry entries, 281–282
    storage, 281
  root elements, 289
  64-bit systems, 289–290
  SRP technology, 281
  versions, 281
  XML, 289
assemblies, 351
Astronomy Picture of the Day (APOD), 73
auditing, 187–191
  UAC, 7–8
    manifests, 208–209
  user actions, 187–191
    administrator privileges, 191
    byte values, 188–189
    configurations, 187–188
    current settings, 191
    documentation, 189
    index value registry, 189
    Local Security Policy console, 190–191
    modifications, 191

registry configuration, 187–188
testing, 190–191
writing code, 188–190
Windows NT security, 187–191
  directories, 195–198
  files, 195–198
  user actions, 187–191
AWE. *See* Address Windowing Extension

## B

Background, 293–327. *See also* trigger-start services
  advantages, 294–295
    diagnostics, 295
    enhanced functionality, 295
    general services, 295
    media support, 295
    monitoring, 295
    protocol support, 295
    security services, 295
    specialized hardware, 295
  application recovery, 319–323
  application restart, 319–323
    Code Pack, 320
    code writing, 320–323
    configurations, 320
    display, 320
    event handlers, 322
    form constructors, 323
    recover mode, 319
    timer definition, 321–322
  applications, 294
    enhanced functionality, 294
    responsiveness, 294
  extended application development, 9
  network list manager, 323–326
    configurations, 324
    connectivity information, 324–326
    network identifiers, 326
    WMI, 323
    writing code, 324–326
  power management, 315–319
    API Code Pack, 315

battery information, 317
configurations, 315
event handlers, 319
information retrieval for, 315–318
monitor states, 317–319
outputting state, 316–318
power sources, 317
queries, 317
UPS, 318
Visual Studio 2010, 319
WPF, 315
system efficiency, 294
trigger-start services, 296–315
  actions, 298
  automatic, 296
  code writing, 300–308
  configurations, 299–300
  data, 298
  definition, 301–303
  devices, 297
  disabling, 296
  domains, 297
  ETW, 297
  event types, 297–298
  firewall ports, 297
  group policies, 297
  installation setup, 300, 310–312
  manual, 296
  network availability, 297
  P/Invoke, 296
  registration, 298
  `ServiceNative.cs` file, 298–300
  Telnet configurations, 308–310, 312–315
  testing, 308–315
  third-party software, 297
background garbage collection, 23
bacronyms, 37
batteries, Background power management, 317
buttons
  Aero Glass, 153
  Multi-Touch Interface, 163–164
  taskbars, 38
    modified, 38
    show desktop, 38

## C

C# language
  cmdlets compiler, 463–464
  taskbar application creation, 48
CAS. *See* Code Access Security
certificate providers, 474
check membership, 235–236
  code creation, 235–236
  configurations, 235
ClickOnce Intranet, 242–245
  configurations, 242–245
  custom policies, 244–245
  debugging, 243–244
  installation, 243–244
  Internet settings, 244
  Windows Firewall, 274
  XML, 244
CLR. *See* common language runtime
cmdlets, 455–467, 469–472
  access ease, 456
  application interfaces, 456, 470–471
  basic, 460–466
    C# compiler, 463–464
    command prompts, 462–463
    executable command, 463–464
    make-shell utility, 464–465
    registry, 465–466
    reverse-string, 460–463, 466
    testing, 465–466
  built-in, 470–471
  complex shell extensions, 456
  custom, 471
  distribution issues, 456
  IIS 7.0, 469
  investment, 456
  resource usage, 456
  scripts v., 455
  security, 456
    enhanced, 456
    specialized, 456
  shell extensions, 457–459
  skill level, 457
  speed, 456
Cobra language, 25
Code Access Security (CAS), 220–222, 232
  configurations, 222
  imperative security, 223–225
  policies, 227
  policy example code, 223–226
code groups, 227
ColdFusion language, 25
Collection Editor, 129–130
COM. *See* Component Object Model
common language runtime (CLR), 222, 238–239
  large-number example code, 358
CommonFileDialogButton, 142
CommonFileDialogCheckBox, 142
CommonFileDialogComboBox, 142
CommonFileDialog ComboBoxItem, 142
CommonFileDialogControl, 143
CommonFileDialog ControlCollection, 143
CommonFileDialogGroupBox, 142
CommonFileDialogLabel, 142
CommonFileDialogMenu, 142
CommonFileDialogMenuItem, 142
CommonFileDialogProminent Control, 143
CommonFileDialogRadio ButtonList, 142
CommonFileDialog RadioButtonListItem, 142
CommonFileDialogSeparator, 142
CommonFileDialogTextBox, 142
Component Object Model (COM)
  .NET Framework 4.0, 25
  Ribbon, 105–106
  Windows Firewall, 248
  Windows Firewall updates, 276
  WMI, 181
concurrent garbage collection, 23
context menu, 41
  Jump Lists, 6, 19
  taskbars, 41, 44
cryptography, 233
culture-sensitive formatting, 24
custom categories, 67–68
custom cmdlets, 471
custom switchers, 6
  taskbars, 45
custom tasks, 68–70
  configurations, 69
  Jump Lists, 69–70
    definitions, 69–70
    entries, 70

## D

DACL. *See* Discretionary Access Control List
Data Execution Prevention (DEP), 348
debugging
  ClickOnce Intranet, 243–244
  parallel processing, 370–371
  script testing, 448–452
  Windows Firewall, 254
  Windows NT security user permissions, 187
  Windows Powershell 2.0, 416
Debug-Process cmdlets, 470
declarative security, 221, 225
defined verification process, 232
DEP. *See* Data Execution Prevention
-Detailed command line switch, 423
diagnostics features, 24
dialog box launchers, 90
direct security, 221
DirectX hardware, 354
Discretionary Access Control List (DACL), 174
Disk Operating System (DOS), 416
DLL hosting. *See* dynamic-link library hosting
DLR. *See* Dynamic Language Runtime
DOS. *See* Disk Operating System
downloads, to Windows 7, 11
Dragon NaturallySpeaking, 159
drivers, Windows 7 compatibility, 18
Dynamic Language Runtime (DLR), .NET Framework 4.0, 25–26
dynamic-link library (DLL) hosting, 353–354
  API Code packs, 354
  AWE, 354
  DirectX hardware, 354
  loading, 353
  memory, 353
  PAE support, 353–354

dynamic-link library (DLL) hosting
    (*continued*)
    16-bit systems, 354
    VDM support, 354
    WOW64, 353

# E

ECMA standards. *See* European Computer Manufacturers Association standards
Elegant Ribbon, 106
ELS. *See* Extended Linguistic Services
Entertainment Software Rating Board (ESRB) rating, 336
environment providers, 474
ESRB rating. *See* Entertainment Software Rating Board rating
ETW. *See* event tracing for windows
European Computer Manufacturers Association (ECMA) standards, 95
event handlers
    Aero Glass file dialogs, 146
    Background
        application restart, 322
        power management, 319
    Multi-Touch Interface, 164, 166–167
        location information, 166–167
        pixel levels, 166–167
        touch measurements, 167
    Ribbon applications, 124–125
    sensor platform, 388–390
        output code, 390
        sensor change response, 389
    thumbnail toolbars, 79
event tracing for windows (ETW), 24
    trigger-start services, 297
evidence-based security, 232
Excel, 64-bit systems, 348
Explorer Browser control, 341–345
    addition, 341–342
    API Code pack installation, 341
    configurations, 342–343
    dialog box, 342
    initial selections, 344–345
    UI, 343–344

Windows Forms, 342
writing code, 343–345
Extended Linguistic Services (ELS), 155–158
    application additions, 156–157
    configurations, 156
    data extraction, 157
    IETF, 155–156
    LCIDs, 155
    map creation, 157
    NLS, 155–156
    purpose, 155–156
    tasks, 155–156
    user language detection, 156–157
eXtensible application markup language (XAML)
    .NET Framework 4.0, 51–53
    Jump Lists, 52–53
    Ribbon, 106
    WPF, 130–132
    taskbars, 57
eXtensible markup language (XML)
    AppLocker, 289
    ClickOnce Intranet, 244
    Office 2010, 97–98
    Ribbon, 111–114
        application commands, 113
        application views, 113–114
        initial files, 112–114
        QAT, 113–114
    64-bit systems, 350
    Windows NT security, 219, 241–242

# F

F# language, 362
file dialogs, Aero Glass, 139, 141–149
    common, 143
    configurations, 143, 145
    controls, 142–143
    custom locations, 145
    default directories, 145
    definitions, 144–147
    event handlers, 146
    filters, 145–146
    limits, 142–143
    overwrites, 148–149
    read-only, 145, 149

save, 147–149
FileSystem providers, 474
filters, Aero Glass file dialogs, 145–146
folders, 329–335
    administrative, 330
    configurations, 332
    `GetDisplayName()`, 334–335
    information display, 332–333
    `KnownFolders` property, 335
    output, 334–335
    purpose of, 332
    special icons, 332
    writing code, 332–333
foreground tasks, 293
frequent categories, 58–59, 64–67
    incoming file requests, 65–66
    `TaskManager` functionality, 66
function providers, 474

# G

galleries, Ribbon, 90
garbage collection, 23
Geosense for Windows, 378–379, 384–386, 388, 390–393
    configurations, 390–393
    privacy issues, 391
    property modification, 391
    SID, 392
    timestamp, 385
Get Location examples, 386–387
`GetDisplayName()`, 334–335
`Get-Event`, 472
`Get-EventSubscriber`, 473
`Get-Process` cmdlets, 470
Global Positioning System (GPS), 375
Globally Unique Identifier (GUID), 178, 282, 284, 289
    ACEs, 178
    sensor platform, 384–385
    trigger-start services, 303–304
GPO. *See* Group Policy Object
GPS. *See* Global Positioning System
Groovy language, 25
Group Policy Object (GPO), 261, 266–274
    applications, 267

additions, 271–273
deletions, 273–274
exceptions, 267
public profiles, 271–274
AppLocker, 281
configurations, 266–267
entry creation, 285–290
ports, 261, 266–274
rules techniques, 267–274
  additions, 271–273
  addresses, 272
  clearing entries, 270
  complexity, 271
  deletions, 273–274
  direction definition, 272
  if statements, 271
  list of, 268–271
  protocols, 267
  TCP, 271
  UDP, 271
services, 267
Windows Forms, 267
Group SID, 177
GroupComponent, 182–183
GUID. *See* Globally Unique Identifier; globally unique identifier

## H

Hardware, Windows 7 compatibility, 18
hash, 220
help functionality, 18
HKEY users, 289–290
HTTP. *See* hypertext transfer protocol
hypertext transfer protocol (HTTP), .NET Framework 4.0 networking support, 28

## I

ICMP. *See* Internet Control Message Protocol
icons
  Aero Glass, 153
  library folders, 332
  overlay, 45
    taskbars, 80–81
  progress bars, 73

taskbars, 40
  action center, 38
  combination of, 42–43
  overload, 80
  thumbnail toolbars, 78–79
IETF. *See* Internet Engineering Task Force
if statements, 271
IIS 7.0. *See* Internet Information Server 7.0
imperative languages, 362
imperative security, 221, 223–225
installation
  ClickOnce Intranet, 243–244
  .NET Framework 4.0, 30–32
    entries, 31
    program features applet, 32
    stand-alone, 30–32
  SDK, 108
  sensor platform, 380–382
  Telnet configurations, 308
  trigger-start services, 300, 310–312
  verification, 311–312
  Windows 7 applications, 11
  Windows XP, 405
Integrated Scripting Environment (ISE), 439–443
  Windows Powershell 2.0, 10, 439–443
  command, 441
  output, 441–443
interactive scripts, 450
International Standards Organization (ISO) package, 108
Internet
  ClickOnce Intranet settings, 244
  Windows NT security, 220
Internet Control Message Protocol (ICMP), 254
Internet Engineering Task Force (IETF), 155–156
Internet Information Server (IIS) 7.0, 469
Interop Library, 162–163
IRibbonForm interface, 110, 121–122
IronPython, 25
  parallel processing, 27, 362
ISE. *See* Integrated Scripting Environment

IsInRole() method, 237–238
ISO package. *See* International Standards Organization package

## J

JavaScript, 25
Jump Lists, 6, 19, 58–73
  Aero Glass support, 141
  custom tasks, 69–70
    definitions, 69–70
    entries, 70
  .NET Framework 4.0, 52–54
    loaded events, 53–54
    XAML, 52–53
  taskbars, 41, 44, 49–50, 58–73
    APOD, 73
    application creation, 49
    code addition, 49–50
    common categories, 59–60, 63
    custom categories, 67–68
    custom tasks, 68–72
    default programs, 60
    destinations, 72–73
    file additions, 63–64
    file extension registration, 60–63
    frequent category, 58–59, 64–67
    .NET Framework 4.0, 52–54
    ProcessStartInfo object, 62
    program identifiers, 61
    recent category, 58, 64–67
    RegistrationHelper, 59
    registry, 58
    64-bit systems, 72–73
  UI, 82–83

## K

kernel patch protection, 8, 172
keyboards
  Ribbon, 87–88
  Windows 7 strategy development, 15
keywords, Windows Firewall, 248–249
KnownFolders property, 335

487

## L

Language Integrated Query (LINQ), 366
large-number example code, 357–359
    CLR, 358
    disassembly, 359
    testing, 358–359
LCIDs. *See* Local Identifiers
libraries, 329–344. *See also* galleries
    additions, 340–341
    API Code Pack, 330
    browser controls, 330
        Explorer Browser, 341–345
    closing, 340
    content, 340–341
    custom collection, 329–330
    default folders, 338
    Explorer Browser control, 341–345
        addition, 341–342
        configurations, 342–343
        dialog box, 342
        initial selections, 344–345
        UI, 343–344
        Windows Forms, 342
        writing code, 343–345
    folders, 329–335
        administrative, 330
        configurations, 332
        `GetDisplayName()`, 334–335
        information display, 332–333
        `KnownFolders` property, 335
        output, 334–335
        purpose of, 332
        special icons, 332
        writing code, 332–333
    lists, 338–339
    non-filesystem containers, 335–337
        API Code pack, 335
        configurations, 336
        entry types, 335
        ESRB rating, 336
        information display, 336–337
        outside data, 337
        writing code, 336–337
    optimization, 340
    64-bit systems, 350
    taskbar application creation, 46–47
    TPL, 367
    user-defined collections, 338–341
        configurations, 338
        lists for, 338–339
        standard, 339
        tasks, 338–339
        Windows Forms, 338
    WPF, 330
LINQ. *See* Language Integrated Query
*LINQ for Dummies* (Mueller), 366
Linux, 171
LISP language. *See* List Processing language
List Processing (LISP) language, 25
Local Identifiers (LCIDs), 155
Local Security Policy console, 190–191
    UAC, 205
LocalIntranet, 220
Locally Unique IDentifier (LUID), 176
location platform, 373–395
    API Code Pack, 374
    compatibility, 374
    devices, 375–379
        AccelerationMeasurement projects, 394
        AmbientLightMeasurement projects, 394
        development of, 394
        WPF, 374
Lua language, 25
LUID. *See* Locally Unique IDentifier

## M

mail header support, 29
malware detection, 173
Managed Extensibility Framework (MEF), 27
    functions, 27
    MMC, 27
manifest tool (MT) utility, 210
manifests, 207–211
    additions, 207
    applications, 207–209
        codes, 208–209
        definition, 207
        execution, 211
    audit actions, 208–209
    command lines, 209
    compilations, 209–210
    configurations, 209
    input tags, 207
    MT utility, 210
    settings, 207
MEF. *See* Managed Extensibility Framework
memory
    DLL hosting, 353
    parallel processing requirements, 365
    64-bit systems, 347–348, 351
        limits, 347
        requirements, 351
        support, 347
    32-bit systems, 347
    trigger-start services, 304
    Windows XP mode problems, 409–412
menu
    Ribbon, 87
    taskbars, context, 41
message boxes, 249
Microsoft Management Console (MMC), 27
    ACLs, 176
    snap-ins, 176
Microsoft Project, 348
MMC. *See* Microsoft Management Console
Model-View-ViewModel (MVVM), 126
monitors, 317–319
MT utility. *See* manifest tool utility
Mueller, John Paul, 95, 366
multiple processors, 368–369
Multi-Touch Interface, 159–168
    API, 160
    as application addition, 162–167
        buttons, 163–164
        configurations, 163–164
        functionality, 164–167

    Interop Library, 162–163
    reference additions, 164
  artistic applications, 160
  editions, 162
  event handlers, 164, 166–167
    location information, 166–167
    pixel levels, 166–167
    touch measurements, 167
  functionality, 164–167
    business logic creation, 164–165
    event handlers, 164, 166–167
  gestures, 162
  industrial applications, 160
  initialization, 165
  Interop Library, 162–163
    Visual Studio, 163
  mobile devices, 160
  Multi-Touch Platform, 160
  in presentations, 161
  tablets, 160
  TouchHandler object, 165
  training cost reductions, 161
  user requirements, 161–162
    operating-system-specific tasks, 161–162
    screen cleaning, 162
    touch device compatibility, 161
MVVM. *See* Model-View-ViewModel
MyComputer, 220

# N

Named Pipes (NP), 258
NAT support. *See* network address translation support
National Language Support (NLS), 155–156
.NET Framework 4.0, 21–33
  applications, 22–23
    compatibility, 22–23
    deployment, 22–23
    speed, 23
    testing, 23
  backward compatibility, 22
  core features, 23–27
    COM, 25
    diagnostics, 24
    DLR, 25–26
    ETW, 24
    performance, 24
    PIAs, 25
    64-bit systems, 26–27
    updated code contracts, 24
  culture-sensitive formatting, 24
  data improvements, 29–30
    ADO.NET, 29–30
    dynamic, 29–30
    WCF Data Services, 29–30
  as download, 30–32
  early versions, 21–22
  extended functionality, 32
  garbage collection, 23
  globalization, 24
  improvements, 24
  installation, 30–32
    entries, 31
    program features applet, 32
    stand-alone, 30–32
  Jump Lists, 52–54
    loaded events, 53–54
    XAML, 52–53
  MEF, 27
  multiple language applications, 21
  necessity of, 22–30
  networking, 28–29
    HTTP header support, 28
    mail header support, 29
    NAT support, 28
    null cipher encryption, 29
    password handling, 29
    percent value conversion/normalization, 29
    security, 28
    SSL support, 29
  parallel programming, 27–28
    IronPython, 27
    PLINQ, 27–28
  resource pages, 21
  security policy levels, 226
  taskbars, 51–54
    code additions, 52–54
    Jump Lists, 52–54
    reference additions, 52
    Visual Studio 2010, 51
    WPF, 51
    XAML, 51–53
  UAC, 202
  Win32 API functionality, 22
  Windows Powershell 2.0, 417
  WPF, 24, 51
NetStat utility, 313
network address translation (NAT) support, 28
network list manager, 323–326
  configurations, 324
  connectivity information, 324–326
  network identifiers, 326
  WMI, 323
  writing code, 324–326
Networking, .NET Framework 4.0, 28–29
  HTTP header support, 28
  mail header support, 29
  NAT support, 28
  null cipher encryption, 29
  password handling, 29
  percent value conversion/normalization, 29
  security, 28
  SSL support, 29
New-Event, 473
NLS. *See* National Language Support
non-filesystem containers, 335–337
  API Code pack, 335
  configurations, 336
  entry types, 335
  ESRB rating, 336
  information display, 336–337
  outside data, 337
  writing code, 336–337
Notepad, 50
  Ribbon, 93
NP. *See* Named Pipes
null cipher encryption, 29

# O

Office 2007, 86
  ECMA standards, 95
  Ribbon, 93–94
Office 2010, 86
  Ribbon, 86, 94–98
    custom elements, 96
    VSTO, 95
    XML, 97–98
    ZIP files, 94–95

Outlook, Ribbon, 94
overlay icons, 6, 45
    taskbars, 80–81
        status information, 81
        UI creation, 83
overload icons, 80
Owner SID, 177

## P

PAE support. *See* physical address extension support
Paint application, 91–92
Parallel Language Integrated Query (PLINQ), .NET Framework 4.0, 27–28
Parallel Language-Integrated Query (PLINQ), 366
parallel processing, 361–372
    advantages, 363
    applications, 366–371
        PLINQ alternative, 366
        TPL, 367
    asynchronous patterns, 367
    color lists, 369
    configurations, 368
    data, 367
    debugging, 365, 370–371
    declarative languages, 362
    example code, 368–369
    extended application development, 8–9
    F# language, 362
    functionality, 363
    imperative languages, 362
    IronPython, 362
    multiple processors, 368–369
    .NET Framework 4.0, 27–28
        IronPython, 27
        PLINQ, 27–28
    overhead, 363
    PLINQ, 366–367
        applications, 366
        .NET Framework 4.0, 27–28
    requirements, 363–366
        coding techniques, 365–366
        compute-intensive applications, 364
        definitions, 361
        memory, 365
        resources, 365
        task length evaluation, 364
        task type evaluation, 364
        team skills, 365–366
    resource contentions, 362
    security, 363
    states, 362
    tasks, 367
    wasted resources, 364
passwords, .NET Framework 4.0 networking, 29
Peek, Aero Glass, 140
peeking, 40
PHP language, 25
physical address extension (PAE) support, 353–354
PIAs. *See* Primary Interop Assemblies
PID. *See* Program IDentifier
P/Invoke. *See* Platform Invoke
Platform Invoke (P/Invoke), 296
PLINQ. *See* Parallel Language Integrated Query
ports, 258–262
    addition, 258–262
    deletions, 258–262
    GPO, 261, 266–274
    Inbound Rules folder, 261
PreviewRibbon, 120–121
Primary Interop Assemblies (PIAs), 25
`ProcessStartInfo` object, 62
Program IDentifier (PID), 394
progress bars, 6, 44–45
    Aero Glass task dialogs, 150
    error state, 75
    indeterminate state, 75
    NoProgress state, 75
    normal state, 75
    paused state, 75
    states, 75–77
        testing, 76–77
    taskbars, 73–77
        application icons, 73
        configurations, 74
        features, 44–45
        functionality, 73
        management, 74–75
        resets, 74–75
        starts, 74–75
        state changes, 75–77
        stops, 74–75
    timers, 74
    user interface, 83
    visual style, 73
    Windows 7, 6
PS Prompt, 452–453
`.PS1XML` file, 445
`.PSD1` file, 444
`.PSM1` file, 444
publishers, 220

## Q

QAT. *See* Quick Access Toolbar
Quick Access Toolbar (QAT), 90–91
    Ribbon, 113–114, 119–121
        customization, 119
        PreviewRibbon, 120–121
        view creation, 119–120
        WPF, 128, 131–137
    WPF, 128, 131–137
        clicks, 135
        event handlers, 136–137
        removing items, 133, 136
        Ribbon, 128, 131–137
        tracking variables, 135
        updates, 133–134

## R

RBS. *See* role-based security
read-only files, Aero Glass, 145, 149
recent categories, 58, 64–67
    incoming file requests, 65–66
    `TaskManager` functionality, 66
`Register-EngineEvent`, 472
`Register-ObjectEvent`, 472
`Register-WmiEvent`, 472
RegistrationHelper, 59
remote administration settings, 254–258
    application addition, 258
    default techniques, 257
    definitions, 256
    global variables, 256
    modifications, 257
    NP, 258
    RPC, 258
    TCP, 258
Remote Procedure Call (RPC), 258

Remote-Event, 473
resource contentions, 362
`ResultCode`, 280
`reverse-string` cmdlet, 460–463, 466
Ribbon, 6–7, 19, 85–137
  as application addition, 105
  application creation, 121–125
    event handlers, 124–125
    framework definition, 122–123
    initialization, 123–124
    IRibbonForm implementation, 121–122
    resource access, 123–124
  COM, 105–106
  configurations, 110–111
    IRibbonForm interface, 110
  controls, 89, 99–102
    attributes, 102–103
  definition, 86–89
  dialog box launchers, 90
  galleries, 90
  graphics, 89
  Interop modules, 105–106
  minimization, 90
  Office 2007, 86, 93–94
  Office 2010, 86, 94–98
    custom elements, 96
    VSTO, 95
    XML, 97–98
    ZIP files, 94–95
  Outlook, 94
  QAT, 90–91, 113–114, 119–121
    customization, 119
    PreviewRibbon, 120–121
    view creation, 119–120
  RibbonLib, 108–110
  SimpleRibbon, 106
  tabs, 89
  UI, 86–89, 111–121
    definition, 111–121
    edit menu, 88–89
    file menus, 114–116
    format positioning, 89
    home tabs, 117–119
    icons, 115
    keyboards, 87–88
    menus, 86
    QAT, 119–120
    scaling policy, 118
    `SizeDefinition` attribute, 118–119
    tabbed interface, 86
    32-bit graphics, 116–117
    toolbars, 87
    Visual Studio, 116–117
    WPF, 127–132
    XML, 111–114
  Windows 7, 6–7, 19, 91–93
    COM, 106
    controls, 99–102
    functionality, 98–103
    Notepad, 93
    Paint, 91–92
    SDK, 106–108
    Text tab, 93
    Windows Media Player, 93
    Wordpad, 87, 92–93
    Zoom group, 92
  Wordpad, 87, 91–92
  as workflow mechanism, 87
  workflows, 90
  WPF, 125–137
    application creation, 132–137
    button events, 132
    Collection Editor, 129–130
    configurations, 126–127
    downloads, 125–126
    MVVM, 126
    properties, 129
    QAT, 128, 131–137
    source code, 125–126
    support templates, 126–127
    techniques, 106
    UI, 127–132
    XAML, 130–132
  XAML, 106
  XML, 111–114
    application commands, 113
    application views, 113–114
    initial files, 112–114
    QAT, 113–114
*RibbonX for Dummies* (Mueller), 95
role-based security (RBS), 178, 221, 233
  declarative security, 221, 225
  direct security, 221
  imperative security, 221, 223–225
  `IsInRole()` method, 237–238
RPC. *See* Remote Procedure Call
Ruby language, 25

## S

SACL. *See* System Access Control List
scripts, 439–454
  basic, 444–447
    mapping network drives, 445–446
    .PS1XML file, 445
    .PSD1 file, 444
    .PSM1 file, 444
  cmdlets v., 455
  company policy definition, 453
  developers, 440
  experimental code, 440
  ISE, 439–443
    commands, 441
    output, 441–443
    Windows Powershell 2.0, 439–443
  low-level access, 440
  short-use code, 440
  speed, 440
  testing, 447–453
    administrator privileges, 449
    debugging, 448–452
    interactive, 450
    PS Prompt, 452–453
  user editing, 440
  Windows Powershell 2.0, 417, 439
    ISE, 439–440
SDK. *See* Windows 7 Software Development Kit
`Searcher` object, 280
secure sockets layer (SSL) support, 29
security. *See also* Windows NT security
  Background, 295
  cmdlets, 456

security. *See also* Windows NT
    security (*continued*)
    .NET Framework 4.0,
        networking, 28
    parallel processing, 363
    64-bit systems, 349
    Windows 7, 18
        address space layout
            randomization, 8
        data execution prevention, 8
        external interaction, 247
        improvements, 7–8
        kernel patch protection, 8
        mandatory integrity levels, 8
        service hardening, 8
Security IDentifier (SID), 174, 177
    descriptors, 177
    Geosense for Windows, 392
sensor platform, 373–395
    API Code Pack, 374
    categories, 375–377
        attached, 377
        external, 377
        integrated, 377
        invalid, 377
    compatibility, 374
    configurations, lists, 379
    connection detection, 383
    devices, 375–379
        categories, 375–377
        development for, 394
        Geosense for Windows,
            378–379, 384–386, 388
        GPS, 375
        software, 378–379
        WiFi, 378
    event handlers, 388–390
        output code, 390
        sensor change response, 389
    functionality, 379
    Geosense for Windows,
        378–379, 384–386, 388,
        390–393
        configurations, 390–393
        privacy issues, 391
        property modification, 391
        SID, 392
        timestamp, 385
    Get Location examples,
        386–387
    GUIDs, 384–385

handling, 388–390
initialization, 387–388
installation, 380–382
lists, 379–385
    configurations, 379
    view location activity links,
        393–394
    PID, 394
    TID, 394
writing code, 380–385
`ServiceNative.cs` file, 298–300
SID. *See* Security IDentifier
Simple Object Access Protocol
    (SOAP) messaging, 479
SimpleRibbon, 106
site domains, 220
16-bit systems, 354
64-bit systems, 347–360
    advantages, 348–350
    AppLocker, 289–290
    assemblies
        requirements, 351
        writing code, 355
    configurations, 355–357
        defaults, 356
    DEP, 348
    development issues, 351–352
    development strategy, 348
    DLL hosting, 353–354
    Excel workbooks, 348
    extended application
        development, 8
    false savings, 349
    graphics applications, 350
    large-number example code,
        357–359
    CLR, 358
    disassembly, 359
    testing, 358–359
    memory, 347–348, 351
        limits, 347
        support, 347
    Microsoft Project, 348
    .NET Framework 4.0, 26–27
    processor-intensive applications,
        350
    programming issues, 352
        VSTO, 352
    registry access, 352–353
        redirection, 352
        WOW64, 353

reliability, 349
requirements, 348
    assemblies, 351
    drivers, 351
    hardware support, 351
    libraries, 350
    memory, 351
    operating systems, 350–351
    register size, 350
    software support, 351
security, 349
speed, 349
taskbars, 72–73
Windows 7 compatibility, 18
writing code, 354–359
    assemblies, 355
    configurations, 355–357
    large-number example code,
        357–359
    Windows Forms, 355
    XML, 350
`SizeDefinition` attribute,
    118–119
Smalltalk, 25
Snap feature, 5–6
SOAP messaging. *See* Simple Object
    Access Protocol messaging
Software Restriction Policies (SRP)
    technology, 281
SRP technology. *See* Software
    Restriction Policies technology
SSL support. *See* secure sockets layer
    support
`Start-Process` cmdlets, 470
Stephens, Rod, 51
`Stop-Process` cmdlets, 470
System Access Control List (SACL),
    174

# T

task dialogs, Aero Glass, 139,
    149–155
    automatic selections, 154–155
    buttons, 153
    configurations, 150–154
    creation, 151–152
    custom controls, 150
    definitions, 151–154
    effective uses, 149–150

icons, 153
information amplification, 150
progress bars, 150, 153
testing, 154–155
tick intervals, 154
uses, 150
Task Parallel Library (TPL), 367
taskbars, 37–55, 57–84
  Aero interface, 37
  API Code Pack, 57
    application creation, 46–48
  application creation, 45–51
    API Code Pack, 46–48
    C# language, 48
    Jump Lists, 49–50
    libraries, 46–47
    Notepad, 50
    references folders, 48–49
    template forms, 48–49
    testing, 50–51
  application settings, 42–43
    icon combination, 42–43
    label display, 42
  buttons, 38
    modified, 38
    show desktop, 38
  context menu, 41
  controls, 38, 81–82
    thumbnails, 41
  features, 39–41
    active, 39
    custom switchers, 45
    progress bars, 44–45
    `TaskManager` functionality, 66
  icons, 40
    action center, 38
    combination of, 42–43
    overlay, 45, 80–81
    overload, 80
  Jump Lists, 41, 44, 49–50, 58–73
    APOD, 73
    application creation, 49
    application identifiers, 61
    code addition, 49–50
    common categories, 59–60, 63
    custom categories, 67–68
    custom tasks, 68–72

    default programs, 60
    destinations, 72–73
    file additions, 63–64
    file extension registration, 60–63
    frequent category, 58–59, 64–67
    .NET Framework 4.0, 52–54
    `ProcessStartInfo` object, 62
    program identifiers, 61
    recent category, 58, 64–67
    RegistrationHelper, 59
    registry, 58
    64-bit systems, 72–73
    UI creation, 82–83
  multiple windows, 39–40
  .NET Framework 4.0, 51–54
  notification area customization, 38
  overlay icons, 80–81
    status information, 81
    UI creation, 83
  overload, 54
  pinned applications, 38–39
  progress bars, 73–77
    application icons, 73
    configurations, 74
    features, 44–45
    functionality, 73
    management, 74–75
    resets, 74–75
    starts, 74–75
    state changes, 75–77
    stops, 74–75
    timers, 74
    UI, 83
    visual style, 73
  properties dialog box, 40
  thumbnails, 38, 40, 45, 77–79
    controls, 41
    peeking, 40
    toolbars, 77–79
    UI, 82–83
  UI creation, 82–83
    Jump Lists, 82–83
    overlay icons, 83
    thumbnail toolbars, 82–83
  `TaskManager` functionality, 66

TCP. *See* Transmission Control Protocol
Telnet configurations, 308–310, 312–315
  installation, 308
  log entries, 314
  NetStat utility, 313
  port events, 313
Text tab, 93
32-bit systems
  memory limits, 347
  Ribbon UI, 116–117
Thread IDentifier (TID), 394
thumbnails
  taskbars, 38, 40, 45, 77–79
    controls, 41
    peeking, 40
    toolbars, 77–79
    UI, 82–83
  toolbars, 6, 77–79
    button icons, 78–79
    creation of, 79
    definition of, 78
    event handlers, 79
  Windows Media Player, 40–41, 77–78
tick intervals, 154
TID. *See* Thread IDentifier
timers, 74
toolbars
  Ribbon, 87
  thumbnails, 6, 77–79
    button icons, 78–79
    creation of, 79
    definition of, 78
    event handlers, 79
`TouchHandler` object, 165
TPL. *See* Task Parallel Library
Transmission Control Protocol (TCP), 258
  GPO, 271
trigger-start services, 296–315
  actions, 298
  automatic, 296
  delayed, 296
  code writing, 300–308
    creation, 301–306
    definitions, 307–308
    GUID, 303–304
    log entries, 307

trigger-start services (*continued*)
    managed memory, 304
    multi-strings, 304
    native, 304–306
    operating system version, 306–307
  configurations, 299–300
    Telnet, 308–310, 312–315
    templates, 299–300
  data, 298
  definition, 301–303
  devices, 297
  disabling, 296
  domains, 297
  ETW, 297
  event types, 297–298
    subtypes, 297–298
  firewall ports, 297
  group policies, 297
  installation setup, 300, 310–312
    verification, 311–312
  manual, 296
  network availability, 297
  P/Invoke, 296
  registration, 298
  `ServiceNative.cs` file, 298–300
  Telnet configurations, 308–310, 312–315
    installation, 308
    log entries, 314
    NetStat utility, 313
    port events, 313
    testing, 308–315
      Telnet configurations, 308–310, 312–315
  third-party software, 297

## U

UAC. *See* User Account Control
UAP. *See* User Account Protection
UDP. *See* User Datagram Protocol
UI. *See* user interface
UNC. *See* Universal Naming Convention
uniform resource locators (URLs), 221
  permissions code, 241–242
Uninterruptible Power Supply (UPS), 318

Universal Naming Convention (UNC), 480
`Unregister-Event`, 472
updates, 43–45
  Aero Glass, 141
  as interaction tool, 43–44
  QAT, 133–134
  status information, 44
  taskbars, 43–45
    as interaction tool, 43–44
    status information, 44
  Windows 7 applications, 11–12
  Windows Firewall, 274–280
    ClickOnce technology, 274
    COM, 276
    configurations, 275
    current settings, 276–278
    feature selection, 278
    levels, 278
    listings for, 279–280
    output information, 280
    registry checks, 274
    `ResultCode`, 280
    `Searcher` object, 280
    settings code, 275–279
    subkeys, 274
    writing code, 279–280
  Windows XP, 398, 406
UPS. *See* Uninterruptible Power Supply
URLs. *See* uniform resource locators
User Account Control (UAC), 201–216
  administrator control, 205
  application development rights, 203
  developer-created application code, 202
  disabling applications, 206
  drivers, 202
  execution, in administrator mode, 211–215
    definition, 211
    external applications, 214
    manifests, 211
    permission entries, 213
    primary application code, 213–214
    secondary projects, 211–213
    as separate process, 211–215

external application interactions, 202
interactions, 203–206
  Local Security Policy console, 205
manifests, 207–211
  additions, 207
  application codes, 208–209
  application definition, 207
  application execution, 211
  audit actions, 208–209
  command lines, 209
  compilations, 209–210
  configurations, 209
  input tags, 207
  MT utility, 210
  settings, 207
MSConfig, 204
.NET Framework 4.0, 202
overrides, 202–203
restrictions, 205
secondary projects, 211–215
  application codes, 214–215
support, 206–215
  manifests, 207–211
third-party libraries, 202
UAP, 204
Vista, 4, 201
Windows 7
  enhanced auditing, 7–8
  permission elevations, 7
Windows NT security, 219
  features, 173
Windows XP, 397
  adjustments, 403–404
  applets, 403
  testing, 404
WMI, 183, 202
User Account Protection (UAP), 204
User Datagram Protocol (UDP), 264–265
  GPO, 271
user interface (UI). *See also* Multi-Touch Interface
  Aero, 17–18
    taskbars, 37
  Explorer Browser control, 343–344
  Ribbon, 86–89, 111–121
    definition, 111–121
    edit menu, 88–89

file menus, 114–116
format positioning, 89
home tabs, 117–119
icons, 115
keyboards, 87–88
menus, 86
QAT, 119–120
scaling policy, 118
`SizeDefinition` attribute, 118–119
tabbed interface, 86
32-bit graphics, 116–117
toolbars, 87
Visual Studio, 116–117
Wordpad, 87
WPF, 127–132
XML, 111–114
taskbars, 82–83
compatibility, 82
Jump Lists, 82–83
overlay icons, 83
progress bars, 83
thumbnail toolbars, 82–83
Windows 7
functionality, 5
improvements, 4–7
testing, 17–18

## V

VDM support. *See* Virtual DOS Machine support
view location activity links, 393–394
Virtual DOS Machine (VDM) support, 354
Vista
compatibility issues, 4
UAC, 4, 201
Windows 7 v., 3–4
graphics, 5
Visual Studio 2008, 294
Visual Studio 2010, 51, 294
Background power management, 319
Multi-Touch Interface, 163
Ribbon UI, 116–117
taskbars, 51
Visual Studio Tools for Office (VSTO), 95, 352
VSTO. *See* Visual Studio Tools for Office

## W

`Wait-Event`, 473
`Wait-Process` cmdlets, 470
WCF. *See* Windows Communication Foundation Data Services
WiFi. *See* Wireless Fidelity
Windows 7. *See also* Background; libraries; Multi-Touch Interface; .NET Framework 4.0; parallel processing; security; taskbars; Windows Firewall; Windows NT security; Windows XP
accessibility, 18
application development, 3
applications
development, 3
testing, 17–18
AppLocker, 281–290
customizations, 6
switchers, 6
driver compatibility, 18
extended application development, 8–9
background processing, 9
parallel processing, 8–9
64-bit applications, 8
help functionality, 18
improvements, 3–12
from developer's perspective, 4–9
security, 7–8
UI, 4–7
Jump Lists, 6, 19
libraries, 329–344
additions, 340–341
API Code Pack, 330
browser controls, 330
closing, 340
content, 340–341
custom collection, 329–330
default folders, 338
Explorer Browser control, 341–345
folders, 329–335
lists, 338–339
non-filesystem containers, 335–337
optimization, 340
taskbar application creation, 46–47
user-defined collections, 338–341
WPF, 330
moving applications to, 10–12, 17–19
advantages, 18–19
application testing, 17–18
compatibility issues, 11
downloads, 11
tool installation, 11
updating, 11–12
overlay icons, 6
Progress Bars, 6
resource access, 18
Ribbon, 6–7, 19, 91–93
COM, 106
controls, 99–102
functionality, 98–103
Notepad, 93
Paint, 91–92
Text tab, 93
Windows Media Player, 93
Wordpad, 87, 92–93
Zoom group, 92
SDK, 106–108
ISO package, 108
web installer, 108
security, 7–8, 18
address space layout randomization, 8
data execution prevention, 8
external interaction, 247
Firewall, 248–274
kernel patch protection, 8
mandatory integrity levels, 8
service hardening, 8
strategy development, 15
64-bit compatibility, 18
Snap feature, 5–6
strategy development, 13–20
application speed, 15
coding limits, 13
common problems, 14
ease of comprehension, 15
functionality, 15
innovative uses, 14
keyboard usage, 15
new requirements, 14–15
reliability, 15
security, 15
training costs, 16

Windows 7 (continued)
    training requirements, 16
    upgrades, 16
    usage requirement definitions, 14–16
    user satisfaction, 17
    for user window comfort levels, 14–16
  thumbnail toolbars, 6
  UAC
    enhanced auditing, 7–8
    permission elevations, 7
  UI, 17–18
  Vista v., 3–4
    graphics, 5
  WordPad, 6
Windows 7 Software Development Kit (SDK), 106–108
  ISO package, 108
  web installer, 108
Windows 32-bit On Windows 64-bit (WOW), 353
Windows 32-bit On Windows 64-bit (WOW64), DLL hosting, 353
Windows Communication Foundation (WCF) Data Services, 29–30
Windows Firewall, 248–274. *See also* AppLocker; Group Policy Object
  application additions, 262–266
    buttons, 262–263
    exceptions, 263–265
    profile levels, 264
    tabs, 265
    UDP, 264–265
  application deletion, 266
  AppLocker
    configurations, 282, 285
    creating entries, 285–290
    GPO, 281
    GUID, 282, 284, 289
    HKEY users, 289–290
    reading entries, 282–285
    registry entries, 281–282
    root elements, 289
    64-bit systems, 289–290
    SRP technology, 281
    versions, 281
    XML, 289
  automatic updates, 274–280

ClickOnce technology, 274
COM, 276
  configurations, 275
  current settings, 276–278
  feature selection, 278
  levels, 278
  listings for, 279–280
  output information, 280
  registry checks, 274
  `ResultCode`, 280
  `Searcher` object, 280
  settings code, 275–279
  subkeys, 274
  writing code, 279–280
COM techniques, 248
debuggers, 254
dynamic keywords, 248–249
example constants, 250
GPO, 261, 266–274
  applications, 267
  configurations, 266–267
  ports, 267
  rules techniques, 267–274
  services, 267
  Windows Forms, 267
ICMP, 254
interactions, 248–249
manager, 254
message boxes, 249
profile types, 254
settings, 249, 255–258
  add ports, 258–262
  deleting ports, 258–262
  modifications, 255–258
  remote administration, 254–258
  RPC, 258
  TPC, 258
status information, 250–254
trigger-start services, 297
verification of status, 249–255
Windows Forms
  Explorer Browser control, 342
  GPO, 267
  64-bit systems, 355
  user-defined collections, 338
Windows Management Instrumentation (WMI), 180–183
  Background network list manager, 323

COM interfaces, 181
  `GroupComponent`, 182–183
  query creation, 182
  UAC, 183, 202
  user interaction, 181–182
  Windows NT security, 219
  WMIC, 181
Windows Management Interface Command (WMIC), 181
Windows Media Player, 40–41
  Ribbon, 93
  taskbars, 40–41
  thumbnails, 41
Windows NT security, 171–199, 217–246
  access levels, 173–174
  ACEs, 177–178
    general access, 177
    object access, 178
    system alarms, 178
    system audits, 178
  ACLs, 174–176
    LUID, 176
    MMC, 176
    user rights, 175
  address space layout randomization, 172
  AppDomains, 227–231, 233
    Called applications, 230
    example code creation, 230–231
    second project definitions, 228–229
  application directory, 220
  auditing directories, 195–198
    configurations, 196
  auditing files, 195–198
    activity codes, 196–198
    configurations, 196
  auditing user actions, 187–191
    administrator privileges, 191
    byte values, 188–189
    configurations, 187–188
    current settings, 191
    documentation, 189
    index value registry, 189
    Local Security Policy console, 190–191
    modifications, 191
    registry configuration, 187–188

testing, 190–191
writing code, 188–190
CAS, 220–222, 232
   configuration, 222
   policies, 227
   policy example code, 223–226
ClickOnce Intranet, 242–245
   configurations, 242–245
   custom policies, 244–245
   debugging, 243–244
   installation, 243–244
   Internet settings, 244
   XML, 244
CLR, 222
   permissions, 238–239
compliance requirements, 173
   business, 173
   regulatory, 173
cryptography, 233
DACL, 174
   descriptors, 177
data execution prevention, 172
declarative security, 221, 225
defined verification process, 232
descriptors, 174, 176–177
   DACL, 177
   flags, 177
   headers, 177
   SACL, 177
   SID, 177
direct security, 221
directory permissions, 192–195
   changes, 193–195
   code, 192–193
   configurations, 192
enhanced applications, 233–242
   zones, 219–221, 234–236
evidence-based, 232
features, 172–173
   additions, 172
   changes, 172–173
   UAC functionality, 173
file permissions, 192–195
   changes, 193–195
   code, 192–193
   configurations, 192
   modifications, 194–195
hash, 220
imperative security, 223–225
internal threat monitoring, 173
Internet networks, 220
kernel patch protection, 172
Linux, 171
LocalIntranet, 220
malware detection, 173
mandatory integrity levels, 172
monitoring, 172–173
MyComputer, 220
names, 220
needs definitions, 231–233
new features, 218–219
NoZone, 220
overloading, 245–246
permissions, 221–226
   CLR, 238–239
   development, 238–242
   legacy security configurations, 222–223
   local codes, 239–240
   URLs, 241–242
   XML, 241–242
personal rights, 174
pipe security, 172
policies, 226–231
   AppDomain configurations, 227–231, 233
   ClickOnce Intranet, 242–245
   code groups, 227
   default, 240
   development, 242–245
   implementation, 242–245
   .NET Framework 4.0, 226
publishers, 220
RBS, 178, 221, 233
   configurations, 236–237
   declarative security, 221, 225
   development, 236–238
   direct security, 221
   example codes, 237–238
   imperative security, 221, 223–225
   `IsInRole()` method, 237–238
redefined permissions, 171
resource control, 173
SACL, 174
   descriptors, 177
service hardening, 172
SID, 174, 177
   descriptors, 177
site domains, 220
traditional features, 218
trusted applications, 220
trusted override, 220
UAC, 219
   features, 173
URLs, 221
   permissions code, 241–242
user permissions, 178–183
   additions, 186
   changes, 183–187
   configurations, 179, 183–184
   debuggers, 187
   elevated rights, 187
   modification code, 186–187
   modification manifest, 185
   system accounts, 180
   WMI, 180–183
   writing code, 179–180
WMI, 180–183, 219
   COM interfaces, 181
   `GroupComponent`, 182–183
   query creation, 182
   UAC, 183
   user interaction, 181–182
   WMIC, 181
XML, 241–242
   serialization, 219
zones, 219–221, 234–236
   application evidence, 234–235
   application functionality, 219
   check membership, 235–236
   code features, 234
   development, 234–236
Windows Powershell 2.0, 9–10, 416–438. *See also* cmdlets
   application configurations, 475–478
   application status information, 473–474
   commands, 424–437
   basics, 418–421
   prompt replacement, 416–418
   debugging, 416
   default providers, 473–474
   descriptions, 422
   `-Detailed` command line switch, 423

Windows Powershell 2.0 (*continued*)
  DOS, 416
  graphical development environment, 10
  ISE, 10, 439–443
    command, 441
    output, 441–443
  names, 421–423
  .NET Framework 4.0, 417
  online assistance, 421–423
  property system, 424–437
  registries, 474–478
    data types, 478
    related commands, 475–477
  related links, 422
  reliability, 416–417
  remarks, 422
  remote location tasks, 478–480
    SOAP messaging, 479
    UNC, 480
  scripting, 10, 417, 439–443
    ISE, 10, 439–443
  synopsis, 422
  syntax, 422
  system events, 472–473
  variables, 474
  WS-Management, 474, 479–480
Windows Presentation Foundation (WPF), 51, 57
  Aero Glass, 140
  Background power management, 315
  libraries, 330
  location platform, 374
  .NET Framework 4.0, 24
    taskbars, 51, 57
  QAT, 128, 131–137
    clicks, 135
    event handlers, 136–137
    removing items, 133, 136
  Ribbon, 128, 131–137
    tracking variables, 135
    updates, 133–134
  Ribbon, 125–137
    application creation, 132–137
    button events, 132
    Collection Editor, 129–130
    configurations, 126–127
    downloads, 125–126
    MVVM, 126
    properties, 129
    QAT, 128, 131–137
    source code, 125–126
    support templates, 126–127
    techniques, 106
    UI, 127–132
    XAML, 130–132
  sensor platform, 374
Windows Remote Management (WS-Management), 474, 479–480
Windows XP, 4, 9, 19, 397–412
  application testing, 19, 404–408
    in virtual environments, 407–408
  compatibility, 399–403
    ACT, 402–403
    functionality, 401
    mode options, 400–401
    recommended settings, 400
    settings changes, 401–402
    troubleshooting, 401
  configurations, 405–407
    installation, 405–406
  mode problems, 408–412
    memory options, 409–412
    resource integration denial, 408–409
    resource permission issues, 408
    virtual environment speed, 409–412
  sound features, 402
  stand-alone applications, 398
  third party modules, 398–399
  UAC, 397, 403–404
    adjustments, 403–404
    applets, 403
    testing, 404
    updates, 398, 406
  as virtual machine, 398
Wireless Fidelity (WiFi), 378
WMI. *See* Windows Management Instrumentation
WMIC. *See* Windows Management Interface Command
Wordpad, 6
  Ribbon, 87, 92–93
WOW64. *See* Windows 32-bit On Windows 64-bit
WPF. *See* Windows Presentation Foundation
Wrox 2009, 20
WS-Management. *See* Windows Remote Management (WS-Management)

## X

XAML. *See* eXtensible application markup language
XML. *See* eXtensible markup language

## Z

ZIP files, 94–95
Zoom group, 92